Friendlyvision

Fred Friendly broadcasting
Footprints in the Sands of Time on
WEAN, Providence, Rhode Island,
around 1937 to 1941.
(Courtesy Roberta Lowe Allen)

Friendlyvision

Fred Friendly and the Rise and Fall

of Television Journalism

RALPH ENGELMAN

Columbia University Press New York

Columbia University Press
Publishers Since 1893
New York   Chichester, West Sussex

Library of Congress Cataloging-in-Publication Data
Engelman, Ralph.
    Friendlyvision : Fred Friendly and the rise and fall
of television journalism / Ralph Engelman.
        p. cm.
    Includes bibliographical references and index.
    ISBN 978-0-231-13690-7 (cloth : alk. paper)
    ISBN 978-0-231-51020-2 (e-book)
    1. Friendly, Fred W.   2. Television producers and
directors—United States—Biography.
    I. Title.

PN1992.4.F695E54 2009
792.4502'32092—dc2
[B]

                         200840432

∞

Columbia University Press books are printed on
permanent and durable acid-free paper.
Printed in the United States of America
c 10 9 8 7 6 5 4 3 2

References to Internet Web sites (URLs) were
accurate at the time of writing. Neither the author
nor Columbia University Press is responsible for
URLs that may have expired or changed since the
manuscript was prepared.

Contents

Foreword by Morley Safer VII

Acknowledgments XI

Prologue: Salesman 1

Introduction 4

1. Ferd 10

2. "My Rhodes Scholarship" 30

3. "Willing to Be Lucky" 48

4. *See It Now* 72

5. Friendly and Murrow 91

6. Encounter with
   McCarthyism 110

7. Aftermath 130

8. *CBS Reports* 139

9. Camelot 157

10. News President 174

11. At the Top of His Game 187

12. Vietnam 198

13. Resignation 214

14. Policy Maker 234

15. Professor 252

16. *PBL* 271

17. PBS 285

18. The Press and the Bar 299

19. Seminar 310

20 Last Years 329

21. Friendlyvision 346

Notes 365
Index 407

Foreword

IN MY FIFTY-SIX YEARS as a working reporter, I have been lucky enough to work for two men who had the most profound and positive influence on broadcast journalism: Fred Friendly and Don Hewitt, who were both at CBS and often at loggerheads. Don, the creator of *60 Minutes*, now in his eighties and in semi-nonretirement, maintains a youthful passion for editing words and pictures together—and letting them tell powerful stories. It is a quality best described by Red Smith in a 1980 essay in which he noted that Pete Rose had "a lascivious love for the game."

Fred Friendly too had that lust, but the objects of his desire were unattainable. He was perfectly aware that commercial television would never be the Mount Parnassus of his imagination—an opera here, a poetry reading there, interrupted only by penetrating documentaries and intellectuals relieving themselves of Great Thoughts and cures for all of humanity's psychic, economic, and political challenges. He was part Candide, wandering optimistically through life's tragedies, and part P. T. Barnum, bellowing at the suckers to come into the tent.

Fred, the long-time associate of Edward R. Murrow, is considered by many to be a demigod of broadcast journalism. It was certainly the case back in 1963 when his emissaries approached me about coming to work for CBS News. It is understatement to say I was at once thunderstruck, flattered, and scared stiff. My only contact in American broadcasting was my friend John Chancellor, then an NBC News correspondent based in London. I tracked him down at 1:00 A.M. in Brussels.

"What should I do?" I asked.

"You have no choice," he said.

So in the spring of 1964 I turned up for work as a foreign correspondent at the legendary CBS News bureau in London. It had been bombed

out of at least three different offices in various BBC premises during the
Battle of Britain, when Murrow's live reporting permanently established broadcast journalism as a vital source of news. At war's end the
bureau moved round the corner from the BBC to a rundown second-floor
walk-up over a pub called the Stag's Head at 26 Hallam Street. On my
first day on the job the bureau chief, Alex Kendrick, showed me to my
desk. Kendrick, a laconic great bear of a man, said simply, "That was
Murrow's desk." This thirty-two-year-old, who had spent ten years knock-
ing around Europe, Africa, and the Middle East for the Canadian Broadcasting Corporation, felt he had won the Lottery of Life.

In my first nine months at CBS, I covered mainly routine political stories, small features, what magazine editors call "back of the book" stuff.
It was something of a letdown. At the CBC, I had reported from Israel
and Egypt during the 1956 "Hundred Hours War," had spent months in
Algeria documenting the last brutal days of the civil war, was in East
Berlin the night the Berlin Wall went up and was arrested and questioned
by the Stasi.

Now I was beginning to believe that the lottery of life had turned into
a penny-ante poker game. But in December 1964 I was summoned to
New York by Friendly. This was our first face-to-face meeting. When I
was hired, his deputies, Ernie Leiser, assistant general manager of news,
and Ralph Paskman, deputy news director, had done all the talking.

Fred, a giant of a man—big head, big nose, big voice—rose from his
desk, offered a big paw to be shaken, and told me I was on my way to
Vietnam . . . that this was going to become the most important story
since the Flood and that it was up to me to not just cover it but to explain
every nuance. The survival of western civilization depended on me. He
punctuated this one-way chat with an outstretched arm at the end of
which was a bent index finger that he used to imprint a virtual punctuation mark at the end of every phrase.

Many years later, when we became good friends, I realized that one of
Fred Friendly's great gifts was an ability to turn the most mundane memo
or reassignment into Henry V's St. Crispin's Day exhortation. Fred's rants,
written or spoken, could both terrify and inspire. When I left his office
that first day, Paskman was waiting to walk me out to a cab.

"How did it go?" he asked.

"He wants me to save the world."

Paskman laughed. "Don't worry, kid, this Vietnam thing will be over
in three months—maximum, six."

Armed with such savvy news judgment, I left for Saigon. In August 1965, I accompanied U.S. Marines on a search-and-destroy mission in a Vietnamese hamlet called Cam Ne. The marines systematically obliterated most of Cam Ne with flamethrowers and Zippo lighters. The broadcast caused a firestorm in Washington—the State Department, Pentagon, Marine Corps, and the White House demanded that CBS fire me. It was just the kind of fight that Fred relished. In *Friendlyvision*, Ralph Engelman describes in fascinating detail Fred's counterattack and the forceful persuasion he used to stiffen a wavering CBS corporate resolve.

Three months later I returned to Saigon from the central highlands of Vietnam, where I'd been covering the first major campaign involving American troops and regular North Vietnamese units. A message from Friendly was waiting for me: "Return NY soonest with all footage for special report Tuesday Nov 30 on campaign for Ia Drang Valley."

I arrived in New York on Thanksgiving Day and worked through the weekend, writing and editing. On Monday I was sitting in a cramped screening booth with a film editor, watching uncut footage of a group of GI's talking about buddies who'd been killed earlier that day. Their voices were soft, their words gentle . . . no anger, no cursing. Just grief. I felt water dripping down my neck and assumed it was a leaky pipe in the rickety CBS Broadcast Center. I turned around. Standing over me was Fred, a Niagara of tears dripping down over that formidable nose. He left the room without uttering a word.

"The Campaign for the Ia Drang Valley" was scheduled for broadcast at 10:00 P.M. on Tuesday, November 30. At 8:00 P.M. I finished taping the studio inserts and sat in the control room watching the director stitch together the film, the studio portions, and the commercials. It was nearly 9:00 P.M. as the last segment of the broadcast—pictures of GI coffins being unloaded—came to a close. Up came the last commercial—a sultry brunette, in revealing negligee, with a voiceover extolling the seductive qualities of Lanvin perfume. The most brutal juxtaposition of images imaginable. A deafening silence in the control room was broken in an instant by a ringing telephone. It was Friendly, screaming, "Kill the commercial!" We did, which meant a frantic forty-five minutes of rewriting and recording to fill the gap. It was clearly the right thing but not the wise thing to do from a corporate bottom-line point of view, the kind of decision that led to Fred Friendly's departure from CBS a few months later.

There are no saints in broadcasting, as Engelman convincingly points out in this admirable biography, and Fred had character weaknesses galore. Everything about him was outsized, including his faults. He had an enormous ego. He could be manipulative, even conniving, and when he left his position of power at CBS, he was guilty of publicly throwing verbal brickbats at his old colleagues, sometimes deserved, sometimes not. Though I must add that he continued to treat me with great kindness and undeserved and excessive praise.

In his last years he mellowed somewhat as a new persona emerged: the kindly, slightly absent-minded professor surrounded by a group of adoring graduate students, many of whom went on to stellar careers in journalism. But he never lost the passion, the lascivious love for the spoken word. Nor did he lose what Hemingway called a shit detector, the ability to spot the false note, the waffling sentence, the lame alliteration.

It is difficult to argue with Ralph Engelman's contention that Fred may have made his greatest contributions to twentieth-century America after he left CBS News. His pioneering work in the creation of the Public Broadcasting Service, his determination and success in teaching and guiding a generation of minority journalists, the wonderfully lively and inventive media and society seminars are all testament to a remarkable man and a remarkable life.

Morley Safer

Acknowledgments

I COULD NOT HAVE WRITTEN this book without the generous support of Ruth Mark Friendly, Fred Friendly's widow and full partner in his professional life following their marriage in 1968. She opened many doors for me—to the Friendly home in Riverdale, to countless associates, and to her husband's thinking and inner life. I examined his papers primarily at their home in Riverdale, before Ruth Friendly deposited almost all this material in the Rare Book and Manuscript Library of Columbia University. I also profited from a series of interviews with the late Dorothy Greene Friendly, Friendly's first wife, who provided invaluable information about the early part of his career. I am greatly indebted to Joseph Wershba, one of the original producer-reporters for *See It Now* and the consultant par excellence on CBS's history for countless authors and filmmakers. Carolene Marks, Friendly's cousin, shared her reminiscences since their childhood. Friendly's six children—three of Dorothy's offspring, three of Ruth's from her first marriage—each offered perspectives on their father.

I have supplemented the vast trove of Friendly's papers with interviews with many of his associates, as documented in the endnotes. In a race against time I was able to speak to important figures in Friendly's life who did not live to see the publication of this volume. These include Norman Fain, his oldest and closest friend since their childhood in Providence, Rhode Island; Robert Trout, the legendary broadcaster who moderated *Who Said That?* the program that marked Friendly's first breakthrough in network broadcasting; Sig Mickelson, who hired Friendly at CBS; Art Buchwald, who befriended Friendly and Dorothy in the early 1950s; Howard K. Smith, who made the transition from Murrow Boy to Friendly Boy during Friendly's tenure as executive producer of *CBS Reports*; Gordon Manning, Friendly's deputy during his presidency of CBS

News and witness to his resignation from the network; James W. Armsey, Friendly's colleague first in the China-Burma-India theater during World War II and later at the Ford Foundation; and Dr. Peter B. Neubauer, friend and psychoanalyst who advised Friendly on family matters.

I owe a debt of gratitude to Roberta Lowe Allen of Providence, Rhode Island, for use of materials and photographs from the papers of her father, Mowry Lowe, Friendly's first broadcasting mentor. Reinhild Silverman, in her capacity as librarian, provided access to the archives of Temple Beth-El, in Providence. Linda Henderson, library director of the Providence Journal Company, made it possible for me to search the morgue of Friendly's hometown newspaper. John McDonough of Kenilworth, Illinois, an associate of Robert Trout's, provided me with materials from Trout's papers before they were transferred to the Center for American History, University of Texas at Austin. Laura Kapnick and Carol Barnes helped me plumb the files of the CBS News Reference Library in New York. I am grateful for the packet of materials sent to me by Tom Connors, curator of the National Public Broadcasting Archives of the University of Maryland. My thanks to Michael Rosen and Karen Herman for the treasure trove of oral histories contained in the Archive of American Television, a project of the Academy of Television Arts and Sciences Foundation, North Hollywood, California. I am grateful for documentation I received from the Avram R. Westin Papers, Mass Communications History Center, Division of Archives and Manuscripts, State Historical Society of Wisconsin, Madison; the Walter Lippmann Papers, Manuscripts and Archives, Yale University Library; and the Edward R. Murrow Collection, Tufts University Digital Collections and Archives. I have drawn on the archives of the presidential libraries of Dwight D. Eisenhower, John F. Kennedy, and Lyndon B. Johnson for Friendly's interaction with these three chief executives and their administrations. Jim Moske provided a detailed index for the Office Files of Fred Friendly, 1945–80, in the Ford Foundation Archives.

I am grateful for the support of my editors at Columbia University Press, Afua Adusei and the late John Michel, and for the diligence of my copy editor, Polly Kummel. I would like to thank Dr. Everette E. Dennis, Felix E. Larkin Distinguished Professor at Fordham University, for his critical reading of the manuscript.

I owe a great debt to Long Island University, where I have taught in the Journalism Department since 1985. The university has generously afforded me the release time and sabbatical leave that made this daunting project feasible. I owe a special debt for the encouragement of my mentors on the George Polk Awards Committee: Dr. Robert Spector, its chair, and Sidney Offit, its curator. I enjoyed the collegiality and stimulation provided by my colleagues in the Journalism Department, professors Donald A. Bird and Jennifer Rauch, as I worked on this undertaking. Professor Stuart Fishelson of the Media Arts Department assisted in the selection and production of photographs. I would also like to acknowledge the help of Sofija Jovic, Alex Lupus, and Ian Smith, student aides in the Journalism Department, and Zena Kennedy, departmental secretary.

An earlier version of chapter 2 was published as " 'My Rhodes Scholarship': Fred Friendly as an Information Officer in World War II," *Journalism History* 30 (2004): 113–22, and is used with permission of the journal's editor, Dr. Patrick S. Washburn. "Send in the Clowns" (from *A Little Night Music*). Music and Lyrics by Stephen Sondheim. © 1973 (Renewed) Rilting Music, Inc. All Rights Administered by WB Music Corp. All Rights Reserved. Used by permission from Alfred Publishing Co., Inc.

Friendlyvision

Prologue Salesman

"HE WAS A SALESMAN," Robert Trout suddenly interjected as he reminisced about Fred Friendly. Trout, the veteran CBS journalist who had introduced FDR's fireside chats, was ninety when I interviewed him; Trout had met Friendly when Friendly broke into network broadcasting in the 1940s. Trout, still elegant and mellifluous, was speaking in 1999 in the midtown Manhattan pied-à-terre he had maintained since retiring to Spain. "Above all," Trout emphasized, "Fred Friendly was a salesman."[1]

As an education officer during World War II, Friendly sold the war effort to troops in the China-Burma-India theater. Then, for forty years he sold a succession of ideas—at CBS, the Ford Foundation, Columbia University—that transformed television journalism in the United States. For example, he was largely responsible for prompting Edward R. Murrow to *do* television journalism, by conceiving and producing the groundbreaking program *See It Now*. Friendly sold the very concept of public television to legislators and the public as an official of the Ford Foundation. He also sold the foundation on a unique kind of seminar that used the Socratic method to explore controversial topics. He sold Columbia University on a groundbreaking program to train minority journalists. What was always for sale, linking the myriad programming initiatives, was *Friendlyvision,* a term used in the 1960s by Harvey Swados for Friendly's ambitious agenda to use broadcast journalism to elevate the national discourse about public affairs.[2] Friendlyvision in large measure shaped television's response to the great political controversies of the United States of the midtwentieth century, especially McCarthyism, the war in Vietnam, and Watergate.

Friendly and his first wife, Dorothy, had seen the original production of Arthur Miller's *Death of a Salesman*—produced by Elia Kazan and starring Lee J. Cobb—soon after it opened in 1949 at the Morosco Theatre in New York. At the time Friendly was unknown, just embarking on his career. Dorothy recalled years later how, after seeing the play, Fred would play the traveling salesman when he entered their cramped apartment on First Avenue in Manhattan at the end of the day. He would slump inside the door, as if weighted down by a bag of goods in each hand but bolstered by "a smile and a shoeshine," a phrase from Miller's play he liked to quote. At Friendly's memorial service a half century later, one speaker noted that Fred liked to call himself "the Willy Loman of the Constitution."[3] Friendly—if only in jest—associated himself throughout his career with the leading representation of a salesman in American literature.

In selling Friendlyvision, Fred Friendly was also selling himself. He was possessed by a soaring ambition, reflected in the extraordinary drive and the violent temper tantrums that became legendary at CBS. Indeed, a remark about the effect of Friendly's ambition made the rounds at CBS: "Fred Friendly is a man of high principles and low practices."[4] This judgment is both harsh and facile. Yet it is necessary to ask whether at times Friendly's ambition put him at cross-purposes with his own values as a broadcast journalist. This may have been the case at the dramatic turning point in his career, his resignation in 1966 as president of CBS News. The resignation had tragic overtones for Friendly, exiling him for the rest of his career from the institution he most loved. His ambition may have set the stage for his separation from CBS: he had assumed the position of news president against the advice of Edward R. Murrow and other close associates. And the resignation itself, a storied act of principle in television history, may have come about, in part, because of a fateful miscalculation on Friendly's part. Nonetheless, Friendly would land on his feet and advance the cause of Friendlyvision and his own career at the Ford Foundation and Columbia University.

Stuart Sucherman, who worked on the Columbia University Media and Society Seminars, marveled at Friendly's power of persuasion:

> All too often, I would sit there in awe as I watched Fred work over some media personality, corporate executive, government official and, yes, even an occasional Supreme Court justice who had come into a meeting totally convinced that under no circumstances would he or she ever appear in this particular seminar or that particular television program. After about 30 minutes of being "Friendly-ized," the victim had not only accepted an appearance, but was inviting his or her friends or relatives.[5]

Sucherman described Friendly's annual presentation of the budget for the seminars before the board of the Ford Foundation as "30 minutes of pure persuasion, gesticulating, roaring, pounding the table so hard that those of us in the back of the room could feel the room shake." After one of these incredible and exhausting performances, Henry Ford II, a member of the board, exclaimed, "That friggin' Friendly, I should have him out selling my goddamn cars!"[6]

Introduction

ANY ASSESSMENT OF the first four decades of television journalism—
and its subsequent development to our own day—must reckon with the
complex figure of Fred Friendly. Friendly remains the single most important person in the development of news and public affairs programming during the first four decades of American television, from the
medium's inception after World War II until well into the 1980s. His
influence endures in countless ways. And the pitched battles he fought
continue to resonate in the troubled world of contemporary broadcast
journalism.

He wielded extraordinary influence on the development of broadcast
journalism through his characteristically tumultuous tenure at three powerful U.S. institutions: CBS, the Ford Foundation, and Columbia University. Friendly was a maverick who used these venerable agencies of the
eastern Establishment for his own purposes, advancing a succession of
bold new models for public affairs programming. These initiatives made
him a key player in television's response to the great controversies of his
era. Friendly's achievement needs to be situated in the complex institutional cultures in which he operated: CBS in its heyday as the "Tiffany
network," the Ford Foundation under the presidency of McGeorge Bundy,
and the Columbia University School of Journalism in an era of student
and institutional unrest from the late 1960s to the 1980s.

At CBS, Friendly was Edward R. Murrow's full partner in the creation
in the 1950s of *See It Now* and in the program's historic response to Mc-
Carthyism. Friendly subsequently presided over a golden age of television documentaries as executive producer of *CBS Reports*. Then came his
presidency of CBS News in the Vietnam era and his storied resignation
from that position because of coverage of the war. Thereafter, as a communications official at the Ford Foundation, Friendly helped create pub-

lic broadcasting as we know it today. To advance that agenda, he created a radical model for public affairs programming, the *Public Broadcasting Laboratory (PBL)*, a now largely forgotten experiment well worth revisiting. Friendly, who had quit CBS because of its refusal to carry live the hearings of the Senate Foreign Relations Committee on Vietnam, helped establish a public broadcasting system that came of age airing the Senate Watergate hearings.

At the Ford Foundation, he created yet another programming model, the media and society seminars; many were broadcast on PBS, the public television network he helped create. The format was based on the Socratic method, with distinguished panelists considering hypothetical questions about topical issues. In addition, he developed the television concentration within the Columbia Graduate School of Journalism. At the end of the 1960s, with U.S. inner cities on fire, he launched a major initiative to train minorities for careers in television news. Friendly's position at Columbia University enabled him to preside over the training of an influential cohort that remains prominently represented in broadcast journalism today.

Indeed, Friendly's career is a prism through which to view the vicissitudes of the first forty years of television journalism. Fred Friendly's dual status as insider and outsider confronts the student of that career with a paradox. He is the quintessential representative of an era of broadcast journalism and also its greatest critic, one who was virtually cast from its midst. In the formative years of broadcast journalism, no individual was as ubiquitous, as apt to put his signature on so many major undertakings, as likely to be on the cutting edge. By using the term *Friendlyvision* as the book's title, I mean to suggest the overarching ideal that gives Friendly's peripatetic journey coherence and meaning. Such a synthesis also enables us to evaluate Fred Friendly's achievement—its scope and limits, and its implications for the future of broadcast journalism.

The passionate, larger-than-life figure of Fred Friendly—who earned the sobriquet Brilliant Monster at CBS—was an object of controversy in his own right. Widely admired, he could be an object of contempt as well. Andy Rooney of *60 Minutes*, an old friend, considered him "the single most important force for good who ever worked in broadcasting." At the other end of the spectrum of opinion about Friendly, John A. Schneider, his last boss at CBS, angrily protested: "Fred Friendly was a fraud." Mili

Lerner, who toiled as a film editor under Friendly's demanding supervision, claimed, "You either had to love him or hate him; there was no in-between with Fred. No in-between. And I loved him."[1]

For the vast majority of former colleagues and members of the fourth estate, Friendly was a heroic figure. Yet some who worked closely with Friendly at CBS—like Frank Stanton and Herbert Mitgang—declined to be interviewed about Friendly, preferring silence to the airing of bitter professional conflicts. Daniel Schorr, who worked under Friendly at CBS, expressed the more typical mix of emotions felt by many of Friendly's former associates. "Fred had his detractors and his admirers," Schorr noted on National Public Radio upon learning of Friendly's death in 1998. "And some of us were ambivalent mixtures of both." Friendly could be brutal in his treatment of subordinates yet also inspire extraordinary loyalty and sacrifice on their part. How are we to weigh the mixed reviews Friendly received from his contemporaries? What are we to make of Friendly's modus operandi, his phenomenal drive, his legendary tantrums? What are we to make of his capacity for histrionics, which led Carl Sandburg to write that "Fred Friendly always looks as though he had just got off a foam-flecked horse"?[2]

Fred Friendly, the man, is no less fascinating than Fred Friendly, the broadcast journalist—as an individual and as an American archetype. Harvey Swados observed in 1967 that in Friendly "you have a man who can pique a novelist's curiosity because of the possibility that he may be an enlargement of a certain type of American." At Friendly's memorial service in 1998, Supreme Court Justice Antonin Scalia compared him to a character out of Herman Melville: "Fred Friendly, for all his experience and sophistication, was an innocent. There was certain boyishness, a Billy Budd quality to him, that came across in all his dealings." Yet there were also layers of complexity, hints of a dark side. Friendly exhibited frightful rage as well as extreme tenderness. He struggled throughout his life to balance soaring ambition and noble ideals. To acknowledge such tensions is not to demean or debunk the figure of Fred Friendly. For, as Erik Erikson wrote, "A man's conflicts represent what he 'really' is."[3]

Friendly's personal as well as professional odyssey is compelling—his inauspicious beginnings as a dyslexic child with a stutter who did poorly at school and lost his father at a young age, and the newsman's beginnings as an information officer in the eastern and European theaters during World War II, when he witnessed firsthand the liberation of the Mauthausen concentration camp and the destruction caused by the bombing of Hiroshima. Friendly's remarkable war experience helped shape the man and journalist he became. We also need to consider his relationships with a succession of mentors, among them, Rabbi William Braude, Edward R. Murrow, Dwight Eisenhower, and McGeorge Bundy, as well as Friendly's two marriages and rich family life.

Dorothy Greene Friendly, his first wife, and Ruth Mark Friendly, his second wife and widow, gave me indispensable assistance in my quest to understand the personal and professional journey of Fred Friendly. Ruth Friendly provided access to her late husband's papers, which overwhelmed the second floor of the spacious Friendly home in the Riverdale section of New York City before their transfer to Columbia University. In his crowded career Friendly did not often appear to look back, but he seemed to save everything—even a full set of his mother's canceled checks. It was a privilege to examine his papers in the very rooms he occupied for nearly half a century, where so many important scenes in his life—both professional and personal—took place.

His extended family of associates, assembled over a lifetime, provided invaluable insight into the singular experience of working with Fred Friendly. For example, Joseph F. Birk, his military aide, described Friendly's adventures during World War II as an information officer in the China-Burma-India theater. The special community of current and former CBS hands offered a particularly rich lode of information. Andy Rooney described an association with Fred Friendly that began when both were army journalists in 1944 and ended in 1998 with Friendly's death. Robert Trout shared his observations about how Fred Friendly started his career in broadcasting, and Sig Mickelson recalled hiring Friendly to work at CBS. Mike Wallace remembered his excitement—and reservations—when CBS named Friendly to be news president. Walter Cronkite discussed, with a lingering hint of resentment, the low point in his career, when Friendly removed him in 1964 as anchor of the Democratic National Convention.

Friendly's enemies at CBS weighed in as well, no one more bitterly than John A. Schneider: their ugly conflict about airing Senate Vietnam hearings led to Friendly's dramatic resignation from CBS. Schneider said of Friendly, "He had to be dealt with as a cripple; he was not a whole person."[4] Recollections by Friendly's associates at the Ford Foundation or by his students at Columbia University differ markedly as well. Yet it would be an evasion merely to present the varying portraits of Friendly, like the changing picture of Oscar Wilde's Dorian Gray. The challenge is to get behind seemingly contradictory testimony to achieve a multidimensional yet cohesive portrayal of a remarkable individual.

Of course, no interviews and documents, however revealing, can write a biography for an author. Daniel Schorr said of Friendly, "Don't ask me to write dispassionately of this passionate man." A biographer of Friendly might make the same request. Moreover, the problem of subjectivity transcends the challenges of specific biographical subjects but is inherent in the undertaking itself. According to Judith Thurman, a biographer of the French author Colette, "There is no objective biography. You are judging in what you choose to describe and the way you choose to structure the story. The question is how conscious you are of your own subjectivity and how much latitude you can allow your subject." That subjectivity is shaped, in part, by the era in which a biographer lives. The British historian E. H. Carr answers the question posed in his classic essay "What Is History?" by defining its study as "a continuous process of interaction between the historian and the facts, an unending dialogue between the present and the past."[5] The weighing and ordering of biographical data is inevitably contingent upon an author's perspective, which is grounded in a different historical moment.

My lifespan overlapped that of Fred Friendly, but we belong to different generations. World War II decisively shaped Fred Friendly's worldview and approach to journalism, whereas the Vietnam War similarly affected the consciousness of my generation and its perception of U.S. institutions. If history is a dialogue between past and present, biography is an imaginary conversation between subject and author. While viewing the subject through the lens of the present, a biographer must continually strive to re-create an individual and era lost in time. Justin Kaplan, the biographer of Mark Twain, exhorted the biographer to refrain from making tenuous interpretations or otherwise engaging in polemics: "Rather, he should try to render the experience of another person living in a world partly governed by contingency and accident. The question for a good biographer is not why but how: how it felt for the subject of the biography to live his life." Friendly would tell his children, "You have to judge the whole man." To do so means navigating between the Scylla of hagiography and the Charybdis of what Joyce Carol Oates called pathography. Biography is a great and elusive adventure. As the English literary biographer Richard Holmes wrote, biography is "a kind of pursuit, a tracking of the physical trail of someone's path through the past, a following of footsteps." He added that you can "never quite catch them. But maybe, if you were lucky, you might write about the pursuit of that fleeting figure in such a way as to bring it alive in the present."[6]

1 Ferd

FRED W. FRIENDLY CAME from a line of German Jews who were salesmen and merchants. His formative years offered hints—significant hints in retrospect but still only hints—of the man he would become. And until his early twenties he was not yet even named Fred Friendly but Ferdinand F. Wachenheimer.

His father, Samuel Wachenheimer, was the son of a locksmith who had raised his family in the East Sixties in Manhattan when the neighborhood was home to many families of German origin. Samuel was the traveling salesman for Wachenheimer Brothers, a jewelry company he owned with his two brothers. The firm made Art Deco silver jewelry with semiprecious stones. The gregarious, cigar-smoking Samuel Wachenheimer, a member of the Far Western Traveling Men's Association, journeyed widely in the United States. On one of his trips out west, he met Samson Hiram Friendly, a wealthy and influential entrepreneur in Eugene, Oregon, who invited Sam to dinner—presumably to meet his daughter Therese, who was then in her early thirties. A lengthy correspondence and courtship preceded their marriage.[1] The announcement of their engagement in a local newspaper described Therese as "an attractive brunette," noting that "her friends are legion in Portland, San Francisco and Los Angeles where she has passed much of her time since finishing school." Rabbi Jonah B. Wise officiated at their marriage, which took place on October 14, 1913, at the Hotel Osburn in Eugene. The newspaper story referred to Therese as a "prominent society girl of Eugene." Her wedding was attended by "a representative group of Eugene's old families, with a goodly number of guests from Portland and elsewhere." The paper reported that following their honeymoon, the couple would make a tour of the United States while traveling east and planned to establish their residence at 248 West 113th Street in Manhattan.[2]

Therese was the last of the three Friendly sisters to wed; her husband occupied a step below her on the social ladder. Friendly would later describe his father as a "lower middle-class businessman." Samuel Wachenheimer and his bride lived in the Morningside Heights section of Manhattan, first at on 113th Street and then on 110th Street. Their only child, Ferdinand Friendly Wachenheimer—he was called Ferd or Ferdie as a child—was born on October 30, 1915. The physically diminutive mother—she was less than five feet tall—produced an imposing baby of nine pounds. According to an album she kept, when he was eight Ferd began attending the Social Motine School on 114th Street in Manhattan and Camp Winslow in the summer. Therese recorded that he adored camp life, especially sports, and won a prize for proficiency in track and basketball. She noted that ten-year-old Ferd broke a finger playing baseball in Riverside Park. He was an avid baseball fan and an admirer of the great Jewish slugger Hank Greenberg. David Schoenbrun, Friendly's colleague at CBS, describes Friendly as "a product of the sidewalks of New York, a tough, ambitious, streetwise fighter." Schoenbrun was born the same year as Friendly and in the same neighborhood, which Schoenbrun describes as German-Jewish Harlem, on the border of Italian and Irish Harlem: "Just trying to get to school safely through roving street gangs was a daily adventure."[3]

A happy childhood memory involved five-year-old Ferd's first exposure to radio in the early days of broadcasting. He remembered that his father came home one day and said, " 'There is a new invention, Ferdinand. It's called a radiator.' He must have said a radio, but I thought a radiator because I have never heard the word before."[4] Samuel told his son they would build a radio receiver so that they could listen to a live ringside broadcast of the Jack Dempsey–Georges Carpentier heavyweight championship fight scheduled to take place on July 2, 1921. The broadcast was organized by the pioneering Westinghouse radio station KDKA in Pittsburgh together with the National Amateur Wireless Association.[5] At the time no radio stations were broadcasting to the general public in the New York area, nor were any ready-to-use radio receivers on the market. The organizers of this highly publicized experiment encouraged amateur operators to build receivers and invite listeners into their homes or into public theaters and halls across the country. Samuel and Ferd assembled a crystal radio set with a copper coil known as a cat's whisker and subsequently listened, each with one earphone, to the broadcast of the fight in which Dempsey knocked Carpentier out in the fourth round. It is estimated that 200,000 people heard the broadcast, significantly more than the approximately 1,000 people who eight months earlier had heard KDKA's historic broadcast of the returns of the 1920 presidential election. The broadcast of the fight was a landmark in generating interest in radio. As the broadcast historian Susan Douglas has written, Ferd and his father had partaken of a special male ritual of the period: "It was men and boys who brought this device into the home, and tinkering with it allowed them to assert new forms of masculine mastery while entering a realm of invisibility where certain pressures about manhood could be avoided."[6]

When Ferd was ten, in the fall of 1926, the Wachenheimer clan moved to Providence, Rhode Island, where the company's jewelry factory was located. Less than a year after the move, Samuel Wachenheimer returned in apparent good health from a business trip out west but by nightfall was taken to a hospital with a severe case of meningitis. He died two days later, on June 6, 1927, at the age of forty-seven; Ferd was eleven. For a period afterward, Ferd imagined catching a glimpse of the back of his father's head at train stations and other public places. Therese never remarried and raised Ferd on her own. When Ferd was three, Sam had written to Therese that, in case of his death, his brother Harry would look out for her interest and make sure she received his share of their business. "Have my darling Ferdinand . . . know that Daddy always loved him," he continued. "If I have had any shortcomings please overlook them. I have always idolized you and may God bless you."[7]

Therese's father, Samson Hiram Friendly, a major figure in the early history of Eugene, Oregon, made an enduring impression on Ferd, although he was only six when his grandfather died. He was born Samson Hiram Freundlich in 1840, the offspring of Bavarian German Jews named Freundlich. In 1865 he settled in Eugene, then a backwater town. He made his mark on his adopted city as entrepreneur, public official, and philanthropist. The motto of this small, inordinately energetic man was "I lead but never follow." By the end of his career, he was of one of Eugene's leading citizens, a remarkable achievement for a Jew on the frontier in the decades following the Civil War. Friendly's general store sold dry goods and clothing and shipped local products like hops, wool, and wheat to other regions. He also owned valuable real estate in Eugene and Portland, including timber and farmlands.[8] He became involved in civic affairs as a Republican, serving as vice president of the Eugene board of trade and two terms as a city council member. In 1893 he was elected mayor of Eugene. He was a leader in the campaign to get a state university established in Eugene and served for twenty years as a member of its board of regents. His daughter Therese—Fred Friendly's mother—became one of the school's first female graduates. When S. H. Friendly died in 1921, fifteen hundred people attended a memorial service funeral on campus. The university named its first dormitory, Friendly Hall, in his memory.

S. H. Friendly was an exemplar of a successful, assimilated Jew in the American West in the late nineteenth and early twentieth century. While proud of his heritage, he relegated his participation in Jewish ritual to his private life. Lengthy obituaries in Oregon's leading newspapers made scant, if any, mention of his religion. Friendly chose to be buried in his beloved Eugene rather than in the consecrated soil of the Portland synagogue. Nonetheless, in a letter to Therese, Rabbi Stephen S. Wise of the Free Synagogue of New York stressed "how much he did to bring honor to the name of his people in Eugene and throughout Oregon."[9] Fred Friendly would later pay tribute to the memory of his maternal grandfather in his home in the Riverdale section of the Bronx. An old top hat, exhibited under a glass dome, adorned a table visible from the living room. The label inside the hat read, "Moyere, Imported from Paris, S. H. Friendly, Eugene, Oregon." Behind the display hung a photograph of the merchant in front of his general store.

Therese Wachenheimer, born in 1878 as the middle of three daughters, grew up in a Gentile milieu. The sisters learned no Yiddish and attended Christian Endeavor social meetings when they were young. As teenagers, Therese and her sisters, unlike the children of more observant Jewish families, also attended the Sweet Sixteen parties of their Gentile classmates. Therese was graduated in 1898 with a bachelor of science degree from the University of Oregon, where she studied Latin, Greek, German, economics, and philosophy. She excelled in calculus and chemistry and played on the women's basketball team. By all accounts, Therese was an extremely confident and highly educated woman. Soon after her husband's death, she and Ferd moved to a two-family home at 395 Lloyd Avenue; it was located in a middle-class neighborhood of Jews and Gentiles on the more affluent east side of Providence, not far from Brown University. The house was owned by the Fisher family, which also occupied the dwelling. Rent was several hundred dollars a month. Zelda Fisher, daughter of the owners, recalled that Therese "was not a wealthy woman, but she was financially comfortable. She lived well, she ate well, but she was careful, she wasn't a spendthrift."[10] The Wachenheimer Brothers jewelry company went out of business during the Depression, but Therese received monthly checks from her sister Rosalie, who had married a successful stockbroker.[11]

Like her father, Therese was short—four feet, ten inches tall. Although she was hard of hearing and had a heart ailment, she was a highly energetic woman with an active life in community affairs. She maintained a high standard in her personal appearance and household. She dressed fashionably: a milliner, for example, designed her hats. A French-Canadian woman kept house during the day. Zelda, the landlord's daughter, remembered Therese as a "very very proper lady." If Therese Friendly Wachenheimer never had a paying job, "she was no hausfrau," according to Ruth Harris, a boarder in the early 1940s who became part of the Wachenheimer extended family. Therese was a voracious reader with great interest in American history and national and international affairs; she retired every night with a Bible and a copy of the day's *New York Times*. As a result of her activity in religious and civic organizations, Therese made a mark both within and beyond Jewish society in Providence.[12]

Therese belonged to a group of German-Jewish families for which the congregation of Temple Beth El functioned as a center of religious and especially social activity. The synagogue served the more prosperous and assimilated Jews of Providence, many of German origin, whereas the religiously conservative Temple Emmanuel had more members of Eastern European origin. In this period, Temple Beth El was the stridently Reform temple of Providence: its members referred to their rabbi as a minister, did not wear yarmulkes, and substituted confirmation for bar and bas mitzvahs. William Gordon Braude, a distinguished Talmudic scholar from Lithuania who in 1932 was named rabbi at Beth El, became a significant presence in Therese's life and that of her son. Ferd was seventeen and sitting in the fifth row at Beth El during the High Holy Days, when he first laid eyes on the twenty-five-year-old Braude. He soon impressed the congregation—and Ferd—with his learning and his dramatic flair. The spirit of tolerance and cosmopolitanism that Braude brought to his Providence rabbinate was reflected in an address he gave in 1955 at the tercentenary service of the Rhode Island Council of Churches, held at the city's First Baptist Church. He hailed the legacy of Roger Williams (who held the charter that created the colony of Rhode Island) and the multicultural makeup of Providence, detailing the contributions of the Yankees, Jews, Italians, Portuguese, Irish, and Armenians. "I love the people making up the many races of this city," Braude said. "I love the promise of their vigor and imagination."[13]

In addition to joining the Beth El Sisterhood, Therese participated in Jewish affairs on the state and national levels. She was actively involved with Hadassah as well as with the Rhode Island League of Jewish Women and the state section of the National Council of Jewish Women. She was a member of the Conference of Jews and Christians, and the *American Hebrew* named her in 1934 to an honor roll of 150 American Jews who had made a significant contribution to U.S. society. Therese did not limit her interests and activities to Jewish affairs. "She was a liberal Democrat, rabidly antiwar," according to Ruth Harris.[14] Therese was an active member of Rhode Island's League of Women Voters, Federation of Women's Clubs, and World Affairs Council. "It was unusual," Harris emphasized, "for Jewish women of that day to be so outspoken and to participate so actively in non-Jewish organizations."[15] Therese worked closely with the legendary Rhode Island social reformer and pacifist Alice Hunt, a direct descendant of Roger Williams. Hunt was once described as "armed with an iron will and the money and status to support her endeavors." As a result of her crusades, Rhode Island enacted the forty-eight-hour workweek and minimum wage laws, abolished child labor and sweatshops, and established a juvenile justice system and a division of women in the state department of labor. Hunt set up the Rhode Island chapter of the League of Women Voters and was one of the founders of the Rhode Island Committee on the Cause and Cure of War. Alice Hunt often met with Therese at her home on Lloyd Avenue.[16]

Therese's support of the League of Nations and antiwar activity earned her the nickname "Peace Wachenheimer." She became a driving force in the Committee on the Cause and Cure of War and organized the antiwar mass meetings held annually in Providence on Armistice Day during the early 1930s—a project she considered her greatest achievement. In recognition of her peace activity Therese received an invitation to attend the ratification of the Kellogg-Briand Pact of 1928, the agreement outlawing war as an instrument of foreign policy that was signed by sixty-two nations. "Ferd absorbed Therese's concern for the world," recalled Martha Kaplan, a childhood friend of Ferd's.[17] Therese Wachenheimer was a liberal, not a radical. Her reform activity was in keeping with her status as S. H. Friendly's daughter, with her standing as a proper upper-middle-class Jewish woman of German origin. Secure in her Jewish identity yet at home in the Gentile world, she did not have the sensibility of an outsider in U.S. society. As such, Therese's civic engagement—and subsequently that of her son—differed from that of the Jews of eastern European origin who grew up in the urban ghettos of America, which Irving Howe later evoked in *World of Our Fathers*. The political sensibility of these Jews was shaped to a greater degree by poverty, violent labor struggles and ideologies of radical social transformation. Ferd grew up observing and absorbing what Kaplan characterized as his mother's ardent yet genteel activism.

In addition to her involvement in community affairs, Therese was a worried and overwhelmed single parent. According to Ferd's cousin Carolene Wachenheimer, Therese the society woman "was left raising a son without a clear idea how to do so." As a child, Ferd seemed bedeviled by a host of physical and learning problems. He did not have a father to ease the transition from adolescence to adulthood. Ferd was tall for his age and physically awkward. Once, during a visit to his grandparents in Oregon, he made two trips to buy a bottle of milk; each time, he dropped and broke the bottles and was chastised as a dummkopf. He also suffered from color blindness and developed a stutter. Moreover, he was dyslexic. Ferd's difficulty in learning to read first became apparent in elementary school in New York City. Only later in life would Friendly understand that dyslexia caused the problems that plagued his formal education. In those days children with learning disabilities were misunderstood, usually chastised as slow and undisciplined—undoubtedly a source of great frustration for a bright child like Ferd. Friendly's widow, Ruth Mark Friendly, suggested that "his dyslexia, to a large extent, made Fred the man he was"—in the sense that it propelled his legendary temper and ambition.[18]

Ferd also had difficulty with spelling and penmanship, important parts of the elementary school curriculum of the day. He could write only block letters. Math remained a lifelong nemesis. Moreover, his color blindness meant the only colors he could recognize were blue and yellow. He was humiliated when, instructed to color a cow brown, he colored it green. "I was labeled," he later recalled. "And I began to think I was stupid." He finally learned to read in the fourth grade, thanks to Margaret Forhan, a devoted teacher at P.S. 165 on West 109th Street to whom he remained eternally grateful.[19]

After the move to Providence and the death of her husband, Therese continued to be preoccupied by Ferd's myriad problems in and out of school. His slight lisp and stammer prompted her to arrange speech therapy at a school in Providence for the deaf and dumb, as such institutions were then called. She strived to keep him on the straight and narrow. Once when he bought some marbles, Fred stole a suede marble bag. When Therese found out, she sent him to return it, telling him, "Son, never lie. You have to be very smart to lie, and you are not smart enough." Because of her son's academic and behavior problems at school, Therese made an appointment for a consultation with an elderly "nerve doctor" when Ferd was twelve or thirteen. During the consultation, the doctor asked Ferd, "Do you abuse yourself?" Ferd did not understand the question but nonetheless replied with an emphatic no. Friendly was struck by— and always remembered—the unpleasant, musty odor of old age in the psychiatrist's office.[20]

In the eighth and ninth grades, the last two years of junior high school in the Providence school system, Ferd did passable work, getting grades primarily in the seventies and low eighties. His highest grade was 85 in American history; the lowest, 63 in French. After he entered Hope Street High School in the fall of 1931, his academic performance progressively worsened. As an eleventh grader, his marks were all in the low sixties and worse: he received a 62 in English, for example, and 49 in advanced algebra.[21]

A classmate at Hope Street High School recalled Ferd's lack of concentration in English class, a sense that he was not sufficiently stimulated, that his mind was racing ahead.[22] Unlike his more academically successful circle of friends, Ferd appeared disengaged in school. However, his lackluster academic performance did not appear to weigh on him. "He was always very charismatic and creative," his cousin Carolene remembered, "but he just didn't like to study, or couldn't or wouldn't." His contemporaries at Hope Street High School remembered him many years later as gregarious and surprisingly self-confident, a prankster with a joie-de-vivre. Dorothy Greene, his first wife, a Providence native, recalled his reputation in this period as "a cutup."[23] Hyperactive and gangly, with oversized hands and feet, he would play the class clown. Zelda Fisher described him as "very outgoing, an extrovert if I ever knew one. Of course, he didn't care about school—period! That bothered Therese very much." Also to Therese's dismay, he would organize pranks outside school. Once, for example, he called in an enormous order at a Piggly Wiggly grocery store and then drove down in his friend Norman Fain's car to watch the order being filled. It was difficult for the diminutive

Therese to discipline her strapping son. On one occasion, he ripped pages out of a book of Shakespeare to stuff into wet shoes. Therese, furious, called for reinforcements: family friend Joel J. (Joe) Pincus came over and punched Ferd. Pincus, who worked at the Outlet Department Store and whose family figured prominently in the life of Temple Beth El, assumed the role of substitute father and disciplinarian during Fred's youth.[24]

Ferd's cousin Carolene was the daughter of Harry and Cordelia Wachenheimer, in whose home Ferd spent considerable time to get away from his mother's anxious scrutiny. Cordelia, called Cordie, had attended college and exhibited a lively interest in literature and current affairs. She and Therese lived near each other in Providence and spoke daily. Cordie was fond of Ferd and supportive of his endeavors when he became older. According to Carolene, "He felt closer to her than he did to his own mother." Carolene, six years younger than her cousin and also an only child, later wrote that they "were like brother and sister, she the adoring younger sister." She also recalled that a sibling-like rivalry developed between them. According to Carolene, Ferd needed to be the center of attention, and often treated her in a bullying manner. In a family setting, he seemed to her to be a very unhappy and angry child, and as he got older he remained "an unpleasant young man to me." Yet his peers saw little of his aggressive side; indeed, they loved him. Most girls found him charming. In retrospect, Carolene attested to his appeal, his sometimes difficult but also endearing personality, his dynamism, and unexpected displays of warmth.[25]

"He never seemed very ambitious to me," Elaine Frank, a high school classmate, remembered. "He always seemed to live in the moment, in the present, rather than to dwell on future plans." Another classmate, Florence Markoff, recalled Ferd many years later as "a gangling, awkward kind of kid, and certainly not the one that you would pick to become as talented and as famous as he became." Nonetheless, "he had a certain self-assurance about him that frankly a lot of boys his age didn't have," according to Alice Fox, who lived across the street from him on Lloyd Avenue. When Ferd was about fifteen, he became her first boyfriend.[26] By all accounts, Ferd was articulate, often the center of attention, popular with his peers. He did not have the sensibility of a misfit and outcast, and he occupied a secure position in a tight-knit group of middle- and upper-middle-class Jews who attended the same high school, synagogue, and dinner parties.

Temple Beth El served as a center for social and cultural as well as religious activity for the upper crust of Providence's Reform community. Here, for example, Ferd participated in plays and first developed an interest in theater. Rabbi Braude was a frequent guest in the Wachenheimer household. Therese cultivated Braude as a mentor for her son, who sustained a lifelong friendship with the rabbi; however, Braude was too much the reflective philosopher to offer Therese practical advice on raising her boisterous adolescent. Braude "had his head up in the clouds all the time," Zelda Fisher said. "He was a scholar. He always had his nose in his books."[27] Ferd would frequently mimic him, parodying his accent and serious moral tone. If Braude could not improve Ferd's academic performance or moderate his boisterousness, as Therese had hoped, the rabbi provided the young man with something more important. As Friendly would reflect many years later:

My own special bond with Bill was unique. He was a scholar and I was not. He had become a legend in the rabbinate—a teacher of teachers, and I, eight years his junior was an underachiever with a despairing mother who constantly sought the Rabbi's affinity with God to determine what would happen to her gangling, awkward Ferdinand. Dyslexia was not a word in our vocabulary in those days. Bill told her not to worry. He seemed to have detected some flair—some hidden drive within me that must have escaped my other bewildered teachers.[28]

Temple Beth El remained an important social anchor for Ferd. The guests at Therese's dinner parties came from the Temple Beth El/Hope Street High School milieu, where Ferd made some of his closest lifelong friends. Among them were Harold Hassenfeld, whose family owned the Hasbro Toy Company, and Norman Fain, son of a prosperous local entrepreneur. The larger Fain household—Norman had a brother and sister—became another home-away-from-home. Ferd and Norman became lifelong friends. Ferd's self-assurance—his problems at school notwithstanding—sprang from a socially cohesive and supportive environment, the first of a succession of close-knit support systems he would replicate throughout his life.

A seemingly happy and secure as a child, Fred Friendly acknowledged late in life that his learning problems affected him more than he had let on during his childhood. In 1995, three years before his death, Friendly spoke about his self-doubts as a child in a talk at a school for students with learning disabilities in Providence. At times, as he recalled, he had sensed that he was just as smart as the other students. "It wasn't easy, though, because I had the feeling that most people thought I wasn't bright at all—and sometimes I began to believe that myself." He worried about the kind of work he would be capable of doing later in life. At the same time he recalled the lure of broadcasting, how he had been an avid listener of radio. He loved listening to Eddie Cantor, the news commentator Boake Carter, and the reports broadcast four times a day from the newsroom of the *Providence Journal*. Friendly recalled that "one thing I could do—I could speak well—and I had a good vocabulary." He described how "I would stand looking out onto the street with an imaginary microphone set on my radiator and I would report the goings-on of the day—or what I saw happening outside—whatever came into my mind." It reassured him, even gave him confidence, to "stand by the window in my bedroom—on the second floor of my house thinking, I could be a radio announcer—I could be on radio."[29] As a boy he dreamed of performing on radio in a way he could not in the classroom.

Ferd first spoke into a live radio microphone when he was in the eleventh grade at Hope Street High School. He read from *The Valiant*, a one-act play by H. E. Porter and R. Middlemass that had been filmed in 1929 and starred Paul Muni. Ferd did the dramatic reading with Elaine Frank. He played a prisoner on death row; she, a visitor who thought that the prisoner might be her long-lost brother. The reading took place in the studio of radio station WJAR, a member of AT&T's original *Eveready Hour* chain and one of the original NBC affiliates; the station was located on the top floor of the Outlet Department Store on Weybosset Street in Providence.[30]

Four years would pass before Ferd began his broadcasting career in earnest. He had not done passing work in the eleventh grade; one of his former classmates speculated that he was asked to leave Hope Street High School.[31] Therese enrolled him in the Roxbury School in Cheshire, Connecticut, to make up courses in the summer of 1933 and attend during the following academic year. Founded in 1794, Roxbury was an all-male preparatory school with a classical curriculum. Under the long-time headmaster Arthur Sheriff, the school's mission was to nurture underachievers through a supportive environment of individual attention and small classes. The school also offered a postgraduate year for students who needed additional study to get into Yale University or another Ivy League school.

At Roxbury, Ferd reversed his academic decline and got passing grades in English (70), physics (70), and American civilization (66) but continued to struggle in math (61) and French (61). Those were his grades as of April 1, 1934, when the Roxbury School sent his transcript to Brown University, which Ferd had designated in the school's yearbook as his "Intended College." One wonders whether he really thought he might be accepted or whether he applied to save face because so many of his fellow students were headed for Ivy League schools. He was graduated that spring, although his quixotic attempt to gain entrance to Brown failed. The quotation that accompanied Ferd's photograph in the yearbook, "Kindness nose no repentance," might have been an anti-Semitic jibe or just a reference to the size of his nose.[32] The yearbook also noted that he was nicknamed "Wacky" and that he played on the hockey team. A lifetime later, in 1989, he would return as commencement speaker at Roxbury, by then renamed the Cheshire School. In his remarks, he thanked the school for enabling him to complete his high school education and strengthen his self-confidence. While there he told a teacher that the individual attention provided by devoted teachers and the required study periods had proved crucial. He also appreciated the warmth of the weekly Sunday night teas in the headmaster's home, although his size and awkwardness made it difficult for him to balance a tea cup on his knees.[33]

Instead of Brown, Ferd attended Nichols College, a two-year business school in Dudley, Massachusetts, from 1934 to 1936. Ferd threw himself fully into extracurricular activities, especially journalism and theater, and established himself as a presence at Nichols. He became editor of the school newspaper and yearbook. Ferd was the driving force behind a revival of student theatrical productions at Nichols. He headed the drama society and produced Ceiling Zero by Frank Wead. Ferd played the role of Jake Lee, a ground commander in the aviation melodrama made into a film that year by Howard Hawks. However, Ferd had barely passing grades. During his first year he got a B+ in journalism, his best grade, and D's in English, economics, and law. He completed his second and final year with three D's and two C's in his principal classes. When Ferd was graduated from Nichols with a two-year degree, a grateful Therese established the Wachenheimer Trophy for the student who contributed most to dramatics at Nichols.[34]

Nonetheless, Therese was alarmed when Ferd, newly purchased makeup kit in hand, returned to Providence with the thought of embarking on a career in the theater. Instead, she arranged through Joe Pincus for Ferd to work in the rug department of the Outlet Department Store, where Pincus was credit manager. It was an improbable career move, given Ferd's color blindness. He continued to be active in amateur theater, especially at Pembroke College, the women's division of Brown University, where male actors were in great demand. He appeared, for example, in *The Front Page*, Ben Hecht's play set in the city room of a Chicago newspaper. Ferd toyed with the idea of starting a local shopping newspaper, then of scriptwriting, before refocusing his energies on radio.

Mowry Lowe, a pioneer in Rhode Island broadcasting, served as Ferd's earliest mentor and role model as a broadcaster.[35] Lowe worked for WEAN, Providence's first commercial radio station, which was originally housed in Shepard's Department Store. John Shepard, who owned department stores in the Northeast, had developed a chain of affiliated radio stations—thirteen by 1936—known as the Yankee Network. Lowe came from a working-class Jewish family and, like Ferd, was a member of Temple Beth El. Lowe had been graduated from Northeastern University with a law degree and began working at WEAN in 1931. In the early days of radio, broadcasters assumed many roles. In his career at WEAN, Lowe worked as an announcer, did sports and general reporting, presided over concerts and quiz shows, and even sold time. He became best known for a daily man-in-the-street show called *Sidewalk Backtalk*, which was broadcast live in front of the Crown Hotel in downtown Providence, where WEAN's studios were located.

Lowe made a great impression when Ferd saw him in person for the first time, apparently in the summer of 1935, before Ferd left Providence for his final year at Nichols College. "Wearing a white suit and white shoes, rimless glasses, holding a WEAN carbon microphone," Friendly later recalled, "he was surrounded by a cluster of adoring women with a few men watching them." Lowe was doing *Sidewalk Backtalk*. Friendly added: "My impression then (I was 20) was . . . that this glamorous, skilled, relaxed communicator was the exact model of what I might aspire to be. . . . He was my first hero, and in-between that first inspiration on Weybosset Street and wherever it was that my career took me." Friendly declared at Lowe's funeral in 1973, "Mowry was at once a father figure, a colleague, and a brother."[36]

That first encounter made an impression on Lowe as well: "I remember him as a tall, awkward, gangling youth who approached me after one of the shows." Ferd expressed his desire to break into radio. The broadcaster invited him to the WEAN studios, where they spoke at length: "I was impressed with his flamboyant manner and dramatic approach—the waving of the arms—the pointing of the hands—the changing expressions in his face—all of which impelled me to help as much as I could." Ferd recognized that in landing a job in the early 1930s at WEAN, Lowe—"hardly the prototype of the WASP cultured announcer that management was looking for"—had crossed a significant barrier and helped paved the way for his own entry into radio.[37]

While he was still working at the Outlet, Ferd approached WEAN's general manager, James Jennison, for a job. Jennison initially turned him down, suggesting that he try to break into broadcasting at less-established stations in the New England area. Ferd unsuccessfully applied for jobs at other stations in Rhode Island and Massachusetts. He then returned to WEAN with an idea: a series of five-minute biographies to be called *Footprints in the Sands of Time*. Joe Pincus's recommendation was decisive in getting Ferd the opportunity for a trial run of his program idea. However, Jennison insisted on a name change. Ferdinand Friendly Wachenheimer adopted his mother's maiden name as his own and became Fred W. Friendly. Although he would change his name legally, family and friends in Providence continued to call him Ferd. (At CBS, he would tell the secretaries to put through immediately any callers asking for "Ferd.") The name of the program came from "A Psalm of Life," a poem by Henry Wadsworth Longfellow, and was suggested by Ferd's aunt Cordie, in whose Providence home he would sometimes rehearse the program in a bellowing voice that could be heard by neighbors.[38] Each episode began with this stanza from Longfellow:

Lives of great men will remind us
We can make our lives sublime,
And, departing, leave behind us
Footprints in the sands of time—

Five mornings a week, listeners were challenged to guess a famous person's identity based on a dramatic recitation of facts about the individual's career. The first broadcast featured Charles P. Steinmetz of General Electric. Early subjects ranged from King Henry VIII to Nicolò Paganini, from Mohandas Gandhi to the Soong Sisters, from J. Robert Oppenheimer to Marion Anderson. The program suggested what became clearer in the course of Fred's career: his fascination with great figures, past and present. These minibiographies forced Friendly to hone his radio production skills. "To tell their stories in five minutes," David Schoenbrun later reflected, "gave Fred invaluable training in tight writing, tight editing, making the most of every second of time."[39]

Mowry Lowe helped Friendly produce *Footprints*, which was first broadcast for six months on a trial basis—without advertisers or a salary for its host. A publicity photograph from the period shows a youthful and uncharacteristically somber Fred Friendly in a three-piece suit sitting before a WEAN microphone, holding a script in one hand and gesticulating with the other, a stopwatch by his side. Lowe finally sold *Footprints* to a Providence laundry company on a five-day-a-week basis. "We both sat there and laughed and laughed and laughed . . . in joy and fulfillment," Friendly later remembered. Fred was paid $20.50 a week, from which Shepard deducted a 15 percent agency fee. After listening to the first broadcast, Joe and Minnie Pincus asked Ferd about a rattling sound they had heard. The noise was caused by Ferd's nervousness—his script shook in his hands. For two years, he would dampen the pages to mute the evidence of his anxiety.[40]

Fred worked out of an office he shared with an architect in the Old Colony Bank Building in Providence. They also shared a secretary, Martha Kaplan, a friend of Ferd's family and a graduate of Radcliffe College, who was paid about $17 a week. Ferd's letterhead read, "Fred Friendly Co., A Radio Production Service to Advertising Agencies." He produced, for example, a series of radio ads with his friend Norman Fain for the Fain family tire business. Fred also did occasional work for the advertising agency of another Providence friend, Bo Bernstein. However, *Footprints* absorbed the bulk of his time. When Fred moved his office to suite 308 of the Biltmore Hotel, he had stationery for *Footprints on the Sands of Time* printed, with small footprints running down the margin on the left. The slogan at the bottom of the page read, "Friendly Scripts Make Friendly Clients." Ferd would research *Footprints* at the local public library and return to the office to write the scripts. "I can still see him pacing back and forth," said Kaplan, who worked for nearly two years as his office manager and editor.[41] She was impressed with his vocabulary and breadth of knowledge. He was incapable of spelling and inattentive to detail but "very inventive, with tremendous curiosity and imagination." She recalled Fred in his mid-twenties as an "explosive character" for whom she enjoyed working. In four years, he broadcast more than a thousand of the five-minute portraits, which became a popular local program in Providence. In 1942 the Decca Company reissued the program on records that were played in other radio markets. Walter Cronkite remembered hearing—as a young man working for an NBC radio station in Oklahoma City—Friendly's raucous voice on *Footprints in the Sands of Time*; Cronkite could hardly have anticipated that its creator would one day be his boss.[42]

While producing *Footprints*, Fred continued his interest in theater. He produced short dramas for WEAN with a circle of actors from Pembroke and Brown. Kaplan, his part-time secretary, emphasized that in this period his interests were eclectic and creative, that he had not yet focused exclusively or even primarily on news and public affairs. She could not recall Friendly's engaging her in discussions of the New Deal or other political issues of the period. Under the tutelage of Mowry Lowe, he took on a wide range of journalistic and nonjournalistic roles at WEAN. He did an occasional announcing stint and often worked with Lowe on *Sidewalk Backtalk*. He also worked on *The Streets of the City*, a program that highlighted Providence neighborhoods. With Fred's assistance, Lowe conducted numerous quiz shows that were carried live on WEAN. For example, in 1938 they broadcast a quiz show called *What's Your Answer?* from various venues, including the RKO-Albee Theater in Providence. The program posed questions about U.S. history and names in the news. Ferd would also occasionally produce a short dramatic piece for broadcast.[43]

Mowry Lowe's work at WEAN included news broadcasts and an occasional news special. A high point in Lowe's career at WEAN was his coverage—with Friendly's assistance—of the devastating hurricane and flood of September 1938 in Rhode Island. WEAN became an indispensable source of information during the storm, which killed more than six hundred, injured thousands, and destroyed countless homes. "It was, I suppose," Friendly later reflected, "the first momentous news event which either of us had ever covered." Their reports were carried throughout New England and beyond. Fred functioned as Lowe's factotum during the twenty-four hours when Lowe broadcast nonstop. WEAN was the only station in Providence able to stay on the air. Friendly remembered seeing Lowe lean out the second-floor window of the Crown Hotel, where the studios were located, to interview stranded flood victims. At one point, Friendly was dispatched to get sandwiches. When he returned, Weybosset Street had turned into a turbulent river, and he had to cross holding the sandwiches above his head. Lowe read bulletins from across the state, identifying the missing. The governor of Rhode Island appeared in WEAN's studio during the night to make a report. "The next day the NBC Blue Network did a round-robin report from many areas of the flood," Friendly recalled, "and Mowry asked me to help him write it. It was the first time either of us had anything to do with an important network news program."[44] Lowe and Friendly also produced minidocumentaries about such topics as the sinking of the *Titanic*, with Lowe simultaneously juggling narration and sound effects.

In 1938, the year of the Munich crisis as well as of the Rhode Island hurricane, Lowe and Friendly produced a documentary on the fall of Czechoslovakia. Three years later, as war raged in Europe and the Far East, Friendly faced the prospect of being drafted. On May 14, in response to a draft notice, he replied with a request for a temporary deferment on both personal and professional grounds. "I have a mother partly dependent upon me," he wrote, noting that she had just had major surgery. "For obvious reasons I don't think it advisable to leave her alone until she has regained her original state of health."[45] In his letter to the draft board, Fred also made a case for giving him a civilian assignment in the propaganda field, based on his experience in broadcasting and in running a radio production company. He exhibited considerable enterprise in attempting to secure the right assignment. "I think you will be interested in knowing," he wrote his draft board, "that I have already contacted General Elio of the War Department in Washington, offering my services and the services of this office in the field we know best." He indicated that he planned a follow-up visit the next week to the War Department in Washington, D.C., so he could seek the "spot where I can best serve my country." In addition, Friendly reported that he had enlisted the Town Criers of Rhode Island, a civic organization, to get the assistance of U.S. Senator Francis Green of Rhode Island in securing an appropriate assignment. "In the event that I am selected or that I enlist," he concluded, "I feel that it is my duty to the clients we serve, to the radio stations . . . that I so arrange our routine that, at least, a part of our activities may continue during my absence."[46] In his appeal for a deferment, Fred by implication embellished the financial support he gave his mother and the magnitude of "Fred Friendly Co." Yet his concern about Therese and desire to put his communications skills at the service of his country were unquestionably sincere.

In July 1941, two months after he sent the letter to his draft board, twenty-five-year-old Friendly got an opportunity to display his prowess as an advocate of democracy and U.S. military preparedness when the U.S. Navy Air Center opened in Quonset, Rhode Island. The Mutual Broadcasting System, of which WEAN was now an affiliate, carried his live report of the commissioning ceremony. He did not limit himself to reporting on the ceremonies and remarks of dignitaries. In an impassioned delivery just short of a shout, Friendly hailed the completion of the ambitious project in less than a year. Listeners learned that enough asphalt was used to build a two-lane highway from Quonset to Boston, enough telephone wires to run a line to California:

> Brick from Barrington joined steel from Bethlehem, and glass from Pittsburgh, and pipe from Everett, and timber from Oregon and Washington, and a city was rising out of swampland. Railroads were built through the heart of Quonset and every day through the dead of winter the old, odd whistle of the locomotive screamed against the winds of the day. Overshoes covered frozen feet, and thick work gloves protected numbed fingers as the hammer kept resounding through the snows of January and the winds of March.

Quonset, he said, was built in a distinctively American way, without directives from a dictator: "This is democracy in action for you who claim that democracy is slow. Here at Quonset is a melting pot of O'Neils, Murphys, Gustafsons, and Joneses, and Cohens and Marinos. America's melting pot." He concluded, "From here, a war may well be won or lost."[47]

More than a half century after the ceremony at Quonset, a 78-rpm vinyl record of Friendly's broadcast turned up at a yard sale in Rhode Island and was played in 1995 on the *Lost and Found Sound* series of National Public Radio (NPR). The report, characterized as "a piece of radio poetry" with "a kind of Sandburgian-Whitmanian flow to it," remains a powerful listening experience, remarkable for its sweeping imagery and passionate delivery.[48] Questioned by the NPR producer about his reportage, the eighty-year-old Friendly replied, "I am dyslexic. Who even dreamed of such a condition in my early days, but that leads me to guess that what I said at Quonset was a combination of spontaneous remarks, notes and writing. I was always a good talker."[49] The chance discovery of a recording with the Quonset story—Friendly had no idea it had been recorded—provides the earliest surviving example of Friendly's work as a broadcast journalist.

In the Quonset broadcast, Friendly is drawing on contemporary journalistic models, especially the newsreel and the documentary film. Newsreel film crews were not equipped to cover breaking news and specialized in ceremonial events like the dedication at Quonset: parades, awards, and ship christenings. Because most film footage was silent except for background music, the newsreel announcer had to add stirring narration to sound effects to make an event come alive. An influential form of the newsreel of the period, with editions for both movie theaters and radio stations, was *The March of Time*. In addition, the Depression years had spawned documentaries like Pare Lorenz's *The Plow That Broke the Plains* (1936), which combined powerful images and the music of Virgil Thompson to generate support for New Deal agricultural policies. Friendly's Quonset report contained the dramatic narrative techniques of *The March of Time* as well as the social thrust of *The Plow That Broke the Plains*. If he drew upon existing journalistic models, Friendly's broadcast also pointed ahead, anticipating the "why we fight" informational productions that followed U.S. entry into World War II. The Quonset broadcast also reflected the pluralistic ideal that Rabbi William Braude would express in his paean to the diversity and tolerance of Providence.

Friendly's report on American preparedness from Quonset came more than six months before Pearl Harbor. It revealed Friendly's seriousness of purpose, as a broadcaster and as a citizen, in the spring of 1941. By that time, he had overcome childhood hardships—especially the loss of his father and serious learning disabilities—to establish himself as a broadcaster in Providence. He had regular work as a freelancer but not as a full-time staff member at WEAN. *Footprints in the Sands of Time* afforded him a substantial local following and modest income, supplemented by occasional radio production work for advertisers. However, his income was not adequate to make him self-sufficient. He continued to be a dependent of his mother, in whose home he still lived. Therese continued to worry about his future professional and financial prospects.[50] He did not receive the draft deferment he requested. For Friendly, 1941 was a year of coming of age, of endings and new possibilities. Many of his childhood friends had established themselves professionally and started families. He learned that Elaine Frank, with whom he read *The Valiant* on WJAR when they were eleventh-graders at Hope Street High School, was getting married. His nostalgic letter of congratulation, written shortly before the Quonset broadcast, evoked their shared childhood. "I remember a little curly-headed kid with the most brilliant red hair I ever saw," Friendly wrote. "I remember a rich clear voice which could always outact my raucous baritone. I remember Saturday night parties and Sunday afternoon teas, and rides out to Deutschland's [ice-cream parlor], and trips to Summer theaters and even an expedition to WJAR."[51]

The increasing possibility of the entry of the United States into World War II contributed further to Fred's sense of impending change. He was drafted in September 1941. "It really broke her heart when he went into the service," Alice Fox said of his mother, the peace activist and anxious parent. Thanks to his radio experience, Fred would eventually be assigned to the Information and Education Section of the army in the China-Burma-India theater. The war would at once interrupt and propel his career in broadcasting. Ruth Harris, the family friend who lived in Fred's room during his absence, was well positioned to observe the impact of the war on him. In retrospect, she insists, it "made him the man he was."[52]

2 "My Rhodes Scholarship"

IN SEPTEMBER 1941, Fred Friendly was inducted into the army. He went to Fort Devens in Massachusetts for basic training and was assigned to KP. He always remembered the unpleasant task of wearing overalls and dishing out liver and onions and how his body afterward reeked of the food. He found this work intolerable and lobbied actively to be reassigned to a position related to his experience in radio.[1] He succeeded: following basic training, Friendly was assigned to the Signal Corps at Fort Monmouth, New Jersey, where he arrived in December 1941, the month Pearl Harbor was attacked and the United States entered the war. The Signal Corps, the military communications arm of the army founded in 1860, had pioneered the use of the telegraph, radio, and radar in combat. Friendly worked as a basic training instructor for army radio operators and telephone linesmen at Fort Girt, about twenty miles north of the main base at Fort Monmouth. He had responsibility for training units of fifteen to twenty men for four to six weeks. He instructed them in drill and exercise, accompanied them to the shooting range, educated them about the mission of the Signal Corps, taught the basics of signal communication, and instructed troops about the origins of the war.[2] In May 1942, he was promoted from corporal to sergeant and subsequently became the chief instructor at the Signal Corps training center. Jerome Corwin, an acquaintance from Providence who also was assigned to Fort Monmouth, recalled how Friendly used his large frame, booming voice, and flair for the theatrical to good effect, how he shrieked "gas attack," for example, to test his unit's ability to use gas masks. "Fred, even at that point," he observed, "made everything very dramatic." Corwin underscored Friendly's high profile at Fort Monmouth despite his relatively low rank: "He was the kind of a guy who, although he was a buck sergeant, was almost *running* the camp." Corwin also remembered Friendly's keen desire to go overseas to an active theater of combat.[3]

Friendly enlisted the help of his superior officers at Fort Monmouth in gaining an assignment with greater responsibilities for orienting recruits for combat. On August 20, 1942, one of his superior officers wrote him a letter of introduction that described Friendly as "an excellent disciplinarian" and "an exceptionally qualified drillmaster." The officer went on to characterize Friendly as "a teacher of unusual ability" with "the ability to communicate his enthusiasm to others," adding that he had exhibited "marked executive ability." That fall, Friendly was transferred to the Western Signal Corps Training Center at Camp Kohler, outside Sacramento. The public relations officer at Camp Kohler, James Armsey, was responsible for creating one of the orientation and information programs for new troops that the War Department in Washington had decided would be an integral part of basic training and the war effort. Armsey selected First Lieutenant Gilbert Edward (Ed) Clark, who had B.A. and M.A. degrees in journalism from Syracuse University, to head the unit. Armsey and Clark went through personnel cards and identified two men at Camp Kohler with radio backgrounds to work under Clark: a radio announcer from Omaha named Russ Baker (no relation to Russell Baker of the *New York Times*) and Fred Friendly. At the end of October 1942, Friendly was appointed to work as a staff sergeant in Clark's unit. Around this time Friendly also received an inquiry from Jack Kapp of Decca Records expressing interest in issuing on vinyl the one thousand segments of *Footprints in the Sands of Time* that Friendly had produced for WEAN. Would he accept a fee of "25 each"? Decca was offering twenty-five *dollars*, not the twenty-five cents that Friendly originally assumed, so the deal produced a windfall of $25,000.[4]

In November 1942, Clark drew on his journalism training to establish an ambitious education and orientation program at Camp Kohler, and Friendly emerged as his chief aide. The premise behind their efforts was that an informed soldier would be a more motivated and effective combatant. Each day recruits heard a fifteen-minute news report broadcast on the base radio station and received mimeographed news reports. Monday nights were devoted to films. A huge wall map in front of the base auditorium displayed colored pins showing battle lines, which were updated every day. Near the end of basic training the troops attended a formal orientation program consisting of ten lectures on such topics as the nature of fascism and Japanese expansionism. In a written evaluation of Friendly, Clark emphasized the great "imagination and histrionic ability" with which Friendly dramatized the background and events of the war. As a capstone for the orientation process, Friendly also developed a program broadcast on the base radio station called *Sergeant Quiz* that drew on his experience producing the quiz show with Mowry Lowe on WEAN. For two hours on Saturday mornings, Friendly would fire orders or questions at four competing groups of ten men representing different platoons. Each team might be asked to perform army routines such as executing foot drills or identifying bugle calls. The men also would stand before oversized maps as Friendly asked questions about geography or about the historical background to the war. *Collier's* magazine did a story on Friendly's program. In the summer of 1943, the Orientation and Publications Section of the War Department in Washington expressed interest in getting information about the work of Clark and Friendly so it might serve as a model for other education and orientation programs. In response Clark praised Friendly's contribution and suggested that Friendly be debriefed in Washington about his innovations at Camp Kohler.[5]

Friendly and Clark developed a close professional and personal relationship at Camp Kohler. The tenor of Clark's interaction with Friendly was collegial despite Clark's standing as superior officer. Clark's widow, Lyla (Lee) Sween Clark, recalled the compatibility of the two men, how they "they both treated one another as equals." Ed Clark was a dynamic young officer who would soon be promoted to major and receive an important assignment overseas. (After the war he would join the State Department and receive postings as U.S. ambassador to Mali, Senegal, and Gambia.) Lee Clark remembered her initial impression of Friendly—a giant of a man, larger than life, bursting with energy and inventiveness: "My husband used to say, 'Fred would have a hundred creative ideas a day, but some of them were really off the wall. Out of those one hundred would come some excellent and effective ideas.'" Friendly frequently socialized with the Clarks in their cottage off base. Friendly was good company; the Clarks enjoyed his sense of fun. Lee Clark fondly recalled their playing charades, with Fred enacting *Love's Labour's Lost*. Her husband became Friendly's mentor and protector during the war. The two men complemented each other. According to Armsey, Ed Clark was "less flamboyant, less propulsive, more thoughtful, more steadied in his views and judgment." Lee Clark emphasized that Friendly was so "dramatic, dynamic, aggressive in a sense . . . that he really couldn't be contained in the normal sense." Armsey characterized Clark's relationship with Friendly as permissive. Ed Clark, for example, let Friendly record *Footprint* biographies that he then mailed to Providence for broadcast on WEAN five mornings a week.[6]

During his stay in Camp Kohler, Friendly also became acquainted with the family of Paul Guttman, a local man who had drawn Fred's name to come to his home to celebrate Passover. Fred, who insisted on washing the dishes, became part of the household. The frequent weekend guest made a strong impression on the Guttmans' daughter, who was then about eleven or twelve years old: "My early memories of Fred were that of this big, confident, boisterous young man . . . showing up at our house on Sunday mornings. We'd find him asleep in a big chair in our living room when we got up."[7] Fred became a lifelong friend of the Guttmans; Paul would assist Fred in one of his first broadcasting ventures after the war.

Ed Clark left Camp Kohler in September 1943, after he and Friendly had worked together for about a year, for a new assignment: information and education officer at the headquarters of the China-Burma-India (CBI) command in New Delhi. Clark, who assumed his new post in late November, requested that Friendly and Russ Baker—his Camp Kohler team—be assigned to his unit. Meanwhile Friendly was contacted by Brigadier General S. H. Sherrill, the former commander of Camp Kohler, who now was in charge of the training center for the aircraft warning unit at Drew Field in Tampa, Florida. Sherrill arranged that Friendly be reassigned to the training center at Drew Field to mount an orientation program like that at Camp Kohler. Sherrill was pleased with the results, thanking Friendly on December 29, 1943, as he was about to leave for India: "Your zeal, initiative, and drive have been an inspiration to us all in this command." He added that he had reluctantly agreed to Friendly's departure from Drew Field only because a commander in an active theater of operations had sought Friendly's transfer.[8]

Clark had had unanticipated difficulties in getting Friendly assigned to his command. When he arrived in New Delhi, Clark had written Lee of his appeals to Washington to get Friendly: "I really want the lad now in the worst way." Friendly, meanwhile, wrote Ed Clark regularly. "I shall save Friendly's letters to show you some day," Clark wrote Lee, "—they are classics." In December Washington rejected Ed Clark's request for Friendly because of a technicality. Clark wrote Lee that he and his superiors were trying several simultaneous approaches to get the decision overturned.[9] Friendly later told Joseph F. Birk how he went to the headquarters of the War Department in Washington, D.C., which exercised direct control over army information activities, to get the decision reversed. Birk was a staff sergeant in the public relations office of the Signal Corps in New Delhi who later worked as an aide to Friendly in the CBI theater. He claimed that Friendly went to the headquarters of General George Marshall to promote his plans for doing orientation and information work in the CBI theater. Friendly "ended up coming to the China-Burma-India Theater *from Washington*," Birk surmised, "because I guess he conned his way into the office of the chief of staff, General Marshall, and Marshall said, 'This is a great correspondent, we'll send him out and let him do his job.'" However, neither Lee Clark nor James Armsey recalled Friendly's ever mentioning an encounter with Marshall. Perhaps Friendly had met with an aide in Marshall's office. Armsey, although skeptical of the story, conceded that a meeting with Marshall could not be ruled out: "Yes, it's conceivable. I think Fred might be able to talk himself into anything. It would be in character."[10]

On January 25, 1944, Sherrill gave Friendly a letter in which the general recommended that Friendly's skills in orientation—"Sergeant Friendly's talents in this line are unique"—be used at points along his route to New Delhi. By the beginning of February 1944, Friendly was on his way to his new assignment—with permission to carry excess baggage of educational materials—as an orientation specialist under Major Clark in the China-Burma-India theater. Friendly, who had been promoted to master sergeant, traveled to India by sea, arriving in Bombay in mid-April en route to New Delhi. He wrote his mother that "no heat will ever impress me as did the scorching weather of that great ship with its load of homesick Yanks. One of the stirring memories I have . . . more memorable than my first day in school, or my first shirt with tails or that Ice Cream Sundae with Alice Fox or the day [F]ootprints was born, is my . . . vibrant recollection of coming down the gang-plan[k] with 200 pounds of gear across my back and seeing the people and buildings and filth of India."[11] Friendly had arrived in Bombay just as two ships loaded with ammunition blew up, causing many casualties and setting off secondary fires and explosions that lasted for three days. He volunteered to do rescue work on the ships throughout the first twenty-four hours, for which he later received the Soldier's Medal. "Displaying marked leadership ability," the citation for the medal read, "Sergeant FRIENDLY organized and, at great personal risk, led details for removing injured and dead, salvaging ammunition and supplies from warehouses, and clearing debris from the deck area."[12]

Friendly called Clark on the telephone, excitedly screaming his report of events in Bombay over the static. "Talked to 'the hulk' today," Clark wrote Lee on April 16, 1944. "He's been in a week and having a mighty exciting time of it." Two days later, Ed Clark celebrated his reunion with Friendly in New Delhi. He expressed pleasure at Friendly's presence, with his signature enthusiasm and countless ideas. Yet he also described Friendly as "temperamental. Moody, and loud—but filled with a million plans, tremendous energy and unquestioned loyalty. The combination of the heat, the strangeness . . . red-tape, etc had him in a bad way a few days. But I talked turkey like I have only done once before to him—and the world is a rosy wonderland now." Clark felt the need to impress upon Friendly that he would not be able to function as a virtual free agent in his new posting. Nonetheless, in the months to come Clark gave Friendly wide latitude. "Technically he was Fred's boss," Birk said of Clark, "although Fred did damn practically anything he wanted."[13]

During his service abroad, Friendly continued to write his mother almost daily and to correspond with Rabbi William Braude and other friends in Providence. Fred's letters to Therese underscored the closeness of their relationship. He frequently evoked—with a note of nostalgia as well as humor—the details of their life in Providence. In a letter dated July 18, 1944, marking six months overseas, he cataloged at length all that he missed, from the sound of their landlord's opening the garage door at daybreak and the lentil soup of a neighbor to the broadcasts from the street with Mowry Lowe for WEAN. And, he continued, "I miss one of the nation's great women—my Mother—to whose home—to whose life and plans and dreams—I shall one day return." The same letter contained a detailed and vivid description of Friendly's experiences and impressions after half a year on the Indian subcontinent. He evoked the sights and smells and shared with her his observations of people from all walks of life and epiphanies of his own. For example:

I have walked with a lovely Burmese Refugee Girl of 20 into a darkened Hindu Temple in the Moonlight and walked amongst more sleeping men—and stood as frozen when a bearded elder awoke—held his well shaped head against his hand and with expressive eyes and a magnificent smile looked at the girl and me and mused—"Moonlight

Sahib"—Ahh—Sweet Moonlight. Moonlight to me from now on in, will always mean—the man in the Temple.[14]

Friendly's activities in Clark's office of information and education were remarkably broad. They ranged, for example, from giving orientation lectures, writing for the army newspaper *CBI Roundup*, and preparing radio reports for the troops to documenting with recordings the air war on the eastern front. Clark also noted Friendly's Herculean efforts to produce *Newsmap*, a publication to help educate troops about the progress of the war. He described Friendly's riding herd on his contributors, his resourcefulness at getting material, his uncompromising perfectionism, the chaotic scene at the Indian printing shop, and his ultimate success at producing a first-rate publication.

Friendly used *Newsmap* in his orientation lectures, for which he drew on his experience at Camp Kohler. Now, however, his presentations took place in the field, throughout South Asia, often in primitive outdoor theaters under tents in remote locales such as Chabua and Hasting Mill in India. Sometimes a film was also shown, or Friendly introduced a guest speaker to the assembled troops. The outdoor theater at Hasting Mill, located twelve miles from Calcutta, with a tarpaulin for a roof and open on the sides, was typical of the makeshift venues where Friendly spoke. It had a wooden platform about four feet high, a screen for movies, and wooden benches. A CBI veteran remembered Friendly as "a dynamite speaker" who appeared before a capacity audience of approximately 350 enlisted men and officers at night. He had a microphone but no podium. "I picture Friendly as having a rugged look and a gruff voice," he reminisces. "He spoke rapidly and with authority."[15] Friendly's popular presentations, together with his articles in *CBI Roundup*, made him a well-known figure in the CBI theater.

In accordance with a new emphasis on broadcasting within the military, Friendly also used the technologies of radio and recording in his work. The army used the radio broadcasts both to provide information for the home front and to boost the morale of troops overseas. For example, the army produced programs like *The Army Hour* and *Yanks in the Orient*, heard weekly on network radio in the United States. *Yanks* was produced by colleagues of Friendly's in the CBI theater, a four-person team that included a former writer for the *March of Time* radio series and Lieutenant Bert Parks, an announcer who later became master of ceremonies for the Miss America Pageant. The Armed Forces Radio Service was established in 1942 for U.S. troops throughout the world. Both permanent and portable transmitters permitted the establishment of far-flung stations, some on the front lines. The army distributed special radio receivers, including "tropicalized" models that could withstand heat and humidity. In addition, the Signal Corps helped design a new compact wire-recorder—it used a spooled reel of steel wire to capture sounds—for reporting from the front lines. Friendly enthusiastically embraced this technology and used it widely in CBI. "Without the wire-recorder," army radio officials later wrote, "it would have been impossible to present a sound-picture of the war to the American public."[16]

Friendly made recordings for broadcast both on network radio in the United States and on the stations of the Armed Forces Radio Service. In addition, his recordings were sent to Washington, D.C., for the historical archives of the army. Beginning in September 1944, for example, Friendly made combat reports for a program called *Around the World in Fifteen Minutes*. Clark praised Friendly's dramatic reports for the show, writing that "Fred is sending us some terrific stuff. 'This is CBI—hello America, we take you now to the trenches outside.'" One report originated from the bedside of a combat pilot undergoing surgery. Friendly held the sterilized microphone an inch from the knife as it cut the man's abdomen. The reports captured the words of the patient, the nurses, and the surgeon, who at the end despaired of saving the patient.[17]

On November 26, 1944, Clark wrote Lee that Friendly was about to leave to accompany combat missions that would surely produce exciting radio reports: "Only it's going to be rugged—and he's tackling things which have never been done before. You might include . . . Fred in your prayers for the next few weeks, darling." Clark noted that Friendly got drunk on Indian gin the night before his departure. Clark, who made amateur 16-millimeter movies, captured on film a picture of Friendly in 1945 as he made a radio report in the thick of combat. Clark wrote Lee, "I have some swell shots from a foxhole, taken at the same time we were broadcasting, Friendly screaming into the mike, artillery firing, our beautiful silver dive bombers coming down . . . right over our heads, Jap positions blowing high into the sky." Early in 1945, Clark's team established a new Armed Forces Radio station, which Clark believed was the closest to the front in any theater. The initial broadcast in the rudimentary facility included a reading of the Gettysburg Address by the actor Melvyn Douglas and entertainment by the crooner Tony Martin and other celebrities on the USO tour.[18]

Friendly wire-recorded live combat from the air (as well as from the ground), accompanying American and British fighter planes on their bombing runs over Burma and Japan from bases in China late in the war. Friendly and his aide, Joseph Birk, would hook up a wire recorder to the intercom of a bomber, and Friendly would supplement the voices of the crew with a play-by-play of the action. Once, to the consternation of the flight crew, Friendly risked an explosion on board by trying to weld a broken wire with a cigarette while in midflight. On at least two occasions Friendly's plane took enemy fire. When he returned to his base in New Delhi, Friendly would transfer the wire recordings to metal disks. Friendly and Birk, who had security clearances, sat in on bombing mission briefings, since they needed advanced knowledge to plan their recordings. Days after atomic bombs were dropped on Hiroshima and Nagasaki, Friendly flew sorties two hundred feet above the ground in reconnaissance plans to view the devastation.[19]

Many of Friendly's activities in information and education in CBI were dangerous. In February 1945, he received a serious injury to his right arm and hand during the famous first convoy to China by way of central Burma of U.S., British, and Chinese forces under the command of General Joseph Stilwell. After recording combat with the Japanese at the front, Friendly moved down the line approaching the Chinese border. His vehicle was accidentally side-swiped by a Chinese ammunition truck, throwing him eight to ten feet out of his vehicle. He landed on his right side. Surgeons in a field hospital operated on his hand twice. Clark accompanied him on the long flight back to New Delhi for further treatment.[20] On February 21, shortly after the accident, Friendly typed a letter to his mother with his left hand and assured her that his injuries were not serious. Now that he was removed from the combat zone and danger, he could report,

> For the past six months I have been constantly in combat. I have been sent with our recording equipment to broadcast a variety of battle scenes. I shudder to think of the expression on your face when you read this, but I have been over Japan three times in B29's, have been over Nanking, Formosa, Rangoon . . . and have come home on less than four engines on occasions. I have slept with the Chinese in

their foxholes, have lived with those wonderful British Infantry men in the Burma jungles, have lived on K and C rations and gone more than my usual one week without a bath. Every minute of it has been sheer drudgery, and at the same time invaluable experience.[21]

Friendly underwent additional operations that enabled him to avoid amputation and to return to the United States. The accident left Friendly with the three last fingers of his right hand frozen in place. "Fred's morale is pretty good," Clark wrote Lee on the same day Friendly wrote his mother, "but inactivity or a discharge would kill him." It may have been during his convalescence that he developed a relationship with Ilse Beale, an Australian nurse whose photograph he kept with his war papers.[22]

On April 19, when he was returning to active duty two months after the accident, he and Clark hatched a new adventure for Friendly. "Fred and I really dreamed up a honey this time," Clark wrote Lee, "and it has the blessing of Uncle Sam."[23] Their plan was to have Friendly report firsthand on the Allied victory in Europe for *CBI Roundup*, by arranging for *CBI Roundup* to exchange reporters with its European counterpart, *Stars and Stripes*. Clark's contacts in the European theater would take care of Friendly. The reporter who switched places with Friendly was Andy Rooney, Friendly's future colleague at CBS. Rooney recalled briefly meeting Friendly upon his arrival in Paris in a four-engine bomber; Rooney would take the same plane back to India. Rooney, sitting in his office at CBS News more than half a century later, recalled his first impression: "A dominating personality. Bombastic. I'm not sure that was the word. He was someone to be reckoned with."[24] Friendly clearly intended to function independently in the European theater, causing Rooney to worry that Friendly would quarrel with the editor of *Stars and Stripes*. However, Clark had made arrangements that ensured that Friendly would have the support and latitude he needed.

On May 5, Friendly wrote his mother an excited letter from Paris describing a population poised to explode in celebration of the German surrender. It would come three days later. Friendly marveled at the French women: "I have neither the blood nor the will power to resist them and as I plow thru a gauntlet of lush femmes, I do not bother to push them away." Fine meals at restaurants were on the house. He made the grand tour of Parisian landmarks.[25] Friendly left Paris to report on the end of the war in Austria and Germany. He had a jeep and driver at his disposal. On May 8, Friendly was driving east from Linz and about to cross the

Danube when he was turned back by U.S. military police. The road had been sealed because General Patton was up ahead, about to meet his Russian counterpart, General Fyodor Tolbukhin. Friendly, sensing a good story, managed to get a pass to attend the triumphant ceremonies of American and Russian officers at a Hapsburg castle on V-E Day. He reported the event for *CBI Roundup* and later wrote a longer account of the adventure, "General Patton and the Chinese $50 Bill," that he intended to submit to *Collier's* magazine.

Friendly's manuscript—it was never published—detailed how he and his driver ran the gauntlet of U.S. and Russian security to gain access to the meeting of the generals. The proceedings in the castle courtyard included the marching of a Russian regiment before a viewing stand and the music of a fifty-piece band. Afterward, Friendly and his driver, who had intended only to peek into the great hall where an elaborate banquet would be held, ended up being seated. Friendly witnessed and partook of endless toasts, observing at one point Tolbukhin and Patton ceremoniously smash their glasses on the floor. There were ballet and musical performances; Patton himself participated in a duet of "This Is the Army, Mr. Jones." Friendly was able to sidle up to the head table and interview Patton, who asked after his old friend General Stilwell and questioned Friendly about events in the CBI theater. Any message for the troops in CBI, Friendly asked? Patton jokingly said yes: Don't win the war until the Third Army and I get there. Friendly then took a Chinese $50 bill from his pocket and gave half to Patton as a keepsake for a future reunion in the Far East.[26]

Friendly traveled in southern Germany, visiting Regensburg, Augsburg, and Munich, where he viewed the site of Hitler's Beer Hall Putsch. "I have seen a dead Germany," Friendly wrote his mother on May 19, 1945, as he "wondered how a civilization could ever again spring from cities as utterly removed from the face of the earth." Yet as he saw what had happened to Jews under Nazi rule, he felt little sympathy for Germans living in a devastated land. Two weeks had passed since he had written his ecstatic letter from Paris. This letter, mailed several days before his return to New Delhi, was infinitely more anguished. It was prompted by a specific event: Friendly's presence at the liberation of the concentration camp at Mauthausen, Austria, by the Eleventh Armored Division of the U.S. Army. Until this point, few grasped or imagined the reality of the Nazi death camps. Friendly was unprepared for what he saw. In the letter to his mother he described the dead, "their emaciated bodies in piles like cords of wood. . . . The stench of death, of decomposition of human flesh, of uncontrolled body fluids, or burned, charred bones."

The reaction of the living inmates unnerved Friendly the most:

> Mother, I walked through countless cell blocks filled with sick, dying people, 300 in a room twice the size of our living room and as we walked in—there was a ripple of applause and then an inspiring burst of applause and cheers and men who could not stand up, and whispered though they tried to shout it—Vive Lamericansky. Vive Lamericansky. The applause[,] the cheers, those faces of men with legs the size and shape of rope, with ulcerated bodies, weeping with a kind of joy you and I will never, I hope, know.

Friendly was touched when a Polish inmate asked if he was Jewish, and he answered that he was. The experience also fed Friendly's sense of national pride. "For," he wrote his mother, "if there had been no America, we, all of us, might well have carried granite at Mauthausen." He declared that witnessing the liberation of Mauthausen aged him ten years, made him aware of why this war had to be fought, unleashed in him a profound rage. He lamented that he had not engaged the enemy more directly: "I envy with a bottomless and endless spirit, the American soldier who may tell his grandchildren that with his hands he killed Germans."[27]

Friendly would later acknowledge that he had not always been proud to be a Jew, that his mother had preached assimilation above all. In regard to his Jewish identity, Friendly would say of Mauthausen, it was "my emancipation." Friendly wrote a lengthy article for *CBI Roundup* about the camp, describing in vivid detail the gas chamber, cremation room, and cell blocks as well as the condition of the inmates and the imprisonment of those Nazi storm troopers who had been unable to escape. Yet he reserved the rawest description and emotion for his mother: "I have met the Germans, have examined the storm trooper[,] his wife and heritage, and I have learned to hate."[28]

In the latter part of May 1945, shortly after the liberation of Mauthausen, Friendly returned to New Delhi to tell his tale of the end of the war in Europe. James Armsey was there. The commanding general assembled all the field-grade officers—that is, majors and above—in the big war room in New Delhi so that Friendly could report on all he had

seen and the details of the surrender. "And he performed like a real master," Armsey recalled. "I'll never forget this. This big, hulking master
sergeant standing there, sounding off to all these generals and majors
and colonels. He just captured the room." Friendly also traveled outside
the Indian capital to speak with GIs in the field. Robert Bernstein was an
air force staff sergeant in intelligence, assigned to drive Friendly to camps
along the Assam Valley. Bernstein watched Friendly use slides and films
to supplement his accounts of what he had witnessed in Europe: "His
talk, as you can imagine, was overwhelming." After one presentation, as
soldiers surrounded Friendly, the base commander invited him to dinner
in the officers' mess. Friendly replied that he thought it appropriate that
he eat with his fellow enlisted men. One of the soldiers wrote years later,
"I always remember that moment and thinking, 'That man is different. I
wonder what he'll do after the war.' "[29]

More than fifty years later, several CBI veterans recalled the lectures
Friendly gave to counter war-weariness after he returned in 1945 from the
European theater. One remembered a presentation at the theater erected in
Chabua, India—Friendly included an earthy description of riding a tank
and crossing a pontoon bridge behind General George S. Patton, who
stopped the convoy to urinate on the side of the road. Another recalled
Friendly's talk at the outdoor theater at Hasting Mill, especially "his description of the tremendous, endless convoys going across Europe to supply troops at the front. He spoke of how proud he felt as an American and
in awe we could produce such an overwhelming force." Soldiers surrounded Friendly after his talk. The CBI veteran at Hasting Mill remembered Friendly as a riveting speaker, adding, "I think his mission was to
tell us the soldiers in Europe had finished their mission and most would
go home, but we were still at war with Japan and we had to stay to finish
our job." Friendly gave two hundred talks throughout the CBI theater
about his European tour.[30]

Friendly spent the remainder of his active duty reporting for *CBI
Roundup* on the final phase of fighting in the Far East. In late July, the
command in the China theater asked that Friendly be dispatched for up
to six weeks to inform troops in Burma and India of the importance of
their support work for the fighting in Manchuria. One of Friendly's dispatches from Mukden, Manchuria, was written the day General Mac-
Arthur accepted the Japanese surrender on the deck of the USS *Missouri*.
Friendly's report included interviews with a hated Japanese guard and a
Japanese officer at the prison camp that had housed captured Americans

in Mukden. Friendly also reported from the USS *Relief,* a navy hospital ship anchored off Okinawa with more than seven hundred former American POWs, as they celebrated news of the capture of the Japanese general who in 1942 had sent them on the infamous death march in Bataan.

Finally, Friendly filed long dispatches from a Tokyo in defeat. One report profiled two key figures in the air war, Major General Kenneth Wolfe, chief of staff of the U.S. Fifth Air Force, and Major General Mitsuo Arimori, technical director of the Japanese Imperial Air Force. Another report provided a panoramic description of the city and people of Tokyo and its U.S. occupiers. Friendly tellingly evoked the sights, sounds, and smells of the Japanese capital, from the Diet and Imperial Palace to the bustling street life and the protocol in geisha houses. The article closed at day's end: "And so the large full moon comes up over Tokyo, the trains stop running to the country, the lights begin to flicker out, soldiers who have missed the last train or truck, start hitching home, a Navy whistle blows in the harbor, an M.P. [Military Police] jeep rumbles four blocks away, a child cries for its Mother, a lost sailor asks directions, and a long day ends in the third largest city in the world."[31]

Friendly's dispatch described Tokyo just as it was beginning the shift to a postwar world, a transition that he, too, would soon make in his return to civilian life. Friendly would later refer to his military service as "my Rhodes scholarship." A self-deprecating reference to his limited higher education, this was also an acknowledgment of the importance to his development of his experience in the CBI and European theaters of operation. He had covered momentous events for *CBI Roundup.* He had been exposed to the larger world of American journalism and entertainment. He interacted, for example, with Ed Katcher of the *New York Post,* Hugh Crumpler of the *New York Herald Tribune,* and Edgar Snow, then war correspondent for the *Saturday Evening Post.* Friendly chaperoned well-known entertainers to the information and education sessions he conducted with troops in the field. Friendly would stay in touch with Melvyn Douglas, who headed an entertainment unit within the office of information and education in New Delhi.[32] Friendly also would establish professional relationships with others who crossed his path in the CBI theater, among them Newton Minow, later chair of the Federal Communications Commission, and Robert Bernstein, the sergeant in air force intelligence, who would become the head of Random House.

In addition to providing Friendly with important contacts, the war enabled him to express his talents on a wider stage. The war thrust Friendly into a world far beyond the confines of Providence, and he flourished in the army in the wider universe of Asia and Europe. His exploits—a litany of Friendly tales of enterprise often bordering on insubordination, exploits that soldiers learned about from his lectures or articles in *CBI Roundup* or by word of mouth—assumed legendary status in the CBI theater. A fellow soldier later wrote about Friendly's wartime persona: "Friendly, by the force of his personality, could command attention anywhere he went. No matter what the place or situation, he always had an audience. One would gather wherever he started to talk." In the far corners of CBI, a visitor would invariably be asked the whereabouts of Friendly or regaled with anecdotes about him. Andy Rooney recalled with amazement: "I went all over. . . . And there was nowhere I went where they didn't tell me stories about Fred Friendly. I got to know more about him then than in the brief time I met him in Paris."[33] Friendly's special standing was reflected in the lead story on the first page of the November 8, 1945, edition of *CBI Roundup*, about his imminent departure for the United States. The article referred to him as "The Man," his nickname in the CBI theater: "The self-styled 'professional G.I.' is a story in himself. He was almost arrested by a general for daring to scoop the civilian press; had the distinction of being awarded the Legion of Merit one minute, and being bawled out for being in improper uniform the next. He has got feeling good [*sic*] with General George Patton, chatted with Uncle Joe Stilwell and Lord Louis Mountbatten, and bummed rides on Lt. Gen. R. A. Wheeler's personal plane."[34]

Praise for Friendly—from the ordinary GIs he lionized to the officers he badgered—was almost universal. However, his associates sometimes expressed ambivalence about the way Friendly worked. Armsey, who knew Friendly both at Camp Kohler and in New Delhi, admired him as "a take-charge man, a fascinating guy." But at the same time, Armsey sensed that Friendly had an inferiority complex, perhaps resulting from his lack of formal education, that fueled a powerful drive for recognition. As a result, Armsey surmised, Friendly became "a total extrovert, very outspoken, very demanding, very much out in front." Armsey recognized that "one of Fred's principal aspects was his tremendous ambition. He wanted to know important people, and wanted to be with important people. And he strove very hard to get to the front of everything, to be the guy in the viewfinder, as it were. Great desire to be important. I think that's what pretty much propelled him in his career." Major Clark, Friendly's greatest protector and booster in the army, also sounded a warning. In the wee hours of the morning of June 2, 1944, after chewing Friendly out for an unspecified offense, an exhausted Clark confided his misgivings in a letter to Lee:

> With all his fine ideas, loyalty, and drive—he worries me. For one thing I don't always like his methods. For another I sometimes question his ethics. Sometimes he really puts me out on a limb, and he does antagonize people. As long as I can watch him—all is well—but leave him on his own and I feel as tho I were sitting on a keg of dynamite. God knows there are enough . . . situations demanding the most diplomatic handling and the utmost integrity, without additional jeopardy.

"Maybe I'm unfair," Clark added as an afterthought. "I'll reserve further opinions."[35]

Friendly's inclination to push the limits notwithstanding, he made his mark and gained invaluable experience in communications in wartime in a way that would have been impossible in civilian life. In a relatively short time, he had developed orientation courses, lectured to hundreds of assembled soldiers, reported for *CBI Roundup*, made radio reports, and recorded the voices and sounds of war from fighter-bombers and the battlefield. Friendly's activities and accomplishments took place against a backdrop of momentous events: he would witness the liberation of Mauthausen and get a bird's-eye view of the devastated Hiroshima and Nagasaki at the dawn of the nuclear age. Friendly emerged from the war with a greater interest in world affairs and a new sense of the possibilities of broadcasting as a journalistic vehicle in the postwar world. He was convinced that the war experience would make Americans greater citizens of the world and would increase their expectations for radio.

In November 1945, Friendly wrote a lengthy memorandum entitled "On Coming Home to Radio Programs." It was addressed to Jack Kapp, the founder and head of the Decca Company, which had reissued recordings of Friendly's *Footprints* broadcasts. In the past, radio had been little more than a crass medium of entertainment. "U.S. Radio has everything but dignity," Friendly wrote. "It's done everything but grow up in the last twenty years." But Franklin D. Roosevelt's fireside chats, the reports of Edward R. Murrow's team of CBS reporters, and now the war experience itself suggested radio's potential as a great national instrument for disseminating information and fostering dialogue about the great issues of the day. Friendly argued that the U.S. soldier was returning home a new man, with greater cosmopolitanism and heightened expectations. Friendly claimed that the media produced by the armed forces—the newspapers and magazines, films and radio programming—often eclipsed the quality of their commercial counterparts' at home. American soldiers from all walks of life had now heard Melvyn Douglas read poetry and Alfred Lunt and Lynn Fontanne perform radio dramas. Friendly predicted that the "tide of returning vets will force itself into every tributary and every stream. It will cleanse and make bright and maybe even beautiful a tired old river which hasn't been dredged since KDKA did its first prizefight," a reference to the historic broadcast he and his father had listened to. Friendly continued: "America has now a bottomless appetite for news. . . . There's a great new United Nations—which radio must serve. Information is our only safeguard for peace, and this great land of ours. Information and entertainment must be fused together by the wonder of radio."

Friendly emphasized the unrealized potential of recordings to bring to radio the voices of the world and to create a permanent record of those sounds. He noted his own experience of recording B-29 raids and of dubbing them for Armed Forces Radio: "The wire recorder is a magic carpet, with no expense and no static, taking a man with a story to Budapest, to the Queen Mary, to the Taj Mahal, and, by golly, maybe even the moon and the stars in our lifetime. I have seen radio stations in France, Germany, India, China, Japan, and Australia, and found the transcription and library service almost unknown. The export possibilities are enormous."[36] Friendly believed that the ability of recording technology to capture the voices of soldiers and sounds of war and to reproduce it for rebroadcast, what was then referred to as "transcription," could revolutionize radio, could help make it an enriched medium for the new postwar U.S. audience. Friendly once dramatically expressed this conviction to Ed Clark on a flight at the end of the war. Clark shared the anecdote with his son Ted, who later became a reporter for National Public Radio. "This is a wire recorder," Friendly said, holding up the apparatus on the airplane, "and it's going to transform the way we do journalism and the way we do news."[37]

The war, including firsthand experience of the liberation of concentration camps and of the dawn of the nuclear age, endowed Friendly with increased seriousness of purpose and a desire to use communication technologies to address the great issues of the day. Ruth Harris had lived in his room at 495 Lloyd Avenue in Providence as a boarder and companion of his mother's during his absence. Harris recalled the distinct impression that he reentered civilian life more self-confident, more focused, more prepared to conquer new worlds. However, Andy Rooney challenged the view that the war transformed Friendly. "None. Zero," Rooney insisted when asked to what extent the qualities Friendly exhibited in his subsequent career in broadcasting can be attributed to his military experience. "Fred Friendly would have been exactly who he was and what he was if he hadn't seen World War II. That's my opinion. It was a great experience for any of us who were there, but Fred had more impact on the war than it had on him."[38] Both judgments, seemingly contradictory, are not mutually exclusive. Master Sergeant Fred Friendly exhibited many of the qualities of his prewar persona: the restlessness and brash self-confidence, the enterprise and ambition. Friendly brought to his military assignments a long-standing fascination with great figures as well as a passion since childhood for the medium of radio. At the same time the war permitted Friendly to come into his own, to become fully himself, in a fashion and tempo that peacetime would not have allowed.

Armsey noted the difficulty of measuring the impact of the war on Friendly's future fortunes but suggested that "it was like a graduate course in what he was going to do." Armsey later worked with Friendly again, at the Ford Foundation. "Fred used to love to say, 'We need to be free to make mistakes,'" Armsey recalled.[39] And the war afforded Friendly a measure of freedom to test himself and his ideas as well as access to resources that otherwise would not have been at his disposal. The position of education and information specialist in the army provided Friendly with a remarkable laboratory, a unique opportunity to improvise and innovate. His fellow soldiers in the CBI theater, impressed with the way he seized that opportunity, did not expect him to fade quietly into postwar America. "'The Man' has had his day out here," *CBI Roundup* concluded in bidding adieu to Friendly. "We prophesy he will have another, and bigger one, back in civilian life."[40]

3 "Willing to Be Lucky"

AT THE END of World War II, Fred Friendly returned to the warm embrace of Providence, where his wartime record was well known through word-of-mouth and periodic reports in the local press. "When Fred got out of the army," Dorothy Friendly recalled, "he was feted in Providence." His letter about Mauthausen had circulated widely in the city's Jewish community. Now Rabbi William Braude invited Friendly to speak at Congregation Beth-El. On January 21, 1946, Friendly gave a talk, "An Intimate Report from Japan," at a luncheon sponsored by the Town Criers of Rhode Island. Mowry Lowe, Friendly's prewar radio mentor, chaired what amounted to a quasi-official homecoming celebration. Bo Bernstein, a family friend and associate of Friendly's from his days as a local radio producer, offered him a position with the advertising agency Bernstein ran, one of several job offers Friendly received in Providence.[1]

However, the thirty-year-old Friendly was determined to seek fame and fortune in New York, the nation's media capital. He moved back into his mother's home on Lloyd Avenue in Providence but made periodic forays to New York. At first, he stayed at the Iroquois Hotel, next to the Algonquin Hotel, a meeting point for New York's literati. In that period, immediately after the war, he would bring his laundry back to Providence to have it done at home. On occasion, when he exhausted all possibilities and felt uncomfortably at sea, Friendly would kill time by seeing a movie during the day before returning to Providence. He began settling in for longer periods in a more modest hotel in midtown Manhattan called the Beaux Arts. "I don't remember any shame," Norman Fain recalled about this period in Friendly's life. "He was determined to succeed in radio." Friendly's professional quest was underwritten by what remained from the $25,000 windfall he had received from Decca Records for his *Footprints* series, supplemented by financial support from family and friends.

"In all the years I knew him," recalled Fain, "he was never restricted by lack of funds. It wasn't flush. But he was never restricted from doing what he wanted."[2] A desire to help his mother, the costs associated with his proposals and pilot projects, as well as normal living expenses meant that Friendly nonetheless experienced financial pressure while he was trying to launch his career in New York after the war.

During the winter of 1945/1946, Rabbi Bill Braude and his wife, Pearl, introduced Fred to Dorothy Greene, a Providence native who was living and working in New York City as a researcher at *Life* magazine. Pearl had been a classmate and close friend of Dorothy's at Hope Street High School. Dorothy, who was graduated in 1935, had not had direct contact with Fred, who was a class ahead and had left Hope High School in the fall of 1933 to attend the Roxbury School. However, she was aware of his reputation as a poor student and class clown and initially expressed skepticism to Pearl, who replied that he had returned from the war a changed man. Dorothy recalled her first impression of Fred, one that was at odds with the man she later came to know. She first saw him coming up the stairs of her apartment building to pick her up for dinner. He was dressed up and wearing a homburg—as she came to know, he normally gave little attention to his clothes and rarely wore a hat. He was also rather quiet at dinner; Dorothy and the Braudes did most of the talking. But Dorothy was impressed with Fred's interest in news and ideas about the potential of electronic journalism. A few days later, Fred picked Dorothy up at her First Avenue apartment in Manhattan for dinner and a movie. Soon they were seeing each other almost daily.[3]

When Fred met Dorothy, she had established herself in New York City as a young professional with a number of entry-level positions in journalism. While studying at the Rhode Island School of Design, from which she was graduated in 1939, Dorothy had written for the women's page of the *Providence Journal*. John Tebbel, then a reporter at the *Journal*, had a contact at *Time* magazine and encouraged Dorothy to apply there for a job. *Time* had no openings, but she found a position at *Iron Age*, a trade magazine published by McGraw-Hill, where she did editorial work such as shortening articles and writing text to accompany photographs. She did eventually move to Time Inc., where she worked in a number of capacities: as a staff member in the letters department of *Time*, as a temporary replacement on the fifteen-minute radio broadcast *Time Views the News*, and finally as a researcher for four years for *Life* magazine, the position she held when she first encountered Fred. When they met, Dorothy had been part of a group, which included John Hersey and Theodore White, that was trying to launch a magazine called *Opinion* as a liberal newsweekly alternative to *Time*.[4] Dorothy introduced Fred to White and other associates of hers at a time when Fred had few contacts in New York. She later surmised that Fred had heard of her work in journalism in New York and had asked the Braudes to introduce him to her: "He was impressed that I was a researcher at *Life*. I think he thought I could be useful to his career."

Dorothy recalled that when she first met Fred, "he was kind of drifting. Time was sort of suspended. He was just beginning to make the rounds." At the same time, she was impressed with his self-confidence: "I wasn't so sure at first, but he had a great deal of faith in his own ability. In the army he displayed an amazing ability to make people do what he wanted them to do. Recording had just been introduced, and he was very excited about experimenting with that." Dorothy immediately became a partner in Friendly's professional probes and schemes. Early in 1946, when Friendly heard that Melvyn Douglas was visiting New York, he arranged to see the actor he had met during the war in the CBI theater. Friendly toyed with the idea of writing a film script for Douglas or of developing a radio mystery series for him. Fred enlisted Dorothy's help in preparing a script summary. "I knew darn well that at the time he couldn't do that kind of writing," she recalled. With Dorothy's help, Friendly prepared the beginning of a script proposal that he showed Douglas over dinner. Douglas, who was personally fond of Friendly, was skeptical about Friendly's gifts as a scriptwriter, feeling that his strength lay in journalism. But Douglas agreed to consider a more fully developed proposal if Friendly would write it up. Friendly did so that winter and spring, together with Dorothy, and decided to travel to the West Coast to deliver it personally to Douglas. Dorothy accompanied Fred, who also planned to visit Carolene Wachenheimer, his cousin in San Francisco, and Paul Guttman, whose family had opened up its home to him when he was stationed at Camp Kohler, outside Sacramento, during the war.

Because Fred and Dorothy were not married, Dorothy's sister went along as a chaperone to make their traveling together more respectable. Dorothy recalled that Fred suggested the arrangement, "a quaint idea even for that time." To cover the traveling expenses for the cross-country trip, Fred drove a car cross-country for Sam and Bella Spewack, the authors of Broadway hits like *Kiss Me, Kate* and *Boy Meets Girl*. Fred and Dorothy visited Rocky Mountain National Park in Colorado. They stayed in a hotel in Salt Lake City, where they got free room and board for four days while their misplaced luggage was recovered. During this hiatus, Dorothy's sister departed and left Fred and Dorothy to their own devices. After they reached California, Dorothy extended her stay from one to two weeks; Fred remained even longer. He cabled Norman Fain, his close Providence friend, asking him to send additional funds.[5]

During the trip, Friendly learned that Ruth Harris had given birth to a son, David. She was the family friend who had boarded in Friendly's room while he was away at war. In a letter dated August 6, 1946, on stationery of the Hotel Mayfair in Los Angeles, Friendly gave the newborn an orientation lecture of sorts, an introduction to life. He began by providing a who's who of the newborn's extended family, of "the odd-looking people who peer into your crib." He then turned to the beautiful world in which the newborn would live, with its wonderful toys and things to eat, with magnificent flowers, trees, and oceans. "But the people—well, kid, an awful lot of the people stink—No not like your diapers . . . that all comes out in the wash, this is a kind of stink that doesn't come out. And these people, some of them in foreign countries, some of them in America, some of them who sit beside you or near you on Yom Kippur, these people are lousing things up . . . for you and me and the kid born in Saarbrucken six months ago."[6] The tenor of these last remarks was in sharp contrast to Friendly's high spirits during his trip out west. The freshness of the war experience may have prompted these ruminations. Or was a darker view hidden beneath Friendly's optimistic bearing?

In Los Angeles, Friendly met as planned with Melvyn Douglas—alone, without Dorothy—to follow up on their dinner meeting in New York. The upshot was a proposal for a radio series written by Fred and Dorothy called DATELINE with Melvyn Douglas. The prospectus said that the inspiration for the show came from a remark by General Joseph Stilwell that something should be done to sustain the spirit of wartime journalism in peacetime. Friendly wrote that Stilwell would probably be willing to make a cameo appearance on the first show. The main character, played by Melvyn Douglas, is an investigative reporter named Mike Lawrence who helps right the wrongs he uncovers as a foreign correspondent. Lawrence is a former war reporter described as a "cross between Richard Harding Davis, Quentin Reynolds and Ernie Pyle." Lawrence fights international gangsters and warmongers in story lines rooted in current events in the postwar world. In one episode, in a small town outside Naples, he helps citizens wrest control of a local government from fascists; in Hiroshima he helps an American-born priest rebuild a church destroyed by the atomic bomb. Friendly promised to take the listener around the world, "to the Scribe in Paris for cocktails, to Raffles Hotel in Singapore, to the Burning Ghats in Calcutta, to Ernie Pyle's grave in Shimma, to Shepard's Hotel in Cairo, and the White House." His depiction of the reporter was romantic and clichéd: "Mike is a crack newspaper man, with a great love of democracy, a brunette named Mary, all blondes, the truth, peace and bourbon with plain water." In a sample script for the first episode, Friendly identified himself as a "radio writer by profession." Friendly—probably with the help of Melvyn Douglas or the Spewacks—lined up some established Hollywood names as participants in the proposed CBS radio series.[7]

DATELINE with Melvyn Douglas never came to fruition. But it was only one of a host of proposals and pilots Friendly had in the works. And he cultivated contacts in the world of New York journalism as well as Hollywood entertainment. Toward this end, Friendly hung out at Louis and Armand's, a well-appointed French restaurant and bar frequented by CBS personnel. Years later, the journalist James Brady recalled how "Ed Murrow, an icon for our generation, did the evening news live and went across 52nd Street to Louis and Armand's and knocked back a few. Young reporters like me went there to drink at the other end of the bar and watch Murrow drink." Friendly began dropping by Louis and Armand's on a daily basis to network.[8] Unable to afford to dine there, Friendly would place an order for eggs Benedict, with just one egg, for $1.25, claiming that he wasn't hungry. During this period, Dorothy encouraged Fred to focus on his interest in news rather than show business. In retrospect, she said,

> I don't think he could have succeeded in the entertainment world, although he had a strong interest in entertainment and drama. But that was not where his talent was. I remember saying to him, "You know, the news always refreshes itself day after day, while in entertainment you have a heck of a time getting new ideas and creating shows." There was this side of him that was purely a showman, and he later applied that instinct very well in news. At the time he was looking for a job, any kind of job, but I think his chief interest was in news.[9]

At Louis and Armand's, Friendly had the good fortune to meet with John G. "Jap" Gude, an encounter that would give Friendly's career a significant boost. Melvyn Douglas apparently connected the two men. Gude—whose nickname, Jap, derived from a childhood bout of jaundice—was a graduate of Brown University who had joined the CBS news department in the mid-1930s, writing publicity releases and editing news broadcasts. Subsequently, he and Thomas L. Stix formed the Stix and Gude agency, which represented top radio news personalities of the day such as Elmer Davis, Robert Trout, and Edward R. Murrow. The agency flourished during World War II, when the radio networks gave expanded attention to news. Trout remembered Gude as genteel, a far cry from the hyperaggressive, cutthroat celebrity agents of today. James Thurber was a client and close friend. Gude was old school, wearing a porkpie hat after it had fallen out of fashion, and was a long-time summer resident in Martha's Vineyard, where he socialized with a group of artists and the literati.

"It was kind of crazy from my point of view," Trout said of the way Gude conducted business at Louis and Armand's. Trout described a typical luncheon consisting of a succession of leisurely martinis and ending with a cursory discussion of the matter at hand along with a rushed order of food and large pots of black coffee. After such meetings, Trout would call the secretary at Stix and Gude to make sure the deal discussed would in fact be consummated. This manner of conducting business notwithstanding, Gude was broadcast journalism's preeminent agent, the representative of the industry's greatest star, Edward. R. Murrow. A close friend of Friendly's once said it was Gude who gave Friendly entrée to CBS and the world of broadcasting—through the door of Louis and Armand's.[10]

As Fred pursued career possibilities in 1946, his relationship with Dorothy intensified. But until their trip to the West Coast, Fred and Dorothy were working partners but not romantically involved. Fred had returned from California several weeks after Dorothy, after which they starting seeing each other every day. Fred began to stay in Dorothy's apartment. Shortly after his return from California, they were in a taxi returning from dinner at the Pen and Pencil restaurant, when Fred suddenly said to Dorothy, "I'm going to make you my wife. What do you think of that?" and kissed her. Dorothy happily agreed, but she was worried about the reaction of Fred's mother, Therese, to the marriage of her only son. Fred and Dorothy decided to inform Therese only three weeks before the wedding so that she would be compelled to accept it as a fait accompli. When they told her, her first reaction was to ask whether Dorothy was pregnant.[11] Therese's unenthusiastic response may have resulted, in part, from her sense of social superiority. Her circle in Providence consisted of the upper-middle-class Jews of German origin who were associated with the Reform Temple Beth-El, whereas Dorothy's family attended the more religiously conservative Temple Emmanuel, whose congregants were primarily of eastern European stock. Over time, Fred's mother softened or at least grudgingly accepted Dorothy. "On the Dorothy situation—," Fred wrote Bill and Pearl Braude, "Therese seems much ready to accept her and that makes things easier."[12] When they got married, Therese told Dorothy she would have to worry about money but not about other women.

The marriage took place in June 1947, at the home of Rabbi Braude. Just Fred's immediate family and Norman Fain and his wife, Rosalie, attended the intimate ceremony. Dorothy was surprised—and disappointed—that Fred did not want any photographs taken. The newlyweds celebrated their honeymoon in Boston and Nova Scotia. Dorothy later recalled that her happiness was tinged by a touch of anxiety. She loved Fred's warm and good-natured personality. And she relished being married to such a dynamic and creative man committed to a career in media, although she had no inkling of the magnitude of his future success. What concerned her was his volatility: his propensity for outlandish ideas, his deep-seated need to be the center of attention. But she was confident that she could help him settle down.[13]

Fred and Dorothy complemented each other as partners. She did not share his boisterousness and bravado. She was a quiet, introspective person with a passionate interest in art—both as a student of art history and as an artist who painted in oil and water color. Dorothy was also well organized. She had helped Fred write scripts and program proposals such as *DATELINE with Melvyn Douglas*. Fred's long-time friend Norman Fain went so far as to say of those early projects, "She did the work; he was the face."[14] Following the trip out west, Dorothy decided to leave Time Inc., when she was transferred to the audience research department because staff members returning from the war were reclaiming their old positions. After briefly exploring other job possibilities, she decided to become Fred's full professional partner. Dorothy's separation pay from Time Inc. and unemployment benefits helped the young couple make ends meet.

Dorothy knew she could continue her painting on her own. For Fred, she would function as part writing coach, part manager, handling their finances as well as refining their scripts. She also sensed, behind the bravado, a fear of not making the grade. "This fear," she emphasized, "was deep inside of him, and it was with him all the time." Despite the appearance of utter self-confidence, he needed "to be told every hour on the hour how wonderful he was." Yet he would not brook any doubts from others. Dorothy recalled saying at one point, "'You just can't make this happen by willing it!' He was offended by this remark, and I never raised this question again." Dorothy welcomed the opportunity to set aside her own career and to become Fred's professional partner as well as his wife. Such a role suited her self-effacing nature: "I had a very modest idea of my own contribution to Fred's work. I never expected to get a lot of credit for it." Norman Fain, however, emphasized Dorothy's impor-tance for Fred in this critical time in his life: "When he came back from the war, he was lost. That is, he knew where he wanted to go, but didn't know how to get there. She pointed the way. She was good for him. He knew it and never forgot it."[15]

In *Here Is New York*, an essay written shortly after the end of the war, E. B. White catches the spirit of adventure, of the quest on which young people like Fred and Dorothy had embarked. White writes that the out-of-towners who came to fulfill a dream shaped New York City's dyna-mism and achievements. An awareness of following in the footsteps of great figures reinforced the sense of great possibilities. White describes his thoughts while sitting in a stifling hotel room in the summer of 1948 with 90-degree heat in midtown:

No air moves in or out of the room, yet I am curiously affected by emanations from the immediate surroundings. I am twenty-two blocks from where Rudolph Valentino lay in state, eight blocks from where Nathan Hale was executed, five blocks from the publisher's of-fice where Ernest Hemingway hit Max Eastman on the nose, four miles from where Walt Whitman sat sweating out editorials for the Brooklyn *Eagle* . . . ; and for that matter I am probably occupying the very room that any number of exalted and somewise memorable char-acters sat in, some of them on hot, breathless afternoons, lonely and private and full of their own sense of emanations from without.[16]

White wrote these lines in the same period in which Fred Friendly, first from the Beaux Arts Hotel and then from Dorothy's cramped apartment, imagined *his* possibilities. "We were happily penniless for a long time," Dorothy would later say, "But we weren't worried. New York was ours." New York City was no less a broadcasting mecca than a literary one, and

Friendly could feel the emanations of radio's luminaries. And as George W. S. Trow has written, postwar New York was about to experience a displacement of the old New York WASP Establishment, a transformation in which the advent of television would play a major role. As Trow puts it, "We New York-Televisioned our way into the media age." Yet Friendly had no guarantee of success. As White writes of the city, "It can destroy an individual, or it can fulfill him, depending a good deal on luck. No one should come to New York to live unless he is willing to be lucky."[17]

Good fortune for Friendly came in the form of a musicians strike in 1947 that left recording companies eager for alternative material. Friendly had proposed to Jap Gude a record project capturing the sounds of the momentous events of the 1930s and 1940s.[18] He told Gude how in 1942, during an earlier musicians strike, Jack Kapp of Decca Records had called him with an offer to put *Footprints in the Sands of Time* on records. At the end of the war, Friendly had declaimed to Major Clark the importance of recorders for the future of communications. Immediately after the war audio technology took a leap forward: the old wire-recording system was replaced by magnetic tape, which created new possibilities for the editing of audio. At the same time the recording industry had developed an improved long-playing high-fidelity 33-rpm record format. The era of rigid electrical wire recorders, transcriptions on aluminum disks, and poor sound quality gave way to new recording technology that made Friendly's idea of an audio documentary possible.

Friendly's proposal struck Gude as an audio equivalent of Frederick Lewis Allen's popular history of the 1920s, *Only Yesterday*. Gude approached the author with the suggestion that he collaborate with Friendly, but Allen was unavailable. Friendly then coyly suggested he could undertake the project on his own so long as he had a world-class narrator, "someone like Edward R. Murrow." Gude responded as Friendly had hoped: he would invite Murrow to a meeting with Friendly in the hope of interesting the CBS correspondent in the venture. The three met for lunch at Louis and Armand's. Friendly made his pitch. Murrow, who spoke of his experience with recorders during the war, quickly agreed. Decca turned the project down, but Goddard Lieberson, head of the classical music division at Columbia Records, gave the go-ahead. There was no precedent for talking records' making much money, but Friendly was soon to be married, and Gude broached the question of an advance. A contract was signed between Columbia Records and the team of Friendly,

Murrow, and Gude; Gude would be listed as the record's producer. Friendly would receive a $1,000 advance. Murrow insisted that Friendly also receive his own $1,000 advance and a higher percentage of the royalties. "He knew I was broke," Friendly later recalled, "and so he gave himself the smaller slice." The contract was signed soon after Fred and Dorothy were married in the spring of 1947. Friendly later wrote that the prospect of a $2,000 advance made it possible for him to remain in New York; otherwise, he would have been forced to return to Providence.[19]

Friendly spent many months listening to five hundred hours and taping one hundred hours of audio actualities—the recorded voices of news makers and collateral background sounds—from the archives of the networks and the Library of Congress. He and Dorothy spent three hot summer weeks at the National Archives and the War Department in Washington. Joe Wershba, a writer and reporter for CBS News, also helped assemble material. Murrow, a gifted editor, helped pare the material to forty-five minutes. Overseeing the production was Joel Tree, the pioneering broadcast engineer for Norman Corwin's renowned CBS broadcasts of the 1930s and 1940s. Dorothy recalled Fred's excitement and pride with regard to the project. On a trip back home to Providence, he gathered family and friends to play about fifteen minutes from the tape recordings he had assembled. Unfortunately, the audio quality was poor, the voices barely audible, so that the session ended up being a letdown for all. Fred was distraught, and Dorothy gently chastised him for trying to impress the hometown crowd with fragments of an incomplete undertaking. "He was upset," Dorothy remembered, "but he got over it quickly and moved on. He got over everything quickly."[20]

"*I can hear it now . . . ,*" *1933–1945*, was released on the Columbia Masterworks label on Thanksgiving Day, 1948. The liner notes, signed by Murrow and Friendly, emphasize that the record is a testament to the importance of radio during the Depression and World War II. It captures historical events as well as entertainment and human-interest stories of the era. The record begins with Will Rogers's remarks on the Depression and Franklin Roosevelt's inaugural speech reassuring the nation that it had "nothing to fear but fear itself." The listener hears, for example, Fiorello LaGuardia speaking to New Yorkers, the report of the *Hindenburg* disaster, Lou Gehrig's farewell speech, and a ringside account of the Joe Louis–Max Schmeling fight. Most of the record is devoted to the war, with excerpts of key speeches by Churchill, Hitler,

Mussolini, and Stalin. Listeners revisit the original reports of the bombing of Pearl Harbor, D-Day, the death of FDR, and the dawning of the nuclear age. The record also captures the sounds of the marching feet and songs of Nazi storm troopers, a London air-raid alarm, the roar of planes during the Normandy landing, and the tolling of the Liberty Bell in Philadelphia.

Murrow, the narrator, links the various reports and provides a brief epilogue. The record differed from earlier sound documentaries, which relied on actors and music, whereas *"I can hear it now . . ."* was based exclusively—or almost exclusively—on original recordings. The papers of Robert Trout and research by broadcast historians suggest that the album was doctored in at least two places. In the first instance, John Daly's announcement of the attack on Pearl Harbor on CBS Radio on December 7, 1941, received what Trout called "Friendly-esque enhancement."[21] To add drama to the announcement, Murrow introduces the segment by noting that at the time the New York Philharmonic was tuning up for a live broadcast. The added sound effects of the orchestra warm-up are followed on the record by "We interrupt this program for a special announcement," after which the listener hears Daly's original Pearl Harbor report. (Daly's "We interrupt this program—" was apparently transposed from Daly's announcement of the death of FDR.) The attempt to create a heightened effect makes it appear that Daly had interrupted a broadcast of the New York Philharmonic to report the attack on Pearl Harbor. A radio historian has written how "the 'I Can Hear It Now' series had penetrated the public consciousness to the point where the fake Pearl Harbor clip had actually become the reality for most people." Friendly always denied that any misleading editing was done in regard to the Pearl Harbor broadcast.[22]

The second instance concerns the announcement on August 14, 1945, by Trout of the defeat of the Japanese and the end of the World War II. The quality of the original recording of the report was poor, so Friendly asked Trout to re-record it. In a note to his wife, Kit, on July 8, 1948, Trout wrote that Friendly wanted him "to record an 18 second announcement of the end of World War II, which I suppose Fred will write, presumably from my own words—more or less." Trout explained, "They're just making some changes to make it more suitable for the album, but no changes that anyone would detect."[23] More than half a century later, in 1999, Trout recalled the re-recording on National Public Radio:

You've probably heard that flawlessly rendered recording many times. It seems to turn up in many documentaries; my greatest hit, as it were. But I have a confession to make. It's a fake. Three years after the war, Fred Friendly and Ed Murrow were assembling . . . *I Can Hear It Now.* . . . Fred asked me to come into the studio and re-create a more sanitized version. Ever since, the re-creation has been taken for the original by nearly everybody, and in the modern tradition of such shocking revelations, I have the tapes to prove it.[24]

In addition, Friendly had pressured David Schoenbrun, a member of Murrow's wartime European team, to ask Charles de Gaulle to re-record his historic broadcast of June 18, 1940, calling on the French people to resist the Nazi occupation. De Gaulle refused and criticized Schoenbrun for making the request. "Friendly was furious when I called to tell him of de Gaulle's refusal," Schoenbrun remembered. "He stormed over the phone, protesting that de Gaulle was a nit-picker, a purist, a holier-than-thou fanatic. Fred was in a tantrum. I simply hung up. It was at this point that I began to have doubts about Friendly's commitment to accuracy. I would have other occasions to confirm this."[25] Several alterations on an album purporting to consist only of original recordings do not detract substantially from its overall value and integrity. However, they reveal Friendly's propensity to let ethical standards slide when it suited his purposes, which had concerned Major Clark during the war.

"*I can hear it now* . . . ," in both the old 78-rpm and new long-playing formats, was an instantaneous critical and commercial success. For example, in the November 22 edition of the *New York Herald Tribune*, John Crosby hailed it as "possibly the first volume of aural history ever produced." Early in 1949, the *New Yorker* paid tribute to the record's achievement and detailed the process by which it was made. Friendly reaped substantial financial benefit. His first royalty payment for the initial six-week sales period ending December 31 amounted to $32,911.12, adjusted for a $22,000 loan that Friendly had taken out as an advance on royalties. Sales continued to be strong after the holiday season of 1948 and reached 250,000 copies in the first year, an unprecedented success for a serious nonmusical recording. Friendly received a second semiannual royalty payment of $12,920.98 for the period ending June 30, 1949.[26]

"I can hear it now . . ." marked a turning point in Friendly's professional fortunes but not solely because of the substantial income it produced. The initial encounter with Edward R. Murrow had a powerful and
enduring impact on Friendly. Friendly later recalled having glimpsed
Murrow for the first time in the lobby of CBS offices at 485 Madison Avenue, where Friendly and Gude had gone to get tapes in preparation for
their initial meeting with Murrow about the record project: "He suddenly
came through the door," Friendly later recalled, "his hair windblown
from driving in his convertible down from the country. He was the most
handsome and magnetic human being I had ever seen, in the prime of
life." Murrow and Friendly were a study in contrasts, physically and tem-
peramentally. A Murrow biographer, contrasting the two figures as they
met for the first time across a table in Louis and Armand's, wrote that
Murrow saw a mastodon of a man:

> Where Murrow was trim and suave, Friendly was simply huge. His
> head was huge. His feet and hands were huge. His features were
> thick, the nose, mouth, and chin. Two men could hardly have been
> less alike, Friendly explosive and Murrow contained; Friendly ebul-
> lient, yet insecure, and Murrow intense, yet poised; Friendly all sur-
> face electricity and Murrow all surface calm; Friendly uneasy with
> his petit bourgeois background and Murrow patrician in spite of his
> background.[27]

For Dorothy Friendly, the core difference was psychological: "Murrow
was so poised, so quietly self-assured, so much in control, impeccably
dressed in his English-tailored suits. Fred was the opposite: big and awkward, invariably rumpled in appearance, his emotions always barely under control." Friendly had approached his first meeting with Murrow
acutely aware of his undistinguished academic pedigree. He was surprised and elated when Murrow responded favorably to the record proposal without inquiring about his credentials. Friendly could hardly believe that "this urbane, sophisticated man saw in *me* a colleague! Me,
rough on the edges, effusive, exuberant."[28]

The advance for *"I can hear it now . . ."* prompted Dorothy to suggest
that they move to larger quarters. She visited Peter Cooper Village, the
housing complex then being completed below Twenty-third Street on the
East Side of Manhattan. For their rental application, Jap Gude doctored
the income figures to make them reach the minimum because Fred and

Dorothy's combined earnings were less than $1,000 a year before he got the advance for the record album. Dorothy was determined to move, although she worried whether she and Fred could handle the $105 rent for their new one-bedroom apartment.[29] It represented a move from quasi-bohemian quarters to a respectable middle-class setting. Friends like Joe and Shirley Wershba moved there as well. Now the Friendlys could entertain their growing circle of professional contacts. Dorothy noted in her diary that March 10, 1949, marked "our first elaborate dinner party at home—The Murrows, [Goddard] Lieberson & wife, the Gudes," adding that "after best part of a decanter of brandy & one of scotch, it was decided to do two news albums—one a sequel—1945–1948."[30]

The great success of *"I can hear it now . . ."* did not resolve Friendly's quest to find work in broadcasting. He feverishly worked toward that end on various fronts in 1947 and 1948, drawing upon Jap Gude's connections and exploiting his new relationship with Edward R. Murrow. In March 1948, while accumulating tapes for the record, he applied for the job of program director at WTOP, the newly acquired CBS station in Washington, D.C. The position was clearly a reach for Friendly, given his limited experience in broadcasting up to that point. Despite having no affiliation with CBS, Friendly had applied for the position using Murrow's office as a personal mail drop, a ploy sure to gain his application additional attention. The response that Friendly received from WTOP's general manager, indicating that the position was being filled internally, was addressed to Friendly, care of Edward R. Murrow at his CBS office at 485 Madison Avenue. The WTOP official softened the blow by writing that "all of us at WTOP, and also at CBS in New York . . . felt definitely that you were the best qualified person for the job, and if it had been possible for us to go outside of the organization, you would have been our choice."[31]

However, another Friendly initiative did pay off in 1948, and it at long last provided his entrée into network broadcasting: a quiz show called *Who Said That?* Friendly drew on his experience with the quiz show format at WEAN and Camp Kohler. Quiz shows had been a staple of radio programming, but Friendly aimed to create a more highbrow version for the listeners who followed current affairs. He apparently borrowed $5,000 from Paul Guttman to prepare the program pilot, offering his friend a share of the venture, which he declined.[32]

On *Who Said That?* a panel of celebrities was asked to identify quotations reported in the previous week from politicians, entertainers, and other figures in the news. On October 13, 1947, Friendly had unsuccess-fully auditioned an earlier version of the program for CBS that would have featured some of its star reporters.[33] Friendly and Jap Gude subse-quently sold the show to NBC. Its radio network began broadcasting *Who Said That?* as a sustaining—that is, unsponsored—summer replacement program from July through September 1948. Friendly, executive pro-ducer and owner of the program, got Robert Trout to be the program's host and John Cameron Swayze to be its regular panelist. Friendly had met Trout, the legendary reporter of historic events in the 1930s and 1940s for CBS, in the course of his work on *"I can hear it now . . . ."* Trout, now employed by NBC, was renowned as an ad-libber: Franklin D. Roo-sevelt would on occasion delay the start of his radio speeches for the plea-sure of listening to Trout's impromptu remarks. Swayze was a well-regarded radio reporter for NBC who would soon help inaugurate television network news. Various celebrity panelists joined Trout and Swayze, the two regulars. These special panelists ranged from politicians and writers to entertainers and included such figures as H. V. Kalten-born, Norman Thomas, Milton Berle, James A. Farley, S. J. Perleman, Moss Hart, Al Capp, and Harold Ickes.

The program was a critical and popular success. John Crosby wrote in his syndicated broadcasting column that the appeal of the news format was heightened by the comments and asides of the participants. *Variety* praised the radio program "since it caters to the intelligence of well-informed listeners" and called it "a refreshing departure from run-of-the-mill entertainment." Friendly also got a rave review from his mother. Rela-tives and family friends assembled at Therese's home in Providence to hear the first broadcast. They ranged from his aunt and confidante Cordie Wachenheimer and his childhood neighbor and classmate Alice Fox to family friend Joel Pincus. One group listened to a radio on the porch; another, to a set in the living room. All thrilled to hear the credits for Fred and Dorothy at the close of the show. Therese wrote that most who knew Fred in Providence listened in their own homes as well.[34] The broadcast represented a triumph for Friendly, Providence's former class clown, whose own mother had worried about his professional prospects.

Robert Trout recalled that almost immediately after *Who Said That?* aired on NBC radio, Friendly campaigned to have the program broadcast on television as well despite initial resistance from network executives. Friendly had become fascinated with the possibilities of the medium that was about to revolutionize communications. He prevailed, and a televised version began airing in December 1948, making it the first quiz show on network television. The radio edition gained a regular slot on NBC's radio schedule in January 1949. For a period in 1950, the television soundtrack was used on radio, one of the earliest simulcasts in broadcasting history. In February 1949, Friendly signed a five-year contract with NBC for *Who Said That?* The level of payment to Friendly would be based on whether the program attracted sponsors, which it eventually did. The radio version would pay $250 a week unsponsored, $1,000 a week sponsored, the television version $250 and $600, respectively, and a simulcast would combine radio and television payments but would reduce the television fee by half.[35] The radio program ended in 1950, while the television edition continued on NBC until 1954 and ended on ABC in 1955. *Who Said That?* was a joint Fred–Dorothy production. In an interview, Friendly gave to the *Providence Journal* during a visit to Providence in 1950, he said it was Dorothy's responsibility to come up with the quotes, which she did by going through dozens of newspapers in their apartment in the Stuyvesant Town complex. Friendly's job consisted of lining up the celebrity panelists and overseeing the production of the program. The couple frequently worked together on the set.[36]

A typed journal maintained by Robert Trout captured both the pleasure and the discomfort he experienced working under Friendly on *Who Said That?* Trout clearly enjoyed the challenge of helping shape the program and adapting it to the medium of television. At the same time, the meticulous, hypersensitive Trout was put off by Friendly's freewheeling and overbearing style. Trout kept lists of how Friendly transposed and edited quotes to render them more pungent for the show. He expressed surprise about Friendly's cavalier treatment of the voluminous mail sent by the audience, farming it out to be read by all manner of people, including his mother on the occasion of a visit she made to watch a broadcast. Trout noted Friendly's propensity to pull ideas out of the blue and then forget them, to change his mind from one minute to the next, to become distracted while attempting to do two things at once. Trout also found Friendly to be a micromanager who chided him, for example, for not being more sociable with the guests before and after the program.[37] In 1950, Friendly told Trout that people felt that he was coasting on the program, being paid well but putting little energy into it on and off the air. Trout responded that he bitterly resented the remarks, that Friendly's accusation was overkill, an attempt to create a "crisis atmosphere" rather than to offer constructive criticism.[38] And yet, despite his discomfort,

Trout retained a grudging respect for Fred Friendly, especially his creativity and his determination in implementing his ideas.[39]

Who Said That? could not fully satisfy Friendly's ambitions as a broadcaster. His memorandum "On Coming Home to Radio Programs," written in 1945, had revealed his lofty agenda for more substantive programming for postwar broadcasting. The memorandum was originally written with radio in mind, but Friendly's interest now embraced television as well. In the summer of 1948, drawing on his new association with NBC, he got credentials to observe in Philadelphia the Republican and Democratic National Conventions, the first to be covered by network television. As *Who Said That?* first went on the air that summer, Friendly was already thinking about his next move—in a journalistic direction.[40] *Who Said That?* was an important step in getting his foot in the door of network television. The need to line up celebrity panelists enabled him to interact with a broad spectrum of influential individuals. February 1950 marked a great coup for *Who Said That?*—a command performance at the annual dinner for the president of the United States given by the Radio Correspondents' Association. A thank-you letter written by Elmer Davis, then head of the association, noted that Truman "has informed us that the show . . . was the best he has ever attended since being president."[41]

Later in 1950, Friendly demonstrated his determination to go beyond the relatively light fare of *Who Said That?* in order to address important historical and contemporary issues in his radio work. In July, the NBC radio network aired in four weekly installments Friendly's *The Quick and the Dead*, a documentary on atomic power. The program was created within NBC's department of news and special events, which was headed by William Brooks, a network vice president. But the program was conceived by Friendly—a firsthand witness to the devastation caused by the bombing of Hiroshima and Nagasaki—who received credit as writer, producer, and director.[42]

Friendly convinced William L. Laurence, the well-connected science reporter for the *New York Times*, to collaborate on the project. His book *Dawn over Zero: The Story of the Atomic Bomb* (1946) served as a primary source for the radio documentary. Laurence had been selected by the head of the Manhattan Project to be the official historian of the development of the atomic bomb; he witnessed its first test explosion in the United States and flew on an observation plane when Nagasaki was bombed. Laurence also wrote many of the official government statements

about the development and use of the atomic bomb for President Truman
and the Department of War. Hence Laurence was in the questionable
position of being a covert participant in events that he covered as a journalist. At any rate, Laurence's expertise and contacts were invaluable for
Friendly's undertaking, enabling him to enlist a remarkable group of
prominent figures to assist or participate in the broadcast—among them,
Albert Einstein and other prominent scientists, the pilots who dropped
the bombs on Japan, and well-known actors like Helen Hayes and Paul
Lukas, as well as the comedian Bob Hope.

Friendly had already exhibited his proclivity to go to the top, to seek
out the big names, whether it was General Patton during the war or Edward R. Murrow in its aftermath. But how could Friendly, still a relative
unknown, sell NBC, Laurence, Einstein, and other prominent figures on
working with him on his radio documentary? Mike Dann, then in the
press department of NBC and a friend of Friendly's, testified to his colleague's extraordinary persuasive powers. Friendly's pitches were so impassioned, detailed, and riveting, Dann recalled, that often the final
product, the actual broadcast, no matter how good, could not fully live up
to Friendly's original description. Dann compared Friendly's articulation
of a proposed program with the power with which Arthur Miller read
from his own work. More than fifty years later, Dann still recalled Friendly's
histrionic description of his plan for dramatizing the first atomic chain
reaction, which was set off on an abandoned squash court under Stagg
Stadium at the University of Chicago. What stood out for Dann was the
incredible physicality with which Friendly made his case in such situations. It was as if, with his towering presence and loud voice and penetrating gaze, he cornered his prey: "He might physically grab you by the
collar and talk to you . . . [and] when he talked to you—in show business
they call it an eye lock—you couldn't turn your head anyplace."[43]

In order to give *The Quick and the Dead* broad appeal—to make the
story of nuclear power informative but also dramatic and entertaining—
Friendly directed his power of persuasion toward a legendary Hollywood
personality. Friendly came up with the idea of using Bob Hope as a narrator who represented an average American citizen confused about the
history and future of nuclear power. (Hope had been one of the subjects
of Friendly's *Footprints* series.) Among Friendly's papers is the outline of
a letter to Hope, apparently drafted by Friendly for NBC vice president
Brooks, marked confidential and for delivery by messenger. The draft
notes the importance of the topic and the lack of knowledge and fear

surrounding the issue of atomic power. It describes "a project which could well be the finest thing that radio has done since the war," one that promised "to win every award in the book." And it adds that William Laurence and Albert Einstein, among others, had agreed to participate in the project: "The project needs but one thing—Bob Hope."[44]

Hope did agree to play the role of the befuddled man-in-the-street posing questions about atomic power. Laurence provided historical and scientific background, interspersed with speeches by Roosevelt and Churchill, interviews with actual participants in the bombing of Japan, as well as dramatic reenactments, with Paul Lukas playing Albert Einstein and Helen Hayes playing the pioneering nuclear physicist Lise Meitner. The development of the bomb was dramatized as a great detective story, with Meitner's forced departure from Germany for Denmark (where, by a chance experiment, she split the atom) and with the arrival of Enrico Fermi in the United States (where he initially failed to interest the military in the atomic bomb). The second program was devoted to the building of the atomic bomb; the third, to the hydrogen bomb; the fourth and final episode, to the future of nuclear power. Jack Gould of the *New York Times* characterized Friendly's approach as "a brilliant use of the showmanship of the entertainment world to explain vividly and simply the most portentous undertaking of the world of science."[45]

As one reviewer of *The Quick and the Dead* wrote, "This tour de force was accomplished by one of writer-producer Fred Friendly's favorite gadgets, the tape recorder." Armed with his recorder, Friendly had traveled across the country, bringing together on tape principals in the story of the atomic bomb. In Florida, for example, he taped an interview with one of the pilots of the *Enola Gay*, the B-29 that dropped the bomb on Hiroshima. Friendly traveled to Chicago to interview the physicist I. I. Rabi; on the train ride back to New York, Friendly encountered Robert Bernstein, his former driver from the China-Burma-India theater with whom he would establish an important personal and professional relationship.[46]

Although the documentary made it appear that Bob Hope and William Laurence were conversing in the same room, Hope's questions and comments had all been taped separately in Hollywood; Hope and Laurence never actually met or spoke with each other. Moreover, Friendly used some inspired aural effects. A newspaper critic wrote, "Of all the voices heard on the first program, the most compelling was that of the neutron counter . . . as it recorded, tick by tick, the first self-sustaining chain reaction." In order to dramatize as authentically as possible the historic event on the squash court in Chicago—the segment he had originally described to Mike Dann—Friendly recorded a real counter measuring uranium at the Columbia University physics laboratory.[47]

Friendly outdid himself in replicating the otherworldly sound of the first test of the atomic bomb in New Mexico, which reverberated between two mountain ranges. All who heard it—no actual recording of the sound was available—recalled the actual explosion as having been preceded by an ominous, violent, drawn-out trembling. Friendly set out to create a sound effect that could be felt before it was heard. Technicians pounded mallets on an enormous vertical drum of stretched leather, six by eight feet, to create an eerie vibration for radio listeners. To simulate the actual explosion, the combined sounds of wire cable whips and sixteen thunder records were played simultaneously and then multiplied eightfold by tape copies. Jack Gould described the effect in the *New York Times* as "the most extraordinary reproduction of the sound of an explosion yet heard on the air. Through Mr. Friendly's recording magic, the listener at home almost felt the explosion's vibration before he could hear its rumble. The effect was startling—and awakening."[48]

Indeed, Friendly's goal for *The Quick and the Dead* was to arouse the U.S. public: "Decisions on the control of atomic energy made in the next few years will affect you and your children's lives." In the final episode, on the future of the nuclear age, Friendly quoted David Lilienthal's criticism of excessive secrecy: "If schemers or fools or rascals ever get this thing out of the people's hands, it may be too late to find out what it's all about." Although he called for increased public discussion, Friendly wished to end on an upbeat note, "with special emphasis on atomic energy as a boon to mankind."[49] *The Quick and the Dead* did not address controversy about the need to drop atomic bombs in Japan or fears about the long-term effects of radiation. The radio series aired in the early days of the nuclear arms race with the Soviet Union.[50] Dissident perspectives voiced by figures like I. F. Stone and Leo Szilard were not incorporated in Friendly's documentary.

Yet if constrained by a climate of opinion that discouraged critical perspectives about atomic power, and by Laurence's role in providing what one historian has called an "official narrative" of the dawning of the nuclear age, *The Quick and the Dead* represented a major breakthrough in the radio documentary. *Time* magazine wrote that it was a miracle that it reached the air at all: "Some network executives protested that it was too controversial; some scientists, fearing sensationalism, were at first reluctant to help; and the cast of 19 had to be tracked from Pensacola to Hollywood with recording equipment."[51]

Friendly's frenzied work on *The Quick and the Dead* left him exhausted. His seven-week crash course on atomic power, travels across the nation with his tape recorder, and ambitious production schedule resulted in a loss of twenty pounds.[52] But the effort gave Friendly the greater recognition he sought for public affairs programming more substantive than his news quiz show. Indeed, the series on nuclear power prompted interest in Friendly at NBC's rival network, CBS, which was seeking new blood for its radio documentary unit. *The Quick and the Dead* had marked the end of one era and the beginning of another in the history of the broadcast documentary. Friendly, standing with one foot in the past, had used the device of dramatization characteristic of the popular radio and newsreel editions of *The March of Time*. However, he had based the reconstructed dialogue on careful research and avoided the histrionics and bathos of the Time Inc. newsreels. Moreover, Friendly had exploited new recording technology—magnetic tape—to capture and edit the actual voices of leading figures in the story of atomic power, pointing to the future of the documentary as an authentic purveyor of information. *The Quick and the Dead* expanded on the techniques used to create the original *"I can hear it now . . ."* album in 1948.

As *The Quick and the Dead* aired in July 1950, and the second volume, *"I can hear it now . . . ," 1945–1949*, went on sale, Sig Mickelson, then director of public affairs for CBS, invited Friendly to dinner at the Chinese Rathskeller on West Fifty-second Street. William Paley and Frank Stanton had recently met with Mickelson to signal their desire to reclaim CBS's prewar primacy in radio documentaries. The establishment of a documentary radio unit in 1946 had not produced the results that CBS's top management desired. Mickelson believed that the brass might also have been acting out of concern that previous contributors were vulnerable to charges of being committed liberals and "soft on communism."[53] Paley and Stanton asked Mickelson to recommend a producer who could capitalize on the new recording technology and provide fresh leadership for the documentary unit. Mickelson had a keen eye for talent; in the early 1950s he would anoint Walter Cronkite as television's first anchor and hire Harry Reasoner and Charles Kuralt. Or, put less charitably by a Murrow biographer, "Like many men who lack fire themselves, Mickelson could feel it in others." In his meeting with Paley and Stanton, Mickelson strongly recommended the hiring of Friendly, citing *The Quick and the Dead* and his collaboration with Murrow on the *"I can hear it now . . ."* album. Paley responded, "Go get him," prompting Mickelson's dinner meeting with Friendly.[54]

At the time Friendly was under a five-year NBC contract that began March 1, 1949, but only as an "independent contractor" to produce *Who Said That?* The critical success of *The Quick and the Dead* made Friendly a rising star and held out the promise of new possibilities in public affairs programming at NBC. Yet CBS had always been Friendly's network of choice. Jap Gude had been conspiring with Friendly to find an opening to CBS, and the agent contacted Mickelson when he heard about a possible opening in the documentary unit.[55] Nonetheless, Friendly wanted to be sure that being hired in the radio documentary unit would not constrain his career at CBS in two critical respects: the opportunity to work with Murrow in the news department and to try his hand in the emerging medium of television.

At the luncheon with Mickelson, attended by both men's wives, Friendly signaled his willingness to work on radio documentaries but stressed that "his long-range goal was to produce a '*Life* Magazine of the Air'" for television. Mickelson said that the idea of a television newsmagazine was premature for a medium still in its infancy but that Friendly would be well positioned and encouraged to participate in such an undertaking when the time was right. As far as Mickelson was concerned, the deal was sealed with a drink at the old Ritz Hotel bar. However, Friendly had not broached with Mickelson his second concern, his desire to work with Murrow, and wanted to meet with Murrow before actually signing a contract with CBS.[56]

In the summer of 1950, Murrow was covering the war in Korea and would return only in mid-August. So while Friendly agreed in principle to join CBS, he decided to await Murrow's return before finalizing the arrangements. Friendly wanted a tacit understanding that they would work together in news, even though Mickelson was hiring him to work in the documentary unit. So Friendly was in limbo, eagerly awaiting Murrow's return from Korea. At the same time, Dorothy was pressing Fred not to postpone a vacation trip to Europe that they had planned. The trip was prompted by a windfall—a check for $24,000—that he received that spring from NBC, his share of the revenues from *Who Said That?* They had worked hard for the past three years, with Dorothy's cramped apartment on First Avenue serving as both home and office for much of that period. She felt strongly that it was time for them to catch their breath, to take pleasure in each other away from the demands of work, and to enjoy the fruits of their initial success. She viewed the trip as a second honeymoon. As an avid student of art history, she was eager to visit the great museums of Europe. But Fred now felt that too much was happening professionally for him to leave the country, and he wanted to cancel the trip. "Jap and Helen Gude came over and tried to convince me not to go," Dorothy later recalled, adding: "Fred would have other people talk to me to say something he didn't want to say himself. I realized at once that Fred put them up to it." But Dorothy persisted and Murrow was unavailable, so Fred reluctantly agreed to take the vacation after all.[57]

Fred and Dorothy took a liner across the Atlantic, and Friendly returned to Europe for the first time since the war. Fred seemed distracted at first, but after arriving in Europe he was able to put work aside sufficiently to enjoy himself during the six-week grand tour. They traveled extensively in Italy, staying in Florence and Pisa and motoring along the coast. Dorothy relished the museum visits, and Friendly networked with U.S. journalists stationed abroad. In Vienna, they saw the CBS correspondent Alexander Kendrick. They traveled on the Orient Express from Vienna to Paris, where David Schoenbrun introduced them to Art Buchwald, who was then writing for the *International Herald Tribune*. The Friendlys hit it off with Buchwald and his future wife, Ann. In a telephone interview years later, Buchwald recalled his first impression of Friendly as "an overpowering guy," adding, "And since he wasn't my boss, I wasn't afraid of him." Dorothy, Buchwald felt, anchored Fred: "I think the key to the whole thing—I hope you got it on tape—was his wife. She brought him down to earth."[58]

Friendly returned to New York in late August eager to see Murrow, preferably at his farm in Pauling, New York, where the two could confidentially discuss CBS's offer. As Dorothy recalled, Friendly did not initially tell Murrow the real reason he wanted to meet in Pauling but said instead that Dorothy was eager to see the farm. At Pauling, Janet Murrow gave Dorothy a tour of the property while the two men talked business. Dorothy distinctly recalled Fred's satisfaction at the outcome of the meeting. "The Murrow factor made him interested in CBS," she emphasized. "He wanted assurance he would work with Murrow—which he apparently got."[59]

Moving to CBS meant that Friendly would have a full-time salaried job for the first time in his life. More important, he would have the opportunity to become a working colleague of his idol, Edward R. Murrow. Five years earlier, Friendly had spurned job offers in his native Providence to see whether he could make it in New York. He had briefly contemplated screenwriting, then focused his considerable ambition and energies on breaking into network broadcasting. For three years he did not earn a cent. If Friendly had any doubts about his prospects, he did not articulate them, even to the woman who became his professional partner and wife during this period.

Years later, Friendly would acknowledge how difficult this time had been for him. The difficulty was more psychological than economic, the unspoken pressure of not knowing whether he would recapture that sense of mastery he had experienced in the China-Burma-India theater: the feeling of being at the center of history, of having extraordinary freedom to do highly innovative and significant work under the protection of a powerful mentor. His first breakthrough was meeting broadcast journalism's top agent, Jap Gude, and Friendly's subsequent collaboration with Murrow on *"I can hear it now . . . ."* A measure of financial success and professional recognition came at the NBC radio network with the quiz show *Who Said That?* and the documentary *The Quick and the Dead*. Finally, in the late summer of 1950 came the job offer from CBS with Murrow's support. In an interview decades later, Friendly recalled the years immediately after the war: "You have to be 'willing to be lucky,'" as E. B. White once said, and I *was* willing to be lucky, but the luck took a long time in coming."[60]

4 *See It Now*

FRED FRIENDLY'S HIRING BY CBS in 1950 marked a watershed in the thirty-five-year-old's life. He was no longer just a talented and ambitious freelance producer from Providence with a successful record, radio quiz, and radio documentary program on his résumé. While the ties to Providence would remain strong, he had now truly made it in New York. Moreover, the older generation in Providence was dying off. A year earlier, Joe Pincus, a substitute father figure during Friendly's childhood in Providence, had died. Dorothy recalled the impact of the news of Joe's death: "It was the only time I remember [Fred] crying."[1] Fred volunteered to pay Pincus's widow a monthly stipend of $40 to help with her living expenses, which the Fain family would supplement. A year after the move to Peter Cooper Village and Fred's hiring at CBS, his and Dorothy's first child, Andrew, was born. While Friendly had never voiced doubts about realizing his ambitions in the years after the war, Dorothy felt that the pressure had made him irritable at times, closed up, hard to get to. After the CBS contract, he became visibly more confident. According to Dorothy, "Success made him easier to live with."[2]

The contract that Fred Friendly signed with CBS is a remarkable document, a testament to the network's belief that Friendly would play a major role as a producer for the new medium of television no less than for the radio documentary unit for which he had been hired. The contract, dated October 30, 1950, notes that Friendly "enjoys a preeminent position in the preparation and production of public affairs and documentary programming." His pioneering efforts in public service, news, and documentary production place him "in a unique position to contribute his experience to the development of television programming in that field." The contract recognizes "that Friendly desires to study and engage in certain experiments respecting the format and presentation of television documentaries." At the same time, the network signals its intention "to provide for Friendly's association with Columbia over a long period of time, not only as producer of public affairs and documentary programs but as an advisor to Columbia in the general field of public service programming." Friendly was hired for a five-year period as a producer for radio and television at a base salary of $22,500 a year, which would be supplemented according to a formula for commercially sponsored programs produced by Friendly.[3]

If the contract marked a breakthrough for Friendly, it proved to be a shrewd step for CBS that would help ease Murrow into the age of television. Murrow had returned from the war highly wary of television. He prepared two articles about television for the *New York Times* and *Atlantic Monthly*.[4] Neither publication chose to print Murrow's pessimistic assessment of television's prospects as a news medium. Murrow feared that its dependence on the visual would sacrifice substance, asking "Will TV regard news as anything more than a saleable commodity?" Yet, paradoxically, Murrow was a natural for television. After watching Murrow on television, a CBS director remarked, "Ed Murrow had on a television screen what Gary Cooper and Spencer Tracy had on the movie screen, the same virility, the same cinematic eyes. And he had that voice, that pure voice."[5] Friendly, enthusiastic about television's potential as a vehicle for news and public affairs programming, wanted to harness Murrow's talent and prestige for the new medium. Friendly would have preferred to launch a television news program when he arrived at CBS, but Murrow was not ready.[6] "Had Murrow wanted it," Murrow's biographer Joseph Persico observed, "the new medium would have been theirs." So Friendly began his partnership with Murrow at CBS on radio. On November 9, 1950, ten days after Friendly signed his contract, the new broadcast team produced for CBS radio *A Report to the Nation—The 1950 Election*. A CBS press release said that the program would be "the first in a series of projected documentary productions which Murrow will do on CBS radio and TV."[7] The statement suggested how quickly and successfully Friendly had staked his claim at CBS to working in television as well as in radio.

The election special served as a launching pad for a weekly hour-long radio news program broadcast at 9:00 P.M. on Friday evenings called *Hear It Now*. CBS said that the documentary series would rely on the revolutionary technique of audio montage pioneered by Murrow and Friendly.[8] As the name *Hear It Now* suggests, the show capitalized on the success of their record album and on the advances in recording technology that could be exploited for radio as well as records. It marked the first opportunity for Friendly to develop a broadcast magazine, a format he had originally conceived for television as a "*Life* magazine of the air." *Hear It Now* covered the news of the previous week using tape recordings of actual events supplemented by live interviews. Friendly was listed as "writer-producer"; Murrow, as "commentator." In addition, Don Hollenbeck did press commentary and Red Barber, sports commentary. Virgil Thompson composed the theme song for *Hear It Now*, which aired on 173 stations.[9]

The first edition of *Hear It Now*, broadcast on December 15, included a wide range of reports: the voices of soldiers under fire in Korea, remarks from the chief U.S. delegate to the United Nations, a biographical vignette of General Douglas MacArthur, reviews of the press and the arts, excerpts from the film *Born Yesterday*, Carl Sandburg reading his poem "The People, Yes," a humorous segment about President Truman's response to a music criticism, and sports. An enthusiastic review the next day in the *New York Times*, "Show Illustrates Drama in the News," said the program "proved that news in the raw can be exciting radio fare." The reviewer wrote that *Hear It Now* exhibited serious journalism and could become a significant audio supplement to print journalism. Only one caveat was expressed: "Unfortunately, Mr. Murrow, in adapting 'March of Time' techniques—high tension delivery, stirring bars of music, vivid adjectives and verbs—forgot that history needs no histrionics." Jack Gould of the *Times* was more critical of *Hear It Now* in the Sunday paper a week later. Gould argued that "sound journalism does not always permit the theatrical touch," and he expressed the hope that the supercharged first run would be followed by a more measured and well-integrated approach. Gould may have been correct in pointing to an initial attempt to do too much but might not have fully understood the implications of the broadcast magazine that Murrow and Friendly were developing as a format distinct from the traditional radio news summary.[10]

While broadcasting *Hear It Now* on radio, Murrow could observe the unmistakable signs of the growth of television as a medium for news as well as entertainment. The migration of radio stars to television and the dramatic increase in viewership set the stage for the decline of the radio networks. In 1948 CBS, like NBC, inaugurated a nightly fifteen-minute network news broadcast; CBS's program was *Television News with Douglas Edwards*. Insiders at CBS believed that Sig Mickelson, the newly named president of television news, had hoped that Murrow, despite his reservations about the medium, would do the program.[11] In addition to the nightly news programs, the networks televised occasional news specials, and one such special made a deep impression on Murrow and Friendly: television coverage in 1950/1951 of Senator Estes Kefauver's hearings on organized crime conducted in different cities throughout the United States. Interest reached a fever pitch in March 1951 during eight days of televised proceedings from New York City that featured fifty witnesses, among them, former mayor William O'Dwyer and the crime boss Frank Costello.

The hearings were carried in nineteen eastern cities—national network interconnection had not yet been established—and viewed by an estimated 30 million.[12] People took off from work; classes were dismissed; department stores, theaters, and restaurants lost business; the streets were empty. The hearings revealed to a fascinated public the scope of the problem of organized crime and prompted a national discussion of solutions. *Life* magazine reported that "never before had the nation been riveted so completely on a single matter" and suggested that television had the potential to reengage Americans in a more direct way in public affairs. It was, *Life* said, "the broadcast from which all future use of television in public affairs must date." Murrow acknowledged that television had not simplified the topic at hand. Friendly was deeply impressed as well: it opened his eyes to the ability of television to give congressional testimony a national forum that would influence public discourse about a significant public policy issue.[13]

In April 1951, a month after the Kefauver hearings in New York City, television covered with fanfare the return of MacArthur from Korea and his address before a joint session of Congress. Slowly, despite his continuing skepticism, Murrow began to reassess his view of television. He began to acknowledge the tremendous potential impact of television in relation to what he now termed "the old-fashioned instruments of radio and print."[14] It was becoming more difficult for him to resist the pressure from Friendly to tackle the new medium. Not long after the Kefauver hearings, Murrow and Friendly decided to end *Hear It Now* after only six months on the air—its last broadcast was on June 15, 1951—and coproduce a new version of the program for television called *See It Now*. As Joseph Persico observed, launching *Hear It Now* for radio in 1950 "had been rather like building the best street lamp at the turn of the century when most people were rewiring their homes for electricity."[15]

Yet, as he was about to embark on this new television venture, Murrow hesitated, even contemplated leaving CBS and the broadcasting field. In the summer of 1951, Murrow received a call from his alma mater, Washington State College, asking whether he would agree to be considered for the position of college president. He surprised the school's search committee by allowing his name to be submitted. Murrow wrote school officials expressing frustration with the professional grind at CBS and with the constraints of raising his son in New York City. He made discreet inquiries about breaking his contract with CBS and met quietly with members of the search committee in Spokane during a trip out west. However, at the end of the summer he withdrew his name from consideration.[16]

As A. M. Sperber's biography emphasizes, Murrow's "entry into television had coincided with a low point in his life, his health, his outlook and output." In general, the transition from wartime London to postwar New York had been difficult for him. CBS had changed: Bill Paley became chairman and was replaced as president and chief operating officer by Frank Stanton, who would become Murrow's archrival within the company. Murrow's unhappy tenure at CBS as vice president and director of public affairs beginning in 1946 lasted only a year and a half; it was marred by the angry departure of an old—now former—friend, William Shirer, amid accusations of censorship and betrayal. Moreover, Murrow was disheartened by the advent of the cold war abroad and anti-Communist hysteria at home. In the summer of 1950, he went to the Far East to cover the Korean War. As he prepared to return to the United States, Murrow raised searching questions about the conflict. For example, on August 14, 1950, less than two months after the outbreak of the war, he spoke of the plight of Korean peasants victimized by a scorched-earth policy. "Will our reoccupation of that fleabitten land lessen, or increase, the attraction of Communism?" Murrow asked.[17] The report never aired because Paley and Stanton believed that it contravened General MacArthur's prohibitions against criticisms of command decisions. Shocked to learn that his final report had been censored, Murrow contemplated resigning from CBS.

The same year, Murrow's daily radio news program lost its national sponsorship. In this period, Murrow became decidedly less outspoken. His bouts of depression and physical exhaustion increased in frequency. Although only in his early forties, Murrow was not in good health. His hard-working, hard-living, and hard-smoking regimen had taken its toll. In the winter of 1950/1951, he began suffering from debilitating colds with spells of shortness of breath and heavy coughing, a harbinger of the lung cancer that would lead to his untimely death. No wonder that on the eve of his entry full force into the medium of television, he entertained the idea of forsaking it all, of abandoning the frenzied world of broadcasting for the pastoral life of academia in his home state of Washington.[18]

Thus Murrow and Friendly began preparations for *See It Now* in markedly different frames of mind. Murrow harbored reservations about the transition from radio to television while exhibiting symptoms of professional and physical burnout. Determined to prove himself, consumed by ambition, possessed by a manic energy, Friendly was acutely aware that *his* career was poised for takeoff. His contract with CBS reflected his dream of pioneering a new form of public affairs programming for a medium that he realized was on the cusp of transforming U.S. culture—a medium he was prepared to embrace. That this experiment would be undertaken at CBS with a living—if ambivalent—broadcasting legend intensified Friendly's excitement and sense of possibilities.

As planning began for the new television show in the summer of 1951, Friendly expressed lofty aspirations for television journalism in an article in *Variety* headlined "Video to Mirror World as 'Mass Information Gazette.'" Friendly wrote about the possibility of creating a new kind of reporting, an original form of television actuality or documentary. It should not be modeled on newsreels or a magazine of the air, he wrote. It should not be a simple hybrid of audio and visual reportage "but an entirely new concept combining these vital human senses in the creation of a new medium." Friendly argued that by depending on recycled radio entertainment, television risked exhausting itself, running itself "as dry as an eroded, wasted wheat field in a Kansas dust bowl." Television could renew itself through regular and substantial coverage of news and educate the public as well: "It will enable the American people to be the best informed people in the world, or the worst, depending upon how well we make use of it." Friendly, in effect, was an evangelist for the potential of television as "the greatest mass information gazette in the history of man."[19]

See It Now, the vehicle for Friendly's agenda for television, was established with a considerable degree of editorial and institutional independence. According to Friendly, Alcoa executives took the initiative in offering to sponsor a televised version of *Hear It Now*. The giant aluminum company sought to use the prestige of a television program featuring Murrow to counter public relations problems caused by antitrust violations. Murrow warned Alcoa's representatives, "Fred doesn't know anything about television and neither do I." Friendly recalled that Alcoa did not even request a pilot program, "and Ed and I agreed to produce the series without quite knowing what we would be doing, or even which end of the camera one looked into." Murrow did know, however, to exact from Alcoa a promise of complete editorial independence.[20]

Murrow also established *See It Now*'s autonomy in relation to the network news operation that was being established under Sig Mickelson, who had been named in August 1951 to the new position of director of CBS-TV News and Public Affairs. Mickelson, who had hired Friendly for the radio documentary unit at CBS and worked with him on *Hear It Now*, assumed that *See It Now* would be situated within the news department. But *See It Now*'s offices were located behind frosted glass on the seventeenth floor of 485 Madison Avenue, walled off from Mickelson's bailiwick. Murrow and Friendly would report directly to Paley and Stanton.[21] CBS announced at the end of October 1951 that *See It Now*, a "Murrow–Friendly News Series," would debut on November 18, with Alcoa sponsorship to begin with the December 2 broadcast. The press release characterized the program airing on Sundays from 3:30 to 4:00 P.M. as "the news magazine of television." CBS underscored the Murrow–Friendly partnership. The program would extend "into the medium of sight and sound the Murrow–Friendly technique of presenting the news through the people who make the news." Murrow was designated "on-camera editor" and Friendly, "collaborating producer."

The CBS press release said that *See It Now* would feature live reports and filmed segments. Topics would range from personal interviews to overseas reports, from documentary features to late-breaking news. CBS noted that the program would draw on an array of sources: *See It Now*'s own four mobile camera-reporter crews, supplemented by regular CBS television news correspondents, plus material from newsreel companies and news agencies. The press release identified Friendly as "a veteran radio producer and writer who, among other notable achievements, wrote and produced the famous documentary on atomic energy, 'The Quick and the Dead.'"[22] Fred Friendly was the driving force in the genesis of *See It Now*. Yet as CBS's press release indicated, his experience in broadcasting was limited to audio—to recordings and radio—except for the televised simulcast of his radio quiz show *Who Said That?*

Friendly had significant precedents in photojournalism, newsreels, and documentary film on which to draw. However, television differed significantly from these media, with its unique set of technological constraints and potentialities. Virtually from the beginning of his relationship with CBS, from his first luncheon with Sig Mickelson and subsequent contract negotiations, Friendly had expressed interest in creating for television a "*Life* magazine of the air." Friendly did not have extensive knowledge of the history of photojournalism. However, he was aware of the remarkable visual impact of the magazine that Henry Luce had founded in 1936, of the power of its great photographers to tell stories and encapsulate issues for a national readership. Time and again in the years to come, Friendly would describe *See It Now*'s approach as providing the "little picture" that illuminated larger truths, an implicit acknowledgment of the great tradition of *Life*'s photojournalism during the preceding fifteen years. Friendly would also draw upon the precedent, as well as the personnel, of the newsreel, the ten-minute prelude to feature films produced by Metrotone, Fox Movietone News, and the Pathé Newsreel. While the production quality of the newsreels shot with 35-millimeter film was high, the journalistic standards were low. The newsreels featured staged events such as ship christenings and press conferences accompanied by bombastic voiceovers, and they lacked the journalistic enterprise or breadth of a fully developed news medium. Another Luce enterprise, *The March of Time*, added a dimension to the newsreel; it existed from 1935 until 1951, the year of *See It Now*'s launch, and gave lengthier treatment to fewer stories, reconstructing and dramatizing events. It also introduced controversy into its newsreels—for example, a critical report on Huey P. Long in which he was ridiculed through clips of his speeches and actions. However, in dramatizing events *The March of Time* used newsmakers and actors to reenact scenes, a practice that undermined its journalistic integrity.[23]

The tradition of documentary film provided the substance lacking in the newsreel. As with photojournalism, Friendly had not previously exhibited a serious interest in documentary film. As a young man in Providence, he briefly considered a career in acting and enjoyed movies but was drawn to conventional Hollywood fare. After the war, when he had toyed with the idea of becoming a screenwriter, he had aspired to write commercial feature films. There is no evidence that Friendly as a young man was familiar with the classic documentary films of the 1920s and 1930s of Robert Flaherty and Pare Lorenz.[24] At CBS, however, Friendly became an autodidact, mounting his own crash course to prepare himself to produce a television newsmagazine. He systematically studied documentaries in the film collection of the Museum of Modern Art. He also reviewed and contrasted the techniques of the different newsreel operations while familiarizing himself with the nuts and bolts of film equipment. In addition to the countless hours he spent viewing this footage, he interviewed documentary film and newsreel professionals in order to better understand the operating methods of the two genres.[25]

Although Sig Mickelson would not have authority over *See It Now*, he closely observed Friendly's preparations for the program. He saw how Friendly's study of the journalistic practice of traditional media provided a host of useful precedents but no definitive model for *See It Now*. Friendly came to realize that the medium of television would transform his notion of a "*Life* magazine of the air" in ways he had barely begun to contemplate, that the model of photojournalism was too static for what he had in mind. Here the documentary film tradition was instructive. Yet works like *Nanook of the North* and *The Plow That Broke the Plains* involved lengthy preparation and an artistic synthesis incompatible with a weekly news program. Newsreels, conversely, were produced on a weekly basis but were usually limited to ten-minute episodes of questionable journalistic value. In addition, Friendly found that the lack of synchronous sound, except for an occasional speech, circumscribed the journalistic potential of newsreels. Friendly counted on the potential technical flexibility of television, especially its ability to combine live and filmed segments, to permit a weekly program of substance. *See It Now* would owe a great deal to the example of the newsmagazine and the radio roundup in form. Mickelson wrote of Friendly, "He began thinking of a new art form that would borrow from print, sound broadcasting, film and live television blended in a way that was unprecedented."[26]

Nonetheless, for a moment Friendly hesitated to take full charge. While making the rounds in preparation of the program, he had asked Bosley Crowther, the film critic of the *New York Times*, to recommend a motion picture director to coordinate and integrate the content of *See It Now*. Crowther advised Friendly against such a hire, suggesting that to do so would tilt the project toward old rather than new approaches.[27] He took Crowther's advice. As Friendly assumed full responsibility, he made a technical decision with far-reaching implications: *See It Now* would use 35-millimeter film instead of the markedly inferior 16-millimeter film. But CBS's rudimentary film facilities were set up for 16-millimeter. Opting for 35-millimeter film required—indeed, enabled—Friendly to go outside CBS to subcontractors for personnel and production facilities, further increasing his control of the program.

Friendly capitalized on cutbacks in the newsreel industry in creating his production team. Hearst Metrotone News/MGM News of the Day subcontracted to *See It Now* camera teams as well as use of a film laboratory on Ninth Avenue and editing and screening facilities at 550 Fifth Avenue. At the outset, CBS paid Hearst, which in turn paid *See It Now*'s technicians. Hence these subcontractors functioned outside the direct purview of the network and were answerable only to Friendly. Friendly hired top camera operators from News of the Day like Martin Barnett, Leo Rossi, and Charles Mack. He also hired seasoned professionals as film editors: Academy Award–winner Gene Milford from Columbia Pictures; William P. Thompson, who had worked with Frank Capra; and an assistant editor, Mili Lerner. In addition, *See It Now* needed a European cameraman-producer as well as reporters and a director. Friendly convinced Bill McClure of the Pathé Newsreel, who was based in Paris but on leave in New York, to join *See It Now*. Palmer Williams, a documentary filmmaker, heard about CBS's new contract with News of the Day and went to see Friendly, who hired him as director of operations in New York.

Friendly added key personnel from within the ranks of CBS, including two reporter-producers from WCBS in New York: Edmund Scott and Joseph Wershba. Scott had formerly written for the liberal New York newspaper *PM*; Wershba had worked on the *"I can hear it now . . ."* record and the *Hear It Now* radio program. For the position of director, Friendly selected Don Hewitt, an associate producer of the original CBS evening network news program with Douglas Edwards. Friendly was astute at determining the talent he needed and finding the right candidates for those positions. He was not afraid to surround himself with talented people; indeed, he realized they would be crucial to his own success. Many members of the original team—for example, Bill McClure and Joe Wershba—would have long and distinguished careers at CBS. Don Hewitt would later produce the first televised presidential debates and create *60 Minutes*. The hiring of Palmer Williams was especially important. During the war, Williams had worked on the *Why We Fight* series and on *The True Glory*, which won an Academy Award. In the postwar period, he had worked with Burgess Meredith and John Houseman, and at one point had suggested to Jap Gude that the *"I can hear it now . . ."* record be put to film. Williams's breadth of knowledge and organizational skills were such that Friendly described him as "our pathfinder as we ventured down an unmarked trail" and "as much my teacher as was Murrow."[28]

The mix of personnel was not without its contradictions and potential tensions, as Bill McClure observed: the team included both the urbane, liberal, veteran CBS correspondents and the newsreel camera operators from the conservative, red-baiting Hearst organization. Privately, Palmer Williams, aware of how difficult a series with weekly deadlines as conceived by Friendly would be, was skeptical that it could be sustained. He underestimated Friendly's determination. After *See It Now* was on the air, Williams recalled Murrow's telling Friendly, "You son of a bitch, you *knew* how tough this was going to be and didn't tell us." Murrow had also been naive about the need for a powerful executive producer to make it all work. Before the initial broadcast, he met in London with David Schoenbrun and Howard K. Smith to introduce them to Bill McClure and go over plans for *See It Now*. Smith asked who would be in charge of the operation. Murrow answered no one, it would be a team effort like that of the Murrow Boys during World War II, a response that Smith found unrealistic.[29]

On November 18, 1951, Murrow opened the program with an acknowledgment that *See It Now* was an experiment, a work in progress: "This is an old team trying to learn a new trade." The old team could be understood as all the associates at CBS who had previously worked with Murrow on radio. Yet Murrow also emphatically and publicly located the new program on the continuum of productions of the Murrow–Friendly team, now facing the challenge of bringing journalistic authenticity to a new medium. Murrow continued:

> Four years ago we began producing the I CAN HEAR IT NOW record album. A year ago we began doing a weekly radio version called HEAR IT NOW. In preparing to do SEE IT NOW on television, we were faced with the problem of "where to do it from." As they say in the trade, "Where do we originate." In the record album and HEAR IT NOW, we had always prided ourselves on the fact that every voice we used was real . . . every sound, raw. . . . No actors; no sound effects. How, then, could we originate our television version on a TV sound stage with sets, props and the usual variety of effects . . . ? There was talk of originating in my office. Even this, they said, would

have to be a duplication of my office and this seemed a bit phony. So, as an experiment, we have decided to try doing the show from where all television shows have to originate . . . the control room. I am talking to you from the control room of Studio 41, for actually, if I have any function on this show, it is really only that of a switcher who occasionally leans over the cameramens' [sic] shoulder to whisper something in your ear.[30]

Viewers saw Murrow in a swivel chair and Don Hewitt, the director, facing four monitors, responding to Murrow's requests to switch from one video line to another.

Sig Mickelson credited Friendly with realizing that a program relying on film need not broadcast from a studio with a set. Mickelson recalled a successful three-minute test run of fitting a bulky television camera into the cramped space of the control room. Don Hewitt would claim that he came up with the idea of broadcasting from the studio. Most likely, the decision reflected to some degree Murrow's desire to dispense with artifice, Friendly's attempt at a creative solution responsive to Murrow's wishes, and Hewitt's technical prowess to make it work. The provenance of the idea was less important than the team's ability to conceive and implement it, for the inspired decision to broadcast from a control room served as number of purposes. It provided an object lesson in the embryonic field of television journalism, revealing the technological underpinnings of *See It Now* as a newsmagazine. At the same time, it provided an ideal setting for Murrow, enabling him to exercise maximum flexibility in integrating live video and audio feeds with segments on film, using his characteristically understated comments and commanding screen presence. A critic for *Saturday Review* suggested that the success of *See It Now* would be rooted in "the program's fundamental premise—Murrow viewing the monitors."[31] The illusion that Murrow together with the audience was seeing something for the first time reinforced the identification of the viewer with Murrow and gave the program a sense of immediacy.

Murrow proceeded to demonstrate the prowess of television at a moment when the coasts had just been linked by a high-frequency coaxial cable. *See It Now* positioned camera crews in San Francisco and New York. In what became iconic images in television history, Murrow asked Don Hewitt to alternate live pictures of the two cities. First came New York. "Now, on monitor two," Murrow asked, "may we have the Pacific coast, please?" Murrow chatted with the two mobile units, asking for a succession of alternating images of the two city's famous bridges, skylines, and harbors. The sequence ended with television viewers looking at the Atlantic and Pacific oceans, which were displayed simultaneously on their screens. Murrow observed, "For the first time in the history of man we are able to look out at both the Atlantic and Pacific oceans . . . at the same time." It was a theatrical, perhaps even gimmicky, technological display. But Murrow underscored the serious intent behind it:

> We are slightly overwhelmed by this television gadget. Reporters in the past have been given great weapons . . . the printing press, the typewriter, the Linotype machine, the teletype, newspapers, radio . . . but no journalistic age was ever given a weapon for truth with quite the scope of this fledgling television. This afternoon, as we begin our shake-down cruise in this staggering new medium, we want you to know that we are aware of the electronic wonder entrusted to our fingers.[32]

Jack Gould wrote in the *New York Times* that before *See It Now*, the potential of television's new national networking capacity had not been exploited: "Never before has television's great power—enabling the viewer to have a sense of being in two places at once—been so simply and vividly detailed."[33]

Murrow and Friendly wished to capitalize on what they considered television's promise as "an instrument of transportation." In addition to the opening images of the coasts, the program included reports from the veteran Murrow correspondents Eric Sevareid in Washington and Howard K. Smith in Paris. At the same time, Murrow and Friendly grasped television's power—like that of photojournalism but increased exponentially—to capture the essence of an individual or an issue by providing a "little picture." The first broadcast of *See It Now* exploited the intimate character of television in several filmed reports. For example, viewers saw a nasty exchange between Soviet and British disarmament negotiators as well as an aged and diminished Winston Churchill giving a speech, "a deeply revelatory picture," in the words of John Crosby of the *New York Herald Tribune*.[34] The broadcast also chronicled the campaign tour of the Republican presidential hopeful Robert A. Taft, including the image of the foolish-looking candidate relishing a laudatory introduction. The filmed segment was followed by a live remote interview with Taft, who was given an opportunity to comment on what he and the audience had just viewed—another playful strategy for exploiting the flexibility of the medium.

The entire fifteen minutes of the second half of the program featured a revealing group portrait of front-line U.S. troops in Korea—specifically, of Fox Company, Second Platoon, Nineteenth Infantry. The report by CBS's Asia correspondent, Robert Pierpoint, dispensed with standard battlefield reports to provide a portrait of the soldiers and their daily routines in Korea when not in combat. "As a piece of editing and camera work," *Variety* wrote about the Korea segment, "it rates superlatives, telling more than tons of Page One material. The viewer was on the spot for a graphic personalization of what a soldier feels. . . . Throughout, the camera work was extraordinary, virtually taking it out of straight news reporting and giving it dramatic impact."[35] In his terse closing, Murrow noted that since the filming, fifty men of the unit had suffered causalities. Years later, Pierpoint recalled the difficulty and sense of improvisation involved in the report. Friendly initially asked Pierpoint, a veteran radio reporter, to do a nighttime report from the battlefront. Pierpoint thought Friendly's assignment would be impossible to realize with a television camera and crew: "I had to be very careful in dealing with Fred, because Fred did not seem to have a clear idea of the difference between news and movies. And television, to some extent, was doing movies. And so I had to explain every step of the way that I could only do certain things with television when I was dealing with the troops during a wartime situation. That was not a happy experience with Fred, but I think he learned."[36] Pierpoint adjusted by reporting on the life of the troops behind the lines, an approach that was seen as original and highly praised by critics. Clearly, Friendly was feeling his way as he pushed his staff to innovate.

Television critics immediately recognized that *See It Now* marked a departure. John Crosby of the *New York Herald Tribune* wrote that *See It Now* represented something other and more important than a roundup of the week's news: "It is, instead, an almost entirely new form of journalism, 'told in the voices and faces' of the people who made the news; a technique that offers a deeper insight into the headlines and the people who make them." As a result, the program was positioned to provide context and interpretation as Murrow and Friendly saw fit. Leading critics viewed the initial broadcast as an important landmark in the development of television journalism. They noted both its substance and showmanship. In the *New Yorker*, Philip Hamburger characterized as "nothing short of spectacular" this first serious attempt to explore the power of television for covering public affairs. This sentiment was echoed by Jack Gould, who described the broadcast in the *New York Times* as "a magnificent achievement—absorbing in its exploitation of video's technical capabilities and human and revealing in its understanding." He also wrote, "Mr. Murrow and Mr. Friendly . . . are bringing to television the one quality for which the medium has been literally starved: original thinking."[37]

The quest to use television to take audiences where they had never been before set the tone for much of *See It Now*'s initial 1951/1952 season. For example, viewers entered the world of coal miners, including the mines themselves, in Grant Town, West Virginia (December 9, 1951). Traveling abroad, *See It Now* conducted a tour of the Suez Canal (May 25, 1952). Friendly had displayed an interest in explaining and dramatizing scientific topics in his radio documentary on atomic power. *See It Now* broadcast segments on such topics as the U.S. Navy's "mechanical brain," a computer system that kept track of airplanes and ships worldwide and filled six rooms at MIT (December 16, 1951). A filmed report on heart surgery was one of many firsts for television (February 17, 1952). A broadcast from a submerged submarine reflected Friendly's zeal to push the limits of television's technical capabilities (January 20, 1952). For a Christmas special, "The Spirit of Yuletide U.S.A" (December 23, 1951), Friendly placed the first television camera atop the Washington Monument in the nation's capital. It was one of thirty-seven cameras used in a broadcast that originated live in ten different American cities to create what CBS called "a sight-and-sound poem" of the nation during the Christmas holiday.[38]

During its first season, *See It Now* focused on displaying the technological prowess of television as a news medium, not on addressing injustices and controversial political topics. "They felt awed by their new medium," the broadcast historian Erik Barnouw writes of Murrow and Friendly's early television broadcasts, "and needed to spend time exclaiming over the wonder of it. And they had to find out, by trial and error, what could be done with it." On February 24, 1952, Pierpoint reported on a case of housing discrimination against a Chinese American family in San Francisco. The segment included a live shot of the Statue of Liberty and a reminder from Murrow that the nation had just celebrated Brotherhood Week. Perhaps, in retrospect, it was a hint of things to

come. But, the CBS News veteran Edward Bliss Jr. notes, "the series began . . . as a half-hour program distinguished by its immediacy and
imagination, not by its bite."[39]

Murrow was breaking new ground in a medium whose technology he
hated. Joseph Persico writes that "Murrow regarded the hardware of
television—the hundreds of pounds of equipment required, the camera,
tripods, film magazines, lights, and batteries, as so many millstones
around his neck. The days of a single microphone in a cubicle in the BBC
basement began to take on a pastoral quality in his memory."[40] Murrow
continued to do his radio program five nights a week. The job of harness-
ing the new technology of television for *See It Now*, of overseeing production logistics, belonged exclusively to the junior member of the Murrow–
Friendly team. The challenge was daunting. CBS's radio studios could
not begin to meet television's technical needs. Union agreements regarding operations within CBS threatened to hamstring Friendly further. He
was forced to set up a host of makeshift facilities spread throughout midtown Manhattan.

See It Now's offices, where Murrow and Friendly would normally meet,
were located at CBS headquarters at 485 Madison Avenue. A laboratory
on Ninth Avenue developed the film that came in from the field. Murrow
prerecorded his off-camera narration at a radio studio near his office.
A loft at 550 Fifth Avenue, at Forty-fifth Street, above Wallach's Men's
Stores, served as the site for the all-important editing and screening facility. When Mili Lerner began working there, she found "the junk room of
the world," filled with discarded reels and boxes of papers and plagued by
rats. Three cramped stations contained noisy Moviola editing machines.
An adjoining room contained a projector and several chairs. The staff
usually worked through the night before the broadcast. There was no
air-conditioning, so in the summer the film would curl from the heat. An
enormous fan blew hot air and added to the clatter of the Moviolas. During the winter, the heat went off at 6:00 P.M. Friendly respected his editors, learned a great deal from them, but was clearly in charge. A perfectionist, he insisted on countless changes. There were arguments about
cuts; breaking news required last-minute changes. When frustrated,
Friendly erupted in violent temper tantrums, throwing pencils at the
staff or kicking equipment or furniture in a rage.

Murrow rarely visited the editing facility at 550 Fifth Avenue and then only to view a nearly complete segment in the screening room. On those occasions, Murrow would watch and leave; any subsequent discussion between Murrow and Friendly was held elsewhere. The cutting room was Friendly's domain.[41] After he viewed film footage, Friendly would write the first draft of a narrative, beginning a series of successive film edits and rewrites. When a rough cut and accompanying text were complete, Friendly's assistant, Natalie Foster, would hand-deliver it to Murrow, beginning a round of rewriting by Friendly and Murrow from Friday until Sunday. On Sunday morning, Foster would go to Murrow's apartment on Park Avenue to type his closing remarks.[42]

From CBS's broadcast studios in Grand Central Terminal, Friendly developed and presided over a complex process to integrate image and sound. In preparing the program, Murrow's narrative, piped by telephone line to the cutting room, would be taped in relation to the images being screened, with Friendly, telephone to his ear, yelling cues to the editors. A separate recorder would be used to integrate Murrow's comments and the audio portion of the film footage on a master audiotape. Friendly insisted on having the superior quality he could get from separate sound and picture tracks, but there was not enough time to integrate the two tracks before broadcast. In a radical departure from newsreel practice, he devised a risky procedure to broadcast film and audiotape separately. At air time, the separate audio and film tracks were broadcast on a tape and projection machine in synchronization—which worked most of the time but not all the time.[43] The program closed with Murrow's tailpiece, or final remarks, carried live.

The fruits of a week of frenetic work, material from the far corners of the nation and the world, processed in a matrix of facilities in Midtown Manhattan, gelled in the hot and crowded control room at Grand Central Terminal at air time. The editors often worked through the previous night; on occasion they added and polished material up to and even during the broadcast. Studio 41 was packed with equipment and personnel. Just before the broadcast, Friendly would review Murrow's run-through of his script. Once the program began to air, Don Hewitt gave orders with hand signals or whispers into a chest microphone. Friendly positioned himself on the studio floor, sitting in a special chair with the legs sawed off, just out of camera range at the feet of Murrow, prompting him by pulling his pants or poking him with a pencil.[44]

Thus Friendly presided over the actual broadcast of See It Now as well as its preparations. He was the driving force integrating the disparate pieces into a whole from start to finish. Friendly's debt to photojournalism, radio reporting, the newsreel, and documentary film was evident. Yet he selectively integrated these elements into something new: a unique blend of image and sound, of live and prerecorded reportage, for a new medium. The great radio writer Norman Corwin emphasized that in the final analysis *See It Now* was not derivative: "Fred and Ed staked out new ground."[45] Friendly molded the chaos into a final form by virtue of his relentless drive. It almost seemed as if he was demanding—willing—that the technologies at hand stretch their capabilities to do his bidding. He similarly placed extraordinary demands on his human resources, the talented *See It Now* team.

Friendly could be equally demanding of CBS correspondents who were called on to contribute to *See It Now*. For example, Robert Pierpoint was exhausted in 1952 after a story he did on three wounded GIs, following them over several days from their evacuation from Korea to their arrival in hospitals in the United States. Friendly then assigned the sleep-deprived Pierpoint to interview the Chinese couple facing housing discrimination in San Francisco. Pierpoint tried to beg off, but Friendly would not take no for an answer. Pierpoint recalls that Friendly told him, " 'Well, this is the kind of story only you can handle,' " and, Pierpont added, Friendly was "very clever at flattering reporters, so under Fred's blandishments and flattery and orders, I managed to get out of bed and meet the camera crew." After the interview, Pierpoint traveled to New York and for the first time met Friendly, who put him up at a good hotel and got him tickets to *My Fair Lady*. Pierpoint appreciated the amenities and was impressed with the imposing figure of Fred Friendly, finding him both "full of himself and full of ideas."[46]

David Halberstam described the producer in Friendly as "driven by an inner fury to be the best." At times, his frenzied drive for excellence intimidated and even frightened his associates. This was especially true when the physically intimidating, six-foot-four, two-hundred-pound Friendly confronted obstacles, provoking his legendary temper tantrums. Joe Wershba, who socialized with Fred and Dorothy in addition to working as one of the two original reporters on *See It Now*, once confided to Murrow his deep-seated fear of Friendly's wrath.[47] Joe Wershba would write in retrospect:

It was not easy working for Fred Friendly. He could be ruthless and brutal. He could also be tender and deeply sensitive to the needs of his writer-reporters, film editors and camera crews. We often speculated that he would wind up with ulcers. "You don't understand," one of our people explained: Fred Friendly doesn't get ulcers—*he gives them.* Once, Fred told me unhappily: "They are going to end up calling me the worst son of a bitch in the business, but we are going to turn out the greatest broadcasts this business has ever known." . . . He called his people "this band of brothers," and never were brothers more bullied, driven, inspired, ennobled and glorified. . . . But they gave Fred everything he demanded.[48]

5 Friendly and Murrow

FRIENDLY'S WORKING RELATIONSHIP with Mili Lerner, a tough and talented young film editor, was illustrative of how he forged the *See It Now* team behind Edward R. Murrow. Lerner grew up in the Bronx, a member of a working-class family of Jewish immigrants that had been on relief during the Depression. Before finding her vocation as a film editor, she had worked at various factory jobs, including at a cannery in Monterey, California, where she helped organize a union. Influenced by her brother's work in theater and film in Los Angeles, she developed a passion for film editing and became the first female member of the editors' craft union in New York. Gene Milford originally offered her a job in the summer of 1951 as an assistant to two editors who worked on the pilot for *See It Now*. Hired to organize the cutting room at 550 Fifth Avenue, she found chaos, with film covering the floor and Friendly ordering people around despite an obvious lack of familiarity with film production. A female staff member who planned to quit warned Lerner: "There's this giant of a man called Fred Friendly. Stay out of his way; he'll kill you. All he does is yell and carry on."[1]

Lerner's relationship with Friendly was testy at first. She told him she wanted to be a full-fledged editor in six months; Friendly expressed doubts she would last that long in the job. Initially, he ignored her. Six months to the day of her hiring, she told him she was ready to be an editor and asked for an assignment. When he declined, she took her coat and started to leave, and Friendly grabbed her. "So he gave me a story," she recalled, "hoping I'd fail, but I didn't." Milford, Lerner's mentor, soon quit, and she went on to edit many of *See It Now*'s most famous programs. Milford, accustomed to Hollywood production protocols, thought quite simply that "Fred Friendly is nuts" and fostered "an insane way to work." Lerner's toughness served her well in her dealings with Friendly. "She never took any lip from Fred," Dorothy Friendly recalled. "And he respected her for standing up to him."[2] Lerner testified to the difficulty of working for Friendly. He knew no boundaries when it came to making demands on his staff. She had to weather his outbursts, once coolly watching as he attacked a file cabinet. At times, she wondered whether he was capable of hurting or even killing someone. The outbursts were, at once, frightening and comical. Danny Kaye, visiting 550 Fifth Avenue for a UNICEF segment for See It Now, mimicked an enraged Friendly behind his back, to the delight of the staff.

Once Lerner crossed Friendly, refusing to edit a segment because the footage was too poor. As punishment, Friendly refused her request to edit a program on Louis Armstrong, but when the assigned editor was not up to the task, Friendly relented. He might hold a grudge but not for long. In addition, Lerner felt that as a woman she had an advantage in her dealings with Friendly. He tempered his outbursts with females, at least insofar as throwing objects at them was concerned. It was not just a question of etiquette. As Lerner recalled, "Fred was always a little afraid of women, and I sensed that."[3] For Lerner, the hardships of working for Friendly did not diminish the excitement and professional satisfaction of being part of his team.

Friendly clearly drove the editorial process, with strong ideas about what he wanted, obsessively pursuing and rethinking how to realize his vision for each segment. Yet he was open to suggestions and even criticisms regarding his approach. The editors, for example, ultimately convinced Friendly of the desirability of cutaways to enhance interviews, despite his inclination to view interviewees as deserving the audience's undivided attention. But challenging him and defending an alternative approach required fortitude. You could change Friendly's mind provided he respected your talent, believed you were loyal to him, and had his best interests in mind. This openness helped make the extreme demands and tantrums tolerable. Then, again, Friendly's histrionics could unleash creative energies in the cutting room as well as inspire fear. "He was a most creative man," Lerner recalled, "and he would scare you at the same time." His creativity was infectious: "He would come out with fresh ideas all the time, and that would stimulate us to go a little further. . . . And he would get excited, and because he got excited, we got excited." For Lerner the sense of creating a new and important kind of television made the sacrifices worthwhile: "Our social life was almost nil. I lost more boyfriends. But we felt we were changing the world."[4]

In turn, Friendly exhibited great loyalty to his staffers. They enjoyed their privileged position within CBS independent of its executives, answerable only to Friendly. He was available to them at any time of day or night. On one occasion in the dead of winter, Friendly received an early-morning call about the bitter cold at 550 Fifth Avenue and arrived shortly before dawn with an armful of heavy sweaters, socks, and gloves. For Lerner, "he was inspirational." Friendly generously acknowledged Lerner's contribution. He singled her out for praise in the book of *See It Now* program transcripts that he and Murrow published in 1955. He wrote in her copy of his memoir, *Due to Circumstances Beyond Our Control . . . ,* "For Mili: Who was a woman among men. Who is part of the Murrow tradition. He loved you, too." As Ed Bliss says of Friendly, "He was one with his people."[5]

If his interaction with Mili Lerner was illustrative of his relationship with an individual staff member, Friendly's stewardship of Korean War specials in 1952 and 1953 revealed his role as the driving operational force of the *See It Now* team. On December 10, 1952, Friendly distributed a six-page single-spaced memorandum for all reporters and camera operators and the CBS Tokyo Bureau spelling out the concept and logistics of the first of two annual specials from the Korean front. The first hour-long *See It Now* program would originate in its entirety from Korea. Friendly began by articulating an overarching vision and strategy:

Although this is a "maximum effort," it is not to be a "tour de force" or an effort to flex our muscles, or to razzle-dazzle with fancy gadgets, exciting switches or over-produced episodes. We are simply going to portray the face of the war and the faces of the men who are fighting it. . . . We like to say that SIN specializes in the "little picture." It is our intention to capture the mood of the combat by coming back with the "little picture." The best picture we could get would be a single GI hacking away at a single foxhole in the ice of a Korean winter, or a guy on an icy road trying to change a flat tire . . . or a doughfoot explaining the science of keeping your feet dry. . . . This is a piece that happens to be done at Christmas but is not primarily ABOUT Christmas. To be sure, it takes place during the few days just preceding Christmas and on Christmas, but this is all secondary to the basic concept. The least useable picture we could get would be twenty bombers flying in formation or a barrage of artillery bouncing off a distant mountain peak, or a correspondent interviewing a

General about strategy and tactics. . . . We want the sights and sounds
of the Korean War. The narrower the focus, the more isolated the
sounds, the better the picture.[6]

Friendly went on to detail the "order of departure" for the large CBS crew
with multiple reporter-camera teams that he had assembled. He specified flight times and destinations, arrangements for the transport of
equipment, and liaison assignments with the U.S. military. In addition,
he assigned stories he wanted covered from various locations en route to
the Far East; these would be aired on *See It Now* on December 21, the
week before the Korea special.

Friendly also outlined a "plan of procedure" upon arrival in Korea. He
spelled out reporting protocols: Murrow would decide where reporter-
camera units would go; otherwise, reporters would have wide latitude
regarding the content of stories. Friendly specified how each spot would
be introduced and concluded—simply and unobtrusively—in order to
make the segues flow cleanly and give the documentary momentum. "As
always," he noted, "we will want the extreme close-up and accompanying cutaways." Additional sections of the memorandum addressed technical matters such as sound equipment. For example, Friendly emphasized that sound quality comes first; a visible microphone is fine but
should not have the CBS logo attached, which would distract from the
picture. A small experimental tape recorder would be used where heavy
sound cameras could not be placed. Murrow would have an Ampex 400
tape recorder so that he could record his 7:45 P.M. radio show and record
nonsynchronized sound for the Korea broadcast. Friendly asked all reporters to keep notes that Murrow could draw on to annotate the remotes.
A separate section specified shipping arrangements, including cable
code words, special stenciled red bags, and flight connections: "This is
where we make it or lose it." Friendly concluded with a Murrowesque
"Good luck and stay in focus."

Friendly's memorandum, a remarkable conceptual and organizational
call to arms, reads like a military operation mounted by Master Sergeant
Friendly. It provided a detailed plan for something new: an unprecedented hour-long documentary for television. Robert Pierpoint recalled
feeling the virtual presence of Friendly in Korea, despite being ten thousand miles away: "Fred's input was clearly crucial." Indeed, Friendly eventually got the shot he wanted to open the program for the second Korea
Christmas special. Murrow found a sergeant on a ridge trying to break

the frozen ground with a shovel. Charlie Mack shot the man's hands, boot, and shovel and the unyielding frozen soil—what has been called the program's most arresting shot and a "wartime TV classic."[7] The camera crews filmed from no-man's-lands, air bases, a hospital ship, small villages, and the streets of Seoul, but in these locales the emphasis was always on the human dimension as revealed by unscripted individuals speaking on camera directly to reporters. The heart of the program portrayed the life of GIs during downtime—eating, sleeping, gambling, joking—against the backdrop of war.

Friendly not only organized the expedition to Korea but had to grapple with the raw product, nearly 20 million feet of film sent in batches with accompanying notes in the designated red bags to New York by way of Tokyo. Joseph Persico emphasizes the achievement of the entire *See It Now* team that Friendly had assembled in creating the Korea specials, how "cameramen with the eyes of poets, several of the finest reporters in broadcasting, Palmer William's mastery of the technology of television, and finally Friendly's capacity to transform great masses of celluloid into a seamless whole—converged into a new art form." On December 29, 1952, the *New York Times* lauded the first Korea documentary as "a visual poem" and "a masterpiece of reportorial artistry."[8]

The point of view of "Christmas in Korea," especially the second Korea special, which was broadcast at the end of 1953, reflected a subtle shift of emphasis in the treatment of the Korean War. One broadcast historian has characterized the perspective as "patriotic but not uncritical." The program did not question the legitimacy of U.S. involvement in the conflict. Yet the broadcast featured a wide spectrum of perspectives. Viewers hear from blacks as well as whites, from women as well as men, from French, British, Irish, and Ethiopian soldiers as well as American GIs. The opinions expressed run the gamut from the need to confront Communism and the necessity of doing one's duty to outright criticism of the war effort. Introducing critical perspectives, even in a highly balanced program that presented the U.S. military in a sympathetic light, represented a departure from standard Korean War coverage and from wartime broadcasting in general. For example, when Robert Pierpoint asks a marine on the western front what he thinks of the war, he pauses and then replies, "Can't see the sense of it." The broadcast focused on the plight of the ordinary soldier far from home—and of the plight of the civilian population as well. In one sequence, Bill Downs reports from a deserted Korean village near the front that has been overrun by opposing armies four times. Looking at an empty thatched hut, he observes, "People used to live there. I have seen the same picture too many times in Russia, in France, in Germany." Murrow closes the program on a jarringly open-ended note: "There is no conclusion to this report from Korea because there is no end to the war."[9]

Murrow and Friendly did not conceive of "Christmas in Korea" as advocacy journalism questioning U.S. foreign or military policy. Nonetheless, its approach was in marked contrast to the daily battle summaries and long-distance battle footage supplied by the military that typified television coverage of the Korean War. Some have discerned an antiwar sensibility, arguing that the program "brought home the horrors of war in a way never seen before. The cameras revealed not fighting machines, but men and boys, scared, lonely, bored, and above all, human."[10] As J. Fred MacDonald emphasizes in his study of television and the cold war, by avoiding "overblown patriotism, fear-mongering, and empty rhetoric," the Korea program shuns the characteristic representations on television of the "simplified emotionalism of the anti-Communist era."[11]

See It Now's distinctive format and voice crystallized in its Korea programming, beginning with Robert Pierpoint's fifteen-minute report on the first *See It Now* program followed by segments on the odyssey of a donated pint of blood, wounded soldiers returning home, and the first account of the release of imprisoned American POWs. The full-length documentary "Christmas in Korea" in 1953 was the crowning achievement. In its first season, *See It Now* had not entirely freed itself from the model of the newsreel and photo essay, had not yet fully integrated these precedents into a new video format for television. Murrow and Friendly were groping for how to move beyond a weekly news report tied to breaking stories so that they could treat topics in greater depth. In the succession of programs about Korea, the new format emerged, one that increasingly led *See It Now* to focus on a single story each week. According to A. William Bluem, a historian of the television documentary, the "Christmas in Korea" program in 1953 "represented the culmination of Murrow's [and Friendly's] search for a proper TV News Documentary [*sic*] form. Thenceforth, *See It Now* moved steadily away from all attempts at hard news as its function became one of providing timely and searching reports ranging over the leading edge of history." As a result, Bluem adds, *See It Now* would be "choosing its own subjects and developing its own conflict-charged treatments of them."[12]

Edward R. Murrow did not watch the broadcast on December 28, 1952, of the first of *See It Now*'s two "Christmas in Korea" specials. He was too sick to do so. In charge of directing coverage in Korea, of realizing the ambitious plan contained in Friendly's memorandum, Murrow pushed himself to his limits in frigid, stormy weather. He developed a severe cold in Korea and became seriously ill. Near collapse, he was brought by ambulance to a hospital near Seattle while the rest of the *See It Now* team returned to New York. He was diagnosed with flu and nervous exhaustion, forbidden to have visitors, and unable to watch the broadcast. The fatigue persisted when he finally returned to New York, where he went into the hospital for another week of tests.[13] Janet Murrow came to resent Friendly, in part because of what she felt were his excessive demands on her husband and the toll they took on his health. When she complained, Murrow would say, "Oh, that's just Fred being Fred." Yet it would be an oversimplification to characterize Murrow simply as a reluctant tool of Friendly's agenda for the medium of television and for what became its leading newsmagazine. Reporter Lou Cioffi thought Murrow seemed happier returning to Korea than working behind a desk in New York, despite the physical demands of being in a war zone.[14]

Murrow was unquestionably the senior partner of the team. Without Murrow's stature, none of his joint ventures with Friendly—the triad of record, radio, and television show—could have come to fruition, Friendly's critical role in these productions notwithstanding. The success of the Murrow–Friendly team resulted from the way they complemented each other rather than their relative importance. *See It Now* would strike a balance between the yin of Friendly's showmanship and hyperbole and the yang of Murrow's gravitas and penchant for understatement. As Joseph Persico writes of Murrow, "The kind of magazine of the air that he wanted to do was *Harpers* or the *Atlantic Monthly*, not *Life*."[15]

The two comrades-in-arms were a study in contrasts, personally and professionally. Murrow, with his Savile Row suits, cut an elegant figure; Friendly was ungainly in appearance and awkward in manner. Murrow had a dark and impenetrable side, in contrast to Friendly's can-do optimism and effusive nature. By the 1950s, Murrow was already a legend with access to high places on both sides of the Atlantic. He did not feel he needed to prove himself, unlike Friendly, who in the early 1950s was just beginning to make his mark. Behind Friendly's bravado lurked a need for recognition. Hence, as David Halberstam emphasizes, "He took great refuge in Murrow's respectability and legitimacy." Dorothy Friendly always felt that "there was always an element of awe" and a deferential quality in Friendly's interactions with Murrow.[16] Friendly looked up to Murrow more as an idealized big brother than a father figure. He epitomized a kind of masculinity and worldliness that Friendly may have felt was beyond his reach. Friendly wanted to measure up to the Murrow standard, in ways large and small. Friendly was unnerved when Murrow drove recklessly over the Blue Ridge Mountains in his Thunderbird convertible en route to their interview with Carl Sandburg and felt impelled against his better judgment to speed as well when he took over the wheel. And when they would leave CBS offices for the Pentagon Bar, Friendly struggled to keep up with Murrow's capacity for alcohol.[17]

Friendly literally sat at Murrow's feet—just out of the camera's reach when *See It Now* aired—and figuratively as well. Murrow never failed to acknowledge how much he relied on Friendly, but at times Murrow became exasperated with his partner. Once during a *See It Now* broadcast, Friendly jabbed Murrow too hard with a pencil and Murrow kicked him right in the face, sending him reeling. Normally, Murrow would not show such frustration or criticize Friendly in front of the staff. Once, however, a staff member saw the two of them walk off together and heard Murrow say, "Fritzl"—a nickname Friendly hated—"don't be such a *maniac*."[18] Murrow appreciated Friendly's flair for the dramatic but was also wary of his associate's willingness at times to stretch the facts for dramatic effect. Like Major Clark, Murrow valued Friendly's brashness and creativity, but at times he felt the need to temper Fred's excesses.

Friendly assumed the role of Murrow's loyal lieutenant at CBS. At times it meant standing guard against the philistines at the network. When the CBS bookkeeper requested the return of a raincoat purchased for $5.08 and used during coverage of an appearance by General MacArthur and of a subsequent tornado in Arkansas, Friendly wrote a hilarious memorandum that made the rounds at CBS and was even read aloud for amusement at a CBS board meeting.[19] Friendly was continually in touch with Murrow, day and night. "When the phone rings at four or five in the morning," Murrow said, "I answer, 'Yes, Fred.'"[20] Friendly often invoked his working relationship with Murrow to get what he wanted. Joe Wershba recalled how "Fred would wake you at three in the morning anywhere in the world and begin with the portentous announcement: 'Ed wants . . .' I found myself saluting the telephone even though I knew it was really Fred wants."[21]

Moreover, Friendly's relationship with Murrow had a possessive quality, which reflected Friendly's need to establish his primacy as Murrow's partner. His wife, Dorothy, was struck by Friendly's desire for an exclusive relationship: "Murrow was *his* Murrow."[22] This was apparent in Friendly's attitude toward *Person to Person*, which went on the air in 1953 and featured Murrow interviewing celebrities in their homes. The format in which Murrow, seated in an armchair in the studio, made small talk with famous people by way of remote feeds from their private quarters—from John and Jacqueline Kennedy to Marilyn Monroe—owed something to the technological innovations of *See It Now*. Indeed, the two producers of *Person to Person*, Jesse Zousmer and John Aaron, had initially worked on *See It Now* until conflicts with Friendly led him to fire them. Murrow had been on good terms with the two producers but upheld Friendly's authority over the program's staff. But Murrow was open to their proposal for *Person to Person* and its creation as a private enterprise in which they and Murrow shared the profits. According to Wershba, "The show almost caused a break in the Murrow–Friendly relationship. Fred pushed Ed too hard, tried to get him to drop the show before it even started. Ed Murrow was not a man to be pushed. He told Fred where to get off. Fortunately, the rift was healed just before 'See It Now' began its series of reports on McCarthyism."[23] *Person to Person* became highly successful and lucrative, unlike *See It Now*, which consistently lost money. Friendly continued to seethe about *Person to Person*. He felt that the show was beneath Murrow, and Friendly resented a second Murrow television program outside his purview.

Friendly also had ambivalent feelings about the Murrow Boys, whose ranks included luminaries like Charles Collingwood, William Shirer, Eric Sevareid, David Schoenbrun, and Howard K. Smith.[24] Murrow shared a sense of camaraderie with a group he had regarded more as a band of brothers than subordinates. For the Murrow Boys, Friendly was an upstart working in a medium they viewed with suspicion. They recognized how the complex technology and heightened importance of producers, who were central to television, would diminish the independence the Boys had enjoyed as radio journalists. In fact, on *See It Now* Friendly consciously sought to limit the role of correspondents, which included those Murrow Boys who were gradually seeking to come to terms with television journalism. When *See It Now* first went on the air, Friendly ordered that Murrow alone would conduct interviews. When that proved impractical, Friendly sought to have footage edited so that it *appeared* that Murrow was doing the interviews conducted by others. Howard K. Smith, among others, found the proposed technique highly objectionable. Eventually, Friendly gave up, but the resentment remained, and his attempts at downgrading the role of renowned correspondents pointed to his sense of competitiveness with Murrow's old guard.

Stanley Cloud and Lynne Olson, in their book *The Murrow Boys*, write of how "consciously or not, [Friendly] seemed to see the Boys as threats that had to be neutralized if his own oversized ambitions were to be fulfilled. He became possessive of Murrow and Murrow's reputation in a way that admitted few others—and none of the Boys." David Schoenbrun expresses the resentment felt by many of the Boys when he writes that "Friendly eventually dominated and twisted Murrow. Fred began almost as Charlie McCarthy sitting on Edgar Bergen's lap, and ended with Ed as Charlie McCarthy sitting on Fred's lap." Friendly would later scoff at the notion that he had felt threatened by the Murrow Boys, suggesting instead that no such collective entity ever existed, that it was a myth. But on his desk was a plaque with lines from *Henry V*—"We few, we happy few, we band of brothers"—appropriating for the *See It Now* team language that had been associated with the Murrow Boys.[25]

Murrow, for his part, dependent now on Friendly, did not intervene in his executive producer's conflict with the Boys, despite their protests. Joe Wershba emphasized Friendly's importance for Murrow:

> Ed Murrow referred to those of us who worked with him as "my colleagues." A touch of British Old Boyism perhaps—but what a sweet compliment. . . .
>
> But there was only one man whom Murrow called: "my partner." That man was Fred W. Friendly. That's the bottom line. . . . It won't satisfy carping critics who insisted that Friendly presumed on Murrow's name and draped himself in Murrow's mantle. . . .
>
> Murrow backed Friendly to the hilt and Friendly brought out the best in Murrow—in a field neither of them knew much about and even feared: television. Friendly swung his weight at CBS—because he had Murrow's prestige to swing.[26]

In his radio broadcasts, Murrow worked virtually alone and felt in control. The medium of television required a strong producer to ride herd over a production team. As David Halberstam writes, the partnership "married Murrow's great broadcasting skills, and very considerable shyness, and totally enviable reputation with Friendly's great ambition and superb technical skills." In addition, "Television, for better or worse, did require a show-business component, and Friendly provided that, marvelously tailored to Murrow."[27] If Murrow felt the first stirrings of professional burnout and declining health, Friendly's manic drive could fill the breach. *See It Now*, under Friendly's stewardship, revived Murrow's career, gave it a new dimension.

The Murrow–Friendly relationship was primarily professional and limited socially. If after the war Friendly's working ties with Murrow eclipsed that of the Murrow Boys, he did not inherit the close personal bonds they had forged with Murrow. Jap Gude said that Friendly was unable to establish a friendship with Murrow outside work: "Fred could never get beyond that barrier."[28]

If a more intimate relationship with Murrow eluded him, Friendly's professional success contributed to a fuller home and social life. He became more confident and upbeat with his success. His social and professional life overlapped considerably. The Friendlys began to entertain more, both at Peter Cooper Village and during summer vacations. Dorothy, who was not a skilled cook, approached the dinner parties with some trepidation, especially when important colleagues of Fred's were invited, but she hired help and enjoyed the interaction with interesting people. Dorothy later recalled how among peers Fred, a great storyteller, was the life of the party. She marveled at his self-confidence, despite his lack of formal education; it seemed to her that he acted as if he knew everything. Fred was especially adamant about his vocation: "It was anathema for anyone to question his work, his programs. Anyone who disagreed with him might be treated to a tirade." In such instances, even his closest friends were not spared. Dorothy would try to smooth over conflicts when he became too argumentative. She felt that despite the expanded social life, "the work came before anything else. And when he was so concentrated on what he was doing, I felt like a shadow."[29]

Fred and Dorothy's first child, Andrew, had been born in 1951, less than two weeks before *See It Now* went on the air. Their second child, Lisa, was born during the summer of 1953, after the show's second season. The Friendly family moved to a larger, two-bedroom apartment in Peter Cooper Village. Fred became, and remained, an enthusiastic and engaged parent, especially when he was able to carve out time from work. In the summer of 1951, the Friendlys rented a summer house on Stillwater Lake in Westchester County. The next summer, Jap and Helen Gude, who had a home on Martha's Vineyard, found a house for the Friendlys to rent. The house belonged to Charles Boni, of the publishing house of Boni and Liveright, and was located near Menemsha Harbor in the town of Chilmark. Al Leventhal of Simon and Schuster was a neighbor and would host visits from Robert and Helen Bernstein. Another neighbor was Leopold Mannes, an inventor of Kodakcolor with George Eastman and a supporter of left-wing causes who was popular with the artists and writers on the island. James Thurber would periodically appear as Jap Gude's guest. The Friendlys enjoyed the big cocktail party scene. Dorothy remembered "wonderful summers."[30]

In the summer of 1952, when the national political conventions took place, the Friendlys were the only family in their circle on Martha's Vineyard with a television set. This may have reflected television's infancy or disdain for the new medium on the part of the Vineyard literati. Friendly, of course, made no apologies for his television work. Instead, he and Murrow continued to refine *See It Now*'s format in order to equip the show to address the burning issues of the day in more direct ways. Murrow as host and Friendly as producer developed interviewing techniques on *See It Now* to explore conflict, whether individual or social. They built on the practice of radio reporting, letting subjects speak their mind while keeping commentary to a minimum. Murrow believed that the most compelling testimony occurred when individuals—whether ordinary citizens or world leaders—spoke extemporaneously about what they knew and believed. "Under the pressure of the moment," Murrow wrote, "and armed with the conviction born of conflict, they composed compelling literature."[31] The program's premise was that a television interview could use both image and word to reveal the complexities of a person's character and beliefs.

Interviews on *See It Now* became increasingly longer in subsequent seasons; at times, an entire half-hour show would be devoted to a single interview. One such interview took place with Carl Sandburg at his goat farm in Flat Rock, North Carolina. Viewers accompanied the seventy-six-year-old Sandburg as he toured the farm. The author revealed his work habits and sang a folk song during the broadcast on October 5, 1954. He reflected on his life and work, his obsession with Abraham Lincoln, and the meaning of patriotism. Following the program, Sandburg's publisher reported a sharp increase in the sale of his books, and CBS received many requests from schools for screenings and transcripts of the program. A. William Bluem has called the Sandburg piece a supreme example of the *See It Now* interview: "What was dramatic and subjective was the man himself and the depth of his character and experience as revealed by the television camera. What was factual and journalistic was his words and opinions. . . . No added dramatic values of sound effects, mood music, camera manipulation, or stylized editing were necessary to sustain these programs as documentary in the best tradition."[32]

Another program devoted to a single interview several months later featured J. Robert Oppenheimer, who had headed the Manhattan Project during the war but lost his security clearance to work at the Atomic Energy Commission in 1953. The interview, which aired on January 4, 1955, does not deal directly with his security clearance but focuses on his role as director of the Institute for Advanced Study in Princeton, New Jersey. Oppenheimer does, nonetheless, criticize secrecy in science and government, and he laments the impact of the Internal Security Act of 1950 on the free movement of people and ideas in the United States. He describes in some detail the work of the institute and its remarkable range of associates such as Albert Einstein, the Swiss psychologist Jean Piaget, the art historian Erwin Panofsky, and the diplomat George Kennan. Sitting at his desk and smoking a pipe, a blackboard filled with calculations behind him, Oppenheimer reflects on a wide range of topics, from the creative process to human prospects in a nuclear age he helped inaugurate.

Philip Hamburger wrote in the *New Yorker* that he "was overwhelmed by the beauty and candor of the program," which he characterized as "a true study . . . in genius—tense, dedicated, deeper than deep, somewhat haunted, uncertain, calm, confident, and full, full, full of knowledge, not only of particles and things but of men and motives, and of the basic humanity that may be the only saviour we have in this strange world he and his colleagues have discovered." Jack Gould of the *New York Times* praised the program for revealing more than what the complex and tragic figure of Oppenheimer said: "The pauses as he groped for the desired phrase, the look in his eye or his pensive reflection were a TV cameo of a mind at work." The broadcast historian Erik Barnouw characterizes "A Conversation with Dr. J. Robert Oppenheimer" as "one of the mightiest hours ever seen on television. There was no hint of the arrogance some scientists ascribed to Oppenheimer; instead there was fragility, dedication, tension, and an unsparing urge to dig to the heart of issues. There were not easy slogans. The reaction among educators was overwhelming; praises showered on the producers and on CBS. Prints of the film remained in demand for years."[33]

See It Now provided a forum for political figures as well as for representatives of the arts and sciences like Sandburg and Oppenheimer. It broadcast, for example, the first substantial television interviews of non-Western leaders like Mahatma Gandhi and Hailie Selassie. A program on the Suez Crisis in 1956 featured an interview with Egyptian president Gamal Abdel Nasser, about which a *Variety* critic wrote: "It was a closeup portrait in which Nasser's personal attractiveness, intellectual sharpness and messianic potential was evoked under Murrow's sharp questioning."[34] An interview with the British foreign minister Selwyn Lloyd countered Nasser's views. *See It Now* also used dialogue captured on film to highlight the views of people with divergent positions on controversial issues as well as to capture the thinking and inner conflicts of individual figures like Sandburg or Oppenheimer. Friendly applied this approach during the 1953/1954 season, for example, in "An Argument in Indianapolis," intercutting two meetings about a local civil liberties controversy. "It was the first time we had edited such conflicting views in juxtaposition," Friendly later observed, "and the film was most effective."[35]

To highlight such conflicts of ideas, Friendly, working closely with his camera operators and film editors, made innovative use the so-called cross-cut interview. As Bluem explains:

> For in terms of production, the primary contribution of [*See It Now*] was the "cross-cut" interview—a device which was always available to theatrical film documentarists but seldom used with flair and imagination. Subsequently imitated by many others in television and film, the technique involved the procedure of recording many interviews at great length and in considerable detail—a certain way to achieve the conviction Murrow and Friendly sought—and then fragmenting them into a series of shorter statements to be "shotgunned" throughout a program. The process permitted not only arresting and rapid flow of visual interest, but a bold juxtaposition of different points of view in short and emphatic bursts.[36]

The cross-cut interview was an invaluable tool in enhancing *See It Now*'s ability to explore controversy.

Yet Murrow and Friendly exercised great caution in exploiting the arsenal of techniques and prestige of *See It Now* to confront the most sensitive domestic issue of the period: the red scare. During its first two seasons, from the fall of 1951 to the spring of 1953, *See It Now* did not treat in any substantive way the problem that came to be known as McCarthyism: the threats to civil liberties posed by loyalty oaths, blacklists, and the witch hunts of congressional committees. Murrow was critical of the Soviet Union and, in the words of one of his biographers, "a conventional anticommunist."[37] Murrow made an exception to his practice of not joining political organizations to become a member of the Committee on the Present Danger, which supported a policy of containment of Communist expansion abroad. Members of the committee included Harvard president James Conant, the labor leader David Dubinsky, and General William "Wild Bill" Donovan, head of the Office of Strategic Services during World War II. On his radio program, Murrow defended the death sentences for Julius and Ethel Rosenberg, arguing that the American public was bound to accept the outcome of what he considered a fair trial.[38] Murrow was not a person of the left but a political moderate, anti-Communist in foreign affairs, liberal in domestic matters, with a general sympathy for the underdog. As a journalist, he valued the protections afforded by the Bill of Rights. While supportive of the policy of containment abroad, he was opposed to self-appointed ultrapatriots and anti-Communist crusaders at home. Murrow used his prestige to come to the defense of targets of the witch hunts in broadcasting.

According to Dorothy, Friendly's political views were largely unformed until his encounter with Murrow. Friendly had absorbed broad humanistic and cosmopolitan values during his upbringing in Providence. His mother's chief political commitment was to the cause of international peace. Rabbi William Braude of Temple Beth El had imbued Friendly with a general vision of the United States as a democratic melting pot. These values were reflected in Friendly's early series of audio biographies, *Footprints in the Sands of Time*, which included sympathetic portraits of figures like Susan B. Anthony, William Jennings Bryan, and Tecumseh. Friendly viewed World War II as a great affirmation of American values, and his experience in the China-Burma-India theater and as witness to the liberation of the Mauthausen concentration camp by U.S. troops reinforced his patriotism. Yet Friendly did not exhibit an active interest in political or social issues before and immediately after the war.

When in Providence, he considered a career in acting, his point of reference was the popular fare of Broadway and Hollywood. He showed no awareness of the revolution in theater in the 1930s led by the Group Theater in New York and the politically engaged playwrights like Clifford Odets who were associated with the company. "Fred had always been interested in current affairs in a casual way," Dorothy later recalled. "Politically, he was not very aware until he was working with Murrow."[39] By the time of *See It Now*, however, Friendly was influenced not only by Murrow but by the more outspokenly liberal milieu in which he now moved. Quick to absorb unfolding events, he shared the outrage at the trial of the Hollywood Ten and the imprisonment of Alger Hiss, who was a friend of Joe Wershba's. However, no one in Friendly's circle of friends in this period was directly affected by the blacklist.

For Murrow and Friendly, the red scare inevitably became an issue in which they had a professional and personal stake. In June 1951, *Counterattack: The Newsletter of Facts on Communism*, published by three former FBI agents, issued *Red Channels: The Report of Communist Influence in Radio and Television*, which accused 151 people of having links to Communist and Communist-front groups.[40] The premise of the report was that international Communism used radio and television to advance its agenda in the United States. Conservative business interests threatened boycotts if the networks did not fire those named in the report. Allies in the press, especially the Hearst newspapers, echoed the charges of the blacklisters. "The book," Erik Barnouw writes, "could be seen as a move to pillory the liberal impulses of two decades as traitorous—and perhaps to control the course of television."[41] The list of 151 names included those of many of the most prominent figures in broadcasting, among them colleagues of Murrow at CBS like Norman Corwin, Joseph Julian, Alexander Kendrick, William Shirer, and Allan Sloane. Although Murrow was not listed in *Red Channels*, in 1952 *Counterattack* devoted an entire issue to Murrow, writing that he "is confused on communist issues and defends those involved in communist causes."[42] Murrow had testified on behalf of the radio actor Joseph Julian in his libel suit against *Counterattack*. Murrow also fought successfully to save the job of Winston Burdett, a correspondent who had admitted to being a former member of the Communist Party.

In response to *Red Channels*, CBS instituted its own screening system. Compensating for its socially conscious programming during the Depression and World War II, CBS now became "purge headquarters."[43] In

December 1950, CBS required all its employees to fill out a questionnaire about affiliation with the Communist Party and its fronts or with any subversive organizations, including those on the attorney general's list of subversive organizations. Most of Murrow's old team of war correspondents viewed the questionnaire as a de facto loyalty oath and a violation of their constitutional rights. At first they refused to sign. They were shocked to learn, however, that CBS vice president Joseph Ream had cleared the questionnaire with Murrow. The civil rights attorney Morris Ernst spent hours trying, without success, to convince Murrow of the necessity that he—given his stature—not fill it out; otherwise, everyone in the news department would be forced to. Murrow responded angrily when Eric Sevareid, Charles Collingwood, and other long-time associates objected to the questionnaire. Murrow told David Schoenbrun, "If you don't sign it, suspicion will hover over you. I'm signing. Do you have more integrity than I do, David?"[44] They all reluctantly signed. The authors of *The Murrow Boys* are at pains to explain Murrow's behavior, speculating about the state of his health, his dark forebodings about the future of the country and television, and his calculation about the limits of his influence at CBS. "He considered McCarthyism a scourge," they write, "but he seems to have sensed that he did not have the clout to move Paley on the 'loyalty oath' question, just as he had been unable to move him during the final act of the Shirer drama." In 1951, CBS went a step further, hiring Daniel O'Shea, a film industry attorney, as vice president for security. O'Shea consulted with the FBI and congressional investigating committees to determine who should be barred from working at CBS. Once again, Murrow voiced no objection.[45]

Fred Friendly had already brushed up against blacklisting at NBC in 1949, when a sponsor of *Who Said That?* created a blacklist of its own that the network rubber-stamped. The list of guests barred from the quiz show included Norman Thomas, Al Capp, Oscar Levant, Henry Morgan, and even several U.S. senators and representatives—"not because they were part of the Communist conspiracy," Friendly remembered being told, ". . . but because in a live, ad-lib broadcast 'they just might say something.'" Friendly had entered into negotiations with Sig Mickelson about coming to CBS in July 1950, the same month *Red Channels* was published. He was working with Murrow on the radio program *Hear It Now* when the CBS questionnaire was distributed. Friendly later proudly claimed that he never filled it out.[46] Don Hewitt later expressed skepticism about Friendly's claim: "It was standard operating procedure. I didn't know of any way to avoid doing it and not lose your job. It was required." Friendly maintained that he just put the questionnaire in his desk, and no one asked for it. Friendly's claim about not signing sounds plausible: he explained his noncompliance in terms of a bureaucratic oversight, not as an act of defiance. And given that Murrow, his mentor, had signed it, Friendly would most likely have had no compunction acknowledging he had done so if that had been the case. Whether he complied with the questionnaire or not, Friendly as producer of *Hear It Now* was forced to take the blacklist into consideration. For example, when Friendly went to a CBS executive to get money to commission original theme music for *See It Now*, and he presented the names of three modern composers, he was told that one of them—presumably, Aaron Copland, who was listed in *Red Channels*—could not be considered.[47]

Allan E. Sloane believed that Friendly did not let him contribute to *Hear It Now* and *See It Now* because his work was too socially engaged. Sloane was a radio writer for CBS; he had been listed in *Red Channels*, and he had appeared before the House Un-American Activities Committee. Sloane and Friendly had crossed paths before the war at the offices of the *Providence Journal and Bulletin*, where Sloane had worked as a feature writer and Friendly had gone to do research for his radio work. After the war, Sloane received critical acclaim for producing a radio documentary narrated by Murrow, *Between the Dark and the Daylight*, which was based on interviews Sloane had conducted in displaced persons camps and pockets of poverty in postwar Europe. One day, Sloane recognized Friendly as he was walking with a fistful of Associated Press wire copy through the news department at CBS, on the ninth floor of 485 Madison Avenue, "his head slightly cocked as if he was listening to voices nobody else could hear."[48]

Once Sloane asked Friendly directly why he could not get assignments from Friendly. Friendly replied, "Okay. You asked for it. You'd better not hold your breath till I call. You don't fit into the operation. I'm trying to put out good radio. But you're trying to change the world with a radio script." Sloane felt that Murrow and Friendly should have openly fought the loyalty questionnaire and blacklist apparatus at CBS. Sloane bitterly charged years later that Friendly was not prepared to risk his job: "I think Fred, way down deep, wanted to get on the picket line of life—but never had the courage—or temerity—to do so." Sloane nonetheless tempered—indeed, reconsidered—his criticism of a person he admittedly disliked. Something other than rank careerism was driving this man whom he had observed obsessively revising and reediting *Hear It Now* late into the night. "And as I think back through the mist of the past," the eighty-five-year-old Sloane reflected in 2000, one year before his death, "I realize that Fred Friendly found his Grail: To go after the truth, and when it is as close to accuracy as the medium can get, put it on the air. And whether he liked it or not, he too was trying to change the world."[49]

6 Encounter with McCarthyism

THE CONFRONTATION BETWEEN Edward R. Murrow and Senator Joseph McCarthy is a celebrated episode in broadcasting history. It received Hollywood treatment in 2005 with the feature film *Good Night and Good Luck*, in which George Clooney played Friendly as a loyal if nondescript aide, someone who was not a major player in the unfolding drama. It is worth revisiting the confrontation in order to weigh Friendly's true role in *See It Now*'s encounter with McCarthyism and in the development of documentary techniques that shaped its outcome.

As early as 1951, Murrow and Friendly expressed interest in doing programs on the FBI, the institution that played a critical—in retrospect perhaps the leading—role in the anti-Communist crusade of the 1950s. Ellen Schrecker, an authority on McCarthyism, has written of the agency and its director, J. Edgar Hoover:

> Had observers known in the 1950s what they have learned since the 1970s, when the Freedom of Information Act opened the Bureau's files, "McCarthyism" would probably be called "Hooverism." For the FBI was the bureaucratic heart of the McCarthy era. It designed and ran much of the machinery of political repression, shaping the loyalty programs, criminal prosecutions, and undercover operations that pushed the communist issue to the center of American politics during the early years of the Cold War.

The FBI provided information for congressional witch-hunting committees as well as personnel for the administration of the blacklist in critical areas of U.S. life, including broadcasting. *Counterattack*, the publication that issued *Red Channels*, was published by three former FBI agents.

The FBI cultivated a reputation of mythic proportions as defender of the U.S. public through an extensive and sophisticated public relations campaign. Hoover paid lip service to civil liberties, denouncing witch hunts and vigilantes. He cultivated a secret and mutually beneficial relationship with Morris Ernst of the American Civil Liberties Union (ACLU), who nonetheless had urged Murrow to challenge CBS's loyalty questionnaire. Ernst was a fervid anti-Communist who gave public support to the FBI and strengthened its legitimacy in the eyes of liberals. Some critics of McCarthy would contrast McCarthy's methods with the "responsible" anti-Communism of the FBI. Schrecker writes that "with only a few demurrals, most Americans, even most liberals, trusted the FBI."[1] In this regard, Murrow and Friendly were no exception. In 1949, for example, Murrow had praised the FBI for refusing to turn the raw files in an espionage case over to congressional investigators, in turn eliciting an appreciative letter from Hoover.[2]

In early 1951, Morris Ernst urged Murrow to do a program on the FBI on *Hear It Now*.[3] Ernst's idea was to do a serious documentary on what he considered the FBI's critical role in American society; the program would supplement the dramatic portrayals of FBI agents capturing criminals. Hoover initially was enthusiastic about the idea. The FBI hierarchy considered Murrow "one of the great voices on the air" and an important potential FBI contact for the future. At the end of June, Friendly traveled to Washington to meet with the FBI's assistant director, Louis B. Nichols, who gave him a tour and backgrounder. According to Nichols's internal memorandum on the meeting, Friendly made the case that "the real philosophy of the Bureau as the guardian of civil rights and the like has never been really told and they would like to do it. . . . [Friendly] wants to tell the real story of the philosophy behind the FBI, who its agents are, the extensive training they receive and why the FBI is not a Gestapo."[4] Friendly's pitch may have reflected his salesmanship, his ability to tell the FBI what it wanted to hear, but it also appears to have represented his true feelings at the time about the agency. Hoover gave his go-ahead for the project.

Prompted by the negotiations, the FBI did a background check on Friendly, designated "urgent," that was completed a month after his meeting with Nichols. Alfred B. Berry, a former FBI agent then working on loyalty investigations at CBS with Daniel O'Shea, network vice president for security, served as a confidential source for the report. Berry characterized Friendly as "a protégé of Murrow who can be expected to follow Murrow's desires in any program he handles." Berry noted that Friendly was advised, perhaps by Ernst—the name is redacted in Friendly's FBI file—to consult with Associate Director Nichols about the advisability of a program on the FBI. The report stated that friends of Friendly, apparently connected with the agency Stix and Gude, "in the past associated themselves with individuals of leftist tendencies." It ended with personal data—Friendly's marriage, residence at Peter Cooper Village, $22,500 salary supplemented by income from *Who Said That?* satisfactory credit rating, and lack of a criminal record—and a recommendation of "no further action."[5]

The *Hear It Now* program on the FBI was never produced. By the time Friendly met with Nichols at FBI headquarters, the radio show was being phased out as preparations commenced for *See It Now*. The failure to produce the program as planned had a chilling effect on Murrow's relationship with Hoover. Friendly subsequently tried to resume negotiations with the FBI, exploring the possibility of something more dramatic for *See It Now* than the original radio documentary proposal, perhaps an FBI versus the Klan story or a live broadcast from FBI headquarters. The FBI responded evasively to this and subsequent approaches by Friendly, whose appeals became more insistent. Friendly wrote Louis Nichols on January 15, 1954, noting that the last time they spoke in late 1953 "you were under such terrific pressure from the Harry Dexter White hearings," a reference to a Senate inquiry regarding accusations that the former Treasury official had engaged in espionage and that the Truman administration had ignored evidence provided by the FBI. "The time is now," Friendly wrote about scheduling a *See It Now* program on the FBI, repeating at the end of his letter, "Please, the time is now." Nichols replied, "Quite frankly, you couldn't hit us at a worse time and with all the matters now pending, I do not see how we possibly could be of any assistance. Perhaps some day the situation will ease." When Friendly expressed his great disappointment, Nichols reminded Friendly of the failure to follow through on the earlier program originally conceived for *Hear It Now*.[6]

Although Murrow was generally respectful of Hoover's authority, there was tension in their relationship during Murrow's brief and unhappy tenure as a CBS vice president and board member. It required him to protect the network in ways—including reporting to Hoover—that Murrow felt compromised his standards as a journalist. David Schoenbrun writes, "It pained him every time he was obliged to write to J. Edgar Hoover . . . to advise him of the substance and themes of new CBS programs, inviting Hoover to express his views on the programs. The 'Murrow boys' knew nothing of his correspondence with Hoover. It would have shocked and saddened us." Schoenbrun adds, "Murrow admitted he felt nauseous when he discovered that President Frank Stanton had also sent a message to Hoover informing him of a new program, 'See It Now,' and invited Hoover to listen to it and tell CBS what he thought of it."[7]

Moreover, since Friendly's initial visit to FBI headquarters, Murrow was becoming persona non grata in the circles driving the anti-Communist crusade. *Counterattack* began attacking Murrow as early as February 1952, during *See It Now*'s first season. His relationship with the FBI deteriorated. Hoover, for example, was deeply offended in 1952 by a radio commentary about his testimony before Congress regarding Harry Dexter White in which Murrow suggested that the FBI's proper role was to supply information to government bodies, not to accuse people publicly of espionage. By 1956, when an invitation was extended to Hoover to appear on *Person to Person*, a celebrity interview show that Murrow was hosting, the director jotted on the bottom of the page, "I will never have anything to do with anything with which Murrow is connected." "The fact that the invitation was sent to Hoover in the first place," Joseph Persico observes, "makes clear that Murrow had no idea of the extent of his pariah status within the FBI."[8] During the early and mid-1950s, the FBI stepped up its scrutiny of Murrow—of his associations past and present, his travels, his responses to loyalty controversies—so that his file ultimately contained more than a thousand pages.[9] Friendly was not a person of interest to the FBI: his FBI file through the 1960s contained only the initial background investigation and his correspondence with Louis Nichols.

Thus the repeated attempts by Murrow and Friendly to do a program on the FBI proved futile. As for the topic of McCarthyism, *See It Now* proceeded with caution. By the end of its second season in June 1953, it had run several brief reports or made references regarding McCarthy but had offered viewers no focused treatment of him or of the witch hunts that had had such a devastating impact on government, education, and the arts. By this time, *See It Now* had the tools to mount such a treatment. The first hour-long Korea Christmas special had aired during the second season, as *See It Now* refined its newsmagazine and documentary format and found its voice. By the beginning of the third season, Murrow was at the peak of his postwar influence, commanding what has been termed a "triple-threat platform": his fifteen-minute weekday radio show, the serious newsmagazine *See It Now* on Tuesdays at 10:30 P.M., and *Person to Person* on Fridays at 10:30 P.M.[10] Moreover, since World War II Murrow had had a close personal as well as professional relationship with William Paley. Given Murrow's popular prestige and special position within CBS, it is not surprising that many of his closest colleagues and friends felt Murrow was well positioned to take on McCarthy.

But while *See It Now* had yet to take on a full treatment of McCarthyism, it had tangled with the senator from Wisconsin. Early in its first season, *See It Now* reported the introduction of a resolution in August 1951 calling for McCarthy's expulsion from Congress by Senator William Benton of Connecticut and planned follow-up interviews with Benton and McCarthy on a subsequent broadcast. McCarthy had retaliated against Benton by accusing him of protecting Communists and distributing lewd works of art during his earlier tenure as an assistant secretary of state in charge of overseas information programs. In Murrow's three-minute interview with McCarthy that aired March 16, 1952, on *See It Now*, the senator from Wisconsin launched a nonstop diatribe against Benton, repeating the charges and calling Benton a coward for hiding behind his congressional immunity in accusing McCarthy of being a liar. A frustrated Murrow felt that he had lost control of the interview and let McCarthy's attack go unchallenged. The following week, when Benton was permitted to respond, Murrow also pointed out McCarthy's misrepresentations as he read quotes from the transcript of the McCarthy interview, noting, "When we began this series of reports, we said that we would try to be the first to correct any errors. . . . That applies likewise to our *guests*."[11]

The Benton episode made clear to Murrow and Friendly that dealing with McCarthy on the air would be difficult. Friendly later faulted himself for not allocating more time for the first exchange and for not juxtaposing the views of Benton and McCarthy in a more substantive way. Murrow's coverage of the Benton–McCarthy conflict may have provoked the attack on him that appeared in the February 1952 issue of *Counterattack*. Murrow made critical asides about McCarthy on *See It Now* in 1953 as well. In one instance, Murrow ended a report on an emotional celebration for McCarthy in Milwaukee by stating that "this was the same man who had accused General Marshall of treason." In another, Murrow and Friendly showed footage of the McCarthy Committee badgering a witness; the same program included a segment on the life and death of Joseph

Stalin. "The juxtaposition of Stalin and McCarthy was not lost on view-ers," Joe Wershba later observed.[12]

See It Now's reports on Senator Benton, the homecoming celebration for McCarthy in Milwaukee, and the juxtaposition of McCarthy and Sta-lin represented significant critical sidebars on McCarthyism—yet they were only sidebars. By the beginning of the third season of See It Now, there was increased pressure on Murrow and Friendly to do something more substantive. Friendly later conceded that during the first two sea-sons, with the exception of programming on Korea, "the missing ingre-dients were conviction, controversy and a point of view." He attributed this to the need for a two-year apprenticeship for what Murrow had termed "an old team trying to learn a new trade." In addition, Murrow and Friendly faced issues of timing and approach. During the spring of 1953, toward the end of the second season, Murrow and Friendly began struggling with the question of how to frame a full-length treatment of McCarthy. Friendly remembered meeting a delegation of civil libertari-ans sharply critical of Murrow for not tackling McCarthy head-on: "Ed and I argued that we weren't going to use our microphones and cameras as a monopolized pulpit from which to preach, but that when there was a news story that dramatized the problem of guilt by association we might be able to make our point legitimately."[13] Such a news story presented it-self in October 1953, early in the third season, a critical moment when McCarthy was beginning to target supposed Communist infiltration of the army. That month, McCarthy began closed hearings at the Signal Corps Center at Fort Monmouth, New Jersey, the very same army base where Friendly had begun his military service during World War II. Un-der pressure, the army released a number of employees accused by Mc-Carthy of being "security risks."[14] The order also ended the guarantee of an impartial dismissal hearing. In the same month as the Fort Mon-mouth investigation, Murrow passed on to Friendly for follow-up a clip-ping from the Detroit News about an air force lieutenant who was being forced out of the military as a security risk (but not a loyalty risk in the peculiar logic of the time) because of charges that his father and sister were leftists. The result would be "The Case of Milo Radulovich, A0589839," broadcast on See It Now on October 20, 1953.

Milo Radulovich, a twenty-six-year-old student at the University of Michigan, had been asked to resign his commission as a meteorologist in the Air Force Reserve because of accusations against his father and sister by unnamed sources. When Radulovich refused to resign, an air force board ordered his separation. Murrow provided the lead; Friendly sent Joe Wershba for a preliminary investigation and then dispatched Charlie Mack to film interviews with Radulovich, his family, and local residents. Forty-eight hours later, Friendly was screening footage, so excited that he asked Murrow to come to 550 Fifth Avenue that night after his radio show. Murrow, moved by what he saw, suggested that they consider devoting the entire program to the topic. He told Friendly to try to get the air force to comment and CBS to do a special promotion for the program, while he worked on his tailpiece: "Leave me enough time because we are going to live or die by the ending. Management is going to howl . . . but we simply can't do an 'on the other hand' ending for this." Murrow deliberately violated the long-standing principle enunciated by Paul White at CBS that the viewer should not be able to discern a broadcaster's own view of a controversial issue receiving coverage. Murrow argued that "some issues are not equally balanced. We can't sit there every Tuesday night and give the impression that for every argument on one side there is an equal one on the other side."[15]

The air force refused to participate; instead, two officers met with Murrow and Friendly to discourage them from doing the program. Murrow realized that the Radulovich program might advance the broadcast journalist's ability to take on controversial issues but that it also threatened the sponsorship and the future of See It Now. CBS executives declined the opportunity to preview or promote the show. A notice for the program in the New York Times did not have the CBS logo but the signatures of "Ed Murrow and Fred Friendly," who personally paid for the advertisement. Editing proceeded through Monday night and Tuesday until shortly before the 10:30 P.M. broadcast. No time remained for a dress rehearsal of the complete program. The See It Now apparatus created by Friendly had produced the program in less than a week. Seconds before air time, Murrow said to Friendly, "I don't know whether we'll get away with this one or not, and things will never be the same around here after tonight, but this show may turn out to be a small footnote to history in the fight against the senator."[16]

In the Radulovich program, See It Now used documentary technique to present a "little picture" with broad implications.[17] As the media scholars Thomas Rosteck and Thomas Doherty have demonstrated, Friendly deftly structured this and subsequent documentaries on McCarthyism in a way that shaped the audience's sympathies and grasp of the issues. The Radulovich program began with See It Now's standard opening: the introduction of the topic by Murrow, who then turns to the monitors, followed by a dissolve and the film itself, transporting viewers from Studio 41 to Dexter, Michigan. Radulovich's hometown is portrayed as a Norman Rockwell embodiment of a middle-American hamlet. The audience sees its shopping district and travels to meet its citizens, who were filmed from the vantage point of a passenger in the front seat of a car. The program is divided into three sections: a portrait of Milo Radulovich, interviews with citizens and Radulovich's family, and Murrow's concluding commentary. Radulovich is presented as everyman: viewers enter his home, meet his wife, and hear his account of the mundane details of his exemplary life. Then they learn how the accusation of being a security risk—because his relatives were said to read subversive publications—turned his world topsy-turvy. "Anybody that is labeled a security risk these days," he observes, ". . . simply won't be able to find employment."[18]

The camera then shifts from the intimacy of the Radulovich home to Selfridge Field, where the hearing took place. Murrow points out that the air force did not produce any witnesses and refused to reveal the contents of a manila folder containing allegations against Radulovich's family. Viewers see a high chain-link fence with barbed wire on top; a police guard motions the camera away. The depersonalized harshness of the air force's Selfridge Field is in stark contrast to the humanity of Radulovich—and of the neighbors who comment on his predicament. A town marshal, an employee of a dry-cleaning establishment, and a beer truck driver who formerly headed the local American Legion post all come to Radulovich's defense. These figures have been described as "an ensemble of flinty small-town types" and a "chorus of citizen-witnesses"—the voice of the people—prompting the sympathy of the audience.[19] Their testimony is followed by an interview in Detroit with Radulovich's father, a Serbian immigrant and naturalized U.S. citizen with a poor command of English. In a halting voice, he reads a letter addressed to President Eisenhower noting that he came to the United States thirty-nine years before and fought in the army in World War I: "My whole life, my whole family, is American. Mr. President, I am writing you because they are doing a bad thing to Milo. They are wrong." He continues: "Mr. President, I am an old man. I have spent my life in this coal mine and auto furnaces. I ask nothing for myself. All I ask is justice for my boy."[20]

Murrow begins his tailpiece by reading from the transcript of the hearing to dramatize its Kafkaesque character. He challenges as absurd the government's contention that Radulovich could be deemed a security risk but not a loyalty risk. Murrow notes that Radulovich's appeal would be considered by Harold Talbott, secretary of the air force. And Murrow invites representatives of the military to appear on the air to correct any errors and to express their views. The program ends with a brief commentary in which Murrow invokes the name of his partner: "Whatever happens in this whole area of the relationship between the individual and the state, we will do it to ourselves—it cannot be blamed on Malenkov, or Mao Tse-Tung, or even our allies. And it seems to us—that is, to Fred Friendly and myself—that that is a subject that should be argued about endlessly."[21]

The program was widely and enthusiastically hailed as a breakthrough in television journalism. Jack Gould wrote in the *New York Times* that for the first time in the medium's history a major network and advertiser "consented to a program taking a vigorous editorial stand in a matter of national importance and controversy." An industry critic characterized the broadcast as "a milestone in the realm of pictorial editorialization which brought to the TV medium a new found [*sic*] respect."[22] "The Case of Milo Radulovich" used the little picture to criticize McCarthyism without invoking the senator's name.

Despite the praise, Murrow and Friendly realized that using documentary technique with a point of view made them more vulnerable to critics within and outside the network. The advertisement in the *New York Times*, as well as the program's tailpiece, signaled that Murrow and Friendly took personal responsibility for the program. CBS executives said nothing about the Radulovich broadcast, either to Murrow and Friendly or to the press. About four weeks after the Radulovich program, on November 17, a McCarthy investigator, Donald Surine, told Joe Wershba that he had evidence that Murrow had been on the Soviet payroll in the mid-1930s, when he worked for the Institute of International Education. The message was clearly intended to signal that McCarthy was collecting information on Murrow and to encourage him to cease doing programs like the Radulovich broadcast. According to Wershba, this threat crystallized Murrow's resolve to begin planning a program on McCarthy. In a quiet rage he said, "The question now is, *when* do I go against these guys?"[23]

A week after Surine's warning to Wershba, *See It Now* would score a victory in the Radulovich case and broadcast another documentary of about the climate of fear in the nation entitled "An Argument in India-napolis." Friendly had worked through the night with his film editors to prepare for the November 24, 1953, broadcast. At 8:00 A.M., he received a call from Murrow saying that the secretary of the air force had requested that a camera crew be sent to the Pentagon so that he could make a state-ment for viewers of *See It Now*. Dorothy got a call at home at 2:00 P.M. from Fred, who told her that Radulovich would be reinstated. She jotted a note that read, "F and I both got too choked up to talk." Viewers saw Mur-row begin the broadcast that night by introducing the secretary of the air force, who read a statement addressed to "Mr. Murrow." Talbott an-nounced that he had cleared and reinstated Milo Radulovich, declaring that "the preservation of our American way of life requires that we must be alert to safeguard our individual liberties."[24] Talbott's appearance on *See It Now* was a remarkable testament to the authority of Murrow and the program, as Thomas Rosteck has emphasized. Murrow and Friendly had made the Radulovich case a national issue. Talbott appeared on the program at the invitation of Murrow and addressed his remarks to Mur-row rather than the audience, underscoring the broadcaster's special sta-tus. Moreover, Talbott adopted the civil libertarian subtext of the program in reinstating Radulovich. Thus, Rosteck writes, television, in the form of *See It Now*, became a participant-observer in the conflict: "This way, *See It Now* is not the mere medium of 'news'; it is a maker of news, itself a part of the story, an element in the resolution of a conflict in the public arena."[25]

"The Case of Milo Radulovich" was the first of a series of five full-length programs that aired over five months in the 1953/1954 season and ad-dressed the phenomenon of McCarthyism. Two weeks after the Radulo-vich program, *See It Now* featured two interviews with targets of Mc-Carthy: George C. Marshall, who had just been awarded the Nobel Peace Prize, and Harry Truman. In a filmed interview, Murrow exhibited great deference to Marshall, whom McCarthy had attacked on the Senate floor as early as 1951. In the second part of the program, a live interview with Truman, Joe Wershba asked the former president about those who had challenged Marshall's patriotism. Truman replied, "The man who made that attack isn't fit to shine General Marshall's shoes." In his final com-mentary, Murrow said that while he had not always agreed with Truman, "certainly we do on the subject of George Marshall, and we are also obliged to applaud Mr. Truman's selection of shoeshine boys." *Variety* commented that the reference to McCarthy was self-evident and that in the journalistic fraternity the senator's enmity for Murrow was well known.[26]

Three weeks later came "An Argument in Indianapolis." On the surface, the program involved a neutral juxtaposition of the views of the American Legion and the American Civil Liberties Union, as the camera shifted back and forth from their respective meetings. The press critic Gilbert Seldes praised the program at the time for its virtually mathematically balanced impartiality. Subsequent content analysis by Thomas Doherty nonetheless suggests that in this broadcast "the surface evenhandedness of video journalism tilts heavily toward civil liberties." The documentary, after all, opens with the secretary of the air force's statement about Milo Radulovich and the importance of freedom of expression. It closes with a local pastor, who came forward to provide the ACLU with a meeting room, affirming the importance of the free exchange of ideas. During the program, members of the American Legion echo attacks on the ACLU made by McCarthy. The framing of images and the lighting underscore the regimented feel of the American Legion's meeting and its representatives, who read from prepared statements. Conversely, supporters of the ACLU speak extemporaneously and project greater warmth and tolerance. The very nature of a program airing conflicting views implicitly affirms the principles of pluralism and open debate. Hence Rosteck characterizes the documentary as "a supposed 'impartial text' that, through depiction, casts McCarthyism in an unbecoming light."[27]

In the trio of broadcasts that addressed the issues posed by McCarthyism from various perspectives—the Radulovich program, Truman interview, and Indianapolis story—the senator's name was not mentioned. The question remained: Would Murrow and Friendly take on McCarthy directly and, if so, when? Having documented the fallout of McCarthyism in a series of little pictures, would they examine the larger picture—that of McCarthy himself? It was common knowledge in television circles that the *See It Now* team had been accumulating footage of the senator's hearings, press conferences, and other public appearances. McCarthy had let it be known that *his* investigators were building *their* file on Murrow, who came under increasing attack by the senator's allies in the press. A clash seemed inevitable.

In the weeks following the broadcast of "An Argument in Indianapolis," staff members of *See It Now* pressed Murrow and Friendly about when they use the film footage of McCarthy that they had been assembling. The deliberations of Murrow and Friendly on the question of the timing of the McCarthy program are impossible to reconstruct. They discussed such matters in private and subsequently said little about their respective positions and how they came to a decision. Daniel Schorr, who joined CBS News in 1953, characterized Friendly as "the one who prodded Murrow to take on Senator Joe McCarthy." Schorr surmised this because "Friendly told me that Murrow sometimes had to be prodded."[28] Yet Murrow would subsequently suggest that he had taken the lead in the matter.

What is clear, at any rate, is that the final decision was Murrow's. Friendly, as Murrow repeatedly stressed, was his full partner on *See It Now*. Yet Friendly was Murrow's *junior* partner, which Friendly freely acknowledged on many occasions. For example, Friendly's brief biography at the end of the book of transcripts of *See It Now* programs that he edited with Murrow says that "he describes his relationship with Murrow as that of being Managing Editor to an Editor-in-Chief."[29] Joe Wershba recalled:

If Murrow was the power, Friendly was the impresario—the prod and the goad. On the tough stories, Murrow was the final word. Ed would take the heat for the editorial content, and Fred would ride the backs of the troops to put on the best possible live-and-film broadcast in an age when film was downright primitive compared to the taped technology of the present day.

That was their mode of operation, whether it was Sen. McCarthy or the Lt. Milo Radulovich story that led up to McCarthy, or the Annie Lee Moss story that followed the week after McCarthy. All the big stories that dealt with McCarthyism . . . were ordered up by Murrow and shepherded onto the air by Friendly.[30]

The final decision of whether and when to do a program on McCarthy was Murrow's to make. Meanwhile, *See It Now* returned to less controversial programming themes after "An Argument in Indianapolis" aired in November 1953. Following the broadcast of the second Korea program a month later, *See It Now* resumed its magazine format of multiple news-related and feature stories. During January and February 1954, topics ranged from the proposed Bricker Amendment, limiting presidential treaty-making powers, and a controversy about rabies inoculations in the

Los Angeles City Council to the role of coffee in U.S. life. *See It Now*, for example, broadcast a speech by Herbert Hoover, interviewed the historian Arnold Toynbee, and documented the economic plight of Lawrence, Massachusetts, since the closing of its textile mills.

During this period, McCarthy's attacks on the Eisenhower administration and the army reached a crescendo. In one hearing in mid-February, McCarthy lost his temper and told General Ralph W. Zwicker, a hero of World War II, that he was "not fit to wear the uniform," a statement that was widely reported and created shock waves.[31] McCarthy's actions began to seem excessive and disruptive to increasing numbers of people in and out of government who up to this point had tolerated his crusade. *See It Now* segments did in fact touch on McCarthyism twice in February: first by examining the Anti-Americanism Committee of a local Connecticut post of the Veterans of Foreign Wars, and then by noting, as part of a report on the Big Four foreign ministers meeting in Berlin, fears in Europe that McCarthy represented a fascistic threat to U.S. democracy. Still, three months after "An Argument in Indianapolis," at a time when McCarthy's escalating attacks made him at once more threatening and more vulnerable, there was no indication of when the long-awaited treatment of the senator by *See It Now* would take place.

After McCarthy's attack on General Zwicker, Murrow asked Friendly to assemble all the accumulated McCarthy footage, which the two men watched for nearly three hours. The decision at the end of February to go ahead, Friendly later recalled, was in part preemptive: "If we waited much longer, history or McCarthy—or both—might run us down."[32] "The tactical command of Operation McCarthy was taken over by . . . Friendly," Wershba recalled. Wershba was pulled off other assignments to work on the connective narrative with Friendly. Murrow concentrated on writing his final commentary. The entire *See It Now* team—now numbering twenty-eight, with four full-time camera crews—was mobilized for the undertaking. Attempts to get film footage of McCarthy's Wheeling, West Virginia, speech in 1950 and attacks on General Marshall were unsuccessful. Friendly considered a rough compilation of the McCarthy footage screened for Murrow on March 1 to be thin, but Murrow felt that the McCarthy clips, together with a strong narrative voice and final statement, would provide the basis for a viable program. The reporters were more hesitant, the film editors more eager, to press ahead. The target date was March 9. The *See It Now* team worked virtually around the clock at 550 Fifth Avenue for the six days leading up to the broadcast. Murrow assumed a greater role than usual in writing the script, which was usually drafted by Friendly and lightly edited by Murrow. As the program neared completion two days before air time, Friendly thought he sensed some uneasiness among the staff, prompting him to call a meeting of the entire team. He wanted to hear any reservations about the program as it was shaping up but also whether any staff members had anything in their background that the senator could exploit in the aftermath of the broadcast. Palmer Williams said his first wife, from whom he was divorced, had been a member of the Communist Party. Wershba described it as "one distressing moment when it seemed we were about to buckle under and play according to McCarthy's witch-hunting rules." "I suppose it was my own uncertainty and fear," Friendly explained somewhat ruefully in retrospect, that led him to question whether "we had an Achilles heel."[33]

The nature of the program had been communicated to CBS management, which followed its protocol for the Radulovich program: no pre-screening of the show and no CBS-sponsored advertisement in the New York Times. Once again, the announcement appeared without the CBS logo and only the names of Murrow and Friendly, who had used their own money for the notice. However, on the morning of the broadcast William Paley called Murrow to say, "I'll be with you tonight, Ed, and I'll be with you tomorrow as well." As the 10:30 P.M. air time approached, Murrow started getting crank calls. As a precautionary measure, Friendly had arranged that uniformed CBS guards be posted at the elevator below and outside Studio 41 on the third floor above Grand Central Terminal. Seconds before air time, Friendly whispered to Murrow, "This is going to be a tough one," to which Murrow replied, "Yes, and after this one they're all going to be tough."[34]

"A Report on Senator Joseph R. McCarthy" is a sophisticated hybrid of two genres: objective reportage and public argument.[35] The opening suggests the conventions of journalistic objectivity: a report told in the words and pictures of the senator, who is offered future air time on See It Now to counter any inaccuracies or bias. Viewers see filmed sequences of McCarthy in a variety of public and private settings. Murrow "trails the Senator like a Greek chorus," in the words of one historian, linking and interpreting the sequences. Murrow uses biting irony in quoting McCarthy against himself, correcting factual errors, reading from editorials, and exposing the senator's use of the half-truth and the congressional investigation. Visual clues reinforce the underlying message. In one instance, the camera pans from an overwrought McCarthy in the Capitol building to a mural of a stately George Washington on the wall of the room. The close-ups of McCarthy are devastating. In a departure from normal documentary technique, the camera lingers beyond the conventional edit at the end of a statement to reveal awkward or unsavory imagery. For example, after McCarthy recounts his meeting with Eisenhower, the sequence continues as the microphone picks up what has been described as "the senator's breathy giggle, which continues, rising in pitch, unnerving. Magnified by the sound track, McCarthy's laugh is eerie, even chilling."[36] Here the skills of Friendly's editors came into play. The program ends with Murrow's famous final commentary, which has rightfully been called "an act of showstopping oratory."[37] Asserting that McCarthy did not create the climate of fear but merely exploited it, Murrow closes by turning the focus away from the senator and calling on the public to reflect on the deeper causes of McCarthyism.

"A Report on Senator Joseph R. McCarthy" was acclaimed by McCarthy's critics. Enthusiastic messages flooding the CBS switchboard included calls from luminaries ranging from Harry Truman to Groucho Marx. Furthermore, and perhaps more important, the program resonated with many in the general television audience. CBS received more than twelve thousand calls in a twenty-four-hour period, with a positive ratio of 15 to 1. Telegrams and letters similarly endorsed the show. The program received rave reviews in the *New York Times*, the *New York Herald Tribune*, and *Newsweek*, among other publications. Nonetheless, some commentators—led by the dean of press critics, Gilbert Seldes, writing in the *Saturday Review*—criticized the program as a dangerous precedent for the use of the powerful visual medium of television for advocacy journalism. In fact, documentary techniques had been used to advance a point of view in the Radulovich and Indianapolis programs, which Seldes had praised for their balance. The calculated framing in the McCarthy program was simply more obvious than the earlier treatments of McCarthyism in symbolic local dramas in Dexter, Michigan, and Indianapolis, Indiana.

Friendly did not dispute the one-sidedness of the program, recalling that he and Murrow were aware that they had "crossed the line into editorial comment," especially in the program's closing statement.[38] McCarthy had the Senate and other forums in which to make his accusations and defend his position. The nature of documentary film and television, in which the selection of visual images inevitably tilts the perspective, defies

simple polarities of objectivity and partiality as posed by Seldes. Moreover, *See It Now* pioneered television documentary in the context of the
battle about civil liberties in the 1950s, impelling Murrow and Friendly
to go further than they ordinarily might have in advancing a point of
view in their cycle of programs on McCarthyism. Reflecting on the Mc-
Carthy program two decades later, Friendly characterized it as an exception to the general rule that broadcast journalists should avoid taking
sides. Under extraordinary extenuating circumstances, "where the future of the republic is involved," an exception can and should be made:
"And if we altered the rules we had set up for ourselves—all rules sometimes have to be broken."[39] Friendly argued that *See It Now* could legitimately present for public consideration a critique of a senator who had
skillfully used for his own ends a press—print and electronic—that re-
flexively reported his charges without routinely examining their veracity:

> And in the final analysis, what if we hadn't done the broadcast? And
> supposing McCarthy had triumphed, as he might well have, then
> where would Mr. Seldes and those who criticized the broadcast be? If
> we had it in our power to counteract the abuses, the one-sidedness of
> Joseph McCarthy and we hadn't used it, if Joseph McCarthy had
> taken this government . . . as he very closely did. I'm not for one mo-
> ment saying we stopped him or that we did it alone, but we helped. . . .
> I think we were balancing what we knew how to do well against what
> he did superbly well, which was to be a demagogue. And I'm sorry
> we had to do it that way. But it was the challenge of a lifetime, a des-
> perate moment for the country, and not to have used it because of
> some series of rules that we would apply to ourselves and that Sena-
> tor McCarthy would abuse to the ultimate would have made history
> judge us very harshly.[40]

Following the McCarthy broadcast, *Newsweek* wrote to CBS management posing a series of questions about the expression of opinion on
television. William Paley and Frank Stanton responded with a carefully
crafted nine-page statement. News programs, they replied, communicate
and illuminate facts through analysis but do not editorialize. Other types
of broadcasts such as the feature or documentary program may contain
opinion, adding that CBS delegates responsibility for program content
and the expression of opinion to those "in whose integrity and devotion
to democratic principles CBS reposes complete confidence" and who are

"bound by the overriding policies of fairness and balance." "As for CBS," they emphasized, "the reaction caused by 'See It Now' will not alter our programming structure or our policies."[41]

The inquiry from *Newsweek* was written a day after *See It Now* aired a follow-up to the McCarthy program, "Annie Lee Moss Before the Mc-Carthy Committee." Murrow began that broadcast by assuming personal responsibility for *See It Now*'s substance within the framework of CBS policy: "This program is a weekly document for television, both live and on film, and is not designed to present hard, fast-breaking news. I and my co-editor, Fred Friendly, have been delegated the responsibility for its content. 'See It Now' operates under the broadcasting policies set by CBS." He announces that Senator McCarthy has accepted the invitation to reply to the previous week's program, which has been identified as controversial. Murrow continues: "Tonight we bring you a little picture of a little woman," Annie Lee Moss, accused, in the course of McCarthy's investigation of the army, of being a Communist while employed as a secret code operator for the Signal Corps. The program consisted almost entirely of footage filmed by a *See It Now* crew at the Senate hearing.[42]

Moss was a diminutive African American woman who appeared before the committee to deny convincingly the charges of membership in the Communist Party. Observers of the hearing laugh when, in response to a question, she asks who Karl Marx is. Viewers see a simple, guileless, and sympathetic figure in a cloth coat who apparently has to be told what the word *espionage* means. It emerges that she might have been the victim of mistaken identity. McCarthy beats a hasty retreat from the hearing room, leaving Roy Cohn, his chief counsel, to answer questions. Senator Stuart Symington states that he believes her testimony and offers to help her find a job if she does not get her army position back. When Cohn later repeats the charges against Moss, Senator John McClellan receives applause when he makes a passionate speech about the right to face one's accuser. Here, as in the Radulovich program, was an ordinary person caught in the larger drama of McCarthyism.

But unlike "The Case of Milo Radulovich" and the other programs on McCarthyism, "Annie Lee Moss Before the McCarthy Committee" did not require Murrow's connective narration and conclusion. It seems to unfold objectively as fact caught on film. Selection of footage and its editing alone shape viewers' perception, as the two-hour hearing was boiled down to less than half an hour. Periodically, images flash on screen of

McCarthy's empty seat and a glum Roy Cohn. A passage from a speech by President Eisenhower about the right of due process is introduced to reinforce McClellan's comments. Gilbert Seldes and other critics felt that the lack of overt editorializing made the Moss documentary more effective than the McCarthy program a week earlier. Murrow and Friendly included its transcript in the book of See It Now programs they issued in 1955, characterizing the episode as "the most unpremeditatedly analytical report that the program attempted. It required no editorial comment at the time, nor does it now." Friendly, who considered the program "one of the best broadcasts ever done by anyone," later went so far as to write, "If we had had the Annie Lee Moss footage earlier I would like to think we never would have done the original broadcast on McCarthy."[43]

Friendly's reflections on the relative merits of the McCarthy and Moss programs notwithstanding, the See It Now programs on McCarthyism need to be viewed as a whole to assess their importance. A debate has developed around whether the engagement of Murrow and Friendly came too late to warrant heroic status in the fight against McCarthy. McCarthy's demagogic crusade began in 1950, whereas the McCarthy and Moss programs aired in March 1954, just a month before the Army–McCarthy Hearings, which led to the senator's censure at the end of the year.[44] Prominent journalists in print and broadcasting like Drew Pearson and Elmer Davis had already taken a strong public stand against McCarthy. Some have argued that Murrow and Friendly entered the fray too late, waiting until McCarthy was already weakened before taking him on. Friendly conceded that he and Murrow received considerable—and, with hindsight, justifiable—criticism for holding back. Friendly later recalled Murrow's saying they should have done the Radulovich program six months earlier. And speaking of the McCarthy program two decades after its broadcast, Friendly said, "In retrospect knowing that we could have taken the risk and the company endured, we now say—I say, we should have done it a year earlier and I think Murrow felt that way, but who was to know that."[45]

The reality was more complex than the debunkers of Friendly and Murrow would have it. Murrow and Friendly had clearly signaled their feelings about McCarthy as early as the first season of See It Now, when Murrow on air pointed out McCarthy's misrepresentations about Benton. Yet Murrow and Friendly delayed making a frontal attack. "I think Murrow felt we had to be careful that we weren't too far ahead of public opinion," Friendly recalled. He added: "Normally, you should be way ahead of public opinion except we were in broadcasting—television, which was a brand new art—a brand new form of journalism, and it had not been established that it could do controversial subjects."[46] Journalists who had already criticized McCarthy did so in print or on radio, including Murrow and his colleagues at CBS. Yet to contemplate doing so on television was especially charged, given its power as a visual medium and the lack of precedents for such provocative programming. Moreover, *See It Now*'s encounter with McCarthyism put the program at odds with television's role in the 1950s as an engine of the cold war and of the consumer boom that followed World War II.

Not surprisingly, CBS management had made clear its discomfort with "The Case of Milo Radulovich," the first of the series of *See It Now* documentaries that addressed McCarthyism, albeit without mentioning McCarthy's name, in October 1953. Murrow and Friendly realized they were placing themselves at risk as television journalists as they prepared for the McCarthy program. Yes, editorial statements condemning McCarthy had appeared in other media. "But," as Edwin Bayley writes in *McCarthy and the Press*, "television had been so cowed by the Red baiters, the blacklisters, and the fearful sponsors that Murrow's cautious courage seemed heroic."[47] Friendly was modest in his claims for the McCarthy program: "To say that the Murrow broadcast of March 9, 1954, was the decisive blow against Senator McCarthy's power is as accurate as to say that Joseph R. McCarthy . . . single-handedly gave birth to McCarthyism." We now know that McCarthy overplayed his hand when he attacked the army and the Eisenhower administration beginning in the winter of 1953/1954. Yet his demise in 1954 assumes a false sense of inevitability in retrospect. McCarthy's public opinion ratings remained high early in 1954. The McCarthy broadcast was only one of a number of variables that ultimately led to McCarthy's censure. Few argue that it was the single most important factor, but it was important nonetheless, given its impact on public opinion by virtue of its television audience. As *Billboard* observed at the time, "What *Time* and *Life* and hundreds of newspaper editorials had failed to do, Murrow achieved by splicing some film together and adding to it his own biting commentary." A broadcast historian, reflecting on what happened, concludes that "Edward R. Murrow may not have singlehandedly slain the dragon of Joseph McCarthy, but he surely defanged the creature." Allan Sloane, the CBS writer, said that while he dreamed of having an impact, Friendly actually did so: "Did a marvelous job on Joe McCarthy—but McCarthy was almost on the ropes by then.

Still—that one show alone changed the world."[48] If Murrow was the grand strategist in *See It Now*'s confrontation with McCarthyism, Friendly was its indispensable tactician who executed the battle plans using the weapons and troops he had assembled in the *See It Now* documentary unit.

7 Aftermath

MURROW AND FRIENDLY had reason to fear the consequences of the programs on Joseph McCarthy. The political smear campaigns and broadcast blacklist were far from dead after the McCarthy and Annie Lee Moss broadcasts in March 1954. That June, the CBS radio reporter Don Hollenbeck, a target of unrelenting attacks by the Hearst television critic Jack O'Brian, committed suicide. "His death weighs on all our consciences," Friendly wrote.[1] He and Murrow felt in retrospect that they might have done more to shield and support Hollenbeck. In the aftermath of the suicide, with Bill Paley's support, they canceled *See It Now*'s arrangement with the Hearst newsreel as a subcontractor for film production.

But a month later, Joe Wershba was forced to leave CBS.[2] An anonymous postcard sent to CBS said Wershba had been a member of radical organizations as a student in the 1930s. When Wershba confirmed the information to Daniel O'Shea, administrator of the CBS blacklist, and refused to name names, Wershba was told he would have to leave the network. It marked the first direct interference with a member of the Murrow–Friendly team. Wershba had been its top reporter-producer, playing a major role in "The Case of Milo Radulovich" and most of the important *See It Now* broadcasts. Murrow spoke on Wershba's behalf to O'Shea, who argued that he was protecting the economic interests of the network, a position that inhibited Murrow from pressing Paley hard on the issue. Meanwhile, Friendly assigned Wershba to auditing tapes. Despite additional appeals by Murrow to O'Shea, CBS management would not budge, and Wershba realized that he would have to resign. Friendly naively believed that Wershba could hang on at CBS. "If you leave—*I* leave," Friendly said, which Wershba interpreted as an expression of emotional solidarity rather than of any serious intention on Friendly's part to resign. When Wershba felt he had no choice but to leave CBS, Friendly angrily said to him that he was making a grave mistake that would end his career as a journalist. Years later, Friendly wrote that he and Murrow should have fought harder on Wershba's behalf and that CBS was wrong in letting him go: "That we let the best producer-reporter at CBS go—it's something I'll always live with."[3]

The third season of See It Now had been a heady period for Friendly. The excitement of that season peaked with the McCarthy broadcast. After the broadcast, and a round of drinks at the Pentagon Bar with Murrow, Friendly and Wershba had shared a taxi to Peter Cooper Village. Friendly, still overwrought, said, "Well, Murrow may be fired—but we'll make him President yet." Wershba, who apparently found the comment flippant, remembered, "I had the urge to open the cab door and push him out." Following the McCarthy broadcast, Murrow became a hero in the eyes of many, and Friendly basked in the afterglow. Friendly could rightfully be proud. He had fulfilled his aspirations, enshrined in 1950 in his initial contract with CBS, "to study and engage in certain experiments respecting the format and presentation of television documentaries."[4] He was the driving force in conceiving and running See It Now, which had broken new ground and achieved a series of historic broadcasts. His partner, whom he idolized, had now gained even greater stature as a broadcast legend. See It Now would have new battles to wage, both internally and externally, as the fates of Don Hollenbeck and Joe Wershba made clear. Yet Friendly's prospects and future at CBS seemed assured.

Friendly returned to work from his summer vacation in the fall of 1954 with renewed confidence and energy. As See It Now returned to the air for its fourth season, a CBS press release noted that in the spring and summer of 1954 alone, the program had received more than twenty awards from a broad range of journalistic, educational, and civic organizations and that Murrow would be receiving in October the prestigious Freedom Award presented by Freedom House. See It Now continued to address a broad range of major topics. For example, Murrow and Friendly tacked the issue of race, at home and abroad. A program on the impact of the decision in Brown v. Board of Education on two southern towns represented the first substantial treatment of the issue of segregation on network television. See It Now also aired the two-part "Report on the Union of South Africa" at a time when the system of apartheid was being instituted. The reporter Howard K. Smith and camera operator

Bill McClure spent six weeks on location, interviewing government officials and native Africans and filming conditions in mines, schools, bush country, and other locales. The program was subsequently shown in movie houses in London and got *See It Now* banned from South Africa. Another two-part series examined the debate about the link between smoking and lung cancer. Jack Gould praised Murrow and Friendly for tackling a subject that inevitably would rankle advertisers, writing that once again *See It Now* "set the pace in TV reporting of controversy."[5]

"Nevertheless," Friendly observed, despite the awards and continuing critical acclaim, "we could feel CBS's support for *See It Now* fading ever so gradually." During the 1954/1955 season, *See It Now* conducted its interviews with Carl Sandburg and J. Robert Oppenheimer at the Institute for Advanced Study in Princeton. At the time of the Oppenheimer broadcast on January 4, 1955, Sandburg was in New York, and Bill Paley arranged a luncheon for the two men together with Murrow and Friendly. According to Friendly, Paley was enthusiastic about the Oppenheimer program, although conservatives objected to the sympathetic treatment of a figure who had been denied a security clearance. "Yet in a strange, disquieting way," Friendly later wrote, "the company that Paley ran found the broadcast disturbing." Friendly noted that for the rest of the 1950s, Oppenheimer was virtually banned from the CBS airwaves; for example, an interview with Oppenheimer by Howard K. Smith during the *Sputnik* crisis in 1957 was ordered cut by CBS management. In the spring of 1955, Alcoa announced that it would stop sponsoring *See It Now* at the end of the season. Dorothy Schiff, writing in the *New York Post*, noted Alcoa's denials that it was dropping *See It Now* because of its controversial programming but speculated that the Oppenheimer program was the last straw.[6]

Murrow was more attuned to the ill omens at CBS than Friendly was. The quiz show *The $64,000 Question* aired for the first time on June 7, 1955, just before the second part of *See It Now*'s series on smoking and lung cancer. Murrow, horrified, turned to Friendly in the control room and asked, "Any bets on how long we'll keep this time period now?" Friendly naively thought that the quiz show would increase the lead-in audience of *See It Now*, making it more attractive to new sponsors. In fact, the network viewed the time slot as potentially lucrative for entertainment fare. Called to Paley's office at the end of the season, Murrow and Friendly learned that *See It Now* would lose its regular weekly time slot. Instead, CBS would broadcast eight to ten one-hour or ninety-minute *See It Now* specials on an irregular basis. Paley argued that the change would facilitate more in-depth programs without the burden of a weekly half-hour show. Murrow and Friendly acknowledged Paley's logic. But they also realized that they were losing a measure of control over content as well as a regular presence on the air. Now individual *See It Now* specials would be originated through a decision-making process involving CBS management, including its sales and scheduling departments. "No longer," Friendly realized, "could we alone decide to do a McCarthy broadcast or a program on South Africa or a report on lung cancer." Yet, Friendly testified, "I must admit that we didn't protest very vigorously."[7]

See It Now aired on CBS in its new, irregular long form for three additional seasons. The first broadcast of the new format in October 1955 was "The Vice-Presidency—The Great American Lottery." In conjunction with Teachers College at Columbia University, a supplementary study guide was prepared for high school classes and civic organizations and distributed by more than a hundred CBS affiliates throughout the country. General Motors had agreed to sponsor *See It Now* but canceled the arrangement out of fear that "The Vice-Presidency—The Great American Lottery" would be a vehicle for attacking Vice President Richard Nixon. Friendly was quoted in the press as complaining about the fear of any potential controversy on television.[8] *See It Now* topics ranged from programs on Israeli-Egyptian relations and a two-part report from Africa to "Two American Originals," affectionate portraits of Grandma Moses and Louis Armstrong. The most controversial of the seven *See It Now* broadcasts during its fifth season was "The Farm Problem: A Crisis of Abundance." It documented the decline of the small farmer in competition with large mechanized agribusinesses. Although Murrow interviewed Secretary of Agriculture Ezra Taft Benson at the end of the program, he and the Republican National Committee asked for time to reply. To the chagrin of Murrow and Friendly, who felt that the issue had been treated in an evenhanded way, CBS acceded to the request.

In 1956/1957, *See It Now* was moved to the less desirable slot of 5:00 P.M. on Sundays for its occasional broadcasts. They included the first substantial television interviews with Zhou Enlai and Marshal Tito; the latter interview prompted a front-page article in the *New York Times* about the Yugoslav leader's remarks. According to Friendly, CBS was embarrassed by these two interviews with Communist leaders and barely tolerated them. *See It Now*'s relationship with CBS management continued to be strained. "When I stopped by Fred's office, late afternoon," Dorothy wrote in her diary several weeks before the Tito interview, "his faced looked tired, & eyes strained. I asked him why. He sort of groaned. Oh I had a three hour lunch. I'll tell you about it."[9]

Important changes in Friendly's personal life took place the three years between "A Report on Senator Joseph R. McCarthy" and the end of the 1956/1957 season of *See It Now*. Fred and Dorothy had moved into the stately house that they had bought early in the spring of 1954, at the time of the McCarthy broadcast. A month after the McCarthy and Annie Lee Moss programs, Friendly's mother died in Providence at the age of seventy-six. Dorothy remembered that when Fred, Therese's only child, got the news on the telephone, he started to say, "If only—" but never finished the sentence.[10] The funeral took place on April 19 at Temple Beth El in Providence. (Three years later, during the Purim festival of 1957, Friendly organized a memorial tribute to his mother, with Rabbi William Braude presiding at Temple Beth El's new building. Tribute was paid to Therese for her involvement in peace activities and civic affairs. A true Friendly production, it featured two luminaries. Edward R. Murrow, who had met Therese once, spoke about the aftermath of the Suez crisis. It became part of temple lore how Murrow motioned from the dais for permission to smoke, which Rabbi Braude granted. Carl Sandburg participated as well, reading from his works and singing folk songs. The twenty-five hundred attendees constituted a who's who of Providence.)[11]

In July 1954, with the tumultuous 1953/1954 season of *See It Now* and their move to Riverdale, New York, behind them, Dorothy and Fred took a luxury cruise to Europe. As with their European holiday in 1950, Dorothy had taken the initiative in planning the trip, and it took Fred time to decompress. During the first two days, Dorothy felt tired and saddened at leaving the children (Andrew was now three; Lisa, one), with whom they spoke by shortwave. "Also Fred wished to speak to no one but to be alone and think and chew over the problems he left behind," Dorothy wrote in her diary. "But these feelings vaporized and left us by the third day." Dorothy relished the escape from everyday life. She marveled, for example, at an elegant meal of turtle soup, sole with white grape sauce, and truffle paté en glace. "It was what I thought 1929 sailings were like—paper

hats, streamers, lots of wine and laughter, the captain throwing balls,"
she noted. There was spirited conversation among an interesting group of
passengers. They included, for example, Niccolò Tucci, an Italian writer
who contributed regularly to the *New Yorker.* "Nico lives and breathes by
Fred's side," Dorothy recorded about their cruise routine. "It's entertaining for all of us as they stimulate each other and there is good talk."
When Tucci showed Fred an article he was writing for the *Atlantic* on the
commercialization of the Appian Way, Fred suggested a segment on *See
It Now* with Tucci as narrator.[12] Fred may have finally been able to relax,
but his work was never far from his thoughts.

Friendly returned to New York and to *See It Now* with growing visibility as Murrow's partner. Following the McCarthyism programs, the *New
York Times* had profiled the "Unseen Man Behind 'See It Now.'" The article noted the popular association of the program with the figure of
Murrow: "But, although he is never in front of the camera, Friendly . . .
places his unmistakable mark—vibrating intensity and freedom from
pretense—on the program." At the outset of the fourth season, a three-
page CBS press release noted that the Murrow–Friendly working relationship dated to their record album six years earlier.[13] Murrow and
Friendly began working on their book of transcripts and photographs of
See It Now programs; they received equal billing as co-editors.

After Fred began working at CBS and Dorothy became a mother, she
relinquished her role of the immediate postwar years as Fred's professional associate. In fact, she had felt a sense of relief when Fred became
less reliant on her—"like when you first let your kid walk to school alone."
She no longer helped with writing and editing, as Fred's own writing
skills had advanced, influenced, in part, by Murrow's prose style. She had
not expected the degree of Fred's success and enjoyed its fruits: "I loved
the excitement of meeting all these people, and I liked giving successful
dinner parties. That was a great deal of fun for me." Entries in Dorothy's
diary in the spring of 1957 reflect the role she played as hostess in Riverdale and organizer of the couple's social life, which revolved to a great
extent around Fred's work. An entry for March 5, for example, describes
a candlelight dinner with two tables that she decorated with coral and
shells from Florida. Guests included close friends Sam Standard (an
eminent surgeon and father figure for Friendly), Robert and Helen Bernstein, and the publisher George Braziller and his wife. Dorothy noted
that the *New York Times,* Simon and Schuster, CBS, and the *New Yorker*

were all represented. "Good talk & good food, unbeatable," she observed. An evening with the Sevareids followed. Several days later, Fred told Dorothy to call Ben Shahn about getting together, perhaps in New York, where Shahn was completing a mural, or Boston, where they could take in a performance by Danny Kaye and hear Shahn lecture at the Fogg Museum.[14]

The Friendly family had grown with the birth of their third child, David, in 1956. Despite his heavy schedule, Fred enjoyed the role of paterfamilias, which included reserving Wednesdays for the household. Dorothy noted with pleasure, for example, Fred's first serious father–son talk with five-year-old Andy, who was upset that his new baseball glove was not a real mitt, because it did not come from Yankee Stadium and was too clean. But while she took pleasure in Fred's professional success and life, Dorothy sought to wean him away from his nonstop preoccupation with his work. In May 1957, she expressed pleasure about an intimate evening with Fred and the hope of tempering his hard-driving, volatile nature: "At night—at last, after sitting tightly at dinner, after pretending to read & to watch a television drama—at long last we clung to each other, and were peaceful together, tender. Today I paint, I write, I garden, easy in all my being. Till when? Perhaps I can pour this sweet ease into him—I will try."[15]

Later that summer, on vacation on Martha's Vineyard, Dorothy experienced a psychological crisis characterized by extreme anxiety and depression. She felt she needed to flee from Martha's Vineyard and return to New York City. Fred turned for advice to Peter Neubauer, a psychoanalyst who also vacationed on Martha's Vineyard. Neubauer recommended that Dorothy see Mortimer Ostow, a prominent psychoanalyst with offices in Riverdale and Manhattan. She began long-term psychotherapy with Ostow. She later remembered him as a remarkable man: "He saved my life." Dorothy remained grateful to Fred for being supportive of her therapy; only later did he complain about its length and expense.[16]

When the troubled vacation on Martha's Vineyard ended, Friendly returned to what would be a difficult season for *See It Now*, although this was not apparent at the outset. The 1957/1958 season included such high points as "Atomic Timetable," on the threat of radiation and peacetime use of nuclear power, and "The Lady from Philadelphia," about the contralto Marian Anderson's tour of Southeast Asia. British Prime Minister Harold Macmillan became the twenty-third foreign head of government to be presented to U.S. audiences on *See It Now*. However, "Statehood for Alaska and Hawaii," featuring supporters and opponents of the entry of the two states to the Union, led to an unanticipated conflict with CBS management. A right-wing member of Congress from New York, who believed Hawaiian statehood was part of a Soviet conspiracy, requested and received air time for a response. Murrow was not consulted in the matter; Friendly was notified, and his objections were ignored. Murrow wrote a letter of protest—"perhaps too strong," in the view of Friendly— suggesting that the action jeopardized the legendary newsman's relationship with CBS and the future of *See It Now*.[17]

When Paley met with Murrow and Friendly at the end of the seventh season, the question of the right to reply to *See It Now* broadcasts was moot. Paley had decided to end the program's run. In a heated meeting Murrow asked, "Bill, are you going to destroy all this? Don't you want an instrument like the *See It Now* organization?" To which Paley replied, "Yes, but I don't want this constant stomach ache every time you do a controversial subject." In recalling the pitched battle between Paley and Murrow, close associates for two decades, Friendly wrote: "It would be inaccurate to say that I was silent during the Paley–Murrow encounter, but I was out of my class in more respects than one." This suggests that Friendly, despite his partnership with Murrow and accomplishments to date, felt inferior—professionally and socially—to the chairman of CBS and his most renowned correspondent. Later that summer, Friendly met alone with Paley to tie up loose ends in the dismantling of the *See It Now* operation. Friendly remembered questioning Paley's actions, "which must have impressed the chairman as sophomoric statements." Paley replied that Friendly was speaking beyond his competence. Friendly tried to storm out of the office, mistakenly entering Paley's private bathroom instead of the exit. "It took me five years to be able to laugh about that," Friendly recalled, "—and it was just about that long before I was in his office again."[18]

On July 8, 1958, the *New York Times* reported that CBS would not renew *See It Now*. The article contained a review of the final program, "Watch on the Ruhr," which had aired the night before and examined the resurgence of Germany since the end of World War II. Jack Gould noted CBS's contention that Murrow and Friendly might continue their partnership in a new programming format. But Gould added that the demise of *See It Now* seemed to signal a fundamental policy change at

CBS. Another critic, hailing *See It Now* as the most important program in the brief history of television, wrote that Murrow's future at the network was uncertain: "He and Friendly will continue somehow, somewhere, but 'See It Now' is finished and with it an era ends."[19]

How would Friendly fare in the new, post–*See It Now* environment at CBS?

8 CBS Reports

FRED FRIENDLY'S future career path at CBS was unclear after *See It Now* was canceled at the end of its seventh season. Murrow continued to do his nightly radio broadcast and *Person to Person*, programs that did not fall under the umbrella of the Murrow–Friendly partnership. *Small World*, hosted by Murrow and produced by Friendly, was a stopgap. The half-hour program consisted of conversations with major figures in politics and the arts—often in unorthodox combinations—from multiple locations in the world. The initiative reflected Friendly's desire to push the limits of communication technology in innovative ways before the advent of communications satellites. Participants could not see one another and conversed through a shortwave-radio hookup. These discussions were simultaneously filmed on location and recorded through overseas telephone lines, then spliced together in New York. The first broadcast on October 12, 1958, for example, featured a dialogue among Thomas E. Dewey in New York, Jawaharlal Nehru in India, and Aldous Huxley in Britain.

Friendly had originally conceived of *Small World* as a vehicle for Eric Sevareid, who had not yet found his niche in television and who would serve as host. Sevareid filmed a pilot under Friendly's direction. But in the spring of 1957 Murrow, sensing that *See It Now*'s future was not secure, began angling to replace Sevareid as host of the planned program. Friendly told Dorothy of his discomfort when Murrow invited him to spend the night at Pawling, ostensibly to talk about *See It Now* but in fact to broach the subject of replacing Sevareid in the new venture. Dorothy recorded in her diary the following day Fred's account of his exchange with Murrow. Murrow began:

"You know, Paley claims the show could be sold in a minute, if I would do it instead of Eric. But I was thinking while I was running

the cat (tractor) this afternoon—I couldn't possibly do that—" with a
pause and an implied "Could I?" on the end. Fred said, no, he guessed
not & went on to other things about [See It Now] but Ed came back
again & again about Small World. . . . Fred says that it was lucky for
him that he is sort of naïve & slow, & really didn't get it that Ed
wanted to do the show himself & wanted support from Fred. I think
Fred did get it in the first instant, but then something blanked in his
mind because he didn't really want to comprehend. . . . Fred finally
had to talk directly to the point, & said that benching Eric would be
the final blow, the final humiliation for Eric—who is ready to quit
radio and TV, but is so excited about this show, and did a really good
job on the test show. . . . Fred said Ed would never be able to live with
himself, & that his name would smell in the industry. Ed agreed, of
course.[1]

Murrow nonetheless did become host of Small World. One program
on the nature of humor, for example, featured James Thurber, Noël Coward, and Siobhan McKenna. Maria Callas in Milan, Sir Thomas Beecham
in Nice, and Victor Borge in Connecticut argued about opera. Ingrid
Bergman, Daryl Zanuck, and Bosley Crowther talked about movies. Senator Everett Dirkson, C. Northcote Parkinson, and Carl Sandburg debated
the legacy of Abraham Lincoln. World leaders discussed religion and international affairs. Murrow played the role of intellectual provocateur,
and the resulting dialogue was lively. Despite its popularity, it was a tame
successor to See It Now. Small World employed about half of the See It
Now unit, but the veteran producers Arthur Morse and Ed Scott and camera operator Marty Barnett, among others, had to seek work elsewhere.
Friendly recalled the period as "a sad time for all of us."[2]

The enormous success of quiz shows and the ensuing scandal provided the context for this transitional period for Murrow and Friendly. In
1958, a colleague in CBS's advertising department had alerted Murrow
and Friendly that the quiz shows might be rigged, but See It Now was
about to end its run, and they did not follow up.[3] Shortly after its final
broadcast in August, word about the rigging filtered out, twenty quiz
programs were abruptly canceled, and television faced the first and most
far-reaching programming scandal in its history. Murrow's famous address on October 15 before the annual convention of the Radio-Television
News Directors Association (RTNDA) in Chicago—three days after the
debut of Small World—was fueled by his dismay about the quiz show de-

bacle and by what he considered the downward spiral of programming. The speech sounded an angry alarm for the future of public affairs programming on television. Murrow criticized the "decadence, escapism and insulation from the realities of the world in which we live" that characterized the prime-time schedule. He warned that the nation would pay a steep price "for using this most powerful instrument of communication to insulate the citizenry from the hard and demanding realities which must be faced if we are to survive." He spoke of the "incompatible combination of show business, advertising and news" and "a clash between the public interest and the corporate interest." Murrow was unforgiving in his criticism of network television's top management, the number crunchers steeped in sales and show business. He lamented "a built-in allergy to unpleasant or disturbing information." "This instrument can teach, it can illuminate; yes, and it can even inspire," Murrow said. "But it can do so only to the extent that humans are determined to use it to those ends."[4] The speech would resonate for a generation of broadcasters, not least among them, Friendly.

Murrow's speech infuriated his superiors at CBS. Paley considered the speech a personal affront: Murrow had always voiced his grievances privately with the CBS chair, with whom Murrow had had a special long-standing relationship. Murrow returned from Chicago feeling spent and deeply depressed. Normally fiercely stoic and independent, Murrow confided in Friendly that he felt deeply out of sorts. Friendly recommended that he speak to Sam Standard, the avuncular surgeon and confidant on whom Friendly relied for advice and support. Murrow had several lengthy conversations with Standard, after which he decided to take a year's leave of absence and travel with his family to Europe. CBS announced Murrow's so-called sabbatical in February 1959, saying that it would begin that July at the end of the 1958/1959 broadcast season. Friendly pleaded with Murrow to continue to do *Small World* while traveling, arguing that he was needed to keep alive a program that employed a core of the old *See It Now* team. Murrow agreed.[5]

On May 6, 1959, Frank Stanton voiced a rejoinder to Murrow's broadside seven months earlier in an effort to control damage from the quiz show scandals. He spoke before the Institute for Education by Radio-Television of his alma mater, Ohio State University, to announce a new public affairs programming initiative. He said that CBS intended to create a new documentary series to be broadcast in prime time that would treat major issues and figures in the news in depth. The show would begin broadcasting during the 1959/1960 season on a monthly basis but eventually would air weekly.

Stanton made the announcement at a time when CBS was on the defensive. The cancellation of *See It Now* had been widely criticized. John F. Kennedy, then a leading contender for the Democratic presidential nomination for the 1960 election, had complained to Louis Cowan, the president of CBS Television, about the state of television programming and CBS's cancellation of "its most consistently outstanding public affairs program, *See It Now*." Senator Warren Magnuson, whose Senate committee oversaw broadcasting, had written Stanton to express concern about further reductions in public affairs programming.[6] Murrow's speech before the RTNDA had kept the controversy about *See It Now* alive. The speech had been widely quoted and endorsed: the *Reporter*, an influential liberal magazine, reprinted the address in its entirety. In early 1959, the Federal Communications Commission announced that it would conduct hearings to examine antitrust issues in the broadcasting industry. The deepening quiz show scandal added to the impetus for greater official scrutiny of the networks. A grand jury investigation in New York was followed by word that late in 1959 Congress would conduct hearings. As a result of these developments, network executives had reason to fear greater regulatory oversight and government control of television. In his Ohio speech, Stanton made no mention of the demise of *See It Now*, Murrow's RTNDA speech, or the quiz show scandals, the confluence of factors providing the impetus for the announcement of a new flagship documentary program. A broadcast historian has challenged Friendly's contention that concern about the ramifications of the quiz show scandals was the primary consideration in establishing the new program.[7] But however one measures the relative importance of the pressures on CBS by 1959, Stanton's announcement of a new flagship documentary program served as a preemptive strike against critics by purporting to demonstrate CBS's commitment to public service.

Murrow and Friendly hoped that Stanton's proposal might represent an attempt to revive the *See It Now* model with greater network control. A month after Stanton's speech, when Sig Mickelson asked to see him, Friendly, worried about his future at CBS, reviewed the provisions of his contract before the meeting. To his surprise Mickelson offered him the position of executive director of the yet-to-be-named series. Mickelson recalled that Friendly was flattered and enthusiastic. Mickelson had been reluctant to recommend Friendly, but Stanton convinced him "that the project needed central direction with the flair that Friendly would give it." Mickelson was surprised that Friendly had the support of Stanton, who was hardly on good terms with the Murrow–Friendly team.[8] Paley would have had to approve the recommendation; most likely it was his idea. The chair of CBS undoubtedly recognized Friendly's gifts as a producer. Moreover, the selection of Murrow's partner for the position would deflect criticism about the cancellation of *See It Now*.

When Friendly said to Stanton and Mickelson that he assumed the offer was being made to the Murrow–Friendly team, he was told in no uncertain terms that that was not the case. Murrow would be leaving for his sabbatical at the end of the year. Moreover, CBS management ruled out any semblance of another autonomous Murrow–Friendly unit. The new program would be produced by—and identified with—the news division of CBS, which would use a group of rotating correspondents led by Howard K. Smith. Stanton and Mickelson sought to break up the decadelong Murrow–Friendly partnership that had produced a groundbreaking recording, radio program, and television show. Friendly faced a painful dilemma about accepting a position that would propel him from post–*See It Now* professional limbo to the top ranks of television journalism. He could do so only by accepting—indeed, by being a party to—the process by which CBS was reducing the status of his mentor. Moreover, going solo would make Friendly more vulnerable as well as more powerful. He would no longer be shielded by Murrow's reputation, visibility, and accountability for the controversial programs they produced together. "It was obvious from his cool reaction," Mickelson wrote of Friendly, "that he was less than enchanted with the prospect of working with unfamiliar production teams and without Murrow's direct participation."[9] Friendly later wrote of his dilemma:

> The options were clear. I could decline the offer and go on co-producing *Small World*, in which case the new assignment would go to others. . . . My other choice was to take the assignment and hope that by the time Ed returned, the corporate mood would have changed and he could assume his proper role. And if I took the job it meant the rejuvenation and even enlargement of the old *See It Now* organization.
>
> Unthinkable though it was to do all this without Ed's full partnership, I *was* thinking about it; what made me feel particularly guilty

was that if the situation had been reversed, Murrow would undoubtedly have rejected the proposal out of hand.[10]

In order to take the next step, Friendly had to engage in an awkward colloquy with Murrow, like the one in Pawling about who would host *Small
World*. But now it was Friendly who was protesting that under no circumstances would he accept a new arrangement without Murrow's encouragement. Murrow did in fact let Friendly off the hook, advising him to go
ahead as long as he received assurances of editorial independence and
access to Stanton and Paley.

Before accepting the position, Friendly insisted on a meeting with
Mickelson and Stanton in Murrow's presence to break a three-week im-
passe in the negotiations and to spell out his role and that of Murrow for
the proposed program. Murrow was about to leave for his European sabbatical, so the meeting took place at 11:00 P.M. on July 8 in Stanton's office. It was agreed that Friendly would serve as executive director for one
year and that future arrangements would be considered when Murrow
returned at the end of the program's first season. In the meantime, Murrow would continue to be the chief correspondent for *Small World* but not
for the new series. Friendly received permission to consult with Murrow
"frequently, if not in fact 'constantly,'" in the language of the memorandum of understanding. Friendly, in turn, agreed that he "would not take
advantage of this privilege unnecessarily." The agreement had some of
the feeling of a military disengagement treaty between CBS and Murrow.
It included other details about the responsibilities of Friendly and Murrow in the year to come and specified that the as-yet-unnamed program
would be the network's preeminent public affairs series. It was agreed
that the program could deal with controversial issues but would not take
editorial positions that would prompt protests and requests for air time
for rebuttals. Mickelson remembered the meeting as much warmer and
less acrimonious than he had anticipated.[11]

Friendly left the late night meeting with what he subsequently termed
a "naïve belief" that the acrimony surrounding Murrow's status at CBS
had been resolved and that a renewed Friendly–Murrow partnership
could resume in a year.[12] However, a week before the first broadcast of
CBS Reports, as the new show was called, the conflict between Stanton
and Murrow spun out of control. In October 1959, it was Frank Stanton's
turn to address the RTNDA convention. He used the occasion, in light of
the quiz show scandals, to outline house-cleaning measures at CBS in

which the network would dispense with all forms of artifice in its programming. In a follow-up interview with Jack Gould of the *New York Times*, Stanton offered Murrow's *Person to Person* as an example of a rehearsed program with a pretense of spontaneity. In London, Murrow was livid when he learned about Stanton's attempt to link him to the tawdry practices of the quiz shows he despised.

According to David Halberstam, CBS's treatment of Murrow reflected the determination of network television's ownership to establish greater control of its news and public affairs offerings.[13] The *See It Now* programs on McCarthy represented both television journalism's finest hour and the end of a short-lived era. Murrow's prestige and power as a journalist were incompatible with the corporate culture of television as it emerged by the late 1950s as the most powerful communication medium in history. CBS diminished Murrow's status incrementally rather than take the heat for firing him. So at first, the network had limited the number of *See It Now* programs, then changed its time slot, and finally canceled it. Murrow was subsequently barred from being chief correspondent and coproducer of the new flagship documentary program, *CBS Reports*, over which his junior partner would hold sway. CBS had in effect broken up the Murrow–Friendly team, but not completely: Murrow would continue to do *Small World* and sporadically serve as correspondent on *CBS Reports*. Murrow's options following his return in a year were ostensibly kept open.

Paley may have conceived the strategy of progressively marginalizing Murrow, but it was implemented by Stanton, who carried out Paley's directives, especially the unpleasant ones. So it was Stanton who administered the next blow, the smear of Murrow's reputation by associating his television work with the ethical violations of the quiz show scandals. In response, Murrow in London issued a statement underscoring the elaborate technical preparations required for the remote broadcasts from private residences on *Person to Person*. Rejecting Stanton's charge that he had misled the public, Murrow said, "My conscience is clear. His seems to be bothering him." Paley and Stanton, deeply offended, sent CBS's general counsel to London to get an apology or a resignation letter from Murrow. Their emissary received neither, and the tense standoff between Murrow and CBS management continued during the eight months remaining in his sabbatical year. Sig Mickelson realized that the intricate negotiations about Murrow's status and *CBS Reports* the previous summer were unraveling: "It was even questionable whether the new rift could be patched over, or whether Murrow would even remain with CBS."[14]

CBS press material about the debut of *CBS Reports* highlighted Friendly's role in the new program. With his assignment as executive producer, "Fred W. Friendly entered a new phase of an award-laden career." Publicity included an overview of Friendly's biography, from his early broadcasts in Providence and his wartime service to his association with Murrow and *See It Now*, which was characterized as a response to the challenge of "a young television medium." Mickelson was quoted as referring to *CBS Reports* as the most important project in the history of the network's news division; he said the program would give Friendly "broader scope than ever for his creativity, energy and skill." *CBS Reports* first went on the air on October 27, 1959, with "Biography of a Missile," completed by Friendly and Murrow before Murrow's departure. The program told the story of a missile from drawing board to what ended as an unsuccessful launch. The eleven programs that aired that season included "The Space Lag" and "The Population Explosion," both narrated by Howard K. Smith. "Biography of a Cancer" documented Dr. Tom Dooley's ordeal at a time when patients were reluctant to speak openly about the disease. Bill Leonard produced "Trujillo: Portrait of a Dictator," about the ruler of the Dominican Republic. "Iran: Brittle Ally" took a critical look at the regime of the shah, who submitted to a lengthy interview. The broadcasts received critical acclaim and a host of prizes, including three Peabody Awards—"and," Mickelson later observed, "CBS, not the Friendly–Murrow team, was receiving the public plaudits."[15]

During the first season of *CBS Reports*, Friendly scored a coup by getting Walter Lippmann sit for an interview for the program.[16] Friendly's interest was prompted by Lippmann's scathing critique of commercial television and the medium's poisonous influence on public taste and discourse. Lippmann advocated the establishment of a nonprofit fourth network, funded by the federal government, to engage in serious public service programming like that of the BBC. Friendly opposed Lippmann's proposal in this period because he felt it could give the commercial networks an excuse to abandon programs like *CBS Reports*, which Friendly considered "television's last best chance" and a potential model for all three commercial networks. Lippmann was a friend of Howard K. Smith, who arranged a meeting at Friendly's request to discuss Lippmann's views on television. Friendly did not make much headway in challenging Lippmann's advocacy of a fourth noncommercial network, but as a result of their encounter Friendly broached the idea of a televised interview. Lippmann was extremely resistant. "He had an intellectual's contempt for commercial television," Lippmann's biographer has written, "combined with an old newspaperman's suspicion of the medium."[17] Over several months, Friendly worked to break down that resistance—through a succession of letters, telephone calls, and lunches at the Metropolitan Club in Manhattan. Friendly would not take no for an answer. He challenged Lippmann by arguing that television needed the involvement of figures like him to change the medium's character and realize its potential. Lippmann finally succumbed, with the understanding that he could preview and veto the program if it were not to his liking. He insisted that he approve the sponsors—no dog food or deodorants, for example—and that no commercials would interrupt the dialogue. A check for $2,000 sealed the deal.[18]

The first part of the interview was filmed in May 1960 in the study of Howard K. Smith's home overlooking the Potomac River outside Washington, D.C. Because nearly two months passed before CBS could find a spot in its schedule for the program, Friendly arranged a follow-up interview on the porch of Lippmann's summer residence in Maine to keep the interview current. "Lippmann on Leadership" aired on July 7, 1960. It contained a far-ranging discussion of foreign policy issues of the day such as the U-2 incident and its impact on U.S.–Soviet relations. The winding down of the Eisenhower administration and upcoming presidential race prompted an extended discussion of leadership, a topic of special interest to Lippmann. Friendly was ecstatic about the exchange, which he felt was comparable in quality to the interview with J. Robert Oppenheimer on *See It Now*. Robert Lewis Shayon wrote in the *Saturday Review*, "To have the sage of Washington up close and ad-libbing revealed not only his urbanity . . . [but] yielded a bonus in the impression of kindliness and personal warmth never apparent in the intense concentration of his logical, impersonal prose." For Friendly, the broadcast reflected two complementary sides of television's promise: exposing Lippmann's thinking to an audience unfamiliar with his books while permitting his readers to *see* the author responding to questions. According to Friendly, Lippmann's appearance on television enhanced and transformed the writer's stature:

What television does superbly is to hold a mirror up to the individual. There is a great difference between what a man says and what he is.

Exploring that difference—that's what television is all about. Take
Walter Lippmann. He's been writing well and successfully for over
50 years. But on the basis of just one television program, the American people got to know him better than they ever had before. The
television camera made him bigger than life."[19]

The Lippmann program generated interest and praise beyond all expectations, including front-page stories and quantities of mail. Paley offered
Friendly his congratulations. Lippmann then agreed to a five-year contract for periodic interviews, what Friendly referred to as "an annual
event, a kind of television chair or fellowship." When the interviews were
published in book form, Lippmann dedicated a copy for Friendly, "the
only begetter, who conceived and produced all this."[20]

Gene DePoris, who produced the Lippmann interviews, witnessed
how assertive Friendly could be with esteemed individuals like Lippmann, how Friendly's behavior could seem impudent and be disarming
at the same time. Once during a lunch break from filming one of the annual interviews, Lippmann began to say, "Let me tell you something
about television—" Friendly interrupted, saying, "Listen, Walter, you take
care of South Asia and I'll handle television." Lippmann at first seemed
taken aback, but then smiled. "Lippmann on Leadership" launched an
important relationship for Friendly. The broadcast increased Friendly's
credibility as the head of CBS Reports. When Friendly teased Lippmann,
saying he had rescued him from the obscurity of print journalism, Lippmann countered, "And I made you respectable, young man." In general,
Lippmann was an important figure in Friendly's professional and intellectual universe. Friendly's correspondence with Lippmann reveals his
cultivation of an important contact but also the deep respect he and his
circle had for the journalist. For example, Friendly forwarded to Lippmann a note he got from Andy Rooney saying that Lippmann's A Preface
to Morals was a book that he kept by his bed and should replace Gideon
Bibles in the hotels of the nation. On another occasion, Friendly praised
a Lippmann column in the fall of 1965, adding, "Your ability to stay two
years ahead of everybody else seems to grow keener with time." In the
same note, Friendly wrote of Bill Paley's interest in inviting Lippmann to
lunch.[21]

By the time the first Lippmann interview was broadcast toward the
end of the first season of CBS Reports, Murrow was back. He had returned in May 1960, four months early, from what had not been a restful

sabbatical.[22] Friendly met him at the airport and immediately informed Murrow that *Small World* was being canceled: its advertisers and staff resources would be shifted to *CBS Reports*, a change initiated by Friendly. Friendly wanted to concentrate on the accelerated schedule of broadcasts of *CBS Reports* in its second season; he received only about $1,000 extra for the *Small World* broadcasts, which drained his energies and those of his staff. The end of *Small World* meant that Murrow no longer had a program of his own. However, Friendly had plans for Murrow to play a leading role in *CBS Reports.* Murrow involved himself immediately, doing two programs in May and June and scheduling an additional eight through the following May. Yet, despite Friendly's efforts to involve and to encourage him, Murrow seemed out of sorts. Friendly was clearly in charge of *CBS Reports* in a changed institutional culture at CBS in which an executive producer's accountability to higher-ups had hardened. Former *See It Now* staffers thought that Murrow seemed disillusioned and uncharacteristically unsure of himself, lost in the new environment. Mili Lerner remembered how "you always felt he'd be more comfortable next door—somewhere else. He was good on the camera or mike—but only when he was working. There was no feeling that this was *his.* When he sat on a chair, it didn't seem to be his. Everything had closed up while he was away, and he was like a displaced person. There was a feeling, too, that Fred didn't fight for him, though we couldn't prove it."[23]

Despite feeling in limbo, Murrow threw himself into his assignments for *CBS Reports* and seemed most comfortable in the field. He committed himself without reservation to the documentary on migrant workers that became "Harvest of Shame." Friendly had given David Lowe, a documentary filmmaker, a small retainer to explore the topic. Friendly realized that the documentary could be a great vehicle for Murrow. Murrow, in turn, found Lowe's assembled footage spellbinding and insisted on traveling with Lowe to the labor camps in the South, despite respiratory problems that fall that were sapping his strength. Murrow, who had hoed corn and experienced hard times in his youth, identified with the plight of the migrants.[24]

The production is vintage Friendly. It opens with Aaron Copland's *Fanfare for the Common Man.* A chaotic scene unfolds: rural black families milling about in a cloud of dust respond to a barker's offer of seventy cents for a day's work and climb into a ramshackle truck. Murrow's voiceover intones: "This scene is not taking place in the Congo. It has nothing to do with Johannesburg or Capetown. It is not Nyasaland or Nigeria. This is Florida. These are citizens of the United States, 1960. This is a shape-up for migrant workers . . . this is the way the humans who harvest the food for the best-fed people in the world get hired. One farmer looked at this and said, 'We used to own slaves. Now we just rent them.'"[25] Then come compelling interviews with the migrants in the fields where they worked and in the hovels where they lived, as they journeyed from the orange groves in Florida and the peach orchards in Georgia to the lettuce fields on Long Island. Murrow asks the fathers, mothers, and children about the details of their lives: what they eat, how much money they have in their pocket, where they sleep, and their toilet facilities. He elicits shocking details of squalor and exploitation but also the aspirations of children—malnourished and in rags—to become teachers and doctors when they grow up. He also speaks with a grower, who claims the migrants have gypsy in their blood and love their work and life. The art of juxtaposition, used so successfully in the McCarthy programs, contrasts the superior treatment of vegetables and cattle in transit and that of the migrant workers. The timing of the broadcast was selected for maximum impact: the day after Thanksgiving.

"Harvest of Shame" drew on the experience and expertise of the *See It Now–CBS Reports* team. Friendly insisted that the odyssey of the migrants be filmed with the unwieldy but high-quality 35-millimeter cameras, operated by the talented Charlie Mack. A vivid portrait gallery of faces, reprised at the close of the documentary, became etched in the viewer's mind. As Bill Moyers recalled, "Fred used to say, 'There is no greater production value than the power of the human face: the way the eyes move, the ways the head tilts, the pauses, the silence. . . .' He loved the human face and the human voice. He didn't go for a lot of fancy or clever engineering or editing. He was very much for 'see it now,' see what it is." In the words of John Schultz, its film editor, "Harvest of Shame" was produced in keeping with "the *CBS Reports*–Murrow-Friendly dogma" of closely integrating image and text through a collaborative process of seemingly endless reedits. "Tighten it up" became Friendly's refrain as he aimed to eliminate the extraneous and to heighten the pace and ultimate effect. Schultz, who had been hired by Friendly during Murrow's sabbatical, found Friendly "very alert to dramatic emphasis." As with "Christmas in Korea," Friendly decided he wanted a specific shot. "David," Friendly told Lowe at one point, "what you need there is a shot of *The Grapes of Wrath*: a family by the side of the road, with a flat tire and no money, and the kids looking out the window." Lowe told Friendly that such a shot could not be simply manufactured, but sure enough they found just such an image in Charlie Mack's footage and used it to good effect. "See, I told you that would work," Friendly said.[26]

According to Schultz, Friendly operated less like a typical television producer than a theatrical director, continually tweaking the performance of the members of his team. Friendly thought he could get the best out of people by pushing and challenging them. The veterans of *See It Now* accepted Friendly's active role in driving a production, often found it inspiring, but others, like David Lowe, experienced him as overbearing. There was no overt hostility between Friendly and Lowe, but the two men were wary of each other. Nonetheless, Lowe relished working with Friendly and Murrow on *CBS Reports*. His only disappointment was that he did not get more credit for "Harvest of Shame," which gained recognition as one of the greatest television documentaries ever produced.[27] In his dealings with Friendly, Lowe could still count on the moderating influence of Murrow. Although Friendly was now unquestionably in charge, Schultz observed a change in Friendly's demeanor in Murrow's presence: "In the screening room, where we all gathered, when Murrow was there, it was a little bit like Fred ceding ground to his father. . . . Fred was a little quieter, and less dramatic. Murrow put him on his best behavior."[28]

As the film took shape, Friendly encouraged Murrow to "do an ending just like the McCarthy program." At the close, as viewers once again see the faces of the migrants he has interviewed, Murrow observes, "The people you have seen have the strength to harvest your fruit and vegetables. They do not have the strength to influence legislation. Maybe we do. Good night, and good luck." Although "Harvest of Shame" included interviews with representatives of the growers and the Farm Bureau as well as the secretary of labor, it had a clear point of view. The historian A. William Bluem terms "Harvest of Shame" an editorial documentary: "It was intended to shock, to make men aware of deplorable conditions under which some Americans must exist—and dictated only one response— direct social action."[29] The program created a sensation, precipitating wide debate and calls for congressional hearings on the plight of farm workers. It was a prime example of the syncretic nature of Friendly's achievement as a television documentarian. "Harvest of Shame" drew on multiple traditions—the muckraking journalism of Ida Tarbell and Lincoln Steffens, the protest literature exemplified by John Steinbeck's *The*

Grapes of Wrath, the photojournalism of Walker Evans and Dorothea Lange—refashioned into a landmark of television reportage. "As a work of television art and a cry for social justice," Joseph Persico has written, "it remains unsurpassed."[30]

Despite protests from the Farm Bureau and its political allies, Stanton had high praise for the program. In a terse conversation in an elevator Paley told Friendly that he, too, liked the program, except its ending. Once again, in the CBS chair's view, Murrow was courting controversy by editorializing. What Friendly called "the long-postponed climax to the Murrow–Stanton dispute" took place shortly after the broadcast of "Harvest of Shame." Prompted by plans to accelerate the transition of *CBS Reports* from a monthly to a weekly program, Friendly initiated a meeting in December 1960 to revisit the question of Murrow's status. Paley, Stanton, and Dick Salant—a lawyer, corporate vice president, and protégé of Stanton who would soon replace Sig Mickelson as head of the news department—attended the meeting. Friendly proposed that *CBS Reports* present documentaries and live debates on topical issues on alternative weeks, with Murrow as coproducer and anchor to give *CBS Reports* continuity and added stature. Paley objected to making *CBS Reports* another Murrow–Friendly joint production, asking, "What do you have against Howard Smith?" The meeting ended without a consensus, and Friendly had contentious follow-up meetings with Salant. When Salant finally said that the proposal for an elevated role for Murrow had been rejected, Friendly threatened to quit as executive director of *CBS Reports*. He got his producers to commit to follow his lead if he resigned and then took Dorothy and their children skiing in the Berkshires.[31]

Murrow was saddened but not surprised when he got the news from Friendly. Once again, Friendly was torn between his loyalty to Murrow and his ambition. He later wrote, "A year before, I had yielded because Ed was leaving on a sabbatical; now my option was to resign or to compromise again so that the Thursday night series could perhaps break new ground for broadcast journalism." The dilemma was resolved when in January 1961 the newly inaugurated John F. Kennedy offered Murrow the position of head of the United States Information Agency. In the weeks separating the December meeting at CBS and the January offer to Murrow, Friendly had not tendered his resignation as work intensified on the new series of weekly *CBS Reports*. Kennedy's people had first offered the position at USIA in mid-December to Stanton, who turned it down and recommended Murrow. Murrow clearly possessed impeccable credentials for the position; but at the same time, it was also an opportunity for Stanton to finesse Murrow's separation from CBS. After Murrow received the offer, he went to New York to confer with Friendly, who apparently was alone in advising Murrow not to take the position, arguing that the roles of journalist and propagandist were incompatible. By this time, Murrow's relations with CBS management had reached their nadir. Earlier that month, he had again attacked the industry in a speech before the Radio and Television Executives Society. And he had gone to England to put out feelers about working for the BBC. Friendly's appeal for Murrow to turn down Kennedy's offer may have been more a symbolic act of loyalty than a viable recommendation. Yet as Friendly revealed years later to A. M. Sperber, a Murrow biographer, he naively persisted in the belief that "we could have ironed it out if he had stayed."[32] Over a closed-circuit-television broadcast to the network and affiliates, Murrow bade farewell to his former colleagues—"more emotionally naked than any of them had ever seen," in the words of Joseph Persico—and entered into what Friendly termed "an eased exile" from CBS.[33]

When Kennedy called to offer him the job, Murrow was on location in the capital of Alabama working with David Lowe on "Who Speaks for Birmingham?" for *CBS Reports*. Murrow felt strongly about the program on the civil rights crisis and asked that Howard K. Smith replace him as chief correspondent on the story. Smith did not harbor any of the resentment of Friendly attributed to some of Murrow Boys. To the contrary, Smith had relished his work as *See It Now*'s chief foreign correspondent, later writing that he "always felt that Fred's guidance back in New York was a guarantee of a superior result."[34] Many viewed the courtly, handsome, and articulate Smith as Murrow's heir at CBS. Before World War II, Smith had studied at Tulane University, the University of Heidelberg, and then Oxford on a Rhodes scholarship. He joined Murrow's wartime news team in 1941, covering Europe, the Battle of the Bulge, and the Nuremberg trials. After the war, he replaced Murrow as CBS's chief European correspondent based in London. When Smith returned to the United States in 1957, he fulfilled a variety of tasks at CBS: commentator on Douglas Edwards's news program and correspondent for *See It Now* and subsequently *CBS Reports*, winning George Polk and Emmy awards for his writing and narration of "The Population Explosion" in 1960. He moderated the televised Nixon–Kennedy debates, for which he received accolades, and in 1961 he was named the head of the CBS Washington Bureau and its chief correspondent.

As Murrow's replacement on the civil rights story, Smith, a South-
erner deeply opposed to Jim Crow practices, was present in Birmingham
in May 1961 when freedom riders received a severe beating with the tacit
approval of police chief Eugene "Bull" Connor. Smith watched the civil
rights activists being beaten bloody with metal pipes and brass knuckles;
one would be paralyzed for life. It reminded Smith of the attacks against
Jews by the Nazis that he had witnessed in Europe. Appalled, Smith
closed "Who Speaks for Birmingham?" by quoting Edmund Burke: "The
only thing necessary for the triumph of evil is for good men to do nothing."[35] The ending was similar in spirit to Murrow's famous ending to
the McCarthy program, with its quotation from Julius Caesar, an implied
call for citizens to assume greater responsibility to counter demagoguery.
CBS management objected to the ending by the man slated to assume
Murrow's mantle. Paley had been concerned about the impact of Smith's
critical commentary on the Little Rock crisis and thereafter on segregation, fearing that southern affiliates might leave the network. Moreover,
Paley had hoped that the departure of Murrow would defuse the problem
of editorializing on the air.[36] Smith recalled that "I was established in
Paley's realm as being a trouble-maker who had to be dealt with firmly. I
don't think they thought of me as being another Murrow, but of being
another Murrow problem."[37]

Concern about Smith's crossing the thin line between an editorial
statement and a more benign commentary or analysis led to a screening
of a rough cut of "Who Speaks for Birmingham?" attended by the vice
president of station relations and a CBS lawyer together with Smith,
Lowe, and Friendly. The screening, which would have been unthinkable
for a *See It Now* program, took place in the dark viewing room with
battered theater seats in the rundown Ninth Avenue film facility that
Friendly had used since 1951. According to Smith, the location had originally been chosen by Murrow and Friendly precisely because "it wasn't
the kind of place a company lawyer would casually drop in on while en
route to somewhere else." Following the screening, the executive declared
that the ending constituted an editorial and would have to be cut. Smith
was livid and argued with the executive at length. "Friendly took almost
no part in the discussion," Smith recalled. "He was [a] scarred veteran of
many such encounters and knew how to economize his interventions to
get the most results." Smith led the fight and did not defer to Friendly or
Lowe. "Fred was neutral, nearly silent about my Burke shot," Smith later
reflected, "but I think it would be unfair to say he had a management

perspective. I think he simply felt he knew from experience that staying out of one fight would leave him strength to win later ones." In supporting Smith's freedom as a journalist yet distancing himself from the decision to use the Burke quote, Friendly said to the CBS executive, "Those pieces belong to the reporters; I get my kicks producing." Otherwise, Friendly said nothing. "I think Fred was a better diplomat than we were," Smith surmised. "He knew how to avoid losing his temper and how to keep relations in order."[38] Friendly's tantrums and histrionics may have been legendary, but his demeanor in the Smith affair suggests that he was capable of shifting gears and being highly circumspect when it was in his interest to do so.

Smith angrily left the meeting on Ninth Avenue, insisting on a summit with Paley to protest what he considered a craven act of censorship. Salant asked Smith to send him a statement of his position, which Salant would go over with Paley. Smith returned to Washington but was suspended as CBS bureau chief. "One day," Smith recalled, "Friendly phoned and in an alarming tone told me, 'Don't come to New York. No matter who calls you or for whatever reason, do not come.' I tried to get the reason behind this message, but he would say no more." Shortly thereafter, Salant called Smith to arrange a luncheon meeting with Paley. Friendly hoped that by keeping a low profile, the controversy might blow over and Smith would save his job. Smith felt that avoiding the luncheon was impossible: he felt too strongly about the issue, as did Paley, who wished to set a clear precedent for the news division in the post-Murrow era. A contentious luncheon meeting with Paley took place, attended by Stanton and Salant but not Friendly. Smith countered Paley's insistence on balance with arguments about the responsibility of journalists to provide both information and opinion on the burning issues of the day. Smith was unyielding and confrontational at the meeting. Paley always avoided firing someone directly but made it clear that Smith's twenty-year career at CBS was over.[39]

Friendly made a last-ditch appeal for retaining Smith as a correspondent for *CBS Reports* while removing him as chief of the Washington bureau. Paley's response had a familiar ring: What's wrong with Eric Sevareid or Charles Collingwood? Smith submitted a letter of resignation on October 31, 1961. In retrospect, Smith assumed responsibility for his separation from CBS, believing that he gave Paley no other option. "His strategy must have been right," Smith wrote of Friendly's nonconfrontational tactics. "He got a pretty good documentary on the air; I got fired."[40]

Friendly nonetheless was extremely uncomfortable that he had witnessed—and survived—the purge of Murrow's heir apparent over a matter of principle less than a year after the departure of Murrow. Friendly later wrote of his thoughts as he walked to meet Smith and tell him there would be no reprieve: "I wondered whether a pattern was developing, and if so why it was that I was always the survivor. Suddenly I remembered a bitter quotation Elmer Davis once applied to another man's moment of decision: 'Yesterday afternoon [the] Senator . . . wrestled with his conscience. He won.' In both the Murrow dispute and the Smith dismissal, I too had wrestled long and hard with my conscience, and for the rest of my life I would wonder who had won." Friendly may not have fully shared his misgivings at the time with Smith, who wrote in retrospect, "If he had any tinge of bad conscience, it was not more than he could handle."[41]

9 Camelot

Dorothy Friendly recalled Fred's anxiety when he first became executive director of *CBS Reports*. He felt insecure without Murrow, who in the course of their collaboration had vetted Friendly's ideas, reviewed the progress of their work, made major decisions, and assumed final responsibility for the outcome. By the end of 1961, Howard K. Smith, Murrow's putative successor, was gone. Friendly suggested to Eric Sevareid that he might be *his* next Murrow. The proposal reflected Friendly's insecurity as well as his respect for Sevareid, who nonetheless found the suggestion offensive, as he told Ed and Janet Murrow.[1] Yet Friendly soon became more comfortable with his new level of independence and authority. After all, the core staff of *CBS Reports* consisted of the loyal and talented team that he had assembled to produce *See It Now*. That *CBS Reports* was not a fiefdom like *See It Now* but an integral part of the news division had a certain advantage for the now Murrow-less Friendly, whose excesses could be tempered and decisions reviewed through the normal CBS chain of command. Yet Friendly found that he was "more or less given carte blanche."[2]

Friendly's demeanor remained the same when he became the sole executive producer of *CBS Reports*: a palpable, driving presence at every level of the operation. John Schultz, hired as an editor during Murrow's sabbatical, recalled his baptism by fire, as Friendly stormed into his cutting booth with a furious outburst. Sensing he was being tested, Schultz countered in kind, and Friendly backed off. Schultz suspected that Friendly sometimes orchestrated his tantrums to get the most out of people: "Fred played a little bit of a game, to put people on edge. They were afraid of his unpredictability. He would throw pencils. . . . He would shout and scream at them. 'This is absolutely unacceptable' was his favorite term."[3] Staff members at every level experienced his single-minded intensity, including, for example, the son of David Lowe, who was hired as a gofer and driver for Friendly. David Lowe Jr. remembered being treated like a nonentity, the target of Friendly's impatient rages, when they would get stuck in traffic. On such occasions, Friendly would tell him he was fired. The first time this happened, Palmer Williams told the dejected young man to ignore the firing since Friendly would not recall it, which proved to be the case. The younger Lowe also recalled a Christmas Eve when he drove Friendly home to Riverdale and then waited for hours in his vestibule for a taxi to pick him up and take him home. If David Lowe Jr. experienced Friendly as a harsh boss, he also saw his compassionate side when he thoughtfully comforted the Lowe family following the death of David Lowe Sr.[4]

Yet Friendly calibrated his management style as circumstances and personnel required. He gave great leeway to Jay McMullen, a producer who specialized in well-researched investigative reports. His first program for CBS Reports in 1959 was "Hoffa and the Teamsters." Friendly recognized McMullen as "a painfully slow worker" and "stubborn and intractable," enabling McMullen to become television's preeminent investigative reporter by freeing him from tight deadlines. McMullen said of his interaction with Friendly, "You proposed ideas and you discussed them with Fred. I never had an idea imposed on me. Fred believed you did better work on something you were interested in personally than on something that did not interest you."[5] Friendly also gave David Lowe a special measure of respect because of his experience as a filmmaker as well as his marriage to the television critic Harriet Van Horne in an era when such critics had considerable clout. Friendly likewise interfered relatively little with the work of the respected veteran television documentary maker Al Wasserman, who directed and produced "Biography of a Cancer" (April 21, 1960) for CBS Reports. Wasserman had worked under Irving Gitlin in CBS's documentary unit, for which Wasserman produced Out of Darkness (1956), a groundbreaking program on mental illness. Wasserman described the large and passionate Gitlin as "Fred Friendly without the temper." Although Friendly gave Wasserman wider latitude than did other producers, Wasserman recalled that "Irv left you alone. Fred couldn't do that."[6]

Friendly added new producers to the CBS Reports staff and steeped them in his meticulous approach to the preparation of television documentaries—especially the interviews of subjects. In a profile that appeared on February 19, 1962, in the New Yorker, Thomas Whiteside described how Friendly put his imprint on *CBS Reports*. Friendly frequently made the final decision in the selection of topics and people to be interviewed. He targeted individuals whose passion and conviction would overcome the intimidating presence of cameras and then helped strategize how to question and photograph that person. Friendly was intimately involved in the deployment of equipment. Before an interview with Dwight Eisenhower, for example, *CBS Reports* used blueprints of the former president's office at Gettysburg to block out the most unobtrusive positioning of cameras, lighting, and recording equipment. On other occasions, Friendly did the opposite, using the presence of cameras to provoke a stronger response from a subject. He was uncompromising in the standards he set for lighting and sound quality, and he refused to use stock footage. Friendly did not hesitate to take direct charge of a shoot. This was the case during filming at the National Aeronautics and Space Administration in Huntsville, Alabama, for "Why Man in Space?" (April 27, 1961), when Friendly led a crew into a crowded and noisy building where a Saturn rocket booster was being assembled, ordering his camera operators, "Get those engines! I want all eight of them in the shot! And I want a pan shot right along here!" Av Westin described Friendly's critical role in the production of "The Population Explosion," which aired on November 11, 1959, and was one of the earliest and most praised programs on *CBS Reports*. "Dailies" from India would be sent to Friendly, who would cable back detailed comments. Friendly seized on footage of a small boy sitting by a communal well and playing a shepherd's flute as the signature image for the program. Westin wrote, "Although I received credit for writing the script on 'The Population Explosion,' it really belongs to Friendly."[7]

Before he came to CBS, John Schultz had been accustomed to creating a rough cut on his own, and he found it disturbing at first when Friendly would continually pop into the cutting room and become directly engaged in the editing process. Friendly used montage to maximize what he thought was television's unique potential to reveal human character. He recognized that television was a small box and that, unlike the movie screen, did not lend itself to the panoramic picture. He believed that close-ups had an almost magical effect of concentrating and magnifying a person's essence while rendering that person larger than life. Whiteside wrote of Friendly's approach: "In the flesh, a man's face is, after all, only part of him, but in a close-up it becomes, suddenly, all of him. Every facial movement or gesture is heightened in effect, and every accompanying vocal inflection is correspondingly stressed." Extreme and medium-range close-ups were supplemented by "grab shots" of revealing details like a hand gesture or an article of clothing. Friendly created "a system of visual and aural punctuation, in which a smile, gesture of the hand, or an ironic laugh may be used in the manner of a comma, a semicolon, or a period." No wonder Friendly characterized the heavy technical apparatus required by television documentaries as his "one-ton pencil."[8]

In many respects *CBS Reports*, during Friendly's five-year tenure as executive director, continued the grand tradition of *See It Now*. The programs constitute an impressive body of work, treating in substantive fashion issues—domestic and foreign—that would loom large in the coming decades. For example, in addition to "Harvest of Shame" and "Who Speaks for Birmingham?" the second season of 1960/1961 featured programs on the international refugee problem, auto safety, space travel, and the Algerian war for independence. The following season included prescient reports on the rise of the radical right and the decline in the number of metropolitan daily newspapers. In addition, *CBS Reports* broadcast a number of multipart series, including "Eisenhower on the Presidency" and "The Balance of Terror," and a three-part examination of the threat of nuclear war and the prospects for disarmament.

CBS Reports broke important ground in investigative reporting with Jay McMullen's "Diary of a Bookie Joint," a program on gambling in Boston that aired on November 30, 1961. Attorney General Robert F. Kennedy had suggested the topic to McMullen as a way to highlight the problem of organized crime, which, to Kennedy's consternation, J. Edgar Hoover claimed was a myth.[9] Hidden microphones and cameras in and outside a locksmith shop in Boston revealed the relationship of local gambling dens, local authorities, and organized crime. In the summer of 1961, CBS cameras filmed raids on the locksmith and other gambling establishments that had been prompted by the evidence supplied by McMullen. Boston authorities and news outlets criticized the collusion of the federal government and CBS in staging an event for television. The program led to 180 grand jury indictments, numerous convictions, and the loss of the mayor's jurisdiction over the police department. Friendly had permitted McMullen to devote two years to "Diary of a Bookie Joint," a landmark in investigative television journalism that pioneered the use of the hidden camera.

Friendly gave a wide-ranging interview about the theory and practice of *CBS Reports* in October 1962, early in the program's fourth season. He took issue with the term *documentary* and said he preferred such terms as *electronic journalism* and *television reports* to describe the genre of public affairs programming that he had developed specifically for video. In this regard, he reaffirmed the emphasis on the "little picture" that he believed best suited the medium: "What television does best is to transport you, the viewer, to a place, a person. Television is, after all, a small black box which is not suitable for the presentation of the big, panoramic view." Friendly also wrote that television is a medium of amplification: When camera focuses on a man in a tiny village in India, his voice is heard around the world. Friendly said the key to the success of *CBS Reports* was a high level of engagement, a visceral involvement in the subject by the entire team, from reporter to camera operator. He noted that when he documented the launch attempt in "Diary of a Missile," Admiral Hyman Rickover said of Friendly's involvement, "You'd almost think Fred made the Polaris all by himself." Asked in the interview if some topics were off limits, Friendly replied, "There isn't anything we cannot do."[10] He would note with pride that many *CBS Reports* provoked the ire of powerful individuals and special interests. For example, Captain Eddie Rickenbacker objected to the treatment of plane crashes in "The Case of the Boston Elektra" (February 16, 1961). The tobacco industry objected to "The Teenage Smoker" (September 19, 1962), the gun lobby to "Murder and the Right to Bear Arms" (June 10, 1964), and the undertaking industry to "The Great American Funeral" (October 23, 1963). An angry senator John D. McClellan unsuccessfully sought outtakes from "McNamara and the Pentagon" (September 25, 1963), which contained allegations of favoritism in the awarding of an airplane contract. Friendly paid tribute to CBS and the program's sponsors for providing a firewall that enabled him to air dissident voices and to challenge vested interests.[11]

Nonetheless, management did sometimes involve itself in issues of content—for example, with "The Berkeley Radicals," broadcast in 1965. The producer, Arthur Barron, sought to use cinema verité techniques for a sympathetic portrayal of the student rebels of the period, focusing on members of the graduating class of the University of California at Berkeley. According to Barron's production memo, their story would be told subjectively, "more a diary than an essay, more an autobiography than a report." Clark Kerr, president of the University of California and a friend of Frank Stanton's, expressed concern as the program was being filmed on campus. Paley and Stanton insisted on advanced screening of the program and negotiated changes with Friendly. Paley and Stanton subsequently ordered additional edits over Friendly's objections, cutting voice-overs and commentary and requiring the insertion of a speech by Kerr. Barron felt that his documentary had been gutted.[12] Barron's subjective and nonlinear approach was at odds with the norms of the television documentary up to that point as established largely by Friendly. A study of the television documentary notes that the competitor of *CBS Reports*, NBC's *White Paper* documentary series, would expand the use of subjective elements, especially "the technique of *involving* the camera," whereas Friendly would "keep essential control of the story in the editing-room." Furthermore, Friendly did not share Barron's enthusiasm for student rebels who challenged the norms—cultural, political, and institutional—of mainstream liberal authorities and institutions. Friendly later wrote that "The Berkeley Rebels" prompted "the only serious reprimand that I ever received from Paley," and that while he objected on principle to management's involvement in the program's content, he essentially agreed with the chair's objections.[13] "The Berkeley Rebels" portrayed a generation of activists taking matters into their own hands, unlike, say, "Harvest of Shame," an appeal to public opinion and political leadership on behalf of a victimized population.

Friendly also faced pressures that were emanating from CBS's affiliates. For example, CBS management exhibited nervousness about programs dealing with race that might not be palatable to southern affiliates; this nervousness had been central to the departure of Howard K. Smith. Many stations in the Deep South chose not to carry *CBS Reports*. Other affiliates expressed concern about programs that affected their locale— Wichita about a program on farming, for example, and Los Angeles about one of its newspapers. As a result, Stanton and Salant piped advanced closed-circuit screenings to the affiliates. Friendly later wrote that this practice led to a degree of self-censorship:

> I found myself subconsciously applying a new kind of conformity to our documentaries. Looking back now, I suppose that I was subtly influenced to do controversial subjects in a noncontroversial manner. We did handle tough subjects and we often did them well, but there were no strong endings such as in the McCarthy, Radulovich or "Har-

vest of Shame" programs, or anything similar to Howard Smith's proposed ending for "Who Speaks for Birmingham?" Our techniques improved through the years, but in balancing arguments rather than objectively weighing them, we were sacrificing one ingredient of good journalism.[14]

Mili Lerner, whose association with Friendly dated to the earliest days of *See It Now*, recognized subtle changes. Program topics became a little safer, fewer risks were taken: "Murrow wasn't there anymore, and he became—for him—a little more conservative, but to anyone else he was still wild Fred."[15]

A less controversial but significant subset of *CBS Reports* of the highest priority for Friendly consisted of presidential specials. Friendly boasted that Eisenhower, upon completion of his second term, became a virtual "part-time correspondent for *CBS Reports*." Eisenhower filmed a series of conversations reviewing his presidential years as well as programs on current international developments. Friendly devoted great energy and resources to a project dear to his heart: "D-Day Plus 20 Years: Eisenhower Returns to Normandy," a commemoration of the anniversary of the Allied landing. In August 1963, Friendly presided over the filming of Eisenhower's return to France. Dorothy Friendly accompanied Fred on an outing that had the feel of an intimate reunion. The CBS delegation in France included Eisenhower's brother and son; Bill Paley, who had worked with Eisenhower during the war; and Walter Cronkite, the program's correspondent. One night, Eisenhower asked Friendly to come to his sleeping quarters after dinner, expressing his concern that his visit the next day with Cronkite to the cemetery at Omaha Beach would strike the right note for viewers whose family members had been killed during the war. For Jack Gould, the program proved "quietly moving" and captured "the personal magnetism of General Eisenhower" when it aired in June 1964. The *Times* added that the *CBS Reports* special avoided controversy and could have been shorter: "But in picture and in word the program evoked the over-all intent of Fred W. Friendly," which Gould characterized as "an experience in nostalgia and a reminder of D-Day's cost, particularly in the closing scene of 9,000 American graves at St. Laurent-on-the-sea." The program was purchased for broadcast in eighteen foreign countries, including Great Britain, West Germany, and Japan.[16]

Friendly also began maneuvering to get Kennedy to appear with Eisenhower for the first broadcast of two U.S. presidents at one time. Friendly broached the idea personally with Kennedy on the day before his inauguration, at a meeting arranged by Blair Clark, general manager of CBS News and a friend of Kennedy's. Both Kennedy and Eisenhower had reservations about a joint appearance. In his meeting with Kennedy, Friendly also made a more general argument that Kennedy should consider substantive discussions on television, modeled on the programs with Walter Lippmann, to supplement traditional presidential speeches and press conferences. The president-elect, who had enjoyed the Lippmann conversations and other *CBS Reports*, promised to give the proposal serious consideration.[17]

The election of John F. Kennedy represented an important marker in the history of television and in Friendly's career. Kennedy owed his election in large measure to his success in the first televised presidential debates, and his administration initiated live broadcasts of presidential press conferences. Satellites launched during the Kennedy years would transform telecommunications. Kennedy embarked on a program of broadcasting reform under the dynamic leadership of Newton Minow, the newly appointed chair of the Federal Communications Commission (FCC). The thirty-five-year-old Minow sent shock waves through the industry on May 9, 1961, with an address to the annual convention of the National Association of Broadcasters (NAB). He characterized television programming as a "vast wasteland" and put broadcasters on notice that license renewals would not be automatic on his watch as FCC chair. In his speech, Minow cited *CBS Reports* as an example of a "marvelously informative" program that was an exception to the rule. The night after the speech, Minow received congratulatory telephone calls from two people: President Kennedy's father and Edward R. Murrow.[18]

Friendly had initiated contact with Minow before the "vast wasteland" speech. In December 1960, soon after the president-elect announced that he was nominating Minow to head the FCC, Friendly arranged an off-the-record evening meeting with Minow at the home of Howard K. Smith for documentary producers from all three networks. Unbeknownst to Friendly, during World War II, Minow had heard Friendly report at an outdoor theater in New Delhi about his tour of the European theater and the liberation of the Mauthausen concentration camp, which Minow remembered as riveting and "a powerful, compelling verbal picture of what he had seen." Now, at Smith's home fifteen years later, Friendly led the meeting, which addressed the obstacles to producing programs on controversial issues. Minow was asked, for example, whether the FCC might be able to compel affiliates to air regularly scheduled network programs such as *CBS Reports*. Someone also asked whether the FCC could require more public affairs and public service programming. Minow was highly sympathetic to these requests but warned that he had to contend with a divided group of FCC commissioners and with legal limits on what the agency could mandate. Nonetheless, the session reinforced Minow's reformist agenda for television and strengthened his resolve to confront the industry in his speech before the NAB. It also initiated a professional relationship between Minow and Friendly that would last for the rest of their careers.[19]

The Kennedy administration's challenge to the television industry worked to Friendly's advantage, ushering in what is now considered a golden age of network documentary programs. If *CBS Reports* originated as a measure of network damage control, it received added legitimacy in a climate in which Minow's FCC was demanding more quality television programming. Once again Friendly seized on technological as well as political developments: New lightweight 16-millimeter cameras, which replaced the bulkier 35-millimeter models, transformed documentary production. A confluence of political, regulatory, and technological factors— plus the social upheavals of the 1960s—gave impetus to the television documentary at NBC and ABC as well as CBS. The *NBC White Paper* series flourished under the tutelage of former CBS staffers Irving Gitlin and Albert Wasserman. ABC entered the documentary field with its *Close-Up!* and *Special Projects* documentary series; here, too, another CBS veteran, John Secondari, played a major role. During the 1961/1962 season, the three networks carried 254 hours of documentaries, a high point in the history of U.S. television. As a broadcast historian has noted, the Minow–Friendly soiree at Howard K. Smith's home paid dividends: "Following a stern word from the chairman about affiliate stations not clearing their networks' public affairs efforts, many local stations quickly changed their ways." Affiliates broadcasting *CBS Reports* increased from 115 to 140 stations.[20] In the dramatic expansion of television documentary across the entire television landscape, Friendly remained its recognized leader and *CBS Reports* the gold standard.

Soon after the inauguration, Friendly sought to ingratiate himself with the new administration. On February 6, 1961, Friendly wrote the president to offer assistance in the administration's use of television: "I am prepared, at your direction and convenience, to come to Washington to discuss: 1. The news conferences thus far — 2. Other methods of utilizing television to communicate ideas to the electorate." Referring to the president's secretary, he added, "I am constantly available to Mrs. Lincoln or [to] a member of your staff at CBS or, at night, at home in Riverdale, New York, Kingsbridge 8-5943." Several days later, Friendly sent a telegram to Pierre Salinger, alerting the president's press secretary to a debate on CBS about Kennedy's health care plan. "Would appreciate it if you would try to watch," Friendly wrote. Murrow, now head of the United States Information Agency, was in a position to champion Friendly's cause within the administration. For example, there was talk in the White House of televising cabinet meetings as a way of developing support for administration policies. Murrow wrote a memorandum in March about the proposal, in which he said, "The success of the venture would, as usual, depend on the Producer-Director. The best man in the business is my old partner, Fred Friendly." (The proposal was never implemented.) Friendly maintained a steady flow of communication with Newton Minow, who wrote after viewing "Eisenhower on the Presidency": "It was a major contribution, I think, to public understanding and represented television at its best."[21]

If Friendly could not get Eisenhower and Kennedy to appear on air together, he was determined to interview them individually. Friendly's cultivation of the Kennedy White House continued unabated, as he put out feelers about getting Kennedy on the air. In August, for example, Friendly wrote Salinger, detailing an ambitious series of programs on disarmament. Friendly closed the letter by writing, "If you think it advisable you might wish to mention this project to the President. Needless to say, we would welcome his participation." By the fall, Friendly was exploring the possibility of a full-length televised interview with the president. In a cover letter to Kennedy's secretary, Friendly wrote, "The attached letter is for the President. I think I do not presume too much when I say I think he would like to see it, and I would be grateful to you if you would show it to him." In the accompanying letter, Friendly reminds Kennedy that they had spoken about the possibility of a televised conversation at the end of his first year of office. Friendly wrote, "Obviously Blair [Clark] and I are for it and the Director of the United States Information Agency says he's for it, and says I can quote him. If the President has appetite for an earlier date, how about Thanksgiving night? Everybody is home then and it might provide just the right mood." Finally, in December 1962, Salinger called Friendly to say that the president had agreed to a one-hour conversation. Kennedy was ending his second year in office with the Cuban missile crisis behind him. The program would be a joint project of the three networks, with a correspondent from each posing questions. However, Kennedy specified that a CBS crew directed by Friendly produce the program. Friendly and Don Hewitt meticulously prepared the broadcast. Two of five cameras were set up to focus on Kennedy from extremely close range, but the cameras were hidden in an alcove to maximize the president's comfort level. Kennedy was asked to forsake his squeaky swivel desk chair for a rocking chair. George Herman of CBS, Sander Vanocur of NBC, and Bill Lawrence of ABC were selected as questioners.[22]

Frank Stanton had initially wanted a continuous hour-long interview rather than an edited composite. Friendly argued strenuously and successfully that a ninety-minute interview edited down to an hour would ensure a more substantive and effective broadcast. But during a break after nearly an hour of taping, Friendly received a call from Blair Clark, who had been monitoring the taping in New York. Clark told Friendly to end the shoot, saying that he and Dick Salant felt he had more than enough material. Friendly angrily replied that this contravened the ground rules agreed on by all and that important domestic issues slated for the second part of the interview had not yet been addressed. When Friendly returned to the Oval Office visibly upset, Kennedy asked, "What's the matter, Fred, you got problems with your brass?" At the end of the taping, Kennedy reviewed some of the footage before the production team rushed to catch a flight back to New York. As Friendly was leaving, Kennedy smiled at him and said, "Let me know if you need a job tomorrow." Friendly and representatives of the other news organizations worked through the night to complete the editing of the interview. The three networks prepared "After Two Years: A Conversation with the President" for national and foreign broadcast on December 17. The next day, Friendly went directly to Stanton to complain about the interference, threatening to resign if he would have to work under such conditions in the future. A conciliatory Stanton appeased Friendly, praising the program and implying that he would not be subjected to such interference again. As the *New York Times* noted in a front-page article, Friendly had achieved another television first, since "no other President has hitherto consented to a television interview while in the White House." Tom Wicker, reporting from the newspaper's Washington bureau, wrote that for Kennedy the broadcast was "a stunning personal success and an effective 'non-political' coup that promised great political return."[23]

As television's preeminent public affairs producer during the Kennedy years, Friendly would take the lead in television's entry into global telecommunications, just as he did with the inauguration of televised presidential dialogues. On July 23, 1962, the three networks planned to pool their resources to produce a fourteen-minute broadcast that would be beamed to Europe, after which Americans would be able to view a return broadcast from Europe. Friendly was selected as the producer in charge. He would preside over network television's inaugural international broadcast transmitted by a communications satellite. "In 1962 I was selected by the three networks," Friendly would later say, "not because I was so skilled but because I was so noisy and aggressive, to produce the first satellite broadcast." Earlier that month, *Telstar I*, the first satellite that could relay television signals along with all other forms of communication, had been sent into orbit.[24] A by-product of competition between the United States and the Soviet Union in the space race, the technology initiated a new era in communications by making possible instantaneous live transmission from around the world. Its debut was compared in importance with Samuel Morse's introduction of the telegraph more than a century earlier.

Friendly was always at the ready to extend the limits of television technology. In 1951, *See It Now* had capitalized on the new national coaxial cable and microwave relay to show the East and West coasts simultaneously on its first broadcast. Now, at the dawn of a new era of satellite communication, Friendly would direct the first transmission demonstrating television's international reach. On July 23, *Telstar* was positioned in the Atlantic Ocean in the line of sight of both Europe and the United States for twenty-two minutes, permitting instantaneous transmission between the two continents for that period of time. (Synchronous communications satellites, positioned at fixed sites around the globe to allow global communication at any time, soon would replace the rudimentary *Telstar*.) As conceived by Friendly, the broadcast—hosted by Walter

Cronkite—echoed and extended the themes of the premiere of *See It Now* a decade earlier, the notion of television as a medium of transport.

The first part of the program transmitted to Europe a live tour of the continental United States, beginning with New York and San Francisco, bracketed by images of the Brooklyn and Golden Gate bridges.[25] The tour—with Cronkite, Howard K. Smith, and Chet Huntley as guides—spanned Niagara Falls and the Canadian border to the north, Detroit in the Midwest, and Texas and the Rio Grande and Mexican border to the south. Friendly went a step further in offering snapshots of life in the United States. For example, Friendly dispatched the CBS producer David Buksbaum to coordinate a segment from Mount Rushmore. Buksbaum's engineer arranged for the CBS affiliate in Rapid City, South Dakota, to be shut down for three days to be retrofitted so that it could send a signal by microwave links from Mount Rushmore to *Telstar*. Friendly called Buksbaum to tell him that he wanted the Mormon Tabernacle Choir to perform at the site. Four planes would be needed to transport the choir, but there was no public airport near Mount Rushmore, so arrangements were made with the Pentagon for use of a Strategic Air Command base nearby. The Forestry Service was prevailed on to build a stage for the performance. Furthermore, Friendly insisted that cameras capture a herd of buffalo as an iconic image of the Wild West. Buksbaum got the superintendent of nearby Custer State Park to traverse the plains in search of a herd, which was then laboriously coaxed for days toward a camera position near an abandoned fort. Buksbaum was warned that that these wild animals were unpredictable and could not be counted on to appear on camera as planned. Friendly, at master control, was listening to the satellite tracker on the telephone report on the satellite's approach for the brief window of time for his broadcast. Av Westin describes the scene at Mount Rushmore at air time:

> Chet Huntley was reading his narration. The sun was out. The Presidents' rocky faces were magnificent against a blue sky. The secondhand on Buksbaum's stopwatch was running. "Cue the buffalo!" he shouted into his telephone. A barrage of dynamite caps and shotgun blasts went off. The herd, startled, paused for what seemed an interminable moment. Buksbaum thought, "Oh, God, all we're gonna get is a picture of that damn hill." Then, one buffalo snout appeared on the horizon, almost as if asking, "Now?" Up over the

rise they came—not the ten or twelve Buksbaum had hoped for but nearly one hundred buffalo—running madly toward the camera in clouds of dust. The Mormon Tabernacle Choir was in full voice! It had worked.[26]

It was vintage Friendly.

In addition, the European audience visited a Chicago Cubs baseball game at Wrigley Field, where the announcer asked fans to let out a cheer for the European viewers. It was the only day game played that afternoon and normally would have been poorly attended, so Friendly got the *Chicago Tribune* to mount a campaign to fill the stands. At Cape Canaveral, viewers met John Glenn, the first American to orbit the earth. During the broadcast, a presidential press conference was in session in the auditorium of the State Department. Friendly had left nothing to chance: Kennedy's podium was rigged so that a red light told him when the session was being transmitted to Europe. The broadcast ended at the prayer chapel of the United Nations, with Howard K. Smith calling on viewers to reflect on the implications of a new age of global communications. "For ten seconds now," Smith said, "our transmitters will be silent in many languages." About three hours later, when *Telstar* was properly situated over the Atlantic, fifty-three cameras provided Americans with images of European life in the second part of the program. The broadcast fascinated the critics and the public. Gilbert Seldes wrote in *TV Guide*, "The first formal transmissions, both ways, were almost unbearably exciting." "The years go by but the magic touch remains," Murrow telegraphed Friendly from the USIA. "Monday's Telstar show was America at its most extraordinary, television at its best, and Friendly at his finest."[27] The interests of network television and the U.S. government were uniquely aligned for the broadcast. Friendly came of age as television's leading public affairs producer during the heady days of Camelot, profiting from the television policies as well as the liberal idealism of the Kennedy administration.

During the 1962/1963 season, *CBS Reports* continued to address a wide range of domestic and foreign issues; shows included "The Teenage Smoker," "Mississippi and the 15th Amendment," "Showdown in the Congo," and "Sabotage in South Africa." In April 1963, "The Silent Spring of Rachael Carson" introduced a wider audience to the dangers of pesticides and other environmental issues. After the Carson program, Newton Minow dashed off a handwritten note: "Fred, Why does no one in educational television have the imagination and drive that you do? Newt." Minow was leading the Kennedy administration's efforts strengthen educational television, the repository of its hopes for the future of serious television. As Friendly had made clear to Walter Lippmann, he was not prepared to give up on network television but nonetheless expressed sympathy with Minow's efforts. In his response to Minow, Friendly wrote that "the crisis in educational television makes me feel like a slacker on the home front while the real fight in going on on the beaches." That season, Minow enthusiastically welcomed a major programming initiative, the three-part series on *CBS Reports* entitled "Storm over the Supreme Court." After the first two installments aired, Minow wrote Friendly that he had spoken with Associate Justice Arthur Goldberg, who was interested in inviting Friendly to have dinner at the Supreme Court and to arrange a private screening of the two programs; Goldberg planned to invite a small group of fellow Supreme Court justices and friends for the off-the-record gathering.[28] The highly praised series marked the beginning of Friendly's growing fascination with the judicial branch of government and its relationship with the press.

CBS Reports came of age with broadcasts like "Storm over the Supreme Court" during John F. Kennedy's presidency. The policies and climate of the Kennedy years helped propel Friendly's career. He capitalized on his contacts within the administration and its space program for a number of major initiatives, including the *Telstar* broadcast. Less than a year after he produced "After Two Years: A Conversation with the President," Kennedy was dead. Because Friendly headed a documentary unit at CBS, he was not directly involved in the network's coverage of the assassination, which he subsequently highlighted in the recording *I Can Hear It Now/The Sixties*. Friendly's relationship with Kennedy's successor, Lyndon Johnson, would be characterized by greater complexity and ambivalence.

By 1963/1964, Friendly's fifth season as executive director of *CBS Reports*, his position at CBS seemed secure. Rumor had it that James Aubrey, head of the CBS television network, had designs on the prime-time weekday evening slot of *CBS Reports*, which would be more profitable if used for entertainment programming. Friendly let it be known that he would resign in such an eventuality.[29] But *CBS Reports*, which had Stanton's support and was an important source of prestige for CBS at the time, was not in danger. In his statement "Looking Ahead," which was distributed by the network, Friendly wrote that there was no shortage of topics and of people with "fire in the belly" willing to speak out about them. He suggested that the success of *CBS Reports* represented a vindication of the integrity of CBS and the network system:

> It is a labor in which we have received the fullest of backing and the freest of hands from the Columbia Broadcasting system. I would be remiss if, in saluting CBS News and the CBS Television Network for the "use of the hall," I did not also salute the sponsors who helped pay for the "hall." No sponsor ever sees *CBS Reports* before it is broadcast, or has any voice in its content. The fact that such important businesses as the Travelers Insurance Company encourage and underwrite our editorial integrity is, I believe, an eloquent testimonial to the health of the television system this country enjoys.[30]

The film editor John Schultz remembered Friendly in this period as exuding a supreme sense of self-confidence. Although he had begun his tenure as executive producer of *CBS Reports* with a degree of trepidation, Friendly had quickly and authoritatively gained his stride. In a May 1961 interview, Friendly came close to disparaging *See It Now* in comparison with its successor: "Those old *See It Nows*—they're nostalgic and amateurish. We made some of them in four or five days. *CBS Reports* has ten full-time producers, and they do about two shows each year. When we did *Harvest of Shame*, David Lowe lived with the migrant workers for a full year." *CBS Reports* had become a prestigious fixture of prime time in 1961 and 1962, when it was scheduled to produce twenty hour-long and four half-hour programs. It was during this third season that Thomas Whiteside of the *New Yorker* profiled Friendly, describing the "big, loose-limbed man of forty-six" as the undisputed leader of the renaissance in television documentaries. His team of ten producers and scores of assistants put him in control of the biggest documentary operation in television, and his mastery of the form made *CBS Reports* the model for the genre as a whole. Friendly presided over his team in what Whiteside described as the "atmosphere of unremitting crisis" that Friendly cultivated. He maintained regular communication with the crews of *CBS Reports* located across the nation and around the globe while fielding telephone calls from prominent figures: "Dr. Jerome Wiesner holding on Six, Mr. Friendly. General Eisenhower on Nine! Walter Lippmann on Seven!" When he was in New York, Carl Sandburg would enjoy quietly sitting in Friendly's office just to watch him in action.[31]

Dorothy's appointment books show that she and Fred enjoyed interacting with many of the prominent figures he had come to know through his work. Some entries from 1959 and 1960 capture the breadth of their social life. In 1959, Fred threw a surprise party for Dorothy on her fortieth birthday; the approximately forty guests included the writers Isak Dinesen and James Thurber, the conductor Eric Leinsdorf, and the painter Chaim Gross. Summer travels in 1960 included visits with the Murrows in Pauling and with the Lippmanns and Rachael Carson in Maine. Later that year, the Friendlys attended a reception for President Sékou Touré in the Guinean Embassy and a party for Marian Anderson.

CBS Reports garnered virtually every major broadcast journalism prize, often in multiples. At the end of the second season in the spring of 1961, Friendly received his tenth Peabody Award for "Harvest of Shame," which meant he had six more than Murrow. A critic for the *New York Journal-American* characterized Friendly as "one of the invisible giants of television." Friendly's direction of all-network productions such as the Kennedy interview and the initial *Telstar* broadcast underscored his status as television's preeminent public affairs producer. In 1962, Friendly received a special George Foster Peabody Award. The citation hailed his influence as a pioneer in a generation of television public affairs producers. "As a result," the tribute continued, "not only CBS News but the news organizations of other broadcasters—and the public—have been vastly enriched by the remarkable journalism of Fred Friendly."[32] But Fred Friendly was always looking for the next challenge. Where would he go from here?

10 News President

In March 1964, Fred Friendly became president of CBS News, then "electronic journalism's hottest spot," in the words Jack Gould, the *New York Times* television critic. Friendly's stewardship of the network's storied but now troubled news division took place at a tumultuous time in Friendly's personal life, in CBS's institutional history, and in the life of a nation increasingly divided over the war in Vietnam.

The appointment came at a time of family upheaval, shortly after his wife, Dorothy, suffered an emotional crisis. She had been her husband's full-fledged partner at the outset of his career in broadcasting but now devoted her full energies to raising three young children—Andrew, Lisa, and David—and maintaining the Friendly household. Dorothy shared the feelings of colleagues at CBS who had to balance Friendly's charm and wrath: "He could be so warm with people. People who worked for him could alternately love and hate him. That was how it was with me, too. He could be as rough with me as with the people he worked with."[1] Dorothy was a highly sensitive, private, and increasingly fragile person. Clearly, Fred's professional success, culminating now in his appointment as news president, created additional stress in their lives. Dorothy found it difficult to live in her husband's highly public and pressure-filled world.

Signs of Dorothy's emotional problems had appeared during the summer of 1963, when she accompanied Fred to France for the program about the twentieth anniversary of the Normandy invasion. Uncomfortable in the presence of Dwight Eisenhower, Bill Paley, and Walter Cronkite, Dorothy became reclusive. In one instance, she disappeared from sight, and Fred found her sleeping in an automobile. In the fall of 1963, after returning from France, Dorothy Friendly had her second and more serious psychological crisis, five years after the first. Dorothy's old friend Barbara Fogel recalled a deep depression. Once during this period Fred and Dorothy came to the Fogels' for dinner, but Dorothy could not bring herself to leave the car and face other people, so they returned home. It was difficult for Dorothy to care for her children. According to Fogel, "There was no affect, no ability to relate to anybody. It was very hard for him." Friendly turned to Peter Neubauer, a psychiatrist he had met on Martha's Vineyard, and asked him to talk to Dorothy. "I saw a very psychotic person," Neubauer remembered. Dorothy entered Montefiore Hospital in November 1963, undergoing electroshock therapy and taking antipsychotic medication under the supervision of Mortimer Ostow, who became her therapist. According to Neubauer, Friendly exhibited great concern but little psychological insight into Dorothy's difficulties; at times, he was uncomprehending and angry about her treatment. Yet he remained steadfastly loyal to her and brushed aside her talk of separation. As Fred became president of CBS News in early 1964, he remained committed to Dorothy's care and to their marriage. However, he had to assume additional responsibility for their three children, and the marriage became increasingly untenable in the months to come.[2]

In 1963 and 1964 the CBS household was also in disarray. Indeed, Friendly owed his appointment as news president to the disorder caused by conflict at the highest level of CBS over NBC's challenge to CBS's preeminence in network news. Since the 1960 party conventions and presidential elections, the NBC team of Chet Huntley and David Brinkley had upstaged CBS News. During the early 1960s, NBC won the ratings war and replaced CBS as the network news leader. This reversal of fortunes was a blow to William Paley, who took great pride in CBS's pioneering role in the development of network news. After the war, CBS may have focused on entertainment programming in the relentless pursuit of profits, but the news operation was meant to perpetuate the company's cachet as the Tiffany network.

The declining fortunes of CBS News exacerbated tensions between Paley and his chief lieutenant, CBS president Frank Stanton. Stanton was a Calvinist from the Midwest: a workaholic and statistician who kept his emotions at bay, a meticulous administrator, the ultimate organization man. Paley, in contrast, was more intuitive and emotional, a hedonist with a taste for beautiful women, fine food, and modern art. Stanton had assumed increasing authority over the day-to-day operations of CBS as Paley became something of an absentee landlord who devoted considerable amounts of time to the world of high society and to his vacation homes on Long Island and Bermuda.

However, in the early 1960s, following surgery and a bout of depression, Paley became reengaged in CBS's affairs, especially in the news department, which he considered his special domain. This created an opening for Friendly, who was lobbying for the position of news president. NBC's primacy in news undoubtedly spurred Paley to action. Resentful of Stanton's status as the embodiment of CBS and as broadcasting's preeminent statesman, Paley began to rethink the understanding that when he reached the mandatory retirement age of sixty-five in 1966, Stanton, seven years his junior, would become head of CBS. As Friendly observed, "Murrow had grown too big for Bill Paley. Now Frank Stanton had too."[3] The tension between Paley and Stanton increased as CBS evolved from a broadcasting network to a communications conglomerate. The management consulting firm of Booz Allen and Hamilton had been hired to study CBS's operations and to recommend changes in its structure and personnel. Black Rock, CBS's sleek new headquarters designed by Eero Saarinen, symbolized a new era in the company's history. It opened in 1964, the same year Friendly replaced Richard Salant as president of CBS News.

Paley had never liked Salant, Stanton's protégé and president of CBS News since 1961. "He never felt comfortable with Dick," Stanton said of Paley. "He didn't try to block the appointment, but he didn't greet it with enthusiasm."[4] A graduate of Harvard Law School, Salant had been hired by Stanton in 1952 as a corporate vice president and became Stanton's chief troubleshooter before replacing Sig Mickelson as news president. (Salant claimed that on becoming news president, Murrow warned him, "Watch out for Fred Friendly. Fred does have fire in his belly. And he's a great producer. But watch out—he doesn't know a fact when he sees one.") On Salant's watch Walter Cronkite replaced Douglas Edwards as anchor of the *CBS Evening News*, which expanded from a fifteen-minute to a half-hour broadcast. However, the program now lagged behind *The Huntley-Brinkley Report*, and Paley insisted that Salant be replaced by Friendly. Stanton believed that in making the change, Paley was influenced by his feelings about the two men as well as the Nielsen ratings. Salant's acerbic, often stubborn, demeanor disturbed Paley, especially when Salant stood up to him. Stanton said of Salant, "When he thought something through and took a position, he was almost unassailable." Paley viewed Friendly "as a man of great vigor who loved to shout and carry on. It was easier to argue and have a kind of verbal duel with someone like that." The chair of CBS may have felt that, compared with Salant,

Friendly was more approachable and perhaps more malleable as well. It was rumored that Friendly was first offered the number-two position under Salant but insisted that he would leave producing only if he became news president.[5]

The replacement of Salant with Friendly was extremely painful for Stanton. Stanton told Salant that he was needed to strengthen CBS's government relations and that the decision was his, not Paley's. Fifteen years later, he would tell Salant the truth. Paley took a calculated risk in the hope that Friendly, who had brought distinction to CBS's documentary division, might reverse the fortunes of the news department as a whole. So Fred Friendly—"brought in fourteen years back as Murrow's junior partner, who had so closely skirted getting sacked but for the one fact, then as now, that he was needed," as A. M. Sperber writes—became president of CBS News. Friendly understood that the move entailed a pay cut, since compensation was generally greater for top producers than for managers. However, in negotiating his new contract, one consideration was paramount for Friendly: the requirement that he have direct access to Stanton and Paley.[6] In making this demand Friendly was mindful of the example of Murrow's personal and professional relationship with Paley and the Murrow–Friendly team's access to both CBS's chair and president.

Yet the figure of Edward R. Murrow cast a dark shadow over Friendly's appointment. By the fall of 1963, Murrow had been diagnosed with lung cancer and had had one lung removed. He resigned as director of the United States Information Agency, effective in January 1964. Following his resignation, Murrow traveled to La Jolla, California, to recuperate at the invitation of Jonas Salk. In lobbying to replace Salant, Friendly had encouraged speculation about a revival of the legendary Murrow–Friendly partnership by voicing his desire to bring Murrow back to CBS. However, at his crowning moment of achievement Friendly did not get Murrow's blessing. Murrow's reservations about Friendly's appointment as news director may have been colored by Murrow's own brief and unhappy experience in the executive suites of CBS as vice president for public affairs. But he also expressed doubts that the fit was right. "I was *appalled*," Murrow wrote his old friend James Seward after hearing the news in La Jolla. "The greatest producer, bar none, but overall news chief?" While Murrow was in La Jolla, Friendly remained in touch with him by telephone. "Of course I discussed the offer of the job with Murrow," Friendly would later write. "He advised me to take it if I thought I could handle it, but not to agree 'to report to any ten-man committee.' "[7] Murrow, aware that Friendly coveted the position in any case, may have muted his opposition in his conversations with his former partner. Friendly's memoir of the period was written in 1966, a year after Murrow's death. Even by Friendly's account, Murrow's counsel—go ahead *if* you think you can handle it—hardly constituted a ringing endorsement.

In March 1964, just as Friendly began his tenure as news president, Paley traveled to La Jolla to visit Murrow. The ailing newscaster was no longer a threat to Paley. A rapprochement took place between the two men, whose friendship and interlocking careers had been forged nearly three decades earlier. When the subject of Friendly's appointment came up, Murrow repeated the doubts he had expressed to Seward. As Alexander Kendrick writes, Murrow "valued his close longtime associate as a producer without peer, but was not so sure that his restless temperament would be compatible with the demands of administration or of corporate conformity." Paley left La Jolla with doubts that Murrow would recover or would ever be able to return to CBS. Murrow was pleased by the reconciliation with Paley and less eager to see Friendly. Sperber, who interviewed both Seward and Murrow's widow, Janet, for her biography of Murrow, describes what happened: "Try to discourage him, Murrow had pleaded with Seward: He couldn't hold Fred's hand again, hadn't the strength; couldn't stand up to the exhaustion of his presence, Murrow's tone for the first and only time taking on the querulousness of the very ill. But he didn't tell Friendly and no one else did and Friendly came anyway, never suspecting that he was anything but highly welcome, exuberant in his new dignity as President of CBS News."[8]

Murrow was not alone among Friendly's associates who sought to discourage him from accepting the job of news president. Joe Wershba, his former *See It Now* colleague and close friend, feared that all would not end well. The job of news chief had proved to be a difficult and ultimately frustrating experience for all five men who had held the position since 1946. Friendly believed—mistakenly—that Stanton as well as Paley wanted him to take the job. In an interview years later, Bill Moyers disagreed with those who had criticized Friendly for seizing a great opportunity: "I think he did the right thing. It was very hard for Fred to work under other people. He was an impulsive and compulsive creator of ideas and explorer of opportunities. You ought to be a leader when you do that, not a seeker. You ought to be able to make the decisions, not ask others to make them." Friendly's ambition, his desire to be at the center of action, and his impulse to take charge gave the position irresistible appeal. The rivalry with NBC stoked his competitiveness. In addition, he was propelled by genuine idealism, by the belief "that the news division could focus that influential eye on the moon and Vietnam, on parliaments and senates, on the slums of Harlem and Johannesburg, and provide our society with knowledge and insight." In June, Friendly traveled to Paris, where CBS's foreign correspondents were summoned to meet with him. Daniel Schorr recalled how Friendly envisaged the dawn of a new era in the history of CBS News. He promised that CBS, whose correspondents were now linked by satellite, would regain its preeminence in news over NBC.[9]

Reaction within the news department was positive, even enthusiastic, although some expressed reservations. "When I came back from Europe in 1966," Daniel Schorr remembered, "[Friendly] proposed to make me New York correspondent. I declined, and he asked why. 'Because you're here,' I said." Les Midgley, a Salant loyalist, was distraught about Friendly's appointment. As executive producer for *Eyewitness*, an outstanding half-hour program on breaking news stories, Midgley had had nasty turf wars with Friendly's *CBS Reports*. After he learned of the appointment, a morose Midgley retired to Costello's, a CBS watering hole, where his friends Ring Lardner and Walt Kelly discouraged him from resigning. That night, Friendly called Midgley, telling him not to resign and to see him in the morning. Friendly offered him any assignment he wished. Midgley suggested a one-hour program on Vietnam with Charles Collingwood. As a result, a thirteen-person CBS team produced a searching documentary, *Vietnam: The Deadly Decision*, and Midgley remained a top producer in Friendly's news department. Midgley was not the only person Friendly had to win over. Members of the news department knew of Friendly's legendary temper tantrums and of his propensity to push his subordinates to extreme lengths. Eric Sevareid was "apprehensive of the wild man taking over." In general, the news personnel were a fractious lot. *Time* magazine noted that although Friendly referred to his colleagues as his "band of brothers," his new position would expose him to a cutthroat environment: "What the brethren call him ranges from 'brilliant slob' to 'self-promoting megalomaniac.' Nice friendly place, CBS."[10]

Yet, as Mike Wallace remembered, many greeted news of the appointment with enthusiasm, even elation. Wallace had felt very much in debt to Salant, who in 1963 had hired Wallace as a news correspondent over objections at the time about his credentials as a serious journalist. Yet despite his loyalty to Salant, Wallace welcomed Friendly's appointment. Thirty-six years later, sitting in his office at *60 Minutes*, Wallace recalled the awe in which he and his colleagues held Friendly, the mythic status of the Murrow–Friendly team. Friendly became president of CBS News exactly a decade after the famous *See It Now* program on Senator Joseph McCarthy. Salant's legal and corporate background paled beside Friendly's journalistic credentials, which held out the promise of a renaissance in the news department. Wallace added that the elation was tempered by concerns about what it would be like working under Friendly, about "his volcanic nature, his unpredictability, his stubbornness." He noted, "We weren't sure about Fred." Yet these concerns, Wallace made clear, did not diminish the sense of excitement within the ranks of CBS News.[11]

Since *CBS Reports* had been a separate unit within the news department, many news department personnel had had no direct contact with Friendly. When he addressed the staff for the first time as its president on March 2, he claimed that his goal was to prove "that I really do not have horns." Yet the tenor of his remarks put the news staff on alert rather than at ease. "I expect *you* to do better," he said. "*I* expect to do better." He warned that he would not always be liked, that indeed he cared little about his popularity with his staff. Yet the tenor of Friendly's remarks suggested he was on a high. He proclaimed that CBS News would do more investigative journalism, shake things up, "teach the country to itch a little more." He also said, "If this isn't fun, I'll be a flop." On March 17, Friendly spoke to CBS affiliates through a final closed-circuit broadcast from Studio 41 above Grand Central Terminal—where *See It Now* had originated—ending his remarks with "Good night, and good luck." He joked to a CBS staff member responsible for special events that his tenure as news president would be rocky: "You can start planning my farewell party."[12]

The appointment received considerable—and largely favorable—national press coverage. Several reports questioned how Friendly would make the transition from the less hurried production of documentaries to the pressures of hard news, given that he "stews, fusses and frets over everything he does." *Newsweek* observed, "For years he had been the arch perfectionist, spending up to a year or more on one hour of TV programming. Running a network news operation won't allow him the same leeway, yet Friendly has put CBS staffers on notice that he expects absolute perfection right down to the briefest news film clip." Jack Gould of the *Times* wondered whether Friendly's penchant for controversy would bump up against the traditional culture of CBS News, the restraints on editorializing, the avoidance of "journalism with passion." Gould juxtaposed CBS's sober reportage and propensity for pompous commentary with NBC's breezier, more informal, style and its greater willingness to interrupt regular programming for breaking stories. Would Friendly have the authority to pull the switch? Gould concluded that "the most intriguing aspect of last week's executive drama in C.B.S. News still lies ahead: what really cooked between Mr. Friendly and Dr. Stanton and what, in turn, are they cooking up for N.B.C.?"[13]

Friendly moved into Dick Salant's former office off the corridor to the right of the ground floor of the CBS Broadcast Center at 524 West Fifty-seventh Street. Secretaries were situated in the middle of the office suite, with offices for two news vice presidents on the left and Friendly's modest-size quarters on the right. Friendly made one change: he added a door directly from his office to the exterior corridor, enabling him to avoid someone in the outer office he did not want to see. (The escape door was subsequently sealed, but the molding on the corridor exterior remains to this day, a kind of archaeological remnant of Friendly's tenure as news president.) Up until recently, all executive offices of CBS had been housed at 485 Madison Avenue, with senior management on the twentieth floor and news executives three floors below. Their proximity facilitated direct contact over the years between CBS's chief officers— Paley and Stanton—and their news department. In the original plan for Black Rock, CBS's new headquarters at 51 West Fifty-second Street, news offices and studios were to be housed on the ground floor. However, Black Rock sat atop the Sixth Avenue subway line, and tests revealed that electrical interference and vibration caused by the subway system would interfere with live cameras on the ground floor. As a result CBS's news division was moved to a squat, four-story former milk-processing plant, nicknamed the Barn, on West Fifty-seventh Street.

The separation marked a change in the culture of CBS. To get from Black Rock to the Barn, one had to walk five blocks north and six long windy blocks west toward the Hudson River, from the elegant East Side of Manhattan to the then seedy-area adjacent to the neighborhood known as Hell's Kitchen. The days when Paley or Stanton could casually ask their news executives to drop by were over. "So Black Rock was East, and 524 West 57th Street was West," Dick Salant observed, "and while it was not true that . . . the twain never met, they met much more rarely than they otherwise would have."[14] Friendly had observed Murrow's close working relationship with Paley and Stanton at 485 Madison Avenue during the heyday of *See It Now*. It remained to be seen whether the new degree of separation between the top executive suites and his own office would help or hinder Friendly's position as news director.

Friendly's launched his tenure as news president with an expression of homage to the Murrow tradition. He declared that "getting Ed back here is my first order of business," which proved an unrealizable goal, given Murrow's failing health. Friendly quickly gave assignments to two Murrow Boys—Eric Sevareid to cover the Jack Ruby trial in Dallas and Charles Collingwood to report on the Vietnam War. Yet Friendly displayed an interest in going outside CBS and in adding journalists with a print background. When Ernie Leiser told Friendly that he wanted to quit as assistant general manager of news, he suggested as his replacement A. M. Rosenthal of the *New York Times*. At Friendly's request, Leiser had lunch with Rosenthal, who expressed interest in coming to CBS. As Leiser recalled with dismay, "He offered Abe the damn job and then changed his mind after offering it to him." For Leiser, who preferred Salant as news president, it was a harbinger of the insecurity, fickleness, and quixotic qualities that Friendly would exhibit in his new position.[15]

Instead of Rosenthal, Friendly selected as his first top staff member Herbert Mitgang, another *Times* recruit, who was named special assistant and executive editor of the news department. Mitgang had contributed scripts to *CBS Reports*, but his chief professional affiliation was with the *Times*, where he had worked for twenty years as a critic and an editor before joining its editorial board. Friendly conceived Mitgang's role as that of a creative coordinator for the various producers and production units in the news department. The appointment reflected Friendly's desire to import some of the prestige of the *Times* to his department and to signal his determination to bring greater depth to CBS's coverage of news and public affairs. The search for a new head of news for the CBS radio network showed how, as in the case of Rosenthal, Friendly could be heavy-handed in his hiring practices. He told Joe Dembo, then director of news at WCBS-AM in New York, that he was considering him for the radio network post and that he should write up a strategic plan for the future. Dembo excitedly worked day and night and submitted his proposal. After several days had passed with no word from Friendly, Dembo went to Friendly, who said he had instead selected Lee Hanna, who now had Dembo's document. Dembo felt used and humiliated.[16]

Friendly quickly put his personal stamp on the news department. If Salant had been somewhat aloof, dubbed the "absentee landlord" by the news staff, Friendly was unmistakably hands-on. By the end of his first day on the job, for example, he had telephoned Washington bureau chief Bill Small half a dozen times; several days later, Friendly flew to Washington to accompany Small on a whirlwind tour of meetings with Secretary of Defense Robert McNamara and Attorney General Robert Kennedy, among others. Small remembered Friendly's wolfing down his meals—"Fred's view of food was that it was fuel"—and showing up at the White House without any identification papers. Friendly brought a frenzied quality to his first weeks on the job as news president. Soon after he assumed his new post, NBC decisively beat CBS in covering an earthquake in Alaska. *The Huntley-Brinkley Report* broadcast film reports on location, while the *CBS Evening News* could offer only rewrites of wire service stories. Friendly raged at subordinates in New York and at CBS news bureaus—and threatened dismissals—for what he theatrically bemoaned as "my Bay of Pigs." Word spread that "he was ripping his shirt and buttons were coming off and he wanted to fire everyone for getting beaten on the story."[17]

Friendly infected the news division with what became known at CBS as "bulletin fever," a trigger-happy increase in interruptions of scheduled programming in the quest to be first with breaking news. Gordon Manning, who became one of Friendly's chief lieutenants, complained that, in the first months of Friendly's tenure as news president, he seemed constantly and indiscriminately explosive, "like a constant volcano on small matters." He continued to make extraordinary demands on his staff, as he had as executive producer of *See It Now* and *CBS Reports*. "He'd call you in the middle of the night, wake you up and say what do you think of this? It would be something that easily could have waited until the next day. He was always on the phone; he loved the phone," Manning recalled with a sense of grudging admiration and even appreciation for Friendly's commitment to reviving the fortunes of CBS News. "He was thoughtless but it was his exuberance, it wasn't conniving." The tantrums continued unabated. When Friendly was angry with someone, he would not wait a day and then call the person into his office. He would come "busting out like a tornado or hurricane," Robert Trout said, "as if he were possessed by the devil." On one occasion, Trout witnessed a distraught Friendly enter the Barn and try to fire the first person he encountered, only to be told that he was a member of the union and could not be dismissed. "Then who the hell can I fire?" Friendly yelled.[18] Yet for Trout, like Manning, the excitement and satisfaction of working for Friendly outweighed the hardships.

Like others before him, Small observed how ideas came tumbling out of Friendly, some good, others bad. But Friendly was open to criticism and quick to jettison dubious proposals. For example, when he assigned Roger Mudd to gavel-to-gavel coverage of the Senate filibuster of civil rights legislation in 1964, Friendly suggested that Mudd not shave to underscore the length of the proceedings. Small convinced Friendly that the idea was gimmicky; instead, a crawl at the bottom of the screen reported the duration of the debate. Mudd's coverage was outstanding, and, thanks to Friendly's assignment, his career received a substantial boost.[19]

Friendly's proclivity for micromanagement as news president extended to his old bailiwick, *CBS Reports*. He appointed Arthur Morse, a respected print and broadcast journalist, as his successor as executive director. Morse moved into the spacious office suite that Friendly had outfitted for himself in the Barn. As Morse's widow recalled, "It was really two rooms with sliding doors in between. One side was a conference room. There were paneled walls with maps of the world, a gorgeous desk, and windows on 57th Street." As news president, Friendly moved to the smaller and simpler office of the spartan Richard Salant. After Friendly visited Morse in Friendly's old quarters for the first time, he quipped, "What's a schmuck like you doing in an office like this?" It was a jest, to be sure, but a jest with an edge, and Morse never forgot it.[20]

Morse was the producer of acclaimed programs for *See It Now* and *CBS Reports* and a personal friend of Fred and Dorothy's. Morse—immediately subjected to a relentless barrage of telephone calls—learned that Friendly would not grant him the same autonomy Friendly had enjoyed in the same job. They argued, for example, over "Cigarettes: A Collision of Interests," a report in which an advertising executive criticized network presidents who permitted cigarette commercials. Friendly also expressed displeasure when Morse did not consult with him before asking Stanton to be interviewed on a program about television ratings. Their differences came to a head when Morse wrote directly to James T. Aubrey Jr., president of the CBS television network, protesting the plan to move *CBS Reports* from the 7:30 P.M. to the 10:00 P.M. slot. The time change undermined Morse's plan with the National Educational Association to encourage teachers to incorporate *CBS Reports* in their classwork. Morse criticized the decision as well as Aubrey's failure to consult him or even inform him before the press reported on the change, a broadside not unlike Friendly's protestations to management in the past in defense of *his* programs. But when Friendly saw the letter, he told Morse, "Now you've done it. I can't protect you anymore." Morse resigned. "All I know," Morse's widow said years later, "is that Arthur felt that Fred had sold out."[21]

Early in his term as news president, Friendly also had to discipline the correspondent Daniel Schorr. On the eve of the Republican National Convention, Schorr had filed a story from Germany saying that Barry Goldwater planned to take a vacation in Berchtesgaden following his expected nomination. Schorr correctly noted that Berchtesgaden had been Hitler's favorite retreat and that German right-wingers were eager to meet with Goldwater. However, Schorr added a sentence in which he suggested that the visit reflected a desire on Goldwater's part to link up with the German far right—an assertion that Schorr could not substantiate and later regretted making. Goldwater, livid about the report, threatened to boycott CBS News during the convention and subsequent presidential race. The Goldwater campaign accused William Paley of being behind the story because of his friendship with Dwight Eisenhower, who was opposed to the Arizona Republican's nomination.[22]

Paley, furious at Schorr for causing him embarrassment, suggested to Friendly that the correspondent be fired. Friendly also feared that his push to have CBS regain an edge over NBC in convention coverage would be stymied by lack of access to the Republican camp. Friendly reprimanded Schorr, yelling on the telephone—in Paley's presence—that Schorr had hobbled his first major project as news president. Friendly asked Schorr to publicly retract the entire report. Schorr felt that Friendly was overreacting and that a clarification and apology for the one inaccurate sentence would be sufficient. Friendly met with his top aides—Bill Leonard, Ernie Leiser, and Herb Mitgang—to discuss whether to reprimand or fire Schorr. When Mitgang opposed any disciplinary action that could be interpreted as succumbing to pressure, Friendly angrily countered, "What do you know about broadcasting?" According to Schorr, Friendly's handling of the matter contributed to Mitgang's estrangement from Friendly. As Leiser remembered, "Fred wanted to fire Schorr, but luckily he was dissuaded." Friendly ended up reprimanding Schorr privately in a cable and requiring him to submit subsequent stories for clearance. Years later, Friendly told Schorr that he never intended to fire him but had to contend with Paley's fury. Friendly said he had been told to come to Paley's hotel room in San Francisco: "I was talking to you with him sitting right there. That was the price I had to pay." In addition, Friendly described how Paley sat at his side in the CBS viewing room at the convention for four straight days, repeating, "'Have you fired Schorr yet?' And I kept telling him that it would destroy the morale of the whole correspondents' corps if a guy got fired for one mistake."[23]

Clearly, the pressures of a presidential election year added immeasurably to the challenges that Friendly faced in 1964 as the new president of CBS News. This was an era when the conventions garnered great public interest, and the success of a network's coverage influenced the standing of its news operation for the four years to follow. Friendly understood that Chet Huntley and David Brinkley had turned the tide in the ratings battle with CBS at the political conventions in 1956. In planning convention coverage, Friendly worked closely with Bill Leonard, the head of CBS's election unit, to reverse the network's fortunes. "I fell under his spell in the late 1950s," the veteran CBS reporter said of Friendly, "and my life has not been the same since." Leonard described the new president of CBS News as "a serious journalist with a Hollywood personality, and that confuses friends and enemies alike. He is a dragon-slayer who outroars the dragons."[24]

11 At the Top of His Game

F RED F RIENDLY AND B ILL L EONARD set out with zeal to slay the two-headed dragon of Chet Huntley and David Brinkley at the 1964 national political conventions. Their quest to revamp the way CBS handled convention coverage precipitated a conflict with Walter Cronkite, anchor of CBS's convention coverage since 1952 and the network's premier newsman. Cronkite was surprised that Friendly insisted on meeting him at the San Francisco airport when he arrived a day before the opening of the Republican conclave. Friendly insisted that they go directly to the convention site. Cronkite learned that a young woman hired away from Huntley and Brinkley at NBC would replace his long-time communications assistant. He was shocked to learn of the scuttling of the communications system used since 1952 to link the anchor desk directly to the director, producer, and floor correspondents. The change, he felt, would hobble his ability to coordinate and direct coverage. In addition, Cronkite would be teamed with the veteran correspondent and commentator Eric Sevareid in the CBS convention booth, further eroding Cronkite's authority as anchor. According to Leonard, Friendly conceived Sevareid's role as "a more reflective sort of 'Brinkley'"; Cronkite exploded when the discussion turned to where Sevareid would be placed in the booth. Cronkite felt blindsided: there had been no discussion of these changes in New York. "Fred came in and totally tore the thing apart," Cronkite observed bitterly years later.[1]

Despite or because of the changes, coverage of the Republican National Convention marked a low point for both Cronkite and CBS News. Cronkite recalled his frustration with the new setup as well as the frantic involvement of Friendly and Leonard: "The two of them were wild-eyed. Leonard would come charging in to the anchor booth every five minutes with a brainstorm." Cronkite resisted the segues to the floor reporters arranged by Don Hewitt, prompting off-air altercations in the booth. According to Leonard, "It was painfully obvious that some of the conflict going on behind the scenes had come through on the air."[2] Cronkite was unnerved by the distractions and later conceded that it represented the worst convention performance of his career. NBC again beat out CBS in the ratings. A full-page story in *Variety* emphasized the magnitude of NBC's victory and predicted its ascendancy in news for the next four years. Leonard had no illusions: the first major initiative of Friendly as news president and Leonard as head of the expanded election unit was a "resounding failure." Back in New York, Paley recommended replacing Cronkite as anchor of the upcoming Democratic National Convention, to be held in Atlantic City, New Jersey. (Cronkite heard that among those criticizing him was the author Truman Capote, a close friend of Paley's wife, Babe, and a fixture in her household.)[3] Paley recommended a new anchor team pairing Roger Mudd, a rising star at CBS, with Robert Trout, who had anchored CBS's radio coverage of every political convention since 1936.

Friendly and Leonard questioned the change but agreed to consider it because Paley remained adamant. A follow-up meeting took place in Friendly's home in Riverdale; Ernie Leiser, a producer for the *CBS Evening News*, joined Leonard to prepare a response to Paley's recommendation. Leiser came away from the meeting with the understanding that Friendly would resist Paley's attempt to preempt the judgment of the news division and remove Cronkite. Yet Friendly, torn between his professional judgment and the wishes of Paley, sought the advice of Dick Salant, his predecessor as news president. Friendly appeared at Salant's office at Black Rock but insisted that they walk toward the broadcast studios on the West Side so that they could speak in confidence. Friendly described his dilemma as they walked through the crowds of pedestrians. Salant recalled that "Bill Paley was a master at making what he wanted done perfectly clear, but he stopped just short of commanding it. . . . Fred asked me what I should do. I told him that I could not answer until he told me what he wanted to do. Fred replied that what he wanted to do was irrelevant, it was Paley's candy store." Salant, feeling that they were talking past each other, turned around and walked back to his office.[4]

Friendly later recalled spending the afternoon walking the streets of Manhattan before deciding to accept Paley's recommendation: "It seemed to me then that I had little choice; I was convinced if I resisted this drastic step, the future of the news division and my authority to make long-range changes . . . would be jeopardized." Leiser felt that Friendly had violated their agreement in Riverdale to oppose the change. "If he had stuck to his guns," Leiser believed, "he could have gotten away with it and would have saved CBS News a hell of a lot of grief." The CBS historian Gary Paul Gates reflects archly: "If he was not overly concerned about losing his job, Friendly was fearful that, in taking a defiant stand now, he might undermine his future. That, really, is what it came down to: Fred Friendly's own ambition."[5]

Friendly and Leonard flew to Los Angeles to break the news to Cronkite, who was vacationing with his family in California following the Republican convention. To Friendly's relief, Cronkite—who retained his position as anchor of the CBS news broadcast—took the news stoically when they met face to face at the American Airlines lounge of the Los Angeles airport. "I admired him for that," Cronkite later said. "He came out to tell me in person, and I don't recall that he invoked anybody else's decision. . . . And then he assured me that I would be continuing as anchor of the evening news." Publicly, Cronkite held his tongue despite a storm of critical press coverage and irate viewer response to his removal as convention anchor. Privately, he remained angry with Friendly and Leonard, the two men who Cronkite felt had failed to defend him, using him instead as a scapegoat for their own misguided attempts to refashion convention coverage. Two years later, Friendly characterized the removal of Cronkite as "my worst blunder as president of CBS News," which he attributed to "a lack of will power and stamina." "I now believe," he added, "that if I had stood firm and refused to substitute anyone for Cronkite I could have prevailed."[6]

Trout was wary of making the transition from radio to television coverage of the convention. Friendly countered that Trout, the historic master of convention coverage, could extend his mastery to video and reestablish his preeminence as a political broadcaster. Trout got the full treatment from Friendly, who was equally adept at effusive praise and devastating criticism. "It was personalized," Trout remembered, "he didn't talk about the company, it was you, you, you." Trout found Friendly's vaunted praise and expectations unsettling, "so that you lose half your confidence because you are worrying that you aren't going to be *that* good." Trout reluctantly agreed, aware that Friendly would be a proactive director of CBS coverage of the convention. Anticipating, for example, the increasingly important role that polling would play in the political process, Friendly arranged for Trout, Mudd, and the rest of the convention team to take a two-day seminar with Lou Harris at the IBM complex in Pleasantville, New York. Once convention coverage began, Friendly remained a presence in the CBS broadcast booth. Trout had been used to having a free hand in CBS's convention coverage on radio, where he felt like a symphony conductor integrating the disparate sounds into a whole for listeners. Friendly and Leonard positioned themselves just out of view of the camera so that they could direct coverage. Sometimes arguments broke out with technicians. Trout was frustrated that he could not direct the cameras to capture the sidebars that spiced convention coverage. As Trout later recalled, "Fred and Bill ran this thing with a heavy hand." Trout was angered, for example, when he was ordered to do a cutaway to a picture of Lyndon Johnson's plane flying toward Atlantic City because it interrupted the emotional high point of the convention, a filmed tribute to John F. Kennedy. Friendly was apparently worried that NBC would show Johnson's plane first. "Why couldn't they at least have used a split screen?" Trout wondered.[7]

Trout and Mudd provided credible coverage of a convention in which the nomination of Lyndon Johnson and Hubert Humphrey was a foregone conclusion. However, the chemistry between Trout and Mudd was not strong, and they did not successfully mount a challenge to the hegemony of Huntley and Brinkley. Indeed, the ratings differential between CBS and NBC was even worse than for the convention in San Francisco anchored by Cronkite.

Following the conventions, Friendly sought to complete his appointments in the news department. Paley offered no resistance when Friendly said he wanted Cronkite to preside over election night coverage. Capitalizing on his authority as news president, Friendly rehired Joe Wershba, who had been forced out of CBS in 1954 because of the blacklist. Robert Trout received a new assignment, as CBS's roving correspondent in Europe. Trout was pleased, but he confided to Jap Gude that Friendly mistakenly believed that he was unhappy with his treatment by CBS. On the eve of his departure for Europe, Trout met with Friendly to clarify the situation. The meeting was vintage Friendly, a mix of reproaches, reassurances, and recommendations that left Trout's head spinning. Trout, as he frequently did, typed out his thoughts and feelings in a diary-like style. "It seems so impossible for me to hold a meaningful conversation with someone like Fred—stating conclusions, saying what I mean, and not allowing statements with which I disagree to go unchallenged or uncorrected," Trout wrote. Trout acknowledged his difficulty in maintaining his equilibrium and a sense of clarity about his own responses in his encounters with the human whirlwind that was Friendly: "Ten or 15 minutes afterward, the entire conversation seems to take on a different perspective. There are new, or at least altered meanings to most of the things that he said and my replies are suddenly revealed to me as all wrong."[8]

Friendly's appointments included naming Bill Leonard and Gordon Manning as his two chief lieutenants. They joined Herb Mitgang, the news department's executive editor, to constitute Friendly's triumvirate of top aides. Leonard, as vice president for soft news, had responsibility for documentaries and live coverage of special events. Leonard was an old CBS hand, well liked by Frank Stanton as well as by his colleagues in the news department. Leonard—low key, willing to give producers creative freedom and to delegate responsibility—complemented Friendly's aggressive style of management. Leiser, an obvious candidate to be Leonard's counterpart for hard news, expressed a preference for the position of executive producer of the *CBS Evening News*, freeing Friendly to go outside the company for his hard news chief. Friendly selected Manning, a print journalist, as vice president for hard news. A veteran of United Press, Manning worked at *Collier's* magazine before moving to *Newsweek*, where he became executive editor. Manning's name first came up when Friendly was distraught at CBS's slow response to the Alaska earthquake. During a luncheon with Pat Weaver, Friendly beseeched the former NBC president for the name of someone who could take charge of breaking news at CBS. Weaver turned for help to Lewis Marcy, a former colleague at NBC, describing Friendly as beside himself about coverage of the Alaska earthquake. "I had lunch with that madman Fred Friendly," Weaver reportedly said, "who gave me a commission to find a newsman before the week is out. Like a fool—because he is so demanding and commanding—I said okay." Marcy recommended Manning, whose hiring was endorsed by Les Midgley and by Katherine Graham, the publisher of *Newsweek*.[9]

Friendly first met Manning for lunch at Louis and Armand's, where Friendly questioned him in detail about strategies for responding to breaking news. Manning was a journalist steeped in the fierce rivalry between the United Press and the Associated Press, a storied struggle in which resourceful UP reporters often prevailed over the better-funded AP apparatus. Manning remembered that the focus of the conversation was "how the game is played, especially the competitive game." Friendly needed someone like Manning to outscoop NBC in the future, to make a serious run in the ratings war. Manning understood Friendly's desire to be educated about the coverage of breaking news. Yet over time, Manning also came to see Friendly's avocation as something other than reporter or editor in the conventional sense: "He was not a working journalist. He was a dreamer and a schemer."[10]

The last key appointment Friendly made at the end of 1964 was the replacement of Don Hewitt with Ernie Leiser as executive producer of the *CBS Evening News*. Hewitt, like Friendly, ranked as a pioneer of television journalism at CBS. Friendly looked down on Hewitt as a lowbrow with a tabloid mentality who was unsuited for the position of executive producer of Cronkite's program. Hewitt's reputation within CBS as a potential loose cannon had been reinforced when he was caught stealing an NBC election handbook during the Republican National Convention in San Francisco. Now the *CBS Evening News*, locked in battle with *The Huntley-Brinkley Report*, was replacing the documentary as the centerpiece of CBS's news department. Cronkite preferred a more serious journalist like Ernie Leiser as his executive producer. Friendly consulted Cronkite, who did not object to the change: Cronkite liked Hewitt personally but shared Friendly's reservations about Hewitt's seriousness and ethics as a journalist. When Hewitt heard rumors of his replacement in December 1964, he spoke to Friendly, who assured him that his position was secure. Later that day, Friendly called Hewitt back to his office to inform him of a "promotion" to develop a new kind of news broadcast, the "live documentary." Only after he left Friendly's office did Hewitt realize that he had been fired as Cronkite's executive producer. "I think," Hewitt reflected years later, "Friendly always thought that CBS wasn't big enough for the two of us." Hewitt remained in a state of limbo in the news department until the inception of *60 Minutes*, when Friendly was no longer at CBS. Friendly remained adamant about the wisdom of replacing Hewitt with Leiser as executive producer of the *CBS Evening News*: "Best decision I ever made."[11]

By the end of 1964, Friendly's team was in place. Friendly had survived his rocky initiation as news president: the burst of bulletin fever, the conflicts with Arthur Morse and Daniel Schorr, and the convention debacles. In fact, Friendly did not emerge from the conventions in a seriously compromised state. He had, after all, counseled Paley and Stanton against the removal of Cronkite as anchor of the Democratic National Convention. As election night anchor, Cronkite made inroads into NBC's ratings on the night of Lyndon Johnson's landslide. Indeed, *The Huntley-Brinkley Report* had reached its apogee in 1964, after which its ratings and prestige declined—and would be overtaken—by the *CBS Evening News with Walter Cronkite*.

By mid-1965, as a result of the rising fortunes of CBS News, Friendly was at the top of his game as news president. In June, he shared his sense of accomplishment and the sheer pleasure he took in his work—as well as the grinding pressure—in a speech in Providence, where he had grown up and launched his broadcasting career. The occasion was a dinner of the Rhode Island Broadcasters Association in honor of Mowry Lowe, the New England broadcasting pioneer who had served as Friendly's earliest radio mentor three decades before. In his speech, Friendly recalled how Lowe had helped him get his first program on WEAN, *Footprints in the Sands of Time.* Friendly noted that initially he did the program without a fee, adding, "I was never successful enough to tell that to anybody until now." He alluded to his family's worries about his professional prospects as a young man and to the challenge of his career path and current responsibilities. Looking out at the audience, which included childhood friends; his wife, Dorothy (a Providence native); Mowry Lowe; and other early associates, Friendly said, "Coming back I realize a great deal of this strength comes from the people in this room."[12]

Friendly remembered how thrilled he was in the old days when WEAN provided a radio feed to New England's old Yankee Network via the radio studio in the Buckminster Hotel in Boston; now he oversaw television feeds at CBS from around the world. He described how his current CBS office looked like a control room, with television sets for CBS, NBC, and ABC. A fourth line-monitor enabled him, with the switch of a dial on his desk, to view—without audio—preparations at any of the sites from which a CBS feed might be originating that day, be it Cape Canaveral or the White House. He emphasized "how impossible, chaotic" his job was, the mad scramble and inner turmoil, for example, when interrupting regular programming for a breaking story. He related how he faced such a dilemma in March 1965, when he suspected that a hastily called White House press conference would address the murder of the civil rights worker Viola Liuzzo in Alabama. CBS had covered a ceremony that morning at which President Johnson had given medals to the *Gemini III* astronauts Virgil Grissom and John Young. NBC covered the parade that followed, but CBS returned to regular programming. Bill Small, chief of the CBS Washington Bureau, alerted Friendly that the president might return to the press room in a few minutes but said that White House officials would not reveal why. Friendly quickly consulted with CBS network executives, who strongly objected to the possibility of yet another interruption of the soap opera *Search for Tomorrow* and a resulting loss of revenue. "Can't this wait until the evening news?" they asked. Friendly tried to reach Frank Stanton, who was unavailable. Friendly then talked to the White House press secretary George Reedy on the CBS tie line in a vain attempt to learn the subject of the press conference.

In New York, Friendly's office was filled with CBS news personnel who urged him to switch to the press conference, while the sales department argued against preempting regular programming. Friendly saw Johnson entering the East Room: NBC switched to the White House; ABC did not. Friendly noticed his hands were trembling: "If you're right and it's an important speech, you're a hero, and if you're wrong you're a bum and should go back to doing *Footprints in the Sands of Time*." Friendly said go, then a millisecond later saw J. Edgar Hoover and Attorney General Nicholas Katzenbach by the side of the president, who announced arrests in the Liuzzo murder. It was the first time the director of the FBI had been seen live on television. This time, Friendly had guessed right. So the local boy who made good had an impossible job, Friendly continued. Sometimes your decisions did not pan out, and sometimes you had to take a stand even if it upset your superiors. No one in his right mind would aspire to such a job: "There isn't enough money in the world to make anybody do what I do. You have to be slightly diseased to want to do it."[13]

Such protestations notwithstanding, Friendly conceded that "I relished the presidency of the news division." The position gave him the freedom to take initiatives large and small. For example, a succession of speeding tickets that required him to undergo driver education led to *The National Drivers' Test*, a discussion of driving safety with a test for viewers that became a popular annual broadcast. *Time* magazine wrote in its review of the program that "when Fred Friendly has a headache, he thinks the whole world is in pain."[14] Friendly often worked at his desk from 7:00 A.M. until 1:00 or 2:00 A.M. He would sometimes interrupt his workday to speed up and down the West Side Highway between Manhattan and Riverdale to fulfill his responsibilities as a father at a difficult time in his household. *CBS Reports*, for which he remained ultimately responsible, continued to flourish. For example, before his untimely death David Lowe produced noteworthy programs for *CBS Reports* in 1965, including "Abortion and the Law" and "The Ku Klux Klan: The Invisible Empire," on the inner workings of the Klan. Cultural documentaries ranged from *The Mystery of Stonehenge* to *Casals at 88*. In addition, Friendly wished to cover stories outside the parameters of the regularly scheduled news and documentary programs. Such coverage involved preempting regular programming, reducing advertising revenue, and usually locking horns with Paley and Stanton. For example, Friendly and Manning provided extensive coverage of Pope Paul VI's appearance in September 1965 in New York, the first of a pontiff to North America. Before giving a reluctant go-ahead, Paley questioned the appropriateness of such extensive coverage of a religious leader and whether the visit warranted the loss of a day's advertising revenue.[15]

A regular Tuesday luncheon hosted by Paley in his private dining room provided the setting in which Friendly would discuss such issues with the CBS chair. Friendly's top aides—Mitgang, Leonard, and Manning—attended, along with Stanton. Here CBS's chief officers could vet Friendly's initiatives and make their own proposals. Friendly's demeanor tended to be subdued and deferential at these sessions, in contrast to his interactions with his subordinates. If Friendly had serious differences with Paley, he would voice them quietly and then press Stanton more forcefully on the telephone after the meeting. Friendly viewed the luncheons as a forum for generating ideas, suggesting that figures like Walter Lippmann and Admiral Hyman Rickover be invited to discuss emerging trends meriting coverage. Friendly also recommended including news staff in the Tuesday luncheons after CBS corporate headquarters moved to Black Rock: "I am most anxious that the CBS News people, particularly the correspondents, feel an identity with the new building. As a starter, would it be possible to invite Walter Cronkite and perhaps Ernie Leiser to a Tuesday luncheon?"[16]

Paley issued a continual flow of memos to his news president in 1965 in which he asked for personal favors or made suggestions for news broadcasts. For example: my friend Jerome Robbins would like footage of the racial conflagrations in Watts, Birmingham, and Harlem for a project of his; can you oblige him? A friend has passed along to me a film produced for the National Gallery of Art; might we broadcast it? Can Mike Wallace's morning news program be fed to affiliates in such a way as to permit five minutes of local news and weather reports at the end? Paley wrote a series of memos regarding potential changes in the way CBS reporters and individuals in breaking stories might be identified through superimposed text on the television screen. In response, Friendly instructed his secretary: "Copies to Manning, Leonard, Mitgang," saying 'I concur what should we do about it. FF."[17]

Paley's missives—his requests for special favors for friends, the occasional attempts to micromanage—could undoubtedly be an annoyance for Friendly. Leonard recalled the unevenness of Paley's judgment "erratic, sometimes brilliant, occasionally a bit off course by our standards." Paley and Friendly had their share of disagreements about issues like the replacement of Cronkite as convention anchor or coverage of the pope's visit. Nonetheless, Friendly welcomed his contact with Paley. Friendly had always been fascinated by prominent figures. And Murrow had advised Friendly to insist on access to Paley as news president. Friendly derived great satisfaction from his interaction with the legendary chair of CBS. Indeed, many testified to Paley's charisma. He was well known as a womanizer but was equally adept, figuratively speaking, at beguiling the men with whom he worked. "He was a smooth piece of work," Stanton once observed. "He could charm the birds right out of the trees."[18] A private meeting in Paley's office at Black Rock—with its plush carpets, antique furniture, and priceless original paintings by Toulouse-Lautrec, Picasso, and other masters that hung on a dark green wall—was a heady experience. In a tête-à-tête with Paley, one would sit opposite the chairman across a small, exquisite antique French gaming table in his office. Beside the table was a life-size wooden Indian holding a hatchet, a relic from the Paley family's cigar business. Friendly, like others, experienced how enthralling a meeting in Paley's enchanted lair could be.[19]

In the summer of 1965, Paley, who was about to travel to Europe, asked Friendly to arrange a meeting in Paris of CBS's foreign correspondents. The meeting would include Robert Trout, Charles Collingwood, and Eric Sevareid, and a more junior cohort represented by Daniel Schorr and Dan Rather. In a memo to Paley in connection with preparations for the meeting in Paris, Friendly attached an upbeat news department progress report dated July 2, 1965, sixteen months after his appointment as head of news. In the area of special events, Friendly noted that CBS had topped NBC in both critical acclaim and ratings in coverage of the funeral of Winston Churchill, the report of the Warren Commission, and the *Gemini III* and *IV* launches. The regular CBS network morning and evening news programs, Friendly continued, had increased the breadth and depth of their coverage. He added that CBS was ahead of the pack in its use of the *Early Bird* communications satellite for rapid transmission of breaking stories. Recent Nielsen reports showed the *CBS Evening News* abreast and even ahead of *The Huntley-Brinkley Report* for the first time. As a result of CBS's triumphs in both special and regular news reporting, Friendly suggested, "NBC is off balance and, for the first time in some years, unsure of itself." *CBS Reports* continued to distinguish itself as the only prime-time program of news specials and documentaries in network television. Friendly pointed to a heightened sense of morale and momentum in the news division. "Last, but not least," Friendly concluded in his report to Paley, "we are attracting more and more attention from sponsors interested in news product, and this is a most encouraging portent for the future."[20]

The baptism of fire behind him, his management team in place, and ratings up, Fred Friendly seemed well positioned as the president of CBS News to direct the network's coverage of the controversy that would dominate—and define—his tenure as news president: the Vietnam War.

12 Vietnam

THE PRESIDENCY OF CBS NEWS gave Fred Friendly greater access to the highest level of politics in the United States: the Oval Office. That entrée was a function of the growing importance of television in American politics. He continued to serve as CBS's unofficial liaison to Dwight Eisenhower. He had developed close ties with the Kennedy White House, a function of his relationship with Newton Minow, the televised conversation with Kennedy, and the *Telstar* broadcast. Now Friendly found himself being courted by Lyndon Johnson. When Friendly began his tenure as news president, he received a congratulatory letter from Pierre Salinger, LBJ's press secretary: "I can think of no one in the entire television industry more qualified for this post and I look forward to our continuing association."[1]

Friendly's relationship with LBJ was reinforced—and complicated—by Frank Stanton's long-standing ties with the president. In 1938, Stanton had agreed to a request from a young Texas congressman that his family's small Austin radio station become a CBS affiliate, which laid the foundation for the Johnson family's wealth. The two men remained close as Johnson moved from the House of Representatives to the Senate and finally to the White House, a relationship that served both men well. When Fred Friendly became CBS News president, Stanton was serving as an unofficial media adviser to Johnson, who was unhappy with his appearance and performance on television. Johnson came to know Friendly when he produced another televised presidential conversation, which aired in March 1964, less than four months into the Johnson administration. Friendly demonstrated that he would not be intimidated by the president, who had said that he did not want to be asked questions about a scandal involving his former aide, Bobby Baker. With the taping seemingly concluded, Friendly insisted that the public would expect that the

Baker affair be addressed and that doing so was in Johnson's best interest. So at Friendly's behest, Johnson and his interlocutors taped an additional segment on the matter that was seamlessly edited into an interview that included discussion of the legacy of President Kennedy, civil rights, and the Vietnam War.

As Bill Moyers recalled, Johnson was looking for a talented press czar who could improve his ability to communicate with the public and became interested in Friendly as a candidate: "Johnson recognized creativity when he saw it, Johnson recognized genius when he saw it. He was struggling with the contrast between his use of television and Kennedy's. . . . He was looking for the cure, for the god who could put things right. I don't know whether Frank Stanton suggested it, or whether other people suggested it, but he got this idea that this guy Friendly was a television genius, and that if he came to the White House he would solve his problems."[2] On Friday, December 18, 1964, Johnson invited Stanton, along with an eye doctor and optometrist, to figure out why he always seemed to be squinting at the camera and fix the problem. LBJ was to be fitted with contact lenses and new eyeglass frames. Stanton asked Friendly to come along for the meeting, which was designated "off record" in the president's daily diary. This meeting took place at a time when the relationship between the press and the presidency was less guarded, before escalation of the war in Vietnam and Watergate would reorient U.S. journalism. CBS was engaged in a delicate balancing act—simultaneously serving and covering a president—that would be considered unacceptable in the years to come.

As Johnson was being fitted for contact lenses, he suddenly asked Friendly if he would consider joining his administration as a media adviser and become a domestic counterpart to National Security Adviser McGeorge Bundy. Friendly expressed surprise that Johnson would make such an offer to a virtual stranger. Johnson replied that he had spoken with Walter Lippmann and Dwight Eisenhower about him. Why don't you do something for your country? the president continued. We can clear it with J. Edgar Hoover today; you'll come to the ranch this weekend; and we'll announce the appointment on Monday. Johnson told a hesitant Friendly that he needed intellectuals in the White House, to which Friendly replied, "I'm not an intellectual. All I can do is produce television shows," adding, "You might not like me. I might not like you." As Moyers observed, "Watching the two of them take each other's measure was like watching King Kong and Godzilla squeeze through the same airport security detector simultaneously." If anything, "They were too much alike; they had egos that filled the same room, leaving no space for anybody else."[3]

Friendly did not reject the offer out of hand. Later that day, Friendly called Murrow, who told Friendly it was a terrible idea: "They'll cut your balls off in four weeks." The presidential aide Jack Valenti wrote a memo for Johnson on Monday, December 21, with a suggested job description for Friendly and the title of executive assistant to the president. Friendly would have broad responsibility to "advise the President on how he should present his actions to the public" through speeches, press releases, and other forms of communication. In addition, he would work with Moyers, who had succeeded Salinger as press secretary, and cabinet officers to improve communication of administration policies in general. Toward that end, Friendly would sit in on meetings of the cabinet and the National Security Council in order to advise how the work of these bodies could best be structured and communicated to the press and public. Johnson followed up with a telephone call to Friendly's office in New York. It was one of those insistent telephone calls for which Johnson was renowned, full of praise for the listener, zeal for the task at hand, and patriotic appeal. Johnson extended another invitation to the LBJ Ranch to discuss the offer further. Friendly still hesitated. Johnson placed a second call later that week, this time late at night to Friendly's home in Riverdale. Now, to Dorothy's chagrin, Friendly dissembled, attributing his reluctance to accept the offer to *her* objections to the reduction in salary and requirement that the family relocate to Washington, D.C.[4]

On December 30, Valenti made a handwritten notation that "Friendly did *not* go to ranch. I have talked with him—and the job offer is dead at this time—Friendly is reluctant to come—thinks the job is too indefinite." Ernie Leiser thought Friendly was wise not to accept the job: "LBJ was even more strong-willed, more unpredictable, and more erratic than Fred." Moyers sensed that Friendly had never seriously entertained the possibility of working for Johnson. Friendly's passion was for journalism, not the management of news for political purposes. And, as Moyers recalled, the mid-1960s were "a great time to be a news executive. In those days it was just three networks, and he was the star of the managers. I don't think he would have seriously considered leaving that job for any political assignment or cabinet job."[5]

Might Frank Stanton have orchestrated the offer from Johnson to Friendly? Friendly's appointment could have served a dual purpose, providing Johnson with the television adviser he needed while easing Friendly, Stanton's foe, out of CBS. Murrow's appointment to the United States Information Agency had served a similar purpose. At any rate, Friendly did not go for the bait. His bond with CBS was deep, and he took great pride in his stewardship of its news division. In 1965, when Moyers expressed his intention to step down as presidential press secretary, Johnson once again dispatched him to fly to New York to feel out Friendly as a replacement. "I'm flattered, Bill," Friendly responded, "but leaving CBS News to come to the White House would be a step down." "Even Friendly's driving ambition had some limits," David Halberstam writes of Friendly's rejection of the offer, "and he sensed the danger ahead."[6] Four months earlier, the administration had gotten Congress to pass the Gulf of Tonkin Resolution to formalize escalation of the war in Vietnam. In the months to come, the war would threaten the broad popular support enjoyed by the Johnson administration and polarize the nation.

Coverage of the war by CBS was problematic enough. Friendly's boss, Stanton, was LBJ's confidant, a member of the board of the USIA, and a hawk on the war. At the weekly news department luncheons with Paley, Stanton reported on complaints he received from Johnson about what the president considered negative coverage of the U.S. effort. The broadcast historian Erik Barnouw notes that in general, network television lagged behind print journalism in offering critical perspectives on the war, and that the administration was acutely aware of the influence of television coverage of the first living-room war. Network executives, seeking to avoid offending government officials, did not question the rationale and tactics of the war effort. Little direct censorship took place; self-censorship was more the norm. Coverage of Vietnam would become the central preoccupation of Friendly's tenure as president of CBS News.[7]

The Gulf of Tonkin Incident of August 2–4, 1964, put into sharp relief the dilemmas faced by Friendly at CBS. The White House claimed that the North Vietnamese had made unprovoked attacks over a two-day period on two U.S. destroyers: the *Maddox* and the *Turner Joy*. In response, Johnson ordered retaliatory bombing of North Vietnamese installations, the first overt U.S. act of the war against the North. On August 6, Johnson used the Tonkin incident to ask for authority to act in Vietnam without a formal declaration of war. The next day, Congress passed the sweeping Tonkin resolution with the support of Senator William Fulbright of Arkansas, chair of the Senate Foreign Relations Committee. No journalists witnessed events in the Gulf of Tonkin, so no one outside the administration could either corroborate or challenge the administration's account. Only later, during a time of growing disenchantment with the war, would reporters and officials revisit what happened in the Gulf of Tonkin. Evidence surfaced that the *Maddox* had been supporting raids by South Vietnamese torpedo boats against North Vietnamese shore installations, and that the U.S. ship had not been hit by any fire on August 2. The second attack, on the *Turner Joy*, it was later discovered, apparently never happened either. In retrospect, it appeared that the Johnson administration manufactured the incident to gain the support of Congress and the public for widening the war. In 1970, Congress would vote to repeal the Gulf of Tonkin Resolution.

After Johnson's televised speech on the Gulf of Tonkin Incident, CBS gave a pro forma two-minute summary, unlike NBC, which devoted more attention to the story. Afterward, Friendly received a jarring call in his office at CBS from Edward R. Murrow. Murrow was terminally ill by then, with less than a year to live, no longer in the government as director of the USIA. As a recent member of the Kennedy and Johnson administrations who had sat in on National Security Council meetings, Murrow was in a position to read between the lines of Johnson's speech and was disturbed by its implications.[8] Years later, after interviewing Friendly, David Halberstam wrote of how

that night as the news unfolded on the screen, Murrow did something he had never done before, he called up his onetime protégé Fred Friendly . . . and tore into him. In the past when Murrow had been angry with Friendly he had handled him quietly. . . . But this time he was in a rage: "By what God-given right did you treat it this way? What do we really know about what happened out there? Why did it happen? How could you not have Rather and the boys do some sort of special analysis?" Friendly was shocked by his anger, and felt a certain guilt because he had that day been on the phone with Dan Rather, and Rather had said that it all smelled a bit tricky, and Friendly had told Rather for God's sake not to say anything along that line on the air. Friendly simply did not know how to cover something as elusive as this, how to raise the questions. He was still, like the country, more hawk than dove, and the whole thing scared him. And he was also in quite close contact with the Johnson administration. There was some talk about coming back on the air later that night—perhaps a midnight special—but that too was dropped.[9]

Friendly must have been stung by the angry call from the person he revered most in the world: he made no mention of it in *Due to Circumstances Beyond Our Control* . . . , the memoir of his CBS years published in 1966. Only later in his career did he feel comfortable talking openly about Murrow's telephone call. Less than a year after that call, on April 27, 1965, Friendly was flying back from a meeting at the BBC in London when he learned from a flight attendant that Murrow had died. Friendly had five hours to reflect in the half-empty aircraft. As the plane approached the United States, Friendly asked the pilot to relay a message to CBS to be distributed to all bureaus and correspondents. In the message, he quoted Murrow's farewell to the English people when he left London after the war: "You lived a life instead of an apology."[10] The telephone call from the ailing Murrow, and now his death, may have steeled Friendly's willingness to buck the pressures from Stanton as the Vietnam War widened in 1965.

Controversy about CBS's coverage of the war soon came to a head. In August 1965, exactly a year after the Gulf of Tonkin Incident, the CBS correspondent Morley Safer delivered an electrifying report from the village of Cam Ne; it was a watershed in television reporting and public opinion about the war. Safer, a Canadian and veteran war correspondent, worked with a Vietnamese camera operator who was fluent in English, French, and Vietnamese. They accompanied U.S. Marines engaged in an action on August 3 against a complex of villages known as Cam Ne, which was said to have aided the Vietcong. Early in the maneuver, the camera operator barely managed to convince marines not to fire a flame thrower down a deep hole from which the voices of women and children could be heard. Safer's report showed a marine using his cigarette lighter to set huts on fire; more than a hundred were burned to the ground. Film footage captured women, children, and elderly men sobbing as their ancestral homes went up in flames. No Americans were injured in the action. Safer immediately filed a story for CBS Radio and prepared a filmed report for television.

Friendly was awakened and informed about the radio report before it aired and about the explosive footage that was in transit to the United States. He was extremely anxious about the decision he would have to make and checked to make sure that Safer had his facts right. According to Halberstam, Friendly did not welcome Safer's story. Friendly immediately called Frank Stanton and alerted Arthur Sylvester, the Pentagon's press spokesman, that Safer's radio report would be broadcast in the morning. CBS reserved a telephone line from Los Angeles so Friendly could view all the footage when it first arrived in the United States. Friendly watched with Walter Cronkite and his executive producer, Ernie Leiser. "It was awesome," David Halberstam writes of the impact the footage made on the three men sitting in a small screening room, "the full force of television, the ability to dramatize, now fastening on one incident, one day in the war, that was going to be shattering to an entire generation of Americans." Early the next morning, after Safer's report on Cam Ne had aired on the *CBS Evening News with Walter Cronkite,* a groggy Stanton received a phone call: "Frank," the caller asked, "are you trying to fuck me?" Stanton asked who was calling. "Frank, this is your President, and yesterday your boys shat on the American flag." Johnson was livid, accusing Safer of being a Communist who had bribed the marine officer at Cam Ne. The administration launched an investigation of Safer and conducted a smear campaign against him. Safer believed that Moyers, Johnson's press secretary, was complicit in that campaign and has never forgiven Moyers.[11]

Friendly, who had been wooed to join the Johnson administration seven months earlier, now had to defend Safer and CBS News from the attacks by the White House and the Pentagon. A week after the Cam Ne story, military authorities accused Safer of a violation of press guidelines and a major security breach in his report on August 10 about U.S. troop reinforcements for the battle raging in the highland city of Pleiku. The report first aired on CBS Radio's *World News Roundup,* with Adam Rafael in Saigon quoting Safer, who had spoken to Rafael by field telephone from Pleiku. On August 12, CBS carried Safer's televised report. That day, spurred by government accusations, Friendly sent the first of two urgent cables to the CBS bureau in the Caravelle Hotel in Saigon:

CBS NEWS COVERAGE OF THE VIETNAM WAR HAS BEEN SO EXCELLENT THAT I REGRET HAVING TO ASK NOW FOR AN IMMEDIATE TELEX EXPLANATION WHY SAFER BELIEVED THE PLEIKU STORY DID NOT INVOLVE SECURITY STOP I HOPE AND PRAY THERE ARE SUFFICIENT REASONS. . . . IF WE DID VIOLATE SECURITY IN THE NAME OF A SCOOP I WANT TO KNOW THAT. . . . THIS BREACH IF IT WAS A BREACH COULD ENDANGER THE ENTIRE CBS RECORD OF EXCELLENCE IN VIETNAM AND I WANT A PERSONAL EXPLANATION IMMEDIATELY.[12]

In his second cable, Friendly emphasized that the

CBS NEWS LONG TRADITION OF COOPERATION WITH UNISTATES GOV-
ERNMENT WILL BE MAINTAINED STOP ALL HANDS MUST EXERCISE
PROPER JUDGMENT IN FULLEST COMPLIANCE WITH GUIDELINES ISSUED
BY UNISTATES MISSION STOP EYE WILL NOT TOLERATE ANY LAPSES BY
CBS NEWSMEN IN THIS CRITICAL AREA.

Friendly wrote Stanton that "my confidential cables to Safer and other hands are perhaps overdue." Friendly unquestionably believed in the principles he set forth in the two cables, but they may have been written as much for Frank Stanton's consumption as for Safer's. On August 14, Safer responded to the two cables with a lengthy telegram in which he documented that no security breach had taken place and that a high U.S. military official—whom he identified by name a day later—had cleared his report. Safer ended the cable by expressing his confidence—or was it his hope?—that "THE SUPERB SUPPORT AND CONFIDENCE GIVEN ME BY CCCBBBSSS EDITORS IN THE PAST WILL CONTINUE."[13]

Since the Cam Ne story, Friendly had been in telephone contact with the Pentagon press spokesman Arthur Sylvester about Safer's reporting. The conversations were testy. At one point, Sylvester questioned the propriety of CBS's use of native personnel: "How much do you pay your Vietnamese cameramen?" Friendly shot back, "How much do you pay your Vietnamese soldiers?" On August 12, Sylvester summarized his criticisms of Safer in a letter to Friendly that contained four attachments, including a lengthy rebuttal of the Cam Ne story by marine personnel and the text of press guidelines for Vietnam. Frank Stanton received a copy. In the letter, which began with the informal salutation "Dear Fred," Sylvester characterized Safer as "a man with a strong anti-military bias." He argued that Safer's Canadian citizenship made him less fit to report on the war, and objected to the use of a Vietnamese cameraman. Sylvester asserted that the marines had exposed the inaccuracy of the Cam Ne report, and he repeated the charge that Safer was responsible for a security breach in Pleiku. Sylvester echoed Lyndon Johnson's accusation that Safer's reports had weakened the war effort.[14]

On August 16, Friendly replied with a ringing defense of CBS News and Morley Safer, who clearly had answered to Friendly's satisfaction the charges leveled against him. Friendly's reply contained detailed, point-by-point refutations of the Pentagon's criticisms of Safer's Cam Ne and Pleiku stories. Friendly placed those stories in the larger context of CBS's overall coverage of the war. Friendly, producer of the *See It Now* programs on McCarthyism, also took issue with the smear campaign and implication of disloyalty on which Sylvester's letter was posited. Friendly deemed the accusations of bias against Safer based on unnamed sources "a shameful tactic." He continued: "Your suggestion that Safer and Hathu can be replaced with an American correspondent and cameraman would be amusing were it made seriously. . . . And, in suggesting that an American correspondent might be more 'sensitive' in his reporting, perhaps what you really mean is that he might be more 'sympathetic' to the official [Department of Defense] position. We continue to prefer the old-fashioned criteria of responsibility and objectivity."[15]

The patriotism of Friendly, a decorated veteran of World War II, could not be impugned. In a cover memo he sent to Frank Stanton with documents in the Pleiku controversy, Friendly wrote: "We are keeping a very close rein on such broadcasts in the future and, although I have not apologized to the Defense Department, nor do I intend to, I think Mr. McNamara and Mr. Sylvester know where we stand."[16] Here Friendly appears to reassure Stanton that, any conflicts about CBS coverage of Vietnam notwithstanding, he personally supported the war's broad objectives and that the administration was well aware of that support. Friendly was no dove but a news executive asserting the prerogatives of the press in reporting on a war in which U.S. troops were engaged. He took a principled position on the Cam Ne controversy in much the same way that he and Murrow had confronted McCarthyism: almost reluctantly, extremely carefully, but ultimately with great force and effectiveness.

The Cam Ne affair ended well for Friendly. Safer cabled Friendly that General William Westmoreland was furious with the marines, not with CBS, after viewing a kinescope of the Cam Ne report. Members of Westmoreland's staff said privately that the report was helpful in prompting U.S. forces to modify procedures in search-and-destroy missions. On August 23, Safer revisited Cam Ne for a second report for CBS News. Now interpreters accompanied the marines, who warned civilians to leave their homes and provided them with shelter, food, and medical attention. The follow-up report can be viewed variously as proof of the salutary effects of independent reporting, as a conscious attempt by CBS News and Safer to showcase their balance, or as the Pentagon's use of CBS for damage control. Probably all these factors came into play. Stanton referred to Safer's follow-up report in an October letter to Senator George Smathers of Florida, who had criticized Safer's report. Friendly forwarded Stanton's strong letter in support of the Safer–CBS News coverage of Vietnam to Gordon Manning and Herb Mitgang with the note "Something for you to cherish." Friendly also sent a flattering memo to Stanton: "I am moved by your response to Senator Smathers. . . . I would hope that someday you would let me share your letter with Safer for, indeed, I believe that this kind of faith in our newsmen is a vital continuing factor in maintaining the morale of the News Division."[17] Friendly was clearly relieved and grateful to have received the support of Stanton, who was trying to square a circle: communicating LBJ's displeasure at Vietnam coverage while serving as the news department's heat shield.

Friendly's effusive praise of Stanton may have derived, in part, from Friendly's desire to cultivate Stanton's backing for the battles ahead about coverage of the war. Friendly later wrote that in the summer of 1965—the summer of Cam Ne—he concluded that broadcast journalism had failed to present the complexities of the war in Vietnam to the American people. Growing conflict with Stanton about Vietnam coverage also dated from this period. Friendly felt that nightly news reports had to be supplemented by reasoned debate by leading writers and officials. To heighten the level of public discourse, Friendly instituted special programming such as the *Vietnam Perspective* series. Bill Small, the CBS Washington Bureau chief, recalled how Friendly developed "an insatiable appetite for as much Vietnam as we could put on the air," and how Vietnam specials caused resentment within the network by bumping regularly scheduled programming.[18] But as Friendly later made clear in response to Stanton's criticisms, he did not intend to give air time or legitimacy to the growing popular protest movement on college campuses and in the streets:

> I believed, for my part, that healthy debates by responsible leaders could build national understanding of the President's position, and that the spectacle of congressional leaders debating the war was far better than the epidemic of one-sided teach-ins and hostile demonstrations that had filled the void in the absence of a national debate. In my opinion, responsible debates and the subsequent Senate hearings actually de-escalated the demonstrations and draft-card burnings that so embarrassed the Administration.[19]

At the behest of McGeorge Bundy, LBJ's national security adviser, Friendly arranged a live televised debate about the war between Bundy and several professors, including the prominent war critic Hans Morgenthau. Bundy had recently canceled at the last minute his participation in a Vietnam teach-in at the University of Michigan that was to have been carried on campuses throughout the nation through telephone lines and filmed for television broadcast. Bundy subsequently approached Friendly with the idea of a more controlled televised debate, with a neutral moderator and a selected studio audience instead of hostile students. Friendly jumped at the opportunity, assigning Eric Sevareid to moderate a debate in a setting that worked in Bundy's favor. The program, *Vietnam Dialogue: Mr. Bundy and the Professors*, originated on June 21, 1965, from Georgetown University. Friendly truly relished such verbal give-and-take. Bill Small remembered Friendly's excitement in the control room and frustration when time was up. Friendly wanted the dialogue to continue and ordered the credits dropped to permit another minute of discussion.[20]

Despite the debate at Georgetown and Friendly's desire to air contending perspectives, Friendly was on a collision course with Stanton about Vietnam, resulting in a succession of skirmishes. For example, when Friendly arranged a meeting at Bill Paley's request with Walter Lippmann, by then a leading critic of the war effort, Stanton snubbed the columnist by boycotting the luncheon. Stanton was enraged when the CBS correspondent Murray Fromson revealed that U.S. military bases in Thailand were being used for bombing runs against North Vietnam. Friendly rejected Stanton's argument that Fromson had revealed military secrets, countering that the North Vietnamese were fully aware of the use of the Thai bases and that only the American public had been uninformed. Friendly saw in Senator William Fulbright, who felt he had been hoodwinked by the Gulf of Tonkin Incident, an important official voice of dissent on the war. When Fulbright finally appeared on *Face the Nation*, Stanton called Friendly and accused him of stabbing President Johnson in the back.[21] The conflict about coverage of Vietnam came to a head over Friendly's desire that CBS provide live coverage of the February 1966 hearings by the Senate Foreign Relations Committee, which Fulbright chaired, into the conduct of the war. The clash marked, for Friendly, the most charged programming decision since the McCarthy program on *See It Now* more than a decade earlier. The outcome would represent a turning point—indeed, a defining moment—in Friendly's career.

A major reorganization of CBS coincided with—and complicated—the

Fred Friendly, born Ferdinand Friendly Wachenheimer, at about two years of age, in New York City during World War I. His mother, Therese, is wearing a Red Cross uniform.
(Courtesy Lisa Friendly)

Friendly (*right*) in Providence, Rhode Island, around the time of his father's death, plays with his cousin Carolene Wachenheimer (*left*) and his friend Ted Golden (*center*).
(Courtesy Lisa Friendly)

Mowry Lowe (*rear right*), Friendly's first broadcasting mentor, on the "set" of *Sidewalk Backtalk* in Providence.
(Courtesy Roberta Lowe Allen)

At Camp Kohler in California, around 1943, Friendly looks over the shoulder of First Lieutenant Gilbert Edward Clark, subsequently his superior officer and mentor in the information and education office of the army in the China-Burma-India theater. (Fred Friendly Papers, Rare Book and Manuscript Library, Columbia University)

In Mukden, Manchuria, in 1945, Master Sergeant Friendly (*right*), with Captain Jerry Cook (*left*) and two Russian crewmen, stands in front of an American-built P-39 fighter plane bearing the Russian red star.
(Fred Friendly Papers, Rare Book and Manuscript Library, Columbia University)

Friendly works on the set of *Who Said That?* at NBC. The quiz show, which marked Friendly's breakthrough in network broadcasting in 1948, became one of the first programs to be simulcast on radio and television.
(Collection of Ruth Friendly)

For his four-part radio documentary on nuclear power, *The Quick and the Dead*, broadcast on NBC in 1950, Friendly got comedian Bob Hope to fill the role of a curious average American. (© NBCU Photobank)

John G. "Jap" Gude, broadcast journalism's preeminent agent in his day, took Friendly under his wing and introduced him to Edward R. Murrow to make the record *"I can hear it now . . . ,"* 1933–1945. (Courtesy of Elizabeth Gude Drezner)

Friendly, who idolized Murrow, shaped his mentor's career in television after World War II. The two are pictured in Friendly's office on October 15, 1954. (© CBS/Landov)

Murrow and Friendly are joined in the screening room at 550 Fifth Avenue by Edmund Scott, a staff reporter for *See It Now*, on October 17, 1952. (© CBS/Landov)

The role of the producer was dramatically elevated in the transition from radio to television journalism. Friendly takes notes during a Walter Cronkite interview for *CBS Reports* on May 25, 1961. (© CBS/Landov)

Dorothy Greene Friendly, Friendly's first wife and professional partner following World War II, and their daughter, Lisa, in Riverdale, New York, 1955.
(Courtesy Lisa Friendly)

Friendly revered Walter Lippmann, convincing him to appear on CBS and forming a close friendship. The two are pictured during the production of "Walter Lippmann, Year End," on *CBS Reports*, December 14, 1961. (© CBS/Landov)

Friendly's extensive contacts with Dwight Eisenhower made him CBS's unofficial liaison to the former president. They are pictured on December 14, 1963, before an interview on *CBS Reports*. (© CBS/Landov)

John F. Kennedy asked that Friendly produce the three-network interview "After Two Years: A Conversation with the President." Don Hewitt stands just behind Friendly during the taping in the Oval Office on December 16, 1962. (© CBS/Landov)

Lyndon B. Johnson, who later tried unsuccessfully to convince Friendly to leave CBS to work in the White House, listens to Friendly during the setup for "A Conversation with the President" on March 13, 1964. (© CBS/Landov)

Friendly took great pleasure in his work with McGeorge Bundy at the Ford Foundation. He and Bundy are pictured during their testimony in August 1966 before the Senate on behalf of the Ford Foundation satellite plan, initiated by Friendly, for funding public broadcasting. (Fred Friendly Papers, Rare Book and Manuscript Library, Columbia University)

Friendly, Ruth Friendly (*center, head turned*), and Greg Jackson (*far right*), one of the instructors recruited by Friendly, speak with students in the first year of the Summer Program for Minority Journalists. Gloria Rojas (*front*) became a pioneering Puerto Rican television reporter in New York. (Fred Friendly Papers, Rare Book and Manuscript Library, Columbia University)

Friendly at a taping of "Public Trust, Private Interests," for the *Ethics in America* series of the Columbia University Seminars on Media and Society, broadcast in 1989 on PBS. He is speaking to Rudolph Guiliani, then a U.S. attorney, and Congressman Newt Gingrich of Georgia. (Fred Friendly Papers, Rare Book and Manuscript Library, Columbia University)

Friendly as paterfamilias, presiding with Ruth over a family of six children from two marriages in his patio in Riverdale: (*clockwise from left*) Richard Mark; Fred Friendly; Andrew Friendly; David Friendly; Jon Mark and his wife, Susan; Ruth Friendly; Lisa Friendly; Michael Mark and his wife, Mary. (Alfred Eisenstadt © Time Inc.)

Friendly in May 1994, holding his honorary degree from Tulane University, with Ruth, full partner in his post-CBS career, who remained the driving force behind the renamed Fred Friendly Seminars after Fred's death. (Fred Friendly Papers, Rare Book and Manuscript Library, Columbia University)

internal battle that Friendly waged to provide live coverage of the hearings. Two factors had prompted a review of how the company was structured: the transformation of CBS as a corporate entity and the question of Paley's status as chief executive officer as he approached the age of sixty-five. By 1966, CBS had expanded from the original radio network to a television behemoth and communications conglomerate whose properties included publishing, toy, and guitar divisions as well as the New York Yankees. CBS contracted with the firm of Booz Allen and Hamilton to study CBS's operations and to recommend changes in structure and personnel. The review was no secret at CBS because the consulting firm conducted extensive interviews with all department heads. Les Brown, then the television editor for *Variety*, had an inside track on Booz Allen and Hamilton's deliberations: a member of the research team was a neighbor of his in Larchmont, New York, and the two would often ride the train together in the morning into Manhattan and talk about CBS. Brown recalls how during one commute the Booz Allen representative asked if he had ever heard of Fred Friendly. Brown recalled that his neighbor said, "'I have a lot of problems with him,' and I said 'really?' 'The first guy who went in to interview him just came out with his hands in the air, saying he just keeps talking about wanting guys with fire in their bellies. I don't know what the hell he's talking about so we're going to have to send another guy in'" to interview Friendly.[22]

One can imagine the culture clash between the explosive Friendly and the management consultant from Booz Allen and Hamilton, who embodied traditional corporate values of efficiency, hierarchy, and the bottom line. Although the Booz Allen consultants had given Friendly low marks as a manager, Brown did not believe that Friendly would be fired as a result. According to Joe Wershba, Jap Gude, Friendly's agent, tipped Friendly that the Booz Allen study would result in a major shakeup and might spell trouble for him.[23] Hence at the time of the fight about live coverage of the Senate hearings, Friendly had a sense of his growing vulnerability as news president.

A regular meeting of the CBS board was scheduled for February 9, 1966. The directors had to address the status of the company's two chief officers—Paley and Stanton—as well as the recommendations for restructuring made by Booz Allen and Hamilton. Paley was scheduled to step down as CEO in September 1966 when he would turn sixty-five. Stanton was slated to succeed Paley as CEO, a position that Stanton coveted and that would crown his career in broadcasting. Preparations for the board meeting took place while Friendly was pressing for live coverage of the Senate Foreign Relations Committee's hearings on the war, which meant preempting regular programming and a loss of advertising revenue. Friendly prevailed on Friday, February 4, when David Bell, head of the Agency for International Development, testified. Unable to debate the war with LBJ, the senators challenged Bell instead. It was, in Friendly's words, "the first bona-fide unstaged Vietnam senatorial debate on television."

On Monday, February 7, Friendly argued with Stanton all day to resume live coverage the next day when Lieutenant General James Gavin, a war critic, was scheduled to testify. Stanton suggested that the testimony instead be edited for broadcast at 10:00 P.M. The regular Tuesday meeting with Paley had been canceled, and with great reluctance Stanton gave Friendly the go-ahead. In addition to broadcasting Gavin's testimony live, on February 8, CBS gave extensive coverage on its evening news show to President Johnson's meeting with South Vietnamese premier Nguyen Cao Ky in Honolulu. CBS broadcast a special at 10:00 P.M. on the Gavin testimony and Honolulu meeting and covered live the return of LBJ to Los Angeles near midnight New York time.

At 1:30 A.M., an exhausted Friendly left the Broadcast Center on West Fifty-seventh Street for his home in Riverdale. As he drove north on the West Side Highway, his satisfaction with the day's coverage of Vietnam was tempered by a queasy feeling about not having heard from CBS's top management all day. The weekly Tuesday meeting with Paley and Stanton had been rescheduled for the next morning. Friendly planned to press for live CBS coverage of testimony later that week by George F. Kennan, the renowned diplomat and political scientist, and for a Sunday Vietnam special recapping the week's developments.[24]

However, Friendly arrived in his office on Wednesday morning, February 9, to learn that the morning news meeting had again been canceled. Stanton instructed Friendly to work out the decision on the Kennan testimony and the Sunday Vietnam special with John A. (Jack) Schneider, president of the CBS television network. Friendly was unaware of the important board meeting scheduled for 1:30 P.M. on the thirty-fifth floor of Black Rock. At the last minute, Paley reversed his decision to step down, forcing Stanton to introduce a resolution at the board meeting requesting that Paley remain as chair and CEO. Then the CBS board restructured the company based on the recommendations of Booz Allen and Hamilton. CBS was reorganized into two divisions: the

Broadcast Group and the Columbia Group. Jack Schneider became head of the Broadcast Group, which gave him responsibility for the news department—Friendly's bailiwick—as well as for the television network, radio network, and CBS-owned television stations. Stanton briefed Friendly before the official announcement, saying that Paley would now be a step removed from broadcast operations and that henceforth Friendly would report to Schneider rather than directly to CBS's chair and president. Friendly asked whether news policy would continue to be made at the weekly news meetings headed by Paley and Stanton. Stanton responded that this would no longer be possible. Friendly reminded Stanton that he had taken the job of news president two years earlier with the understanding that he—like Murrow before him—would report directly to Stanton and Paley. Friendly raised the possibility of his resignation in light of the new ground rules. According to Friendly, Stanton encouraged him to appeal directly to Paley to reconsider the changed line of responsibility for news.[25]

At the same time Friendly needed to address the immediate question of live CBS coverage the next day—Thursday, February 10—of Kennan's testimony before the Senate Foreign Relations Committee. When Friendly returned from Black Rock to his office on Wednesday afternoon and briefed his staff about the changes, they doubted that Schneider would go against the wishes of the news department on his first day on the job as head of the Broadcast Group. Friendly wrote a memo to Schneider making a case for live coverage of the testimony of Kennan as well as of that of Secretary of State Dean Rusk and General Maxwell Taylor the following week:

> Broadcast journalism has, once or twice every decade, an opportunity to prove itself. Such an opportunity were the events leading up to World War II; such was the McCarthy period. The Vietnam war—its coverage in Asia and in Congress—is another such challenge. I am aware of the financial burden that such coverage places upon the Television Network. . . . But I consider these hearings as a matter of conscience for this company and this executive. This is public service in the most basic sense.[26]

At 4:00 P.M., Schneider called Friendly to inform him that CBS would not carry Kennan's testimony live. The new group vice president argued that revenue would be lost, that opinion leaders would not be watching during the day, and that the predominantly female audience was not interested in Vietnam.

Friendly argued with Schneider, accusing him of using business criteria to make a news judgment. Friendly said he could not fulfill his responsibilities in such circumstances and would seek a meeting with Paley to clarify his status as news president following the reorganization at CBS. In response to the memo that Friendly then wrote to Paley, Friendly received a call from the chair's secretary to confirm an appointment for noon the next day. Friendly and the news staff still held out the hope that CBS management would reconsider before his meeting with Paley and allow the broadcast of the hearing. After all, it was CBS's turn to provide pool facilities for the live broadcast. Friendly instructed Small to have Eric Sevareid and Roger Mudd ready to go on the air at 10:00 A.M. NBC announced that Chet Huntley and David Brinkley would anchor live coverage of the hearings. The CBS news department was noncommittal when asked by the press about its intentions. That night, Friendly asked Gordon Manning, his vice president for hard news, to press Schneider about the Sunday Vietnam special, for which Schneider gave his approval. However, when Manning broached the subject of the Kennan testimony, he was rebuffed. Manning ended the conversation with Schneider by saying that the final decision could be left open until air time, when the hearings could be carried on the network by the touch of a button.

Friendly and his staff held out the hope that Paley or Stanton might overrule Schneider at the last moment. Friendly later described a chaotic scene in his office that morning. His CBS monitor carried reruns of *I Love Lucy*, *The Andy Griffith Show*, and *The Real McCoys*, while the NBC monitor showed Kennan making his opening statement and his interrogation by Senators Fulbright and Wayne Morse. A management consultant was present by appointment to interview Friendly about the distribution of CBS filmed reports to foreign broadcasters. News staff members came in to voice their dismay that CBS was not broadcasting the hearing. Friendly called Schneider, and the two men had a testy conversation. Friendly lauded the hearings and complained that CBS had missed the boat but offered the possibility of a thirty-minute or hour-long edited special that night. Schneider said he had been too busy to watch the hearings but would call back with a decision on the rebroadcast that night. Friendly felt that the Kennan episode represented a dangerous precedent for denying the news department freedom to seize the initiative on major stories.[27] In the words of Gordon Manning, it was a turning point: "Take a stand here, otherwise we are going to be constantly denied air." More than three decades later, Manning recalled Friendly's confidence about the ultimate outcome: "Fred took [Bill] Leonard and me aside and said, 'I can win this battle. They will come to one of you and offer you my job. I want your word that you won't take it. That you'll stick with me and we will win this because we have public opinion on our side.'" Friendly was agitated and passionate but did not exhibit the histrionics of previous news crises. At this point, Manning believed, Friendly thought that he would regain his prerogatives as news president and that his separation from CBS was unimaginable: "Fred was an exuberant, positive-minded guy. He always believed that he was an indispensable man."[28]

13 Resignation

FRED FRIENDLY ENTERED Bill Paley's office at noon on Thursday, February 10, 1966, fearful that the reorganization of CBS might weaken his authority as news president. Friendly began the meeting by expressing pleasure that Paley would remain as chairman beyond his sixty-fifth birthday. As he said it, Friendly later recalled, "it occurred to me that I sounded like all organization men talking to all chairmen of the board. But I meant every word." He then reminded Paley of his promise that as news president Friendly would always have direct access to him and Frank Stanton. Paley countered that organizations like CBS and their chains of command inevitably change. Friendly said he had no objection to reporting to Jack Schneider on budgetary and other administrative matters but argued that the new group vice president did not have the competency to make news judgments. Friendly offered as an illustration Schneider's decision to overrule continuing live coverage of the Senate hearings on Vietnam—Kennan was testifying as they spoke. (And Kennan was making news: the man who had helped shape Truman's containment doctrine was challenging Dean Rusk's testimony that the United States was countering Russian expansion by fighting in Vietnam.) Paley sought to reassure Friendly: Schneider, new on the job, would undoubtedly rely heavily on Friendly's experience and judgment.[1]

Friendly asked for a mechanism for the final appeal of a news decision, suggesting that the Tuesday news meetings might continue to serve such a purpose. Paley, now committed to remaining chair beyond his sixty-fifth birthday but wishing to withdraw more from day-to-day responsibilities, was reluctant to continue the Tuesday sessions. According to the CBS historian Gary Paul Gates, Paley and Stanton had grown increasingly irritated with Friendly's constant complaints, demands, and requests for meetings: "In the early weeks of 1966, Paley and Stanton saw their chance to give themselves a little insulation, and they took it."[2] Schneider would serve as a useful buffer. Friendly told Paley that without some recourse to top management, he would consider resigning. Paley expressed the hope that Friendly would not quit, especially in light of his accomplishments during the previous two years. The meeting ended inconclusively, as Paley urged Friendly to meet with Stanton and try to work out an acceptable arrangement. But to permit negotiations to go forward, Paley cautioned Friendly to hold his tongue—"Whatever you do, don't talk about it"—advice the emotional and garrulous Friendly would have difficulty following.[3]

Following his meeting with Bill Paley on February 10, Friendly stopped by Stanton's office, but he was out to lunch. By the time Stanton tried to call him back, Friendly was en route to Washington, D.C., to attend the White House Radio-Television Correspondents Association dinner. Friendly called Stanton from Washington to make an appointment to see him the next morning, promising not to discuss publicly his dispute with Jack Schneider. At a reception after the dinner hosted by the CBS Washington Bureau, Friendly received a call from E. Kidder Meade, a CBS corporate publicist, informing him of rumors in the press that Friendly would resign and join NBC. Friendly received a second call from Ben Kubasik, his publicist in the news department, who read him an article by Jack Gould in the early edition of the next day's *New York Times* headlined "Schneider and Friendly Split on Vietnam-Hearing Telecasts." Schneider reportedly said that relatively few viewers would have watched the live broadcast of Kennan's daytime testimony and that it was more important to extract hard news from the hearings for the evening news. Schneider went a step further in an interview with the *New York Post*, suggesting that unedited live coverage of the hearings could confuse rather than clarify the issues. He denied that advertising revenue—about $175,000 was lost when regular daytime programming was preempted—was a factor in his decision not to broadcast the hearings live.[4]

In his report in the *Times*, Gould described a network in disarray, with rumors of Friendly's resignation and unconfirmed reports of efforts at conciliation. Gould, who had met Friendly for lunch earlier in the week, wrote that Friendly had remained incommunicado throughout the day. Gould noted Friendly's position, that full live coverage of the Senate hearings represented an opportunity to add substance to the national debate about the Vietnam War.[5] As Friendly listened to Ben Kubasik read the *Times* article, he was angered that Schneider had spoken to the press about their dispute—a point he made when he met with Stanton at 10:30 A.M. on Friday. "We talked for the better part of two hours," Friendly said of his meeting that Friday with Stanton, "and got nowhere." Stanton told Friendly that Schneider's decisions, whether right or wrong, had been made in good faith and that Friendly and Schneider should try to find a working arrangement acceptable to them both. Stanton suggested that no decisions be made until after the weekend.[6]

Friendly then went to lunch at Patsy's Restaurant to talk things over with his three chief lieutenants: Gordon Manning, Bill Leonard, and Herb Mitgang. Friendly's appointment book shows that after the luncheon, at 3:00 P.M., he and Kubasik met in Friendly's office with Gould, followed at 5:30 P.M. by Les Brown of *Variety*. Friendly, no longer incommunicado, was making his case to the two most important television critics in the nation. It appears that Friendly had not made a final decision to resign, although he had drafted a letter of resignation earlier in the week. But by the end of the day he was pessimistic about his prospects for remaining at CBS. At 7:30 P.M., he met his close friend Robert Bernstein, the head of Random House, for dinner at the Ground Floor, the restaurant off the lobby of Black Rock. Bernstein recalled feeling during dinner that Friendly—who seemed spent, calm but sad—had all but given up hope of remaining at CBS. They walked back to Friendly's office on West Fifty-seventh Street, where Friendly started to remove some memorabilia from the wall. Bernstein remembered wondering whether Friendly was on the verge of resigning or being fired, a question Bernstein never resolved in his own mind: "I remember very clearly wondering, did he go or was he pushed? And I never really knew."[7]

During the weekend, Friendly's mood shifted and he became more hopeful about the possibility of a negotiated settlement. Saturday's *New York Times* ran a story under the headline "Stanton Said to Be Hopeful on Schneider–Friendly Issue." Three vice presidents and several press officers in other divisions of CBS called Friendly at home—perhaps at the behest of Stanton—to express sympathy with his position but to discourage him from rocking the boat at a time of corporate reorganization. The news division, Friendly felt, was in his corner. Heads of two affiliates called, one in support, the other in opposition to continued broadcast of the hearings. Friends inside and outside CBS weighed in as well. Les Brown, *Variety*'s television critic, recalled distinctly that amid the frenzied telephone calls, Friendly felt that he might yet prevail: "Fred was very hopeful that they would not accept his resignation and that they would work things out." Ben Kubasik called Friendly periodically from Brown's home in Larchmont to see whether his boss had heard from Stanton. Brown surmised that Friendly did not believe that Stanton and Paley would accept his resignation. Friendly displayed confidence that the crisis would be resolved in his favor, although Manning allowed that his boss may not have confided all his thinking and maneuvering to his subordinates.[8]

On the morning of Monday, February 14, Friendly held a news department staff meeting attended by Stanton, who praised a Vietnam debate and Maxwell Taylor's appearance on *Face the Nation* that had aired on Sunday. Friendly was further encouraged at midday by what he felt was a sympathetic hearing he received when he spoke with John Reynolds, Schneider's successor as network president, about carrying live the testimony of Maxwell Taylor and Dean Rusk at the end of the week. According to Friendly, he met alone with Stanton at 4:45 P.M. and hoped that he would receive approval for the Taylor and Rusk broadcasts as well as a modified reporting arrangement involving access to Stanton and Paley. Friendly described his disappointment in the far-ranging discussion, which ended without a resolution of his principal concerns. He remembered criticizing Stanton and Paley for relinquishing their responsibility to make news policy and for relying on efficiency experts to restructure CBS. Friendly asserted that CBS News would be judged by how it covered Vietnam. He seemed to couch his position with Stanton's relationship to Johnson in mind: "I happen to believe that the President has little choice but the one he is pursuing. But I am convinced that one of the reasons there is such uneasiness about the war is that the debate has been so bottled up. These hearings and our Sunday shows give us a chance to ventilate the struggle. It might even prevent the war from escalating any further and give the President ammunition against his critics."[9]

Stanton conceded little. Friendly would have to deal directly with Reynolds and Schneider on the question of continued live broadcasts of the Senate hearings and of future requests for preempting regular programming. The corporate restructuring was a given; perhaps some form of the Tuesday executive news meetings could be reinstated. Friendly complained: "If I keep compromising over important matters, I won't be Fred Friendly at all—I'll be a flabby mutation." Stanton laughed but cautioned that Friendly was painting himself into a corner. Stanton offered to arrange a meeting with Schneider. In case an agreement could not be reached, Stanton read a draft announcement of Friendly's departure, which was attributed to CBS's reorganization. Friendly asked that the dispute about the Vietnam hearings be added and then read a paragraph from his own draft letter of resignation. Stanton agreed that, after speaking with Schneider, Stanton would meet with Friendly the next day.[10]

Accounts by Friendly and Stanton of their meeting on Tuesday diverge in critical respects. According to Friendly, he went to Stanton's office at 12:30 P.M. assuming that they would have their usual Tuesday lunch, but Stanton seemed distant and said he had another engagement. When Friendly noted that he had not yet heard from Schneider, Stanton repeated that Friendly had painted himself into a corner, and Stanton said he saw no way out. According to Friendly, a CBS press officer was waiting outside Stanton's office with an announcement of Friendly's resignation. Friendly then handed Stanton a copy of his letter of resignation. Although he had written the letter, Friendly seemed unprepared for this turn of events at his final meeting with Stanton: "I said that I was sorry to leave and that I thought they were making a mistake. My last words were: 'Someday you may ask me back.'"[11]

Friendly wrote that he was resigning because of the failure of CBS News to broadcast George Kennan's testimony—a business decision had overridden the unanimous recommendation of the news department. He lamented the decline of the news department as a quasi-autonomous entity responsible directly to the chair and president of CBS. He decried the ultimate authority of Jack Schneider despite his limited news credentials. Friendly continued: "My departure is a matter of conscience. At the end of the day it is the viewer and the listener who have the biggest stake in all this. Perhaps my action will be understood by them. I know it will be understood by my colleagues in news and I know Ed Murrow would have understood." Friendly quoted Murrow's 1958 speech before the Radio-Television News Directors Association and expressed the hope that "my leaving will help insure the integrity and independence of the news operation." He noted John F. Kennedy's claim in *Profiles in Courage* that individuals often leave their ultimate mark through great unrealized undertakings. Friendly ended the letter by bidding farewell after sixteen years to CBS's great news department and to the network's two chief officers, Bill Paley and Frank Stanton.[12]

Around 2:00 P.M., Friendly spoke by telephone with Bill Paley, who was in Nassau. Paley was livid that Friendly had quoted Murrow's speech: "You had no right to do that," Paley said. "He is dead."[13] Paley accused Friendly of breaking his word to not go public about the controversy.

Friendly replied that he had made the promise before Jack Schneider spoke to the press. In retrospect, Friendly thought it a mistake to have made the promise and also regretted failing to inform Paley of his resignation letter before its release. Friendly remembered that Paley ended their conversation by suggesting that Friendly's own behavior had ultimately precluded a negotiated settlement.[14] It must have been a crushing conversation for Friendly, who had great respect for Paley.

"It came as a surprise," Bill Small said, describing his initial reaction to the resignation. "I thought he was dumb to quit. . . . I didn't think it was an issue worth quitting over, and I and many others would have loved for Fred to have stayed." As word of Friendly's departure spread within the Broadcast Center, top CBS news executives—David Klinger, Bill Leonard, Gordon Manning, Herb Mitgang, Ralph Paskman, Lee Hanna, and Bob Chandler—issued a telegram deploring the loss of Friendly and imploring CBS management to find a means for him to resume his leadership of the news department. News producers circulated a petition in the same spirit. The sixteen signatories included many members of the *See It Now* and *CBS Reports* old guard, among them Palmer Williams, David Buksbaum, Joe Wershba, Gene DePoris, Jay McMullen, Bill McClure, and Arthur Barron. The appeals had symbolic value but no practical impact. Indeed, as one reporter wrote, "Friendly's exit closes the Edward R. Murrow era at CBS."[15]

The next day, Wednesday, February 16, the *New York Times* printed the full text of Friendly's letter. The headline on Jack Gould's front-page story read: "Friendly Quits C.B.S. News Post in Dispute over Vietnam Hearing." The report noted that Schneider's authority, as much as Schneider's decision, precipitated the crisis. A *Times* editorial entitled "Vietnam vs. Lucy" concluded, "Mr. Friendly will be missed, and the circumstances of his resignation speak ill for C.B.S.'s sense of news responsibility." Friendly received sympathetic coverage in the national press and broadcasting trade publications. The columnists Ted Lewis in the *New York Daily News* and Harriet Van Horne in the *New York World-Telegram and Sun* speculated that Lyndon Johnson, in collusion with Frank Stanton, might have had a hand in the controversy within CBS about broadcasting the Vietnam hearings. Les Brown reported Friendly's resignation as a reflection of the central dilemma of U.S. broadcasting, the conflict between its commercial nature and its public service obligations. Brown wrote that CBS had "put Mammon before its obligation to humanity."[16] As news president, Friendly ultimately faced a conflict between company loyalty and his own conscience. Mindful of the impact of the Army–Mc-Carthy Hearings, he believed that televised coverage of the Senate hearings on Vietnam could provide a platform to resolve policy dilemmas and reunite the nation.

As a result of the cumulative effect of Friendly's eloquent letter, favorable press coverage, and the account in his memoir, Friendly's resignation has assumed mythic proportions in the annals of U.S. broadcasting history. An alternative version of the final sequence of events—the meetings with Frank Stanton on February 14 and 15—did not surface until decades later, after the tight-lipped Stanton had retired. According to Friendly's account, on Monday, February 14, he had an inconclusive meeting with Stanton and on Tuesday, February 15, to his surprise, was told that his resignation would be accepted. Stanton's version of the final deliberations—communicated to his subordinates, several authors, and an oral history project—is sharply at odds with Friendly's account in one critical respect. According to Stanton, Friendly was forced to resign in the course of negotiations with CBS when Stanton learned that Friendly had given the press a resignation letter in anticipation of the possibility of his quitting. Friendly then reportedly offered, in vain, to withdraw the letter from circulation.

This additional information, based on interviews with Stanton and others, was contained in Sally Bedell Smith's biography of William Paley, published in 1990. Smith noted that despite giving a detailed account of the resignation in *Due to Circumstances Beyond Our Control . . .* , Friendly "skirts his premature release of the resignation letter, an action that WSP [Paley], FS [Stanton], and EKM [chief CBS publicist E. Kidder Meade] all vividly recall as a decisive factor in FWF's [Friendly's] departure." In 1997 Corydon B. Dunham, a communications attorney, further detailed Stanton's version in a book based on interviews with the former CBS president. According to this account, Winnie Williams, Stanton's secretary, interrupted his meeting with Friendly on February 14 to tell him that Jack Gould was in the outer office and urgently needed to talk to him. "And I said to Fred, 'What the hell does Jack Gould know? Does he know that you are having this conversation?' 'No, no, nothing about it,'" Friendly replied.[17] When Stanton went out to see Gould, the *New York Times* television critic showed him a copy of Friendly's draft letter of resignation. Stanton recalled:

I went back in and I said to Fred, "Jack's got your letter of resignation. You told me nobody knew about this." "Well," [Friendly] said, "I was just talking with Jack about it." That was a terrible day. That was about 11:30 and just before I was going to lunch I got a call from his lawyer. . . . He came over and said to me, "Fred is sorry for what he has done. He understands he can't behave this way," and so forth. And I said, "No way I'll take him back in that position." And he said, "Fred can handle Jack Gould, he can get the letter back," and I said, "I know Gould is too good a journalist to ever let a thing like that happen."[18]

The memoirs of Richard Salant, published posthumously in 1999, echo Stanton's version of the encounter, including the last-ditch attempt of Friendly's attorney, Ed Fogel, to revive negotiations about a reporting arrangement that would permit Friendly to remain at CBS. Salant concluded: "Fred, I am sure, did not really want to resign—as he later wrote; he loved the job. But the letter was out; it was too late—the point of no return had passed." Near the end of his life, Stanton gave two lengthy interviews for the Archive of American Television, a history project sponsored by the Academy of Television Arts and Sciences Foundation. In the course of the interview on May 22, 2000, Stanton reviewed the final meeting with Friendly on Monday, February 14. After describing his secretary's interruption of the meeting to say Jack Gould had appeared in the outer office and Stanton's brief conversation with Gould, Stanton said: "We had agreed on Friday afternoon that we, neither of us, would talk to anybody. I wasn't gonna talk to Paley or Schneider or anybody, it was just that we were freezing the conversation and picking it up on Monday. I went back in the office and I said, 'Fred, that was Gould, he's got your letter.' 'Oh,' he said, 'that doesn't mean anything.' He said that was just tentative in case I did it, I wanted him to have a copy. I said you can't play that game and we parted company."[19]

Friendly most likely gave Gould the resignation letter when they met in Friendly's office at 3:00 P.M. on the Friday preceding his final meeting with Stanton on Monday. By Friday evening, as Friendly indicated to Robert Bernstein, he held out little hope for remaining at CBS. However, during the weekend Friendly's mood seemed to change, as he allowed himself to hope that he might reach an understanding with Stanton. Perhaps he thought that the resignation letter he gave to Gould would be moot if a deal were struck by Monday. It is unlikely that Friendly gave the letter to Gould on an off-the-record basis with an understanding that it could only be used if and when he announced his resignation. The *Times* critic died in 1993; his son strongly doubted that he would have "burned Friendly" by betraying a confidentiality agreement. Moreover, Friendly never subsequently exhibited any animus toward Gould; to the contrary, he nominated Gould for a Pulitzer Prize in 1969 and called him "the conscience of the industry" upon Gould's retirement in 1972.[20] It is therefore inconceivable that Gould would have betrayed Friendly's trust. The question remains why Friendly did not specify the conditions under which Gould could reveal the existence of the letter to Stanton and to the public.

Friendly's secretary, Hazel Layton, recorded and circled "FWF Resigned" in his appointment book under the entry for his scheduled 1:00 P.M. appointment with Stanton on Tuesday, February 15. If the alternative scenario is to be believed, Friendly—after threatening to resign—was forced to step down in the course of negotiations with CBS management, after attempting to withdraw his prematurely distributed letter of resignation. While Friendly's account made no mention of Gould's appearance at Stanton's office, it did quote Paley's closing remark during their subsequent telephone conversation, an oblique acknowledgment of Friendly's early release of the letter: " 'Well, if you hadn't put out that letter, maybe we could still have done something.' I answered that my letter was 'after the fact, long after.' "[21] However, Friendly's story line blurred the timing and importance of the letter's release.

More than two decades later, Les Brown of *Variety* expressed regret at reporting Friendly's version at face value. In particular, Brown faulted himself for focusing primarily on the issue of the Vietnam War: "He wanted all of us who were writing about this to represent it as his having resigned on a matter of principle, not as his having resigned because he didn't want to report to Schneider—and the Kennan hearing was just an excuse. So I must say that Gould wrote about it that way and so did I." Brown speculated that Friendly made the two appointments with Gould and Brown on the afternoon of Friday, February 11, in the hope of getting favorable press that would put pressure on Stanton and Paley to back down or, failing that, to put a positive spin on his resignation:

> The thing about Fred—I certainly learned it from that episode—is that he was a very good journalist with very high standards, and only bent the truth when he bent the truth for himself. He could actually be dishonest and manipulative, which he was in this case. So everybody let it play that, dammit, he was a martyr, and he left because

they wouldn't let him put on the Kennan hearings, and CBS played *I Love Lucy* instead, and everybody liked that, that he had the moxie to have done that, which made him quite a hero.[22]

Brown eventually left *Variety* to become television correspondent of the *New York Times* from 1973 to 1980, after which he launched two media magazines and wrote seven books. In 2000, the lanky and soft-spoken writer, a youthful seventy-two, revisited his coverage of Friendly's resignation. He expressed uncertainty about why he joined the Friendly bandwagon instead of engaging in more rounded reporting, calling the episode "one of the bits of reporting at that time in my life that I really regret."[23] Brown was at a loss to explain his lapse in journalistic standards, whether he succumbed to Friendly's persuasiveness that Friday or to his antipathy for Stanton. Brown's discomfort at withholding from Friendly his knowledge of the Booz Allen and Hamilton report may have come into play: "I don't know, I can't even tell you, we sort of liked the idea that he was a champion, a guy going out on a matter of principle. And also I would have had to disclose my source."[24]

Friendly's resignation had reverberations for the careers of other associates who, like Brown, continued to harbor strong and in some cases unresolved feelings about the event. One such figure was Gordon Manning. Retired and a widower living in an old farmhouse in Connecticut in 2000, he recalled how during negotiations Friendly had exacted a promise from his two news vice presidents to reject any offer to replace him as news president. Following the resignation, Manning in fact did turn down such an offer from Jack Schneider, citing his fidelity to Friendly. Schneider, who concluded that Manning lacked an institutional loyalty to CBS and could not be trusted, was instrumental in the eventual firing of Manning from CBS. During the struggle about the Vietnam hearings, Manning believed that Friendly, while maneuvering to salvage as much autonomy as news president as possible, genuinely thought he could negotiate a modus vivendi that would permit him to remain at CBS. Manning wondered whether Friendly's naiveté led to unrealistic hopes that the negotiations could succeed and suggested yet another level of intrigue: "Maybe, Fred never realized what a villain Stanton was. That there was a plot to get rid of him . . . that was fueled by Salant, who was ambitious to get back and prove that he was fired unjustly." Yet Manning was also aware that he might not have had full knowledge of Friendly's intentions and dealings: "Of course, he didn't confide everything in Leonard and me;

there may have been other voices, other rooms." Manning emphasized that "Fred was a mystery man. He worked many sides of the street."[25]

Jack Schneider never forgave Friendly for casting him as the heavy in the conflict that ended in Friendly's resignation. Up until his collision with Friendly, Schneider, who was thirty-nine in 1966, had been something of a CBS management wunderkind, working his way up as general manager at WCAU-TV in Philadelphia and WCBS-TV in New York. In the latter capacity, Schneider first clashed with Friendly—about coverage of the election results in November 1964. Friendly resisted Schneider's argument for regular five-minute cutaways every half hour so that affiliates could report on local races. As Schneider recalled, Friendly seemed concerned almost exclusively about the presidential election and suggested that a senatorial contest should be given attention only if it had national political implications: "He couldn't be bothered about the presumption that there was some yahoo in Albuquerque who didn't have Fred's vision of what was important. Didn't have Fred's priorities. Didn't have those megastars who brought rare and special insight into things. They were just those affiliates."[26]

As Gary Paul Gates observes, Schneider was more sympathetic to the news division than Jim Aubrey had been but handled the controversy about the Vietnam hearings disastrously. Schneider made a gaffe in arguing that the daytime audience of housewives, whose sons were serving in Vietnam, had little interest in the war. "Why were NBC's housewives interested?" Friendly asked in his letter of resignation. Moreover, Schneider's claim that advertising revenue was not a consideration in the decision to carry reruns instead of Kennan's testimony was transparently false. Friendly portrayed Schneider as a philistine, a bean counter with little understanding of public affairs, ill equipped to preempt the role of Paley and Stanton in making major news decisions. According to Gates, the true cause of Friendly's distress was the reorganization of CBS, not the appointment of Schneider, who served as a "convenient villain."[27]

In 2000, the seventy-three-year-old Schneider, sitting in the Indian Harbor Yacht Club in Greenwich, Connecticut, reflected on his conflict with Friendly. In 1966, Jack Gould had predicted that Friendly's resignation "may dog the rest of [Schneider's] days in the media." "I did not find it disabling," countered Schneider, who remained a top executive with CBS until 1978 and then served as president of Warner Amex Entertainment from 1979 to 1984. Schneider remained convinced that it made more sense for CBS to distill and interpret Kennan's testimony in its news reports than to broadcast the Senate hearings live. He kept in his possession several personal letters from CBS news staff in 1966 supporting the position he took. He continued to resent the notion that Friendly represented "a priesthood and the rest of us were money changers in the temple." "Well, that was a long time ago," Schneider said, "and you can tell I am still mad." Schneider especially resented how Friendly's version resonated in the press and subsequently in broadcasting history. Schneider accused Friendly of taking cheap shots and distorting the record in his attacks on him, although at the time Schneider elected to remain quiet and avoid what he termed a "pissing contest" that would have prolonged the controversy.[28]

According to Schneider, the fight about Kennan's testimony represented a maneuver on Friendly's part to establish a measure of autonomy from the new group president, but Friendly overplayed his hand, especially with the premature release of his resignation letter, which sealed his fate. "We weren't trying to throw Fred out," Schneider insisted, "we were trying to get Fred under control." The clash involved temperament as much as policy. Schneider, a highly organized and disciplined executive, expressed repulsion at Friendly's theatrics, going so far as to say that "he had to be dealt with as a cripple; he was not a whole person":

> Fred led, as far as I can tell, a kind of fantasy life about how important he was to the life of the United States. How important he was to everything he touched, how it was always a very important mission, the end of the world as we know it today. He was very dramatic. Everything about him was melodramatic. I think you will find that reflected in recollections of other people. But it was high, not just high drama, it was high melodrama . . . you had a picture of Fred always perspiring, and waving his arms, and, God, it was just awful, wonderful, awful and wonderful, nothing in between.[29]

After 1966, Schneider would always resent how Friendly had subjected him to a public row, as well as how Friendly continued to identify himself professionally with CBS as Murrow's partner and the network's former news president. Schneider went for the jugular in 1974 when he printed and sent his nemesis a batch of business cards that read, "Fred W. Friendly, Former President, CBS News."[30]

Stanton remained unwilling to talk to a biographer of Fred Friendly. In a 1996 letter, Stanton, then eighty-eight, initially agreed to talk about

Friendly. However, he soon had second thoughts, citing the sale of his residence of forty years and the overwhelming task of discarding the papers, books, and personal effects accumulated over a lifetime. Approached in 1999 before a luncheon at which he received a career award from the Deadline Club, the New York City chapter of the Society of Professional Journalists, he again declined an interview, stating tersely, "Fred Friendly and I did not get along." In response to a final appeal for an interview through an intermediary, Stanton said that he reserved the right to take certain memories to the grave.[31] He died in 2007.

If Friendly's departure from CBS created turmoil for his associates, it marked for him a momentous turning point. Countervailing impulses impelled Friendly to remain at CBS and to quit; they explain his shifting moods and seemingly contradictory behavior in the days leading up to his resignation. CBS, to be sure, had a strong hold on Friendly. It was the setting for his collaboration with Edward R. Murrow, the most important figure in his life. It was the venue for the legendary broadcasts of *See It Now*, *CBS Reports*, and the groundbreaking programming on Vietnam. At the Providence dinner honoring Mowry Lowe in 1965, Friendly had made clear that he relished the job of news president at CBS. The same year, he told Bill Moyers that a move from CBS to the White House would have been a step down. Moreover, Friendly took pride in the significant progress in the fortunes of CBS News under his leadership. On one level, his departure from CBS must have been virtually unthinkable for him.

Yet developments at CBS forced him to reconsider his sixteen-year relationship with the network. As a precondition of accepting the position of news president, Friendly insisted that he report directly to Frank Stanton and Bill Paley. He was not driven by conceit but by an impulse to go to the top, a core instinct, his approach to his work as a journalist and executive. In addition, Friendly was aware that the reorganization of CBS might put his position as news president at risk. According to Les Brown, the removal of Robert Kintner as operating head of NBC at the end of 1965 had seemed to spark a premonition: "Friendly recalled that such men as Ed Klauber, Paul White and Edward R. Murrow, all of whom had made an indelible mark on broadcast news, were also in one way or another ticketed out of positions of influence while they seemingly were still in their prime." Moreover, Friendly had gotten wind that the Booz Allen report had been highly critical of his administrative skills. Years later, Friendly would advise a public television executive, "If you think you are going to be fired, quit first."[32]

A sense that Friendly had already compromised too much at CBS also weighed on him. He questioned whether he had fought hard enough in 1959 to make Murrow—then at odds with Stanton and Paley—a full partner of his at *CBS Reports*, when Friendly negotiated to become its executive director. Soon thereafter, Friendly agonized whether his opposition to the departure of Howard K. Smith had been sufficient. Friendly also regretted not insisting in 1964 on keeping Walter Cronkite as anchor of the Democratic National Convention. In addition, in 1965 an ailing Murrow had chastised Friendly as news president for CBS's failure to take a closer and more skeptical look at the incidents prompting the Gulf of Tonkin Resolution. The memory of Murrow, who died less than a year before the controversy about Kennan's Senate testimony, may have troubled Friendly's conscience and inspired his actions.

Thus a host of opposing factors and feelings pulled at Friendly in February 1966 as he struggled to determine his future at CBS. He was an extrovert, someone who exploded rather than imploded, who tended to follow his instincts rather than to be self-reflective. Hence it was especially hard for him to consciously sort out all the factors, to carefully weigh his thinking and course of action. This explains the shifts in his moods—for example, his feeling at the end of the day, on Friday, February 11, that all was lost, followed by his renewed hope during the weekend that he and CBS management could come to terms. His inner turmoil may also explain Friendly's apparent lapse in failing to exact an agreement with Gould that the existence of his letter not be divulged until his decision to resign was final. (Or did Friendly hope that Stanton would learn of the letter's existence and become more accommodating in their negotiations?) Nearly a year after the resignation, on January 10, 1967, over lunch with Sig Mickelson, Friendly acknowledged his own confusion about his departure from CBS. Mickelson, who had first hired Friendly at CBS, had worked as the network's first news president until 1961, when Dick Salant replaced him. In late 1999, four months before his death, Mickelson remembered thinking during that 1967 luncheon, at which he and Friendly discussed the end of their respective tenures as news president: "[Fred] doesn't know whether they put him into a position where they assumed he'd retire or whether they actually fired him." Mickelson vividly recalled Friendly's uncertainty about whether, in the final analysis, he quit or was terminated.[33]

On Wednesday evening, February 16, 1966, the day after Friendly resigned, a reporter found Friendly sitting at home with a six-inch stack of telegrams of support and a copy of John F. Kennedy's *Profiles in Courage*, which twelve-year-old Lisa Friendly had given her father the night before. Friendly expressed a jumble of thoughts and feelings. "I don't want to be a hero—really," he said but also declaimed, "Do you know it cost me about a half million dollars to resign?" He again attributed the refusal to broadcast Kennan's testimony to a shortsighted concern about lost revenue. Friendly recalled how he had responded once to Jim Aubrey, then president of CBS television, who was protesting that all he wanted to do was save money. Friendly replied that all *he* wanted to do was save the conscience of the company. Now Friendly wondered whether his irrevocable breach with CBS had been necessary: "All I wish right now is that I could turn the clock back a week. Maybe I wasn't forceful enough."[34]

By Friday, when Jimmy Breslin of the *New York Herald Tribune* visited Friendly's Riverdale home, Friendly exhibited a greater degree of acceptance of his separation from CBS. That morning, dressed in a brown sports jacket and a blue shirt open at the collar, he sat comfortably in a leather chair before a television set tuned to CBS on the second floor of his home. As a step in damage control after Friendly's resignation, the network had reinstated live coverage of the Senate hearings on Thursday and Friday. Friendly excitedly watched Senator Wayne Morse question General Maxwell D. Taylor and accuse the Johnson administration of misleading the public. According to Friendly, this moved the Vietnam debate to a proper venue: "Now we have it, and now we won't hear so much about draft card burners or a lot of people going out in the streets, exhibitionists. Now the debate is in the hands of responsible people on television, where the country can watch and this is where it belonged from the start."[35] Friendly could not contain himself: he called out for the "tele-ops" identifying various figures at the hearings, as if he were in the CBS control room. A smaller television was tuned to ABC, which was not carrying the hearings.

As he watched the proceedings, Friendly kept punching the four buttons on his telephone at his feet and talking to well-wishers. Admiral Lewis Strauss called and asked about Friendly's plans: "No, I don't know. What am I doing? I'm watching the Senate hearings on my alma mater. You ought to watch. They're fascinating." When a technician called to shut down the CBS tie line, Friendly expressed relief that one of his children had not answered the call. Nonetheless, he did not express bitter-

ness toward Paley and Stanton but, surprisingly, a rationale for their behavior: "They want everything for television that I want. Believe me they
do. But they're caught in a system. Some day, 10 years from now, 50 percent of television will be news. Right now it isn't. Somebody had to do
what I did." When the morning session of the hearings ended, Friendly
went downstairs for a sandwich, a scotch and soda, and a walk. Asked if
he was glad he resigned, he quietly replied, "Of course not."[36]

Friendly received a wide range of letters of support—from notables,
colleagues, and personal friends. One of the first came from Dwight
Eisenhower, who had coincidentally telephoned Friendly on Tuesday, February 15, during Friendly's final meeting with Stanton when the breach
became irrevocable. "When we were talking on the phone this morning,"
Eisenhower wrote from Indio, California, "I was so shocked by the news
of your resignation that I fear I failed entirely to make you understand
how truly distressed I am." Eisenhower suggested that the turn of events
might cause him to rethink his special relationship with CBS:

> I have been partial to CBS because of my friendship with Bill Paley
> and later with Frank Stanton. Then, when I came to know, and work
> with, you and Walter Cronkite my partiality became truly pro-
> nounced. For a long time you have known that I found my associa-
> tion with you and Walter to be particularly pleasant; so much so that
> I almost lost all interest in any working arrangements with another.
> Now I have to review my own situation. But this is nothing com-
> pared to my feeling of regret that you felt it necessary to resign from
> CBS. . . . I will be deeply interested in whatever move you now
> make.

Eisenhower also expressed the hope "that one of these days we can get together in a renewal of the personal contacts that have meant much to me."[37]

In his reply, Friendly joked that he was writing as one former president to another. He strongly encouraged Eisenhower to maintain his
allegiance to Paley and Stanton—"both honorable men, broadcast
statesmen"—and to remain inside the CBS tent. Friendly confided that
he could not imagine working for a competing network. Noting that he
had long-standing plans to take a family vacation out west in the spring,
Friendly expressed interest in meeting with Eisenhower during the trip
"to see you and perhaps seek your advice on future plans."[38] Eisenhower

replied that he would welcome such a meeting. "I cannot help from feeling," he added, "that your separation from the two men that you admire so much, Bill Paley and Frank Stanton, is nothing less than a personal tragedy."[39]

Friendly also received a letter from Eisenhower's former vice president, Richard Nixon, who wrote of how much he had enjoyed working with Friendly on CBS broadcasts: "You were always unfailingly thoughtful and considerate and I valued the wise counsel you gave me on several occasions. Whatever your future association may be I hope we will have the opportunity to work together again."[40]

Friendly received many letters from colleagues within and outside CBS. For example, Bill McClure, the veteran camera operator, wrote from the CBS London Bureau that the Murrow–Friendly era at CBS already seemed prehistoric. He included a clipping of an editorial from the *Times* of London, noting that "the 'play' has been in the direction you intended." Another member of the old Murrow team, Av Westin, described the new climate at CBS News: "The excitement has gone completely these days and worse, the fun has gone with it. The 'killer instinct' is difficult to maintain. . . . We're inundated with a sea of memoranda with copies to everyone." Westin added an afterthought: "If you ever plan to light some fires, I'd like to hold the matches for you." A distraught note calling Friendly "a casualty of the war in Vietnam" came from a young member of the CBS news department. "You and Murrow," he wrote, "were the reasons I came into this field and choose to remain in it." John Dunn, managing editor of NBC's *Today* program, wrote: "To give up a job at the summit must have been a tremendously difficult decision to make, but to us in the trade it was not unexpected from a man who had the courage to tackle Joe McCarthy at the peak of his power." Tom Wicker, Washington correspondent for the *New York Times*, sent Friendly a handwritten letter. "I am most disturbed," he wrote, "that for the time being at least this takes such a vital force . . . as yours out of television news. We can't afford that kind of loss and I really hope that you will live again to fight another day. We need you in this bloody business of ours." The comedian Godfrey Cambridge also weighed in with what he called an unabashed fan letter: "In an industry where to quote George Jean Nathan, 'testicles tinkle' it is refreshing to hear a loud clang every once in a while." Friendly received so many letters that his responses often contained a stock reply: "I happen to believe that with the possible exception of Vietnam, television is more important than any story we cover. The fact that both issues were joined . . . gave me no course of action other than the one I chose."[41] A succession of letters also came from childhood friends and associates in Providence, including his mother's landlady and the widow of Joel Pincus.[42]

Friendly's tenure as news president, beginning with his unexpected appointment and ending with his dramatic departure, lasted two brief but eventful years. His colleagues at CBS were sharply divided in their assessment of his performance as head of the news department. Gordon Manning remembered the excitement of that period: "I mean, we were winning. We brought that news division back and we took Huntley and Brinkley's measure. . . . It was challenging." Roger Mudd, who made great strides at CBS under Friendly's tutelage, felt similarly: "Generally speaking, his leadership, as I look back on it, was exciting, inspiring at times, turbulent, volcanic on occasions."[43]

Yet other colleagues, both friend and foe, felt that Friendly had made a fatal mistake in becoming a news executive. Ernie Leiser was not especially fond of Friendly and had opted to leave the post of assistant general manager of CBS News to become Walter Cronkite's executive producer, in part to remove himself from Friendly's direct purview. At the same time, Leiser had great respect for Friendly's gifts as the executive producer of *See It Now* and *CBS Reports*. But he felt that Friendly was out of his element as news president, that his volatility and histrionics rendered him ineffective as a manager. Recalling Friendly's remark that NBC's scoop of the Alaska earthquake story was his Bay of Pigs, Leiser countered, "His Bay of Pigs was the day he took over as president of CBS News from Salant." Joe Wershba, Friendly's colleague from *See It Now* and a good friend, similarly took exception to Friendly's assertion that removing Cronkite from covering the Democratic National Convention in 1964 had been his biggest mistake: "Wrong, Fred. Your worst decision was to accept Bill Paley's offer of President of CBS News, which Murrow warned you against. Your strength was when you were in an adversarial relation to management. Once you became a top executive, you were one of 'them.' You had to trim your sails. You had to conform to company interests." Friendly later reflected, "I thought I'd have all the power that Ed had. Ed didn't think so. He said, 'Don't take it. They'll cut off your balls.' He was right."[44]

Yet, as Bill Moyers asked, how could anyone in broadcast news, and especially Friendly, have turned down the opportunity to be president of CBS News in the mid-1960s? Bill Leonard, Friendly's former deputy, mused:

> It may be true that by temperament Friendly was not destined to stay at CBS News much longer anyway. If it had not been that blowup, then surely, one could imagine, it would have been another. Indeed it took all the reasoned calm of Dick Salant to guide CBS News through the troubled waters of Watergate, of "Hunger in America," of "The Selling of the Pentagon." Even so, if Fred's future did not lie in CBS News, I was—and still am—sorry that an editor and producer of such extraordinary talent wasn't working somewhere at the core of the business, in the thick of the action during the sixties and seventies.[45]

Before he resigned from CBS, Friendly had intended to join his family for a vacation in California in March after a visit to the CBS bureau in Vietnam. He decided to take his family out west as planned, meeting en route with Eisenhower to discuss career options. Then the family traveled to San Francisco, where Fred's cousin Carolene threw a party for him that he thoroughly enjoyed. The final leg of the tour was Los Angeles. Friendly booked an overnight train for the trip; he wanted his children to experience the excitement he felt as a child when he took sleeper trains across the country with his mother to visit her family on the West Coast. Dorothy Friendly recalled that at the time of the trip Fred did not seem depressed—at least on the surface—but upbeat and energized.[46] While in Los Angeles, Friendly took his family to Disneyland. Then Friendly, together with his family, returned to New York to begin a new life.

For the second time, a trip to California marked an interregnum in Fred Friendly's personal and professional life. In 1946, he had traveled to California with his bride-to-be in his quest to launch a career. He was then thirty-one and fresh out of the army. Twenty years later, the marriage was on hold. Dorothy had suffered from depression and undergone electroshock therapy not long before Fred was named CBS News president. She found the marriage difficult to sustain and began raising the possibility of separation. Fred opposed the idea out of a sense of responsibility to his fragile spouse, although some of his closest friends urged him to consider it. In the period of Fred's resignation from CBS and the family's trip to California, Dorothy recalled that she did not want to push the issue: "I wouldn't have left him at that point when he was in such a vulnerable position."[47] Would they remain married, or would Fred embark on a new personal and family life? As he returned from California, Friendly was at a professional crossroads as well. He was fifty-one and had seemingly reached the pinnacle of his profession at CBS. Would F. Scott Fitzgerald's adage, that there are no great second acts in American life, hold for Friendly? Could Friendly continue to be an innovator and player in television journalism?

14 Policy Maker

FOLLOWING HIS RESIGNATION from CBS, Friendly carefully weighed—indeed, plotted—his next career move. Press speculation included a report that he might be hired by ABC to expand the weakest of the three network news divisions. Friendly, however, told the *New York Times* that although he had received calls from "high places" (which he did not identify), he was keeping his options open. He added that it was unlikely that he would join another network, because he did not want to compete with the CBS News department he had helped build. During his trip to the West Coast in March, it was reported that he had received offers from NBC, the BBC, a dozen major television stations, and an unidentified person who wanted to finance a series of documentary programs.[1] But Friendly wanted to top, not simply replicate, his past positions and accomplishments.

On April 6, 1966, seven weeks after his resignation, came the announcement of an unusual dual appointment: television adviser to the Ford Foundation and professor of journalism at Columbia University. The two positions were linked. In addition to hiring Friendly, the Ford Foundation was funding a new chair at Columbia, the Edward R. Murrow Professorship in Journalism, so that it could be filled by the former president of CBS News. Friendly could draw on a powerful circle of contacts in charting his future professional course. While out west he had met with Dwight Eisenhower, who still wielded influence at Columbia as a former president of the university. And Friendly's relationships with McGeorge Bundy and Walter Lippmann were instrumental in his employment at the Ford Foundation. Immediately following his resignation, Friendly had received a telephone call from Bundy at the White House. Bundy said he would be leaving the Johnson administration to become president of the Ford Foundation and wanted to meet with Friendly.

Bundy told Friendly that he had gotten his telephone number from Lipp-mann, who "planted the seed that you might have some ideas about non-commercial television."[2]

The television industry had assumed that Friendly would find another position in broadcasting, not in teaching and public policy. Friendly explained to the press that he had decided he could have a greater impact on the outside. As a result, he was prepared to forgo a high salary; he said that the pay for the two new jobs would not approach the $125,000 he had earned as president of CBS News. He expressed a desire to instill in journalism students the values of Edward R. Murrow. In addition, he emphasized that the satellite was at the center of a revolution in media technology and that in the coming years someone would have to write an "electronic magna carta" for the future of communications. Asked whether this meant he had produced his last documentary, Friendly replied, "I wouldn't say that. Let's wait and see."[3]

The Ford Foundation, soon to move, was still located at 477 Madison, just down the street from CBS's old offices at 485 Madison Avenue. Friendly brought with him his devoted secretary, Hazel Layton, and Ben Kubasik, who had been his publicist at CBS News. Friendly's intention to assert his authority immediately became apparent to James Armsey, Friendly's old colleague from the information section of China-Burma-India theater, who had been administering Ford's grants to educational television for the past decade. When Friendly first came by his office, Armsey moved from behind his desk so the two men could speak more informally in chairs in front of the desk. During the conversation, Friendly got up, paced, and gesticulated as he spoke and then sat down behind the desk—a clear indication to Armsey that he would now be Friendly's subordinate. In their dealings at the foundation, Armsey would refer to Friendly as "Fred," while Friendly addressed Armsey as "major" rather than "Jim." Armsey had held the rank of major in the CBI, superior to Friendly's grade as master sergeant. Armsey felt that Friendly was saying, in effect, "Look, you were a major and I was a sergeant, but I was a hell of a lot more important than you were, and I'm a hell of a lot more important *here* than you are." Armsey soon went to McGeorge Bundy to tell him that after ten years of working on educational television, he was ready to move on to other projects. Many educational broadcasters were pleased that a man of Friendly's stature would be devoting his considerable energies and ambition to the cause of noncommercial television. But as the veteran educational broadcaster James Day recalled,

"His appointment . . . sent a shudder through the system: Ford's money and Friendly's style . . . were an awesome, and to some a fearsome, combination."[4]

While he was beginning two new jobs, Friendly undertook a third task: writing a book that would chronicle his years at CBS and his agenda for the future of television. After his resignation from CBS, he mentioned to Jimmy Breslin that he was considering writing a memoir. Breslin shipped him a wooden box with 150 reams of paper.[5] Friendly wrote the manuscript at breakneck speed, completing it in eight months. In March 1967, *Life* magazine carried two installments of the book, *Due to Circumstances Beyond Our Control . . .*, which was published by Random House. The volume contains, at once, a reflective memoir of Friendly's experiences at CBS, a history of the birth of the television documentary, a discussion of television coverage of the Vietnam War, a critique of network television, and a prescription for the medium's future. The first part is devoted to his collaboration with Murrow and the glory days of *See It Now*. Entire chapters devoted to the "The Case of Milo Radulovich, A0589839" and "A Report on Senator Joseph R. McCarthy" provide background and details for *See It Now*'s historic confrontation with McCarthyism. The chapters "The Strange Death of *See It Now*" and "The Strange Birth of *CBS Reports*" follow, providing an account of Murrow's conflict with CBS management and Friendly's emergence as sole producer of *CBS Reports*. Friendly reviews his tenure as executive producer of *CBS Reports* and as president of CBS News and offers an account of his resignation from the network.

On the basis of his experience at CBS during a sixteen-year period, he advances a broad critique—one of the earliest and most trenchant—of commercial broadcasting in the chapter "Common Stock vs. the Commonweal." It contains a historical analysis of the evolution of commercial sponsorship, from tentative beginnings to a dominating role. Friendly also examines the history of government regulation, making a convincing case for the inadequacy of the Communications Act of 1934—and the Federal Communications Commission it established—to protect the public interest in the use of the airwaves. He reviews the development of a network and affiliate system that prized short-term profitability over innovative and controversial programming. He also laments how the growing cross-fertilization of Hollywood and the networks threatened to render television a medium of entertainment and escapism. Yet the broadcast industry hypocritically used the First Amendment as a shield to protect its monopoly and profits. For Friendly, the system he describes is beyond repair "due to circumstances beyond our control," a play on the words that appeared on television screens in television's early days when programming was interrupted by technical problems. Attempts at change from within the system were futile. Instead, Friendly ends by calling for sweeping federal legislation to reverse broadcasting's trajectory—"a Magna Carta of broadcasting"—enabling television to fulfill its potential as a public resource.[6] Friendly concluded that a new noncommercial television system—which McGeorge Bundy had brought him to the Ford Foundation to develop—represented the hope of the future.

Friendly criticizes the commercial broadcasting system but not its top officers. He portrays William Paley and Frank Stanton more as victims than villains, their best intentions stymied by the economic structure of network television: "Paley and Stanton looked on while programs proliferated which assaulted their sense of taste, and even decency; they seemed incapable of stopping the inexorable flight from quality." In addition to absolving Paley and Stanton from responsibility for CBS's shortcomings, he treats them with great deference. This is especially true when Friendly writes about Stanton, Murrow's nemesis. For example, Friendly characterizes Stanton's speech at Ohio State University in 1958— an exercise in damage control, following Murrow's address to the Radio-Television News Directors Association—as "perhaps the most eloquent of his career." Friendly assumes a position of neutrality in the bitter Stanton–Murrow rivalry, implying that the conflict was largely personal in nature. Friendly writes, for example, that when Stanton infuriated Murrow by linking the practices of the quiz show scandals to the preparations for *Person to Person*, Murrow's response "was as excessive as Stanton's." Friendly also writes that "I don't believe that there was any determined plot on the part of Bill Paley to whittle Murrow's influence and independence." When Paley criticized "The Berkeley Rebels" program and told Friendly that his job was to keep CBS News holy, Friendly describes it as "the most inspiring sentence the chairman of the board ever said to me."[7]

Critics commended Friendly for taking the high road, for emphasizing the structural issues plaguing the broadcast industry rather than the behavior of individual executives. Yet the accolades Friendly bestowed on CBS's chief executives had a cloying quality. Would Friendly have written about the Stanton–Murrow conflict in such neutral terms had Murrow, who had died a year and a half earlier, still been alive? Friendly's final words to Stanton had been "Someday you may ask me back"; only six months had elapsed when Friendly completed his manuscript.[8] The flattery of Stanton and Paley may have derived from a mix of genuine sentiment and a calculated attempt to avoid burning his bridges to CBS.

Friendly's memoir can be viewed as an apology—in the classical sense of a formal explanation or justification—for his resignation from CBS. His career at the network, from the great achievements with Murrow to the ascendancy of the money changers over the news department, served as a prologue for his dramatic departure. The epilogue pointed to public television's potential to overcome the restraints that had led him to quit CBS. Friendly's book was widely reviewed and praised. The historian Eric Goldman described the volume as "tartly analytical, astute, passionate and disturbing. No one can read it without a sharply heightened sense of the tragedy of American television." Walter Goodman, one of the few to express reservations, wrote in the *New York Times* of "smudges of self-congratulation peeping mischievously through the cosmetic modesty." If *Due to Circumstances Beyond Our Control . . .* provided an epitaph for an era of commercial television, it also set the stage for Friendly's next great project: public television. When the book was published, Friendly sent inscribed copies to a host of notables, among them, high government officials, prominent figures in broadcasting, and opinion leaders.[9] He kept a supply of signed copies in his office in the Ford Foundation and would freely dispense them to visitors. *Due to Circumstances Beyond Our Control . . .* was a public relations tour de force. As a critic wrote in the *Saturday Review*, "If this is a feat of showmanship, he *is*, after all, a showman."[10]

Friendly's memoir looked ahead as well as back. Its final chapter contains a bold plan for the future of noncommercial television that Friendly was advancing at the Ford Foundation. Friendly's entry into the affairs of what was then called educational television occurred at a time when National Educational Television (NET) was a poorly funded, marginal hundred-odd station association with a tape duplication and distribution system based in Ann Arbor, Michigan. NET could not afford to rent the telephone lines that could provide the interconnection that would make it a true network. Instead, NET "bicycled" programs, sending copies through the mail to NET stations to be broadcast on an irregular basis. NET lacked outlets in key cities like New York, Los Angeles, and Washington, D.C. Friendly was among the first to conceptualize the possibility of "educational television" as an expanded national system of "public television." It entailed a vision of an innovative fourth network for the quality programming in the arts and public affairs that CBS, NBC, and ABC were incapable of providing in a sustained fashion. Soon after his separation from CBS, Friendly developed a comprehensive program for addressing noncommercial television's lack of funding, programming, and interconnection.

Friendly's first assignment at the Ford Foundation was to read a series of papers on the future of educational television commissioned from figures like Edward R. Murrow, Newton Minow, and Irving Gitlin. Friendly immediately realized that none of the submissions addressed the critical question of the source of funding that would make a fourth network viable. At their first dinner meeting in New York City following their respective departures from the White House and CBS, Bundy told Friendly that he wanted to complete Ford's investment in educational television by establishing a permanent, self-perpetuating infrastructure for a fourth network, securing its financial independence and an exit strategy for the foundation. Shortly thereafter, Friendly began toying with an idea for a permanent source of funding for noncommercial television. In the spring of 1966 he began considering the possibility that synchronous satellites might provide the magic potion for the fourth network.

Friendly had pioneered in the application of communications satellite technology to broadcasting from the outset. In 1962, he had produced the inaugural demonstration broadcast of *Telstar*. As president of CBS News in 1965, he was one of several broadcast executives who met in London to establish the protocols and rates for use of the *Early Bird* satellite. The costs of the first communications satellites were prohibitive. But Friendly was quick to grasp that the growing use of synchronous communications satellites would result in substantial savings for broadcasters and transform the communications landscape. The new generation of satellites, held by gravity in fixed positions in synchronous orbit 22,300 miles above the earth, promised to supplant the patchwork of telephone lines and microwave relay stations used by the broadcast networks. The satellite system, once established, would provide a higher quality interconnection at a fraction of the cost. Friendly also realized that the synchronous satellite system would have a synergistic impact on the future development of other new communications technologies, especially cable television, which was still in its infancy. His idea was that a nonprofit entity would administer the satellite system and that a relatively small portion of the immense savings and profits generated by satellites for commercial interests should be set aside to constitute a permanent source of funding for noncommercial television, the fourth network. Friendly wrote that 1966 marked the year "when satellites promise to change television as much as television altered radio." It was a critical moment, because the FCC was soliciting proposals, and Congress was planning hearings, on the establishment of a domestic communications satellite system. James Day says of Friendly's idea of using emerging satellite technology to both fund and interconnect a new public broadcasting system: "It was a brilliant leap of the imagination, a concept worthy of one of television's most creative minds."[11]

When Friendly first approached Bundy with the idea, Bundy asked whether the satellite proposal was technically feasible. Friendly, about leave for a West Coast vacation with his family, volunteered to meet in California with Harold Rosen, a physicist employed by Hughes Aircraft who had been instrumental in the development of synchronous satellites. Friendly met with Rosen, who came to New York two weeks later to meet with Bundy. After the meeting, Bundy committed himself to organizing a major foundation effort to develop a response to the FCC's call for proposals on ownership and governance of the next generation of satellites. Bundy and Friendly organized a crash program to prepare a position paper by the FCC's deadline of Monday, August 1. In doing so, Bundy used his extensive contacts in academia and government to recruit high-powered experts to examine the legal, economic, and scientific implications of the proposal. Preparation for the FCC submission, undertaken in secrecy, reached a frenzy in July. "In the thirty days prior to our submission," Friendly recalled, "the eleventh floor of the Ford Foundation looked more like a newsroom just before election than a philanthropic institution." Participants experienced a strong esprit de corps. Executives and secretaries worked through the final weekend. Ben Kubasik worked the press on behalf of the proposal, priming editors for a major announcement. Bundy directed the effort.[12] But the idea had Friendly's imprint; and in introducing and nurturing it he was, for a moment, transforming the normally staid Ford Foundation into something more akin to a *See It Now* production working on deadline.

At 10:30 A.M. on August 1, the eighty-page Ford Foundation proposal was submitted, with a cover letter from Bundy, to the FCC in Washington, D.C. The plan recommended that a nonprofit corporation operate the satellite system, leasing lines to commercial channels and realizing a profit that would fund educational television. In addition, the satellite would provide free interconnection to noncommercial stations. The Ford Foundation linked the development of a satellite system and a noncommercial television network as national goals. In his cover letter, Bundy characterized the financial support to be afforded noncommercial television as "a people's dividend, earned by the American nation from its enormous investment in space." At 11:00 A.M., a half hour after the proposal was submitted to the FCC, Bundy addressed a crowded press conference at the Ford Foundation's headquarters in New York; Friendly stood at the back of the room. As a historian of communication satellites notes, "The satellite plan was greeted with attention rarely paid to briefs filed in obscure regulatory proceedings." Bundy and Friendly quickly followed up by reaching out to Congress. First Friendly and then Bundy briefed Senator John O. Pastore of Rhode Island, who chaired the Subcommittee on Communications of the Senate Commerce Committee. Pastore would refer to the Ford proposal as a bombshell and convened hearings on August 10 on space communications and the Ford Foundation proposal.[13]

On August 17, Bundy and Friendly testified before televised hearings of Pastore's subcommittee. After a short opening statement Bundy turned to Friendly, asking him to elaborate on the rationale and logistics of the proposal. Friendly began with a reference to Edward R. Murrow's speech in 1958 before the RTNDA. When Pastore asked him to read his prepared statement, Friendly said he preferred to ad lib. "All right," the senator replied. "You are one of the best ad libbers I know." Friendly repeated his oft-stated contention that the commercial television system short-changed the public. It denied the American people vital information at a time when "what they don't know can kill them," a phrase he would use time and again. "Not only what they don't know about Southeast Asia," he continued, or "solid fuels or liquid fuel or great urban sprawls in Harlem and Watts and even in Johannesburg, but it denies them a kind of yeast and cultivation of their own intellect, which comes from an open window. And television, like radio, is an open window." Drawing on his experience at CBS, he described the technological and financial constraints of the current system of interconnection by telephone lines and what he described as a bucket brigade of microwave relay stations. Shifting metaphors, he said that satellites could transform television from a capillary system of communications into a "mighty jugular vein." For Friendly and Bundy, the satellite proposal would make it possible for public television to foster the informed citizenry that Walter Lippmann believed was a pre-requisite for a modern democracy. In his prepared statement, Friendly emphasized that the dawn of the age of communications satellites pre-sented an opportunity that must be seized now or lost forever: "America must weigh this last best chance for a noncommercial television system that can run on its own solar engine, while at the same time benefiting its commercial partners."[14]

In his testimony, Bundy made clear Friendly's importance in conceiv-ing and articulating the significance of the satellite plan. Senator Hugh Scott of Pennsylvania commended Friendly for being "an emotional man" with a sense of mission. Countervailing forces opposed to the Ford plan were also at work, as subsequent testimony at the hearings made clear. They ranged from telecommunication giants like AT&T, ITT, and Western Union to the networks, whose objections were voiced by Frank Stanton. Friendly wrote after the hearings, "I am rash enough to believe that some satellite system benefiting noncommercial television is going to emerge in the coming months."[15] But the FCC and Congress, suc-cumbing to pressure from vested commercial interests, let the Ford pro-posal die.

Friendly had promoted the satellite proposal with his characteristic élan. Despite the plan's ultimate failure, Friendly had helped raise public awareness about the development of domestic communications satellites. At the same time, he had placed on the national agenda the key issues of funding and interconnection for the soon-to-be-established public broad-casting system. The Ford plan also got Friendly's relationship with Mc-George Bundy off to a strong start, confirming the foundation president's belief that he had picked the right man to be his television adviser.

Bundy and Friendly were a study in contrasts. Bundy was a product of Groton, Yale, and Harvard. As a Harvard dean, he had compiled a mixed record in addressing the threat posed by McCarthyism to academic free-dom during the period Friendly produced See It Now.[16] In his capacity as national security adviser to presidents Kennedy and Johnson, Bundy was one of the architects of U.S. policy in Vietnam; Friendly had produced the television show in 1965 in which Bundy had defended the war against critics in academia. Bundy was known for a keen intellect and emotional control that shaped a coldly rational style of examining public policy is-sues. Friendly, a middle-class Jew, had barely been graduated from high school and a two-year business college. If Bundy was cool, Friendly was hot, a man capable of being overcome by extreme enthusiasm or fury. These two disparate figures became good friends and forged a professional relationship that would have a lasting impact on the nation's telecommunications landscape.

In 1967, early in Friendly's tenure at the Ford, the foundation moved into its own building at 320 East Forty-third Street. Inside its sleek modernist exterior was an enormous atrium eleven stories high, with a pathway past trees and bushes to a bubbling pond.[17] Glass offices overlooking the atrium were furnished with mahogany desks, parquet floors, and marble fixtures; wall decorations included Belgian linen and original lithographs by Miró and Picasso. The building was a monument to the world of the eastern Establishment, the universe that produced McGeorge Bundy, but Friendly would create a comfortable niche within its walls. McGeorge Bundy was given a mandate to break with the cautious leadership of his predecessor, Henry Heald, and to shake things up at the Ford Foundation. He was secure enough to appoint and delegate authority to a talented group of iconoclastic and innovative vice presidents. Bundy operated in turn like a Harvard dean, fostering the atmosphere of a seminar with a free give-and-take of ideas, and like a U.S. president, meeting with his cabinet to develop policy together with high-powered specialists. Stuart Sucherman, who later worked under Friendly at Ford, remembered the mix of patrician WASPs and the new blood brought in by Bundy, intent on using the foundation's clout to promote change in bold and innovative ways. "It was an incredible place to be for the seven years I was there, because there was no idea that was off limits. You could literally walk into Mac Bundy's office and say, 'I have this idea about X.'"[18]

Willard Hertz, a foundation staff member, said that hiring someone like Friendly would have been unthinkable in years past. "To me," Hertz said of the Bundy era, "it was a golden age of the Ford Foundation. Fred was very much a potent and brilliant and influential member of that group."[19] With his joint appointment at Columbia University, Friendly was barred from officially being named a vice president because he did not work full time at the foundation. For this reason, he received the title "adviser on television," later broadened to "adviser on communications." But his ability to hire his staff, his reports to the board of trustees, and his relationship with Bundy made him a de facto vice president. James Day writes of how his colleagues in noncommercial television viewed the Bundy–Friendly relationship:

Few among us understood the symbiosis that drew them together, unless perhaps it fulfilled their mutual needs. Bundy drew heavily for counsel on Friendly's street smarts, not only about television but about other Ford initiatives as well, partly out of respect for Friendly's skills at selling an idea and infecting everyone within earshot with his own contagious enthusiasm. Friendly, for his part, probably found in Bundy a substitute for the departed Murrow and a link with the Establishment—someone who gave his presence respectability and status in those quarters where the self-made Friendly felt most uncomfortable.[20]

Sucherman remembered the banter of an affectionate relationship: "Mac kidding Fred about his outrageous ideas. . . . Fred kidding Mac about 'oh, you wouldn't understand this kind of thing where you come from.'" A visitor passing the president's office might see Friendly talking with his feet on Bundy's desk. Bundy relished Friendly's creativity and spontaneity, even his outlandishness, which might have offended the sensibilities of foundation old-timers. A social relationship developed, in which Friendly would invite Bundy and his wife to dinners and family gatherings in Riverdale. On these occasions. Bundy felt comfortable enough to have some stiff drinks and unwind. Hertz emphasized how "Bundy loved him so much, and I use the term 'loved' advisedly." Sucherman agreed: "I really think they loved each other."[21]

Bundy relied on Friendly's expertise as a result of his professional record, referring to "his unsurpassed experience as a broadcast professional" before one congressional committee and as a statesman in his field before another.[22] At the same time. Bundy understood—as did others before him—that he needed to differentiate the good from the bad in the constant flow of ideas generated by Friendly. Hertz, who as assistant secretary from 1973 to 1979 took minutes at board meetings, observed: "If Fred went a little bit too far, then Bundy would say, 'Aw, Fred, you don't really mean that, do you?' Or, 'Fred, we'll take a little more time for that maybe,' or, 'let's talk about that later.' But Fred got his way sooner or later at just about everything he wanted to do."[23]

From Sucherman's perspective "it was pretty much equal. Fred would push Mac, Mac would push back. It was not a 'roll over' kind of thing. And Fred pretty much got what he wanted to get." Friendly worked the foundation board in unconventional, sometimes brazen, ways, establishing a personal license not shared by others. Once, in response to yet another request for funding for public broadcasting, Henry Ford asked Friendly if he saw any light at the end of the tunnel. Friendly replied, "I see light there, Henry, but you know, at the end of the tunnel it could be New Jersey, and you don't want me to stop in New Jersey, do you?" Bundy and the board roared with laughter. Hertz got the impression that Friendly "often prepared his statements very well—even his wisecracks and jokes—ahead of time. He was well prepared in this sense for board meetings. I had the very distinct feeling that he gave the impression quite often of shooting from the hip, but he really wasn't. It was carefully rehearsed."[24]

A big test came when Friendly, along with the de jure vice presidents, had to present his annual budget request to the board. Friendly had a difficult time preparing these submissions. Hertz, assigned to assist Friendly, said of him, "He had no sense at all for figures, for statistics, for how much money he wanted, how much money he had."[25] The presentation would take place in the imposing boardroom on the lower level. Bundy and the board chair sat in the middle of an elongated table; directly across from them was the hot seat for vice presidents. Board members were arrayed around the table, and staff aides sat in the "bleachers," the second row of chairs along the wall. Friendly usually followed the budget proposals of the international division, whose presentation was supplemented by charts, slides, and detailed written reports that filled the gargantuan table in the boardroom. "So, picture him sitting at this table," his aide Stuart Sucherman said:

No slides, only a single piece of paper with some notes written in that strange scrawl of his. Then he would begin. He would expound: thirty minutes of pure persuasion, gesticulating, roaring, pounding the table so hard that those of us in the back of the room could feel the room shake. None of it quite made any sense, but it sounded good. When he stopped, there would be this stunned silence, with a few mouths agape. Then some poor soul like Bob McNamara or Andy Brimmer would attempt to ask a very tough, penetrating question, and Fred would say, "That's a good question," and he would be off again for another ten minutes of rhetorical flourish that never quite answered the question but, again, sounded good. After a couple of these, the board, emotionally exhausted, would simply give up and approve our budget of sixty million bucks.[26]

To be sure, Bundy had made the Ford Foundation a less formal and stuffy place. Yet Friendly's approach to being its television adviser, whether calculated or not, was still over the top. It was a pattern in his life—in the army, at CBS, and now at the foundation—to challenge the institutional culture in which he worked to advance his role and agenda.

The Friendly–Bundy plan for public broadcasting had a competitor, the Carnegie Commission on Educational Television, which issued its report, *Public Television: A Program for Action*, in January 1967. Nominally an independent body established by the Carnegie Corporation of New York, the commission had close ties to the Johnson administration.[27] The establishment of the Carnegie Commission represented an end-run around the old guard of educational broadcasting—NET and its patron, the Ford Foundation—based in New York. The Carnegie initiative was essentially a Cambridge/Boston operation in its personnel and geographical center of operations. The idea for what became the Carnegie Commission had first been proposed by Ralph Lowell, who had been instrumental in the establishment of WGBH-FM and WGBH-TV in Boston. The Carnegie Commission was chaired by James R. Killian Jr., the chair of MIT's corporation. Killian was a prominent representative of the Cambridge–Washington axis of intellectuals who moved back and forth between MIT and Harvard and the federal government. The Carnegie Commission prompted mixed feelings on the part the Ford Foundation. Bundy and Friendly welcomed a report that promised to lead to a permanent source of funding and infrastructure for public broadcasting. Such an outcome would mark a crowning achievement for Ford's investment in noncommercial television and the end to the foundation's burdensome role as primary funder. At the same time, the blueprint for the future system was being drawn largely outside the purview of the historic leadership of noncommercial broadcasting at Ford and NET, whose influence on the final report was limited to testimony delivered during a Carnegie Commission visit to New York.

Two fundamental differences separated the Carnegie and Ford approaches. The first involved plans for the structure of the public television system. Friendly favored an authentic fourth network with a strong national reach in public affairs programming. The members of the Carnegie Commission envisaged a more decentralized member organization. Friendly argued that "the price of autonomy need not be the emasculation of a live NET network at birth. Crucial issues such as Vietnam, space and national politics require a national news organization with depth of personnel and facilities—and ability to get on the air: *nationally and immediately.*"²⁸ The second difference concerned funding. Friendly feared that direct government funding would foster undue caution, political pressure, and even censorship. Hence he and Bundy had advanced the satellite plan as a source of funding without recourse to either governmental appropriation or a special tax, thereby insulating the system from political pressure. The report of the Carnegie Commission recommended an excise tax on the sale of televisions to fund public broadcasting, a variation on the method by which the BBC was financed in the United Kingdom.

To Friendly's chagrin, the Johnson administration seemed prepared to settle for congressional appropriations as the means for funding the proposed Corporation for Public Broadcasting. Friendly's concern was reflected in "The State of Television," a speech he gave on April 5, on the eve of his and Bundy's scheduled testimony before Congress on proposed legislation for public broadcasting. The occasion was a dinner in Friendly's honor at Brown University that was followed by a panel discussion. Panelists included Nicholas Johnson, an FCC commissioner; Richard K. Doan, a television critic for *TV Guide*; and Ralph Lowell, scion of the Boston Lowell family and head of the Lowell Institute, an educational foundation in Boston. WGBH-TV videotaped the entire program for broadcast in Boston and distribution by NET. It was another in a series of Friendly's triumphant returns to Providence, where he had grown up and gotten his start in broadcasting. In the course of his remarks, he caught the eye of Minnie Pincus, the widow of Joe Pincus. He interrupted the speech to relate how in 1937 her husband had gotten the Outlet Department Store to sponsor his series of five-minute biographies, *Footprints in the Sands of Time*. He noted how he had received $8 per episode and how his hands had shaken so violently at first that listeners could hear the sound of crackling paper on the air. Friendly clearly basked in the glory of his subsequent achievement. He proudly described, for example, looking for a cab in the *See It Now* days in the company of Edward R. Murrow, J. Robert Oppenheimer, and Carl Sandburg. He was trying to shield these celebrities from a curious onlooker, who finally came up to *him* and said, "Excuse me, but aren't you Fred Friendly?"²⁹

Friendly joked from the podium with Lowell about differences in their origins and institutional loyalties: "Mr. Bundy told me before I came up, 'Tell Ralph Lowell I'm his second cousin.' I think all you Presbyterians are each other's second cousins, Mr. Lowell, but I am sort of Mr. Bundy's third cousin by satellite shot-gun marriage, so we're related to each other, and I'm glad that the Friendlys and the Lowells are finally talking." Friendly then reiterated the case for the Ford satellite plan as the foundation for the interconnection and financing of public television, especially its news and public affairs programming. During the panel discussion, Doan expressed doubts about the interest of Americans in public television, and he asked Friendly's view on the argument that a decentralized system might provide the best means of political insulation for the new system. Friendly countered that public broadcasters needed to cultivate and reconstitute a national audience that had been corrupted by commercial appeals to the lowest common denominator. "I'm much more worried about Poor Brother than Big Brother," he added. He acknowledged the importance of strong local stations like WGBH in Boston and KQED in San Francisco. Nonetheless, he added, "I think we need a national network." Lacking a strong interconnection, he insisted, public broadcasting could not provide a meaningful journalistic and cultural alternative to commercial television. He described public television's potential as unlimited and called for a collaboration involving academia, major thinkers and artists, and talented broadcasters to forge a new form of television that would be a vital resource in the life of the nation. Friendly noted that the Ford Foundation had appropriated $10 million to create a live Sunday program for the 125 noncommercial stations that would serve as a demonstration project for television's unrealized potential as a social and cultural instrument.[30]

Friendly understood that Ford and Carnegie shared a concern for insulating funding from government influence, even if their preferred mechanisms for doing so—the satellite plan and the recommendation for an excise tax on the sale of televisions—differed. He viewed the Johnson administration's support for direct funding by Congress as a threat to the new system's independence, especially in regard to coverage of politics and international affairs. Friendly alluded to the Senate hearings on public television that would be broadcast the following week: "It will be one of the great debates of our time, for . . . television will determine what kind of people we are, and there is no story, Vietnam possibly excluded, more important than television itself." Friendly expressed his belief that television journalism in the space age could deliver news quickly enough to permit a greater degree of public consideration of issues as they unfold rather than after the fact. He reiterated his belief in television's potential as "the greatest teaching tool that's ever been handed down since Johannes Gutenberg and moveable type and the first printing press."[31]

In his testimony before the Senate Subcommittee on Communications a week later, on April 12, Friendly gave qualified support to the report of the Carnegie Commission and to the proposed Public Broadcasting Act. But he told the assembled senators that he wanted to sound an "early warning" about the danger of establishing a dedicated trust fund with annual federal appropriations: "Of one thing we can be certain: public television will rock the boat. There will be—there should be—times when every man in politics—including you—will wish that it had never been created. But public television should not have to stand the test of political popularity at any point in time. Its most precious right will be the right to rock the boat." Overwhelming reliance on government money would constitute a "license to fail." He reiterated the case for the satellite plan and consideration of other mechanisms for protected revenues. When pressed, he said he would support the bill as then drafted, with reliance on federal funding—in order to launch the system, and in the hope that there would be substantial modifications in the future. Friendly subsequently testified in a similar vein before a subcommittee of the House of Representatives, reiterating his vision of public television as an "electronic preserve" comparable to the federal park system and as "broadcasting's last best chance."[32]

Friendly's appearance on April 12 before the subcommittee was one of a series of high-profile interventions he made about the future of noncommercial broadcasting. After leaving CBS, Friendly had emerged as the most visible individual champion of an expanded public television system. In 1966, following the development of the Ford satellite plan, Friendly had secured funds from the Ford Foundation for an ambitious programming initiative to which he had alluded in his speech at Brown University. It would be called the *Public Broadcasting Laboratory* (*PBL*). The program was conceived as a cutting-edge public affairs and cultural magazine that would be carried live by noncommercial stations for three hours on Sunday evenings. For Friendly, the program would serve multiple purposes: to strengthen the noncommercial television network, provide a new programming model for realizing television's potential, and give impetus to efforts to create a new public television system.

Plans for *PBL*, and Friendly's role as public broadcasting's leading evangelist, prompted a lengthy cover story in the *New York Times Magazine* on April 23, 1967, less than two weeks after his Senate testimony. The author of the article, the writer Harvey Swados, noted Friendly's complexity and expressed great ambivalence about Friendly the man and "Friendlyvision," a term that had been used in *Variety* to characterize Friendly's agenda for television. Swados averred that the novelist in him was drawn to Friendly's extremes and contradictions as well as to a sense that he was an American original. Swados reviewed Friendly's entire career from military service through the CBS years and characterized Friendly as one of the era's great salesmen—of ideas and of himself. Interviews with former colleagues revealed sharply divided assessments. Some testified that working under Friendly was the high point of their career. Others spoke of his egotism and cruelties to subordinates. Friendly recounted castigating a subordinate and then reflecting that he must be getting soft because he did not make the person cry. Many people in the industry interviewed about Friendly expressed fear of being quoted by name. In speaking with Friendly, Swados was impressed by his willingness to concede his faults and by his considerable charm. "It's been said by one of your detractors," Swados began. "I have *detractors?*" Friendly interrupted, eyes widening in mock astonishment.[33]

Swados wrote that Friendly, an evangelist for elevating the political and cultural substance of television, was not a true intellectual and noted Friendly's reliance on clichés about "fire in the belly" and "what you don't know can kill you." An unnamed NBC executive conceded that the example of Friendly's programming achievements at CBS helped elevate standards at the other networks. "But," Swados added,

> this same executive has severe reservations about the frenzy, the razzle-dazzle, the fascination with Big Names, that in his view make Friendly both an example and a victim of the "Washington syndrome"— the seductive talk about the national purpose, the awe of the celebrity and the abject reliance on "the world's leading authority," the belief that The New York Times is the sole criterion not only for news but for intellectual significance. . . . [The executive added:] "Behind all the high-flown talk resides the kind of belligerent low-brow who is fascinated by technique and by the 'wisdom' symbolized by a handful of sages, and who knows nothing of an entire world of art and intellect."[34]

Friendly welcomed the article, despite the penetrating criticism that accompanied considerable praise. He expected an element of negativity as a function of long-standing skepticism about broadcast journalism on the part of the *New York Times*. At the same time, in the words of Tom Bettag, his graduate assistant at Columbia, "I think Fred loved the attention. . . . The first reaction was 'Look, we got big play in the *Times*, and that's important.' To a certain extent, his efforts were getting recognized, he had broken through. . . . The fact that the *Times* was paying attention was what he most cared about, not the slights that came with it."[35]

Swados had concluded that Friendly's contribution overshadowed his foibles, that even his intellectual shortcomings and personal excesses ended up serving the public interest. Although no intellectual, Swados wrote, Friendly was possessed by "the intellectual's desire to please himself above all as well as by the craftman's passion for perfection":

He has never lost that wide-eyed amazement about significant ideas and important people that is the common property of the very young and the very creative; and his most passionate desire is for the right use of a marvelous new medium. Despite failures, failings, and falterings, he is committed in his own way to . . . one of the essentials of democracy: informing the public. In the course of his career, he has already left his imprint upon our history, and he is now committing his ferocious energy to forcing open, and holding open, a door to the future.[36]

15 Professor

IN 1966, FRIENDLY ASSUMED the role of professor at Columbia University as well as policy maker at the Ford Foundation. He had an equally ambitious agenda at Columbia: to build a dynamic broadcast journalism program in a school with a historic emphasis on print. The hiring of a controversial figure lacking a bachelor's degree represented an unorthodox appointment at an Ivy League institution. The university administration hoped to shake up a stodgy program that it felt had not adjusted sufficiently to the age of electronic journalism. The dean of the Graduate School of Journalism, Edward W. Barrett, told university president Grayson L. Kirk, "This whole undertaking is a gamble, but I think we agree that it is a damned good gamble."[1] At the time, only Murrow's widow voiced an objection. According to a former Columbia journalism professor, Janet Murrow called Louis Cowan, the former CBS-TV president who was then director of special programs at the journalism school, urging that the faculty not approve Friendly's appointment. Janet had always found Friendly to be intrusive and overbearing in his relationship with her husband. After Murrow's death, she once told Dorothy Friendly how she resented Friendly's "trading in Ed's name."[2]

The tenured faculty of the School of Journalism approved Friendly's appointment, and Columbia's announcement described his duties as chairing the broadcast curriculum committee and developing a television workshop in addition to teaching. Columbia and Ford announced Friendly's joint appointments on April 6. It was reported that Friendly's combined salary would be $40,000; at CBS, he had received $75,000 as news president and $100,000 as executive director of *CBS Reports*. Acknowledging that he would be taking a pay cut, he told Richard K. Doan of the *New York Herald Tribune*, "There's nothing in the Constitution or the Bill of Rights that says Friendly has to make a lot of money *every year*."

Columbia had become something of a redoubt for former CBS hands. In addition to Louis Cowan, the former chief CBS European correspondent David Schoenbrun became a Carnegie Fellow at the journalism school. (In addition, William Paley was a university trustee.) But Friendly would clearly be given much greater latitude than Cowan and Schoenbrun to build a broadcast journalism program. Dean Barrett also encouraged Friendly to consider producing an occasional television program on the order of the interviews with Walter Lippmann. Friendly left the possibility open. However, he emphasized that his two new posts were not intended to provide a hiatus before a return to network television: "I expect to do this the rest of my life. This is no temporary thing. I think the two jobs together will give me a chance to do more for broadcasting on the outside than I could do on the inside."[3]

Friendly moved with characteristic speed. In his first semester, in addition to a Monday lecture and two Thursday seminars, he joined the broadcasting curriculum committee. At the same time, he began to develop plans for a public television laboratory at Columbia that would produce a weekly program for educational television. By the spring semester, he had assumed responsibility for eight masters' theses and a broadcasting practicum in which twenty students produced a weekly half-hour news program over a closed circuit. The students would be up until 3:00 A.M. the day before, editing actualities and interviews they had shot and writing accompanying copy. Friendly made notes and later assessed the contribution of each student. He told an observer, "I wish someone had told me about teaching before, it's such a fantastic experience."[4] He sparked an upgrade of the broadcasting laboratory on the sixth floor of the journalism building, which included donated equipment from CBS, completed during his second year. He hired new faculty for the broadcasting track like John M. Patterson, a veteran CBS radio reporter, and later John Schultz, who had edited "Harvest of Shame."

Friendly selected Martin Clancy as the first in a succession of talented teaching assistants he recruited from the pool of journalism school graduates. The use of these aides, critical to Friendly's teaching methods, would cause resentment among some of its faculty. Tom Bettag, his second-year assistant, a straight-laced Midwesterner who combined a keen intelligence with attention to detail, recalled how Friendly astutely picked assistants with attributes that complemented his own. Friendly's aides at Columbia, like those at the Ford Foundation, came to experience the alternately terrifying and rewarding experience of working under Friendly.

Stuart Sucherman, who worked under Friendly at Ford, said of Friendly's uncompromising demands:

> It made people extraordinarily nervous, almost physically sick some-
> times, it was so powerful. I was a relatively shy kid growing up and
> had never seen anything like it in all my life. Scary. In order to deal
> with it you had to sort of physically . . . be prepared for it. Like box-
> ing, you had to get ready for that first punch so it doesn't overwhelm
> you. Some people were petrified and would literally go out of their
> way not to have a meeting with him. Sometimes I would be delegated
> to go in and tell him bad news because I could handle it, but it took
> me a while.[5]

Once on the job, Bettag found Friendly to be a hard-driving but needy boss, grateful for the help his assistants gave him. Beneath the bluster was "a lot of underlying humility and insecurity." Sometimes Friendly would read his notes on a legal pad while fighting for words. Bettag was taken aback at first when Friendly would pound the pad and remonstrate, "What is it I want to say here? Come on. You know. Tell me what it is I'm trying to say." Despite Friendly's public bravado, Bettag recalled, "I think Fred was always conscious of what he didn't know and did not consider himself to be a well-educated man—he was a self-educated man—and was always questioning, 'Do I know what I'm doing?' And I think one of his hallmarks was surrounding himself with people whom he consid-ered to be smart." Once you became part of his team, Bettag added, "he trusted you, he relied on you, he believed in you, believed in you more than any reasonable person should. . . . I could do no wrong—except, of course, when I did. Fred would tear my head off."[6] Friendly the professor, like Friendly the producer at CBS, maximized his impact by surrounding himself with gifted assistants.

Friendly became a popular instructor. He illustrated his presentation of the principles of journalism with dramatic accounts of his own experi-ences at CBS. He relished the opportunity to perform before a large audi-ence of journalism students. Bettag, a student during the first year that Friendly taught at Columbia, recalled him as "absolutely inspirational." To supplement his classes, Friendly would invite journalism luminaries like Walter Cronkite and Mike Wallace to speak. Friendly's invitations crossed ideological boundaries and included William F. Buckley Jr. and even Roy Cohn. Friendly would preside over special election-night radio programming for which wire service copy would be fed into the broadcast laboratory, and students would work through the night—with Friendly present—as other students in the field called in reports. A postmortem took place the next day. According to John Schultz, "He was re-creating what he did at CBS election night. It was very exciting." David Kuhn, who took part in one such exercise, later told Friendly that "the Election Night exercise was one of your more ingenious ideas, for it created such demands on the students that they might just as well have been on the air. They certainly tried as hard. We were better than most local commercial stations, I now know—certainly we had more reporters in the field. I recall the excitement and triumph as our man in [George] Wallace headquarters reported by phone, and we cross faded into a network pickup of his concession. Hot stuff!"[7] The excitement generated by Friendly was such that a growing number of students who had come to the journalism school intending to focus on print switched to the broadcasting track.

Friendly nonetheless had an influence on students in the print track as well. Eileen McNamara remembered how he recoiled at the notion that any assignment was impossible, dismissed her complaints of the logistical obstacles to a thesis project that would take her out of state, and brought her to his home in Riverdale to lend her a family car. Friendly impressed upon her the importance of grappling with ethical issues: "Pacing, challenging, demanding, Friendly trained journalists as if democracy itself depended on the results of his work. To answer 'I don't know' to an ethical dilemma he posed in that room would bring his fist down on the seminar table. 'You need to know; you have to know,' he'd shout. When you leave here, there will be no time on deadline to ask what's right. You need to know it here.'" A quarter of a century later, Nc-Namara, a Nieman Fellow who would win a Pulitzer Prize at the *Boston Globe*, wrote that Friendly "did not give his students jobs. He gave us his conscience and pointed us toward the highway." According to Bettag, some students recoiled from Friendly and his histrionics. But the majority of students embraced his teaching. Av Westin, Friendly's former colleague at CBS, said of his relationship with students, "I know how tremendously they stimulate him. . . . Friendly is really getting turned on by those kids. I myself think that he can communicate with them more easily than he can with his own generation." Early in Friendly's tenure as a journalism professor, Dean Barrett wrote to Columbia president Kirk that their gamble appeared to be paying off: "Fred Friendly is proving to

be (1) a dynamic teacher and lecturer, (2) a strong advocate of broad liberal education, (3) a 'de-emphasizer' of techniques and hardware in relation to content."[8]

In the early 1970s, Friendly began team-teaching a seminar, "Journalism and the First Amendment," with Benno C. Schmidt Jr., then a young
law professor at Columbia Law School. Schmidt recalled first meeting
Friendly and being "immediately impressed and charmed by the ebul-
lient energy, the flow of great stories." It was the beginning of a long
professional relationship for Schmidt, who would later become president
of Yale University. The course scrutinized major First Amendment cases.
According to Schmidt, "Fred approached the class the way a great television producer would approach a documentary." Friendly would present
the original material that prompted the case, seize on its dramatic elements, and force the students to weigh competing claims and principles.
Whenever possible, Friendly would invite litigants and judges in the
cases being studied to appear in class. To Schmidt's amazement, few
seemed able to resist his invitation. To facilitate these encounters, Friendly
got funding from the Markle Foundation and the New York State Bar Association. Schmidt was struck by how Friendly questioned distinguished
guests in the same irreverent and provocative way that he challenged
students. This included his colloquies with judges accustomed to being
treated with great deference. Friendly got away with this in part by plead-
ing ignorance, by asking for an explanation for something he could not
understand. Moreover, his sense of humor was disarming. "Fred had the
ability to charm people even if he irritated them a lot," Schmidt observed.
"It was always understood that his heart was in the right place and was
just Fred being Fred."[9] The class—originally restricted to journalism
students, later opened to law students by popular demand—became the
journalism school's most sought-after seminar.

In addition to building the broadcasting track, Friendly launched the
Summer Program for Minority Journalists in the spring of 1968. The
initiative represented a response to the recommendations of the National
Advisory Commission on Civil Disorders, established by Lyndon Johnson
and chaired by Governor Otto Kerner of Illinois. A section of its landmark report criticized print and broadcast journalism for reinforcing racial divide in the United States by failing to report adequately on urban
disorders and on African American life in general. The report contained
a broad indictment of U.S. journalism's coverage of race relations and
hiring practices: "News organizations must employ enough Negroes in

positions of significant responsibility to establish an effective link to Negro actions and ideas and to meet legitimate employment expectations." It underscored the importance of broadcast journalism, noting that "television is the formal news source most relied upon in the ghetto." In April 1968, a month after the publication of the Kerner report, riots broke out in more than a hundred cities following the assassination of Martin Luther King Jr.

While shaving and ruminating one morning that April, Friendly decided to call off a planned trip to Europe during what promised to be a tense, hot summer in New York. "We could open the J School this summer," Friendly said, "—get competent minority applicants who can't make it into our graduate school through the usual route . . . maybe an eight-week program—the way the Army did it—those 90-day wonders it produced. We'll get grants, pay the students and get media organizations to hire them at the end of the course and bring minorities into the media and mainstream." The Ford Foundation provided a $122,000 seed grant for the pilot project for twenty students at Columbia that summer.[10] Using his extensive contacts in the television industry, Friendly got the networks and television stations to sponsor individual students, who were guaranteed jobs upon completion of the program. Participating stations helped underwrite expenses for continuing or prospective employees enrolled in the program. Students received room and board, expense accounts, and family allowances. The coalition of institutions that Friendly forged to support the program included the New York Urban Coalition and the Center for Urban Minority Affairs at Columbia in addition to CBS and NBC.

Participants used the new broadcasting laboratory that had been completed just in time for the first training program. Friendly appointed as administrator Richard Kwartler, a former deputy director of public affairs for the Human Resources Administration in New York, and hired a blue-ribbon faculty made up of broadcast professionals and journalism school instructors. Friendly arranged for celebrity guests like Walter Cronkite, as well as a wide range of writers and officials, to speak to students. The first summer, for example, Friendly invited John Hersey, who had just published *The Algiers Motel Incident*, an account of the police killing of three black youths and brutal beating of nine others at the time of the Detroit riots in 1967.[11]

The annual summer program continued into the mid-1970s, expanding to include a faculty of eighteen with thirty-five students. Geraldo Rivera, sponsored by WABC-TV in New York, belonged to the summer 1970 cohort. He later described the climate in which Friendly launched and directed the program: "The Upper West Side streets enclosing Columbia University were an exciting, revolutionary place to be in the summer of 1970. The campus was in a kind of shambles. The riots of two years earlier were over, but sheets emblazoned with antiwar slogans and minority demands still draped the campus's wrought-iron fences, and hung from dormitory windows. The air was thick with protest, reefer, Black Power, and free love." The flashy and ambitious Rivera was a Friendly favorite that summer. Rivera was romantically involved with another star student, Michelle Clark; she later worked for a short period at CBS News before she was killed in an airplane crash in 1972, after which the program was renamed in her memory. Years later, Rivera recalled his skepticism before Friendly's introductory talk to the group, Rivera's expectation of "another old white guy who's gonna tell me how lucky I was to get a chance to be just like him." Then Friendly appeared, "a big guy and not bad-looking, with that sharp tomahawk face of his and that posture that kind of reminded me of the Statue of Liberty." His remarks surprised Rivera:

> The "You should be grateful" or "You have the opportunity of a lifetime" speech never came. It was about the riots, and about the cities going up in flames. . . . It was about disconnection and discontent and about how he hoped and prayed, along with his partners here at Columbia and the Ford Foundation, that our class of minority novices might see something that the almost all-white corps of reporters had perhaps failed to see. What the hell was igniting all those fires, igniting all that rage?[12]

Program participants came from a wide range of backgrounds. Some were already working as journalists; others had neither reporting experience nor a college degree. The second-year summer class of 1969, for example, numbered thirty-six: twenty-five men and eleven women ranging in age from twenty-one to forty-one. The ethnic mix consisted of thirty-one African Americans, four Puerto Ricans, and one Mexican American. At the conclusion of the program, a former consultant to health organizations went to work at CBS, a former salesman got a job at the *Wall Street Journal*, and a former postal clerk was hired at the *Denver Post*. The group's graduation luncheon was held in the Crown Room at Columbia's John Jay Hall. The program provided invaluable training to journalists of color and continued to nurture successful careers.[13]

A year after he participated in the 1970 summer program, Geraldo Rivera received an award from the New York State Associated Press Broadcasters Association for a three-part series he did for WABC-TV in New York called *Drug Crisis in East Harlem*. A year later, he shocked the nation and won a Peabody Award for his exposé of conditions at the Willowbrook State School mental institution in New York City. Rivera credited the Columbia summer program for training him, adding that it was "a little too idealistic" in regard to broadcast journalism's potential to effect change, a cherished tenet of Friendly's. Another Latino, J. J. Gonzalez, who was a former associate of the Young Lords, became a reporter and an assignment editor at WCBS-TV in New York. The program launched new careers in print journalism as well, enabling Edgar Henry, for example, to go from being a food salesman to a financial reporter at the *Wall Street Journal* and allowing Laura Blackwell to leave a teaching career for a position as a reporter at *Newsday*.[14]

Many students valued highly Friendly's experience and counsel. Some viewed him with bemused skepticism. Subtle racial tensions and misunderstandings were perhaps inevitable. Al Donaldson, a member of the 1970 program along with Geraldo Rivera and Michelle Clark, recalled Friendly's volubility, "a line of palaver that could stretch from Morningside Heights to The Village and back—twice." Donaldson continued: "As one of the brothers said: 'Damn, Fred Friendly can sho nuff talk. He means well, but when I see his [sic] coming, I'm splitting for an assignment. I can't afford to blow a half-hour listening to his rap.'" Friendly would regale participants with stories about his collaboration with Edward R. Murrow and lecture them about journalism ethics. According to Donaldson, most participants tolerated Friendly's foibles since he was the linchpin that made the program possible. Donaldson learned a great deal during assignments that often took him to what he called New York's hell holes in locales like the South Bronx and Bedford-Stuyvesant. He felt that Friendly was much more interested in the broadcast students and merely tolerated those on the print track. At the end of the program, Friendly invited the entire class to his home in Riverdale for a farewell party:

We were all loaded into a bus and shuttled to his backyard, where he, for some unknown reason, decided to serve fried chicken and watermelon. Most of the students chalked this gaffe up to un-coolness rather than insensitivity, but several made dark threats, up to and including "burn, baby, burn." Friendly's honored guest that evening was Ramsey Clark, the former U.S. attorney general. He joined some of the brothers in a basketball game and got smoked. . . . After he caught his breath, I talked to him. He sort of half-hinted that if the circumstances were right, he would consider running for president. I knew he was floating a trial balloon at me and I should've questioned him in depth. But since I had to keep a good eye on a couple of the brothers who were still seething about the evening's menu, I figured I would be better served to get out of Dodge in one piece instead of talking to a sweating Ramsey Clark about his political ambitions.[15]

Earl Caldwell, then a reporter for the *New York Times*, was among those who lauded the program and Friendly's support for the professional development of journalists of color. At the time Caldwell was resisting attempts by the Department of Justice to force him to reveal his sources in the Black Panther Party to a grand jury; the matter eventually would be decided by the Supreme Court as part of a landmark case regarding protection of news sources. As Caldwell recalled, Friendly reached out to him in 1971 in connection with the summer program at Columbia:

> Fred was a staunch advocate of First Amendment issues. He became a sort of guru to me. He'd invite me to NYC to talk about [the Summer Program for Minority Journalists], but we'd spend hours talking media and the law. He introduced me to a whole spectrum of power figures at the top—in the foundation community, publishing, and in network TV. He figured the contact would help me in the struggle I was involved in, and also he believed these were people I ought to know. On some occasions, he'd host a dinner at his home. Another time, it would be in a restaurant. Or at the Ford Foundation or Columbia.[16]

Caldwell would speak to Friendly's classes and, later, participate in the Columbia University Seminars on Media and Society, developed in the mid-1970s, including one in England. When Caldwell was considering writing a book about his court case, Friendly invited him to dinner with his friend Robert Bernstein, president of Random House. Caldwell emphasized that after the Kerner Commission's scathing indictment of the press, "Fred Friendly—and in many ways, Fred Friendly alone—developed a plan, rolled up his sleeves and did something about it. He had the kids at his home because he cared." When in 1972 Friendly asked him to run the summer program, Caldwell recommended that Robert Maynard also be involved. Maynard had been a Nieman Fellow at Harvard and was working as a national correspondent for the *Washington Post*. Caldwell and Maynard became codirectors and with Friendly's support brought into the program as teachers talented minority journalists like Charlayne Hunter-Gault of WRC-TV in Washington, D.C., John Dotson of *Newsweek*, and Frank Sotomayor of the *Los Angeles Times*. Although Friendly delegated authority to Caldwell and Maynard, he continued to play a mentoring role. "Once he sat Maynard and me down," Caldwell recalled, "to tell us about his life and what it meant to be Jewish and why he changed his name. He opened himself to us and he did it so that we would have the benefit of his experience and to make with it what we could in our journey."[17]

The minority training program at Columbia University was yet another astutely timed and productive Friendly initiative, responsive to an acute crisis in race relations. Structuring job placement into the program assured that the program would meet its own goals. The timing was propitious in that the mainstream media desperately needed ethnic reporters to cover communities where white reporters had limited access and trust. The minority training program suffered as the momentum of black revolt waned. The final session of the program took place in the summer of 1974. During the six years of its existence, it trained 225 journalists of color and placed them in broadcast and print newsrooms across the country. Maynard said that many would interpret its termination to mean that "now that there are no riots, we can't get any action."[18] The program's demise was also protested in *Deadline*, the weekly newspaper produced by the program's newspaper track.

A critical factor in ending the summer program at Columbia was growing resentment on the part of faculty and students in the graduate journalism program. The regular faculty became estranged from the minority program as outsiders brought in by Caldwell and Maynard replaced them. Graduate students protested what they considered the privileged position of those in the summer program. The grad students paid $5,000 in tuition and got no job guarantees, whereas the summer interns got scholarships and commitments for employment despite, in some instances, not having an undergraduate degree.

At the emotional final graduation ceremony that summer, Friendly said he had seen Michelle Clark die once and did not want the program commemorating her to disappear without a trace. He promised to see that the effort would continue in another form and helped Maynard and Caldwell establish the Institute for Journalism Education. "Fred got us established, showed us how to raise money, helped us define our mission," Caldwell remembered.[19] The institute found a home at the University of California at Berkeley. Friendly continued to support it as an unofficial adviser. Renamed the Maynard Institute after Robert Maynard's death in 1993, the institute continues to play a leading role in the professional development of journalists of color and in the promotion of diversity in the newsroom.

Unease on the part of the journalism faculty about the special status of the Summer Program for Minority Journalists was only one factor complicating Friendly's relationship with his colleagues at Columbia University. Penn Kimball, a long-time faculty member, felt that Friendly had created a schism: "He took the broadcast faculty and split it off under his dominion, away from the rest of the school. So they all voted together at all faculty meetings." According to Kimball, Friendly "would hold secret meetings and then he would take his caddies, his assistants, with him and poison their minds against the rest of the faculty." Kimball, a Princeton graduate and former Rhodes Scholar who had had a distinguished career in print journalism before coming to the School of Journalism in 1958, had given enthusiastic support to Friendly's hiring; Kimball subsequently considered it "the biggest mistake of my life. He was divisive and he was self-promoting."[20]

In addition, there was lingering resentment about Friendly's response to the student occupation of the Columbia campus in 1968. Student activists, led by Students for a Democratic Society (SDS), protested the university's plan, despite opposition from the local community, to build a gymnasium in a park bordering Harlem; at the same time, they opposed government-sponsored research related to the Vietnam War at the school's Institute of Defense Analysis. A ban on demonstrations precipitated the occupation of administration offices in Low Library and other buildings on campus for more than a week in April 1968. The New York City police forcibly ended the occupation, injuring more than two hundred students. Lawrence Pinkham, a member of the journalism faculty, immediately resigned as director of the broadcast program under Friendly, explaining, "I cannot in good conscience carry out duties connected in even a remote way with a University administration whose top officers are responsible for the calculated brutality wrought by police on our students last night."[21]

The journalism building was not one of the buildings seized during the occupation. Journalism faculty and students decided to meet off campus and give the top floor over to protesting students for use as a media center. Pinkham recalled that "Fred Friendly was very much against the SDS and the occupation of those buildings." Joshua Friedman, then a student of Friendly's and years later a member of the Columbia journalism faculty, remembered how Friendly served as an unofficial media adviser to the administration, seeking to counter the sympathetic coverage of the protesters. According to Melvin Mencher, another faculty member, "Friendly was the only one, so far as I can recall, who sided with the administration and tried to keep the building open." Mencher claimed that Friendly served as an adviser to the administration during the crisis and that at one point the students hung a banner in the school deriding him.[22]

Although the journalism faculty had given the protesters use of its facilities, Friendly arranged for his students to do an interview in the journalism laboratory with David Truman, a vice present at Columbia, that WNET-TV would broadcast live. Pinkham objected vociferously, arguing that such use of the laboratory constituted strikebreaking and threatened to lock the door if necessary to prevent it. Friendly met with his student David Kuhn, who was producing the program, and a decision was made to move the production downtown to Channel 13's studios. In early May, Friendly oversaw staff members of the *Spectator*, Columbia's student newspaper, as they produced a special eighty-page publication, *The Crisis at Columbia*. By that time, New York City police had forcibly ended the occupation of five buildings; the campus remained polarized as SDS and allied faculty sought to continue the strike. The purpose of the booklet was to present a nonpartisan account of the conflict on campus. It contained reports from the previous thirteen issues of the newspaper as well as an analytical magazine supplement, "Columbia in Upheaval." Under Friendly's direction, the publication was produced within ten days. Ten thousand copies were printed in Worchester, Massachusetts, and brought to New York in a small U-Haul truck driven by Kuhn. Boxes of the booklets were brought into Journalism Hall under cover of darkness. The *Times* and other news organizations got prerelease copies that night, before a news conference held the next day. Kuhn would later tell Friendly: "You orchestrated . . . the release of the book beautifully."[23]

A major factor in Friendly's opposition to the occupation was that, in his view, it preempted reasoned face-to-face dialogue about the issues. Mark Harrington was a student of Friendly's who was supportive of the student protests. When Friendly invited him to dinner, Harrington thought it was so he could meet his family. In fact, Friendly also invited a member of the Columbia board to set the stage for a debate at the dinner table. Harrington recalled being pitted "in defense of all student protest against a university trustee who wanted to end it all with a police truncheon." He added, "It was my introduction to life with the Friendlys, and life was never quite the same again."[24]

Early in 1969, Friendly joined Jacques Barzun and a hundred other Columbia faculty members who signed a statement opposing amnesty for students involved in the disturbances the previous spring and urging strong disciplinary measures against any further protests that would disrupt classes. Friendly nonetheless took issue with both critics of student demands like Barzun and supporters of SDS, referring to himself as "a dues-paying member of the radical center."[25] He wished to steer a middle course between student radicals and academic traditionalists. Hence Friendly criticized Barzun's concept of the university—advanced in his book, *The American University* (1968)—as an ivory tower whose classical curriculum should be shielded from demands for greater relevance to contemporary problems.

In a speech on November 28, 1968, before the National Council of Teachers of English in Milwaukee, Friendly suggested that Columbia's very geographic location, bordering the black population of Harlem and the dissidents of the Upper West Side, made its engagement in a society in crisis inevitable: "Between Morningside Heights and Broadway the generation gap, the race gap all intersect. It was in the conflict over a gymnasium between Columbia and its neighbors that the explosions of last spring found their fuse. But nowhere in this scholarly work of Barzun's do the words Harlem, or black, or Negro appear. Yet race is as actively germane to Columbia, and to all universities in urban surroundings, as the atomic bomb is to world peace."[26] Friendly noted with sympathy the alienation of a generation of college students who felt that their elders had failed to take responsibility for the inequities in U.S. society as well as American policy in Vietnam. Remedies were needed for what Friendly considered the understandable but inchoate responses of student radicals. He lamented the separation of liberal arts and the professional schools; for example, no one at the journalism school taught courses in the undergraduate college. Why, he added, should the social sciences and the law school exist in separate realms? Friendly advocated sweeping educational reforms in higher education to create an interdisciplinary curriculum to address the great issues of the day. American journalism, like the university, needed reform. Friendly would concede that "my journalism students at Columbia feel that time after time broadcasters of my generation misjudge the youth movement and the black movement." He called for a citizenry better served by the two key American institutions with which he was engaged: academia and television.[27]

Despite his desire to steer a middle course, there was something visceral in Friendly's aversion to the student revolt. He became apoplectic when his son David let his hair grow long in college. Andrew Friendly, whose defense of his brother led to a shoving match with his father, recalled how "That 'Afro' really drove him nuts." Tom Bettag thought that Friendly's political misgivings about the student revolt and occupations might have had a psychological as well as political foundation. Bettag suspected that Friendly dreaded the prospect of mass hysteria, which he associated with Nazism and his searing experience as a witness to the liberation of Mauthausen. Friendly, in general, hated crowds. Bettag sensed in him "an inherent feeling that mob psychology can take over and can become very dangerous. . . . Whether linking it to the Holocaust is right or not, I don't know, but it is a fear that ran deep."[28] Friendly made a career of challenging institutions like CBS and Columbia University—but from the inside, not from the vantage point of an oppositional culture critical of established institutions.

Tension between Friendly and the journalism faculty was not merely the result of resentment at the expansion of the broadcasting track or his opposition to the student strike of 1968. Friendly's general operating style inevitably clashed with faculty mores. He hated the numerous faculty and committee meetings, the petty squabbling, and the resistance to change characteristic of academic life.[29] Conversely, some faculty— Melvin Mencher, for example—found Friendly to be high-handed and disruptive. Mencher was a former print journalist and the author of the standard college textbook on newswriting. As Mencher recognized, Friendly "came from an industry where the top dog had absolute authority. He was impatient with discussion and deliberation, and often contemptuous of those who differed from him." Friendly got low marks for collegiality. John Schultz recalled a faculty meeting at which Friendly noted his greater reputation in an argument with Penn Kimball, who replied, "That may be, Professor Friendly, but I'm smarter than you." Mencher and Kimball became especially critical of Friendly. They resented Friendly's special status, which gave him dispensation to hold two jobs simultaneously. (His designation as television "consultant" at the Ford Foundation was designed to circumvent the university's ban against multiple employers.) Friendly was the only member of the journalism faculty with teaching assistants, or caddies, as Kimball derisively called them. Mencher and Kimball accused Friendly of dereliction of duty as a professor, claiming that he relied excessively on his graduate assistants in grading students' papers and writing his books. Mencher wrote of Friendly's relationship with students, "Some found him an inspiration, a role model, some a bully."[30]

Lawrence Pinkham had a more complex experience as Friendly's colleague than Mencher and Kimball. Pinkham, a graduate of the journalism school, had worked with United Press before joining the faculty in the late 1950s. He collaborated with Friendly in developing the broadcast track and did not share the resentment of the print diehards. He and Friendly became close, driving to work and lunching together. Pinkham thought the opposition to Friendly was the inevitable result of introducing "a very powerful force into the middle of a fairly static situation." For Pinkham, Friendly was a great colleague; Pinkham would savor their collaboration for the rest of his life. Nonetheless, a disagreement would alter their relationship. When in 1968 Friendly was planning the Summer Program for Minority Journalists, he asked Pinkham to administer it. Pinkham felt that the stipend Friendly offered was inadequate and demurred. Friendly never forgave him. "We were very, very close," Pinkham recalled, "and it was a betrayal to him." Pinkham quickly realized that "you don't really cross Fred more than once, if whatever involved is important to him." To Pinkham's regret, their relationship became strained and distant. Another bone of contention in 1968 between Pinkham and Friendly was the student revolt on the Columbia campus. Pinkham began walking up eight flights to his office to avoid encountering Friendly in the elevator. Nonetheless, when in 1972 Pinkham left Columbia for the University of Massachusetts, he and Friendly parted on a cordial note. As he looked back on their relationship, Pinkham emphasized the qualities that had originally endeared Friendly to him: "I admired him and loved him. . . . He was a big, powerful man, capable of great, great feeling."[31]

Willard Hertz thought that Columbia was a less hospitable institutional environment for Friendly than the Ford Foundation. Hertz, who worked with Friendly at Ford, was a graduate of the journalism school and got reports on his clashes with faculty from Professor Richard T. Baker. Hertz noted that under McGeorge Bundy "the Ford Foundation was in the business of institutional change. . . . And, generally speaking, university faculty is more resistant to change." Bundy gave Friendly much wider latitude at Ford than the journalism dean could provide at Columbia. Yet for Friendly, the pleasure of teaching made up for all the conflict and frustration. John Schultz, who worked closely with him, first at CBS and then at Columbia, said of Friendly's experience with students at the journalism school, "He held forth there. He was in his glory."[32]

A year after his departure from CBS, having established himself as a force to be reckoned with both at the Ford Foundation and Columbia University, Friendly said in an interview, "At 51 I have found a whole new life." Friendly was referring in March 1967 to his professional life on the occasion of the publication of *Due to Circumstances Beyond Our Control . . . .* However, his private affairs were in a state of flux. Dorothy's psychological problems made it more difficult for her to sustain her role as Fred's personal and professional partner. She became the polar opposite of her husband's gregarious and commanding public persona. The psychiatrist Peter Neubauer viewed Friendly as a gifted extrovert endowed with a remarkable élan vital, someone who was not highly introspective and psychologically attuned. Neubauer found Friendly's reaction to Dorothy's condition to be sympathetic and supportive but also somewhat uncomprehending. As a result of Dorothy's illness, Fred had to assume primary responsibility for the upbringing of their three children, two of whom were experiencing the turbulence of adolescence. In 1967, Andrew would turn sixteen; Lisa, fourteen, and David, eleven. According to one observer, "All of them were a mess. They were angry kids, depressed, sad. Andy was having terrible trouble at school. Lisa would come home and Dorothy would be in bed all the time. [Lisa] would go marketing with Fred, go to Bloomingdale's and pick out dishes." Dorothy was not in a position to nurture her children, whereas Fred realized he had neither the time nor the wherewithal to give them all that they needed.[33]

Fred and Dorothy had become increasingly estranged over the years. The long working hours of Friendly and Murrow permitted both men to escape problems at home. Friendly came to understand that his union with Dorothy had been more a marriage of convenience than an affair of the heart. He would later advise a young man living with his girlfriend, "Don't make the same mistake I did. I fell into a marriage. We were together. I didn't know how to say no." Nonetheless, Fred resisted at first Dorothy's desire for a separation. His closest friends encouraged him to consider divorce. Fred felt loyal to Dorothy, the indispensable partner for the launch of his career after the war, a debt Friendly would always readily acknowledge. He also recognized her pain and vulnerability. "Leaving her," he felt, "would be like abandoning a sinking ship." In 1966, they agreed to a trial separation. Fred remained with their children in the house in Riverdale, and Dorothy moved into the Hotel Adams on East Eighty-sixth Street in Manhattan. Friendly soon realized the inevitability of the breakup and the desirability of a divorce rather than a legal separation. On the advice of his closest friends, Friendly said he would grant a divorce only on the condition that he could keep the house and get custody of the children. Dorothy agreed, fearing the turmoil of a conflict. "I finally persuaded myself that it would be better for the children," she recalled. "They would go to the best schools, go on great trips with Fred, meet stimulating people. I took it for granted that Fred would marry someone who would be good for the children. I concluded it would be best if they lived in that beautiful house." The divorce was finalized in January 1968. "The next five or six years were hell for me," Dorothy said.[34]

The situation took its toll on Friendly, too. Although he was enjoying his new career at the Ford Foundation and Columbia University, those close to him detected a sense of sadness at unguarded moments. Friendly was slow to start seeing other women. Robert and Helen Bernstein came forward to play the role of matchmaker. In December 1967, they invited Friendly to a dinner party to introduce him to Ruth Weiss Mark, a recently widowed schoolteacher from Scarsdale. "You told me how a hostess had arranged a meeting between you and a school teacher at a party," Tom Bettag reminded Friendly years later. "You hadn't been consulted beforehand, and you said you weren't one bit happy about that sort of arrangement."[35] Also attending the dinner party were Bennett Cerf, the chairman of Random House; Theodor Geisel, better known as Dr. Seuss; and the actor Kitty Carlisle. Helen Bernstein arranged for another couple from Scarsdale to drive Ruth to the dinner in Manhattan and hoped that Friendly would drive her home. Ruth and Fred, seated next to each other, hit it off. She was impressed, recognizing immediately that he was "a larger-than-life guy." They spoke about their children. "He was quiet . . .

a little down, subdued," Ruth recalled. "It was a difficult time for him. I think his social self-confidence was shaken—not in terms of his work but his social relationships." Fred did in fact drive her home in his red Mustang. Early in the courtship, Fred said, "My intentions are honorable," which sounded to Ruth amusingly formal and Victorian. Fred later claimed that Ruth jokingly answered, "Let's set the date."[36]

Ruth, an intelligent and attractive blonde with blue eyes, was forty-three; he was fifty-two. She had grown up in Pelham, New York, the daughter of Herman Weiss, a vice president of and general counsel for Bloomingdale's. She was graduated from Smith College and received a master's in elementary education at Teacher's College, Columbia University, after which she taught school and raised her family. Her husband, an engineer, had died suddenly of a heart attack nine months before she met Friendly.[37] Fred and Ruth's courtship was whirlwind; within a week, they had spent several evenings together. Fred had to cancel a third date but sent flowers and a poem. "It was a big romance very quickly," Ruth recalled. "We probably knew within a month that we were going to get married." Once during the 1967 Christmas holidays, Fred and Ruth were in the second-floor study of his home, where he was showing Ruth scrapbooks from the war, when his daughter, Lisa, unexpectedly came home with some friends to make hot chocolate. Ruth offered to come down and help, but Fred asked her to stay upstairs because he had not yet told his children about their relationship. But Lisa saw Ruth's coat downstairs. Fred said it was nobody's and claimed the next day that it belonged to a reporter. Later, when Fred and Ruth reminisced about their courtship, Lisa would say, "I hated that coat" because her father had lied to her.[38]

Fred and Ruth were married in June 1968 at the home of the Bernsteins. Ruth had three children: Jonathan, twenty; Michael, eighteen; and Richard, twelve. In deciding where the merged family would live, Fred and Ruth had to choose between her house in Scarsdale with more land and his house in Riverdale with more bedrooms; they opted for the latter. "An enormous merger, the merger of the century," she later joked. "We merged furniture, guinea pigs, silver, children, stereos." Fred would embrace Ruth's children as if they were his own. He reveled in his role as paterfamilias in his new expanded family. Dorothy would visit the children once or twice a week; sometimes she would bring them to her apartment on the West Side of Manhattan to do homework, go skating, or attend a show. "Once I picked up David around the time the divorce was being finalized," Dorothy recalled. "He was at the table with Ruth and ran over to give me a big hug. I felt crushed at the moment. Fortunately, they were comfortable with Ruth. Otherwise, that would have been devastating."[39] Ruth used her considerable charm and social skills to make Dorothy feel as comfortable as possible. There was no rivalry between the two women, and Ruth interacted with Dorothy more than Fred did.

Despite their differences, Dorothy and Ruth shared a feature in their marriages to Fred: involvement in his work. "Before you knew it," Ruth observed, "I was pulled into what he was doing." She began proofreading what he wrote. "Don't microread it, macroread it," he proclaimed, meaning that he wanted her reactions to his ideas rather than her corrections of his writing. Ruth became progressively more engaged in Fred's professional activities. She would accompany him on his research trips for his books, taking notes and functioning as an all-purpose aide. She become a de facto associate producer when he started organizing seminars. She did not have a title or salary; working with Fred was for her a stimulating and integral part of their marriage. Once again in Friendly's life, marriage coincided with a burst of collaborative work, only this time he was also truly smitten with his new partner, as Tom Bettag observed. After 1968 Friendly experienced a sense of renewal in his private, no less than his professional, life. According to Bettag, "I think that he was enormously troubled about his children, and Ruth brought all that around and brought her three children in. I think he loved having six happy kids and watching his children blossom." After Friendly remarried, Bettag recalled, "the sadness largely went away." After leaving CBS in 1966, Friendly had become a professor at Columbia University and a policy maker at the Ford Foundation, capitalizing on the synergy of the two positions to become the most powerful force in broadcast journalism working outside the profession. Now, with Ruth as his personal and professional partner, he could truly say, "I have found a whole new life."[40]

WHEN FRIENDLY FIRST JOINED the faculty of the graduate journalism program at Columbia, he planned a major programming initiative called the University Broadcast Laboratory, a weekly show to be carried live on Sunday nights by National Educational Television (NET). He conceived the program as a joint project of a consortium of two dozen universities; it would have a magazine format that would permit a full range of programming about politics, international affairs, and the arts and sciences. Friendly recruited his former colleague at CBS, Av Westin, to become the project's executive director in early 1967. The plan sought to capitalize on the synergy that could be created by joining the resources of the academy and the untapped possibilities of the medium of television, a dream of Friendly's and of his intellectual mentor Walter Lippmann's.

A "fact sheet" about the project issued in mid-1967 reflected an intention to use the academy as a staging area from which, in effect, to " 'publish' in television terms, the work of professors, diplomats, scholars, artists." The University Broadcast Laboratory, like the Ford communications satellite plan, reflected Friendly's agenda of promoting the creation of an authentic noncommercial broadcasting network. The fact sheet characterized interconnection—the technology permitting simultaneous broadcast by all stations in a network—as "the single most important contribution television has to offer—speaking to one nation at one time about meaningful issues."[1] At the same time, Friendly designed the experimental program with a local component: during cutaway time in the national broadcast the 125 local noncommercial stations would address the local ramifications of national issues. The University Broadcast Laboratory promised to create noncommercial television's first live weekly show, a demonstration project for system interconnection and programming excellence. At the same time it would enable Friendly to return to his first love and once again have a hand in television production.

At Friendly's behest, the Ford Foundation set aside $10 million for the experimental program development at Columbia, a clear demonstration of the advantages of Friendly's affiliation with both institutions. The initiative received front-page coverage in the *New York Times* and an editorial endorsing the venture as "an exciting test of educational TV's potentialities" and Friendly and Westin as the right people to direct the venture.[2] However, Columbia's board of trustees, reportedly unhappy that Friendly had publicized the project before its formal consent, gave Friendly a qualified approval accompanied by a ten-page document of restrictions. It included a prohibition against raiding the staffs of the commercial networks or duplicating their programming; these stipulations probably reflected the hand of Columbia trustee Bill Paley. The trustees clearly worried about a proposed television program that could create unwanted controversy for the university in the political and cultural cauldron of the late 1960s. Journalism dean Edward W. Barrett, appalled by the restrictions, entered into contentious negotiations with the trustees, threatening to resign in frustration. As Westin recalled, the Columbia trustees came to realize "that what Fred was talking about, what I was talking about, was a kind of information program which . . . could take political positions, economic positions that the trustees of Columbia didn't necessarily want to endorse. So we took care of that. We were out of there."[3]

As a result, Friendly and Barrett shelved plans for Columbia to house the experimental program in the school of journalism. Now Friendly and Westin deemphasized the academic component of the proposed program and highlighted its potential influence on the future of public television. In a memorandum to McGeorge Bundy dated March 13, 1967, Westin emphasized how an independent broadcasting laboratory associated with NET could become the news and public affairs arm of the public television system that was being established on the heels of the Carnegie Commission report issued two months earlier. The University Broadcast Laboratory became the *Public Broadcasting Laboratory* (*PBL*), an independently incorporated entity and autonomous unit of NET. For a moment Friendly considered yet another career change, to head *PBL*, but he had second thoughts about casting aside the positions at Ford and Columbia for an exciting but unproved programming venture.[4] Friendly's vision would be implemented by his surrogate, Av Westin. Despite Friendly's lack of direct responsibility, an observer wryly noted that "it is quite possible that, if pressed, he might give Westin the benefit of occasional criticism and advice."[5] A committee of the NET board was given authority to select the executive director of *PBL* but only with the advice and consent of the president of the Ford Foundation, so that Bundy and Friendly exercised ultimate control over the choice and could reaffirm the selection of Westin. Nonetheless the relationship with NET would exact a price. A twelve-member board would oversee programming, and Friendly could attend meetings only as a guest in a nonvoting capacity.

Jack Gould wrote that *PBL's* design as a centerpiece for a "fourth network" contrasted with the Carnegie Commission's blueprint for a decentralized public television system. Friendly calculated that if he designed *PBL* as a riveting live weekly program—a new *See It Now*—it could foster the creation of a television system with national clout in public affairs programming. According to James Day, "Friendly saw *PBL* as the answer to public broadcasting's need to grow up, to become *real* television." At the same time, Friendly was going to show the commercial networks what they could have had. According to *TV Guide*, "Insiders say Friendly saw it as a chance to show what he could have done at CBS if the brass there had only given him free rein." In the summer of 1967, Friendly suggested in testimony before Congress that the type of programming proposed for *PBL* would force the networks to improve their public affairs programming: "Were I still in commercial broadcasting, I would consider that the gauntlet had been thrown down and would strive to do even better."[6]

Friendly decided that the program should air live and in color for two and a half hours on Sunday evenings, a time when many educational stations did not broadcast because they did not have the money to do so. According to its fact sheet, *PBL* would eschew commercial television's rigid formats and arbitrary time constraints, giving a topic three minutes or three hours as needed. It would break new ground in network–affiliate interchange. It would mark a new departure in broadcast journalism by creating a "desk system" for cultural affairs, national affairs, social sciences, and physical sciences. The producers of *PBL* would ignore the ratings system and would value quality over quantity of audience. Hence *PBL* "provides the possibility of disseminating to important but numerically small segments of the population a wide range of 'unpopular' broadcasts—thoughtful discussions of fundamental public issues, noteworthy music and theatre, sophisticated treatment of new scientific developments, Congressional hearings on significant issues, coherent conversations among great scholars and specialists ... and other offerings of a type not often available on commercial stations," according to the fact sheet. "Here comes the Millennium, hippity-hoppity, into our living rooms," C. H. Simonds wrote in the *National Review*, "to save us from boredom, ignorance, despair and whatever else Fred W. Friendly happens to think is ailing the body politic." Simonds charged that "the Uplifters have, by embracing [public television], abandoned the common man to his imagined hopeless boobery: what they now propose is essentially elite television for the elite and to hell with everyone else." A historian of public broadcasting struck a similar note thirty years later: "Although it dropped its formal Columbia connection and strove to speak to Everyman, *PBL* could barely cloak its elitism: a heavy portion of its on-screen experts had some connection to an Ivy League university."[7]

Friendly had little faith in the capacity of the personnel of educational television and in NET as an institution to fulfill *PBL*'s ambitious mission. NET officials objected to a highly promoted program that would be carried by its affiliates but by-pass its own producers. The affiliates, in turn, were wary about being required to air a controversial program that might offend local sensibilities. Two entities funded by Ford, NET and *PBL*, were linked by a shotgun marriage, while in reality they were being pitted against each other. In a memo to Friendly on April 4, 1967, Westin detailed his attempts to defuse tensions about *PBL* at NET. Six weeks later, Bundy signed a memorandum of understanding formalizing the arrangement by which an editorial policy board appointed by the NET board would oversee *PBL* programming.[8] The NET board would jealously guard its oversight of programming. Its minutes for August 16, 1967, for example, state that "Mr. Friendly, who was present as a guest, suggested the possibility of a very special extended (beyond three hours) treatment of the civil rights issue for the opening show. The Board seemed to favorably incline but did not officially approve or disapprove." On September 13, the board conducted a detailed review of a rough cut of what would be *PBL*'s initial broadcast and pointedly suggested improvements.[9]

The selection of Av Westin as executive director of *PBL* reflected Friendly's reservations about the old guard in educational broadcasting. Westin had worked with Friendly and Murrow on *Hear It Now* and *See It Now* and become one of Friendly's most trusted television directors. At CBS, Westin had relished the "aura of excitement about Fred" and bemoaned the blandness of the post-Friendly CBS News department.[10] Now, two years after Friendly's resignation, Westin—the winner of Peabody, Polk, Emmy, and Lasker awards—jumped at the chance to implement Friendly's bold vision for *PBL*. Other recruits from the networks joined Westin's team. Tom Kennedy and Gerald Slater, for example, also came from the ranks of CBS. So did Stuart Sucherman, later an aide to Friendly at the Ford Foundation. Edward P. Morgan, ABC's senior correspondent, considered an "anchor in the Murrow tradition," was chosen as the program's host.[11] Morgan was joined by two veteran NBC-TV correspondents, Tom Petit and Robert MacNeil. Many staff members had print journalism backgrounds, among them, Robert McCabe of *Newsweek*, a science editor from *Look* magazine, and John Wicklein, a national affairs editor from the *New York Times*. A network of stringers and experts was established to report on breaking stories across the nation. A team of sixty staff editors, working at *PBL*'s offices on Madison Avenue in New York City, prepared for the program's debut in November 1967.

Friendly was acutely aware of the convergence of forces that made his experimental broadcast laboratory timely. In January 1967, President Lyndon Johnson called for the transformation of educational television into a major national broadcasting system in a speech carried live on seventy affiliates by a hookup funded—not surprisingly—by a special grant from the Ford Foundation. The report of the Carnegie Commission on Educational Television appeared shortly thereafter. Congressional hearings on the structure and financing of public broadcasting considered legislation based on the recommendations of the Carnegie Commission during *PBL*'s planning stage. *PBL*'s first broadcast would take place two days before Johnson signed the Public Broadcasting Act of 1967, which established a rudimentary structure for a new radio and television service. *PBL* was in a position to provide a programming model, a public affairs focus—and popular support—for a public television system yet to be defined. "If successful," *Newsweek* reported before *PBL* went on the air, "the experiment could push forward the whole plan for a system of public television passed hesitantly by Congress this fall."[12]

PBL intended to address the political and cultural crisis of the period in order to fulfill its mission as the model for a new kind of public affairs program: "It will be free to be unconventional and controversial, to deal with subjects that are normally taboo," its fact sheet stated. The escalation of the war in Vietnam had spawned a growing antiwar movement and political polarization in the nation. In addition, black power replaced integration as the rallying cry of the civil rights movement. The nation experienced a cultural as well as political breakdown that included generational revolt and a multifaceted counterculture.[13] For example, teach-ins and the alternative press challenged mainstream journalism just as off-Broadway and street drama challenged established theater. Network television epitomized the commercial culture rejected by the countercul-ture. A 1967 Lou Harris poll revealed that a sharp decline in television viewership by the college educated constituted a growing de facto boycott of commercial television.

Westin spoke of his intention "to stir things up, to challenge the status quo of both commercial and educational television." John Tebbel sug-gested in the *Saturday Review* that *PBL* "may be the most significant step in television's brief, cluttered history." *Harper's* magazine anticipated "an experiment which could change the whole nature of American broad-casting." Edward P. Morgan acknowledged the pressure caused by such high expectations: "I don't mind saying," he declared, "I'm scared to death at this point."[14] As *PBL* prepared to go on the air, Friendly wrote Westin a memorandum:

> Don't be afraid to fail sometimes or you will fall into that ancient pat-ter of safe ideas, the pursuit of the obvious. . . . We expect you to be fair but not so balanced to every side on every subject that you be-come predictable. As a viewer I expect to be made to feel uncomfort-able. . . . As a former producer, I expect to feel on numerous occa-sions that "I could have done it better," but I promise never to say it to you. . . . Good luck . . . you and your other associates are the ones who must put their professional reputation where our mouths are. The way for me to thank you is to leave you alone.[15]

Friendly generally believed in taking risks and living with the conse-quences. He kept a photograph in his office of Babe Ruth striking out as a reminder that even the great must fail on occasion.[16] Friendly also warned Westin to steel himself for unsympathetic treatment from televi-sion critics.

PBL first aired on November 5, 1967. The focus of the broadcast was racial conflict. It opened with reports on mayoral elections in Gary, Indi-ana; Cleveland; and Boston that all took place in a context of racial con-flict. The next segment consisted of a tour of black Chicago, filmed and narrated in cinema verité style by Russell Meeks, a local black national-ist. James Ledbetter described Meeks's film this way:

His minidocumentary bombarded viewers with one disturbing image after another: children eating out of dumpsters, bombed-out buildings, a convulsing dog dying in the street in front of an abandoned lot where children played baseball. . . . Meeks called King's nonviolence strategy "the philosophy of the fool," and declared himself part of a new breed of activists who would "rather die on our feet than live on our knees." In his film, white merchants were "exploiters of the people"; the police were "gestapo."[17]

Then Meeks, together with a moderate black minister and a white liberal, engaged in a heated debate about racial conditions in Chicago that was broadcast live from the studios of the city's educational television station. Both the filmed segment and the debate had a raw and unmediated quality rarely seen on the television screen.

The principal and most controversial part of the premiere was a presentation of the Negro Ensemble Theater's successful off-Broadway play *Day of Absence*. In the drama, blacks disappear from a southern town, which becomes paralyzed and implores their return. African American actors in whiteface caricatured the town's dependent citizens, a reversal of blackface performances of the past. As a result of its controversial content the initial broadcast was not carried by 29 of the 119 NET affiliates, mostly in the South. The program also featured two "anti-commercials" on the marketing of aspirin and cigarettes that the *Nation*'s critic described as a powerful "satirical exposé of the cant and hypocrisy of our advertising-saturated, self-deceiving culture."[18]

The Johnson White House reportedly expressed unhappiness after seeing an advance copy of the first program's script, which included a commentary by Edward P. Morgan questioning the claim of the United States to be fighting for a free Vietnam when the promise of democracy had not been realized for African Americans at home. A segment of the second *PBL* show challenged the official account of the Gulf of Tonkin Incident, which Murrow had criticized Friendly for failing to do when he was president of CBS News. Westin recalled the ire of *PBL*'s Editorial Policy Board: "I was called a Communist. I was called an enemy sympathizer. It was practically, 'Where is the Vietcong flag in your closet?' "[19] Erik Barnouw has written that the initial broadcasts set the tone for the programming to follow on *PBL*: "Mindful of its function as an alternative voice, it dipped into work of fringe theaters, cabarets, and underground films, and inevitably reflected the angry subculture. The thrust of the message was anti-war, anti-racist, and anti-establishment." *PBL* did not hesitate to present a critical, even radical, point of view. But it also aired the right-of-center perspectives of Ronald Reagan, Herman Kahn, and Henry Kissinger before the conservative revolution that would give them national reputations.[20]

As Friendly had predicted, *PBL's* premiere received critical reviews. Some critics seemed eager to puncture the balloon of the much-heralded experiment. In the *New York Post*, Harriet Van Horne characterized the program as "bombast, pretense and warmed-over sludge." Jack Gould wrote in the Sunday *New York Times* on November 12 that despite *PBL's* considerable financial and human resources, the premiere was a "blight of awkward confusion and dullness." Responding to the program's hyperbolic promotion by Friendly and Westin, Gould added, "Supporters of public broadcasting will hope that *PBL* will acquire the virtue of modesty and now stop suggesting that all others in noncommercial broadcasting were sad sacks until the laboratory crashed into the breach."[21] Friendly was quoted in the press as saying that the first show was just a beginning but that he, too, had been disappointed. He had not expressed criticism when he called Westin immediately following the broadcast. "I was surprised to learn later that he said to people that he thought it was a disaster," Westin recalled. "I steamed ahead thinking things were okay. He was evidently listening to his buddies, and not mine, and putting out a different line, buying himself some protection. I thought that was what we were supposed to do—to experiment."[22] Michael Arlen, the television critic of the *New Yorker*, responded favorably to the broadcast and chided Friendly for his critical remarks:

> I see by the *Times* ("TV Laboratory's First Venture Gets Largely Adverse Reaction") that Fred Friendly, TV consultant to the Ford Foundation, regards last Sunday's first appearance of the Ford Foundation-backed Public Broadcast Laboratory's two-and-a-half-hour news program as "disappointing." . . . It seems like only yesteryear that Mr. Friendly was being disappointed by the Columbia Broadcasting System, in whole or in part, and here he is not entirely satisfied with the debut of P.B.L., and right now I don't know what there is for any of us to do except just get back to study hall and work a whole lot harder for the rest of the term. For my part, I thought that P.B.L.'s first show was pretty damned good.[23]

PBL continued to get mixed reviews for its twenty-six broadcasts during the 1967/1968 season. High points included an exposé of the meat-packing industry and the television premiere of Harold Pinter's *The Dwarfs*. A PBL film crew had been trailing Martin Luther King Jr. when he was assassinated in the spring of 1968. A PBL photographer, Joe Louw, was staying at the Lorraine Motel in Memphis and took pictures of the slain leader's body and King's associates immediately after the slaying. Three days after King's death, PBL produced what *Newsweek* called "television's most eloquent memorial to the slain civil rights leader." However, PBL did not sustain a uniformly high level of programming and continued to receive severe criticism, from television critics to its own Editorial Policy Board. *Saturday Review* wrote of "hypothesis trouble."[24] Its board sent a memorandum to NET at the end of the season complaining that PBL had failed to live up to its mission as an innovative program, that many of its segments were heavy-handed, and that the board's recommendations had too often been ignored. The board recommended canceling the second season if substantive changes could not be made, including the replacement of Westin as executive director.

The board also took a swipe at Friendly, noting the "strong entrepreneurial hand" of the Ford Foundation in the creation of PBL and adding: "Looking to the future, however, we believe that a more normally remote relationship between foundation and grantee would be good for PBL—and, indeed, for the Foundation." It has been said that Friendly's "involvement in virtually every phase of PBL policy-making and operations was quiet and profound." Westin countered any suggestion that Friendly sought to micromanage PBL covertly. During his tenure at PBL, Westin recalled meeting with Friendly in his office at the Ford Foundation two or three times at most and doubted that Friendly ever visited the program's offices on Madison Avenue. The vision of PBL was Friendly's, to be sure, but he delegated its implementation to others. As for Friendly's expression of disappointment during the first season, Westin said, "I never felt betrayed by him."[25]

In 1967, in addition to PBL, Friendly assumed responsibility for another major television initiative. New York City mayor John Lindsay asked him to chair his Advisory Task Force on Cable Television in New York City. At this time, cable television was a new and untested medium, at a stage of development comparable to broadcast television following World War II. New York City, which had one of the earliest rudimentary cable television franchises, had to renegotiate its contracts with the cable companies serving Manhattan. Lindsay turned to Friendly to conduct an exhaustive study with recommendations for a comprehensive cable television system. "Electronics will dramatically change the method by which people get their TV in the next 10 years," Friendly said in accepting the assignment. Up until this point, the Ford Foundation had given scant attention to cable television. However, a week before his appointment to the mayor's task force, in testimony before the committee of the House of Representatives considering the Public Broadcasting Act of 1967, Friendly had stated that cable television could "revolutionize television as much as satellites and as much as television has revolutionized radio" while warning about the danger of "electronic ghettos."[26]

The "Friendly Report," issued in September 1968, contained a bold plan for a wired city, including the creation of a new Office of Telecommunications that would report directly to the mayor. The report based the proposed system on the principles of diversity of ownership, the notion of cable operator as a common carrier, the reservation of channels for municipal use, and broad public access. In an article in the *Saturday Review* in 1970, Friendly spelled out his vision for cable television's potential. Friendly imagined "a two-way, feedback system linked to our schools, hospitals, libraries and businesses." Such a system could be accessed by digital display screens, which could also serve as portals for such features as multiple audio channels for music and electronic newspapers and libraries. The synergy of cable and satellite technology made new forms of national as well as local television possible. Most important for Friendly, the additional channels could revolutionize televised news and public affairs programming by ending the virtual monopoly of the three broadcast networks and the finite amount of available air time. But Friendly sounded a warning: the danger that once again, as with radio and television in the past, commercial interests would hijack an opportunity to develop a new communications technology to strengthen the public discourse vital to a modern democracy.[27]

At a tumultuous public hearing in July 1970, Friendly criticized the failure of New York City to implement the recommendations of his report in its new franchise agreements with cable companies. "Cable television is too important, its potential too great," he said, "to be dealt away in a series of private, closed door negotiations without the kind of public participation and public analysis of the present operation which the task force felt was essential."[28] Yet despite his disappointment, the "Friendly

Report" was instrumental in making New York City's cable system—especially its public channels—a model for the rest of the nation. Friendly's leadership of the Advisory Task Force on Cable Television, undertaken at the same time he launched *PBL*'s first season, helped launch public access and the community television movement.

At the end of the first season of *PBL*, all parties called for its reorganization. Westin bitterly complained to Friendly about the Editorial Policy Board and the burden of programming by committee, recommending instead a closer working relationship with NET. The television critic for the *New York Daily News* reported on June 18, 1968, that Friendly once again had toyed with assuming direct control of *PBL* but decided against it. The article added that Friendly had brokered a reorganization ensuring a second season before he left for Bermuda for his honeymoon with Ruth. The Editorial Policy Board was to be disbanded and replaced by an advisory committee with no teeth. Westin would remain as executive director but would report to the chair of NET's board, enhancing NET's involvement as Westin had recommended to Friendly. "The sure winner was NET," *Newsweek* reported, noting NET's resentment of the special status that Ford had originally given *PBL*.[29]

For the second season, Westin would be forced to share his authority with Frederick M. Bohen, a former aide in the Johnson White House who became *PBL*'s executive editor. Westin agreed to relinquish a substantial measure of authority in the hope of providing a better institutional framework for *PBL*. He wrote Friendly that he would cede to Fred Bohen "ultimate responsibility and final authority over the overall shape and composition of the series and general content and editorial thrust of each broadcast segment." Bohen, together with Westin, would report to the chair of the NET board. *Newsweek* reported that Friendly had been the first choice of many *PBL* staffers to head its second season. Bohen was a surprising alternative: he was a thirty-one-year-old urban affairs specialist and well-connected administrator with virtually no experience in journalism or television. Clearly, the greater dependency on NET and the appointment of Bohen represented a tactical retreat on Friendly's part to keep *PBL* alive. In addition, the format of the show was downsized and simplified, shifting from two hours to ninety minutes and from a magazine to a single-topic format. Following the reorganization, senior staff went to Saratoga, New York, for a retreat to brainstorm about the following season—without Friendly, who would now be less involved in charting *PBL's* course because Westin, his protégé, would have diminished authority. *PBL's* long-term prospects did not seem bright to Westin: "I had seen the handwriting on the wall, and that March [1969] left for ABC. But that second season was well laid out and was quite successful."[30]

Arthur Barron, who had worked under Friendly at CBS, made "Life and Death," a documentary on the cycle of human existence that received critical acclaim during *PBL's* second season. The film juxtaposed the death of a middle-aged man and the birth of a child using the Lamaze method of delivery. *PBL* broadcast the first of Frederick Wiseman's documentaries to air on television, an inside look at the world of the Kansas City police department. *PBL* also introduced press criticism to television, providing early scrutiny of television news and of the fledgling cable television industry. Nicholas Johnson of the Federal Communications Commission praised this initiative, writing to Westin about "how much I enjoyed the PBL piece on decision-making in television news—it is a subject that was really untouchable before." Yet *PBL* could still be subjected to harsh criticism and even ridicule when, for example, an experimental Polish theater company's play was broadcast in Polish without subtitles. *PBL* ended its two-season run in April 1969. Critics agreed that the program fell far short of Friendly's aspiration to reinvent television. "We did two years and never delivered on its promise," said Westin, whose departure for ABC-TV marked the beginning of a distinguished career in its news department. "I felt it was one of my gross failures," Westin said, looking back at his experience at *PBL*. Soon after Westin's departure, the eight largest noncommercial television stations called for *PBL's* replacement by a new Sunday series, a final blow to the hope that it would evolve into a flagship program for the new public television system.[31]

At its best, *PBL* served its purpose: to demonstrate public television's potential to become a vital interconnected network driven by cutting-edge programming. Its critics were ungenerous, not taking kindly to a television experiment with the inevitable failures that Friendly had warned about in his memorandum to Westin. As Bill Moyers observed, "*PBL* was what Fred thought it should be: daring and bold and making mistakes and picking up and moving on." *PBL* did not receive the credit it deserved for addressing the generational revolt and cultural wars of the period, which the commercial networks were unwilling or unable to do. As usual, Friendly was ahead of others in anticipating what needed to be done, even if the execution was flawed. Moreover, by the late 1960s television had created audience expectations for what had become recognizable formats. The launch of *See It Now* had taken place in the formative period of a new medium, so that the earliest experiment in public affairs programming was projected onto a tabula rasa. In seeking to develop a new programming breakthrough, Friendly oversold *PBL*. On paper, his vision for *PBL* was inspired. James Day, from his vantage point as general manager of San Francisco's educational station and then president of NET, characterized *PBL* as a "victim of its own hype." What a critic wrote about *PBL*'s initial broadcast could be applied to the series as a whole: "The performance did not live up to the promise, largely because the promise was so magnified."[32] It brings to mind Mike Dann's observation, made in regard to the radio documentary *The Quick and the Dead*, that Friendly's dazzling description of a proposed program often outshined its outcome, even when the outcome was very good.

In retrospect, Westin's self-criticism seems too harsh. *PBL* must be evaluated in terms of the scope of its ambitions as well as its extreme range of triumphs and failures. The program transcended the limits of network television—qualitatively and quantitatively—in addressing the crisis in race relations in the late 1960s. It treated this and other issues by providing a live platform in which a wide range of participants could express their views in remarkably frank and raw exchanges, of which some would inevitably be more substantive than others. The program also became a venue for independent filmmakers who could make important personal and political statements; this was the case, for example, with *Can This Be America?* a series of five short films about the United States during the 1968 elections. In championing *PBL*, warts and all, Michael Arlen noted the sorry state of journalism on the commercial networks, which he characterized as excessively cautious, superficial, and formulaic. Arlen insisted that "PBL has been the most consistently interesting and substantial public affairs program right now in American broadcasting."[33]

PBL made significant contributions not readily apparent at the time of its demise in the spring of 1969. Together with the Ford satellite plan, it was another important step in the creation of an interconnected public broadcasting system that was Friendly's cause célèbre. *PBL* assembled a cohort of talented producers and journalists who would make a major contribution to that system for many years to come. At the same time, it provided a template for the launch in 1968 of a tamer and more formulaic variant, *60 Minutes*, the most successful newsmagazine in television history. It inspired other journalists, among them Bill Moyers, who at the time *PBL* aired had left the Johnson White House and would subsequently embark on a career in television journalism. He believed *PBL* represented a creative breakthrough that could "have shaped the future of public broadcasting" and become a flagship program like the BBC's *Panorama* if it had been given the time and support needed to work out the kinks. For Moyers, *PBL* "was not like anything else on television," a program that "really opened up the creative potential of what television could be." Elie Abel, who succeeded Edward Barrett as dean of the Graduate School of Journalism at Columbia, told a congressional subcommittee that "if *PBL* has to be accounted a failure, it must be one of the most influential failures of recent times. I say we need more of them."[34]

THE *PUBLIC BROADCASTING LABORATORY* had gone on the air just days before Lyndon Johnson signed the Public Broadcasting Act of 1967. *PBL* represented a strategic intervention on Friendly's part to give the embryonic public television system a programming model and a strong news and public affairs identity. As its first season came to a close in 1968, Friendly opened another front in his campaign to shape the new system, moving from a major programming initiative to the bureaucratic maneuvering that would shape public broadcasting's infrastructure. Passage of the Public Broadcasting Act led in March 1968 to the creation of the Corporation for Public Broadcasting (CPB) as a nonprofit, nongovernmental agency. However, the president would appoint the CPB board with the advice and consent of the Senate. CPB would disburse congressional appropriations to foster the development of public broadcasting but was expressly forbidden from operating a public television network. While the Friendly and McGeorge Bundy's satellite plan for funding public television had been rejected, how the stations within the system would operate in relation to CPB was still undecided. The structure of the public television network would of necessity be determined by a complex process of negotiation involving many parties.

Friendly realized he needed aides whose skills in organization and negotiation complemented his ability to set an agenda and to use his position at the Ford Foundation as a bully pulpit. In the spring of 1968, as CPB was being established and the first season of *PBL* was ending, Friendly recruited David M. Davis to take charge of the Office of Public Broadcasting at the Ford Foundation. From 1956 to 1967, Davis had been station manager at WGBH-TV, the flagship educational station in Boston. A gifted producer of cultural programming, he had also proved himself to be a highly skilled administrator and politician in the fractious world of noncommercial broadcasting. At the time, Davis was on leave from WGBH and working as the director of programming instruction at the Television Trust in Tel Aviv. One day in April 1968, he was surprised to receive a cable in Israel: "How do I reach you by telephone? Fred Friendly. Ford Foundation."[1] Davis cabled back, and Friendly called him on a Monday to say that he needed a senior executive to advance the Ford Foundation's agenda for public television. Could he meet for lunch on Wednesday at the foundation in New York? Davis received the full Friendly–Ford Foundation treatment. Hazel Layton, Friendly's secretary, quickly arranged for first-class round-trip tickets to New York and a room in the Waldorf Towers. Davis remembered entering the foundation's new building on East Forty-third Street that Wednesday, a beautiful spring day when the magnolia trees in the courtyard atrium were in bloom. He was whisked up to the stately dining room on the eleventh floor, where he had lunch with Friendly and Howard Dressner, the foundation secretary. At 3:30 P.M., Bundy shook hands with the foundation's newest employee. Davis became Friendly's highly circumspect and trusted aide-de-camp. Ward Chamberlin, who would work closely with Davis in the creation of public television's infrastructure, found this enigmatic figure, "a quiet man with an elusive personality," to be a highly effective behind-the-scenes operator.[2]

In 1969, Friendly added Stuart Sucherman to his Ford team. Sucherman was a dynamic young attorney who had been assistant general counsel at NET and had worked briefly at CBS before becoming head of business affairs and administration at PBL. It was the beginning of a long and fruitful professional relationship for Friendly and Sucherman. The two hard-working aides—the secretive Davis and more gregarious Sucherman—complemented each other. They would prove to be exceptionally able operatives, familiar with the world of educational television but committed to Friendly's quest to transform it into a new and dynamic form of public broadcasting. Friendly's ability to surround himself with talented personnel with just the right skills had been a key ingredient in his successes at CBS; his gift for spotting the talent he required would continue to serve him well. Armed with the resources of the Ford Foundation, and with Davis and Sucherman in place, Friendly was in a position to play an important role in the creation of an institutional framework for the public television network.

Friendly would inevitably play a critical role in determining whether NET would remain the networking arm for the new system. NET, responsible for both production and distribution of educational television, was dependent on Ford funding. In the spring of 1969, James Day, then the manager of KQED-TV in San Francisco, learned how Friendly wielded the foundation's power. When Day was in New York for an NET affiliates meeting, he received an invitation from Friendly for breakfast that felt like a "royal summons." A black Lincoln limousine owned by the foundation brought him to Friendly's home in Riverdale, where Friendly discussed the possibility of Day's replacing John F. (Jack) White as president of NET. Day was surprised that Friendly and the Ford Foundation were making the approach because NET had a search committee for that purpose. Friendly seemed annoyed at Day's naiveté. Day expressed reluctance to accept the offer, saying he preferred to work at the station level. Friendly countered that perhaps the New York and Washington, D.C., affiliates could be put under NET's control, so that he would have jurisdiction over those stations as well as over NET. Day remembered thinking that the foundation did not have the legal power to transfer the licenses and that there would be widespread opposition to such a plan. The formal offer of the presidency—which Day accepted—came a week later from Norman Cousins, chair of the NET search committee.[3]

Friendly became the point man in negotiations about interconnection that would lead to the creation of the Public Broadcasting Service (PBS) at the end of 1969. Frank Pace Jr., chair of CPB, was a former secretary of the army and former CEO of General Dynamics; John Macy Jr., president of CPB, had chaired the Civil Service Commission under Presidents Kennedy and Johnson. Pace and Macy relied heavily on the broadcasting expertise of Friendly and his staff at the Ford Foundation. Friendly felt compelled to obscure his role in the negotiations and that of the foundation from both NET and the Nixon administration. He had concluded that a new Washington-based entity—PBS— should operate the interconnection, which would prove to be a bitter disappointment for NET. At the same time, Friendly did not want to provoke the ire of the Nixon administration, which came to office in 1969 deeply suspicious of the Ford Foundation as an arm of the eastern Establishment.

A detailed study in 1979 of the creation of PBS revealed the critical role played by the Ford Foundation behind the scenes, contrary to official accounts of PBS's genesis as a product of negotiations between CBP and representatives of the local stations. The study demonstrates that "although station representatives were included in the deliberations leading to PBS, Ford's role appears to have been in many ways of far greater significance." David Davis observed that many players were formally involved in deliberations, "but the staff work was really being done at my shop."[4] Davis met regularly over an eighteen-month period with Ward Chamberlin, CPB's vice president and general manager. The study concluded that "these two, more than any others, were responsible for creating PBS as it finally emerged." Chamberlin had a business background as associate counsel at General Dynamics when Frank Pace was its CEO; Chamberlin had no experience in broadcasting and looked to Friendly for guidance. Chamberlin recalled an early meeting with Friendly in his office at the Ford Foundation, where four television sets were turned to the networks and educational television: "He kept looking over at the TV sets and suddenly picked up a nearby book and threw it at the CBS set and broke the picture. He was upset at what CBS was broadcasting. I thought to myself—this man really cares. I had seen nothing like this in my previous corporate life."[5]

Jack White, the long-time head of NET, would never forgive Davis and Friendly for what he considered their betrayal in replacing NET with PBS as the administrative arm of the new public television network. "When the history of this period is written," White said, "the blackest page will belong to Fred Friendly." Davis, in retrospect, felt that the NET old guard misjudged Friendly's intention and role. According to Davis, Friendly was sensitive to NET's position and valued its strengths as a source of programming. For this reason, NET was initially given a preferred place as a supplier of programming to PBS, and James Day, White's successor as head of NET, was placed on PBS's board. But Friendly realized that the Public Broadcasting Act called for the separation of production and distribution, which NET traditionally combined. Furthermore, political realities ruled out NET's continuing role as the leading force in either administration or programming. Shortly after the creation of PBS, CPB chair Pace met with a Nixon aide in the White House who said that increased funding for CPB was contingent on the development of station-based production centers that would eventually replace NET.[6] Pace accepted the proposition but said that phasing out NET would take several years. Pace kept this discussion secret from the CPB staff but undoubtedly shared it with Friendly, with whom he worked closely in charting public television's future. Friendly felt that NET had to be integrated into the new system, against its will, if necessary; otherwise, it would be isolated and wither on the vine.

In 1970, NET merged with WNDT/Channel 13 in New York to create WNET. The merger of the two Ford-funded entities, engineered by Friendly, represented a creative solution to a set of vexing problems. Channel 13's financial woes and mediocre programming were an embarrassment to Bundy and Friendly, given its location in the nation's media capital, where most Ford Foundation board members lived. NET's continued existence as an independent institution represented an anomaly in a public broadcasting system whose national programming was based in production centers located within the largest public stations. According to Day, "Friendly believed that a marriage of NET's production skills with Channel 13's audience reach could make the flagship station the showpiece of the public medium." Another round of delicate negotiations ensued involving the merger of two independent-minded boards. Day became president of WNET/Channel 13. To seal the deal, Friendly had the Ford Foundation grant $2 million for WNET's local programming. Friendly told Day to remove producers doing national programming and to improve coverage of the New York metropolitan area dramatically and quickly. "He exploded," Day recalled, "when I told him the results might not be apparent on the screen for at least a year: 'We can't wait a year!' (But he did and, with characteristic generosity, said later that the wait had been worth it.)"[7]

The merger and infusion of funds fostered what came to be a renaissance of local programming on WNET. Jack Willis, coexecutive producer of NET's *Great American Dream Machine,* was hired to head public affairs programming, and Robert Kotlowitz of *Harper's* magazine took charge of cultural affairs. In 1970, a series called *Free Time* provided live interviews with offbeat and controversial figures three nights a week. A mobile unit began covering local events such as the Knapp Commission hearings on police brutality. In 1971, *Up Against New York* began an irreverent look at coping with everyday life in the Big Apple. *Behind the Lines* cast a critical eye on the New York press before becoming a national program. Day knew that Friendly, "the palpable presence in the wings," also wanted a nightly news program. WNET met the challenge with a landmark program, *The 51st State,* which often outscooped the local dailies, challenged the ratings of local network news shows, and won major awards. In general, Friendly's $2 million infusion of funds permitted WNET's programming to take a quantum leap forward. Friendly played a similar role in supporting the turnaround of WETA, the weak but strategically located public television station in Washington, D.C. Ward Chamberlin recalled that the first thing he did on being offered the position as WETA's president and general manager was turn to Friendly: "I talked about it with Fred and Dave Davis. I said: 'Fred, I can only succeed if I get some real money to turn that situation around.' 'How much do you need?' he asked. I said: '1.5 to 2.0 million dollars.' He said right away: 'Okay, we will loan WETA 1.5 million with no interest and if you succeed in a period of three years, we'll forgive repayment.' And that is how it worked out."[8]

Friendly became one of the chief architects of the public broadcasting system despite a variety of constraints. Forced to temper his instinct to create a centralized system, he would forgo the notion of a fourth network in favor of a public broadcasting *service*. Friendly nonetheless tried to resist what he considered excessive localism, chastising public broadcasters who objected to national production centers' being situated at the seven largest stations. The Public Broadcasting Service was in essence a membership organization that administered the network but was forbidden to fund or produce programming. As Ward Chamberlin recalled, Friendly "would have much preferred a stronger centralized PBS with much more authority and not so dependent on station acceptance. No question about that. He reluctantly accepted the PBS we created as being the best we could do."[9] Nonetheless, the creation of PBS represented a landmark in the development of a public television system, for which Friendly was largely responsible. Friendly was probably right in scuttling NET's aspirations to provide interconnection in light of opposition from both the local stations and the Nixon administration, and the shotgun marriage he ordered between Channel 13 and NET proved to be a successful union. Friendly, the wild man with fire in his belly, was also an astute realist who understood when he needed to compromise.

Despite the attempt to downplay the influence of the Ford Foundation, Friendly's role became a flashpoint for criticism. The conspiracy-minded Nixon administration viewed Bundy as a Kennedy and Johnson Democrat, NET as a New York–based bastion of liberalism, and Friendly as the force behind its programming.

While Ford grants clearly had an impact on the direction of programming, they entailed neither a single-minded political agenda nor control over actual programming content, as the Nixon administration believed. Key initiatives often resulted from requests from the stations. This was the case, for example, when Friendly came up with an emergency grant for *Newspaper of the Air* after James Day called him during a San Francisco newspaper strike. "His response to my single telephone call," Day remembered, "was vintage Friendly: no questions asked, just a demand that we do our best and 'let everyone know you're doing it.'"[10] After the strike, Day applied for funding of a successor called *Newsroom*. Inspired by its success, Friendly set aside money to encourage other stations to undertake regular daily local news shows under the *Newsroom* rubric. Three additional public stations—in Dallas, Pittsburgh, and Washington, D.C.—used Ford money to fund their own *Newsroom* programs. *Newsroom* became an important entry point for journalists in public broadcasting: Jim Lehrer, for example, anchor of PBS's *NewsHour with Jim Lehrer*, worked on the KERA edition of *Newsroom* in Dallas.

A critical distinction needs to be made in regard to Friendly's impact on programming. Friendly wielded influence on the origination and continuation of specific programs by virtue of Ford grants but not on actual production of the programs once the grants had been made. To insulate the production process, Ford money was given in the form of "block grants" to institutional entities like NET or stations rather than directly to producers. In addition, Friendly instituted a rule—for himself as well as Davis and Sucherman—barring intervention in a Ford-funded production in progress or prescreening of the final product. "That the Foundation had an important hand in our public-affairs programming was clear," Day later wrote, "but it was a hand that fostered the genre without dictating its content. . . . The Nixon forces were convinced that if the Foundation was paying the piper, the Foundation must be calling the tune."[11]

The administration became convinced, for example, that Friendly had been personally involved in the firing in April 1970 of William Woestendiek, the editor of the WETA-TV edition of *Newsroom* in Washington, D.C., following the appointment of Woestendiek's wife as press secretary to Martha Mitchell, the outspoken wife of Attorney General John N. Mitchell. The general manager of WETA was quoted as attributing Woestendiek's removal to "pressures from outside."[12] The firing became a cause célèbre and the object of heated speculation in Nixon administration circles. Suspicions about the source of external pressure centered on Friendly and on Max Kampelman, chair of the WETA-TV board and a close associate of Hubert Humphrey's. A week later, on April 27, 1970, Friendly was invited to appear before the House Subcommittee on Communications and Power to address the accusation that he had engineered Woestendiek's removal. With David Davis at his side,

Friendly read a prepared statement angrily denying the charges. He said that WETA management had called to inform—but not consult—him about the firing: "Our advice on this course of action was not solicited, and it was not given. . . . We have stayed out of the newsroom, out of the control room and out of the Board room."[13] Woestendiek, an old friend of Friendly's, later said of his firing, "I don't think Fred was responsible for it at all," and attributed the rumor to political machinations.[14]

As James Day said, despite such denials, suspicions persisted:

> Whenever an idea's paternity was in doubt, fingers generally pointed to the brass-and-glass headquarters of the Ford Foundation—if not to its resident expert Fred Friendly, then to one of his colleagues in the Office of Communications, David Davis or Stuart Sucherman. The Foundation tried to play its part in key decisions with quiet discretion. Occasionally, however, decisions announced in the name of the Corporation [CPB] had Ford's fingerprints all over them. Such was the case with the birth of an organization called NPACT.[15]

The National Public Affairs Center for Television (NPACT) was launched in Washington, D.C., in the summer of 1971. The product of a Ford Foundation initiative, NPACT was designed to serve as the new public affairs arm of the Public Broadcasting System. The establishment of NPACT precipitated a major conflict involving the Nixon White House and the Ford Foundation that would have disastrous consequences for public television. The fight took place in the context of the Nixon White House's attack on network broadcasting, signaled by Vice President Spiro Agnew's widely reported speech in November 1969. Agnew complained that after Nixon's speech on Vietnam a week earlier, "his words and policies were subjected to instant analysis and querulous criticism . . . by a small band of network commentators and self-appointed analysts, the majority of whom expressed, in one way or another, their hostility to what he had to say."

Friendly watched Agnew's address on television in his office at the Ford Foundation in the company of William Woestendiek. "He was furious," Woestendiek remembered. "We sat there together and fumed." The networks were cowed; William Paley ordered that CBS drop the practice of instant analysis. Friendly responded to Agnew's speech in an article in the *Saturday Review*. He wrote that Agnew's broadside had the virtue on putting a necessary—if skewed—spotlight on the state of broadcast journalism. Friendly expressed agreement with Agnew's criticism of the monolithic character of network news, although Friendly attributed it to the maximization of audiences and profits rather than to ideological factors. Yet Friendly also associated Agnew's speech with the demagoguery of Joseph McCarthy, paraphrasing Edward R. Murrow in asking, "When the record is finally written it will answer the question, who helped the American people better understand the dilemma of Vietnam—the administration or the American journalist?" Friendly took issue in particular with objections to instant analysis of presidential speeches, emphasizing "our crying need for more, not less, interpretive reporting." Friendly noted his own failure to fulfill this obligation as president of CBS News in August 1964 at the time of the Gulf of Tonkin Incident. "In spite of the pleas of our Washington Bureau," Friendly revealed, "I made the decision to leave the air two minutes after the President had concluded his remarks." Friendly now openly recalled how Murrow "called minutes after the Johnson speech to castigate me and CBS for not having provided essential analysis of the meaning of the event." Friendly wondered if fuller coverage of the Gulf of Tonkin Incident might have altered the course of the Vietnam War. He expressed the hope that the new public television system—as yet in its infancy and untested—would transcend the limitations of commercial television in providing background and analysis of breaking news.[16]

NPACT, conceived by the Ford Foundation and CPB with the political realities of the period in mind, would weaken the role of NET as a producer of public affairs programming, as the White House had insisted. In the spring of 1971, Friendly summoned James Day to the Ford Foundation for a meeting with John Macy, Davis, and Sucherman. Day received an order: PBS would be better served by a Washington production center for public affairs independent of NET. Until then, NET had a well-regarded Washington bureau headed by James Karayn. Under the plan, the NET bureau would be reconstituted as NPACT. The new entity would share production studios with WETA, whose board chair would oversee NPACT. Karayn would remain as general manager of NPACT. Day argued against situating public television's national news division at the doorstep of the federal government and was surprised that Friendly did not support his objection. A week after the meeting, Day received a letter from CPB president Macy confirming the establishment of NPACT with "the concurrence of our colleagues at the Ford Foundation," an acknowledgment of the decisive role played by Friendly.[17] The separation of NPACT from

NET, and the location of the new entity in Washington, D.C., could be seen as attempts to mollify both local public television stations and the Nixon administration. At the same time, the consolidation of NPACT and WETA-TV promised to create a greater presence for public television in Washington, as the merger of NET and Channel 13 had done in New York.

Friendly sought to expand public television's infrastructure in a politically attuned manner in a hostile political environment. However, NPACT provoked the ire of the White House as a result of James Karayn's choice of a star reporter to serve as NPACT's news anchor during the 1972 presidential campaign. In September 1971, Karayn announced the hiring of Sander Vanocur, a highly regarded fifteen-year veteran of NBC; Vanocur had been NBC's correspondent for the JFK interview that Friendly had produced in 1962. In addition, Karayn hired Robert MacNeil, who had had substantial experience reporting for the Canadian Broadcasting Corporation, Reuters, and the BBC and had worked at *PBL*. According to James Day, the selection of Vanocur and MacNeil had the support of Friendly. An article in *TV Guide* later asked, "Was Vanocur's hiring a Friendly plot?"[18] Friendly and Karayn adamantly denied discussing the hiring of Vanocur in advance. At any rate, Richard Nixon's reaction to the choice was apoplectic. Nixon considered Vanocur a political enemy, a Kennedy acolyte whose reporting contributed to his—Nixon's—defeat in the 1960 presidential election. The president could not bear the notion that Vanocur would be given an anti-Nixon platform in Washington at government expense. Nixon wanted to cut all funding for public broadcasting immediately. His aides convinced Nixon that to do so would be draconian and politically impractical. He was convinced instead that a series of steps could be taken, coordinated by the White House Office of Telecommunications Policy (OTP), to bring public television under White House control.[19]

The counteroffensive began a month later, on October 20, 1971, when Clay Whitehead, head of the White House OTP, addressed the forty-seventh annual convention of the National Association of Educational Broadcasters (NAEB) in Miami. The speech contained a broad attack on public television for not adhering to the principles of decentralization and diversity in programming. Friendly and the Ford Foundation were singled out in no uncertain terms. Whitehead accused the assembled public broadcasters of centralizing news programming in NPACT because "someone" thinks that regional autonomy leads to duplication.

"How different will your network news programs be from the programs that Fred Friendly and Sander Vanocur wanted to do at NBC?" Whitehead asked, adding, "Even the commercial networks don't rely on one sponsor for their news and public affairs, but the Ford Foundation is able to buy over $8 million worth of this kind of programming on your stations." Whitehead concluded by saying that long-term, multiyear funding would not be forthcoming as promised unless changes were made in accordance with the wishes of the Nixon administration.[20]

The campaign to discredit NPACT and public television included publicizing the salaries of Vanocur and MacNeil, prompting congressional hearings on public television's pay scales. The assault came to a head in 1972, when Nixon vetoed a two-year authorization bill for public broadcasting passed by broad margins in Congress. Scaled-down funding would be contingent on changes required by the Nixon White House. As a result of the veto, CBP president John Macy and his chief aides resigned; CPB chair Frank Pace was replaced by Thomas B. Curtis, a former Republican member of the House. The CPB board, dominated by Nixon administration appointees, rescinded a commitment for multiyear funding for NPACT and voted to discontinue funding for all public affairs programming except *Black Journal*.

The veto also upset the delicate balance between CPB and PBS, precipitating a conflict in which the authority of PBS—the system interconnection Friendly had labored so hard to establish—was diminished. A hobbled NPACT did not have the resources or independence to provide in-depth coverage of the 1972 presidential campaign, as intended at the time of its creation. Peter Kaye, a former Nixon press aide, was added to the roster of NPACT correspondents. In the words of James Day, public television entered a period of "obeisance to the whims of Washington."[21] In 1973, the CBP board voted to diminish PBS's authority significantly, including ending its final authority over the financing of program acquisition and distribution, and decided to conduct pre- and post-broadcast review of program balance. Only after the administration established its control over public broadcasting did Nixon sign a two-year authorization bill for CPB.

The system for which Friendly had such great aspirations, and had devoted seven years to build, seemed in shambles. In September, a hostile article on Friendly by Richard K. Doan in *TV Guide* bore the headline "Public TV's Most Powerful Friend . . . May Also Qualify as Its Worst Enemy." The article characterized Friendly as the powerful eminence grise of public broadcasting. "But," it continued, "he is almost certainly headed for humbling defeat in his passionate attempt to make public television an important force as a national-affairs forum." The author posited that Friendly's influence on programming, personnel, and content, if indirect, was often decisive. Doan attributed Friendly's agenda to a desire to outshine the public affairs programming of the commercial networks. Doan argued that Friendly was stymied in achieving this goal in large measure because of the resentment he provoked in many quarters, from public broadcasters to the Nixon administration. The former viewed Friendly as "the Big Wheel from Commercial TV who was going to tell them how to run their business." The latter considered Friendly, along with Bundy, as political foes who had long-standing ties to Presidents Kennedy and Johnson and the Democratic Party. Friendly's ego and overbearing personality, Doan suggested, kept him from making the necessary adjustments to realize his agenda. Ford's diminishing funding of public broadcasting could result in the end of Friendly's usefulness and employment at the Ford Foundation. Doan predicted that Friendly would be remembered "as a domineering force who treated public TV as if it were his private domain, who encouraged politically liberal bias in its programming, and who ultimately contributed, at least indirectly, to its downgrading as a national force."[22]

The putative obituary in *TV Guide* of Friendly as a force in public broadcasting proved to be premature. Ironically, PBS's coverage of the Senate Watergate hearings—by NPACT, no less—brought public television the largest audiences in its history and provided the system with a new lease on life. The networks broadcast the initial hearings, but only PBS carried them in their entirety. Witnesses ranging from high Nixon officials to burglars and bagmen became compelling actors in a national drama. As John Dean, one of the lead witnesses, recalled years later, "It was an ongoing soap opera. No one knew how it was going to turn out. And it drew massive audiences."[23] Robert MacNeil of NPACT anchored the broadcast of the hearings from WETA-TV in Washington; some PBS stations carried them live, others rebroadcast them in their entirety at night, and a few did both.

It was fitting that PBS's coverage of the Senate Watergate and House impeachment proceedings marked a turning point for the beleaguered public television system. The broadcasts, a great televised civics lesson, were a perfect illustration of Friendly's vision of what television could be. He understood that broadcasting such government proceedings could be great theater as well as a great public service. After all, he had been deeply impressed by the Kefauver hearings on organized crime early in his career, had been transfixed by the Army–McCarthy Hearings, and had quit CBS after the network failed to carry Senate hearings on Vietnam. Friendly had seen another demagogue, Joseph McCarthy, brought down with the help of television. The broadcast of Watergate deliberations by NPACT on PBS—two institutions that owed their existence largely to Friendly—represented a vindication for Friendly as well as for public television as a whole. In the aftermath of the Watergate hearings, he proposed that Congress open its chambers to public television, beginning in the bicentennial year of 1976, an idea realized in 1979 by the nonprofit C-SPAN cable network.

The Watergate scandal and the resignation of Nixon ended the White House campaign to purge public television of public affairs programming and the influence of Friendly and the Ford Foundation. After 1974, the number of PBS affiliates and the size of their audience grew significantly. The Public Broadcasting Financing Act of 1975 sought to address the need for increased funding. Nonetheless, public television did not emerge from the Nixon assault unscathed. The experience accelerated the retreat from the experimental and controversial programming of the late 1960s and early 1970s. The funding system that Friendly had criticized in 1967 as providing an insufficient political firewall remained intact. Reliance on congressional appropriations would continue to make public broadcasting vulnerable to political pressure and to have a chilling effect on controversial public affairs programming.

Nonetheless, public broadcasting expanded and achieved an institutional equilibrium during the Ford and Carter administrations. In 1976, the Ford Foundation issued a report in which it celebrated public broadcasting's coming of age after a quarter century of the foundation's support. The foundation said that it would scale back its leadership role in public broadcasting while continuing to give smaller strategic grants to complete its initiatives in national programming, satellite interconnection, and audience research. Although it would maintain a "small contingency fund for public television," the foundation's communications office would henceforth focus on policy issues, journalism education, and international issues. Did Friendly's influence in public television wane beginning in the mid-1970s? "Yes," according to Ward Chamberlin, "but that was because the major structural framework of [public television] was in place, and we know he played a major role in bringing that about."[24]

Friendly remained a major force in PBS programming through 1980. He supported the *NewsHour*'s change to a full hour and saw to it that

Ford money continued to support programs like *Washington Week in Review*, *Bill Moyers Journal*, and *Firing Line*, as well as flagship musical and theatrical series. In 1977, Friendly grilled in his office at Ford a thoroughly intimidated, scruffy South African producer in a black leather jacket named David Fanning before giving him a seed grant for *World*, the documentary series that evolved into *Frontline*. Friendly also continued to speak about public television when so moved. This was the case, for example, when *In Hiding: America's Fugitive Underground—An Interview with Abbie Hoffman* aired in 1975 on WNET/Channel 13. The program had been produced by the WNET TV Lab, an experimental unit funded in part by the Ford Foundation that had paid Hoffman $2,500 for the interview. Friendly was furious about this example of checkbook journalism and threatened to reconsider the foundation's grants to WNET. Broadcast of the interview on PBS was canceled. Friendly added to his criticism of the payment his belief that Hoffman was not a newsworthy subject. A video historian reviewing the controversy suggested that Friendly's "self-righteous views on journalistic standards" clashed with PBS's journalism guidelines, which affirmed the importance of airing dissenting views.[25]

At any rate, the controversy about the Abbie Hoffman interview was a sidebar. By 1975, public television had survived the Nixon attack and solidified its infrastructure to become a permanent part of the U.S. television landscape. It may not have been the bold fourth network that Friendly had dreamed of, but it was a considerable achievement nonetheless. Now the focus of the Ford Foundation—and of Friendly—could shift elsewhere. The fifty-seven-year-old Friendly dismissed an interviewer's suggestion that his tenure at Ford might end as the foundation ceased being a primary player in public broadcasting. Friendly saw unmet needs and new challenges ahead: "I see myself," he said, gesturing dramatically, "having *still another career.*"[26]

18 The Press and the Bar

A TURNING POINT in Fred Friendly's professional focus at Columbia University and the Ford Foundation came in 1974. By this time, several major projects had come to fruition. An expanded broadcast journalism track and facility were in place at the journalism school. The Summer Program for Minority Journalists had ended a successful seven-year run on campus; its work would be continued by the Institute for Journalism Education on the West Coast. He continued to enjoy teaching responsibilities that nonetheless had become more routinized. At Ford, he had placed interconnection of noncommercial television on the public agenda with the Ford satellite proposal and then had played an instrumental role in its implementation through the creation of PBS. Public broadcasting had weathered Nixon's assault to achieve a level of institutional equilibrium and permanency. Friendly's dream of a centralized, financially independent fourth network with cutting-edge programming in news and public affairs may have eluded him. Yet he had been in the thick of educational broadcasting's rocky and imperfect but ultimately successful transition to public television. He would continue to build on his contribution to broadcast journalism at Columbia and to nourish public television through the Ford Foundation, but he was ready for new challenges. Friendly, now approaching his sixtieth year as energetic, creative, and restless as ever, had never been one to contemplate retirement.

Throughout his career, Friendly instinctively tackled large, seemingly impossible tasks. In the years immediately after his departure from CBS, he aspired to nothing less than using public broadcasting to rescue television as a news medium. Now he turned to another momentous task, addressing the growing crisis in press and government relations that in his view imperiled democracy in the United States. According to Benno Schmidt, with whom Friendly had been teaching the Columbia seminar on communications law, "Fred had a sense that government and journalism were becoming antagonistic in a way that was unprecedented in his lifetime."[1] Friendly had been a target of the Nixon attack on the press; he also recognized how the Pentagon Papers case, *New York Times Co. v. United States* (1971), signaled a breakdown in trust regarding press coverage of national security. Disputes about protecting news sources further exacerbated relations between the press and prosecutors.

Friendly did not hold the press blameless in its conflict with the judiciary, as he said in a speech, "The Nervous Breakdown of the First Amendment," that he delivered on January 10, 1974, before the Federal Communications Bar Association in Washington, D.C. He cited federal appellate judge J. Skelly Wright on the difficulty of distinguishing "the good guys from the bad guys" in current First Amendment cases.[2] Friendly excoriated the press policies of the Nixon administration. He lamented the precipitous increase in the use of restrictive gag orders directed at the press by trial judges to limit pretrial publicity in court cases. Copyright law was being expanded to limit the fair use of unpublished material of legitimate public interest. Friendly also noted how a flood of subpoenas issued against journalists threatened confidentiality of news sources. For example, Friendly pointed to the subpoena issued to Earl Caldwell for his coverage of the Black Panthers for the *New York Times*; Caldwell's challenge of the subpoena reached the Supreme Court, which in 1972 issued an opinion that substantially weakened the protection of news sources.[3]

At the same time, Friendly made a stinging critique of news organizations for weakening First Amendment protections by invoking them in inappropriate and self-serving ways. He offered as an example network claims that the fairness doctrine, designed to ensure the broadcast of opposing viewpoints on controversial issues, violated the First Amendment. He criticized the *Miami Herald* for refusing on First Amendment grounds to reprint the rejoinder of a local politician who had been criticized in its pages, which prompted the Supreme Court case *Miami Herald v. Tornillo* (1974)—in which the Court held for the paper. He chastised the newspaper industry for successfully lobbying for passage of the Newspaper Preservation Act of 1970, offering a First Amendment rationale for an end-run around antitrust laws that weakened competition and facilitated consolidation and higher profits in print journalism. He suggested that "those who would hide behind some self-serving absolutism in its law distort the Amendment's history and cloud its future." Friendly identified other shoddy practices on the part of the news media. In a subsequent report for the Ford Foundation, Friendly and Martin A. Linsky, an attorney, reiterated a concern about "the festering conflict between the press and the bench" and the failure of the two sides to engage in "reasonable discussion" to address their differences.[4]

Friendly aspired to initiate such a reasonable discussion as both author and producer. In 1975, he published an article that bore the headline "What's Fair on the Air?" and in 1976 the book *The Good Guys, the Bad Guys and the First Amendment: Free Speech vs. Fairness in Broadcasting.*[5] The study examined in detail *Red Lion Broadcasting v. FCC*, a case involving the fairness doctrine that was heard in 1969 by the Supreme Court. In framing the issues raised by the *Red Lion* case, Friendly acknowledged the influence of Walter Lippmann's *Public Opinion*, "scripture to me in both newsroom and classroom," adding that Lippmann had encouraged him to write the book not long before his death in 1974. The *Red Lion* case highlighted the problematic requirement of the fairness doctrine that broadcasters provide individuals who are the target of personal attacks the opportunity to respond over the airwaves. The case was prompted by a vituperative political assault on the muckraking journalist Fred Cook by the right-wing radio evangelist Billy James Hargis that was carried in 1964 by WGCB, a radio station in the town of Red Lion, Pennsylvania, owned by the Red Lion Broadcasting Company. Hargis's hero was Joseph McCarthy; he had been at the senator's side when he died. Cook had roused the ire of the right by writing a book critical of Barry Goldwater and a lengthy exposé, "Radio Right: Hate Clubs of the Air," which appeared in 1964 in the *Nation.*[6]

Following Hargis's attack, Cook wrote to the Red Lion Broadcasting Company requesting free air time to respond, as required by the fairness doctrine. When his request was denied, Cook appealed to the Federal Communications Commission, setting into motion a case that ultimately came before the Supreme Court. Cook and his allies argued that he had a First Amendment right of access to the airwaves to respond to a personal attack. The owners of WGCB countered that the authority of the FCC, a government agency, to determine programming content by requiring air time for Cook violated their First Amendment rights. Both sides wrapped themselves in the First Amendment. The Supreme Court unanimously upheld the constitutionality of the fairness doctrine, arguing that the scarcity of spectrum space justified regulating broadcasting to ensure diversity of perspectives.[7]

The decision seemed to have resolved the issue—but not for Friendly, who would challenge conventional thinking in a detailed reexamination of the case. The question of balance and editorial independence in broadcasting had been a contentious issue during Friendly's tenure at CBS. He and Murrow had volunteered to give McCarthy an opportunity to reply to the See It Now program about him. But CBS's insistence that a congressional critic of the See It Now program on statehood for Alaska and Hawaii be given air time had been a major blow to See It Now. The charge of editorializing had led to the departure of Howard K. Smith from CBS. Many in broadcasting saw the fairness doctrine as a mixed blessing, fostering blandness in programming and arming executives with an argument for avoiding controversy.

In the preface to his book, Friendly wrote that the case provided a "little picture" to illuminate broad First Amendment issues. He interviewed every important player in the case, including Billy James Hargis, whose right-wing agenda combined anti-Communism and anti-Semitism. Fred and Ruth interviewed Hargis at the American Christian College in Tulsa, Oklahoma, which Hargis had founded as an alternative for Christian parents who did not want their children to come under the influence of Jews in secular schools. Ruth recalled seeing a room that seemed to be as big as an airline hangar full of literature that Hargis distributed throughout the nation; she also recalled being apprehensive as they sat down to talk. Friendly would begin such interviews by saying, "Mr. Hargis, you and I disagree about many things, but one thing we don't disagree about is the First Amendment."[8]

Friendly also interviewed Wayne Phillips, a staff member of the Democratic National Committee, and became convinced that Cook's request for air time was part of a concerted effort on the part of the Kennedy and Johnson administrations to silence right-wing radio broadcasters. Friendly discovered that the Democratic National Committee had directed a flood of requests for rebuttals to discourage radio stations from carrying the broadcasts of Hargis and his ilk, and that the DNC had even put Cook up to writing the book about Goldwater and the article about hate radio. Hence the Democrats, as well as the right-wing broadcasters, were using the First Amendment for their own partisan purposes. Friendly was disturbed by what he saw as liberals trying to exploit the fairness doctrine in order to squelch rather than extend free speech.

Friendly characterized the *Red Lion* decision as ambiguous and unsatisfactory. He expressed concern that the fairness doctrine gave government the potential to abuse First Amendment rights. At the same time, he felt that the doctrine's repeal would not be in the public interest because it would permit broadcasters to shirk their responsibility to provide comprehensive coverage of news and public affairs. Friendly recommended a two-part compromise to resolve the dilemmas posed by *Red Lion*. First, he argued that the FCC should cease examining specific programs in relation to fairness but evaluate a station's overall performance in this regard at license renewal time. Second, he used the model of newspaper op-ed pages to argue that broadcasters should develop new formats in which viewers could express their views. In addition, he voiced the expectation that the growth of cable television systems with a multiplicity of channels would eventually bring to an end the scarcity of channels that necessitated the fairness doctrine in the first place. "The networks failed to listen to Friendly ten years ago," a reviewer wrote in the *New Republic*. "One hopes they have the sense to listen now."[9]

Carey McWilliams, editor of the *Nation*, angrily denied that Cook's article for that magazine was a Democratic Party dirty trick and accused Friendly, who had interviewed him as well as Cook and Phillips for the book, of distorting and misusing the information that they gave him. In response, Friendly noted that his history showed that he was no apologist for the broadcast industry or for the views aired by representatives of the radical right on radio: "But the right of broadcasters who choose to carry their programs to do so without fear of harassment or intimidation is still another matter." In contrast, Everett C. Parker, the director of the Office of Communications of the United Church of Christ, characterized Friendly's revelation about the secret campaign of the Democratic Party against right-wing radio as "a reportorial tour de force that adds a revealing footnote to American politics of the nineteen-sixties." However, Parker seemed skeptical of Friendly's hope that the problem would be resolved in part by measures taken by the broadcast industry.[10]

Despite largely positive reviews, some critics complained about an anticlimactic conclusion in which Friendly failed to either embrace or reject the fairness doctrine decisively. The headline on a brief article in *Variety* read, "On the Other Hand, Fred Friendly Finds That Fairness Is Fair." However, reviewers praised the accounts of interviews that Friendly conducted with virtually all the principals in the case, from

Billy James Hargis and Archibald Cox, the former Watergate prosecutor who was one of the attorneys in the *Red Lion* case, to Clay Whitehead, Friendly's former nemesis in the Office of Telecommunications of the Nixon White House. "The book comes alive," a critic wrote in *Business Week,* "when Friendly abandons the court records and lets people talk." The interviews necessitated extensive travel by Friendly and his team. His wife, Ruth, to whom he dedicated the book, served as his constant companion and aide-de-camp. Friendly also generously acknowledged the contribution of three teaching assistants. Dan Werner, a graduate of Columbia Law School as well as of the journalism school, recalled "driving with Ruth down a steep Pennsylvania hill as we tried to follow the tail lights of the car ahead" for a late-night rendezvous and, in general, "one hell of a lesson in journalism." Martha Elliott collated the extensive source material, among other tasks, and Jennifer Siebens wrote critiques of the early chapters. Elliott recalled copy editing drafts of early chapters for Friendly and later fleshing out sections after Friendly jotted down ideas or a rudimentary outline on a yellow legal pad, what he called his hieroglyphics. As Elliott recalled, "Fred was a great storyteller, especially for television, but he wasn't as good a writer when it came to organizing a book. He would start out with a yellow pad and write out thoughts, ideas, paragraphs. I would take it and try to put it together and add to it—especially with legal research because he wasn't the kind of person who would go in a law library and look up a case. It wasn't his thing." However, Elliott added, "Fred liked to do the personal research, do the hands-on kind of research, talk to people. That was his greatest power."[11]

The important role played by Elliott and the other graduate assistants led Melvin Mencher and Penn Kimball—his antagonists in the print track at Columbia—to accuse Friendly of not writing his own books. It was an unfair accusation that reflected a failure to understand how Friendly worked. Despite the collaborative process, *The Good Guys, the Bad Guys and the First Amendment* bore Friendly's imprint from its inception to its publication. It is telling that Friendly referred to the book as a documentary and acknowledged a legion of associates who assisted in its completion. Perhaps he was more the book's executive producer than its author in the conventional sense. "He used to say that he was the engine and everyone else was the train," Elliott recalled. "And it's true: he was the engine that made everything happen." Recalling his participation in the project, Werner emphasized Friendly's authorship: "It was his book. He wrote it. He thought it through. . . . Fred liked to be edited, he liked to argue back. But the important thing about the book is that it was his."[12]

Friendly had been the engine that pioneered the art of the television interview, of the dramatic juxtaposition of ideas, for *See It Now*. Friendly's treatment of the fairness doctrine might have worked better as a television documentary than as a book. Imagine filmed interviews with the radical right-wing reverend Billy James Hargis, the muckraking journalist Fred Cook, the Democratic Party operative Wayne Phillips, the distinguished attorney Archibald Cox, and other players in this complex political and legal drama. At any rate *The Good Guys, the Bad Guys and the First Amendment* would not be the exclusive or even primary means by which Friendly would address the larger crisis in press–judicial relations.

In 1974, together with his staff at the Ford Foundation, Friendly was groping for a more sustained treatment of the problem, brainstorming with a variety of contacts. The line between Friendly's positions at Ford and Columbia had always been blurred. Friendly's law class with Benno Schmidt was now held in the foundation's boardroom. Friendly continued to explore ways to take the issues he dealt with in the classroom onto a larger stage. Lloyd Morrisett of the John and Mary Markle Foundation suggested that Friendly use his position at Ford to mount a national conference on the subject; Friendly did not think it would work.[13] Shortly thereafter, Friendly had lunch with a Massachusetts judge and Tom Winship, editor of the *Boston Globe*, during which he reiterated his desire to do something about the breakdown in relations between the media and the courts. Winship suggested that Friendly contact Martin Linsky, an editorial writer for his newspaper who was also an attorney and a former member of the Massachusetts House of Representatives.

Friendly called Linsky, who came to New York to have dinner with Fred and Ruth. In their first encounter, Friendly struck Linsky as a figure larger than life, appearing even taller than his six-foot, four-inch frame. Linsky found Friendly to be "an incredible networker with an endless Rolodex, almost impossible to say no to, and very, very passionate about his interests."[14] On the basis of his discussion with Friendly, Linsky wrote a proposal for a series of seminars in which representatives of the Fourth Estate and the bar would use Socratic dialogue to discuss the issues that divided them. Linsky drew on his experiences at Williams College and Harvard Law School in designing a structured discourse. The format suggested by Linsky consisted of an off-the-record session in which about twenty people would sit around a U-shaped table answering questions posed by a moderator about a hypothetical case. Friendly and Stuart Sucherman followed up by attending a class of Professor Arthur Miller's at Harvard Law School to examine his use of the Socratic method and to approach him about getting involved in the project. Friendly and Linsky would later spell out the rationale for such seminars in Lippmannesque terms for the Ford Foundation. They wrote of the need for a "new kind of forum" to address the growing frictions between the press and society, adding, "The news media are part of the problem and part of the remedy; from the words and images they decide to write, edit, and transmit, the citizenry forms a view of reality on which it can act."[15]

As Friendly had recommended, the Ford Foundation underwrote an experimental weekend seminar from June 7 to 9, 1974, when fifty New England lawyers, judges, and journalists convened in Chatham, Massachusetts, on Cape Cod. Fred, Ruth, and Sucherman had attended David Friendly's graduation from high school the previous day, so they flew to Cape Cod for the meeting in a private plane. The event was cosponsored by the *Boston Globe* and the Nieman Foundation at Harvard. Linsky invited Miller and Charles Nesson of the Harvard Law School and Dean Abraham Goldstein of the Yale Law School to act as facilitators. Sucherman recalled a measure of discomfort and skepticism among the participants, especially from the journalistic side. At the opening session, James C. Thomson, head of the Nieman Foundation at Harvard, infuriated Friendly when he got up and said, "I don't know why we are all here." Linsky attributed Thomson's reaction to a reluctance to acknowledge that journalists were players in the world of public affairs, not just neutral observers—a key issue that Friendly wanted the seminar to address.[16]

"As maestro," Linsky wrote of Friendly, "both at Chatham Bars Inn and subsequently, he was a ubiquitous presence, opening and closing the event, graciously thanking everyone who participated, and very much the MC and producer of it all." Friendly was pleased by what he and other participants found to be a highly productive exchange of perspectives. As they traveled back to New York, he turned to Ruth and asked, "Do you think this wine would travel?" Ruth was skeptical that such an event could be replicated, but Friendly felt he had hit on something that could be further developed. Linsky also judged the initial session a success: "My sense and recollection is that there was widespread enthusiasm for the event, its drama and intensity captured attendees' imagination."[17] As an outgrowth of the Chatham seminar Harvard University's Institute of Politics and the Nieman Foundation established the New England Conference on Conflicts Between the Media and the Law, which in September 1974 held the first of a series of follow-up seminars.

A retreat in Virginia become the venue for Friendly's second major test conference, held on March 7 to 9, 1975, and cosponsored by the *Washington Post*. Participants included Supreme Court Justice Potter Stewart, who became noticeably agitated as he listened for a second day to complaints about the judiciary's treatment of the Fourth Estate. Friendly noticed that Stewart's fists had become clenched; his knuckles, white. Stewart then asked, "Where, ladies and gentlemen [of the press], do you think these great constitutional rights that you were so vehemently asserting, and in which you were so conspicuously wallowing yesterday, where do you think they come from? The stork didn't bring them. These came from the judges of this country, from these villains here sitting at the table." Stewart noted that the brevity and ambiguity of the language in the First Amendment regarding freedom of the press had made possible passage of the Alien and Sedition Acts at the end of the eighteenth century. "And if these laws were still on the books," he added, "Richard Nixon would still be president of the United States . . . and all of you people would probably be in prison." Stewart argued that it took a succession of court decisions in the nineteenth and twentieth centuries to define and extend the guarantee of freedom of expression. Stewart was clearly angry, and his outburst was followed by a stunned silence. It was broken by Daniel Schorr, who asked, "But what have you done for us lately?" After a moment of silence, everyone laughed, including Stewart.[18] The intensity of the first two sessions suggested that what Friendly and Linsky had developed transcended the limits of traditional conferences or programs featuring talking heads. The success of the two pilot conferences led to the establishment of the Ford Foundation Seminar Program on Media and Society.

For each subsequent seminar, a dramatic hypothetical situation carefully crafted in advance became a vehicle for raising critical issues. The format owed a great deal to the way Friendly ran his Columbia seminars as well as Linsky's experience with the Socratic method. Dan Werner recalled that Friendly used a classroom large enough to set students in a circle with a large center arena. "Crossing that center in random rages," Werner later reminded Friendly, "you put your students to the test." For the seminars, the moderator would describe the scenario in some detail: the principal characters, the political or institutional setting in which they operated, and the developments that had brought them into conflict. The moderator would then confront seminar participants with vexing ethical and legal questions posed by the situation. For example, a seminar on court orders restricting press coverage of trials and the protection of news sources revolved around a hypothetical tale of suburban scandal. After describing successive stages in the unfolding case, which involved gag orders and subpoenas to the press, the moderator asked how panelists would respond in their professional capacities and then continued the narrative and posed additional questions. Another seminar dealt with a hypothetical situation involving national security that created conflicts between government officials and the press. In this case, the occupation of a nuclear power plant by ecoterrorists leads to requests for a news blackout and other restraints to which the panelists representing the press must respond.[19]

During the seminars, Friendly's team of moderators, eminent lawyers skilled in the art of cross-examination, relentlessly posed vexing questions. During a seminar, its moderator moved freely within the open space in front of the U-shaped table like a prosecuting attorney, confronting individual panelists with probing questions. The Socratic dialogue revealed the decision-making process of the panelists and explored dilemmas and inconsistencies in their responses to a specific set of hypothetical circumstances. Most important, the exchanges forced the assembled journalists and jurists to come to grips with the legitimate interests and concerns of their counterparts. Friendly and Linsky defined the process with language that would become a mantra for Friendly. This method, they wrote, discouraged polemics and oratory "by forcing participants to respond to situations where the agony of decision making is so intense that they can only escape by thinking."[20] Charles Seib testified to the intensity of the second seminar hosted by the *Washington Post*. Seib, the *Post*'s ombudsman, wrote soon after:

> The press and the law confronted each other in the Virginia mountains a few weeks ago. It was eyeball to eyeball and sometimes claw to claw. . . . At the end, there was a sense of exhaustion; the Socratic method is draining for those who participate and even for those who watch. There was also evident a sense of mutual understanding and respect among the participants. . . . As they departed, a neutral ob-

server might have observed that the press was waving the First Amendment just a bit less defiantly and that the judges had lowered slightly, but not furled, their restraining orders. The conference was only the beginning in what must be a long dialogue before there is any broad understanding between the judiciary and the press.[21]

As Friendly later explained, "What we sought to do was to ask judges and lawyers to put themselves in reporters', editors' and producers' seats, and to ask journalists to place themselves behind the bench."[22]

In designing the format, Friendly and Linsky opted for settings or retreats removed from day-to-day pressures whenever possible. This would preclude interruption and permit both formal and informal interaction among participants. As originally conceived, the seminars were deemed off the record in order to encourage maximum openness. Friendly understood the critical role of the skilled moderator. Benno Schmidt, of Columbia Law School, soon joined Miller and Nesson of Harvard; the three would serve as moderators for 90 percent of the seminars, which they helped develop as well as lead. Each had the insight and rhetorical skill required, in the words of Friendly and Linsky, "to engage leading professionals in a structured dialogue where humor, hard thinking, and candor prevail over rhetoric and pretense." Friendly, the driving force behind the seminars, directed their overall production—usually opening and closing each session—but rarely served as moderator. According to Schmidt, "His personality was too dominant. . . . To be a good moderator, you have to ask provocative questions, but you have to step back, you have to let people answer. The ideal point in a program like that is when the participants take over the questioning. . . . Fred was just a little too assertive." Schmidt believed that Friendly's awareness of this led him to rely on his three star moderators. As Schmidt observed, "Fred would never have been patient enough to be Socrates."[23] But he was equipped to be Socrates's producer—that is, to produce a new kind of compelling Socratic seminar for the U.S. press and judiciary and, subsequently, for television audiences as well.

19 Seminar

AFTER NEARLY A DECADE of teaching and making policy, Friendly had returned to his first love: producing. The two conferences hosted by the *Boston Globe* and the *Washington Post* in the mid-1970s became prototypes for a nationwide series of traveling seminars under the rubric of the Conference on the Media and the Law. The scope was broadened beyond the courtroom to include media practices in relation to book publishing, business, human rights, privacy rights, city government, medical ethics, and the family. In 1976 and 1977, for example, Denver, Chicago, New York, Detroit, Seattle, Philadelphia, Tucson, and Nashville hosted seminars, which were mounted at a rate of more than once a month. Usually, three seminar sessions with about fifteen panelists and an invited audience of as many as a hundred people took place over a weekend at a hotel or retreat. Cocktails and dinner provided an opportunity for informal give-and-take among panelists and guests. These seminars typically cost about $30,000 each; usually, the Ford Foundation and cosponsoring local organizations divided the expense.

The first attempt to organize a seminar for broadcast—The Anglo-American Conference on News and the Law—took place in 1977 in England, where Friendly had long-standing contacts. Sir Denis Forman, chair of Granada Television, invited Friendly to organize a seminar in England on the law and the press that would be filmed and edited for broadcast. Among the cosponsors was the *Times* of London; its editor, Harry Evans, was a good friend of Friendly's who had attended the very first seminar in 1974. Other sponsors included the *Observer*, the *Scotsman*, Reuters, and the International Press Institute. Brian Lapping, a producer at Grenada, made the case to the three lead seminar moderators—Benno Schmidt, Arthur Miller, and Charles Nesson—that the seminars would make good television. As Schmidt recalled, "It was Brian and the three of us who had to persuade a very skeptical Fred to try this. Fred agreed to try this as a kind of experiment." According to Ruth Friendly, her husband had initially expressed concern that U.S. judges might refuse to participate on the record in televised programs; that was why he had begun the seminars as quasi-private affairs. The initial British seminar became the first in a series of seminars produced by Lapping that were aired throughout the Commonwealth to popular and critical acclaim. In retrospect, Linsky believed that Friendly intended to broadcast the seminars in the future but wanted to establish and perfect the format first. Ruth agreed with Linsky: "Fred was always thinking of doing the seminars on television. He was a television person. But he didn't want to try to do it and not have it work." James Day recognized immediately that the seminars had the elements of good television: celebrity panelists, the drama inherent in the hypothetical plot lines, and the element of the unknown in the panelists' spontaneous responses.[1] However, Friendly would not devote his full attention to televising the seminars in the United States for two more years, until his working arrangements at Columbia University and the Ford Foundation changed.

In 1979, Friendly retired as a full-time member of the journalism faculty at Columbia University. Columbia had already become less of a focal point for him. He continued to select a star graduate of the journalism school to be his "teaching assistant," but Jonathan Landman, chosen for 1978/1979, was paid by the Ford Foundation, where he did most of his work. "By the time I got there, Columbia was really a smaller part of his life," Landman remembered. "Columbia was a place where he taught a course and not much more, although he used that course as a laboratory to experiment a little bit for the other things he was doing." Friendly had had his fill of the academic infighting and the hostility of colleagues in the Graduate School of Journalism; he complained that he was tired of being "nibbled to death by ducks." Friendly had forged his deepest ties with his teaching assistants, the talented group of his aides and acolytes. In 1975, on the occasion of his sixtieth birthday, a group of former teaching assistants had presented Friendly with an affectionate booklet of war stories about working for him. Now, four years later, when he retired as the Edward R. Murrow Professor of Journalism, fourteen former students and assistants celebrated the event at a dinner party, where they presented him with a television screen mounted in wood with their signatures. The day after the party, Friendly distributed an emotional letter to the group. He said he would never forget their work together in the broadcast laboratory, which at its best was "a distant signal of what broadcasting, perhaps because of you, may yet become."[2]

After 1979, Friendly continued to lecture part time as the Murrow professor emeritus. However, he was no longer in charge of the broadcast curriculum. Friendly told the *Washington Journalism Review* that "my days on the payroll there are over"; he would continue to give lectures and courses only by invitation. Columbia's president, William McGill, and the new journalism dean, Osborn Elliott, said they would nonetheless continue to look to him for advice. Friendly said he would do anything they asked of him: "It's no secret that I love the school and that I identify with it." Friendly's days as an employee of the Ford Foundation were numbered as well. In 1979, Franklin A. Thomas replaced McGeorge Bundy as president of the Ford Foundation. Bundy had been the indispensable mentor for Friendly's second career, just as Murrow had been for his first. Thomas's more traditional administrative style precluded the easy-going banter and brainstorming that Bundy had encouraged. It was clear that there would be less room for Friendly's free-wheeling style and that his initiatives and requests for funds would be scrutinized more carefully. According to Willard Hertz, his colleague at Ford, Friendly, who would turn sixty-five at the end of 1980, was not fired or asked to leave: "I think Fred just felt his heyday was over and then he left." However, according to Ruth, Friendly's relationship with Franklin Thomas was good, and retirement at sixty-five was Ford Foundation policy.[3]

Whether his departure was mandated or not, Friendly retired in December 1980 after fourteen years as communications adviser at the Ford Foundation. The position had given him tremendous leverage in the development of public television and communications policy in general. At sixty-five, Friendly's health, ambition, and work ethic remained undiminished. What would he do next? The *New York Times* reported that the Ford Foundation was dropping its official sponsorship of Friendly's seminars, although it was still considering partial funding of a revamped university-based seminar program. A reporter for the *Daily News*, who interviewed Friendly as he cleaned out his office a day before his farewell party at the foundation, found Friendly in a ruminative mood. While going through his desk, Friendly came upon Jack Schneider's cruel joke, the mock business cards bearing the title "Fred W. Friendly, Former President, CBS News." The reporter observed that "the most vivid memory of his life, it seems, is still that resignation 15 years ago." In reflecting on his post-CBS career, Friendly expressed regret for overhyping *PBL*, but he took credit for helping to establish and protect public television during its early years. He expressed pride in the Summer Program for Minority Journalists, which he had mounted at Columbia with the help of Ford Foundation money. During the interview, Friendly referred to himself several times as a "mangy old lion." He said that at his funeral he wanted his family to play the song "Send in the Clowns." At one point, Friendly said of his tenure at Ford and Columbia, "I'm happy to be retiring." But moments later he expressed his reluctance to leave the public arena, saying, "I probably should retire, but I can't."[4]

Friendly's retirement from Columbia and Ford hardly left him bereft of projects. Indeed, in 1980, before he left Ford, he was engaged in a number of undertakings as well as negotiations about future ventures. That year, for example, he was busy completing his book *Minnesota Rag*, about *Near v. Minnesota* (1931), the first press censorship case heard by the Supreme Court.[5] His curiosity about the background of the case had been piqued by a luncheon with Irving Shapiro, chairman of the board of DuPont, who as a boy in Minneapolis had witnessed his father being beaten by the racketeers who were exposed in Jay Near's newspaper, the *Saturday Press*. The story of the case, from its obscure origins in the wild boom years on the Mesabi Iron Range to its consideration by the Supreme Court, became the fourth and most successful of Friendly's books. It told a compelling tale of an anti-Semitic, antiblack, antilabor journalist whose scurrilous paper became the vehicle for a landmark First Amendment case.

Friendly traveled widely to research the book. He went to Chicago to document the role of Colonel Robert R. McCormick, the publisher of the *Chicago Tribune* who provided legal and financial support for the defendants. Friendly met with former associates of McCormick and got a tour of his old office. Friendly illuminated the role and character of other players in this drama, such as Roger Baldwin of the American Civil Liberties Union, and brought to life the Supreme Court justices of the era, supplementing archival research with interviews with their descendants. As in Friendly's other ventures, the *Minnesota Rag* project represented a team effort. Ruth was his indefatigable assistant and companion; their son Richard Mark, a student at Columbia Law School, helped as well. Current and former graduate assistants also contributed, among them, Landman and Karen Gannett. Friendly used the language of documentary making to acknowledge the contribution of two "associate producers," John Guthmann and Martha Elliott, writing of the latter, "Her mark is on every page."[6] Friendly consulted with eminent lawyers and scholars as well.

Yet once again the project, in its conception and ultimate execution, was all Friendly's. It added a dimension to the conversation between the press and the law that had given rise to the media and society seminars. For Friendly, the *Near* case was an example of the legal system's historic defense of First Amendment rights that might be instructive in a period of tension between jurists and journalists. The book was published on the fiftieth anniversary of the *Near* decision and the tenth anniversary of the decision in the Pentagon Papers case, in which *Near* had been cited no fewer than ten times. The result of Friendly's efforts, in the words of one critic, was "a grand book," a short but compelling account of a monumental case in First Amendment law.[7] However, Lyle Denniston, who covered the Supreme Court for the *Washington Star*, offered some critical perspectives. He questioned Friendly's attempt to reconstruct the secret discussion of the case among the justices. Denniston made a more fundamental critique of what he considered excessive cheerleading about the *Near* decision that masked some of its troublesome aspects in regard to the First Amendment. "Ultimately," Denniston wrote, "*Minnesota Rag* is rather superficial and too light hearted. It is not enough these days for those who speak for the press . . . to leave judges with the impression that the press is uncritically thankful for constitutional gratuities grandly dispensed (albeit, with qualifications) by the courts."[8]

In 1980, as he was completing *Minnesota* Rag, Friendly began work on another book, which required periodic trips to England. The subject was a journalistic controversy in connection with a strike against the British Steel Corporation, the first national strike in fifty years, which also spread to the privatized steelworks and lasted for nearly fourteen weeks. During the strike, an unnamed source in the company had given a reporter confidential documents on company management and the machinations of the government of Margaret Thatcher that were disclosed on Granada Television. British Steel sued Granada in a highly publicized case to get the name of the "mole" within the company. Harold Evans, editor of the *Times* of London, and Sir Denis Forman, chair of Granada, encouraged Friendly to write a book about the court case that dealt—in a British political and legal context—with the issue of protection of news sources, a topic of great interest to Friendly. Friendly flew to London in July to observe discussion about the strike and court case in the House of Lords. He met with key players, including the British minister of labor. Evans arranged a clandestine meeting with the "mole," who was later revealed to be a British Steel records officer named Dougal MacKenzie. By the end of January 1981, Friendly wrote Brian Lapping that the book was virtually finished, and in February he sent off the manuscript, "The Mole, the Judges, and the Rule of Law." However, British libel law led his publisher, Collins, to withdraw the book, and it was never published.[9]

The disappointing decision did not cause Friendly to break stride. He had other projects in various stages, and the book project itself was part of a larger agreement between Granada Television and Friendly. Forman had offered Friendly a contract to serve as both seminar producer and consultant at large in the United States for Granada at an annual salary of $40,000. The agreement was signed in late September, with an effective date of January 1, 1981, the day after Friendly's official termination at the Ford Foundation.[10]

In his correspondence with Forman in the fall of 1980, Friendly explained that his role as head of the media and society seminars was in limbo. Ford had decided to relinquish direct control of the seminars and planned to make a major transitional grant that would permit the seminars to continue in a university setting. Proposals were solicited from Harvard and Northwestern as well as Columbia University. Friendly wrote Forman in September 1980 that continuation of the seminars, as well as his stewardship, remained "very conjectural." In the interim, Friendly transferred the seminar offices to the School of Journalism. Osborn Elliott, who became dean in 1979 and was a strong proponent of involving prominent public figures in the school, valued Friendly's contacts and seminars as a source of prestige for the university. Friendly became the director of the rechristened but provisional Columbia University Seminars on Media and Society. The program's future hinged on which university would receive the Ford grant. Friendly was reluctant to lobby the Ford trustees. Harold Howe II, a vice president at Ford, was known to favor his alma mater, Harvard. On a Sunday morning toward the end of 1980, Friendly received a call at home from Alexander Heard at Ford, a Friendly ally, who asked Friendly point-blank whether he wanted the grant to go to Columbia. Friendly said yes, and his request was approved, despite a recommendation by foundation staff that the seat of the seminars be moved to Harvard.[11]

In January 1981, Columbia University sent Friendly the draft of a letter to the Ford Foundation gratefully accepting responsibility for administering "Fred Friendly's" media and society seminars. Also enclosed was a letter from Dean Elliott outlining the university's ambitious plans for the seminars. "Confidentially," Friendly wrote to Forman of the Ford grant to Columbia, "this was a reversal of a staff recommendation, and I know of no such action in a matching grant." Friendly had landed on his feet once again. He would run the seminar program out of the journalism building while remaining independent of the journalism school. He assumed direct ownership of the Ford Foundation project while forging a new relationship with Columbia University, where he would now be a free agent, unfettered by faculty politics. In April 1981, Columbia University officially announced a three-year series of seminars funded by grants from Ford and a consortium of sponsors. Richard M. Clurman, a former chief of correspondents for Time-Life and cultural affairs commissioner of New York City, became chair of the series' board. Friendly agreed to offer a seminar in the fall at Bryn Mawr, which would require a weekly commute of nearly five hours from Riverdale. Friendly's capacity for a frenetic schedule appeared undiminished. As Friendly told an interviewer in 1981, he had difficulty saying no to offers he found appealing, and at sixty-five he was flunking retirement.[12]

In 1981 and 1982, Friendly conducted more than a dozen seminars throughout the nation similar to those formerly held under the aegis of the Ford Foundation. A fortuitous telephone call as Fred and Ruth were having dinner at home opened up the possibility of transforming the seminars from professional workshops to public events that would be broadcast on television in the United States. Up to that point, nearly a hundred taped seminars had been used as instructional tools in settings such as newsrooms, bar association meetings, colleges, and medical society meetings. The telephone call came from Robben Fleming, the former chancellor of the University of Michigan and president of the Corporation for Public Broadcasting (CPB). Fleming was serving as a consultant in the planning stages of a new initiative in educational broadcasting. In 1981, the Annenberg School had announced that it would dispense $150 million over a fifteen-year period for what was called the Annenberg/CPB Project: Educational Excellence Through Telecommunications. Its mission was to support ventures using communications technology for higher education and lifelong learning for the general public. CPB cosponsorship meant that Annenberg programs intended for television would be broadcast on PBS.

Friendly and Fleming knew each other through their involvement in public broadcasting during their respective tenures at Ford and CPB.

Fleming was familiar with the long-distance learning projects of the BBC as well as Friendly's seminars. He turned to Friendly to launch the Annenberg initiative by producing "some early, high-quality product." Eager to initiate a series of programs with a common theme worthy of academic credit, Fleming decided to approach Friendly with the idea of a series on the Bill of Rights as the Constitution approached its two-hundredth anniversary. During his call, he asked Friendly, "Do you think you can teach the people of this country the Constitution on television with your format?" Ruth Friendly remembered Fred's instant reply: "Yes, if I can get Independence Hall, two million dollars, and Potter Stewart." It reminded Ruth of Fred's spontaneous response when he got the idea for the Summer Program for Minority Journalists while shaving. Friendly and Fleming struck a tentative deal, after which Friendly formally applied for the job. He had an inside track, given his relationship and understanding with Fleming. In addition, another figure driving the Annenberg/CPB Project, Newton Minow, was a great admirer of Friendly.[13]

While Friendly was working on the Annenberg/CPB Project, television audiences got to see several media and society seminars. In 1982, public television stations carried the two-part series *Eyeball to Eyeball: Dilemma in the Newsroom*. "As the discussions proceed," a critic wrote, "many of the smiles turn to frowns of irritation. Black and white situations are more than balanced by areas of gray. The questions are serious and a good many defy easy answers."[14] A three-part series of seminars, *Eye on the Media*, began airing on CBS in 1983. It dealt with issues in press–business relations, invasion of privacy, and coverage of terrorism. The first program in the CBS series featured an angry colloquy between Dan Rather and the public relations guru Herb Schmertz in response to questions about news management. Participants in the early televised seminars were challenged and stimulated by the exercises. Geraldo Rivera described the experience as "a cross between a street fight and my old days of moot court in law school." Mike Wallace noted how "you are forced to think on your feet, to justify the reportorial techniques that you use, to face up to the excesses with which you have been charged by critics." Marvin Kitman, television critic for *Newsday*, became an early champion of the televised seminars, emphasizing that they were entertaining and dramatic as well as instructive.[15]

In October 1982, the Annenberg/CPB Project announced initial grants totaling $3.5 million, half of which would go to a new subset of media and society seminars, a thirteen-part series of hour-long programs on the

Constitution on PBS. The Annenberg Project gave the seminars a new dimension, replacing the Ford Foundation as a primary sponsor and ensuring a quantum leap in their visibility and impact. Friendly later gratefully noted that Robben Fleming was "in very many ways the godfather" of the Constitution series, which would put the media and society seminars on the television map. Fleming, in turn, acknowledged Friendly's indispensable assistance in launching the Annenberg/CPB Project. Fleming wrote of the initial two-day seminar at Independence Hall: "It was also helpful that Fred, being the showman that he is, made an occasion out of the live filming by inviting a number of important guests, including the Annenbergs, to sit in the audience." In 1983, PBS broadcast the first four installments of *The Constitution: That Delicate Balance*, shot in Independence Hall in Philadelphia and produced in collaboration with WNET in New York and WTTW in Chicago. Before the ninety-minute premiere, Friendly said, "Except for 'Sesame Street,' we've never fulfilled television's potential as an educational tool. It's never been done for adults."[16]

The blue-chip roster of panelists on the first program—"National Security and Freedom of the Press"—ranged from the civil liberties attorney Floyd Abrams to the conservative U.S. Court of Appeals judge Robert Bork, from Griffin Bell, Jimmy Carter's attorney general, to Senator Orrin Hatch of Utah. Friendly included former government officials and prominent journalists who in their professional capacities had a direct stake in the issues posed by the seminar. They included James Schlesinger, a former CIA director and secretary of defense, and William Webster, then director of the FBI. They were joined by Dan Rather of CBS and Brit Hume of ABC as well as representatives of the *Washington Post*, *Baltimore Sun*, and *New York Times*, among others. The hypothetical involved how the press and government would deal with a leaked story about a secret CIA operation in Latin America. Friendly introduced the program; his one-on-one colloquies with Potter Stewart were edited in to amplify key points. The program revealed Friendly's desire to dramatize constitutional issues in the context of contemporary controversies. This broadcast, for example, took place at a time of debate about covert operations in El Salvador and Nicaragua during the Reagan administration. A subsequent seminar demonstrated how revealing and explosive the exchanges on such topics could be. NBC's John Chancellor was furious, for example, when James Schlesinger said, "The age of Ernie Pyle is dead, regrettably," suggesting that reporters could no longer be trusted to keep a military action secret. The livid Chancellor noted the impediments facing American war correspondents, adding, "But to imply that Ernie Pyle was a patriot and the rest of us are not—I won't accept that." As Floyd Abrams observed, "It is really extraordinary to see heavy hitters from government and powerful journalists talk seriously about what animates them—and to be caught off-guard, with their nerve-centers exposed."[17]

The initial televised seminars on the Constitution dealt with such issues as affirmative action and reverse discrimination, school prayer and gun control, and the conflict between the president and Congress over war powers. The panels were made up of a cross-section of prominent actors in the controversies under review. Participants in the seminar on affirmative action ranged from the neoconservative writer Irving Kristol to Alvin Poussaint, an African American psychology professor from Harvard. They were joined by, among others, Judge Bork and Eleanor Holmes Norton, a Georgetown law professor and former chair of the Equal Employment Opportunity Commission. The program on criminal justice featured the combative former mayor of Philadelphia, Frank Rizzo, and FBI director Webster as well as William Raspberry of the *Washington Post*, a sharp critic of the treatment of minorities by the criminal justice system. The seminars, which approached the Constitution as a living document, used the Socratic method to address both contemporary controversies and broad principles.

Nine additional seminars in the *Constitution* series aired in 1984. Programs focused on key provisions rather than the Constitution as a whole; nine of the thirteen installments dealt with the Bill of Rights. Seminar topics highlighted constitutional factors in debates about executive privilege and congressional authority, immigration reform, campaign spending, abortion, and the right to die. The eighty-five participants in the thirteen seminars constituted a who's who of American public life, including two former presidents and former and current members of the Supreme Court. The seminar format meant that, instead of being treated with deference, these luminaries were pressed to think on their feet and explore the contradictions in their thinking. The series had a significant afterlife as a widely used teaching tool in high schools and colleges. The Annenberg/CPB Project produced curriculum materials to supplement the videos. Soon after the broadcast of the series, more than two hundred colleges acquired a set of the videocassettes. In addition, the Annenberg/CPB Project funded a related telecourse. Several years later, Friendly proudly noted that $800,000 worth of tapes had been sold.[18]

In 1984, Friendly and Martha Elliott produced a book—also entitled *The Constitution: That Delicate Balance*—designed to complement the seminar series. At a book signing in Riverdale, Friendly stressed the synergy of print and video: "A book is a great teacher, but television is also a teaching tool." He added that their sum "should be more than their individual parts."[19] Subtitled *Landmark Cases That Shaped the Constitution*, the book reviewed sixteen controversies, from *Barron v. Baltimore* in 1833 to the War Powers Act of 1973. The volume provided background information for many of the issues addressed in the televised seminars. Friendly and Elliott emphasized the stories of the often-forgotten litigants whose initiatives were critical to the development of constitutional rights in American history.

While preparing the manuscript, Friendly would spontaneously depart on a research trip when his curiosity was piqued. For example, he became fascinated by John Barron's suit against the city of Baltimore, the first case involving the Bill of Rights to be heard by the Supreme Court. Friendly traveled to Baltimore to visit the site of Barron's wharf and to look up local records about Barron and his litigation. Friendly's research yielded graphic portraits of Barron and the seventy-five-year-old chief justice, John Marshall, a recent widower, "frail and graying, his body still weak from a bladder operation the year before." To research the roots of the insanity defense, Fred and Ruth traveled to England to meet with a judge of the Old Bailey, who unrolled old sheepskin documents for them. They went to Ohio to interview Dollree Mapp, the defendant in *Mapp v. Ohio* (1961), a case involving possession of obscene materials; to Florida to speak with Haitian refugees whose quest for asylum raised constitutional questions about the rights of illegal aliens; and to California to discuss the affirmative action case *Regents of the University of California v. Bakke* (1978) with university officials. Friendly even tracked down Norma McCorvey, the poor Texan who was the pseudonymous Jane Roe of *Roe v. Wade* (1973), and invited her to stay in his home in Riverdale for her first visit to New York. Ruth recalled picking her up at the airport: "When I put my arm around her, I could feel her shaking." According to Martha Elliott, the human story behind an issue was what Friendly always found most compelling and revealing: "That was his thing, the little picture. He was always interested most in the human side of it. He was never as interested in the concepts."[20]

Yet Friendly was enthralled by the U.S. legal system as well. Cynthia

McFadden, who in 1984 became executive producer of the media and society seminars, remembered how Friendly was uncharacteristically tentative in his first and unsuccessful attempt to get Associate Justice Harry Blackmun to participate in a seminar: "Fred was . . . I wouldn't say 'cowed,' but he wasn't his usual bomb-throwing self. If Fred had outsized admiration for anyone or anything, I would say it was for the Supreme Court. He really revered the role that the Court played in the history of the nation. He found it mystical and magical." Friendly gave McFadden permission to go back to Blackmun with a second, more assertive, and typically Friendlyesque appeal, which proved successful. Elliott recalled that when she and Friendly went to Washington and first visited the original Supreme Court chamber in the Capitol, and later when they listened to oral arguments in its current premises, "Fred acted as if we were in a church, a temple, a shrine."[21]

Telecasts of *The Constitution: That Delicate Balance* marked Fred Friendly's resurrection as a television producer. Other televised seminars followed: the two-part *Anatomy of a Libel Case* would air on PBS in 1984; the three-part *The Military and the News Media*, in 1985. Moreover, Friendly made plans to use the seminar format in subject areas that were less journalism-specific such as health care and ethics.

Friendly took great care in preparing a seminar for broadcast. He began by selecting a topic for a hypothetical situation that, more often than not, represented a thinly veiled reference to a contemporary controversy. The fictional scenario for a seminar dealing with press–government conflicts in wartime, for example, had striking parallels with the U.S. invasion of Grenada, when reporters were forcibly prevented from accompanying front-line troops. Once a topic was selected, the producer and moderator drafted a hypothetical story line and related questions.[22] Friendly took the lead in the casting process. His approach was to begin by getting a commitment from a high-profile figure whose presence would attract other panelists. Participants did not receive any payment, yet few turned him down. Associate Justice Antonin Scalia, for example, had been dead set against judges' making public appearances and adhered to a personal policy of not appearing on television: "But Fred got me to do his Constitution series four times, and it was in connection with that enterprise that I met him and was quickly conquered by him." Who else but Friendly could get Gerald Ford to role-play how he would, as president, react to a hypothetical situation—or get Potter Stewart to explain the thinking of a justice of the Supreme Court or Admiral Bobby Inman that of the director of the CIA?[23]

Friendly met with potential panelists to make sure that they understood how the seminar worked and that a diversity of perspectives would be represented, but he did not reveal the hypothetical scenario before taping in order to ensure spontaneous responses. After a script was written, the moderator did a test run with stand-ins for the panelists. Friendly insisted that the edited program show what he called an "agony quotient," when a participant would struggle visibly with a question, every five to seven minutes. "We show the long, uncomfortable pauses," Stuart Sucherman told an interviewer. "My God, some of the pauses are the best moments."[24] In taping the seminars, six or seven cameras were used to get spontaneous, authentic reaction shots, as opposed to the practice of inserting fake visuals taped after the actual discussion. Editing was in sequence only: Friendly would not allow segments to be rearranged or statements to be compressed in order to heighten the effects. The format of the seminars, and the critical role of the moderators, obviated the need for slick editing techniques.

Marvin Kitman wrote of the moderator's role: "He is like a stage manager who puts the light on his characters one at a time, then turns it off as the plot thickens." The *Newsday* critic characterized the seminars as the first major format innovation in public affairs programming on television since Frederick Wiseman's cinema verité documentaries: "It is the 'Playhouse 90' of public affairs programming, a Pirandello play with the real-life characters moving in and out of reality." Friendly referred to the programs as "theater of the mind." Another critic argued that the hypotheticals fostered greater insights than traditional television news formats: "The show manages to use props and make-believe to coax out of news makers more intense flashes of honesty, more substance, than straightforward TV news gathering can ordinarily achieve."[25]

Sucherman said, "I'm unapologetic about the drama. We're doing theater in a public policy context, bringing the audience to complex questions in a way that is not threatening." Sucherman served as executive director of the seminars from 1981 to 1984; Kitman called him "the most original thinker in TV today." As usual, Friendly surrounded himself with a strong supporting cast. Cynthia McFadden, who began working as a producer before taking over as executive producer of the seminars in 1984, had studied law at Columbia University, taken a course with Friendly, and done research for Benno Schmidt for the *Constitution* series. When she got her law degree, McFadden was offered a job at a Manhattan law firm but accepted the position working with Friendly on the seminars. The law firm offered to consider her time with Friendly as a judicial clerkship, so that she could join the firm as a third-year associate if the arrangement with Friendly did not work out.[26] McFadden nonetheless remained with Friendly until 1991, after which she embarked on a career as a correspondent and an anchor in network journalism. During her tenure with the seminars, PBS broadcast more than thirty programs, including series on the military, terrorism, and ethics. Martha Elliott functioned as an indispensable researcher-editor-writer and factotum. The media and society team inevitably became part of Friendly's extended family. The lines between office and home were blurred: Friendly would frequently plan seminars over dinner and review tapes with his staff over takeout from the local delicatessen in the sun room of his home in Riverdale.

Friendly brought to the Columbia University Seminars on Media and Society much of the same intensity and perfectionism that he had to *See It Now* and *CBS Reports*. According to McFadden, Friendly was the de facto executive producer of the seminars, although he gave her that title to compensate for her modest salary. As in his CBS days, Friendly could treat the members of his team—even Ruth—harshly. Once, while viewing a rough cut of one of the Constitution seminars in Riverdale, Ruth expressed an opinion that Friendly dismissed. McFadden later viewed the tape with Friendly and, unaware of what had happened earlier, expressed a view similar to Ruth's. Friendly blew up at McFadden. Elliott said his treatment of McFadden was unacceptable, a favorite reproach of Friendly's, which pushed him over the top. He fired McFadden and Elliott on the spot. The next day, Elliott got a call from Friendly's secretary, Natalie Foster, who said, "Martha, Fred tells me you were mean to him yesterday and that you quit." She replied, "That's not what happened, he was screaming at us and he fired us." "Well, that's not what he said," Foster continued. "I was hoping you would come by the office today and we could get everything going smoothly again, because he feels terrible about the way you treated him." Elliott and McFadden resumed their work on the media and society seminars. "Fred yelled at you," Elliott acknowledged, "but he yelled mainly at people he cared about. Usually because he wanted the best for you and the best out of you."[27]

Friendly introduced each program at the beginning of the broadcast, a major step for him. Tom Bettag sensed that although Friendly loved to speak on radio or before live audiences, he had felt constrained by a sense that his physical appearance did not lend itself to television. That sentiment changed as Ruth advised him about his attire and grooming and helped him overcome a feeling of awkwardness. Friendly began to take satisfaction at becoming an on-screen presence.[28] In addition to introducing the seminars on air, Friendly would personally moderate another offshoot of the media and society seminars, a series of lively roundtable discussions of journalism controversies called *The Other Side of the News*.

Friendly increasingly relied on Ruth's judgment as an experienced teacher in regard to program content and on her social skills in their interactions with others. In an arrangement separate from the media and society seminars, he and Ruth signed up with the Leigh Bureau, which booked them for private seminars for a variety of organizations. The fees ranged from $3,500 to $10,000, after agency expenses. Hence in addition to their collaboration on book projects and media and society broadcasts, Fred and Ruth became a traveling act, bringing the seminar techniques to live audiences across the nation. Bettag recalled how Ruth's role grew:

> He was the correspondent, the great bringer-together of people, but she was the one who was the producer in many ways, with the patience to hold people's hands, explain what Fred really meant. When people would get a little exasperated, she'd come over and say, "Oh, come on, you know how Fred is." So she was the handler of people. . . . She was also the person who made sure the details got done. . . . She was a good ear. She was also Fred's traveling companion when he spent four to five days a week on a plane and so made it possible for him to have a life while doing this.

Benno Schmidt recalled that "I saw Ruth almost as much as I saw Fred. That was the way in which Fred handled his professional relationships."[29] Friendly relished his collaboration with Ruth, a sense of shared adventure that he and Dorothy had experienced early in his career. Fred and Ruth's teamwork fostered a personal and professional rejuvenation well into his seventh decade.

Although the media and society seminars were housed at Columbia, the seminar program enjoyed a semiautonomous status at the university— similar to *See It Now*'s relationship to CBS News—that maximized

Friendly's independence. His interaction with former presidents, sitting Supreme Court justices, and other notables enhanced his status at Columbia as he established his own production team for the broadcasts of the seminars. Bettag observed how the televised seminars energized Friendly. He sensed that Friendly relished being back in the mainstream of public affairs, doing important work. After all, Bettag noted, "Laying down real broadcasts that went on the air was how he measured things." David Schoenbrun suggested that "at last he had realized his ultimate dream, a program with no correspondents, no executive overseers, no writers, no one but Fred Friendly himself. Fred did it all, à la Orson Welles." Schoenbrun quickly added: "In all fairness, as one of the men who clashed often with Fred over his dictatorial behavior, let me say that he did it surpassingly well."[30]

Despite widespread praise, a few critics chastised the seminars for sacrificing substance for theatricality. Warren E. Burger, chief justice of the Supreme Court, became the only participant to walk out on a seminar. At a morning session in 1980, Charles Nesson asked panelists how they would respond to a hypothetical situation in which a judge was impaired because of his drug use. At lunchtime, Burger went to Friendly's table and told him he considered the suggestion absurd, like an episode of a situation comedy. "Socrates should sue you," Burger said, before storming out. Michael Stern, a critic at the *Los Angeles Times*, similarly accused Friendly and Elliott of a watered-down television version of issues in their approach to the Constitution. He challenged a "relentlessly upbeat" approach to the Bill of Rights that ignored a continuing legacy of inequality and discrimination. Reviewing the companion book to the series *The Constitution: That Delicate Balance*, Stern wrote, "Each chapter sets up a dramatic conflict between radically oversimplified ideas abstracted from their historical context and proceeds to resolve—or pretend to resolve—it with clichés. The end of each chapter reads like a network correspondent's end-of-story on-camera stand-up."[31]

Others complained that, although the seminars dealt with controversial issues, their structure precluded the kind of advocacy contained in many programs that Friendly had produced for *See It Now* and *CBS Reports*. The heyday of the television seminars coincided with the ascendancy of conservatism in the Reagan years. During this period, the television documentary form pioneered by Friendly and Murrow was in retreat on the networks, and even on public television, with the notable exception of the *Frontline* series on PBS. Furthermore, Tom Bettag recalled, Friendly had personally begun to question certain liberal pieties. Bettag said of the seminars: "I think he saw it as a great way not to do the documentary, to break out of old forms, and create a new form." Sucherman conceded that the dialogues provided a nonthreatening format for the presentation of issues. "I don't give a damn which way minds change," Friendly said. "I just want people to *think*." James Day, Friendly's colleague during the public broadcasting wars of the late 1960s and early 1970s, referred to Friendly's new programmatic design as an "attack-proof" format. Day was quick to add, however, that the substance of the seminars made them "more than a means of juggling a hot issue without the danger of first degree burns."[32]

The seminars clearly represented a departure from the more partisan Murrow–Friendly documentaries on McCarthyism and migrant workers. The new format featured leading figures in U.S. public life, but the ordinary Americans who had been so important in providing the little picture in the documentaries—the individual GI in Korea, Milo Radulovich, the unnamed migrant worker—were largely absent from the seminar table. The pedigrees of certain seminar funders and participants suggested how times had changed since the 1950s. The Hearst Corporation, in celebration of its centennial, gave $1 million to underwrite the seminar series *The Presidency and the Constitution*. During the 1950s, the Hearst press had been among the McCarthy's greatest champions and Murrow's sharpest critics. The changed relationship with the FBI was equally dramatic. During his CBS years, Friendly's approaches to get J. Edgar Hoover on the air had been rebuffed. Friendly had had a run-in with Hoover as late as 1971. That year, the FBI had interviewed Friendly about Daniel Schorr, whose name was on the Nixon White House's enemies list, under the pretext that Schorr was being considered for a high government post. When the *Washington Post* exposed the ploy, Friendly wrote an angry letter to Hoover demanding an explanation. Friendly noted, "In the past twenty years, I have been responsive to more than twenty such queries on a variety of public figures ranging from John Eisenhower to Edward R. Murrow." However, in 1981 Friendly got William Webster, now head of the FBI, to participate in a seminar on terrorism and the media. Webster became an enthusiastic admirer of the seminars and of Friendly.[33]

Friendly's development of the seminars cannot be reduced to a calculated desire for a safer format than the documentary in a conservative political climate. He genuinely relished a debate, the exchange of ideas, whether in his personal or his professional life. "He challenged everyone in his vicinity constantly," McFadden remembered. "It was impossible to have a meal with him and not have a seminar." In explaining why Friendly would invite Roy Cohn to his classes at Columbia, Elliott emphasized that "Fred was the kind of person who always wanted both sides of everything." According to Sucherman,

> Fred was a liberal but not an ideologue. He loved to debate people and argue; there was never a boring dinner conversation at the Friendly table. He definitely had a liberal bent, but he loved the clash of ideas. If you look at his and Murrow's work on *See It Now*, there were very few things that were right of center. By the time the seminars started, I think that he had evolved in his mind that things weren't as simple as that. What we wanted to do with the seminars is something that TV doesn't do, which was to take complex issues and show how complex they are.

A newspaper critic emphasized that the role of the seminar moderators was not to deliver a knockout punch and that a critical dimension was often implicit. "It is enough," he wrote, "that they have punched through the protective layers of specialization to reveal the often short-range and shallow views of many of these important people about the principles that underlie their professions." Friendly's ethos remained, in the words of Tom Bettag, a "journalism of engagement" in the sense that he wished to compel citizens to become involved in the burning issues of the day in a substantive way.[34]

While the seminars were a creative new format, there were also continuities with the Murrow–Friendly documentary tradition. Many of the legendary *See It Now* programs represented an attempt to open up an issue for more discussion. Characteristically, at the end of "The Case of Milo Radulovich, A0589839," Murrow said that the case raised important questions about the relationship of the individual to the state, adding, "And it seems to us that—that is, to Fred Friendly and myself—that that is a subject that should be argued about endlessly." "An Argument in Indianapolis" dramatically juxtaposed perspectives on civil liberties. Programs like the long-form interviews with Carl Sandburg and J. Robert Oppenheimer sought to expand television's potential as a medium of ideas. Some *See It Now* and *CBS Reports* programs were widely used by educational institutions. After all, Murrow's professional background had been in education before his career in broadcasting. The broadcast of the media and society seminars by Friendly was in keeping with Murrow's admonition that television can teach and illuminate. While extending the Murrow–Friendly tradition, the seminars liberated Friendly from the classroom and the boardroom, returning him to the arena of current affairs and broadcast production. The Columbia University Seminars on Media and Society rekindled Friendly's journalistic passions and gave him the direct access to high officials and newsmakers that he had missed since leaving CBS. No wonder that during the final phase of his career, in the words of Stuart Sucherman, "the seminars became his cause."[35]

20 Last Years

Following *The Constitution: That Delicate Balance* in 1984, for the next six years the production team for the televised Columbia University Seminars on Media and Society continued to address critical issues for the press and government. The two-part *Anatomy of a Libel Case* aired on PBS later in 1984; the three-part *The Military and the News Media*, in 1985; and the three-part *Campaigning on Cue: The Presidential Election of 1984* in 1986. In the Constitution's bicentennial year of 1987, Friendly produced a seven-part series, *The Presidency and the Constitution*. The programs focused on the myriad ways the modern presidency uses the authority assigned by the Constitution. For example, individual programs—"The Nuclear Balance of Terror," "The Budget Crunch," and "The Making of a Justice"—explore the president's role in particular areas. In "The Making of a Justice" viewers see Jimmy Carter explaining how a president decides on a Supreme Court nominee and being challenged by senators, legal scholars, and journalists.

In 1989, Friendly produced the ten-part *Ethics in America*, his second major series in collaboration with the Annenberg/CPB Project. Viewers could enroll and receive college credit for a telecourse based on the series that included a reader with an introduction by Friendly.[1] The series sought to examine ethics in all areas of national life in the wake of government and corporate scandals of the 1980s, such as the Iran-Contra controversy, the sex scandal that scuttled Gary Hart's presidential campaign, and revelations about the practices of corporate raiders and insider traders. At the end of 1988, to meet Annenberg's requirement that a sufficient number of colleges use the series in their curriculum, Friendly moderated local seminars on ethical issues as part of a national tour to preview and promote the series. For example, he hosted a seminar in December at the University of California at San Diego that was cosponsored by the local public television station. To the delight of the audience, he opened the session by asking the editors of the two major San Diego dailies—one of the editors was the former Nixon aide Gerald Warren—whether they had ever lied. At another point, Friendly interrupted one panelist to ask, "What, are you going to be like Wernher von Braun? 'I just build the rockets?'" Discussion was interspersed with ten-minute clips from the *Ethics in America* series, which was scheduled to begin national broadcast early in the new year. According to a press account, "Friendly was the challenging ringmaster, cutting panelists off whenever they fell into their natural rhythms of rhetoric . . . producing responses that were often surprising."[2]

The national broadcast of *Ethics in America* began at the end of January 1989. The first installment, "Do unto Others," focused on personal ethics and featured Associate Justice Antonin Scalia, Surgeon General C. Everett Koop, and the presidents of the Hastings Center, Union Theological Center, and the University of Utah. The moderator, Charles Ogletree of Harvard Law School, told an interviewer, "People who have reached a certain prominence in their lives often think they've thought all the issues through, that there are no surprises. But they haven't been challenged to examine their principles." A reviewer wrote, "There's something extraordinary about observing a famously conservative Supreme Court justice as he grapples with the question of whether he'd turn in his own son for cheating." The remainder of the programs addressed ethical questions in different professional settings. For example, "The Human Experiment" dealt with scientific research; the program produced a heated and revealing exchange between the physician-in-chief of Memorial Sloan-Kettering Cancer Center and the editor of the *New England Journal of Medicine* about the ethical dilemmas in testing AIDS drugs. Another high point was the two-part "Under Orders, Under Fire," which dealt with the moral implications of a range of decisions made by journalists and others on the battlefield. "Anatomy of a Hostile Takeover" pitted then–U.S. Attorney Rudolph Giuliani against Frederick Joseph, chief executive officer of the investment banking house Drexel Burnham Lambert. A particularly compelling exchange between Peter Jennings and Mike Wallace concerned potential life-and-death conflicts of journalists in war situations. They struggled with the questions, hesitated, reversed themselves, and were criticized by General William C. Westmoreland and a marine officer before Brent Scowcroft, a former general in the air force and national security adviser to Presidents Nixon and Ford, came to the journalists' defense. The *Quill*, the journal of the Society of Professional Journalists, devoted a cover story to the exchange.[3]

Both praise and criticism of *Ethics in America* focused on the mix of substance and entertainment in the series. Asked about the seminar format, Friendly responded, "People ask me, 'Where did you get the idea?' I say, 'From Socrates and Phil Donahue.'"[4] A writer in *Commonweal* magazine asked of the series, "Ethics or classy bull sessions?" Most critics agreed that the drama inherent in the discussion of the hypotheticals was often gripping. Whatever was sacrificed to showmanship was necessary to present serious issues to a wide audience. "For those who allow themselves to be pulled into its vortex," a reviewer wrote of the series in the *Chicago Tribune*, "it offers a wild roller-coaster ride through some of the most stupendous ideas and concepts and some of the most nettling conflicts and conundrums of the 20th century."[5]

From 1988 to 1990, in addition to producing the seminars, Friendly hosted *The Other Side of the News*, the series on press issues. Two installments focused on high-profile cases that raised difficult questions about how journalism practices can be distorted by the prism of race. The first, "Tawana Brawley and the Press," examined an incident in which the press gave credence to a black teenager's false claims of abuse in New York. The second, "The Boston Hoax," involved the false claim of a white man that his wife had been killed by an African American; it inflamed racial tensions in Boston before being exposed as untrue. For the discussion of the Boston story, Friendly assembled a group of print and broadcast journalists who had covered the story, as well as the Harvard psychiatrist Alvin Poussaint and an NAACP official, to examine the coverage and journalistic complicity in the hoax. "Television and Terrorism—Who Calls the Shots?" dealt with press–police interaction during a hostage situation in Berkeley, California. Several programs cast a critical light on the medium of television. For example, at a meeting of the Council for Advancement and Support of Education, Friendly moderated and taped for broadcast a discussion entitled "Athletics and Academics: An Uneasy Alliance." The panel—which included college presidents, coaches, and sports reporters—probed the corrosive impact of television money on college athletics and higher education, and the failure of sports journalism to address such issues. In producing *The Other Side of the News*, Friendly did not always get cooperation from the industry he scrutinized with a critical eye. For "Tawana Brawley and the Press" he could not secure the participation of two key players in the controversy: WCBS-TV and the *New York Times*; the latter canceled the appearance of E. R. Shipp of its Brawley investigative team two days before taping. A program on the proposed merger of the *Detroit News* and the *Detroit Free Press* had to be canceled when both newspapers refused to participate.[6]

Friendly taped "Entertainment News or Entertainment?" in 1989 at the annual meeting of the American Society of Newspaper Editors. Morton Downey Jr., Larry King, Phil Donahue, Geraldo Rivera, and Don Hewitt represented the hybrid form of tabloid television. They were joined by a high-powered cross-section of broadcast executives, print journalists, and television critics for what proved to be a combative exchange. Friendly punctuated the discussion by showing video excerpts from the panelists' shows: Downey thrusting his armpit in the face of an antagonist, Donahue wearing a dress for a program on cross-dressing, Rivera asking for details about a sex surrogate's efforts to cure sexually dysfunctional clients. Donahue spoke of his need to build his audience to permit him to do his more serious work. Rivera claimed that he was "democratizing" the news. Hewitt countered that ratings and profits were the paramount factors; he added that newspaper chains owned many of the stations that were broadcasting the tabloid television shows of which print journalists were so contemptuous. The exchanges were heated and revealing. In this and the other programs in *The Other Side of the News* series, Friendly presented to the general public in a compelling way critical issues in journalistic practice that otherwise were addressed only by journalism reviews and schools.

"Entertainment News or Entertainment?" had a personal dimension for Friendly, given his past associations with two panelists: Geraldo Rivera and Don Hewitt. Friendly was unhappy with Rivera's recourse to sensationalism, chiding him, for example, about a program he had done on satanism. Rivera defiantly defended his work in response to the criticism of "my professor," as he repeatedly referred to Friendly. Friendly had always been interested in the dramatic dimension of news coverage, but he felt that Rivera, one of the star students of the Summer Program for Minority Journalists at Columbia, had succumbed to crass sensationalism. Friendly would remain a critical but also forgiving mentor for Rivera. Hewitt's participation in the televised panel discussion was more muted than Rivera's. At CBS, Friendly, who had viewed Hewitt as anti-intellectual and a loose cannon, had fired him as the executive director of the *CBS Evening News with Walter Cronkite*. Hewitt once complained to a reporter that Friendly had an exaggerated sense of his self-importance.

"He's not the First Amendment or the Constitution," Hewitt said. "Nobody died and left him in charge."[7] Now Hewitt was executive director of *60 Minutes*, the most profitable program in the history of television news. The program format drew, in part, on Friendly's *PBL* experiment. The success of *60 Minutes*, and of the other public affairs magazines it inspired, contributed to the eventual demise on network television of *CBS Reports* and the full-length documentary, a form that Hewitt considered too highbrow and lacking popular appeal.

Friendly was highly skeptical of *60 Minutes* when it was launched in 1968, although he came to have a grudging respect for some of its reports. Nonetheless, in 1973 Friendly signed for Mike Wallace, a star of *60 Minutes*, a copy of the *See It Now* book that Friendly had coedited with Murrow. The flattering inscription reads, "For Mike, who keeps the S.I.N. tradition alive."[8] Friendly avoided public criticism of *60 Minutes*, where close former associates like Wallace, Palmer Williams, Joe Wershba, and Andy Rooney worked. Privately, however, Friendly expressed grave reservations to confidants about *60 Minutes*. According to Tom Bettag, "He thought it was an appeal to the lowest common denominator, that it was dangerous and pandering, that Don was taking the cream off the news but giving none of the substance." Friendly regarded Hewitt as an impresario more than a journalist and *60 Minutes* as light news, a program that, as Bettag put it, "sucked up most of the oxygen and most of the good people out of the documentary units." The problem for Friendly was not *60 Minutes* per se but that it became a substitute for more serious and in-depth coverage of public affairs. He also disapproved of the reliance of newsmagazines on producers to do the reporting and interviewing, with on-air correspondents only marginally involved in the story. Friendly characterized this practice as "approaching the level of monumental fraud." Friendly noted that the program's enormous success depended on a group of aging correspondents and other variables. "It is, in my judgment," he said, "a very perishable product. And it won't always be there, by the way. Because nothing ever is."[9]

Hewitt was aware of Friendly's true feelings about *60 Minutes*. He would later ask rhetorically in an article in the *Washington Journalism Review*, "Fred, am I sore at you for firing me off the 'CBS Evening News' back in the 1960s? Not so much as I am for your continually putting your arm around me and saying, 'Ed would have been proud of you' when we both know you don't mean it." And in response to Friendly's statement that no journalist should require a salary in the millions of dollars at the expense of a news budget, Hewitt responded, "No journalist requires anything but a respite from Fred Friendly."[10]

Beginning in the 1970s and reaching a crescendo in the 1980s, after his retirement from Ford and Columbia, Friendly assumed the mantle of the leading critic and conscience of broadcast journalism. In addition to using the forum that the seminars provided, Friendly expressed his views in countless hearings, articles, press interviews, awards ceremonies, and meetings of professional organizations. The impact of broadcast deregulation provided added impetus to his desire to speak out. He had exposed the problematic side of broadcast regulation in his book on the fairness doctrine but nonetheless believed that the Federal Communications Commission had an important role to play in holding broadcasters to a public interest standard. Deregulation in his view marked the final abdication of television to the money changers. He expressed pride—and concern—about the future of the public broadcasting system he helped bring into being. At a PBS convention in Cincinnati in late June 1981, he praised public television for often putting the networks and cable channels to shame. He expressed regret that the Ford Foundation was no longer providing major support and that the future of PBS was hardly assured. He nonetheless said that it was time for PBS to take new initiatives—such as a nightly ninety-minute news and public affairs program modeled on NPR's *All Things Considered*. In an interview featured in *TV Guide* a month later, Friendly conceded that he had been overambitious in his expectations of public television in its first years—an oblique reference to *PBL*—but he hailed programs like *Sesame Street* and the *MacNeil/Lehrer NewsHour* as having no equivalent on commercial television. When asked where Murrow would be if he were alive the 1980s, Friendly thought he would be working at NPR or doing a program like the *NewsHour* on PBS.[11]

Friendly criticized the norms of news programming, on both network and local television. For example, he called for a halt to the disturbing trend toward dramatic reenactments of news events on network news and magazine programs. He also chastised local news for being personality driven and focusing on soft news. "All the 'happy talk' makes me sick to my stomach," Friendly told one interviewer. "I don't want journalists kidding around with the weatherman."[12] He expressed disgust with the dismal quality of most local news programming but also praised stations that maintained high standards, like WCVB-TV in Boston, KSL-TV in Salt Lake City, and WBBM-TV in Chicago. Satellite technology created new opportunities for local stations to draw on a variety of news sources and ad hoc networks. Friendly also held out a measure of hope for the future of nonbroadcast television: "I believe that cable will change television as much as television changed radio." Friendly suggested that the networks might in the future operate multiple cable channels, giving them freedom to fulfill their unrealized promise in public affairs and cultural programming. However, to meet immediate needs Friendly waged a campaign—which he advanced in speeches, articles, and interviews—to convince the commercial networks to expand their nightly news broadcast to a full hour.[13] By the latter part of the 1980s, however, he increasingly despaired of the prospects for reform of network television, and he stressed the potential of local television stations that devoted a substantial amount of time to news. He said in 1986 that he was convinced that "the next Murrow, Cronkite or Rather will emerge at the local level and then choose to stay there, where he or she has the air time and resources to do good work."[14]

Friendly also spoke out about the crisis in libel litigation facing the press in the mid-1980s, which was highlighted by General Westmoreland's suit against CBS for its Vietnam War documentary *The Uncounted Enemy*. Friendly chastised CBS for shoddy journalism and for its refusal to grant Westmoreland's request for air time to respond. In accepting an award at a newspaper convention in Tucson, Arizona, in November 1983, Friendly suggested that the landmark libel case *New York Times v. Sullivan* (1964) was not the First Amendment victory many believed. Confusion about its "actual malice" standard had led to a destructive cycle of litigation that had a chilling effect on First Amendment freedoms. Friendly proposed broad reform of libel law, including limiting or eliminating punitive damages and requiring news organizations to provide greater opportunities for reply. When a final settlement in *Westmoreland v. CBS* (1985) was finally announced, with both parties claiming vindication, Friendly examined the outcome in an op-ed article in the *Washington Post*. He argued that claims of victory on both sides notwithstanding, the public had been the loser. "Perhaps the bloodiest casualty is hardhitting journalism, which remains under siege," he wrote. The expense and turmoil exacted by the case would discourage even the occasional public affairs documentary on network television. In April 1985, not long after the *Westmoreland* settlement, Friendly proposed at an awards ceremony at the University of Missouri–Columbia that the television networks underwrite a weekly television forum in which newsmakers could respond to what they considered inaccurate or unfair coverage.[15]

The *Westmoreland* case was of special interest to Friendly because it involved a CBS broadcast. Following the settlement, Friendly was asked to coach the staff of WCBS-TV, the local New York station owned and operated by the network, about protecting news sources and how to avoid running afoul of libel law. He expressed the fear that the television foreign correspondent was becoming an endangered species. Friendly speculated that network news might one day merely serve as an outlet for video news feeds from organizations like the Associated Press, BBC, or CNN. He criticized CBS News in 1987 for firing fifteen correspondents and a total of two hundred people while a dozen high-profile reporters earned $800,000 a year or more, a reflection of the emphasis on star appeal and profits instead of content. He made such criticisms while maintaining open lines of communication with the television industry's top executives, noting that he was on cordial terms with CBS's new CEO, Lawrence Tisch. "Ruth and I have known Larry Tisch for the past 25 years, and we like him," Friendly said. "But firing 200 people at CBS News in two weeks has got to be wrong."[16]

Despite such criticism, Friendly continued to regard CBS as the standardbearer in network news. In 1987 he said, "I guess I feel as I always did—that CBS News is the preeminent broadcast news organization in the United States and in the world."[17] Friendly continued to portray William Paley—no longer chair but still on the CBS board—as a prisoner of Wall Street, a victim rather than an agent of network television's decline. Friendly even defended Frank Stanton in response to an HBO documentary about the Stanton–Murrow conflict, writing that Stanton's refusal years later to give a House committee outtakes and notes for *The Selling of the Pentagon* "was as courageous an act as anything Murrow ever did." Despite Friendly's severe criticisms of network television, he would never make a clean break—professionally and psychologically—from the industry and network he had left in 1966. In 1986, he acknowledged the ambivalence he felt about CBS, telling an interviewer for *Broadcasting*, "I mourn because I left all of my heart and much of my youth at a network. I mourn what is happening there, but every time I read a story, or see the demise of the documentary and special events, you don't have much hope any more. That situation seems to degrade day by day."[18]

Friendly had taken satisfaction in the mid-1970s in the association of Bill Moyers with *CBS Reports*, Friendly's old documentary program. Viewing *See It Now* as a young man had been an important factor in Moyers's decision to embark on a career in public life. The two men had become close in the years following their interaction during the Johnson administration. Moyers recalled that Friendly

> still worshipped at the altar of *CBS Reports*. He was very pleased when I became the senior correspondent, but he was very troubled that it [the broadcast] was irregular, and he knew that its fate was probably sealed because of the forces that were at work at [CBS headquarters at] Black Rock and in the business as a whole. His only consistent advice was, "Never pass up any opportunity for air time," and, second, "Always make sure you are in charge of your material." The third was, "Never go against your journalistic instincts." "Wherever you are," he said, "you can do a good job under the limited circumstances of today's broadcasting world."

Friendly continued to support Moyers when he left CBS for PBS, making behind-the-scenes calls to promote Moyers's successful application for a grant from the MacArthur Foundation to start his own independent production company. When Moyers embarked on a weekly program on a single topic on public television, his star producer was Martin Clancy, Friendly's first graduate assistant at Columbia. Whether at CBS or PBS, Moyers invariably got a telephone call after his broadcast from Friendly, providing feedback—often enthusiastic, sometimes critical. Once, after one of Moyers's documentaries aired, he stood up, and his wife asked him where he was going. " 'To answer the phone,' I said. 'It's not ringing,' she said. 'It will,' I said. And it did. Fred was calling, and Ruth. They were so often on the line together." Sometimes, Moyers added, Friendly would call to comment on the sorry state of broadcast journalism, "on what, to him, was television's own harvest of shame."[19]

Moyers recalled Friendly's ultimate frustration with the public broadcasting system he helped establish. The localism of the system meant that it was impossible to schedule the media and society seminars at the same time throughout the PBS network, making them difficult to promote beyond telling viewers to "check your local listings." His disenchantment grew as he found it increasingly hard to get PBS to commit to distributing the seminars at all on a regular basis. He felt that many of public television's problems stemmed from the lack of adequate long-term funding, the very problem he had sought to address twenty years earlier with the Ford Foundation satellite plan. "You've created an illegitimate child," Friendly said in 1988 in his final testimony before a congressional committee on public television. "You have disinherited him and made him into a begging pauper." Friendly said he supported a transfer tax on the sale of television stations as a funding mechanism but held out little hope for its adoption.[20]

Nor did Friendly consider the advent of twenty-four-hour cable news, inaugurated by CNN in 1980, an antidote to the decline of broadcast journalism. From the vantage point of the mid-1980s, the Cable News Network represented a quantitative but not qualitative improvement. Friendly was quoted as saying, "I do not consider CNN a first-class news organization. . . . The best you can say is, CNN is there whenever you want the news." The bottom line was trumping all other considerations in both network and cable news, Friendly told Sander Vanocur in a 1987 interview for the News Leaders series of the Poynter Institute for Media Studies. "My theory," he said, "is that Harvard Business School and the Columbia Business School and the Stanford Business School have taught American industry and American broadcasting how to institutionalize their greed."[21]

Friendly's dark view of the future of broadcast journalism was reflected in a speech he gave on August 29, 1986, when he accepted the Paul White Award at the annual convention of the Radio and Television News Directors Association. It was the same platform from which, twenty-eight years earlier, Edward R. Murrow had made the famous speech that had so angered CBS management. Friendly began with the opening lines of Murrow's address and quoted freely from his mentor's remarks. Friendly repeated and synthesized his oft-voiced criticisms of broadcast journalism. He lamented the triumph of profits over service and entertainment over information, the decline of network news, its failure to expand to an hour-long broadcast, and the enormous salaries of the star anchors at a time of cutbacks in their news departments. He said that by failing to provide what Walter Lippmann called a picture of reality on which citizens can act, the networks risked becoming as obsolete as the newsreels. Friendly said, "I am constantly asked will there ever be another Murrow?" He stressed that in 1986 Murrow could hardly enjoy the air time and creative freedom he had exercised at the dawn of television journalism. "Sadly," Friendly continued, "I find myself saying I'm not sure Murrow could be Murrow today." The title of Friendly's speech was "If I Had My Career in Broadcast Journalism to Start Over Again in August, 1986 . . ." The seventy-four-year-old man on the podium seemed to be suggesting that he, too, could not have made a mark if he had started out in the current television environment.[22]

After his official retirement from the Ford Foundation and Columbia University, Friendly continued his frenetic pace, at work and play, well into his seventies. But in 1979, he became ill while he and Ruth were playing in a mixed-doubles tennis tournament in the Berkshires, where they had their vacation home. Ruth had noticed that he looked exhausted when they reached the quarter finals, but he had insisted, "I will *not* leave this court!" After they lost the match, Fred told Ruth he was seeing double and experiencing severe chest pain. Tests at a local hospital revealed atrial fibrillation, a temporary bout of irregular heartbeat precipitated by his exertions on the tennis court. He had not had a heart attack. And he remained irrepressible. While he was being monitored in intensive care, Friendly began posing hypothetical questions about medical ethics to the staff. He also wrote an article for the *Berkshire Eagle* about the incident, which he called "a small story about signals and how to read them." He concluded: "The lasting lesson is that the human body, even a strong one, has a limited capacity that cannot always answer the greedy demands of a competitive libido. This is not the first time I have made a fool of myself— nor probably the last. But I have learned to try to act my age."[23]

Five years later, on July 15, 1984, Friendly experienced a more serious medical event. Stuart Sucherman had arrived at the Friendly residence to go over an opening that Friendly had taped for a seminar. Sucherman found Friendly rubbing his left hand and saying that he felt numb on his left side. They surmised that he was having a stroke, contacted Ruth, and called an ambulance. Then, to Sucherman's surprise, Friendly suggested that they watch the tape while waiting for the ambulance. Sucherman, preoccupied with Friendly's condition, feigned concentration. When Friendly asked what he thought, Sucherman mumbled something like "pretty good." "Now," Friendly asked, "you're not just saying that because I'm having a stroke, are you?" New York University Medical Center kept him for a week and determined that his stroke had been mild. Friendly quickly resumed his regular schedule.

Three days after he was discharged, he attended a luncheon meeting. A week later, Ruth said, they were back on the road, to Albany, New York, and Columbus, Ohio. In a letter to William Webster, he made light of what he called his "medical accident."[24]

On January 4, 1990, Friendly made a video addendum to his living will. It was taped spontaneously during a break while he and a crew were working at FBI headquarters in Washington, D.C. Noting that he had done a program called "The Sovereign Self: Right to Live, Right to Die" (part of the *Constitution* series), Friendly underscored his insistence that extraordinary measures not be taken to preserve his life if his faculties were seriously compromised. "Make no doubt about it. I want to preserve my life," he said. "I don't want to preserve my death." He ended by saying, "Enjoy this life. Hope you never have to see this tape. Maybe I'll die in an airplane accident."[25]

Eleven months later, the seventy-five-year-old Friendly collapsed after videotaping a lengthy interview for the Video History Project of the Museum of Jewish Heritage in New York. During the interview, he had discussed in detail his experience during World War II and especially the excruciating experience of witnessing the liberation of the Mauthausen concentration camp. He said that when he heard applause at Tanglewood Music Center near his summer house in the Berkshires, it triggered flashbacks to the soft clapping sounds that U.S. troops heard when they entered the camp. "That sound still resonates in me," he said. He grew visibly tired by the end of the interview, repeating himself and rambling a bit before declaring, "I think you got everything out of me that's in me." After the interview, he skipped lunch, went off to buy some gloves, and passed out in the leather goods store. An ambulance took him to New York Hospital, where Floyd Abrams visited him and they discussed seminar projects. Ruth recalled that his collapse was attributed to low blood sugar and atrial fibrillation.[26] Shortly after his release from the hospital, he conducted a seminar in Santa Barbara, California.

He made no adjustments in his schedule. His commitments for private seminars, many arranged by the Leigh Bureau, would have exhausted a person half Friendly's age. In March 1991 alone, he and Ruth held programs at LaGuardia Community College in New York, Brown University in Providence, and Tulane University in New Orleans. Month after month, Fred and Ruth mounted programs for judicial conferences, colleges, and professional organizations. In August, for example, they led programs in Sun Valley, Idaho; Atlanta; and Hartford, Connecticut. In October, their travels took them to Clinton, Mississippi; Corvallis, Oregon; and Wilmington, Delaware. At the same time, Friendly continued to mount the televised seminars for PBS. For example, the two-part series on education, *America's Schools: Who Gives a Damn?* was broadcast in 1991.[27]

In late September, Friendly traveled to California again to tape a seminar for broadcast at Stanford University, *Safe Speech, Free Speech and the University*. The program examined controversies about racism, sexism, bans on hate speech, and political correctness on campuses. It was one of the few seminars based on a hypothetical situation that Friendly himself moderated. As the seminar was to begin, Friendly experienced chest pains. The assembled panelists included the presidents of Stanford, Yale, and the American Civil Liberties Union; prominent print and broadcast journalists; lawyers; activists; and students. Friendly refused to consider canceling the taping, saying, "I have seven cameras here and I'm going to do the show." Two cardiologists from Stanford's medical school came to Friendly's dressing room with a cardiogram machine; they compared the test results with the records of Friendly's internist in New York by telephone. They agreed to let Friendly do the program with the stipulation that he be hospitalized afterward for a check-up, and the two doctors stood by during the taping. Afterward, he checked into Cedars-Sinai Medical Center in Los Angeles, where it was determined that his gall bladder, not his heart, was the issue. He left the hospital on a Monday to do another seminar in Santa Barbara and returned Wednesday to have his gall bladder removed.[28]

That December, Friendly blacked out momentarily at a holiday party and got a pacemaker a few weeks later. In January 1992, he taped the segues for *A Decade of Hard Choices: A Retrospective with Fred Friendly*, a compilation of seminar broadcasts. His hoarse voice intimated the decline in his health. Later that month, testing at New York Hospital determined that he had suffered a small stroke. But then his condition deteriorated and became life threatening, perhaps because of a bad reaction to medication. He recovered slowly, remaining in the hospital for about a month.

When Friendly was discharged, he was finally and irrevocably forced to scale down his activity. He continued to go to the office of the media and society seminars, but he stopped directing and introducing them on tape. He would still give an occasional class or guest lecture. John Schultz remembered Friendly standing before a class and saying, "I'd like to apologize. I had a stroke, so I have problems." Ruth would sit in the front row, providing a word, name, and or date when Fred faltered. "It was like a train going off track," Ruth recalled, "—push it back on and . . . off he went, continuing his remarks." Schultz recalled Friendly's striving valiantly to overcome the effects of the stroke: " 'I'm trying to get electrodes through my brain matter—now, who was the producer of such and such a documentary? Don't tell me, don't tell me.' He'd be constantly testing himself." Joshua Friedman—a former student of Friendly's, later a Pulitzer Prize–winning reporter and a professor at Columbia—recalled that after 1992 Friendly "was a wounded person." Cynthia McFadden remembered Friendly's frustration: "He was just in a rage. He couldn't believe that his body was not cooperating with him." She added, "He didn't know how to operate at anything less than 100 percent. I think the challenge of the stroke was that he didn't have any frame of reference. . . . I had never seen Fred in idle, or neutral, or even in second gear." Ruth, concerned about his dark moods and outbursts, arranged for him to see a psychiatrist, Gary L. Lefer, but Friendly did not take to therapy.[29]

Not long after his second stroke, Friendly visited the offices of CBS News for the last time. The occasion was a memorial service for Frances Arvold, a long-time and beloved makeup artist at CBS who had died in October 1992. In passing the office of the president of CBS News, Friendly could see the outline of the back door that he had installed as news president so he could escape from unwelcome visitors ensconced in the waiting room. After 1992, Friendly receded from the public stage. In addition to ending his role as director of the media and society seminars, he ceased speaking out as broadcast journalism's de facto public ombudsman. Nonetheless, in 1994 Friendly received a plaudit during Marlon Brando's appearance on *Larry King Live* on CNN. While criticizing the state of contemporary journalism, Brando paid tribute to I. F. Stone and to "Fred Friendly, who is still alive, who is still throwing punches, still going three rounds." During this period, Friendly's role as beloved paterfamilias became primary. His son Andrew remembered this time as "just sweet, bittersweet days and nights filled with simple things we did together when I was a kid." The family watched movies, attended Knicks and Yankees games, and had quiet dinners in Riverdale and reflective moments by the lake in Stockbridge.[30]

Early in 1997, Friendly was felled by a devastating stroke, which Ruth described in a letter to Lee Clark, the widow of Friendly's commanding officer during World War II: "Fred had a nasty knock in January—first a heart attack and then a more serious stroke, but the first two were minor compared to this. Fred is able to get around some; the real damage is in the cognition, reasoning, thinking area, a terrible blow for this great communicator."[31] Ruth's letter was in response to a package of wartime memorabilia that Lee Clark had sent, including Friendly's citation for heroism for his actions during the Bombay fire, photographs, and correspondence. Ruth wrote that Fred devoured the material and asked her to reread Lee's letter several times. Once, when Tom Bettag visited, they watched the video of Friendly's interview for the Museum of Jewish Heritage about his wartime experiences. Since his long-term memory was relatively intact, he especially enjoyed visitors with links to the glory days at CBS. One of his visitors was Mili Lerner Bonsignori, his film editor for *See It Now*. "The last time I saw him," she recalled, "he'd already had a stroke. But he'd say, 'Tell me, tell the story.' And I'd tell him stories of what happened at *See It Now*. And he'd say, 'Right, that's right.' He made me cry."[32]

At moments, inchoate fury welled up in Friendly, as it does in many stroke victims. Of course, rage had always been a part of his makeup, driving his ambition and perfectionism. He once said of Murrow, "His anger was his greatest weapon, but he knew how to control it." In Friendly's prime a host of factors, professional and personal, tempered and channeled his rage. Now, immobilized by a devastating stroke that weakened all restraints, Friendly would sometimes lash out at those closest to him; afterward, he might shyly apologize. Friendly's family and friends lamented that in his last year he was denied so many of the qualities that had made him a giant in his field and a beloved figure for his friends and family. At the end, Andy Rooney could not bear to visit him.[33]

Friendly died at home in Riverdale on March 3, 1998, at the age of eighty-three. Three days later, a funeral service was held at Riverdale Temple.[34] Among his colleagues, Dan Rather, Andy Rooney, Tom Bettag, and Martha Elliott spoke. However, the family took center stage, as his children recalled the ways their father challenged and loved them. Jonathan Mark, the oldest, spoke of Friendly's qualities as a man and a father. Andrew Friendly recalled an early-morning fishing expedition when he was seven and his father refused to allow his shivering and crying son to return to shore until they caught a fish. The children had often been tested at mealtime. David Friendly said, "Dinner was often a test-run for his latest hypothetical, and God forbid you came in unprepared."

"Sometimes you would go to dinner," Richard Mark noted, "and find yourself on the menu." Lisa Friendly evoked an image of his hand, the last three fingers fused in place by his wartime injury, "frozen forever in a gesture of urgency and emphasis." The children also celebrated a loving father and the family traditions he had established, such as cooking the Thanksgiving dinner on the barbeque and invariably ending his good-nights to them with "It's good to be your dad."[35]

The public memorial service for Friendly took place on April 23, 1998, in the Kathryn Bache Miller Theater at Columbia University, located only blocks from where he had been born eighty-two years before. The service, with Dan Rather presiding, was sponsored by the Columbia University Graduate School of Journalism and CBS. Andrew Hayward, president of CBS News, acknowledged Friendly's enduring influence on CBS's newsroom, marking a final homecoming to the network where he often said he left much of his youth and heart.[36]

The service felt like a Fred Friendly production because of the extraordinary range of prominent eulogists and the substance of their remarks, which were supplemented by tapes of Friendly as he reflected on journalism and life. Indeed, the day was marked by his spirit of irreverence and joy, as expressed by his family, friends, former colleagues, and students.

Robert Bernstein told the story of Friendly's politely declining to have dinner with a commanding officer, with Friendly explaining that he felt he should eat with the enlisted men. "'That man is different,'" Bernstein remembered thinking, "'I wonder what he'll do after the war.'" Sucherman described classic Friendly performances at Ford Foundation board meetings. Cynthia McFadden spoke of the immense challenges and satisfaction that came with working for Friendly. She stressed "the terrifying, free-floating anxiety which only Fred Friendly could inspire. He truly believed that being thrown off balance made you think harder and better." She also recalled that

> "unacceptable!" was one of Fred's favorite sentences. His standard for producers was that they produce anything he wanted. He called it "walking through walls." Now, Fred felt that many things that you or I might consider entirely acceptable weren't. Consider, for example, Floyd Abrams' entirely acceptable reason for backing out of a seminar: the chicken pox. "Unacceptable," roared Fred. You can watch the reruns of Floyd's memorable performance on that program late at

night on your local public television station, pox and all. Or the U.S. senator who said he had to attend his father's funeral. "Unacceptable" rang throughout the land, and the senator, of course, showed up.[37]

Antonin Scalia talked about the media and society seminars, relating how Friendly had broken down the conservative justice's resistance to appearing on television. Scalia also emphasized Friendly's "boyish innocence," manifested in his belief that he could improve the state of journalism, foster greater understanding of the Constitution, and strengthen the democratic process: "He believed all that, as a teenager might, and when you listened to Fred, you believed it, too." Friendly had a habit of giving out small copies of the Constitution to his students, and a special edition was distributed at the memorial service. But while Scalia emphasized Friendly's optimism, Bill Moyers underscored Friendly's disenchantment with the direction of broadcast journalism: "He would appreciate the irony, I think, that so many of us who now sing his praises once broke his heart . . . as he watched once-kindred spirits turn journalism into one more branch of the national entertainment state."[38]

Before she thanked the participants, Ruth Friendly asked, "And where is he when I need him the most?" She was determined to keep the media and society seminars going—and did; they were renamed the Fred Friendly Seminars not long after his death. She also made sure that, as her husband had repeatedly requested, Michael and Mary Mark, Friendly's stepson and daughter-in-law, sang "Send in the Clowns."

21 Friendlyvision

"I WAS AN UNDERACHIEVER as a child, and an overachiever professionally," Fred Friendly observed in an interview when he was seventy-five.[1] He was gangly and awkward as a youth, stuttered, and did poorly in school as a result of undiagnosed dyslexia. His mother turned for help to the upper-middle-class Jewish community of Providence, the center of which was Temple Beth El, which embraced her son and gave him a sense of support and belonging. When he became a young man, she feared that he would be unable to support himself. "Who'd ever have thought," Dan Rather said at Friendly's memorial in 1998, "that Ferdie Friendly Wachenheimer, the colorblind, dyslexic kid who spent his early years on 110th Street and in Providence, Rhode Island, who couldn't pass a math test to save his life, would someday be head of CBS News? Or would be spending time with presidents of the United States and Supreme Court justices?"[2]

During his childhood, Friendly developed a fascination—indeed, an obsession—with radio. He had been introduced to the medium when he and his father built a wireless receiver in order to listen to KDKA's broadcast of the Dempsey–Carpentier fight in 1921, when Friendly was five. (Years later, he was thrilled to meet Graham McNamee, who had called the bout.)[3] After the move from New York to Providence, the death of his father, and while struggling in school, Friendly would escape by speaking into an imaginary radio microphone in his living room, a practice that seemed to hold his demons at bay. As a young man, he attached himself to Mowry Lowe, a pioneering Rhode Island broadcaster, the first of a succession of big-brotherly mentors. Friendly idolized Lowe, who attained in Friendly's eyes the enviable status of man-about-town in Providence by virtue of his radio work.

Certainly Friendly's early years provide fertile ground for the psychohistorian. To be sure, the frustration of being stymied in incomprehensible ways by dyslexia contributed to the rage and ambition that carried him to the highest reaches of broadcast journalism. Can we discern a lifelong quest for recognition in the succession of triumphant returns to his native Providence and in the continual quest for new challenges? Toward the end of his career, when he could have disappeared into a comfortable retirement, Friendly criss-crossed the nation, giving seminars at an Olympic pace. "He was incredible, constantly on the go," Stuart Sucherman recalled. "In fact, I always thought that one of his issues was that he had to keep moving, that if he ever stopped and slowed down, he would go into a depression, and I once said that to him. I thought he was going to hit me." Yet Peter Neubauer, Friendly's friend and a psychoanalyst, cautioned against psychological reductionism in regard to Friendly, especially insofar as it would discount the remarkable élan vital that seemed part of his DNA and constituted his most characteristic trait.[4]

Friendly manifested that élan in his service during World War II. Up to that point, he had had a modest career as a part-time broadcaster and advertising producer while living at home. He more than met the challenge of serving in the information and education section of the China-India-Burma theater, attaching himself to his second mentor, Major Ed Clark. Friendly repeatedly exhibited physical courage, rescuing troops in Bombay, accompanying bombing missions, and traveling with the Stilwell convoy to China. Friendly was equally bold about pushing the limits of radio and wire recorders during the war in settings ranging from the battlefield and fighter-bombers in flight to the operating room of a military hospital. Friendly placed himself at the center of action, accompanying U.S. troops at the liberation of the Mauthausen concentration camp and flying over Hiroshima and Nagasaki a few days after they had been hit by atomic bombs. "The Man," as Friendly came to be known in the CBI theater, actively shaped his war experience and in doing so challenged military protocol, just as he would later challenge the cultures of other institutions. Friendly's war experience, his "Rhodes scholarship," became a practicum in which he could test and refine his talents.

Friendly continued to exhibit remarkable drive and self-confidence as he explored professional possibilities in New York after the war. He was starting from scratch, living off his savings, staying in a modest Manhattan hotel, preparing a series of trial balloons in radio broadcasting. His professional and personal partner, Dorothy Greene, became his wife. What seemed remarkable to her was Friendly's inexhaustible energy and apparently unshakable confidence that he would prevail and find great success. In E. B. White's words he was "willing to be lucky." Friendly's voluntarism, his determination to will his achievements, was a central element in his character. At the end of the war, he sensed that U.S. broadcasting was on the cusp of a dramatic revolution, the introduction of television, and that he could become a player in its development. His lack of credentials and contacts did not stop him from enlisting the participation of prominent figures in order to realize his ambitions. For his first programming breakthrough, the quiz show *Who Said That?* the unknown Friendly got as host Robert Trout, a legendary figure in radio news. *Who Said That?* in turn permitted Friendly to interact with leading figures in U.S. politics, journalism, and entertainment. He exhibited great enterprise in seeking out prominent figures for *The Quick and the Dead*, his four-part documentary on the atomic bomb that aired in 1950 on the NBC radio network. As a patron of the CBS hangout Louis and Armand's, Friendly got to know J. G. "Jap" Gude, the preeminent agent of broadcast journalists of his day. Through Gude, Friendly initiated his partnership with Edward R. Murrow, who—after Mowry Lowe and Ed Clark—became Friendly's third major patron.

Friendly was enthralled by big names but not intimidated in their presence. Friendly's expertise as a producer, of course, served as a valuable commodity to people in public life. But his intelligence and assertiveness, together with a beguiling impudence, put him on a more equal footing with U.S. presidents and other luminaries. A grandson recalled being admonished to "show how confident you were so that they will respect you." Once Cynthia McFadden brought Katharine Hepburn to Riverdale to meet Friendly, who started the conversation by asking, "I always wondered: Are all actors stupid?" The ice was broken, Hepburn was not fazed, and the two went on to have a delightful conversation. McFadden felt that Friendly was aggressive in such situations to establish that he would not be dazzled. "Of course," she reflected, "he *was* dazzled, all the time."[5]

Friendly's entrée into the highest reaches of broadcast journalism hinged in large measure on his ability to anticipate the importance of new communications technologies and to apply them in original ways. (Friendly's first biography for the *Footprints in the Sands of Time* series was of the great electrical engineer Charles P. Steinmetz of General Electric.) Friendly seized on the advent of magnetic tape to make the groundbreaking recording "*I can hear it now . . . ,*" *1933–1945*, which initiated his collaboration with Edward R. Murrow. When television was a new medium, Friendly conceptualized and produced *See It Now*, the founding program in the history of public affairs programming. The show represented a synthesis of elements of photojournalism, documentary film, and radio reporting applied to the technological possibilities of television, which Friendly pushed to the limit.

Friendly also was a leader in anticipating the revolutionary implications of communications satellites and cable television. As Stuart Sucherman observed, one can only imagine what creative use Friendly might have made of the Internet. "Fred's greatest gift," Martha Elliott suggested, "was to be able to envision something that didn't exist. People can criticize him for his shortcomings, but very few people have that kind of foresight." Moreover, what enabled Friendly to wield great influence was his capacity to anticipate the emergence of critical issues as well as new technologies—indeed, his ability to apply television technologies to the elucidation of major developments and controversies. Jonathan Landman noted Friendly's prescience, his ability to sense what was going to be important in both the substance and technology of news. "He didn't come to it analytically," Landman emphasized, "he didn't sit down, read a book and write reports. He was a gut guy, and he had an all-time epic gut."[6]

Friendly was a fervent autodidact, eager to learn from the expertise of others. If Friendly willed his successes, he did not do so in isolation. He relentlessly enlisted the expertise, insights, and assistance of others. Hence he would interview, for example, CBS's master radio editor Joel Tall to learn about magnetic tape, Hearst newsreel camera operators in preparation for *See It Now*, and the physicist Joel Rosen for the Ford Foundation satellite proposal. Friendly turned his lack of formal education into an advantage. He would seek out information from others and then apply that information in original ways, unfettered by traditional practices. According to McFadden, "He used his lack of education and his ignorance as a tool. He was not afraid to say he didn't know or understand." Friendly furthermore relied heavily on the talented teams he assembled around him throughout his career. He had a great gift for identifying and assembling gifted professionals—"generally made up of people who could not have been more unlike him," as Tom Bettag said—who played an indispensable role in Friendly's accomplishments. Think, for example, of the *See It Now* team with Palmer Williams and Mili Lerner, among others; the *CBS Reports* team with Jay McMullen and David Lowe; the

Ford Foundation team with Stuart Sucherman and David Davis; the Columbia University Seminars on Media and Society team with Benno Schmidt and Cynthia McFadden. Friendly's style as boss harked back to his days as a master sergeant, as Stuart Sucherman explained: "It was like going to basic training: You came out of it tougher, and more knowledgeable. . . . He was a perfectionist and tremendous taskmaster, and he would push way beyond where you thought you could possibly perform at. That was very unpleasant at times, but I think in the long run he made everyone better."[7]

Tom Bettag emphasized that despite Friendly's reputation as an impossibly demanding taskmaster, his approach also involved a great capacity to reach out to others for help:

> It started, for me, the day I became his teaching assistant. "I have a hundred ideas a day. You have to find the two good ones." "How could you have let me do that?" "You have to make this work." This was a man of unparalleled strength. That he could be so open about his vulnerabilities made him seem even bigger. . . .
>
> Over the next 30 years, I learned there was no one he wouldn't ask to help. He was pursuing ideals and principles he *knew* were important and doing what he *knew* was right. To producers, to cameramen: "You have to help me." But television was too important to be left just to television people. So, to Supreme Court justices, to presidents: "You have to help me." Television would shape the kind of nation we are. So, to Republicans and Democrats, to whites, African-Americans, Hispanics, Asians: "You have to help me."[8]

Friendly exhibited great loyalty to the universe of people who assisted him. Upon becoming president of CBS News, for example, he rehired Joe Wershba, who had been forced to leave CBS during the McCarthy period. When the son of his long-time secretary, Hazel Layton, was severely injured in a diving accident in the early 1970s in the Caribbean, Friendly arranged for a medical evacuation plane, and he and Ruth spent a week beside the young man's deathbed; afterward, Layton stayed for three weeks with the Friendlys in Riverdale. Friendly periodically traveled to a nursing home on Martha's Vineyard to visit Jap Gude, who had initiated Friendly's association with Murrow. Time and again, Friendly exhibited great loyalty to his extended family of colleagues and friends. He could even display constancy with old adversaries: at a *National Review* dinner on December 5, 1985, he made a point of paying his respects to Roy Cohn, who was sitting in an alcove sick with AIDS and less than a year to live.[9]

Friendly always acknowledged, publicly and privately, his debt to his wives, Dorothy and Ruth. Dorothy served as an indispensable partner when he began his career. Ruth became a critical factor in the renewal of both his personal and his professional life two decades later, following his departure from CBS. While presiding over a merger of two sets of children in Riverdale, she assumed a wide range of responsibilities in Friendly's undertakings, among them the role of research assistant and trusted critic. In the mounting of seminars, her social skills complemented Friendly's driving, sometimes abrasive, style. "Without Ruth it would have all turned to rage," McFadden reflected in retrospect. "Ruth helped him channel his rage into some very productive years. She was magic with him."[10] In 1970, after two years of marriage, Friendly acknowledged what Ruth meant to him in a combination birthday card and love letter that he scrawled with a Magic Marker:

> A magic marker for my magic Mark. . . . My Willis Reed or poetry in motion. . . . My gentle friend & critic who never says your socks were too low or your sights were too high. . . . Who is mutually admired by Frank at the deli, [Howard] Dressner at the [Ford] Foundation and 104 students at the [Journalism] school . . . who is at home at Shea [Stadium], the [Madison Square] Garden, the Opera, Cal Tech, Oregon State & [British Prime Minister] Harold Wilson's . . . who makes old men young, young men mature. . . . A fixer, a lover, an angel, a cook, a driver. . . . Bringer of cheer . . . 24 hours every day, every week, every month, every year . . . life saver, life giver . . . an American original. . . . My darling, patient, dearest, darling, patient. . . . –Ruthie—Ruthie . . . I love you. I love you.[11]

Few boundaries existed between Friendly's life at home and in the office. David Friendly said that his father bonded with his children less by entering into their world than by including them in his own. Neubauer, the psychoanalyst and family friend, once remarked that Friendly operated as executive director in all spheres of his life. He was, of course, the executive director of programs like See It Now and the media and society seminars. But, Neubauer suggested, he was also executive director of his social life. Neubauer recalled his discomfort at being summoned to dinner in Riverdale with McGeorge Bundy and being incorrectly introduced by Friendly as Bill Paley's therapist. (In fact, Paley's wife, Babe, was Neubauer's patient.)[12] For Neubauer, Friendly was, moreover, the executive director of his family and ultimately of his own persona. His life could be viewed as a Friendly production. To be sure, Friendly's emotionality—his spontaneity and explosive nature—precluded any possibility of charting his destiny according to a highly calculated game plan. Yet if there is an element of truth in Neubauer's suggestion that both the private and public Friendly constituted an artful construct, the production was brilliant, and Friendly became one with the character he created.

At times, Friendly's actions and principles seemed in conflict. He hung on his wall in Riverdale, and liked to quote, a cartoon from the October 24, 1953, issue of the *New Yorker* in which a man and woman are stranded on an island. They can have sex without anyone's knowledge, but the woman says, "I'd know. That's who'd know."[13] It became one of his stock phrases. He used it, for example, in his book *Due to Circumstances Beyond Our Control . . .* , whose dedication read, "For the professionals at CBS NEWS: 'I'd know—that's who'd know.'" Friendly would hold students and colleagues to the highest ethical standards and rail against deceptive practices in journalism. The *Ethics in America* series marked the crowning achievement of the Friendly seminars.

Yet Friendly could doctor parts of the first *"I can hear it now . . ."* album, which purportedly contained only original recordings. His behavior could prompt objections to unethical practices on his part by two of his mentors, Ed Clark and Edward R. Murrow. David Schoenbrun recalled Friendly's once telling him, "Don't talk to me about morals, I've got the morals of a mink." Schoenbrun reflected, "Accurate and moral, or not, Fred in his own field, was close to being a genius. He had every quality except balance and total news integrity." The chasm on occasion between his principles and actions led David Halberstam to write of Friendly that he was "at once a creator of his own legend and a destroyer of it." Yet Martin Clancy, his former graduate assistant, noted Friendly's ability to acknowledge his own foibles: "That, too, is the essence of Friendly . . . the ability to admit of the Emperor's lack of clothing."[14]

Friendly recognized the aspect of performance in television production, with all the vagaries associated with the stage, including elements of artifice and the absurd as well as the inevitable gaffes. This may explain why Friendly, the class clown at Hope Street High School, embraced the Stephen Sondheim song "Send in the Clowns." Friendly spoke about the special meaning of the song for him on December 2, 1979, on

Lloyd Moss's radio program, *This Is My Music*, on WQXR-FM in New York City. He told Moss, "It does seem to be almost the story of my life. . . . And there is one lyric in it that I would like to think, when they lay me out, whenever that time comes . . . it's almost an epitaph for me. It's 'Isn't it rich? / Isn't it queer? / Losing my timing this late / In my career? / And where are the clowns? / There ought to be clowns. / Well, maybe next year . . .' "[15] Friendly suggested that Murrow—"the most urbane, handsome, sophisticated person that I ever knew intimately"—was his opposite. Friendly confessed that "awkwardness is sort of my style," that his timing could be off, and that his exuberance could get him into trouble.[16] He repeated his wish that "Send in the Clowns" be sung as his funeral. The title of the Stephen Sondheim song has its roots in vaudeville and the circus, when the call would be made to "send in the clowns" to distract from a terrible performance or an unforeseen accident. Two of the verses read:

Just when I'd stopped
Opening doors,
Finally knowing
The one that I wanted was yours,
Making my entrance again
With my usual flair,
Sure of my lines,
No one is there.

Don't you love farce?
My fault I fear.
I thought that you'd want what I want—
Sorry, my dear.
But where are the clowns?
Quick, send in the clowns.
Don't bother, they're here.[17]

The sensibility of a jester served Friendly well. There was a method to his madness. As Dostoyevsky wrote, "The cleverest of all, in my opinion, is the man who calls himself a fool at least once a month."

Friendly's histrionics and myriad projects were linked to an agenda for television, a vision of the medium as a great national resource for American democracy. This vision had multiple, complementary sources. His experience as an information officer in World War II shaped Friendly's view of broadcasting—first radio, then television—as a great democratic instrument. As he came to view the medium of broadcasting as providing a great national classroom, *Sergeant Quiz* moved to a larger stage. Friendly spelled out what he considered U.S. broadcasting's untapped potential as early as 1945, in his letter to Jack Kapp, the head of Decca Records: "Information is our only safeguard for peace." Friendly's perspective was reinforced and extended through his partnership with Murrow, who had worked in international education before becoming a broadcaster. In his speech in 1958 before the Radio-Television News Directors Association, Murrow advocated that the medium of television be mobilized for the "battle to be fought against ignorance, intolerance and indifference."[18] Murrow's speech can be seen as a touchstone for Friendly's career, as Friendly suggested when he in turn addressed the RTNDA nearly three decades later.

For Friendly the writings of Walter Lippmann fleshed out the ethos voiced in Murrow's RTNDA speech and played a critical role in Friendly's conceptualization of his life work. In his classic work *Public Opinion* (1922) and its sequel, *The Phantom Public* (1925), Lippmann had expressed alarm about the deterioration of public discourse after World War I. In his view, the refinement of propaganda techniques, and the growth of the advertising and public relations industries, threatened the theory and practice of American democracy, which is based on a well-informed citizenry.[19] Instead, Lippmann lamented that Americans had become captives of the "pictures in our heads," of stereotypes and simplistic views of complex issues that were advanced by mass media. The emergence of television a quarter century later reinforced Lippmann's fears. He believed that only an elite of experts could frame and address the complex problems of modern society and called on mass media to assume the task of explaining the thinking of leaders in the social and natural sciences for a public otherwise incapable of making informed judgments. It has been said that "the media ideal, according to Lippmann, was not a broad marketplace of ideas, good and bad, informed and ignorant, true and false, but an instrument of mass education—not a mirror but a molder of society."[20] Friendly would frequently quote Lippmann's statement that "the purpose of journalism is to give information on which the citizen can act."[21] Thus Friendly aspired to produce public affairs programming that would enable citizens to consider the pressing issues of the day in an informed fashion. In his view, network television could assume a critical role in elevating the low level of American public discourse.

This is not to say that Friendly took a studious interest in Lippmann's books. Tom Bettag doubted that Friendly ever read *Public Opinion* in its entirety. He noted that Friendly was not a big reader, perhaps a function of his dyslexia: "I can't envision this huge, restless man sitting down and reading many books. He was too restless for that; he was a doer." Ruth Friendly confirmed that he would typically browse through a book, taking from it what he needed. (Nonetheless, Lisa Friendly remembered her father as a voracious reader later in life.)[22] At any rate, Friendly's gift was not systematic analysis or exegesis; instead, he was able to seize on ideas and make them his own in a creative way. The essence of Friendlyvision was the application of Lippmann's ideas to television. Throughout his career, Friendly reiterated his conviction that the very future of democracy hinged, in large measure, on whether television fulfilled its potential as a primary source for information and analysis of news and public affairs.

By the same token, Lippmann provided a rationale for Friendly's desire to produce seminars with prominent figures that would expose the public to complex contemporary issues from different perspectives. Despite Lippmann's emphasis on expertise, Bill Moyers insisted it would be a mistake to characterize Friendly as interested exclusively in the perspectives of elites. As Moyers noted, Friendly helped give voice to ordinary people like Milo Radulovich and the migrant workers portrayed in "Harvest of Shame." "I never thought of him as a populist," Moyers said, "but I don't think of him as an elitist, either. I think of him as someone who believed in the checks and balances of the system." Yet the presence of ordinary people and the downtrodden was more characteristic of Friendly's early work in partnership with Murrow than of the media and society seminars he produced in the latter part of his career. Friendly's instinct as a producer, to highlight the thinking of leading authorities— what one colleague described as "important people saying important things"—became more pronounced over time.[23]

Lippmann's thinking confirmed Friendly's instincts, providing a theoretical basis and added legitimacy for his agenda for public affairs programming on television. Lippmann could help Friendly conceptualize, for example, how a Joseph McCarthy could manipulate public opinion, and how important it was to provide an alternative set of images through a platform like *See It Now* that would expose the demagogue's true nature. Friendly came to understand the broadcast journalist's role as that of an intermediary between leading authorities—political and professional—and the broader population, defining issues and providing information to enable the American people to participate meaningfully in public life. A link existed between the core problem explored in *Public Opinion* and Friendly's agenda for public affairs programming on television. Friendly shared with McGeorge Bundy a veneration for Lippmann. In 1980, Bundy gave Friendly a copy of the 1922 edition of *Public Opinion* that had belonged to Bundy's father. Bundy's inscription thanks Friendly for teaching him the lessons contained in the book. Lippmann, who was deeply skeptical about television, had personally inscribed a later edition of the book for Friendly and had also dedicated a collection of his television interviews to Friendly, congratulating him as "the only begetter, who conceived and produced all this."[24] In 1974, when Lippmann was dying in a nursing home in New York, Friendly and Ruth visited him several times a week. Friendly also arranged for Lippmann's funeral service to be held in the auditorium of the Ford Foundation, where clips were shown from the Lippmann interviews produced by Friendly.[25]

Friendly, like Lippmann, was no populist. Friendly assumed the mantle of nonconformist but played that role *within* the establishment institutions toward which he gravitated. He always managed to carve out a special, semiautonomous niche within those centers of influence. *See It Now* operated independently of CBS News, and the Columbia University Seminars on Media and Society operated outside the purview of the graduate journalism program. There were limits to Friendly's criticisms of major U.S. institutions and their leaders. For example, although he was a civil libertarian he rarely, if ever, publicly criticized the FBI and its egregious record of violations of the Bill of Rights. He cast William Paley as a victim of the economics of network broadcasting. (To the contrary, David Halberstam, in *The Powers That Be*, characterizes Paley as *the* chief architect of a network broadcasting system based on maximizing profits through mass entertainment and an unforgiving ratings system.)[26] Moreover, Friendly's frustration with the role of ratings did not extend to a deeper criticism of the culture of consumerism and the market economics that drove commercial broadcasting. He sought to reform broadcast journalism by personal example and by moral exhortation, and he placed his hopes in an ancillary public broadcasting system. His dogged hopes for the possibility of change within the system were perhaps as much a function of his Billy Budd–like innocence—evoked by Justice Antonin Scalia at Friendly's memorial service—as of his centrist politics.

Friendly instinctively distrusted mass movements, which he felt discouraged rational discourse. Hence he was not sympathetic to the demonstrations against the Vietnam War. He viewed those demonstrations as the unfortunate result of a failure of the media to address the issue of the war in a fuller and more compelling way, as he explained to Frank Stanton during his unsuccessful fight to broadcast George Kennan's testimony. Nor was Friendly sympathetic to the student revolt on the Columbia campus in the late 1960s. Friendly's political views were generally characteristic of the liberalism of the cold war era that Arthur Schlesinger Jr. characterized as the "vital center." Friendly once referred to himself as "a dues-paying member of the radical center."[27] Friendly did not seem troubled that McGeorge Bundy had had a mixed record of standing up to McCarthyism when he was a dean at Harvard University or that Bundy was an architect of the war in Vietnam. Friendly's preoccupation with the Vietnam War resided in improving the quality of its coverage, not in speaking out about the conflict as a public figure.

Friendly's commitment was to the First Amendment and informing the public, not to a political agenda. As Jonathan Landman said, "He wanted to influence people, but he was interested in ideas, not power."[28] Friendly thoughtfully juxtaposed, especially in the seminars, differences of thinking among leading figures in American public life. Yet dissenting or radical voices outside the mainstream—outside the confines of established authorities or of Democratic and Republican politics—were rarely heard. The legacy of such Friendlyesque dialogue, of its undeniable substance but also its self-defined limits, could later be seen on programs like *Nightline* on ABC and the *NewsHour* on PBS.[29] Lippmann, the embodiment of Friendly's journalistic ideal, was a consummate insider. Lippmann relished his wide access to the nation's decision makers and role as adviser to presidents, from Woodrow Wilson to Lyndon Johnson. Lippmann—and by extension Friendly—represented the antithesis of a crusading outsider like I. F. Stone. Indeed Stone's biographer, Myra MacPherson, contrasted Lippmann and Stone as "Jews from opposite sides of the ghetto" with markedly different relationships to established authority. She quoted the observation of *Nation* editor Carey McWilliams that "Izzy enjoyed not being on a first-name basis. Not going to the dinners. Not being Walter Lippmann."[30] Friendly could not lay claim to the purity of Stone's autonomy and muckraking role; Friendly was too fascinated by great figures and the centers of power. Stone's outsider status was the source of his influence and success. However, Friendly's remarkable accomplishments were of a different order; he realized them by virtue of his association with centers of influence at CBS, the Ford Foundation, and Columbia University.

Friendly's achievements at CBS are landmarks in broadcasting history. *See It Now*, the first major public affairs and documentary series on television, was his creation. The program would exert broad influence on the development of various forms of public affairs programming on television, from foreign and war reporting and the long-form interview to magazine and documentary formats. In addition, *See It Now* became the vehicle for a cycle of historic programs on McCarthyism, culminating in 1954 in "A Report on Senator Joseph R. McCarthy." It was only one of a series of high points in Friendly's career. "But I knew," Friendly told an interviewer twenty years later, "that I would never [again] have anything to do with anything this important in my life and I never did."[31] Friendly nonetheless continued to break new ground at CBS. As executive director of *CBS Reports*, he presided over the golden age of television documentaries. In the same period, he produced the first international network broadcast carried by a communications satellite and the first lengthy network interviews with sitting presidents, John F. Kennedy and Lyndon Johnson. Subsequently, Friendly revived the fortunes of CBS News as its president. He presided over increased programming about the Vietnam War and strongly defended Morley Safer's explosive report in 1965 from Cam Ne, a turning point in television reporting on the war.

In retrospect, the denouement of Friendly's separation from CBS was more complex than generally understood. It involved, to be sure, a protest against CBS's refusal to carry live George Kennan's testimony on Vietnam. Les Brown wrote that "Friendly felt that it was in the power of American TV and radio . . . to save the world from World War III." However, Friendly seized on the issue of Kennan's testimony as part of an attempt to shore up his weakened position as news president as a result of CBS's reorganization. While seeking a modus vivendi with Stanton and Paley, Friendly prematurely released his resignation letter, a tactical error that sealed his fate. The affair included a degree of posturing and confusion on Friendly's part. And yet, despite all the ambiguities surrounding his resignation, Friendly's deepest instincts pushing him toward the precipice were sound. Requiring him to report to Jack Schneider represented an omen, an early sign of a sea change in the status of news in network television. The final transformation of broadcast news from loss leader to profit center would not take place for another decade, but the Tiffany network was taking a step down that road. The path would lead over time to slashed network news budgets, a plethora of formulaic news-magazines, infotainment, and so-called reality television. Friendly's departure in 1966 from CBS was traumatic. "I think he never got over the days of glory of *See It Now* and *CBS Reports*," Ernie Leiser said. "Those were his best days, and I think if he were still alive he would still feel that way."[32]

Yet to leave it at that would be to ignore Friendly's remarkable second career—indeed, multiple, overlapping post-CBS careers—in which he equaled, and perhaps exceeded, his record of innovation at CBS. As he left the world of commercial broadcasting dominated by CBS, NBC, and ABC, he set his sights on establishing a fourth *noncommercial* network. Doing so marked the point of departure for his second career. Friendly was a key player in the transformation of educational into public broadcasting by virtue of his position as television consultant to McGeorge Bundy at the Ford Foundation. Friendly's satellite plan was a farsighted if unsuccessful attempt to ensure public television's funding and independence that placed the revolutionary technology of synchronous communications satellites on the public agenda. Friendly presided over the merger of Channel 13 and National Educational Television into WNET-TV in New York and over the transformation of WETA-TV into a major production center in Washington, D.C. He conceived and arranged funding for the *Public Broadcasting Laboratory* (*PBL*), a groundbreaking, if imperfect, programming experiment for the emerging public broadcasting system.

In addition, Friendly was instrumental in the creation of the Public Broadcasting Service (PBS) together with his aides at the Ford Foundation, Stuart Sucherman and David Davis. Friendly, who became a prime target in the Nixon administration's attack on public broadcasting, helped the system to survive the assault, and saw to it that the Ford Foundation continued to fund PBS's signature programming. Friendly, the producer par excellence, exercised great restraint in not meddling in the productions funded by the Ford Foundation. Yet he was clear-eyed about public television's excessive bureaucracy and lack of daring programming. Once he stunned Sucherman by saying, "Public television is like a whorehouse in which everyone wants to play the piano, and no one wants to fuck."[33] Friendly nonetheless was instrumental in the creation of PBS's best public affairs programs. The *NewsHour* remains the only hourlong network newscast on television and *Frontline* the only regularly scheduled investigative documentary series. "He anointed me," emphasized *Frontline*'s executive director, David Fanning, in acknowledging Friendly's critical early support.[34]

At Ford, Friendly was also a pioneer in the development of cable television. At the same time, in response to what he saw as a growing chasm of misunderstanding separating the Fourth Estate and the judiciary, he created the media and society seminars. Based on the Socratic method, this innovative format permitted the consideration of complex journalistic, legal, and ethical issues in a compelling and accessible fashion. It was as original, and as responsive to the temper of the times, as *See It Now* and *PBL* had been in their day. After his departure from the Ford Foundation, Friendly expanded the media and society seminars and their broadcast on PBS; his record as its founder and executive producer constituted his third career.

His position as Edward R. Murrow Professor of Journalism at Columbia University provided the foundation for his fourth career. He played a decisive role in developing the broadcasting track in one of the foremost graduate journalism schools in the nation. He initiated interdisciplinary courses with faculty of the Columbia University Law School. In a period of urban unrest he established the school's Summer Program for Minority Journalists, the single most important initiative to integrate broadcast journalism; its work continues to this day through its successor organization, the Robert Maynard Institute. Earl Caldwell, the African American reporter for the *New York Times* who helped run the summer program, said after Friendly's death, "I was deeply hurt and disappointed when he died that all that he did to bring about some diversity in the newsrooms was completely overlooked."[35]

Friendly also influenced a generation of students in the graduate journalism program at Columbia. This is particularly evident in regard to his graduate assistants, whom he assisted in beginning successful careers. Jonathan Landman, for example, recalled his good fortune at being part of what he called Friendly's orbit, the universe of a journalistic sun king with its concentric circles of people around him, and how this helped Landman get his first newspaper job under James Hoge at the *Chicago Sun-Times*. "He grabs me by the scruff of the neck and he grabs Hoge by the scruff of his neck and bangs our heads together," Landman remembered. "In his bombastic way he tells Hoge, 'You must hire this young man.'" Landman went on to a career in print journalism at the *Daily News* and *Newsday* before going to the *New York Times*, where he became metropolitan editor, editor of the Week in Review section, and a managing editor. "He wasn't a conventional mentor, either," Landman emphasized. "Just a fascinating, original, and extravagantly generous boss and friend."[36]

Landman was part of a group of former students and graduate assistants who feted Friendly at the home of Tom Bettag in June 1979, when Friendly retired from full-time teaching at Columbia and became professor emeritus. Many would make a mark in broadcast journalism. Edward Hersh, for example, worked for CBS Radio and later become senior vice president for documentaries and specials at Court TV. Mark Harrington helped launch MSNBC. Martin Clancy, Friendly's first graduate assistant, worked for Bill Moyers before doing investigative journalism and serving as a senior producer at *20/20*, the ABC-TV newsmagazine. Jennifer Siebens worked in a number of capacities at CBS: as a foreign correspondent for the *CBS Evening News with Walter Cronkite* and later with Dan Rather, and subsequently as CBS bureau chief in Paris and in Los Angeles. Not surprisingly, some joined the ranks of public television. David Kuhn worked on documentaries for *Nova* and *Frontline* before his death in an auto accident. After working at *CBS Reports*, Margaret Drain assumed the posts of executive producer of *The American Experience* and vice president of national programming at WGBH-TV in Boston. Dan Werner became associated with PBS's flagship news program as associate executive director of the *NewsHour with Jim Lehrer* and executive producer of McNeil-Lehrer Productions. Bettag spent twenty-two years at CBS News, where he served as producer for *60 Minutes* and executive producer of the *CBS Evening News with Dan Rather*, before becoming the long-time executive producer of ABC's *Nightline*. (Cynthia McFadden, who was not present at the Bettag party, also ended up working at *Nightline* as coanchor; she previously was senior legal correspondent at ABC.) The graduate assistants were Friendly's star students, but he trained other graduates of the journalism school as well, among them Steve Croft, correspondent for *60 Minutes*. Hence in addition to the example of his programs at CBS and his role as policy maker at the Ford Foundation, Friendly influenced broadcast journalism through a cohort of talented former protégés and students.

Friendly had a final, fifth career: critic. After his departure from CBS, but especially in his last years, he railed against the decline of standards in broadcast journalism. He did so in a variety of ways: through speeches to professional organizations, congressional testimony, op-ed articles, and television programs like *The Other Side of the News* series. Friendly traced a continuum between the issue that had caused his separation from CBS—the subordination of news and public affairs programming to the dictates of ratings and revenues—and the triumph of infotainment in the subsequent two decades of his life. He also expressed disappointment in public television's failure to become a greater force in broadcast journalism. Bill Moyers recalled that, at the end of his life, Friendly felt personally betrayed by the increasing difficulty in getting his media and society seminars funded and aired by the public television system he helped establish. Friendly suggested that public radio was proving to be the superior journalistic instrument. Harking back to his radio roots, Friendly suggested that NPR, more than PBS, had fulfilled its mandate.[37]

When Friendly left CBS in 1966 for Columbia University and the Ford Foundation, he still believed the young medium of television had vast potential as an educational and democratic instrument. As the years progressed, he became less sure that television would fulfill its promise. According to Bill Moyers, "He wasn't bitter; he was broken-hearted and deeply saddened." Yet Friendly would not give up hope. This would have been against his nature and convictions, against his faith in the Constitution and U.S. institutions. Otherwise, Friendly could not have sustained his lifelong professional crusade, including the last campaign he waged as critic and conscience of broadcast journalism. Given the opportunity, he would have pressed on with his characteristic creativity and determination. Like Stuart Sucherman, we can only imagine how Friendly might have exploited the possibilities of the Internet, digitalization, and the convergence of communication technologies for yet another new programming paradigm.

Friendly's formidable historic role in the first thirty-five years of broadcast journalism—as programmer, policy maker, teacher, and critic—is beyond dispute. The shape of his legacy is more questionable, as Bill Moyers has suggested. Moyers's television career was rooted in the Murrow–Friendly tradition of *See It Now*, and Friendly became his adviser and confidant. Moyers has said of Friendly, "He was my greatest inspiration in the early phase: his life, his work, and his principles." Later, Moyers added, "He became a kind of guru, kind of a mentor." Yet Moyers regretfully concluded:

There are no legacies in television. Television is like great movements of lava from many sources that soon overtakes, overwhelms,
covers up anyone who is important at a particular time. One's legacy
lasts only as long as you are in the mind of the last person who knew
you. There is no institution in television that survives because of any
of its founders. Networks are just infrastructure; they are not filled
with the passion or the spirit of the founders. . . . The last of Fred
Friendly's students will die and that legacy will be over. This is a hot,
boiling medium that swallows everything, including memory.

Moyers acknowledged Friendly's great achievement and influence in his
day: "But I don't know that there is any place left for a Fred Friendly in
American broadcasting."[38]

It might be said that Friendly and his triumphs belong to a bygone era.
An oft-told story about Friendly suggests something of a cultural divide
between him and his students when he was still teaching at Columbia.
He admonished a student who was working on a television film about
Vietnam War protesters to explain the slogan "Make Love Not War." The
young woman responded that the trouble with Friendly's generation was
that it did not understand the difference between making love and getting laid. Friendly shared the conversation with Lippmann, who replied
that it was an excellent example of the generation gap but asked what
"getting laid" meant. Friendly could not wait to relate the exchange with
the author of *Public Opinion* to a class at Columbia, only to have a student
ask, "Who is Walter Lippmann?"[39]

Today students might ask, "Who is Fred Friendly?" Can his example
still inspire others? There could never be another Fred Friendly; he was
clearly one of a kind. Nor could there be another career in broadcast
journalism like Fred Friendly's, because television was a new and as yet
undefined medium rife with possibilities when he entered the field.
The nation and world have changed in significant ways since Friendly's
heyday. In his era, centrist institutions were stronger, and the legal profession was less irrevocably politicized. During his lifetime, the Internet had not staked its claim as the future's paramount agent of information and commerce. How the television screen and the computer
monitor converge, how the ability to stream the news is exploited, will
now largely determine the future of broadcast journalism (and print as
well).

To point to the changing media landscape is not to diminish the scope and continuing relevance of Friendly's accomplishments. He was the greatest innovator and producer in the history of television journalism. Who can match his record as the pioneer of the television documentary, as the wizard who demonstrated the revolutionary impact of satellite and cable technology, as the policy maker instrumental in the establishment of public television, as the teacher of an influential cohort of journalists, as the producer of seminars that Dan Rather called "investigative reporting on ideas"? Clearly, others cannot seek to replicate what Friendly achieved. Yet the next generation of reformers and innovators would be wise to look back at the example of Fred Friendly. There is a crying need for broadcast journalists with Friendly's ambition for great initiatives in public affairs programming on television. Friendly embodied thinking big and thinking outside the conventions of the television box. As David Halberstam wrote of Friendly, "The bigger the show, the more difficult the idea, the better he responded—he was excited, not frightened, by big challenges."[40]

To be sure, those who would build on Friendly's achievements cannot limit themselves to working largely within the establishment institutions that he favored and often bent to his will. They will have to rely less on elites and to engage a broader spectrum of the population. They will need to explore the journalistic possibilities of the digital age in relation to alternative as well as mainstream media, perhaps in the spirit of Friendly's *PBL*, which sought to bridge both worlds. At the same time, they should seek to transcend the splintered, hyperspecialized nature of much new media and their discrete audiences: Friendly's quest to mobilize television to promote a substantive *national* conversation on the challenges before us—the essence of Friendlyvision—is more relevant now than ever. Those who wish to rejuvenate television journalism must build on Friendly's bold agenda as well as his capacity for passionate advocacy. As a character says in the Requiem at the end of *Death of a Salesman*—the play that so deeply touched Fred Friendly early in his career—a great salesman must have a great dream: "It comes with the territory."[41]

Notes

Dorothy Greene Friendly, Fred's first wife, and his widow, Ruth Mark Friendly, graciously sat for multiple interviews. Dorothy, to whom I will refer throughout the notes as DGF, was interviewed in New York City on December 21, 1998; February 4, 1999; June 22, 1999; August 31, 2000; and May 9, 2001. Ruth, identified throughout the notes as RMF, was interviewed in Riverdale, N.Y., on July 30, 1998; June 15, 1999; September 30, 1999; January 4, 2000; November 16, 2001; October 21, 2005; and August 15, 2006.

Other abbreviations used throughout the notes are FWF (Fred W. Friendly) and FP (Friendly Papers, held by the Rare Book and Manuscript Library, Columbia University, New York).

Prologue

1. Robert Trout, interview by author, New York City, February 5, 1999.
2. Harvey Swados, "Fred Friendly and Friendlyvision," *New York Times Magazine*, April 23, 1967, 31, 102–104, 109, 114–21.
3. DGF interviews; Arthur Miller, *Death of a Salesman* (New York: Viking, 1971), 138; Cynthia McFadden, in *Memorial Service for Fred W. Friendly* (New York: Columbia University Graduate School of Journalism, 1998), 38 (booklet of eulogies for the service, held on April 23, 1998, New York).
4. Quoted in Swados, "Fred Friendly and Friendlyvision," 114.
5. Stuart Sucherman, in *Memorial Service*, 25–26.
6. Ford, quoted in ibid.

Introduction

1. Remarks by Andy Rooney, tribute to Fred W. Friendly, International Press Freedom Awards of the Committee to Protect Journalists, October 23, 1997, http://www.cpj.org/dangerous/spring98/FriendlyObit.html (accessed October 18, 2000); John A. Schneider, interview by author, Greenwich, Conn., March 15, 2000; Mili Lerner Bonsignori, interview by Michael Rosen, Kissimmee, Florida, Archive of American Television, Academy of Television

Arts and Sciences Foundation, North Hollywood, California, December 11, 1998, videocassette. This and many other interviews in the academy's archive are available at www.emmytvlegends.org.

2. Daniel Schorr, *Weekend Edition*, National Public Radio, March 7, 1998; Sandburg, quoted in Thomas Whiteside, "Profiles: The One-Ton Pencil," *New Yorker*, February 17, 1962, 41–42.

3. Harvey Swados, "Fred Friendly and Friendlyvision," *New York Times Magazine*, April 23, 1967, 31; Antonin Scalia, in *Memorial Service for Fred. W. Friendly* (New York: Columbia University Graduate School of Journalism, 1998), 20; Erikson, quoted in Irving Howe, *The World of Our Fathers* (New York: Harcourt Brace Jovanovich, 1976), 527.

4. Schneider interview.

5. Schorr, *Weekend Edition*; Judith Thurman, "The Secret Lives of Biographers," *New York Times Book Review*, October 17, 1999, 11; Edward Hallett Carr, *What Is History?* (New York: Knopf, 1963), 35.

6. Justin Kaplan, letter to the editor, *New York Times*, September 13, 1999, A18; Andrew Friendly, telephone interview with the author, June 21, 2007; Holmes, quoted in Hermione Lee, "Tracking the Untrackable," *New York Review of Books*, April 12, 2001, 53.

1. Ferd

1. For Friendly's family history, I have relied on Natalie Brooks Friendly, *The Friendly Family: The Descendants of the Freundlichs of Bavaria*, with a foreword by Uri D. Herscher (Boston: Newbury Street Press, 1998), esp. 322–27; on Samson Hiram Friendly, see also Steve McQuiddy, ed., *Full of Life: The History and Character of Eugene's Masonic Cemetery* (Eugene, Ore.: Eugene Masonic Cemetery Association, 1999), 10. Information about Friendly's early childhood was also provided by Friendly's cousin, Carolene Wachenheimer Marks, interview by author, San Francisco, December 28, 2000, and the handwritten "Memory Book" containing text and photographs made by Carolene Marks and given to Lisa Friendly in 1982, as well as the DGF and RMF interviews.

2. "The Bride's Book," unidentified newspaper clipping, wedding album, FP.

3. FWF, interview by Sander Vanocur, February 25, 1987, News Leaders series, Poynter Institute for Media Studies, St. Petersburg, Fla., videocassette, FP; "Baby Book," album, FP; David Schoenbrun, *On and Off the Air: An Informal History of CBS News* (New York: Dutton, 1989), 58.

4. Marks, "Memory Book"; FWF interview by Vanocur.

5. For background on the broadcast of the Dempsey–Carpentier fight, see "July 2nd Fight Described by Radiophone," *Wireless Age*, July 1921, "Old Radio" Web site, http://www.eht.com/oldradio/arrl/2002-06/Dempsey.htm (accessed October 26, 2006).

6. Susan Douglas, "Early Radio," in David Crowley and Paul Heyer, eds., *Communication in History: Technology, Culture, Society* (Boston: Allyn and Bacon, 2003), 215.

7. DGF interviews; Samuel Wachenheimer to Therese Wachenheimer, April 15, 1919, FP.

8. McQuiddy, *Full of Life*, 10.

9. Stephen S. Wise to Therese Friendly Wachenheimer, undated, FP.

10. Zelda Fisher Gourse, telephone interview by author, March 23, 2000.

11. Marks interview.

12. Gourse interview; Ruth Harris Wolf, telephone interview by author, October 2, 1998.

13. FWF, "Rabbi William Braude: A Very Personal Reflection," Temple Beth El, Providence, R.I., February 28, 1988, text of eulogy, FP; Rabbi William G. Braude, Tercentenary Service of the Rhode Island Council of Churches, First Baptist Church, February 6, 1955, Archives of Temple Beth-El, Providence. Braude became a conservative on some social issues, but he marched with Martin Luther King in Selma. See Herman J. Blumberg, "Rabbi William Gordon Braude: Legacy of Challenge," *Jewish Advocate*, March 31, 1988.

14. Wolf interview.

15. Seebert J. Goldowsky, *A Century and a Quarter of Spiritual Leadership: The Story of the Congregation of the Sons of Israel and David (Temple Beth-El) Providence, Rhode Island* (Providence: Congregation of the Sons of Israel and David, 1989); Therese Friendly Wachenheimer, obituary, *Providence Journal*, April 18, 1954.

16. Martha Smith, "Women in R.I. History Marking a Difference: 'A Thrilling Life' Devoted to Reform," *Providence Journal*, March 25, 1994, A-02; "Alice Hunt, 96, Dies," *Providence Journal*, April 18, 1954; Gourse interview.

17. Therese Friendly Wachenheimer obituary; Martha Kaplan Paisner, telephone interviews by author, November 16, 1998, and December 15, 1999.

18. Marks interview; for Friendly's childhood problems, I have relied on RMF interviews.

19. RMF interviews; FWF, text of speech, Wheeler School, Providence, R.I., April 7, 1995, FP; FWF, introduction to *America's Schools: Who Gives a Damn?* Columbia University Seminars on Media and Society, PBS, April 1–2, 1991, videocassette, FP.

20. RMF interviews.

21. For a set of transcripts of Friendly's grades from the eighth grade through high school, see Ferdinand Wachenheimer, School Record, Roxbury School, Cheshire, Conn., FP.

22. Elaine Frank Lieberman, interview by author, Providence, R.I., November 20, 1998.

23. Marks interview; Alice Fox Silbert, interview by author, Providence, R.I., November 21, 1998; DGF interviews.

24. Gourse interview; RMF interviews; DGF interviews.

25. Marks interview; Marks, "Memory Book."

26. Lieberman interview; Florence Markoff, interview by author, Providence, R.I., March 22, 2000; Silbert interview.

27. Gourse interview.

28. FWF, "Rabbi William Braude," 4.

29. FWF, Wheeler School speech.

30. Lieberman interview.

31. Mildred Sydney Marks, interview by author, Providence, R.I., November 21, 1998.

32. *Rolling Stone*, 1934 yearbook of the Roxbury School, 72.

33. Steve Balser, e-mail to author, November 14, 2006.

34. Student's Record for Ferd Wachenheimer, 1934/1935, 1935/1936, Nichols Junior College, FP; *Nicholas Alumnus*, March 1949, 4.

35. On Lowe's career, see the booklet *WEAN: Providence, Rhode Island* (Peoria, Ill.: National Radio Personalities, 1940).

36. FWF, "Mowry," eulogy for Mowry Lowe, October 3, 1973, Temple Beth El, Providence, R.I., papers of Mowry Lowe, courtesy Roberta Lowe Allen, Providence, R.I.

37. Mowry Lowe, "The Golden Age of Radio," in Phillips D. Booth, ed., *Rhode Island Yearbook* (Providence: Rhode Island Yearbook Foundation, 1971), 221–22; FWF, "Mowry."

38. Lieberman interview.

39. Schoenbrun, *On and Off the Air*, 58.

40. FWF, "Mowry"; FWF, "The State of Television: Address by Fred W. Friendly at Brown University," April 5, 1967, Providence, R.I., CBS News Reference Library.

41. Paisner interview.

42. Meg Dooley, "Escape Only by Thinking," *Columbia: The Magazine of Columbia University*, summer 1992, 37; Walter Cronkite, remarks at the celebration of Friendly's seventy-seventh birthday, October 29, 1992, Lincoln Center Campus of Fordham University, videotape courtesy Joseph Dembo.

43. Paisner interview. Miscellaneous script fragments and other programming materials are contained in the papers of Mowry Lowe.

44. FWF, "Mowry."

45. FWF to Selective Service Local Board No. 1, Providence, R.I., May 14, 1941, FP.

46. Ibid.

47. "1941 Mutual Broadcasting System Recording of Fred Friendly Covering the Inauguration of the Quonset Naval Marine Air Station in Rhode Island," rebroadcast on *All Things Considered*, National Public Radio, October 1, 1999, audiocassette, FP.

48. David Gullette, *All Things Considered*, National Public Radio, October 1, 1999.

49. FWF to David Gullette [copy], September 12, 1995, FP.

50. Wolf interview.

51. FWF to Elaine Frank, April 19, 1941, courtesy Elaine Frank Lieberman, Providence, R.I.

52. Silbert interview; Wolf interview.

2. "My Rhodes Scholarship"

1. FWF to William and Pearl Braude, September 8, 1944, FP; RMF interviews.
2. Major Boyd B. Hill, Signal Corps, memorandum, August 20, 1941, FP.
3. Colonel Edgar L. Clewell, Signal Corps, Fort Monmouth, Appointment Certificate, May 12, 1942, Army of the United States, FP; Jerome Corwin, telephone interview by author, March 5, 1999.
4. John M. Ryan, letter of introduction, August 20, 1942, FP; James Armsey, telephone interviews by author, June 26, 2002, and March 25, 2005; Brigadier General S. H. Sherrill, Camp Kohler, Appointment Certificate, Army of the United States, October 31, 1941, FP; RMF interviews.
5. Lieutenant Gilbert E. Clark, Efficiency Report Concerning Tech. Sergeant Fred Friendly, August 10, 1943, FP; "R.I. Radio Producer Gives Army Novel Training Test: Fred Friendly's 'Sergeant Quiz' Wins Wide Praise," *Providence Evening Bulletin*, October 30, 1943, 11; Innis Bromfield, "Sergeant Quiz," *Collier's*, November 6, 1943, 79; Lieutenant Colonel Gilbert E. Clark to Lieutenant Colonel Robert H. George, July 20, 1943, FP.
6. Lyla (Lee) Sween Clark, telephone interview by author, June 2, 2002; Armsey interviews; "Rhode Islander in U.S. Army Still Conducts Radio Shows," *Providence Journal*, March 28, 1943.
7. Rhoda Guttman Klitsner, e-mail to author, May 26, 2000.
8. Brigadier General S. H. Sherrill, Memorandum of Commendation, December 25, 1943, FP.
9. Gilbert E. Clark to Lee Clark, December 29, 1943, and February 23, 1944. Correspondence between Gilbert and Lee Clark courtesy the late Lee Clark and their son Ted Clark, Washington, D.C.
10. Joseph Birk, telephone interview by author, November 17, 1999; Armsey interviews.
11. S. H. Sherrill, letter of recommendation, January 25, 1944; Lieutenant Colonel Arthur C. Farlow, memorandum, January 28, 1944; and FWF to Therese Wachenheimer, July 18, 1944, all in FP.
12. Brigadier General Vernon Evans, deputy chief of staff, United States Army Forces, China Burma India, General Orders Number 137, October 20, 1944, FP.
13. Gilbert E. Clark to Lee Clark, April 16 and April 24, 1944; Birk interview.
14. FWF to William and Pearl Braude, September 8, 1944, and FWF to Therese Wachenheimer, July 18, 1944, both in FP.
15. Harry G. Staffone to author, November 20, 1998; William S. Culbertson to author, December 17, 1998.
16. Edward M. Kirby and Jack W. Davis, *Star-Spangled Radio* (Chicago: Ziff-Davis, 1948), 20.
17. Birk interview; Gilbert E. Clark to Lee Clark, September 20, September 26, and October 4, 1944.

18. Gilbert E. Clark to Lee Clark, November 26, 1944, and March 12 and February 24, 1945.

19. Birk interview; Gilbert E. Clark to Lee Clark, April 2, 1945; FWF, *Due to Circumstances Beyond Our Control . . .* , 2nd ed., with a new introduction by Dan Rather and Tom Bettag (New York: Random House, 1998), xix.

20. Gilbert E. Clark to Lee Clark, March 18, 1945.

21. FWF to Therese Wachenheimer, February 21, 1945, FP.

22. Gilbert E. Clark to Lee Clark, February 21, 1945. Beale later became a doctor. She and Friendly became reacquainted years later at a conference in Australia. A reference to Beale's work with the World Council of Churches and her photograph appear in *World Call*, April 1948, 3.

23. Gilbert E. Clark to Lee Clark, April 19 and May 5, 1945.

24. Andy Rooney, interview by author, New York City, October 5, 2000.

25. FWF to Therese Wachenheimer, May 5, 1945, FP.

26. FWF, "General Patton and the Chinese $50 Bill," typewritten manuscript marked "For Collier's Weekly," with the author identified as "CBI Roundup Correspondent, Retired," FP.

27. FWF to Therese Wachenheimer, May 19, 1945, FP.

28. FWF, interview by Toby Blum-Dobkin, Video History Project, Museum of Jewish Heritage, New York City, November 20, 1990, videocassette, FP; FWF, "Friendly Visits Nazi Butchershop," *CBI Roundup*, undated clipping, FP; FWF to Therese Wachenheimer, May 19, 1945.

29. Armsey interviews; Robert Bernstein, in *Memorial Service for Fred W. Friendly* (New York: Columbia University Graduate School of Journalism, 1998), 13–14.

30. Staffone to author; Culbertson to author, November 20, 1998; confidential memorandum from COMGENIB to CONGENCHINA CHUNGKING, July 27, 1945, FP.

31. Four typed manuscripts of undated articles for *CBI Roundup* following the Japanese defeat, all in FP.

32. Joseph E. Persico, *Edward R. Murrow: An American Original* (New York: Dell, 1988), 285; Hugh Crumpler to author, undated; Melvyn Douglas and Tom Arthur, *See You at the Movies: The Autobiography of Melvyn Douglas* (Lanham, Md.: University Press of America, 1986), 129–43.

33. Boyd Sinclair, "Some Generals and One GI," *EX-CBI Roundup*, May 1954, 18; Rooney interview.

34. "Friendly Leaves for States; Lauds Stilwell, Narrates Anecdote About Cheves," *CBS Roundup*, November 8, 1945, 1.

35. Armsey interviews; Gilbert E. Clark to Lee Clark, June 2, 1944.

36. FWF, "Memo to Mr. Jack Kapp from Fred Friendly: On Coming Home to Radio Programs," November 1945, FP.

37. Ted Clark, telephone interview by author, June 2, 2002.

38. Ruth Harris Wolf, telephone interview by author, October 2, 1998; Rooney interview.

39. Armsey interviews.
40. "Friendly Leaves for States," 1.

3. "Willing to Be Lucky"

1. DGF interviews; Town Criers of Rhode Island, printed flyer, FP; Norman Fain, interview by author, Providence, R.I., November 22, 1998.
2. DGF interviews; RMF interviews; Fain interview.
3. DGF interviews.
4. *Opinion*, cover proposal, FP.
5. DGF interviews.
6. FWF to David Wolf, August 6, 1945, courtesy Ruth Harris Wolf, Providence, R.I.
7. FWF, "DATELINE with Melvyn Douglas," sample script, FP.
8. James Brady, "A Town with the Write Stuff," *New York Post*, November 14, 2001; DGF interviews.
9. RMF interviews; DGF interviews.
10. Carolene Wachenheimer Marks, interview by author, San Francisco, December 28, 2000; Robert Trout, interview by author, New York, February 5, 1999; Joseph Wershba, interview by author, Manhasset, N.Y., July 8, 1998.
11. DGF interviews.
12. FWF to William and Pearl Braude, undated, FP.
13. DGF interviews.
14. Fain interview.
15. DGF interviews; Fain interview.
16. E. B. White, *Here Is New York* (New York: Harper, 1949), 10–11.
17. William Wolf, *Providence Journal-Bulletin*, March 2, 1965, clipping, FP; George W. S. Trow, *My Pilgrim's Progress: Media Studies, 1950–1998* (New York: Pantheon, 1999), 4; White, *Here Is New York*, 9–10.
18. For background on *"I can hear it now . . . ,"* see A. M. Sperber, *Murrow: His Life and Times* (New York: Freundlich, 1986), 321–22; Alexander Kendrick, *Prime Time: The Life of Edward R. Murrow* (Boston: Little, Brown, 1969), 316–17; and Joseph E. Persico, *Edward R. Murrow: An American Original* (New York: Dell, 1988), 287–88.
19. Sperber, *Murrow*, 321; Persico, *Edward R. Murrow*, 287; FWF, *Due to Circumstances Beyond Our Control . . .* , 2nd ed., with a new introduction by Dan Rather and Tom Bettag (New York: Random House, 1998), xix. The two $1,000 checks were paid to Friendly on February 18, 1948 (Columbia Records Check Voucher Numbers 6718 and 3736 for $1,000 each, FP).
20. *Providence Journal*, undated clipping, FP; DGF interviews.
21. Trout, quoted in Jim Widner, "Radio News Broadcasts—World War II: John Daly Pearl Harbor Broadcast," Old Time Radio Newsgroup, March 17, 2000, http://members.aol.com/jeff1070/war.html (accessed October 18, 2000).

22. Elizabeth McLeod, "Radio News Broadcasts—World War II: Farewell to Studio 9/Pearl Harbor," Old Time Radio Newsgroup, July 13, 1999, http://members.aol.com/jeff1070/war.html (accessed October 18, 2000); postings of McLeod, April 3, 1998, and March 16 and 23, 2000; Eric J. Cooper, June 15, 1999; and Chris Chandler, March 14, 2000, to the Old Time Radio Newsgroup; RWF interviews.

23. Robert Trout to Catherine (Kit) Trout, July 8, 1948, courtesy John McDonough, who helped Trout organize his papers before their deposit as Robert Trout Papers, 1930–1999, Center for American History, Media History Archives, University of Texas, Austin.

24. *All Things Considered*, National Public Radio, July 9, 1999.

25. David Schoenbrun, *On and Off the Air: An Informal History of CBS News* (New York: Dutton, 1989), 60–61.

26. "Runaway," *New Yorker*, January 15, 1949, 22–23; Columbia Records Check Voucher 298, FP; Columbia Records Check Voucher 869, FP.

27. Persico, *Edward R. Murrow*, 287.

28. DGF interviews; FWF, quoted in Persico, *Edward R. Murrow*, 287.

29. Lucille Elfenbein, "From Producer, to Housewife," *Providence Evening Bulletin*, December 29, 1953, FP; DGF interviews.

30. DGF, 1949 diary, courtesy DGF.

31. Maurice B. Mitchell to FWF, March 19, 1948, FP.

32. Rhoda Guttman Klitsner, e-mail to author, May 26, 2000; DGF interviews.

33. "May We Quote You on That?" script, October 13, 1947, with Quincy Howe, Larry Lesseur [*sic*], Ned Calmer, and Don Hollenbeck, Columbia Broadcasting System, FP.

34. John Crosby, "'Who Said That?' Hits Bullseye," *Washington Post*, July 25, 1948, L4; *Variety*, July 7, 1948; Therese Wachenheimer to Dorothy and Fred Friendly, undated, FP.

35. Trout interview; John Dunning, *On the Air: The Encyclopedia of Old-Time Radio* (New York: Oxford University Press, 1998), 721; contract, February 10, 1949, between the National Broadcasting Company and Fred Friendly, FP.

36. G. Y. Loveridge, "Now They Can Afford Omelets Anytime," *Providence Journal*, April 2, 1950.

37. Trout entries: "Fred Friendly, the effect of words on him" and "Add Fred Friendly & His Way with Words," undated; "Character, Add Fred Friendly," September 16, 1948; "Add Fred Friendly," October 1948, Trout Papers.

38. Robert Trout to FWF, April 18, 1950, Trout Papers.

39. Trout interview.

40. DGF interviews.

41. Elmer Davis and William Henry to FWF, February 13, 1950, FP.

42. Dunning, *On the Air*, 558.

43. Michael Dann, telephone interview by author, November 8, 2002.

44. FWF to Bob Hope, undated draft, FP.

45. Jack Gould, "Radio and TV in Review," *New York Times*, July 7, 1950, 40.

46. Frederic Jacobi, "About 'The Quick and the Dead': A Look Behind the Scenes at N.B.C.'s Series on the Atom," *New York Times*, July 16, 1950, X7; DGF interviews; Robert L. Bernstein, in *Memorial Service for Fred Friendly* (New York: Columbia University Graduate School of Journalism, 1998), 14.

47. Jacobi, "About 'The Quick and the Dead'"; "Radio and Television: The Biography of the Atom," *New York Herald Tribune*, July 13, 1950, 23.

48. Jacobi, "About 'The Quick and the Dead'"; Gould, "Radio and TV in Review," 40.

49. "The Quick and the Dead: A Biography of the Atom Bomb and the Hydrogen Bomb," NBC press release,1950, and script for *The Quick and the Dead*, pt. 4, 1950, 20, both in FP.

50. Paul Boyer, *By the Bomb's Early Light: American Thought and Culture at the Dawn of the Atomic Age* (Chapel Hill: University of North Carolina Press, 1994).

51. Robert A. Rabe, "The Atomic Bomb, the 'Official Narrative,' and American Newspapers, 1945" (paper presented at the annual convention of the Association for Education in Journalism and Mass Communication, July 30–August 2, 2003, Kansas City); "The Mushroom Cloud," *Time*, July 17, 1950, 66.

52. "Research Takes Weight off Fred Friendly," *Providence Journal*, undated clipping, courtesy DGF.

53. Sig Mickelson, *The Decade That Shaped Television News: CBS in the 1950s* (Westport, Conn.: Praeger, 1998), 45, 44.

54. Persico, *Edward R. Murrow*, 288; Mickelson, *Decade That Shaped Television News*, 45.

55. Sperber, *Murrow*, 352–53.

56. Mickelson, *Decade That Shaped Television News*, 45; Sig Mickelson, telephone interview by author, November 24, 1999; DGF interviews.

57. DGF interviews.

58. Art Buchwald, telephone interview by author, September 24, 2003; Art Buchwald to FWF and DGF, October 4, 1950, FP.

59. DGF interviews.

60. FWF, interview by Lloyd Moss, *This Is My Music*, WQXR-FM, December 2, 1979, audiocassette, FP.

4. *See It Now*

1. DGF interviews.

2. Alfred A. Fain to FWF, October 25, 1949, FP; DGF interviews.

3. Agreement between Columbia Broadcasting System, 485 Madison Avenue, New York City, and Fred Friendly, October 30, 1950, FP. Friendly signed a separate contract on the same date with Columbia Records to make additional *I Can Hear It Now* recordings.

4. Joseph E. Persico, *Edward R. Murrow: An American Original* (New York: Dell, 1988), 294; A. M. Sperber, *Murrow: His Life and Times* (New York: Freundlich, 1986), 354.

5. Sperber, *Murrow*, 354, 283.

6. John Dunning, *On the Air: The Encyclopedia of Old-Time Radio* (New York: Oxford University Press, 1998), 313.

7. Persico, *Edward R. Murrow*, 4; "Edward R. Murrow, Candidates for Offices to Be Heard in 'A Report to the Nation—The 1950 Elections,'" CBS press release, November 6, 1950, FP.

8. "Edward R. Murrow, Candidates for Offices."

9. Dunning, *On the Air*, 313.

10. M. S., "Show Illustrates Drama in the News," *New York Times*, December 16, 1950, 20; Jack Gould, "News Summaries: 'Hear It Now' and 'Voices and Events,'" *New York Times*, Arts and Leisure section, December 24, 1950, 51.

11. Persico, *Edward R. Murrow*, 300.

12. Alexander Kendrick, *Prime Time: The Life of Edward R. Murrow* (Boston: Little, Brown, 1969), 70.

13. "It Is Positively the Most Wonderful Thing I Ever Saw," *Life*, April 2, 1951, 22–23; RMF interviews.

14. Murrow, quoted in Kendrick, *Prime Time*, 333.

15. Persico, *Edward R. Murrow*, 301.

16. Persico dates Murrow's withdrawal of his name to August 1951 (*Edward R. Murrow*, 300–301), whereas Kendrick writes that it occurred in September (*Prime Time*, 333–34).

17. Sperber, *Murrow*, 337; Murrow, quoted in J. Fred MacDonald, *Television and the Red Menace: The Video Road to Vietnam* (New York: Praeger, 1985), 35. For details of the Murrow–Shirer falling-out, see Persico, *Edward R. Murrow*, 251–56.

18. Sperber, *Murrow*, 346–48, 357–58. For Murrow's career during the period 1946 to 1950, see 262–350.

19. FWF, "Video to Mirror World as 'Mass Information Gazette,'" *Variety*, July 11, 1951, 45.

20. Joel Kisseloff, *The Box: An Oral History of Television, 1929–1961* (New York: Viking, 1995), 375; FWF, *Due to Circumstances Beyond Our Control . . .* , 2nd ed., with a new introduction by Dan Rather and Tom Bettag (New York: Random House, 1998), xix.

21. Sperber, *Murrow*, 373–74.

22. "Television News from CBS," press release, October 29, 1951, CBS News Reference Library.

23. On the newsreel, see A. William Bluem, *Documentary in American Television* (New York: Hastings House, 1965), 33–40. Bluem provides an interesting defense of the practice of reenactment by *The March of Time*.

24. DGF interviews.

25. Sig Mickelson, *The Decade That Shaped Television News: CBS in the 1950s* (Westport, Conn.: Praeger, 1998), 45.

26. Ibid., 43–49.

27. FWF, *Due to Circumstances*, xix.

28. Ibid. For the creation of the original *See It Now* team, see also Mickelson, *Decade That Shaped Television News*, 46–47, and Sperber, *Murrow*, 377–78.

29. Sperber, *Murrow*, 378; Murrow, quoted in Edward Bliss Jr., *Now the News: The Story of Broadcast Journalism* (New York: Columbia University Press, 1991), 235.

30. Quotations of Murrow's on-air remarks are from a reproduction of the teleprompter text of the program, CBS News Reference Library. Except for those in brackets, the ellipses appear in the original.

31. Mickelson, *Decade That Shaped Television News*, 47; Sperber, *Murrow*, 356; Robert Lewis Shayon, "TV and Radio," *Saturday Review*, December 15, 1951, 37.

32. Reproduction of teleprompter text.

33. Jack Gould, "Video News Coverage: 'See It Now' Proves a Major Contribution," *New York Times*, November 25, 1951, sec. 2, 11.

34. Edward R. Murrow and Fred W. Friendly, eds., *See It Now* (New York: Simon and Schuster, 1955), xi; John Crosby, "Radio and Television: Two Oceans at Once," *New York Herald Tribune*, November 23, 1951, 21.

35. Rose, "Television Reviews: *See It Now*," *Variety*, November 21, 1951, 29.

36. Robert Pierpoint, telephone interview by author, July 6, 2005.

37. Crosby, "Radio and Television," 21; Philip Hamburger, "Television: Salute," *New Yorker*, December 8, 1951, 147; Jack Gould, "Radio and Television: Edward R. Murrow's News Review, 'See It Now,' Demonstrates Journalistic Power of Video," *New York Times*, November 19, 1951, 32; Gould, "Video News Coverage," 11.

38. "The Spirit of Yuletide U.S.A.," CBS press release, December 18, 1951, CBS News Reference Library, 1.

39. Erik Barnouw, *Tube of Plenty: The Evolution of American Television*, 2nd rev. ed. (New York: Oxford University Press, 1990), 171–72; Bliss, *Now the News*, 236.

40. Persico, *Edward R. Murrow*, 323.

41. Mili Lerner Bonsignori, interview by Michael Rosen, Kissimmee, Fla., December 11, 1998, Archive of American Television, Academy of Television Arts and Sciences Foundation, North Hollywood, Calif. In researching this book, I used videotapes and transcripts from the archive, but most interviews now are available on line at http://www.emmytvlegends.org.

42. Sperber, *Murrow*, 378–79.

43. Mickelson, *Decade That Shaped Television News*, 47; Sperber, *Murrow*, 372.

44. Sperber, *Murrow*, 381.

45. Norman Corwin, telephone interview by author, September 17, 2003.

46. Pierpoint interview.

47. David Halberstam, *The Powers That Be* (New York: Knopf, 1979), 136; Joseph Wershba, interview by author, Manhasset, N.Y., July 8, 1998.

48. Joe Wershba, "Fred W. Friendly: Towering Figure in the Evolution of Television News," *Silurian News*, May 1998, 4, 6.

5. Friendly and Murrow

1. Mili Lerner Bonsignori, interview by Michael Rosen, Kissimmee, Fla., December 18, 1998, Archive of American Television, Academy of Television Arts and Sciences Foundation, North Hollywood, Calif., videocassette.
2. Mili Lerner Bonsignori, telephone interview by author, March 1, 2005; DGF interviews.
3. Bonsignori interview by author.
4. Ibid.
5. Bonsignori interview by Rosen; Edward R. Murrow and Fred W. Friendly, eds., acknowledgements in *See It Now* (New York: Simon and Schuster, 1955), x; Edward Bliss Jr., *Now the News: The Story of Broadcast Journalism* (New York: Columbia University Press, 1991), 236. In his acknowledgments in the *See It Now* book, Friendly singles out Palmer Williams, Dorothy Greene Friendly, Natalie Foster, and Edward Jones. Murrow's handwritten dedication in Bonsignori's copy of the book reads: "For Mili—who knows a good story as well as any man—with biding affection."
6. FWF, memorandum to All "See It Now" reporters, cameramen, and the CBS Tokyo News Bureau, NOT TO BE PUBLISHED, December 10, 1952, FP.
7. A. M. Sperber, *Murrow: His Life and Times* (New York: Freundlich, 1986), 393.
8. Joseph E. Persico, *Edward R. Murrow: An American Original* (New York: Dell, 1988), 322; *Times*, quoted in Sperber, *Murrow*, 396.
9. J. Fred MacDonald, *Television and the Red Menace: The Video Road to Vietnam* (New York: Praeger, 1985), 36; Murrow and Friendly, *See It Now*, 2, 9, 29.
10. Joel Kisseloff, *The Box: An Oral History of Television, 1929–1961* (New York: Viking, 1995), 351.
11. MacDonald, *Television and the Red Menace*, 36–37.
12. A. William Bluem, *Documentary in American Television* (New York: Hastings House, 1965), 94, 96.
13. Sperber, *Murrow*, 396
14. DGF interviews; Persico, *Edward R. Murrow*, 321.
15. Persico, *Edward R. Murrow*, 293.
16. David Halberstam, *The Powers That Be* (New York: Knopf, 1979), 136; DGF interviews.
17. RMF interviews.
18. Sperber, *Murrow: His Life and Times*, 379. For Don Hewitt on the Friendly–Murrow relationship, see 381.
19. On the raincoat, see memos from Henry S. White to Edmund Scott, April 11, 1952, and FWF to Henry S. White, April 15, 1952, FP; Don Hewitt, telephone interview by author, May 6, 2003.

20. Murrow, quoted in "Murrow and Friendly and 'See It Now': An Enthusiastic Partnership and a Deadline-Type of Operation Yields a Unique Program," CBS press release, September 1, 1954, CBS News Reference Library.

21. Joe Wershba, "Fred W. Friendly: Towering Figure in the Evolution of Television News," *Silurian News*, May 1998, 4, 6.

22. DGF interviews.

23. Wershba, "Fred W. Friendly," 4, 6.

24. For Friendly's relationship to the Murrow Boys, I have relied on Stanley Cloud and Lynne Olson, *The Murrow Boys: Pioneers on the Front Lines of Broadcast Journalism* (Boston: Houghton Mifflin, 1996), 284–99.

25. Ibid., 293–95.

26. Wershba, "Fred W. Friendly," 4.

27. Halberstam, *Powers That Be*, 135.

28. Gude, quoted in Sperber, *Murrow*, 379.

29. DGF interviews.

30. Ibid.

31. Murrow, quoted in Bluem, *Documentary in American Television*, 96.

32. Bluem, *Documentary in American Television*, 96–97.

33. Philip Hamburger, "Television: Dr. Oppenheimer," *New Yorker*, January 15, 1955, 85–87; Jack Gould, "Television in Review," *New York Times*, January 9, 1955; Eric Barnouw, *Tube of Plenty: The Evolution of American Television*, 2nd rev. ed. (New York: Oxford University Press, 1990), 181.

34. Herm., "SEE IT NOW With Ed Murrow," *Variety*, October 10, 1956, 33.

35. FWF, *Due to Circumstances Beyond Our Control . . .* , 2nd ed., with a new introduction by Dan Rather and Tom Bettag (New York: Random House, 1998), 18.

36. Bluem, *Documentary in American Television*, 99.

37. Persico, *Edward R. Murrow*, 355–36.

38. Radio broadcast of February 13, 1953, in Edward Bliss Jr., ed., *In Search of Light: The Broadcasts of Edward R. Murrow, 1938–1961* (New York: Knopf, 1967), 234–36.

39. DGF interviews.

40. On *Red Channels* and the broadcasting blacklist, see David Caute, *The Great Fear: The Anti-Communist Purge Under Truman and Eisenhower* (New York: Simon and Schuster, 1978), 521–38, and Barnouw, *Tube of Plenty*, 121–28. Friendly's discussion of *Red Channels* is in *Due to Circumstances*, 23–26. See also Ellen Schrecker, *Many Are the Crimes: McCarthyism in America* (New York: Little, Brown, 1998).

41. Barnouw, *Tube of Plenty*, 124.

42. *Counterattack*, quoted in Persico, *Edward R. Murrow*, 339.

43. Barnouw, *Tube of Plenty*, 130.

44. Murrow, quoted in Cloud and Olson, *Murrow Boys*, 302, who provide the best account of Murrow's response to the CBS questionnaire (301–4). See also Sperber, *Murrow*, 361–65.

45. Cloud and Olson, *Murrow Boys*, 302.

46. FWF, *Due to Circumstances*, 25; RMF interviews.

47. Hewitt interview; RMF interviews; FWF, *Due to Circumstances*, 23–24.

48. Allan E. Sloane to author, March 29, 2000.

49. Ibid. On Sloane's blacklisting see "C.B.S. Halts Scripts by Accused Writer," *New York Times*, November 3, 1952. Sloane later testified voluntarily before the House Un-American Activities Committee, as reported in United Press, "Film, Video Writer Tells of Being Red," *New York Times*, May 11, 1954, 14. Sloane eventually returned to work at CBS, where he won three Emmy Awards, six Peabody Awards, and two Writers Guild Awards. See his obituary in *Washington Post*, May 14, 2001.

6. Encounter with McCarthyism

1. Ellen Schrecker, *Many Are the Crimes: McCarthyism in America* (Boston: Little, Brown, 1988), 203–4, 219, 220. The pervasive influence of the FBI is detailed in the chapter "'A Job for Professionals': The FBI and Anticommunism," 203–39.

2. Joseph E. Persico, *Edward R. Murrow: An American Original* (New York: Dell, 1988), 332.

3. For an account of negotiations about the program and dealings of Murrow and Friendly with the FBI based on agency files, see Persico, *Edward R. Murrow*, 332–35, and A. M. Sperber, *Murrow: His Life and Times* (New York: Freundlich, 1986), 371.

4. Sperber, *Murrow*, 371; FWF, quoted in Persico, *Edward R. Murrow*, 333.

5. Federal Bureau of Investigation, FBI Document 94-43788-1, July 6, 1951. I obtained materials in Friendly's FBI files on January 3, 2004, as a result of requests under the Freedom of Information and Privacy Act, FOIPA no. 1006836-000. Most of those documents are available at "APBnews: Fred Friendly FBI File," http://www.apbnews.com/media/gfiles/friendly/friendly-report_1.html (accessed August 25, 2000).

6. FWF to Louis B. Nichols, January 15, 1954; Nichols to FWF, January 22, 1954, FBI Document 94-43788-2.

7. David Schoenbrun, *On and Off the Air: An Informal History of CBS News* (New York: Dutton, 1989), 70.

8. Persico, *Edward R. Murrow*, 334, 335.

9. Sperber, *Murrow*, 459–60.

10. Thomas Doherty, *Cold War, Cool Medium: Television, McCarthyism, and American Culture* (New York: Columbia University Press, 2003), 168–69.

11. Murrow, quoted in Sperber, *Murrow*, 382.

12. FWF, *Due to Circumstances Beyond Our Control . . .* , 2nd ed., with a new introduction by Dan Rather and Tom Bettag (New York: Random House, 1998), 5; Murrow and Wershba, quoted in Doherty, *Cold War, Cool Medium*, 169.

13. FWF, *Due to Circumstances*, 3, 4.

14. Thomas Rosteck, *"See It Now" Confronts McCarthyism: Television Documentary and the Politics of Representation* (Tuscaloosa: University of Alabama Press, 1994), 58–59.

15. For an account of the making of the program, see FWF, *Due to Circumstances*, 5–22. For the Murrow quotes, see 10.

16. Ibid., 3–4.

17. I am relying on the structural and rhetorical analysis in Rosteck, *"See It Now" Confronts McCarthyism*, 55–82.

18. Ibid., 63, 64.

19. Ibid., 64; Doherty, *Cold War, Cool Medium*, 169; Rosteck, *"See It Now" Confronts McCarthyism*, 66.

20. Radulovich's father, quoted in Rosteck, *"See It Now" Confronts McCarthyism*, 71.

21. Murrow, quoted in Rosteck, *"See It Now" Confronts McCarthyism*, 75.

22. Gould, quoted in FWF, *Due to Circumstances*, 16; trade industry critic, quoted in Rosteck, *"See It Now" Confronts McCarthyism*, 77.

23. Joseph Wershba, "Murrow vs. McCarthy: See It Now," *New York Times Magazine*, March 4, 1979, 31–38.

24. DGF, handwritten notes on the Radulovich affair, November 24, 1953, courtesy DGF; FWF, *Due to Circumstances*, 19–20.

25. Rosteck, *"See It Now" Confronts McCarthyism*, 89.

26. Doherty, *Cold War, Cool Medium*, 171. Doherty adds the program of Marshall and Truman interviews to the pantheon of *See It Now*'s anti-McCarthy shows.

27. Doherty, *Cold War, Cool Medium*, 170; Rosteck, *"See It Now" Confronts McCarthyism*, 110. I have relied on the detailed and comprehensive analysis of documentary techniques used to advance a point of view in Rosteck, *"See It Now" Confronts McCarthyism*, 83–111.

28. Daniel Schorr, *Weekend Edition*, National Public Radio, March 7, 1998; Daniel Schorr, e-mail to author, October 5, 2005.

29. Edward R. Murrow and Fred W. Friendly, eds., *See It Now* (New York: Simon and Schuster, 1955), 210.

30. Joe Wershba, "Fred W. Friendly: Towering Figure in the Evolution of Television News," *Silurian News*, May 1998, 4, 6.

31. Doherty, *Cold War, Cool Medium*, 173.

32. FWF, *Due to Circumstances*, 30. For accounts by *See It Now* principals of preparations and the actual broadcast, see FWF, *Due to Circumstances*, 23–67; Wershba, "Murrow vs. McCarthy"; and Joseph Wershba, "Edward R. Murrow and the Time of His Time," http://www.evesmag.com/murrow.htm (accessed June 6, 2005).

33. Wershba, "Murrow vs. McCarthy," 34; FWF, *Due to Circumstances*, 33.

34. FWF, *Due to Circumstances*, 35, 36.

35. I rely here on Rosteck's rhetorical analysis of the program in *"See It Now" Confronts McCarthyism*, 112–41. See also Doherty, *Cold War, Cool Medium*, 172–77.

36. Doherty, *Cold War, Cool Medium*, 173; Rosteck, *"See It Now" Confronts McCarthyism*, 123.

37. Doherty, *Cold War, Cool Medium*, 173, 176.

38. FWF, *Due to Circumstances*, 34.
39. Michael D. Murray, "Television's Desperate Moment: A Conversation with Fred W. Friendly," *Journalism History* 1, no. 3 (1974): 69.
40. Ibid., 71.
41. William Paley and Frank Stanton, response to letter of March 17, 1954, from *Newsweek*, 2–3, 8, CBS News Reference Library.
42. Murrow and Friendly, *See It Now*, 55.
43. Ibid., 54; Murray, "Television's Desperate Moment," 71.
44. For a critique of the "legend" of the McCarthy show, see Brian Thornton, "Published Reaction When Murrow Battled McCarthy," *Journalism History* 29, no. 3 (2003): 135–36.
45. FWF, *Due to Circumstances*, 4.
46. Murray, "Television's Desperate Moment," 71.
47. Bayley, quoted in Rosteck, *"See It Now" Confronts McCarthyism*, 221n.74.
48. FWF, *Due to Circumstances*, 23; Doherty, *Cold War, Cool Medium*, 178, 188; Allan E. Sloane to author, March 29, 2000.

7. Aftermath

1. FWF, *Due to Circumstances Beyond Our Control . . .* , 2nd ed., with a new introduction by Dan Rather and Tom Bettag (New York: Random House, 1998), 65.
2. For Wershba's departure from CBS, I have relied on the account by A. M. Sperber, *Murrow: His Life and Times* (New York: Freundlich, 1986), 473–75.
3. Sperber, *Murrow*, 475.
4. Joe Wershba, "Fred W. Friendly: Towering Figure in the Evolution of Television News," *Silurian News*, May 1998, 6; Michael D. Murray, "Television's Desperate Moment : A Conversation with Fred W. Friendly," *Journalism History* 1, no. 3 (1974): 70; Agreement between Columbia Broadcasting System, 485 Madison Avenue, New York City and Fred Friendly, FP.
5. "Edward R. Murrow's 'See It Now' Starts Fourth Season Aug. 31," CBS press release, August 19, 1954, CBS News Reference Library; FWF, *Due to Circumstances*, 69; Jack Gould, "TV: Cigarettes and Cancer; Murrow Gives First of Two-Part Report on Controversy on His 'See It Now,'" *New York Times*, June 1, 1955, 67.
6. FWF, *Due to Circumstances*, 68, 75; Dorothy Schiff, "Dear Reader by Dorothy Schiff," *New York Post*, June 19, 1955.
7. FWF, *Due to Circumstances*, 77, 78; Val Adams, "TV's 'See It Now,' Sponsorless, to Be Seen Only Now and Then," *New York Times*, July 22, 1955.
8. "Columbia University Group Prepares Guide for Teachers Linking 'See It Now' Broadcast on the Vice Presidency with Lessons in U.S. History, Civics, Social Studies," CBS press release, October 19, 1955, CBS News Reference Library; Jay Nelson Tuck, "On the Air," *New York Post*, October 20, 1955.
9. FWF, *Due to Circumstances*, 86; DGF, diary entry, May 23, 1957, courtesy DGF.

10. DGF interviews.

11. Ted Holmberg, "Sandburg and Murrow Captivate Audience," *Providence Evening Bulletin*, May 18, 1957; Seebert J. Goldowsky, *A Century and a Quarter of Spiritual Leadership: The Story of the Congregation of the Sons of Israel and David (Temple Beth-El) Providence, Rhode Island* (Providence: Congregation of the Sons of Israel and David, 1989), 386–87.

12. DGF, diary entry, July 8, 1954.

13. Bernard Stengren, "Unseen Man Behind 'See It Now,'" *New York Times*, Sunday Arts section, April 17, 1955, X15; "An Enthusiastic Partnership and a Deadline-Type of Operation Yields a Unique Program," CBS press release, September 1, 1954, CBS News Reference Library.

14. DGF interviews; DGF, diary entries, March 5, May 8, and May 11, 1957.

15. DGF, diary entries, May 21 and May 8, 1957.

16. DGF interviews; Peter Neubauer, interview by author, New York, November 20, 2005.

17. FWF, *Due to Circumstances*, 91.

18. Ibid., 93.

19. Jack Gould, "TV: 'See It Now' Finale: Program Unexpectedly Ends Run of 7 Distinguished Years on CBS," *New York Times*, July 8, 1958, 55; John Crosby, "The Demise of 'See It Now,'" *New York Herald Tribune*, July 11, 1958, sec. 2, 1.

8. CBS Reports

1. DGF, diary entry, May 15, 1957, courtesy DGF. For the history of *Small World*, see Joseph E. Persico, *Edward R. Murrow: An American Original* (New York: Dell, 1988), 431–32, and A. M. Sperber, *Murrow: His Life and Times* (New York: Freundlich, 1986), 517, 534–37.

2. FWF, *Due to Circumstances Beyond Our Control . . .* , 2nd ed., with a new introduction by Dan Rather and Tom Bettag (New York: Random House, 1998), 93.

3. Ibid., 97–98.

4. The full text can be found at http://www.rtnda.org/pages/media_items/edward-r.-murrow-speech998.php (accessed May 23, 2008).

5. Persico, *Edward R. Murrow*, 435–36; FWF, *Due to Circumstances*, 104.

6. James L. Baughman, "The Strange Birth of *CBS Reports* Revisited," *Historical Journal of Film, Radio and Television* 2, no. 1 (1982): 32.

7. Ibid., 27–38.

8. Sig Mickelson, *The Decade That Shaped Television News: CBS in the 1950s* (Westport, Conn.: Praeger, 1998), 167; Sig Mickelson, telephone interview by author, November 24, 1999.

9. Mickelson, *Decade That Shaped Television News*, 168.

10. FWF, *Due to Circumstances*, 107.

11. Ibid., 108; Mickelson, *Decade That Shaped Television News*, 169.

12. FWF, *Due to Circumstances*, 108.

13. David Halberstam, *The Powers That Be* (New York: Knopf, 1979), 130–57.

14. Mickelson, *Decade That Shaped Television News*, 172; Murrow, quoted in FWF, *Due to Circumstances*, 111.

15. "Biography: Fred W. Friendly," CBS press release, September 15, 1959, FP; Mickelson, *Decade That Shaped Television News*, 172.

16. On Friendly and Lippmann, see FWF, *Due to Circumstances*, 116–19, and Ronald Steel, *Walter Lippmann and the American Century* (Boston: Little, Brown, 1980), 516–19.

17. FWF, *Due to Circumstances*, 116; Steel, *Walter Lippmann and the American Century*, 516.

18. Steel, *Walter Lippmann and the American Century*, 517.

19. Robert Lewis Shayon, "TV and Radio: Today and Tomorrow on TV," *Saturday Review*, July 23, 1960, 34 ; Tim Galfas, "The Friendly Persuasions: How the Much-Abused TV Documentary Can Rise to a Uniquely Lofty Level of Dramatic Insight. Some Wise Words from Fred W. Friendly," *Show*, October 1962, 81.

20. FWF to Richard B. Anderson, August 13, 1960, MS 326, box 72, folder 836, Walter Lippmann Papers, Manuscripts and Archives, Yale University Library, New Haven, Conn.; FWF, *Due to Circumstances*, 119.

21. Gene DePoris, telephone interview by author, February 6, 2006; FWF, *Due to Circumstances*, 118; Andy Rooney to FWF, January 17, 1966, box 72, folder 836, Lippmann Papers; FWF to Walter Lippmann, September 8, 1965, Lippmann Papers.

22. For the circumstances of Murrow's return, see Sperber, *Murrow*, 591–94; Persico, *Edward R. Murrow*, 453–54.

23. Sperber, *Murrow*, 592.

24. For the background to "Harvest of Shame," see Sperber, *Murrow*, 594–95.

25. Persico, *Edward R. Murrow*, 460–61.

26. Bill Moyers, interview by author, New York, November 29, 2005; John Schultz, telephone interviews by author, October 22 and November 9, 2004.

27. David Lowe Jr., telephone interview by author, January 24, 2006.

28. Schultz interviews.

29. Sperber, *Murrow*, 604; Persico, *Edward R. Murrow*, 462; A. William Bluem, *Documentary in American Television* (New York: Hastings House, 1965), 104.

30. Persico, *Edward R. Murrow*, 462.

31. FWF, *Due to Circumstances*, 122, 123, 125.

32. Ibid., 125; Sperber, *Murrow*, 611, 612–13, 618.

33. Persico, *Edward R. Murrow*, 467; FWF, *Due to Circumstances*, 126.

34. Howard K. Smith to author, November 9, 1998.

35. FWF, *Due to Circumstances*, 127.

36. Sources for the conflict about the Birmingham program include FWF, *Due to Circumstances*, 126–28; Sally Bedell Smith, *In All His Glory: The Life of William S. Paley* (New York: Simon and Schuster, 1990), 417–18; Stanley Cloud

and Lynne Olson, *The Murrow Boys: Pioneers on the Front Lines of Broadcast Journalism* (Boston: Houghton Mifflin, 1996), 344–49; Howard K. Smith, *Events Leading Up to My Death: The Life of a Twentieth-Century Reporter* (New York: St. Martin's, 1996), 272–76; and Smith's correspondence with the author, esp. letters of August 21 and November 9, 1998.

37. Smith to author, November 9, 1998.
38. Smith to author, November 9 and August 21, 1998.
39. Smith, *Events Leading Up to My Death*, 274.
40. Smith to author, August 21, 1998.
41. FWF, *Due to Circumstances*, 128; Smith to author, August 21, 1998.

9. Camelot

1. DGF interviews. DGF said that Janet Murrow told her of Sevareid's displeasure.
2. FWF, *Due to Circumstances Beyond Our Control . . .* , 2nd ed., with a new introduction by Dan Rather and Tom Bettag (New York: Random House, 1998), 132.
3. John Schultz, telephone interviews by author, October 22 and November 9, 2004.
4. David Lowe Jr., telephone interview by author, January 24, 2006.
5. FWF, *Due to Circumstances*, 137; Schultz interviews; McMullen, quoted in Joel Kisseloff, *The Box: An Oral History of Television, 1929–1961* (New York: Viking, 1995), 396.
6. Lowe interview; Wasserman, quoted in Kisseloff, *Box*, 395.
7. Thomas Whiteside, "Profiles: The One-Ton Pencil," *New Yorker*, February 17, 1962, 42; Av Westin, *Newswatch: How TV Decides the News* (New York: Simon and Schuster, 1982), 182–83.
8. Schultz interviews; Tim Galfas, "The Friendly Persuasions: How the Much-Abused TV Documentary Can Rise to a Uniquely Lofty Level of Dramatic Insight. Some Wise Words from Fred W. Friendly," *Show*, October 1962, 81; Whiteside, "One-Ton Pencil," 54, 62.
9. On "Diary of a Bookie Joint," see Kisseloff, *Box*, 397–98, and FWF, *Due to Circumstances*, 136–44.
10. Galfas, "Friendly Persuasions," 81, 137.
11. On McClellan, see FWF, *Due to Circumstances*, 132–34; on the firewall, see FWF, "Looking Ahead," *CBS Reports 63/64*, CBS press release, CBS News Reference Library.
12. Alan Rosenthal, *Writing, Directing, and Producing Documentary Films and Videos*, rev. ed. (Carbondale: Southern Illinois University Press, 1996), 44; Todd Gitlin, *The Whole World Is Watching: Mass Media in the Unmaking of the New Left* (Berkeley: University of California Press, 1980), 64–66; Michael D. Murray, *The Political Performers: CBS Broadcasts in the Public Interest* (Westport, Conn.: Praeger, 1994), 91–95.

13. A. William Bluem, *Documentary in American Television* (New York: Hastings House, 1965), 117; FWF, *Due to Circumstances*, 196.

14. FWF, *Due to Circumstances*, 134–35.

15. Mili Lerner Bonsignori, telephone interview by author, March 1, 2005.

16. FWF, *Due to Circumstances*, 129, 130; Jack Gould, "TV: Omaha Beach, as It Was and Is," *New York Times*, June 6, 1964, 53; Val Adams, "Eisenhower Show for TV in Demand," *New York Times*, May 20, 1964, 87.

17. FWF, *Due to Circumstances*, 145.

18. Newton Minow, "Television and the Public Interest" (speech presented to National Association of Broadcasters, May 9, 1961, Washington, D.C.), http://www.americanrhetoric.com/speeches/newtonminow.htm (accessed August 20, 2007); Newton Minow, telephone interview by author, June 9, 2005.

19. Minow interview.

20. Mary Ann Watson, *The Expanding Vista: American Television in the Kennedy Years* (New York: Oxford University Press, 1994), 135.

21. FWF to President John F. Kennedy, February 6, 1961; FWF, telegram to Pierre Salinger, February 9, 1961; and Edward R. Murrow, memorandum for Mr. Frederick G. Dutton, March 7, 1961, all in John F. Kennedy Presidential Library and Museum, Boston; Newton Minow to FWF, marked PERSONAL, October 16, 1961, Newton N. Minow Papers, 1954–1965, State Historical Society of Wisconsin, Madison.

22. FWF to Pierre Salinger, August 22, 1961; FWF to Evelyn Lincoln, October 18, 1961; FWF to President John F. Kennedy, October 18, 1961, all in JFK Library. Friendly's account of the background of the Kennedy taping is in *Due to Circumstances*, 145–51.

23. FWF, *Due to Circumstances*, 150; "Kennedy to Span First Two Years in Television Interview Monday," *New York Times*, December 14, 1962, 1; Tom Wicker, "Kennedy on Television," *New York Times*, December 24, 1962, 11.

24. FWF, "The State of Television: Address by Fred W. Friendly at Brown University," April 5, 1967, Providence, R.I., CBS News Reference Library. On *Telstar I*, see Erik Barnouw, *Tube of Plenty: The Evolution of American Television*, 2nd rev. ed. (New York: Oxford University Press, 1990), 308–15.

25. For accounts of the broadcast, see Westin, *Newswatch*, 24–26; FWF, "State of Television"; and Watson, *Expanding Vista*, 206–208.

26. Westin, *Newswatch*, 25–26.

27. Watson, *Expanding Vista*, 208; Edward R. Murrow, telegram to FWF, undated, FP.

28. Newton Minow to FWF, April 12, 1963, courtesy DGF; FWF to Newton Minow, April 15, 1963, and Minow to FWF, March 25, 1963, both in Minow Papers.

29. FWF, *Due to Circumstances*, 153.

30. FWF, "Looking Ahead."

31. Schultz interviews; "TV-Radio: How to Get Involved," *Newsweek*, May 8, 1961, 64; Whiteside, "One-Ton Pencil," 41; DGF interviews.

32. Harold Bender, "Fred Friendly: TV's Invisible Man," *New York Journal-American*, October 25, 1959; "CBS Reports 1959–1964," CBS press release, 1964, FP.

10. News President

1. Jack Gould, "Friendly Rival: Head of C.B.S. News Seeks TV Lead," *New York Times*, Arts and Leisure section, March 8, 1964, X27; DGF interviews.

2. RMF interviews; Barbara Fogel, telephone interview by author, July 12, 2004; Peter Neubauer, interview by author, New York, November 20, 2005.

3. Gary Paul Gates, *Air Time: The Inside Story of CBS News* (New York: Harper & Row, 1978), 108–9; Friendly, quoted in Sally Bedell Smith, *In All His Glory: The Life of William S. Paley* (New York: Simon and Schuster, 1990), 420.

4. Smith, *In All His Glory*, 416.

5. Richard S. Salant, *Salant, CBS, and the Battle for the Soul of Broadcast Journalism: The Memoirs of Richard S. Salant*, ed. Susan Buzenberg and Bill Buzenberg (Boulder, Colo.: Westview, 1999), 35, 50; Paley's view of Friendly comes from Smith, *In All His Glory*, 420.

6. Smith, *In All His Glory*, 421; A. M. Sperber, *Murrow: His Life and Times* (New York: Freundlich, 1986), 690; FWF, *Due to Circumstances Beyond Our Control . . .* , 2nd ed., with a new introduction by Dan Rather and Tom Bettag (New York: Random House, 1998), 159.

7. Sperber, *Murrow*, 690; FWF, *Due to Circumstances*, 159.

8. Alexander Kendrick, *Prime Time: The Life of Edward R. Murrow* (Boston: Little, Brown, 1969), 505; Sperber, *Murrow*, 690.

9. Joseph Wershba, interview by author, Manhasset, N.Y., July 8, 1998; FWF, *Due to Circumstances*, 159; Bill Moyers, interview by author, New York, November 29, 2005; Daniel Schorr, *Clearing the Air* (New York: Berkley Medallion, 1977), 9–10.

10. Daniel Schorr, e-mail to author, October 5, 2005; Leslie Midgley, *How Many Words Do You Want? An Insider's Story of Print and Television Journalism* (New York: Birch Lane Press, 1989), 163, 180–81; Leslie Midgley, telephone interview by author, December 8, 2000; William Small, telephone interview by author, March 19, 2001; "The Reason-Why Man," *Time*, March 13, 1964, 62.

11. Mike Wallace, interview by author, New York, February 2, 2000.

12. "Bulldozer," *Newsweek*, March 16, 1964; "CBS Television Network Closed Circuit," transcript, March 17, 1964, CBS News Reference Library; "Reason-Why Man."

13. "Reason-Why Man"; "Bulldozer," 56; Gould, "Friendly Rival," X27.

14. Salant, *Salant, CBS*, 131.

15. "Bulldozer," 56; Ernie Leiser, telephone interview by author, October 27, 2000.

16. Val Adams, "Mitgang Joins C.B.S.," *New York Times*, April 21, 1964, 75; Joseph Dembo, interview by author, New York, March 20, 2001.

17. Small interview; Gates, *Air Time*, 109–10; Gordon Manning, interview by author, Westport, Conn., October 27, 2000.
18. Gates, *Air Time*, 110; Manning interview; Robert Trout, interview by author, New York, February 5, 1999.
19. Small interview.
20. Joan Morse Gordon, telephone interview by author, November 9, 2000.
21. Bill Leonard, *In the Storm of the Eye: A Lifetime at CBS* (New York: Putnam, 1987), 128; Harvey Swados, "Fred Friendly and Friendlyvision," *New York Times Magazine*, April 23, 1967, 116; Gordon interview.
22. Gates, *Air Time*, 385–86.
23. Ibid.; Schorr, *Clearing the Air*, 8–9; Leiser interview.
24. Leonard, *In the Storm of the Eye*, 73.

11. At the Top of His Game

1. Walter Cronkite, telephone interview by author, November 22, 1999; Bill Leonard, *In the Storm of the Eye: A Lifetime at CBS* (New York: Putnam, 1987), 108–9.
2. Gary Paul Gates, *Air Time: The Inside Story of CBS News* (New York: Harper & Row, 1978), 111; Leonard, *In the Storm of the Eye*, 109.
3. FWF, *Due to Circumstances Beyond Our Control . . .* , 2nd ed., with a new introduction by Dan Rather and Tom Bettag (New York: Random House, 1998), 186; Leonard, *In the Storm of the Eye*, 110; Cronkite interview.
4. Gates, *Air Time*, 112–13; Richard S. Salant, *Salant, CBS, and the Battle for the Soul of Broadcast Journalism: The Memoirs of Richard S. Salant*, ed. Susan Buzenberg and Bill Buzenberg (Boulder, Colo.: Westview, 1999), 52.
5. FWF, *Due to Circumstances*, 187; Ernie Leiser, telephone interview by author, October 27, 2000; Gates, *Air Time*, 113.
6. Cronkite interview; FWF, *Due to Circumstances*, 185.
7. Robert Trout, interview by author, New York, February 5, 1999.
8. Robert Trout Papers, 1930–1999, American News Media History Archives, Center for American History, University of Texas, Austin.
9. Gordon Manning, interview by author, Westport, Conn., October 27, 2000; Gates, *Air Time*, 135.
10. Manning interview.
11. Gates, *Air Time*, 119–22; Cronkite interview; Don Hewitt, interview by Michael Rosen, New York, April 15, 1997, Archive of American Television, Academy of Television Arts and Sciences Foundation, North Hollywood, Calif., videocassette; Donovan Moore, "60 Minutes," *Rolling Stone*, January 12, 1978, 14.
12. FWF, speech before the Rhode Island Broadcasters Association in honor of Mowry Lowe, Providence, R.I., June 1965, audiotape courtesy Roberta Lowe Allen, Providence.
13. Ibid.
14. FWF, *Due to Circumstances*, 189, 190.
15. Ibid., 175–78.

16. Manning interview; FWF, memorandum to William Paley and Frank Stanton, December 8, 1965, FP.

17. FWF to William Paley, November 5 and September 17, 1965; Paley to FWF, September 17, 1965; FWF to Paley, September 11 and October 4, 1965; and FWF, handwritten note on memo from Paley to FWF, October 4, 1965, all in FP.

18. Leonard, *In the Storm of the Eye*, 122; Sally Bedell Smith, *In All His Glory: The Life of William S. Paley* (New York: Simon and Schuster, 1990), 399.

19. Joseph Dembo, interview by author, New York, March 20, 2001.

20. FWF to William Paley, July 2, 1965, 4–5, FP.

12. Vietnam

1. Pierre Salinger to FWF, March 3, 1964, WHCF file, container 271, Lyndon B. Johnson Library and Museum, Austin, Texas.

2. Bill Moyers, interview by author, New York, November 29, 2005.

3. Daily diary, White House, December 18, 1964, container 3, LBJ Library; David Halberstam, *The Powers That Be* (New York: Knopf, 1979), 431–32; Bill Moyers, in *Memorial Service for Fred W. Friendly* (New York: Columbia University Graduate School of Journalism, 1998), 43; Moyers interview.

4. Murrow, quoted in Halberstam, *Powers That Be*, 432; Jack Valenti, memorandum to Lyndon Johnson, December 21, 1964, WHCF file, LBJ Library; DGF interviews.

5. Notation dated December 30, 1964, Valenti to Johnson, December 21, 1964, Fred Friendly/WHCF file, LBJ Library; Ernie Leiser, telephone interview by author, October 27, 2000; Moyers interview.

6. Moyers, in *Memorial Service*, 43; Halberstam, *Powers That Be*, 432.

7. Halberstam, *Powers That Be*, 441; Erik Barnouw, *Tube of Plenty: The Evolution of American Television*, 2nd rev. ed. (New York: Oxford University Press, 1990), 380–82.

8. A. M. Sperber, *Murrow: His Life and Times* (New York: Freundlich, 1986), 694–95.

9. Halberstam, *Powers That Be*, 444.

10. FWF, *Due to Circumstances Beyond Our Control . . .* , 2nd ed., with a new introduction by Dan Rather and Tom Bettag (New York: Random House, 1998), 210.

11. Halberstam, *Powers That Be*, 489–90; Morley Safer, interview by author, New York, October 26, 2000.

12. FWF, cablegram to Sam Zelman et al., CBS Saigon Bureau, April 12, 1965, FP.

13. FWF, cablegram to Sam Zelman, CBS Saigon Bureau, August 12, 1965; FWF, memorandum to Frank Stanton, August 13, 1965; and Morley Safer, cablegram to FWF, August 14, 1965, all in FP.

14. Jimmy Breslin, "Friendly's Day," *New York Herald Tribune*, February 18, 1966, 21; Arthur Sylvester to FWF, August 12, 1965, FP.

15. FWF to Arthur Sylvester, August 16, 1965, FP.

16. FWF to Stanton, August 13, 1965.

17. Morley Safer, cablegram to FWF, August 16, 1965; Frank Stanton to George Smathers, October 16, 1965; and FWF, memorandum to Stanton, October 25, 1965, all in FP.

18. FWF, *Due to Circumstances*, 214–15; William Small, telephone interview by author, March 19, 2001.

19. FWF, *Due to Circumstances*, 217.

20. Kai Bird, *The Color of Truth: McGeorge Bundy and William Bundy: Brothers in Arms* (New York: Simon and Schuster), 320–21; Small interview.

21. Halberstam, *Powers That Be*, 441.

22. Les Brown, interview by author, New York, September 28, 2000.

23. Ibid.; Joseph Wershba, interview by author, Manhasset, N.Y., July 8, 1998.

24. FWF, *Due to Circumstances*, 222, 224–29.

25. Ibid., 230–31.

26. Ibid., 232.

27. Ibid., 232–35.

28. Gordon Manning, interview by author, Westport, Conn., October 27, 2000.

13. Resignation

1. FWF, *Due to Circumstances Beyond Our Control . . .* , 2nd ed., with a new introduction by Dan Rather and Tom Bettag (New York: Random House, 1998), 236.

2. Ibid.; Gary Paul Gates, *Air Time: The Inside Story of CBS News* (New York: Harper & Row, 1978), 124.

3. FWF, *Due to Circumstances*, 238.

4. Ibid., 240.

5. Jack Gould, "Schneider and Friendly Split on Vietnam-Hearing Telecasts," *New York Times*, February 11, 1966, 67.

6. FWF, *Due to Circumstances*, 241.

7. FWF, *Saturday Review* Executive Desk Diary, 1966, February 11, FP; Robert Bernstein, interview by author, New York, June 8, 2000.

8. "C.B.S. Executives Confer in Shifts; Stanton Said to Be Hopeful on Schneider–Friendly Issue," *New York Times*, February 12, 1966, 55; FWF, *Due to Circumstances*, 241; Les Brown, interview by author, New York, September 28, 2000; Gordon Manning, interview by author, Westport, Conn., October 27, 2000.

9. FWF, *Due to Circumstances*, 241–42, 244.

10. Ibid., 245–46.

11. Ibid., 251, 248.

12. Ibid., 249–53.

13. Paley, quoted in Sally Bedell Smith, *In All His Glory: The Life of William S. Paley* (New York: Simon and Schuster, 1990), 451.

14. FWF, *Due to Circumstances*, 253.

15. William Small, telephone interview by author, March 19, 2001; Bill Greeley, "Plea re Friendly Wired to Mgt. by CBS News Execs," *Variety*, February 16, 1966, 33.

16. Jack Gould, "Friendly Quits C.B.S. News Post in Dispute over Vietnam Hearing," *New York Times*, February 16, 1966, 1; "Vietnam vs. [I Love] Lucy" [editorial], *New York Times*, February 16, 1966, 42; Ted Lewis, "Capitol Stuff," *Daily News*, February 15, 1966, 4; Harriet Van Horne, "What TV Would Have You Believe," *New York World-Telegram and Sun*, February 18, 1966, 37; Les Brown, "Friendly's Exit Cues Reappraisal of Company Loyalty vs. Conscience," *Variety*, February 23, 1966, 34.

17. Smith, *In All His Glory*, 704; Corydon B. Dunham, *Fighting for the First Amendment: Stanton of CBS vs. Congress and the Nixon White House* (Westport, Conn.: Praeger, 1997), 48.

18. Dunham, *Fighting for the First Amendment*, 48.

19. Richard S. Salant, *Salant, CBS, and the Battle for the Soul of Broadcast Journalism: The Memoirs of Richard S. Salant*, ed. Susan Buzenberg and Bill Buzenberg (Boulder, Colo.: Westview, 1999), 55; Frank Stanton, interview by Don West, New York, May 22, 2000, Archive of American Television, Academy of Television Arts and Sciences Foundation, North Hollywood, Calif.

20. Lewis L. Gould, telephone interview by author, July 23, 2003; FWF, quoted in Lewis Gould, "Introduction: Portrait of a Television Critic," in Lewis L. Gould, ed., *Watching Television Come of Age: The New York Times Reviews by Jack Gould* (Austin: University of Texas Press, 2002), 22.

21. FWF, *Saturday Review* Executive Desk Diary, February 15, 1966, FP; FWF, *Due to Circumstances*, 254.

22. Brown interview.

23. Ibid.

24. Ibid.

25. Manning interview.

26. John A. Schneider, interview by author, Greenwich, Conn., March 15, 2000.

27. FWF, *Due to Circumstances*, 250; Gates, *Air Time*, 125.

28. Jack Gould, "TV: Friendly's Farewell," *New York Times*, February 17, 1966, 43; Schneider interview.

29. Schneider interview.

30. Gates, *Air Time*, 127.

31. Frank Stanton to author, July 8 and August 19, 1996; Frank Stanton, interview by author, New York, February 10, 1999; George A. Fox, interview by author, New York, June 11, 2001.

32. Brown, "Friendly's Exit," 34; James Day, telephone interview by author, April 27, 1998.

33. Sig Mickelson, telephone interview by author, November 24, 1999.

34. Pat Smith, "Friendly Tells How Much It Cost Him to Quit CBS," *New York World-Telegram and Sun*, February 17, 1966, 1, 4.

35. Jimmy Breslin, "Friendly's Day," *New York Herald Tribune*, February 18, 1966, 1, 21.

36. Ibid.

37. Dwight Eisenhower to FWF, February 15, 1966, FP.

38. FWF to Dwight Eisenhower, February 18, 1966, FP.

39. Dwight Eisenhower to FWF, March 2, 1966, FP.

40. Richard Nixon to FWF, March 9, 1966, FP.

41. William McClure to FWF, March 11, 1966; Av Westin to FWF, March 24, 1966; Peter Davis to FWF, February 17, 1966; John H. Dunn to FWF, February 17, 1966; Tom Wicker to FWF, March 1, 1966; and Godfrey Cambridge to FWF, February 18, 1966, all in FP. Copies of FWF's responses are in FP.

42. Benedict Alper to FWF, March 2, 1966; Ida Fisher to FWF, undated; Rabbi Albert T. Bilgray to FWF, February 28, 1966; Minnie Pincus to FWF, undated; and Arthur J. Levy to FWF, February 17, 1966, all in FP.

43. Manning interview; Roger Mudd, telephone interview by author, January 6, 2006.

44. Leiser interview; Joe Wershba, "Fred W. Friendly: Towering Figure in the Evolution of Television News," *Silurian News*, May 1998, 6; FWF, quoted in Joel Kisseloff, *The Box: An Oral History of Television, 1929–1961* (New York: Viking, 1995), 386.

45. Bill Leonard, *In the Storm of the Eye: A Lifetime at CBS* (New York: Putnam, 1987), 138.

46. DFG interviews.

47. Ibid.

14. Policy Maker

1. Atra Baer, "TViews: Friendly Going to ABC?" *New York Journal-American*, February 17, 1966, 11; Val Adams, "N.B.C. Schedule Next Season Eyes a 'Girl from U.N.C.L.E.,'" *New York Times*, February 18, 1966, 67.

2. FWF, *Due to Circumstances Beyond Our Control . . .* , 2nd ed., with a new introduction by Dan Rather and Tom Bettag (New York: Random House, 1998), 302.

3. Lawrence Laurent, "Radio and Television: TV Rebel Friendly Is Going Academic," *Washington Post*, April 7, 1966, D24.

4. "Kubasik Leaves CBS for Ford Foundation," *New York Times*, September 7, 1966; James Armsey, telephone interviews by author, June 26, 2002, and March 25, 2005; James Day, *The Vanishing Vision: The Inside Story of Public Television* (Berkeley: University of California Press, 1995), 99.

5. William Wolf, "'At 51 I Have Found a Whole New Life,'" *Rhode Islander* [Sunday magazine of the *Providence Journal-Bulletin*], undated clipping, 1967, FP.

6. FWF, *Due to Circumstances*, 298.

7. Ibid., 168, 104, 109, 78, 197.

8. Frank Stanton, interview by Don West, New York, May 22, 2000, Archive of American Television, Academy of Television Arts and Sciences Foundation, North Hollywood, Calif.; DGF and RMF interviews; FWF, *Due to Circumstances*, 248.

9. See, for example, Friendly's exchange of letters about his book with Eisenhower: Dwight Eisenhower to FWF, March 21 and April 7, 1967, and FWF to Eisenhower, April 12, 1967, both in FP.

10. Eric F. Goldman, "The Tragedy of American Television," *Book Week*, March 26, 1967; Walter Goodman, "Broadcasting Business," *New York Times*, Sunday International Economic Survey, March 26, 1967, 265; Daniel J. Leab, interview by author, New York, July 11, 2005; Robert J. Landry, "Behind the Screens at CBS," *Saturday Review*, April 1, 1967, 30.

11. FWF, *Due to Circumstances*, 298; Day, *Vanishing Vision*, 102. For Friendly's account of the Ford Foundation satellite proposal, see *Due to Circumstances*, 301–25.

12. FWF, *Due to Circumstances*, 311.

13. Ibid., 315; M. E. Kinsley, *Outer Space and Inner Sanctums: Government, Business and Satellite Communication* (New York: Wiley, 1976), 131; FWF, *Due to Circumstances*, 301.

14. Senate Committee on Commerce, *Progress Report on Space Communication: Hearings Before the Subcommittee on Communications of the Committee on Commerce*, 89th Cong., 2nd sess., August 17, 1966, 78–117, esp. 83, 84, 87.

15. Ibid., 111; FWF, *Due to Circumstances*, 323.

16. On Bundy's response to McCarthyism at Harvard, see Kai Bird, *The Color of Truth: McGeorge Bundy and William Bundy, Brothers in Arms* (New York: Simon and Schuster, 1998), 121–33; Robert N. Bellah, "McCarthyism at Harvard" [letter to the editor], *New York Review of Books*, February 10, 2005, 42–43; and Eric Pace, "Sigmund Diamond, 79, Professor at Columbia" [obituary], *New York Times*, October 25, 1999, A29.

17. For a description of the building, see Bird, *Color of Truth*, 376–77.

18. Stuart Sucherman, interviews by author, New York, June 25, 2002, and December 5, 2005.

19. Willard J. Hertz, telephone interview by author, April 4, 2005. I have relied on interviews with Hertz, Stuart Sucherman, and RMF for Bundy's leadership style and relationship with Friendly.

20. James Day, *Vanishing Vision*, 104.

21. Sucherman interviews; Hertz interview.

22. Senate Committee on Commerce, *The Public Television Act of 1967: Hearings Before the Subcommittee on Communications of the Committee on Commerce*, 90th Cong., 1st sess., April 12, 1967, 171; House Committee on Interstate and Foreign Commerce, *The Public Television Act of 1967: Hearings Gefore the Committee on Interstate and Foreign Commerce*, 90th Cong., 1st sess., July 18, 1967, 407.

23. Hertz interview.

24. Sucherman interviews; Hertz interview.

25. Hertz interview.

26. Stuart Sucherman, in *Memorial Service for Fred W. Friendly* (New York: Columbia University Graduate School of Journalism, 1998), 26.

27. Carnegie Commission on Educational Television, *Public Television: A Program for Action* (New York: Bantam, 1967). For the origins and makeup of the Carnegie Commission on Educational Television, see Ralph Engelman, *Public Radio and Television in America: A Political History* (Thousand Oaks, Calif.: Sage, 1996), 155–59.

28. Friendly, quoted in John McLaughlin, "The Public Broadcasting Corporation," *America*, July 1, 1967, 13.

29. Joseph Day, "Friendly Assails Johnson Plan for Public TV," *Providence Journal*, April 6, 1967; FWF, "The State of Television: Address by Fred W. Friendly at Brown University," April 5, 1967, Providence, R.I., CBS News Reference Library, 6.

30. FWF, "State of Television," 6, 7.

31. Day, "Friendly Assails Johnson Plan"; FWF, "State of Television," 11.

32. Senate Committee on Commerce, *Public Television Act of 1967*, 172, 171, 185; House Committee on Interstate and Foreign Commerce, *Public Television Act of 1967*, 378–79.

33. Harvey Swados, "Fred Friendly and Friendlyvision," *New York Times Magazine*, April 23, 1967, 31, 114.

34. Ibid., 109.

35. Tom Bettag, telephone interviews by author, July 18 and August 22, 2005.

36. Swados, "Fred Friendly and Friendlyvision," 121.

15. Professor

1. Barrett, quoted in James Boylan, *Pulitzer's School: Columbia University's School of Journalism, 1902–2003* (New York: Columbia University Press, 2003), 163.

2. Melvin Mencher to author, January 15, 2005; DGF interviews.

3. Val Adams, "Friendly Named to 2 New Posts; Will Be Columbia Professor and Ford Foundation Aide," *New York Times*, April 6, 1966, 86; Richard K. Doan, "Friendly: The Academic Life," *New York Herald Tribune*, April 6, 1966, 23.

4. Harvey Swados, "Fred Friendly and Friendlyvision," *New York Times Magazine*, April 23, 1967, 121.

5. Stuart Sucherman, interviews by author, New York, June 25, 2002, and December 5, 2005.

6. Tom Bettag, telephone interviews by author, July 18 and August 22, 2005.

7. Ibid.; John Schultz, telephone interviews by author, October 22 and November 9, 2004; David Kuhn, in *Happy Birthday, F.W.F.* (pamphlet issued and presented to Friendly on the occasion of his sixtieth birthday, October 30, 1975, by his past and present teaching assistants at the Columbia University Graduate School of Journalism), unpaged.

8. Eileen McNamara, "The Fred Friendly Impact," *Nieman Reports*, spring 1998, 76; Swados, "Fred Friendly and Friendlyvision," 119; Boylan, *Pulitzer's School*, 164.

9. Benno C. Schmidt Jr., telephone interview by author, April 25, 2006.

10. Kerner Commission, *Report of National Advisory Commission on Civil Disorders*, "History Matters: The U.S. Survey Course on the Web," http://history-matters.gmu.edu/d/6553 (accessed March 27, 2006); RMF, "Life with Fred" (speech delivered at Smith College, Northampton, Mass., 1970), FP. For the inauguration of the summer program at Columbia, see George Gent, "Columbia to Train Minorities for TV," *New York Times*, June 19, 1968, 95, and Boylan, *Pulitzer's School*, 172. For a report on the program's first year, see Graduate School of Journalism, "1969 Summer Program in Broadcast and Print Journalism for Members of Minority Groups," Columbia University, 1969.

11. FWF, "The Present-Minded Professor" (Ford Foundation Reprint of address to the National Council of Teachers of English, Milwaukee, November 28, 1968), 3.

12. Geraldo Rivera with Daniel Paisner, *Exposing Myself* (New York: Bantam, 1991), 87; Geraldo Rivera, in *Memorial Service for Fred W. Friendly* (New York: Columbia University Graduate School of Journalism, 1998), 29–30.

13. Thomas A. Johnson, "Ebony Editor Sees Black Revolt as Challenge to the News Media," *New York Times*, August 30, 1969, 24; George Gent, "Columbia Aids Minorities to Posts in Broadcasting," *New York Times*, July 10, 1971, 49.

14. John J. O'Connor, "Television: He's at Home in the City Jungle," *New York Times*, November 21, 1971, D21; Gent, "Columbia Aids Minorities."

15. Al Donaldson, "Friendly Dissuasion," *Pittsburgh Post-Gazette*, March 8, 1998, C4.

16. Earl Caldwell, e-mail to author, March 30, 2006.

17. Earl Caldwell, e-mail to author, April 4, 2006.

18. Nathaniel Sheppard Jr., "Minority-Journalists' Program Closes," *New York Times*, August 17, 1974, 24.

19. Earl Caldwell, e-mail to author, March 28, 2006.

20. Penn Kimball, telephone interview by author, March 18, 2005.

21. Pinkham, quoted in Boylan, *Pulitzer's School*, 169.

22. Lawrence Pinkham, telephone interview by author, April 15, 2005; Joshua Friedman, interview by author, New York, October 26, 2006; Mencher letter; Melvin Mencher, e-mail to author, February 4, 2005.

23. See the account of Kuhn, who became Friendly's graduate assistant the following year, in *Happy Birthday, F.W.F.*, unpaged; see also " 'Crisis at Columbia' Traced in a Volume by *Spectator*," *New York Times*, May 12, 1968, 68.

24. Mark Harrington, in *Happy Birthday, F.W.F.*, unpaged.

25. David Bird, "One Hundred on Columbia Faculty Urge Strong Action to Halt Disruptors," *New York Times*, March 11, 1969, 44; FWF, "Present-Minded Professor," 9.

26. FWF, "Present-Minded Professor," 9.

27. FWF, "Some Sober Second Thoughts on Vice President Agnew," *Saturday Review*, December 13, 1969, 75.

28. Andrew Friendly, eulogy at Riverdale Temple, Riverdale, N.Y., March 6, 1998, audiocassette, FP; Bettag interviews.

29. Bettag interviews.

30. Mencher letter; Schultz interviews.

31. Pinkham interview.

32. Willard J. Hertz, telephone interview by author, April 4, 2005; Schultz interviews.

33. William Wolf, " 'At 51 I Have Found a Whole New Life,' " *Rhode Islander* [Sunday magazine of the *Providence Journal-Bulletin*], undated clipping, 1967, FP; Peter Neubauer, interview by author, New York, November 20, 2005; RMF interviews; Bettag interviews.

34. RMF interviews; Bettag interviews; DGF interviews.

35. RMF interviews; RMF, e-mail to author, April 26, 2006; Tom Bettag, introduction to *Happy Birthday, F.W.F.*, unpaged.

36. RMF interviews.

37. For biographical information about Ruth, see Jerry Talmer, "At Home with Fred and Ruth Friendly," *New York Post*, June 30, 1973, 33.

38. RMF interviews.

39. Talmer, "At Home with Fred and Ruth," 33; DGF interviews.

40. RMF interviews; Bettag interviews; Wolf, " 'At 51 I Have Found a Whole New Life.' "

16. *PBL*

1. Richard Kellerman, "The Public Broadcasting Laboratory: A Fact Sheet," August 14, 1967, microfilm 932, reel 1, Avrum R. Westin Papers, Division of Archives and Manuscripts, State Historical Society of Wisconsin, Madison. All material that I cite from the Westin Papers in this chapter may be found on microfilm 932, reel 1.

2. Jack Gould, "Columbia Will Start University Network of Educational TV," *New York Times*, February 7, 1967, 1; "Experiment in Educational TV" [editorial], *New York Times*, February 8, 1967, 30.

3. Westin, quoted in James Ledbetter, *Made Possible by . . . the Death of Public Broadcasting in the United States* (New York: Verso, 1997), 47.

4. Av Westin, memorandum to McGeorge Bundy, March 13, 1967, Westin Papers; Jack Gould, "Columbia News Lab Will Shift to NET," *New York Times*, March 17, 1967, 1, 81.

5. John Fisher, "The Easy Chair: Happening on the Night of November 5th," *Harper's*, November 1967, 16.

6. Gould, "Columbia Will Start University Network," 1, 79; James Day, *The Vanishing Vision: The Inside Story of Public Television* (Berkeley: University of California Press, 1995), 101; Richard K. Doan, "Public TV's Most Powerful

Friend . . . May Also Qualify as Its Worst Enemy," *TV Guide*, September 15, 1973, 9; House Committee on Interstate and Foreign Commerce, *The Public Television Act of 1967: Hearings Before the Committee on Interstate and Foreign Commerce*, 90th Cong., 1st sess., July 18, 1967, 405.

7. "Goals and Operating Principals of PBL," December 15, 1967, 4, 2, Westin Papers; C. H. Simonds, "Turn On, Tune In, Yawn," *National Review*, October 17, 1967, 1128–29; Ledbetter, *Made Possible*, 52.

8. Av Westin, memorandum to FWF, April, 4, 1967, and McGeorge Bundy, memorandum of understanding, May 1967, both in Westin Papers.

9. Minutes, Editorial Policy Board meetings of the Public Broadcast Laboratory, August 16 and September 13, 1967; Av Westin's response to suggested changes in his memorandum and attached letter to FWF, November 2, 1967, all in Westin Papers.

10. Av Westin, interview by author, New York, February 20, 2004.

11. Day, *Vanishing Vision*, 106.

12. "*PBL* on the Brink," *Newsweek*, November 6, 1967, 102.

13. "Goals and Operating Principals of PBL," 3; Ralph Engelman, *Public Radio and Television in America: A Political History* (Thousand Oaks, Calif.: Sage, 1996), 151.

14. John Tebbel, "Latest Hope for Television—PBL: The Great Experiment," *Saturday Review*, November 11, 1967, 87, 85; Fisher, "Easy Chair," 16; "*PBL* on the Brink," 104.

15. Friendly, quoted in Day, *Vanishing Vision*, 108–9.

16. Stuart Sucherman, interviews by author, New York, June 25, 2002, and December 5, 2005.

17. Ledbetter, *Made Possible*, 48.

18. John Horn, "Television," *Nation*, November 27, 1967, 574.

19. Ledbetter, *Made Possible*, 242n.31, 49–50.

20. Erik Barnouw, *Tube of Plenty: The Evolution of American Television*, 2nd rev. ed. (New York: Oxford University Press, 1990), 396–98; Ledbetter, *Made Possible*, 52.

21. Van Horne and Gould, quoted in Day, *Vanishing Vision*, 109.

22. Westin interview.

23. Michael Arlen, "The Air: P.B.L.," *New Yorker*, November 18, 1967, 54.

24. Av Westin, memorandum to Messrs. [Everett] Case, [Howard] Dressner, [Fred] Friendly, and [John F.] White, "Subject: Photographs—Dr. Martin Luther King," April 16, 1968, Westin Papers; "NET Moves In," *Newsweek*, July 1, 1968, 79; Robert Lewis Shayon, "TV and Radio: PBL: Hypothesis Trouble?" *Saturday Review*, December 9, 1967, 37.

25. Network Project, *The Fourth Network* (New York: Columbia University, 1971), 12; Westin interview; Editorial Policy Boarad, quoted in Day, *Vanishing Vision*, 110–11.

26. Robert E. Dallos, "City Weighs Operation of Own CATV," *New York Times*, July 26, 1967, 79; House Committee on Interstate and Foreign Commerce, *Public Television Act of 1967*, 408.

27. FWF, "Asleep at the Switch of the Wired City," *Saturday Review*, October 10, 1970, 58–59.
28. Fred Ferretti, "City Delays Its Decision on CATV Policy," *New York Times*, July 24, 1970, 63.
29. Westin interview; Matt Messina, "News Around the Dials: Friendly Refuses TV Post," *Daily News*, June 18, 1968, 29; "NET Moves In," 79.
30. Av Westin, memorandum to FWF, June 7, 1968, Westin Papers; "NET Moves In," 79; Westin interview.
31. Nicholas Johnson to Av Westin, February 6, 1969, Westin Papers; Westin interview; Jack Gould, "Eight TV Stations Ask Replacement of P.B.L. by New Sunday Series," *New York Times*, March 9, 1969, 1, 2.
32. Bill Moyers, interview by author, New York, November 29, 2005; Day, *Vanishing Vision*, 112; John McLaughlin, "*PBL*'s Premiere," *America*, November 18, 1967, 621–22.
33. Michael Arlen, "The Air: Something Live," *New Yorker*, December 30, 1967, 54.
34. Moyers interview; Abel, quoted in Ledbetter, *Made Possible*, 52.

17. PBS

1. For an account of Davis's hiring by Friendly, see David Davis, interview by James Robertson, in Public Television's Roots, oral history project, Mass Communication History Center, State Historical Society of Wisconsin, Madison.
2. Ward Chamberlin, e-mail to author, March 14, 2006.
3. James Day, *The Vanishing Vision: The Inside Story of Public Television* (Berkeley: University of California Press, 1995), 128–29.
4. Robert K. Avery and Robert Pepper, *The Politics of Interconnection: A History of Public Television at the National Level* (Washington, D.C.: National Association of Educational Broadcasters, 1979), 3; Davis interview, 45. For Ford's involvement, see Avery and Pepper, *Politics of Interconnection*, 2–22.
5. Avery and Pepper, *Politics of Interconnection*, 4; Ward Chamberlin, e-mail to author, March 13, 2006.
6. John White, interview by author, October 14, 1982; Davis interview, 45; John Witherspoon and Roselle Kovitz, *A History of Public Broadcasting*, with an update by Robert K. Avery and Alan G. Stavisky (Washington, D.C.: Current, 2000), 37.
7. Day, *Vanishing Vision*, 193, 201; James Day, interview by author, April 27, 1998. For Day's account of the NET–Channel 13 merger, see *Vanishing Vision*, 191–201.
8. Day, *Vanishing Vision*, 205; Chamberlin e-mail, March 13, 2006. For more on the renaissance in local programming, see Day, *Vanishing Vision*, 201–11.
9. Day, *Vanishing Vision*, 140; Ward Chamberlin e-mail to author, March 14, 2006.
10. Day, *Vanishing Vision*, 55.

11. Stuart Sucherman, interviews by author, New York, June 25, 2002, and December 5, 2005; Day, *Vanishing Vision*, 219.

12. Richard D. Lyons, "Husband of Mrs. Mitchell Aide Ousted," *New York Times*, April 19, 1970, 71.

13. FWF, quoted in "News from the Ford Foundation," press release, April 27, 1970, CBS News Reference Library.

14. William Woestendiek, telephone interview by author, March 6, 2006.

15. Day, *Vanishing Vision*, 141.

16. Spiro Agnew, "Speech on the National Media," November 13, 1969, Des Moines, Iowa, http://faculty.smu.edu/dsimon/Change-Agnew.html (accessed May 30, 2008); Woestendiek interview; FWF, "Some Sober Second Thoughts on Vice President Agnew," *Saturday Review*, December 13, 1969, 61, 62.

17. Day, *Vanishing Vision*, 141–44.

18. Ibid., 215; Richard K. Doan, "Public TV's Most Powerful Friend . . . May Also Qualify as Its Worst Enemy," *TV Guide*, September 15, 1973.

19. Day, *Vanishing Vision*, 215–24

20. Les Brown, "Files of Nixon White House Show Bid to Control Public Broadcasting," *New York Times*, February 24, 1979, 1, 9; Whitehead, quoted in David M. Stone, *Nixon and the Politics of Public Television* (New York: Garland, 1985), 104–5.

21. Day, *Vanishing Vision*, 221.

22. Doan, "Public TV's Most Powerful Friend," 7, 9.

23. For PBS's plans to cover the Senate Watergate hearings, see "Public TV Plans Coverage of Hearings on Watergate," *New York Times*, April 19, 1973, 85, and Les Brown, "Public TV to Cover Watergate on Nightly Basis through Tape," *New York Times*, November 6, 1973, 75; Dean, quoted in Mike McDaniel, "'Watergate Plus 30': And the Lesson Is . . . ?" *Houston Chronicle*, July 30, 2003, 8.

24. *Ford Foundation Activities in Noncommercial Broadcasting, 1951–1976* (New York: Ford Foundation, 1976), 22; Chamberlin e-mail, March 14, 2006.

25. David Fanning, interview with author, New York, April 24, 2008; Deirdre Boyle, *Subject to Change: Guerrilla Television Revisited* (New York: Oxford University Press), 137; for background on the Hoffman broadcast, see 128–38.

26. Doan, "Public TV's Most Powerful Friend," 10.

18. The Press and the Bar

1. Benno C. Schmidt Jr., telephone interview by author, April 25, 2006.

2. Les Brown, "Media Are Scored by Fred Friendly," *New York Times*, January 12, 1974, 67; FWF, "The Nervous Breakdown of the First Amendment" (speech to the Federal Communications Bar Association, Washington, D.C., January 10, 1974), CBS News Reference Library.

3. *United States v. Caldwell* was one of four cases decided as *Branzburg v. Hayes*, 408 U.S. 665 (1972).

4. *Miami Herald v. Tornillo*, 418 U.S. 241 (1974); FWF, "Nervous Breakdown of the First Amendment"; Fred W. Friendly and Martin A. Linsky, introduction

to *The Seminars on Media and Society, 1974–1980: A Summary and Casebook* (New York: Ford Foundation, 1980), 5.

5. FWF, "What's Fair on the Air?" *New York Times Magazine*, March 30, 1975; FWF, *The Good Guys, the Bad Guys and the First Amendment: Free Speech and Fairness in Broadcasting* (New York: Random House, 1976).

6. *Red Lion Broadcasting v. FCC*, 395 U.S. 367 (1969); FWF, *Good Guys*, 257.

7. *Red Lion Broadcasting v. FCC*.

8. FWF, *Good Guys*, xiv; RMF interviews.

9. P. J. Ognibene, " 'The Good Guys, the Bad Guys and the First Amendment' by Fred W. Friendly," *New Republic*, July 3–10, 1976, 30.

10. Carey McWilliams, "Letters: Assigned, Not Arranged," *New York Times Magazine*, April 27, 1975, 69; FWF, "Letters: Fred Friendly Replies," *New York Times Magazine*, April 27, 1975, 69; Everett C. Parker, "Letters: A Matter of Motive," *New York Times Magazine*, May 11, 1975, 84.

11. "On the Other Hand, Fred Friendly Finds That Fairness Is Fair," *Variety*, June 9, 1976, 56; Ephraim Lewis, "Books," *Business Week*, June 21, 1976, 13; Dan Werner, in *Happy Birthday, F.W.F.* (pamphlet issued and presented to Friendly on the occasion of his sixtieth birthday, October 30, 1975, by his past and present teaching assistants at the Columbia University Graduate School of Journalism), unpaged; Martha Elliott, telephone interviews by author, February 1 and February 6, 2006.

12. FWF, *Good Guys*, 259; Elliott interviews; Dan Werner, telephone interview by author, July 17, 2006.

13. Martin A. Linsky, e-mail to author, April 15, 2006.

14. Ibid.

15. Friendly and Linsky, *Seminars on Media and Society*, 5.

16. Stuart Sucherman, interviews by author, New York, June 25, 2002, and December 5, 2005.

17. Linsky e-mail; RMF interviews.

18. Fred W. Friendly and Martha J. H. Elliott, *The Constitution: That Delicate Balance* (New York: Random House, 1984), xiii; RMF interviews.

19. Werner, in *Happy Birthday, F.W.F.*; Friendly and Linsky, *Seminars on Media and Society*, 26–31.

20. Friendly and Linsky, *Seminars on Media and Society*, 6.

21. Seib, quoted in ibid., 6.

22. Friendly and Linsky, *Seminars on Media and Society*, 6.

23. Ibid., 8; Schmidt interview.

19. Seminar

1. Benno C. Schmidt Jr., telephone interview by author, April 25, 2006; RMF interviews; Martin A. Linsky, e-mail to author, June 27, 2006; James Day, *The Vanishing Vision: The Inside Story of Public Television* (Berkeley: University of California Press, 1995), 283.

2. Jonathan Landman, telephone interview by author, April 25, 2006; Martha Elliott, telephone interviews by author, February 1 and February 6, 2006; FWF to former students and teaching assistants, June 10, 1979, FP.

3. James Boylan, *Pulitzer's School: Columbia University's School of Journalism, 1902–2003* (New York: Columbia University Press, 2003), 202; "Friendly: 'I Love That School and Identify with It,'" *Washington Journalism Review*, April–May 1979, 43; Willard J. Hertz, telephone interview by author, April 4, 2005; RMF interviews.

4. Deirdre Carmody, "Friendly Retiring as Ford Fund's Advisor on News," *New York Times*, December 14, 1980, 60; William Henry III, "Fred Friendly Signs Off," *Daily News*, December 8, 1980, M3.

5. *Near v. Minnesota*, 283 U.S. 697 (1931); FWF, *Minnesota Rag: The Dramatic Story of the Landmark Supreme Court Case That Gave New Meaning to Freedom of the Press* (New York: Random House, 1981).

6. FWF, *Minnesota Rag*, 181.

7. Michael Gartner, "A Famous Fight for a Freer American Press," *Wall Street Journal*, June 24, 1981, 30.

8. Lyle Denniston, review of *Minnesota Rag*, by Fred W. Friendly, *Washington Journalism Review*, September 1981, 57.

9. FWF, "The Mole, the Judges and the Rule of Law" [copy], FP; for Friendly's work on the project, see Sir Denis Forman to FWF, October 22, 1980, and FWF to Forman, December 31, 1980, and February 4, 1981, all in FP.

10. Sir Denis Forman to FWF, February 15 and October 22, 1980; FWF to Forman, September 22, 1980; and contract between FWF and Granada Television, all in FP.

11. FWF to Forman, September 22, 1980; Boylan, *Pulitzer's School*, 202; RMF interviews.

12. Columbia University to Ford Foundation [draft]; Osborn Elliott to FWF, January 8, 1981; and FWF to Sir Denis Forman, March 4, 1981, all in FP; Wolfgang Saxon, "Columbia Seminars to Study Press and Society," *New York Times*, April 27, 1981, B5; Sandy Rovner, "Fred Friendly's Court Report," *Washington Post*, June 24, 1981.

13. Robben W. Fleming, *Tempests into Rainbows* (Ann Arbor: University of Michigan Press, 1996), 267; RMF interviews.

14. John J. O'Connor, "TV Weekend," *New York Times*, March 26, 1982, C26.

15. Marvin Kitman, "The Shows That Put the Press in the Hot Seat," *Washington Journalism Review*, November 1983, 44, 40.

16. Fred W. Friendly and Martha J. H. Elliott, acknowledgments to *The Constitution: That Delicate Balance* (New York: Random House, 1984), 330; Fleming, *Tempests into Rainbows*, 267; Marianne Costantinou, "Television Week," *New York Times*, January 2, 1983, A3.

17. Michael I. Meyerson, "The Incredible Thinking Heads," *Channels*, September–October 1985, 35; Kurt Andersen, "Talking Heads with Body Language," *Dial*, September 1984, 25.

18. Ann Hodges, "'Presidency and the Constitution' Series Lets Guests Do the Talking," *Houston Chronicle*, April 28, 1987.

19. Susan Heller Anderson and Maurice Carroll, "New York Day by Day: Mixed Media," *New York Times*, November 5, 1984, B3.

20. FWF, *Minnesota Rag*, 11; RMF interviews; Elliott interviews.

21. Cynthia McFadden, telephone interview by author, April 28, 2006; Elliott interviews.

22. For the production of the media and society seminars for television, see Kitman, "Shows That Put the Press in the Hot Seat"; see also Meyerson, "Incredible Thinking Heads," 35–36, and Andersen, "Talking Heads," 21–25.

23. Antonin Scalia, in *Memorial Service for Fred W. Friendly* (New York: Columbia University Graduate School of Journalism, 1998), 20.

24. Sucherman, quoted in Andersen, "Talking Heads," 22.

25. Kitman, "Shows That Put the Press in the Hot Seat," 42, 55; Andersen, "Talking Heads," 24.

26. Andersen, "Talking Heads," 24; Kitman, "Shows That Put the Press in the Hot Seat," 40; McFadden interview.

27. McFadden interview; Elliott interviews.

28. Tom Bettag, telephone interviews by author, July 18 and August 22, 2005.

29. RMF interviews; Bettag interviews; Schmidt interview.

30. Bettag interviews; David Schoenbrun, *On and Off the Air: An Informal History of CBS News* (New York: Dutton, 1989), 182.

31. Michael Stern, "Whig-Wagging at Constitutional Issues," *Los Angeles Times*, September 26, 1984, F8; Berger, quoted in Carmody, "Friendly Retiring," 60.

32. Bettag interviews; Day, *Vanishing Vision*, 282–83; Friendly, quoted in Andersen, "Talking Heads," 21.

33. FWF to J. Edgar Hoover, November 12, 1971, and Hoover to FWF, November 18, 1971, Federal Bureau of Investigation, APBnews: Fred Friendly FBI File, 9–11, http://www.apbnews.com/media/gfiles/friendly/friendlyreport_1.html (accessed August 25, 2000). On the incident, see Daniel Schorr, *Clearing the Air* (Boston: Berkeley Medallion, 1977), 71–86. Included in Friendly's FBI file is a memorandum from J. D. McKenzie, "Request of Mr. Fred W. Friendly Former President of CBS News to Meet with the Director, 7/1/81," and follow-up documentation, FBI Document 94-43788.

34. McFadden interview; Elliott interviews; Stuart Sucherman, interviews by author, New York, June 25, 2002, and December 5, 2005; Walter Goodman, "TV View: Making Talking Heads Really Talk," *New York Times*, January 2, 1983, A19; Bettag interviews.

35. Edward R. Murrow and Fred W. Friendly, eds., *See It Now* (New York: Simon and Schuster, 1955), 41; Sucherman interviews.

20. Last Years

1. Lisa H. Newton, ed., *Ethics in America Study Guide* (Englewood Cliffs, N.J.: Prentice Hall, 1989).

2. Kevin Brass, "A Friendly Foray into the Realm of Ethical Dilemmas," *Los Angeles Times*, San Diego County edition, Entertainment Desk, December 9, 1988, 1.

3. Terry Kelleher, "Watch Some Tough Guys Squirm: The Questions on 'Ethics in America' Go for the Throat," *Newsday*, January 29, 1989, 6; Mike More, "Divided Loyalties: Peter Jennings and Mike Wallace in No-Man's Land," *Quill*, February 1989.

4. Kenneth R. Clark, "Racking the Mind: Ten-Part 'Ethics in America' Is Sure to Strike a Few Nerves," *Chicago Tribune*, January 31, 1989, 2.

5. Ambrose Cleary, "Ethics in America: Where Else?" *Commonweal*, February 24, 1989, 119; Clark, "Racking the Mind," 2.

6. Walter Goodman, "Review/Television: "The Role of Journalists in the Stuart Case," *New York Times*, January 25, 1990, C22; Michael Fleming, Karen Freifeld, and Susan Mulcahy, "Inside New York: Broadcast Legend Snubbed by Media," *Newsday*, November 4, 1988, 11.

7. "Tele-tiff," *New York Post*, November 27, 1985, 5.

8. Friendly added to the inscription, "With Affection, Fred," and the date, June 19, 1973. The inscribed copy is in the library of Joe Wershba.

9. Tom Bettag, telephone interviews by author, July 18 and August 22, 2005; Kevin Goldman, "Who Really Gets the Story?" *Variety*, June 20, 1984, 43; "How Fred Friendly Sees It Now: The Changing Face of TV Journalism" [interview], *Broadcasting*, August 25, 1986, transcript, http://find.galegroup.com. cwplib.proxy.liu.edu/itx/retrieve.do?contentSet (accessed December 6, 2008).

10. Don Hewitt, "No Journalist Requires Anything Except a Respite from Fred Friendly," *Washington Journalism Review*, May 1987, 21–22.

11. "How Fred Friendly Sees It Now"; "Friendly Rallies Pubcast Troops: 'Don't Give Up,' *Variety*, July 1, 1981, 40; FWF, "CBS: The First 60 Years" [interview], *Broadcasting*, September 14, 1987, 92.

12. FWF, "On Television: News, Lies and Videotape," *New York Times*, August 6, 1989; Eric Siegel, "Some Friendly Criticism on Broadcasting," *Newsday*, November 14, 1982.

13. "An Outspoken TV-News Pioneer Airs His Views on the State of Broadcast Journalism Today," Q&A, *TV Guide*, August 1, 1981, 28. On Friendly's campaign, see, for example, "Friendly's Push for Longer News," *Broadcasting*, March 15, 1982, 186; Hank Ezell, "Public 'Deceived, Shortchanged' by 1/2-Hour TV News, Friendly Says," *Atlanta Journal and Atlanta Constitution*, March 28, 1982, 7B; and FWF, "Let's Have an Hour of Network News," *Advertising Age*, April 26, 1982, M9, M38–M39.

14. Diane Mermigas, "Friendly Criticism," *Electronic Media*, June 16, 1986, 27.

15. "A View from a News Veteran," *Broadcasting*, November 21, 1983, 48 (*New York Times v. Sullivan* may be found at 376 U.S. 254 [1964]); FWF, "After the

Westmoreland Case: How Can the People Talk Back?" *Washington Post*, February 20, 1985, A21; United Press International, "Friendly Backs a TV Forum," *Los Angeles Times*, April 26, 1985, 24.

16. Colby Coates, "The Insider," *Electronic Media*, May 9, 1985; FWF, "CBS," 92; Ann Hodges, " 'Presidency and the Constitution' Series Lets Guests Do the Talking," *Houston Chronicle*, April 28, 1987, 1.

17. FWF, "CBS," 89.

18. Kay Gardella, "Friendly Criticism of CBS," *Daily News*, June 13, 1986, 80; Jay Sharbutt, "Friendly Jabs Network News," *Los Angeles Times*, January 21, 1986, pt. 6:1, 10; "How Fred Friendly Sees It Now."

19. Bill Moyers, interview by author, New York November 29, 2005; Bill Moyers, in *Memorial Service for Fred W. Friendly* (New York: Columbia University Graduate School of Journalism, 1998), 45–46.

20. Associated Press, "Friendly Offers Plan to Fund Public TV," *Los Angeles Times*, April 28, 1988, 14.

21. Hodges, " 'Presidency and the Constitution' Series"; FWF, interview by Sander Vanocur, February 25, 1987, News Leaders series, Poynter Institute for Media Studies, St. Petersburg, Fla., videocassette, FP.

22. FWF, "If I Had My Career in Broadcast Journalism to Start Over Again in August, 1986 . . . ," http://www.rtnda.org/resources/speeches/friendly (accessed November 30, 2005).

23. RMF interviews; FWF, "From Intense Tennis in Stockbridge to Intensive Care at BMC," *Berkshire Eagle*, July 28, 1979, 17.

24. Stuart Sucherman, in *Memorial Service*, 27; RMF, e-mail to author, October 12, 2006; FWF to William Webster, August 21, 1984, and Webster to FWF, September 18, 1984, Federal Bureau of Investigation, FBI Documents 94-43788-6 and 94-43788-7, APBnews: Fred Friendly FBI File, 19–20, http://www.apbnews.com/media/gfiles/friendly/friendlyreport_1.html (accessed August 25, 2000).

25. FWF, addendum to living will, in *Memorial Service*, 32–33. An edited version was played at the service.

26. FWF, interview by Toby Blum-Dobkin, Video History Project, Museum of Jewish Heritage, New York, November 20, 1990, videocassette, FP; RMF e-mail.

27. Spreadsheet guide for Professional Activities/Seminars, FP.

28. For descriptions of Friendly's medical condition, I have relied on RMF interviews.

29. John Schultz, telephone interviews by author, October 22 and November 9, 2004; RMF, email to author, October 12, 2006; Joshua Friedman, interview by author, New York, October 26, 2006; Cynthia McFadden, telephone interview by author, April 28, 2006; RMF interviews.

30. RMF interviews; Marlon Brando, on *Larry King Live*, December 28, 1994, CNN, LexisNexis Academic, Transcript 1317; Andrew Friendly, eulogy at Riverdale Temple, Riverdale, N.Y., March 6, 1998, audiocassette, FP.

31. RMF to Lee Clark, May 4, 1997, FP.

32. Tom Bettag, eulogy at Riverdale Temple, March 6, 1998, audiocassette, FP; Mili Lerner Bonsignori, interview by Michael Rosen, Kissimmee, Fla., December 11, 1998, Archive of American Television, Academy of Television Arts and Sciences Foundation, North Hollywood, Calif.

33. FWF, "A Conversation with Fred Friendly" (transcript of comments at seminar with Nieman class of 1981, Cambridge, Mass.), *Nieman Reports*, winter 1999–spring 2000, 162–66, http://proquest.umi.com/pqweb (accessed February 28, 2006); McFadden interview; Martha Elliott, telephone interviews by author, February 1 and February 6, 2006; Andy Rooney, interview by author, New York, October 5, 2000.

34. RMF interviews; Andrew Friendly, eulogy.

35. David Friendly, Richard Mark, and Lisa Friendly, eulogies at Riverdale Temple, March 6, 1998, audiocassette, FP.

36. Andrew Hayward, in *Memorial Service*, 7.

37. Cynthia McFadden, in *Memorial Service*, 36–37.

38. Antonin Scalia, in *Memorial Service*, 21; Bill Moyers, in *Memorial Service*, 46.

21. Friendlyvision

1. FWF, interview by Toby Blum-Dobkin, Video History Project, Museum of Jewish Heritage, New York, November 20, 1990, videocassette, FP. On another occasion Friendly said, "I am what I am, a great overachiever" (Joseph E. Persico, *Edward R. Murrow: An American Original* [New York: Dell, 1988], 312).

2. Dan Rather, in *Memorial Service for Fred W. Friendly* (New York: Columbia University Graduate School of Journalism, 1998), 8.

3. FWF, "A Conversation with Fred Friendly" (transcript of comments at seminar with Nieman class of 1981, Cambridge, Mass.), *Nieman Reports*, winter 1999–spring 2000, 162–66, http://proquest.umi.com/pqweb (accessed February 28, 2006).

4. Stuart Sucherman, interviews by author, New York, June 25, 2002, and December 5, 2005; Peter Neubauer, interview by author, New York, November 20, 2005.

5. Noah Mark, eulogy at Riverdale Temple, Riverdale, N.Y., March 6, 1998, audiocassette, FP; Cynthia McFadden, telephone interview by author, April 28, 2006.

6. Sucherman interviews; Martha Elliott, telephone interviews by author, February 1 and February 6, 2006; Jonathan Landman, telephone interview by author, April 25, 2006.

7. McFadden interview; Tom Bettag, in *Memorial Service*, 17; Sucherman interviews.

8. Bettag, in *Memorial Service*, 18–19.

9. RMF interviews.

10. McFadden interview.

11. FWF to RMF [handwritten], February 9, 1970, FP.

12. David Friendly, telephone interview by author, December 3, 2007; Neubauer interview.

13. Joan Konner, "Publisher's Note: Fred Friendly, 1915–1998," *Columbia Journalism Review*, May–June 1998, 6.

14. David Schoenbrun, *On and Off the Air: An Informal History of CBS News* (New York: Dutton, 1989), 62; David Halberstam, *The Powers That Be* (New York: Knopf, 1979), 135; Martin Clancy, in *Happy Birthday, F.W.F.* (pamphlet issued and presented to Friendly on the occasion of his sixtieth birthday, October 30, 1975, by his past and present teaching assistants at the Columbia University Graduate School of Journalism), unpaged.

15. FWF, interview by Lloyd Moss, *This Is My Music*, December 2, 1979, WQXR-FM, New York, videocassette, FP.

16. Ibid.

17. "Send in the Clowns" (from *A Little Night Music*). Music and Lyrics by Stephen Sondheim. © 1973 (Renewed) Rilting Music, Inc. All Rights Administered by WB Music Corp. All Rights Reserved. Used by permission from Alfred Publishing Co., Inc.

18. Edward R. Murrow, speech to Radio-Television News Directors Association, October 15, 1958, http://www.rtnda.org/pages/media_items/edward-r.-murrow-speech998.php (accessed May 23, 2008).

19. On Lippmann's thinking about public opinion and the press, see Christopher Lasch, "Journalism, Publicity and the Lost Art of Argument," *Gannett Center Journal*, spring 1990, 1–10, and Ronald Steel, *Walter Lippmann and the American Century* (Boston: Little, Brown, 1980), 171–85, 211–19.

20. Jack W. Mitchell, *Listener Supported: The Culture and History of Public Radio* (Westport, Conn.: Praeger, 2005), 9–10.

21. Quoted in Konner, "Publisher's Note," 6.

22. Tom Bettag, telephone interview by author, July 18, 2005; RMF interviews; Lisa Friendly, telephone interview by author, July 31, 2007.

23. Bill Moyers, interview by author, New York, November 29, 2005; Gordon Manning, interview by author, Westport, Conn., October 27, 2000.

24. Walter Lippmann, *Public Opinion* (New York: Harcourt, Brace, 1922); below the signature of Harvey H. Bundy and the date of June 26, 1922, is the inscription to Friendly signed by Bundy and his wife and dated October 31, 1980, FP. Lippmann's inscription in the later edition of *Public Opinion* (New York: Free Press, 1965) is dated December 1968. Friendly notes Lippmann's dedication to him of Lippmann's book of interview transcripts, *Conversations with Walter Lippmann* (Boston: Little, Brown, 1965), in *Due to Circumstances Beyond Our Control . . .* , 2nd ed., with a new introduction by Dan Rather and Tom Bettag (New York: Random House, 1998), 118.

25. FWF, "Conversation with Fred Friendly"; Steel, *Walter Lippmann and the American Century*, 599.

26. Halberstam, *Powers That Be*, 21–33.

27. FWF, "The Present-Minded Professor" (Ford Foundation Reprint of address to the National Council of Teachers of English, Milwaukee, November 28, 1968).

28. Landman interview.

29. For an analysis of the guest lists for the two programs, see "FAIR Issues New Study on PBS's MacNeil/Lehrer and ABC's Nightline," http://www.fair.org/index.php? (accessed July 16, 2007).

30. Myra MacPherson, *All Governments Lie! The Life and Times of Rebel Journalist I. F. Stone* (New York: Scribner, 2006), 140.

31. Michael D. Murray, "Television's Desperate Moment: A Conversation with Fred W. Friendly," *Journalism History* 1, no. 3 (1974): 70.

32. Les Brown, "Friendly's Exit Cues Reappraisal of Company Loyalty vs. Conscience," *Variety*, February 23, 1966, 34; Ernie Leiser, telephone interview by author, October 27, 2000.

33. Sucherman interviews.

34. David Fanning, interview by author, New York, April 24, 2008.

35. Earl Caldwell, e-mail to author, March 28, 2006.

36. Landman interview.

37. Moyers interview.

38. Ibid.

39. Steel, *Walter Lippmann and the American Century*, 578–79.

40. Dan Rather, in *Memorial Service*, 19; Halberstam, *Powers That Be*, 194–95.

41. Arthur Miller, *Arthur Miller's Collected Plays* (New York: Viking, 1957), 1:222.

Index

Aaron, John, 99
ABC (American Broadcasting Company), 165, 194, 228, 234, 275, 282, 357, 361
Abel, Elie, 284
Abrams, Floyd, 318, 319, 340, 345
ACLU. *See* American Civil Liberties Union
advertising, 194, 195, 209, 211, 215, 224
Advisory Task Force on Cable Television, 279–80, 281
affiliates, 162, 165–66, 198, 274
"After Two Years: A Conversation with the President" (television documentary), 167–70
Agnew, Spiro, 292–93
Air Force, U.S., 115–17, 119
Alcoa, 77–78, 132
Alien and Sedition Acts, 307
All Things Considered (NPR), 334
Allen, Frederick Lewis, 56
American Broadcasting Company. *See* ABC
American Civil Liberties Union (ACLU), 111, 120, 313
American University, The (Barzun), 264
Anderson, Marian, 136, 173
Anglo-American Conference on News and the Law, 310–11
Annenberg/CPB Project: Educational Excellence Through Telecommunications, 316–19, 329–31, 352

"Annie Lee Moss Before the McCarthy Committee" (television documentary), 126
Anthony, Susan B., 105
"Argument in Indianapolis, An" (television documentary), 104, 119–20, 121
Arimori, Mitsuo, 43
Arlen, Michael, 278, 283
Armed Forces Radio, 37–38, 46
Armsey, James, 31, 33, 34, 41–42, 44, 47, 235
Armstrong, Louis, 92, 133
Army, U.S., 30–47, 115; and CBI theater, 33–39, 41–44; and FWF in Europe, 39–41; and FWF's development, 43–45; Signal Corps, 30, 34, 37, 115, 126. *See also* Armed Forces Radio
Army Hour, The (radio program), 36
Around the World in Fifteen Minutes (radio program), 37
Arvold, Frances, 342
Atomic Energy Commission, 103
atomic power, 64–66, 67
Aubrey, James, 171, 184, 185, 224, 228
audio montage, 73

Baker, Bobby, 198–99
Baker, Richard T., 267
Baker, Russ, 31, 33
Baldwin, Roger, 313
Barber, Walter "Red," 74

Barnett, Martin, 81, 140

Barnouw, Erik, 86, 103, 106, 201, 277

Barrett, Dean, 253, 255–56

Barrett, Edward W., 252, 272, 284

Barron, Arthur, 161–62, 219, 282

Barron, John, 320

Barzun, Jacques, 264

Bayley, Edwin, 128

BBC (British Broadcasting Corporation), viii, 153, 234, 247

Beale, Ilse, 39

Beecham, Thomas, 140

Bell, David, 210

Bell, Griffin, 318

Benson, Ezra Taft, 133

Benton, William, 114

Bergen, Edgar, 100

Bergman, Ingrid, 140

"Berkeley Radicals, The" (television documentary), 161–62

Berle, Milton, 62

Bernstein, Bo, 24, 48

Bernstein, Helen, 102, 135, 268

Bernstein, Robert, 102, 135, 260, 344; and FWF's army experience, 42–43, 66; and FWF's resignation from CBS, 216, 221; as matchmaker, 268–69

Berry, Alfred B., 111–12

Bettag, Tom, 270; and FWF's final days, 333, 343; as FWF's teaching assistant, 251, 253–55, 265, 268, 349–50, 361; and Seminars on Media and Society, 323–25, 326, 327

Between the Dark and the Daylight (radio documentary), 108

Bill of Rights, 105, 320, 325, 356; seminars on, 317, 319. See also First Amendment

Birk, Joseph F., 7, 34, 38

Black Rock (CBS headquarters), 176, 181, 195–96

blacklisting, 105–8, 110, 130

Blackmun, Harry, 321

Blackwell, Laura, 259

Bliss, Edward, Jr., 87, 93

Bluem, A. William, 96, 103, 151

Bohen, Frederick M., 281

Boni, Charles, 102

Booz Allen and Hamilton (firm), 209, 210, 223, 226

Borge, Victor, 140

Bork, Robert, 318, 319

Brady, James, 52

Brando, Marlon, 342

Braude, Pearl, 49, 54

Braude, William, 105, 134; and FWF's early career, 35, 48, 49, 54; as FWF's mentor, 7, 19; and Therese Wachenheimer, 14–15

Brawley, Tawana, 331–32

Braziller, George, 135

Breslin, Jimmy, 228, 236

Bricker Amendment, 121

Brimmer, Andy, 245

Brinkley, David, 175, 186, 187, 212

British Broadcasting Corporation. See BBC

Brooks, William, 64–65

Brown, Les, 209, 216–17, 219, 222–23, 226, 358

Bryan, William Jennings, 105

Buchwald, Art, 70

Buckley, William F., Jr., 254

Buksbaum, David, 169–70, 219

Bundy, McGeorge, 199, 240, 274, 357; at Ford Foundation, 4, 234–35, 237, 239, 242–44, 246, 267; as FWF's mentor, 7, 312; and Vietnam War, 208

Burdett, Winston, 106

Burger, Warren E., 325

Burke, Edmund, 154, 155

Cable News Network. See CNN

cable television, 239, 279–81, 338, 349, 360

Caesar, Julius, 154

Caldwell, Earl, 260, 261–62, 300, 360

Callas, Maria, 140

Cam Ne (Vietnam), 203–7, 358
Cambridge, Godfrey, 230
cameras, hidden, 160–61
"Campaign for the Ia Drang Valley,
    The" (television documentary), ix
Cantor, Eddie, 20
Capote, Truman, 188
Capp, Al, 62
Carlisle, Kitty, 268
Carnegie Commission on Educational
    Television, 249, 272, 273, 275; and
    Ford Foundation, 246–47
Carpentier, Georges, 11, 346
Carr, E. H., 8
Carson, Rachel, 170, 173
Carter, Boake, 20
Carter, Jimmy, 297, 329
"Case of Milo Radulovich, A0589839,
    The" (television documentary),
    115–20, 126
CBI. See China-Burma-India theater
CBI Roundup (army newspaper), 36, 39,
    40–44
CBS (Columbia Broadcasting System),
    93, 94, 201, 344; affiliates of, 162,
    165–66, 198, 274; and blacklisting,
    105–8, 110, 130; breaking news at, 183,
    192, 293; and controversy, 116, 154,
    218–20, 224; culture at, 149, 181;
    facilities at, 87–88, 91–92, 176, 181,
    195–96; FWF at, 4–7, 68–69, 71,
    130–38, 167–68, 336; FWF's contract
    with, 72–73, 77, 79; FWF's resigna-
    tion from, ix–x, 2, 4–5, 7–8, 211,
    214–33, 358–59; and McCarthy/
    McCarthyism, 4, 99, 105, 108, 110,
    113–14, 115–20, 122–29, 130–38, 145,
    302, 355–56, 358; and NBC, 175, 177,
    179, 183, 187–88, 190, 192, 196–97;
    reorganization of, 144–45, 208–9,
    210–11, 214, 216, 217, 218, 224, 358
CBS News, vii–viii, 4, 53, 78, 192, 197;
    FWF as president of, 179–86, 193–94,
    201, 212–13, 226, 231, 293; and LBJ,
    204–5; and national conventions

(1964), 187–90, 227; tensions at,
    174–78
CBS Radio, 203–4
CBS Reports (television program), 4,
    139–56, 358; and affiliates, 162,
    165–66; and documentary technique,
    158–59; FWF as executive director of,
    142–44, 146, 157–61, 162, 171–72, 184;
    growth of, 194–95; less controversial
    episodes of, 163–64, 170–71; and
    Lippmann interview, 146–49; and
    Murrow–Stanton conflict, 144–45, 152;
    as news documentary, 141–45; and
    presidential specials, 163–64, 166–68;
    success of, 146, 161, 172, 173, 194, 197
censorship, 162, 247, 313–14
Cerf, Bennett, 268
Chamberlin, Ward, 286, 288, 289–90,
    297
Chancellor, John, vii, 318–19
Chandler, Bob, 219
China-Burma-India (CBI) theater, 33,
    34, 105; FWF's activities in, 1, 7, 36,
    38, 44, 347; FWF's return to, 41–43
"Christmas in Korea" (television
    documentary), 93–97, 113
Churchill, Winston, 57, 66, 84, 196
cinema verité, 161–62, 322
Cioffi, Lou, 97
civil liberties, 105, 111, 120, 125, 153–54
civil rights movement, 275–76
Clancy, Martin, 253, 337, 352, 361
Clark, Blair, 164, 167
Clark, Gilbert Edward (Ed), 46; in CBI
    theater, 34–39; and FWF, 31–33; and
    FWF's ethics, 45, 59, 352; as FWF's
    mentor, 32–33, 45, 347
Clark, Lyla (Lee) Sween, 32, 34, 342–43
Clark, Michelle, 258, 259, 262
Clark, Ramsey, 260
Clark, Ted, 46
Clooney, George, 110
Cloud, Stanley, 100
Clurman, Richard M., 316
CNN (Cable News Network), 338

Cobb, Lee J., 1

Cohn, Roy, 126–27, 254, 327, 350

Collingwood, Charles, 99, 107, 155, 179, 182, 196

Columbia Broadcasting System. *See* CBS

Columbia Records, 56, 57, 73

Columbia University, 1, 252–70, 272; broadcast laboratory at, 252–53, 255, 257; FWF at, 2, 4, 234–35, 243, 299, 360; FWF's retirement from, 311–13; student protest at, 262–65

Columbia University Graduate School of Journalism, 4, 5, 252–53, 311, 344

Columbia University Seminars on Media and Society. *See* Seminars on Media and Society

Communications Act (1934), 236

Communist Party, 76, 105–6, 123; and CBS, 106–7; and Moss, 121, 126–27

Conant, James, 105

Connor, Eugene "Bull," 154

Constitution: That Delicate Balance, The (Friendly and Elliott), 320, 325

Constitution: That Delicate Balance, The (television program), 318, 321

Constitution, U.S., 317–19, 325

controversy, 137, 152, 165, 274, 277, 297, 302; and CBS, 116, 154, 218–20, 224; and journalism, 123, 124, 128; and public affairs programming, 104–5, 132–33, 297; and *See It Now*, 104–5, 132–34; and Senate Foreign Relations Committee, 7, 219–20, 224

Cook, Fred, 301, 302, 303, 305

Cooper, Gary, 73

Copland, Aaron, 108, 149

copyright law, 300

Corporation for Public Broadcasting (CPB), 247, 285, 288, 292, 293

Corwin, Jerome, 30–31

Corwin, Norman, 57, 89, 106

Costello, Frank, 75

Counterattack: The Newsletter of Facts on Communism, 106, 110, 113–14

Cousins, Norman, 287

Cowan, Louis, 142, 252–53

Coward, Noël, 140

Cox, Archibald, 304, 305

CPB. *See* Corporation for Public Broadcasting

Crisis at Columbia, The (student publication), 263

Croft, Steve, 361

Cronkite, Walter, 25, 163, 174, 229; and election night coverage, 190, 192–93; as guest lecturer, 254, 257; and JFK interview, 168–69; and national conventions (1964), 186–90, 227; as news anchor, 7, 68, 176

Crosby, John, 59, 62, 84, 85

Crowther, Bosley, 80, 140

Crumpler, Hugh, 43

C-SPAN, 297

Curtis, Thomas B., 295

Daly, John, 58

Dann, Mike, 65, 67, 283

DATELINE with Melvyn Douglas (radio program), 51–52, 54

Davis, David M., 285–86, 288, 291–93, 350, 359

Davis, Elmer, 53, 64, 127, 155

Dawn over Zero: The Story of the Atomic Bomb (Laurence), 64

Day, James, 273, 283; and educational television, 235–36, 243–44, 287–89; and FWF's seminars, 311, 326; and public television, 240, 291, 292, 294, 295

Day of Absence (play), 277

"D-Day Plus 20 Years: Eisenhower Returns to Normandy" (television documentary), 163–64

de Gaulle, Charles, 59

Dean, John, 296

Death of a Salesman (Miller), 1–2

Decca Records, 25, 31, 45, 48, 56

Dembo, Joe, 182

Democratic National Committee (DNC), 302–3

Democratic National Convention (1964), 186–90, 227

Dempsey, Jack, 11, 346

Denniston, Lyle, 314

DePoris, Gene, 148, 219

Dewey, Thomas E., 139

"Diary of a Bookie Joint" (television documentary), 160

Dinesen, Isak, 173

Dirkson, Everett, 140

Doan, Richard K., 247–48, 252, 295–96

documentaries, radio, 56–59, 67–68

documentaries, television, 4, 120, 162, 327; disappearance of, 325–26; on Korean War, 93–97; on migrant workers, 149–51; and point of view, 118, 124–26, 151; and technological advances, 110, 165, 349; tradition of, 79–80. *See also specific productions*

Doherty, Thomas, 116, 120

Donahue, Phil, 331, 332

Donaldson, Al, 259

Donovan, William "Wild Bill," 105

Dooley, Tom, 146

Dostoyevsky, Fyodor, 353

Dotson, John, 261

Douglas, Melvyn, 38, 43, 46, 50, 51, 52–53

Douglas, Susan, 12

Downey, Morton, Jr., 332

Downs, Bill, 95–96

Drain, Margaret, 361

Dressner, Howard, 286, 351

Dubinsky, David, 105

Due to Circumstances Beyond Our Control . . . (Friendly), 93, 203, 220, 236–37, 238, 267, 352

Dunham, Corydon B., 220

Dunn, John, 230

Dwarfs, The (Pinter), 279

Eastman, George, 102

editorializing, 181, 302; at CBS, 125–27; by Murrow, 152, 154

educational television. *See* public television

Edward R. Murrow Professorship in Journalism, 234, 360

Edwards, Douglas, 74–75, 81, 153, 176

Einstein, Albert, 65, 66, 103

Eisenhower, Dwight D., 117, 122, 127, 174, 185; and FWF, 7, 198, 199, 229–30, 232, 234; interviews with, 159, 163, 164

Eisenhower, John, 326

Elliott, Martha, 323, 327, 343, 349; as FWF's writer, 304, 313–14, 320–21

Elliott, Osborn, 312, 315–16

Erikson, Erik, 6

Ernst, Morris, 107, 111, 112

ethics, 310, 312, 323, 329, 330, 339; and FWF, 45, 59, 63, 98, 222–23, 352; in journalism, 192, 255, 259, 352

Ethics in America (television program), 329–31, 352

Evans, Harold, 310, 314–15

Evans, Walker, 152

Face the Nation (television program), 208, 217

Fain, Norman, 17, 19, 24, 48–50, 54–55, 72

Fain, Rosalie, 54

fairness doctrine, 300–303, 305

Fanfare for the Common Man (Copland), 149

Fanning, David, 298, 360

Farley, James A., 62

Farm Bureau, 151, 152

"Farm Problem: A Crisis of Abundance, The" (television documentary), 133

FBI (Federal Bureau of Investigation), 110–13

FCC (Federal Communications Commission), 142, 164–65, 236, 240–41, 301, 303, 334

Fermi, Enrico, 66

film, 80–81, 150

First Amendment, 307, 335; and censorship, 313–14; and Democratic National Committee, 302–3; and FWF, 256, 260, 302, 357; protections

First Amendment (*continued*)
  under, 105, 260, 300–301, 308, 314; as
  shield, 236–37
Fisher, Zelda, 13–14, 17, 19
Fitzgerald, F. Scott, 233
Flaherty, Robert, 79
Fleming, Robben, 316–18
Fogel, Barbara, 174–75
Fogel, Ed, 221
Fontanne, Lynn, 46
Footprints in the Sands of Time (radio
  program), 23–25, 31, 33, 45, 48, 56,
  105, 193–94, 247, 348
Ford, Gerald, 297, 321–22
Ford, Henry, II, 3, 245
Ford Foundation, 234–51, 267, 295, 299;
  and Carnegie Commission, 246–47;
  and commercial broadcasting,
  236–38; FWF at, 1–5, 47, 266, 285,
  312–13; and funding, 248, 272, 275,
  290–91; and Nixon, 287, 288, 292;
  and *PBL*, 249–50, 278, 279; and PBS,
  286–88; and public affairs program-
  ming, 246–47, 291; and satellite
  communications, 241–42, 247–48,
  285; and Seminars on Media and
  Society, 5, 306–7, 315–16; Sucherman
  at, 244, 245, 286, 292–93, 350
Forhan, Margaret, 16
Forman, Denis, 310, 314–15, 316
Foster, Natalie, 88, 323
Fourth Estate. *See* journalism; news
Fox, Alice, 18, 34, 62
Frank, Elaine, 18, 20
Freedom of Information Act (1966), 110
Friedman, Joshua, 263, 342
Friendly, Andrew, 72, 101, 134, 136, 265,
  267, 342, 343
Friendly, David, 136, 265, 267, 269–70,
  306, 343, 351
Friendly, Dorothy Greene, 1–2, 7, 17, 48,
  163, 200; career of, 49–50, 54; divorce
  of, from FWF, 268–70; emotional
  problems of, 136, 174–75, 267–68; and
  European grand tour, 69–70; and

FWF–Murrow relationship, 98, 106;
  and FWF's moods, 72, 92, 134, 157;
  marriage of, to FWF, 53–54, 57, 99,
  175, 232–33, 267–68, 347; and
  middle-class move, 60–61, 134; role
  of, 54–55, 135, 193, 351; and *Small
  World*, 139–40; social life of, 101–2, 173
Friendly, Fred (Ferdinand Friendly
  Wachenheimer; FWF), 4–9; anxieties
  of, 54, 137; as boss, 63, 97, 253–54;
  creativity of, 86, 92, 199, 349; as
  critic, 334–38; death of, 343–45; early
  career of, 20, 23–29, 48–71; early
  family life of, 10–16; education of,
  16–22, 346; ethics of, 45, 59, 63, 98,
  222–23, 352; funeral of, 313, 345, 352,
  353; health of, 16, 38–39, 339–43;
  influence of, vii–x, 4–5; late career of,
  329–33; learning problems of, 6, 16,
  19–20, 346, 347, 355; marriage of, to
  Dorothy, 53–54, 57, 99, 175, 232–33,
  267–68, 347; marriage of, to Ruth,
  268–70, 306, 323–24, 340–45; and
  mentors, 7, 19, 22–26, 32–33, 45, 48,
  71, 81–82, 226, 271, 312, 346, 347, 348,
  354–55, 357; as parent, 101, 136, 194,
  267–70, 343–44, 351; personality of, x,
  6, 8, 18–19, 35, 39, 44, 47, 50, 54,
  89–90, 97–98, 176–77, 180, 182, 225,
  227, 267; as salesman, 1–3; self-confidence of, 172, 269, 347–48; Soldier's
  Medal of, 34–35; temper of, viii, 2, 6,
  16, 59, 87, 89, 91–92, 101, 157–58,
  174–75, 179, 183, 250, 342–43, 347;
  turning point of, 212–13, 226
Friendly, Lisa, 101, 134, 228, 267, 269,
  344, 355
Friendly, Rosalie, 14
Friendly, Ruth Mark, 7, 16, 268–70, 304,
  311, 313, 351; and FWF's final days,
  340–45; and Seminars on Media and
  Society, 306, 323–24, 345
Friendly, Samson Hiram, 10, 12–13
Friendly, Therese. *See* Wachenheimer,
  Therese Friendly

"Friendly Report," 280–81
Friendlyvision, 1, 5, 250, 346–64
Fromson, Murray, 208
Frontline (television program), 326, 360
Fulbright, William, 201, 208, 212

gag orders, 300, 308
Gandhi, Mahatma, 104
Gannett, Karen, 313
Gates, Gary Paul, 189, 214, 224
Gavin, James, 210
Gehrig, Lou, 57
Geisel, Theodor, 268
Gitlin, Irving, 158, 165, 239
Giuliani, Rudolph, 330
Glenn, John, 170
Goldberg, Arthur, 171
Goldman, Eric, 238
Goldstein, Abraham, 306
Goldwater, Barry, 185, 301, 302
Gonzalez, J. J., 259
Good Guys, the Bad Guys and the First Amendment: Free Speech vs. Fairness in Broadcasting, The (Friendly), 301–2, 304–5
Good Night and Good Luck (film), 110
Goodman, Walter, 238
Gould, Jack, 84, 145; and FWF at CBS, 163, 180–81; and FWF's early career, 66, 67, 74; and FWF's resignation from CBS, 215–16, 219, 220–22, 224, 227; and *PBL*, 273, 278; and *See It Now*, 86, 103, 118, 132, 137
Graham, Katherine, 191
Granada Television, 314, 315
Grapes of Wrath, The (Steinbeck), 151–52
Greenberg, Hank, 11
Grissom, Virgil "Gus," 193
Gross, Chaim, 173
Gude, Helen, 70, 101–2
Gude, John G. "Jap," 56, 101–2; and FWF at CBS, 52–53, 69, 190, 209; and FWF's early career, 60–62, 70–71, 81
Gulf of Tonkin Incident, 201–3, 208, 227, 277, 293

Gutenberg, Johannes, 249
Guthmann, John, 313
Guttman, Paul, 33, 50, 61

Halberstam, David, 89, 98, 100, 145, 201–2, 204, 352, 356, 364
Hamburger, Philip, 86, 103
Hanna, Lee, 182, 219
Hargis, Billy James, 301, 302, 304, 305
Harrington, Mark, 264, 361
Harris, Lou, 190, 276
Harris, Ruth, 14, 15, 47, 51
Hart, Gary, 329
Hart, Moss, 62
"Harvest of Shame" (television documentary), 149–52, 172, 173, 355
Hassenfeld, Harold, 19
Hatch, Orrin, 318
Hawks, Howard, 21
Hayes, Helen, 65, 66
Hayward, Andrew, 344
Heald, Henry, 243
Hear It Now (radio program), 73–74, 75, 108, 109, 111, 112
Heard, Alexander, 315
Hearst Corporation, 106, 130, 326
Hearst Metrotone News/MGM News of the Day, 81, 82
Hecht, Ben, 22
Henry, Edgar, 259
Hepburn, Katharine, 348
Herman, George, 167
Hersey, John, 50, 257
Hersh, Edward, 361
Hertz, Willard, 243, 244, 245, 266–67, 312
Hewitt, Don, 188, 192, 332; at CBS, vii, 107–8, 167; and *See It Now*, 83, 88; and *60 Minutes*, vii, 81, 333–34
Hiroshima, 7, 38, 64, 347
Hiss, Alger, 106
Hitler, Adolf, 57
Hoffman, Abbie, 298
Hoge, James, 360–61
Hollenbeck, Don, 74, 130

Holmes, Richard, 9

Hoover, Herbert, 122

Hoover, J. Edgar, 110–13, 160, 194, 199, 326

Hope, Bob, 65–66

House Subcommittee on Communications and Power, 291–92

House Un-American Activities Committee, 108

Houseman, John, 81

Howe, Harold, II, 315

Howe, Irving, 16

Hume, Brit, 318

Humphrey, Hubert, 190, 291

Hunt, Alice, 15

Hunter-Gault, Charlayne, 261

Huntley, Chet, 169, 175, 186, 187, 212

Huntley-Brinkley Report, The (television program), 176, 183, 192–93, 197

Huxley, Aldous, 139

"I can hear it now . . . ," 1933–1945 (record), 56–62, 68, 81–82, 349, 352

I Love Lucy (television program), 212, 223

Ickes, Harold, 62

Inman, Bobby, 322

Institute for Journalism Education, 262

interconnection: and NET, 238, 290; and noncommercial television, 239, 241–42, 248, 271, 287, 295, 299

Internal Security Act (1950), 103

Jennings, Peter, 330

Jennison, James, 23

Johnson, Lyndon (LBJ), 201, 217, 219, 242, 246, 256, 277, 357–58; and Cam Ne report, 204–5; and CBS, 190, 193, 210, 228; and FWF, 171, 198–201, 296; and public television, 247, 248, 275, 285

Johnson, Nicholas, 247, 282

Joseph, Frederick, 330

journalism, 248, 283, 298, 364; and controversy, 123, 124, 128; investigative, 160–61, 180; and judiciary, 299–309, 329, 360; and minorities,

x, 1, 256–62; objectivity in, 125, 206; photography in, 79, 80, 349; point of view in, 118, 124–25, 151, 278; subjectivity in, 8–9; and wire recorder, 37, 38, 46

journalism, broadcast, 164, 237; at Columbia University, 252–53; FWF's criticism of, 334–35, 361–62; FWF's beginning in, 20, 23–29, 61–63, 348; FWF's goals for, 356–57; FWF's influence on, vii–x, 4–5

journalism, television, 1, 64, 77, 82, 85–86, 118, 145

"Journalism and the First Amendment" (seminar), 256

Julian, Joseph, 106

Kahn, Herman, 278

Kaltenborn, H. V., 62

Kampelman, Max, 291

Kaplan, Justin, 8

Kaplan, Martha, 15, 24, 25

Kapp, Jack, 31, 45, 56, 354

Karayn, James, 293–94

Katcher, Ed, 43

Katzenbach, Nicholas, 194

Kaye, Danny, 92, 136

Kaye, Peter, 295

Kazan, Elia, 1

KDKA (radio station), 11–12

Kefauver, Estes, 75

Kellogg-Briand Pact (1928), 15

Kelly, Walt, 179

Kendrick, Alexander, viii, 70, 106, 178

Kennan, George, 103, 210, 211, 215; testimony of, 212, 214, 218, 223–25, 357, 358

Kennedy, Jacqueline, 99

Kennedy, John F. (JFK), 164–66, 218, 228, 242; and CBS, 142, 190, 358; and FWF, 167–70, 198, 296; idealism of, 170–71; and Murrow, 99, 152–53, 170

Kennedy, Robert F., 160, 183

Kennedy, Tom, 275

Kerner, Otto, 256

Kerner Commission, 256, 260–61

Kerr, Clark, 161–62

Killian, James R., Jr., 246

Kimball, Penn, 262, 265–66, 304

King, Larry, 332

King, Martin Luther, Jr., 257, 277, 279

Kintner, Robert, 226

Kirk, Grayson L., 252, 255–56

Kissinger, Henry, 278

Kitman, Marvin, 317, 322

Klauber, Ed, 226

Klinger, David, 219

Koop, C. Everett, 330

Korean War, 69–70, 76, 93–97, 113

Kotlowitz, Robert, 289

Kristol, Irving, 319

Kubasik, Ben, 215–17, 235, 240

Kuhn, David, 255, 263, 361

Kuralt, Charles, 68

Kwartler, Richard, 257

Ky, Nguyen Cao, 210

LaGuardia, Fiorello, 57

Landman, Jonathan, 311, 313, 349, 357, 360–61

Lange, Dorothea, 152

Lapping, Brian, 310–11, 315

Lardner, Ring, 179

Laurence, William L., 64–65, 66–67

Lawrence, Bill, 167

Layton, Hazel, 222, 235, 286, 350

Ledbetter, James, 276–77

Lefer, Garl L., 342

Lehrer, Jim, 291

Leinsdorf, Eric, 173

Leiser, Ernie, viii, 182, 185, 200; at CBS, 188–89, 191–92; and FWF at CBS, 231, 359

Leonard, Bill, 146; and FWF at CBS, 216, 219, 232; as FWF's aide, 186, 187, 191; and national conventions (1964), 187–90; and Paley meeting, 195–96

Lerner, Mili, 149; and FWF, 91–93, 163, 343, 349; as FWF's editor, 5–6, 81, 87

Levant, Oscar, 107

Leventhal, Al, 102

Lewis, Joe, 57

Lewis, Ted, 219

libel law, 335–36

Lieberson, Goddard, 56

Life (magazine), 75, 79, 80

"Life and Death" (television documentary), 282

Lilienthal, David, 67

Lincoln, Abraham, 102, 140

Lindsay, John, 279–80

Linsky, Martin A., 301, 305–9

Lippmann, Walter, 164, 199, 208, 242, 301, 363; and FWF, 234, 354–56; FWF's interview with, 146–49, 253; as FWF's mentor, 271, 354–55, 357

Liuzzo, Viola, 193–94

Lloyd, Selwyn, 104

Long, Huey P., 79

Longfellow, Henry Wadsworth, 23

Lorenz, Pare, 79

Louw, Joe, 279

Lowe, David, 149–54, 158, 172, 194–95, 349

Lowe, David, Jr., 158

Lowe, Mowry, 22–26, 32, 35, 48, 193, 226, 346

Lowell, Ralph, 246, 247–48

loyalty oaths, 105, 107–8, 111

Luce, Henry, 79

Lukas, Paul, 65, 66

Lunt, Alfred, 46

MacArthur, Douglas, 42, 74, 76

MacDonald, J. Fred, 96

Mack, Charles, 81, 95, 116, 150–51

MacKenzie, Dougal, 315

Macmillan, Harold, 136

MacNeil, Robert, 275, 294, 295, 296

MacPherson, Myra, 357

Macy, John, Jr., 287, 293, 295

Magnuson, Warren, 142

Mannes, Leopold, 102

Manning, Gordon, 195; at CBS, 183–84, 191–92, 207, 213, 231; firing of, from CBS, 223–24; and FWF's resignation from CBS, 216, 219
Mapp, Dollree, 320
March of Time, The (newsreel), 79
Marcy, Lewis, 191
Mark, Jonathan, 269, 343
Mark, Mary, 345
Mark, Michael, 269, 345
Mark, Richard, 269, 313, 344
Mark, Ruth Weiss. *See* Friendly, Ruth Mark
Markle, John, 305
Markle, Mary, 305
Markle Foundation, 256, 305
Markoff, Florence, 18
Marshall, George, 34, 119, 122
Marshall, John, 320
Martha's Vineyard, 101–2, 136
Martin, Tony, 38
Marx, Groucho, 124
Marx, Karl, 126
Mauthausen (concentration camp), 6–7, 40–41, 48, 105, 265, 340, 347
Maynard, Robert, 261–62
Maynard Institute. *See* Institute for Journalism Education
McCabe, Robert, 275
McCarthy, Charlie, 100
McCarthy, Joseph, 110–29, 293, 297, 301. *See also* McCarthyism
McCarthy and the Press (Bayley), 128
McCarthyism, 1, 106, 107, 357; and fear, 119, 124; and Moss, 121, 126–27; and *See It Now*, 4, 99, 105, 108, 110, 113–14, 115–20, 122–29, 130–38, 145, 302, 356, 358; and witch hunts, 105, 110
McClellan, John, 126, 127, 161
McClure, Bill, 81–82, 132, 219, 230
McCormick, Robert R., 313
McCorvey, Norma, 320
McFadden, Cynthia, 361; and FWF's health, 342, 344; and Seminars on

Media and Society, 320–21, 322–23, 327, 350
McGill, William, 312
McKenna, Siobhan, 140
McMullen, Jay, 158, 160, 219, 349
McNamara, Eileen, 255
McNamara, Robert, 183, 206, 245
McNamee, Graham, 346
McWilliams, Carey, 303, 357
Meade, E. Kidder, 215
Meeks, Russell, 276–77
Meitner, Lise, 66
Mencher, Melvin, 263, 265–66, 304
Meredith, Burgess, 81
Miami Herald v. Tornillo (1974), 300
Mickelson, Sig, 83, 227; and *CBS Reports*, 145–46; and FWF at CBS, 7, 68–69, 79, 80, 107, 142–43; and Murrow–FWF partnership, 143–44; as news director, 75, 78, 152
Middlemass, R., 20
Midgley, Les, 179, 191
Milford, Gene, 81, 91
Miller, Arthur, 1–2, 65, 306, 309, 310–11
Minnesota Rag (Friendly), 313, 314
Minow, Newton, 43, 164, 239, 317; and educational television, 170–71; and FWF, 165, 166, 198
Mitchell, John N., 291
Mitchell, Martha, 291
Mitgang, Herbert, 6, 182, 185, 195, 207, 216, 219
"Mole, the Judges, and the Rule of Law, The" (Friendly), 315
Monroe, Marilyn, 99
Morgan, Edward P., 275, 276, 277
Morgan, Henry, 107
Morgenthau, Hans, 208
Morrisett, Lloyd, 305
Morse, Arthur, 140, 184, 185, 192
Morse, Samuel, 168
Morse, Wayne, 212, 228
Moss, Annie Lee, 121, 126–27
Mount Rushmore, 169–70
Mountbatten, Louis, 44

Moyers, Bill, 150, 201, 204, 345, 361, 362–63; and FWF at CBS, 178, 226, 231–32, 337, 355; and LBJ, 199, 200; and *PBL*, 282, 284

Mudd, Roger, 184, 188–90, 212, 231

Muni, Paul, 20

Murrow, Edward R., 53, 118, 237, 239, 293; at CBS, 76, 139, 141, 143–45, 152–53; and CBS loyalty question-naire, 107–8, 111; and *CBS Reports*, 149, 227; editorializing by, 152, 154; and FWF, vii, 61, 134, 152, 202–3; as FWF's mentor, 7, 71, 82, 226, 348; health problems of, 76–77, 97, 101, 149, 177, 182; and Hoover, 112–13; and *"I can hear it now . . . ,"* 56–59; influence of, 2, 52, 86, 105, 131, 145, 151, 235, 277; and JFK, 99, 152–53, 170; and Korean War, 69–70, 76, 94, 96–97; and McCarthy, 107, 110, 114, 119–21, 124, 128–29; and Paley, 114, 178; partnership of, with FWF, 69, 70–71, 78, 82, 91–109, 121, 131, 135, 143–44, 157, 225, 259, 348–49, 352, 354; personality of, 60, 97–98, 202–3; and radio, 45–46; and RTNDA speech, 140–41, 142, 218, 338, 354; sabbatical of, 141, 143–44, 148–49; and Schoenbrun, 99, 100, 112–13; and *See It Now*, 1, 4, 75–77, 82–83, 85, 91, 137–38; and *Small World*, 140, 144; and television history, 83–84; and television journalism, viii, 1, 73, 75–76, 87–88; at USIA, 152–53, 166, 201

Murrow, Janet, 70, 97, 178, 252

Murrow Boys, 99–101, 113, 153

Murrow Boys, The (Cloud and Olson), 100, 107

Nagasaki, 38, 64, 347

Nasser, Gamal Abdel, 104

Nathan, George Jean, 230

National Advisory Commission on Civil Disorders. *See* Kerner Commission

National Association of Broadcasters (NAB), 164–65

National Broadcasting Company. *See* NBC

National Educational Association, 184–85

National Educational Television (NET), 238, 246, 273, 277, 289; and NPACT, 293–94; role of, 274, 281, 286–87, 288; and University Broadcast Laboratory, 271–72

National Public Affairs Center for Television (NPACT), 292–95

National Public Radio. *See* NPR

NBC (National Broadcasting Company), 62, 107, 176; and CBS, 175, 177, 179, 183, 187–88, 190, 192, 196–97; FWF's contract with, 63, 64, 69, 234

NBC Radio, 62, 64, 71, 348

Near, Jay, 313

Near v. Minnesota (1931), 313, 314

Nehru, Jawaharlal, 139

Nesson, Charles, 306, 309, 310–11, 325

NET. *See* National Educational Television

Neubauer, Peter, 136, 175, 267, 347, 352

New England Conference on Conflicts Between the Media and the Law, 307

New York City, 48, 57; and cable television system, 279–81; postwar, 55–56

New York Times Co. v. United States (1971), 300, 314

New York Times v. Sullivan (1964), 335

news, 4–5; breaking, 183, 192, 293; documentary, 141–45; on film, 79, 80, 81; FWF's criticism of, 334–35, 361–62; on television, 62, 74–75, 80, 86; and *Who Said That?*, 62–63. *See also* public affairs programming

news sources. *See* First Amendment

NewsHour (television program), 291, 297, 334, 357, 360, 361

Newsmap (publication), 36

Newspaper Preservation Act (1970), 300

newsreels, 79, 80, 81

Newsroom (television program), 291

Newsweek (magazine), 125–26

Nguyen Cao Ky. *See* Ky, Nguyen Cao

Nichols, Louis B., 111, 112, 113

Nichols College, 21, 22

Nixon, Richard, 133, 230; attacks on FWF by, 300, 359; and Ford Foundation, 287, 288, 292; and public television, 294–95, 297, 299–300; suspicions of, 290–91, 294

Norton, Eleanor Holmes, 319

NPR (National Public Radio), 58–59, 334, 362

Oates, Joyce Carol, 8

O'Brian, Jack, 130

Odets, Clifford, 106

O'Dwyer, William, 75

Office of Telecommunications Policy, White House (OTP), 294

Ogletree, Charles, 330

Olson, Lynne, 100

"On Coming Home to Radio Programs" (Friendly), 64

Oppenheimer, J. Robert, 103, 132, 147, 327

O'Shea, Daniel, 107, 111, 130

Ostow, Mortimer, 136, 175

Other Side of the News, The (television program), 331–32, 362

Pace, Frank, Jr., 287, 288, 295

Paley, Babe, 188, 352

Paley, William, 107, 154, 155, 162, 163, 174; at CBS, 68–69, 209, 210, 212, 214, 292; and *CBS Reports*, 143–45; as Columbia University trustee, 253, 272; and Cronkite replacement, 188–89; and editorializing, 125–27; and FWF's resignation from CBS, 214–15, 217, 219, 220, 222, 229; influence of, 195–96; and Murrow, 114, 178; and NBC, 175, 177; and Schorr, 185–86; and *See It Now*, 76, 78, 130, 132–33, 137, 148; and *Small*

World, 139–40; and Stanton, 175–76, 195–96; as victim , 237, 336, 356

Panofsky, Erwin, 103

Parker, Everett C., 303

Parkinson, C. Northcote, 140

Parks, Bert, 36–37

Paskman, Ralph, viii, 219

Pastore, John O., 241

Patterson, John M., 253

Patton, George S., 40, 42, 44

PBL. See *Public Broadcasting Laboratory*

PBS (Public Broadcasting Service), x, 5, 285–98, 359; and Ford Foundation, 286–88, 290–93, 295, 297; and *Frontline*, 326, 360; and NET, 286–90, 294, 298; and Seminars on Media and Society, 336–37

Pearson, Drew, 127

Pentagon Papers, 300, 314

Perleman, S. J., 62

Persico, Joseph, 73, 75, 87, 95, 97, 113, 152

Person to Person (television program), 99, 113, 139, 145

Peter Cooper Village, 60–61, 72, 101, 131

Petit, Tom, 275

Phantom Public, The (Lippmann), 354

Phillips, Wayne, 302, 305

photojournalism, 79, 80, 349

Piaget, Jean, 103

Pierpoint, Robert, 85, 86, 89, 94–95, 96

Pincus, Joel J. (Joe), 18, 21–22, 23, 24, 62, 72

Pincus, Minnie, 24, 247

Pinkham, Lawrence, 262–63, 266

Pinter, Harold, 279

point of view, 118, 124–25, 151, 278

Porter, H. E., 20

Poussaint, Alvin, 319, 331

Powers That Be, The (Halberstam), 356

Preface to Morals, A (Lippmann), 148

Presidency and the Constitution, The (television program), 329

Profiles in Courage (Kennedy), 218, 228

protest movements, 4; and civil rights,

275–76; FWF's opposition to, 262–65, 357; and Vietnam War, 207, 275

Providence (Rhode Island), 48, 346; FWF's family in, 12, 19; and FWF's honor, 193–94, 247; FWF's ties to, 48, 57, 72, 105–6, 347; multiculturalism of, 14–15; Therese Wachenheimer in, 53–54, 134

public affairs programming, 86, 142, 161, 349; and controversy, 104–5, 132–33, 297; and Ford Foundation, 246–47, 291; and FWF, 4–5, 68, 168, 170, 173; and *PBL*, 273, 275–76, 283; possibilities in, 69, 354–55

public broadcasting, 4–5, 248, 273, 285; funding for, 242, 245, 246; and FWF, 290, 337; and Nixon, 297, 299–300. *See also* public television

Public Broadcasting Act (1967), 249, 275, 280, 285, 288

Public Broadcasting Financing Act (1975), 297

Public Broadcasting Laboratory (*PBL*; television program), 5, 271–84, 285, 359, 364; as controversial, 275–78, 279, 282–84; demise of, 283–84; and Ford Foundation, 249–50, 278–79; reorganization of, 281–82. *See also* University Broadcast Laboratory

Public Broadcasting Service. *See* PBS

Public Opinion (Lippmann), 354–56, 363

public policy, 75, 234–51

public service programming, 146, 211, 219–20

public television, 238–40, 241, 290–92, 359, 362; attack on, 294–95; and Carnegie Commission versus Ford Foundation, 246–47; and FWF, 1, 249–51; and informed citizenry, 241–42; and LBJ, 247–48, 275, 285; potential of, 238, 282; turning point for, 296–97; and White House control, 294–95, 297, 299–300. *See also* PBS

Public Television: A Program for Action (Carnegie Commission), 246–47

Pyle, Ernie, 318–19

Quick and the Dead, The (radio program), 64, 65–66, 67, 68, 69, 71, 78, 348

quiz shows, 32, 61–64, 107, 132, 140–42, 145, 348, 354

Rabi, I. I., 66

race relations, 256–57, 261, 283

radio: documentaries for, 56–59, 64–69, 71, 78, 108, 348; FWF's beginning in, 11, 22–26, 346; interest in, 12, 20, 46, 57, 74; and Murrow, 45–46; programs on, 22, 25, 73; quiz shows on, 61–64, 107, 348; right-wing, 302, 303; series on, 51–52, 54; and simulcasts, 63; sound effects for, 66–67. *See also* Armed Forces Radio; CBS Radio; *Footprints in the Sands of Time*; *Hear It Now*; NPR, WEAN

Radio-Television News Directors Association (RTNDA), 140–41

Radulovich, Milo, 115–20, 126, 128, 326, 355

Rafael, Adam, 204

Raspberry, William, 319

Rather, Dan, 196, 202, 317–18, 343–44, 346, 361, 364

Reagan, Ronald, 278, 325

Ream, Joseph, 107

Reasoner, Harry, 68

Red Channels: The Report of Communist Influence in Radio and Television, 106–8

Red Lion Broadcasting v. FCC (1969), 301, 303, 304

Reedy, George, 194

Regents of the University of California v. Bakke (1978), 320

"Report on Senator Joseph R. McCarthy, A" (television documentary), 122–26

Report to the Nation—The 1950 Election, A (radio documentary), 73

Republican National Convention (1964), 187, 192
Reynolds, John, 217
Rickenbacker, Eddie, 161
Rickover, Hyman, 161
Rivera, Geraldo, 257–59, 317, 332
Rizzo, Frank, 319
Robbins, Jerome, 195
Roe v. Wade (1973), 320
Rogers, Will, 57
Rooney, Andy, 5, 7, 39, 47, 148, 333, 343
Roosevelt, Franklin D., 1, 45, 57, 58, 62, 66
Rosen, Harold, 240
Rosen, Joel, 349
Rosenberg, Julius and Ethel, 105
Rosenthal, A. M., 182
Rossi, Leo, 81
Rosteck, Thomas, 116, 119, 120
Roxbury School (Cheshire School), 20–21
RTNDA. *See* Radio-Television News Directors Association
Ruby, Jack, 182
Rusk, Dean, 211, 214, 217
Ruth, George Herman "Babe," 276

Saarinen, Eero, 176
Safer, Morley, vii–x; report of, from Cam Ne, 203–7, 358
Salant, Richard, 152, 155, 162, 181, 221, 232; and FWF's replacement, 176–77; interference from, 167–68; as news chief at CBS, 180, 183, 188
Salinger, Pierre, 166, 167, 198, 200
Salk, Jonas, 177
Sandburg, Carl, 6, 74, 98, 102–3, 132, 134, 140, 172, 327
satellites, communication, 168–70, 179, 280, 335; *Early Bird*, 196, 239; and noncommercial television, 241–42; potential of, 235, 239–40, 349, 359; *Telstar I*, 168–70, 171, 198, 239
Scalia, Antonin, 6, 321, 330, 345, 357
Schiff, Dorothy, 132

Schlesinger, Arthur, Jr., 357
Schlesinger, James, 318–19
Schmeling, Max, 57
Schmertz, Herb, 317
Schmidt, Benno C., Jr., 256, 299–300, 305, 309, 310–11, 324, 350
Schneider, John A. "Jack," 215; as FWF's boss, 5, 211–13, 214, 217, 218, 219, 358–59; FWF's conflict with, 7–8, 312; and FWF's resignation from CBS, 223–25
Schoenbrun, David, 82, 253; at CBS, 11, 107; and FWF, 24, 59, 70, 325; and Murrow, 99, 100, 112–13
Schorr, Daniel, 6, 121, 179, 185, 192, 196, 307, 326
Schrecker, Ellen, 110, 111
Schultz, John, 150–51, 157, 159, 172, 253, 265, 267, 341–42
Scott, Edmund, 81, 140
Scott, Hugh, 242
Scowcroft, Brent, 330
SDS (Students for a Democratic Society), 262–64
Secondari, John, 165
See It Now (television program), 86, 112, 118, 125, 130–38, 160, 283; autonomy of, 76–78, 356; at CBS, 79–81, 83, 88, 93, 104, 126, 137–39, 142; controversy in, 104–5, 132, 133–34; interviews on, 102–4; from Korea, 85, 93–97, 113; and Lerner, 91–93; and McCarthy/McCarthyism, 4, 99, 105, 108, 110, 113–14, 115–20, 122–29, 130–38, 145, 302, 356, 358; and Murrow, 1, 4, 75–77, 82–83, 85, 91, 137–38; and new technology, 168–69; as newsmagazine, 77, 78, 83, 85, 97; and Paley, 130, 132–33, 137, 148; and Radulovich, 115–20; team for, 81–84, 91, 92, 95
Seib, Charles, 308–9
Selassie, Hailie, 104
Seldes, Gilbert, 120, 124–25, 127, 170
seminars, 310–28; on Bill of Rights, 317, 319; and documentaries, 326–27;

private, 311, 324, 340. *See also*
    Seminars on Media and Society
Seminars on Media and Society (Fred
    Friendly Seminars), 315–29; and
    Columbia University, 2–3, 5, 260,
    315–16, 323–25, 328, 329; and Ford
    Foundation, 5, 306–7, 315–16; and
    FWF, 2–3, 5, 315–16, 360; at PBS,
    336–37; and Ruth Friendly, 306,
    323–24, 345
Senate Foreign Relations Committee,
    on Vietnam War, 218, 228; contro-
    versy over, 7, 219–20, 224; hearings
    of, 5, 208–13, 214–15, 216, 217, 225
Senate Subcommittee on Communica-
    tions (Senate Commerce Committee),
    241, 249
"Send in the Clowns" (Sondheim), 313,
    345, 352, 353
Sergeant Quiz (radio quiz show), 32, 354
Sevareid, Eric, 84, 136, 196, 208; at CBS,
    107, 155, 157, 179, 187, 212; and
    Murrow, 99, 182; and *Small World*,
    139–40
Seward, John, 177
Shahn, Ben, 136
Shapiro, Irving, 313
Shayon, Robert Lewis, 147
Shepard, John, 22, 24
Sheriff, Arthur, 20
Sherrill, S. H., 33, 34
Shipp, E. R., 332
Shirer, William, 76, 99, 106
Sidewalk Backtalk (radio program), 22, 25
Siebens, Jennifer, 304, 361
"Silent Spring of Rachel Carson, The"
    (television documentary), 170–71
Simonds, C. H., 274
simulcasts, 63
60 Minutes (television program), vii, 81,
    180, 192, 283, 333–34
$64,000 Question, The (television quiz
    show), 132
Slater, Gerald, 275
Sloane, Allan E., 106, 108–9, 128

Small, Bill, 183, 184, 193–94, 207–8, 219
Small World (television program),
    139–40, 141, 143–44, 149
Smathers, George, 207
Smith, Howard K.: at CBS, 143, 146,
    152–56; departure of, from CBS, 162,
    227, 302; and Murrow, 99–100; and
    See it Now, 82, 84, 131, 132; and *Telestar*
    program, 169, 170
Smith, Sally Bedell, 220
Smith, Walter "Red," vii
Snow, Edgar, 43
Socrates, 309, 325, 331
Socratic method, 305–6, 307, 308, 309,
    319, 360
Sondheim, Stephen, 352–53
Sotomayor, Frank, 261
Sperber, A. M., 76, 153, 177, 178
Spewack, Bella, 50, 52
Spewack, Sam, 50, 52
Stalin, Joseph, 58, 114–15
Standard, Sam, 135, 141
Stanton, Frank, 113, 155, 162, 177, 242;
    and Cam Ne report, 203–7; at CBS,
    68–69, 125–26, 142, 143, 208–9;
    FWF's conflict with, 6, 357; FWF's
    defense of, 237–38, 336; and FWF's
    resignation from CBS, 214–15, 216,
    217, 221, 225–27, 229; interference
    from, 167–68; and LBJ, 198, 199,
    200–201; and Murrow, 76, 78, 141,
    153; and Murrow–FWF partnership,
    143–45; and Paley, 175–76, 195–96;
    and Vietnam War, 207–13
Steffens, Lincoln, 151
Steinbeck, John, 151–52
Steinmetz, Charles P., 23, 348
Stern, Michael, 325
Stewart, Potter, 307, 317, 318, 322
Stilwell, Joseph, 38, 40, 44, 51
Stix, Thomas L., 53
Stone, I. F., 67, 342, 357–58
"Storm over the Supreme Court"
    (television documentary), 171
Strauss, Lewis, 228

Students for a Democratic Society. *See* SDS

Studio 41 (CBS), 83, 88

Sucherman, Stuart, 275, 339; at Ford Foundation, 244, 245, 286, 292, 293, 350; and FWF, 243, 254, 286, 306, 344, 359; and Seminars on Media and Society, 2, 322, 326, 327, 328, 347

Suez Crisis (1956), 104

Summer Program for Minority Journalists, 266, 299, 313; and faculty resentment, 261–62; as FWF innovation, 256–62, 360

Supreme Court, 260, 300, 301, 313, 321

Surine, Donald, 118

Swados, Harvey, 1, 6, 250–51

Swayze, John Cameron, 62

Sylvester, Arthur, 203–4, 205–6

Symington, Stuart, 126

Szilard, Leo, 67

Taft, Robert A., 84–85

Talbott, Harold, 118–19, 120

Tall, Joel, 349

Tarbell, Ida, 151

Taylor, Maxwell, 211, 217, 228

teaching, 234–36, 252–70, 299

Tebbel, John, 49, 276

technology, 87–89, 139; coaxial cables, 83–84, 168; magnetic tape, 56, 68, 348–49; microwave relay, 168–69; simulcasts, 63; tape recorder, 66, 68, 74, 94; wire recorder, 37, 38, 46. *See also* satellites, communication

Tecumseh, 105

telecommunications, 164, 168–70

television, 63, 142, 201, 250, 332; and controversy, 133, 137, 146–47; history of, 56, 83–84, 145, 236; and JFK, 165–66; network, 237, 248, 276, 335, 336; as news medium, 62, 74–75, 80, 86; potential of, 77, 80, 84, 85, 128, 198, 328, 362; and simulcasts,

63; and *Who Said That?*, 62–63. *See also specific networks and programs*

television, noncommercial: funding for, 239–40; future of, 249, 359; and interconnection, 239, 241–42, 248, 271, 287, 295, 299. *See also* public television

Thatcher, Margaret, 314

theater, 21–22, 25

Thomas, Franklin A., 312

Thomas, Norman, 62, 107

Thompson, Virgil, 74

Thompson, William P., 81

Thomson, James C., 306

Thurber, James, 53, 102, 140, 173

Thurman, Judith, 8

Tisch, Lawrence, 336

Tolbukhin, Fyodor, 40

Touré, Sékou, 173

Toynbee, Arnold, 122

Tracy, Spencer, 73

Tree, Joel, 57

Trout, Kit, 58

Trout, Robert, 1, 7, 53, 196; at Democratic National Convention, 188–90; and FWF, 63–64, 183–84; on NPR, 58–59; on *Who Said That?*, 62, 348

Trow, George W. S., 56

Truman, David, 263

Truman, Harry S., 64, 65, 74, 112, 119, 124, 214

Tucci, Niccolò, 135

United States Information Agency (USIA), 152–53, 177

University Broadcast Laboratory, 271–72

Valenti, Jack, 199

Van Horne, Harriet, 158, 219, 278

Vanocur, Sander, 167, 294, 295, 338

"Vice Presidency—The Great American Lottery, The" (television documentary), 133

"Vietnam: The Deadly Decision" (television documentary), 179

Vietnam Dialogue: Mr. Bundy and the Professors (television debate), 208

Vietnam War, viii–ix, 1, 8, 174, 198–213, 275, 277; CBS coverage of, 4–5, 197, 201, 203–4, 207–13, 215, 217; course of, 201, 293; and FWF, 197–213, 357; FWF's specials on, 207–8, 210; and Gulf of Tonkin Resolution, 201–3; Senate Foreign Relations Committee on, 5, 7, 208–20, 224, 225, 228

von Braun, Wernher, 330

Wachenheimer, Carolene, 16, 17, 18, 50, 232

Wachenheimer, Cordelia, 18, 23, 62

Wachenheimer, Ferdinand F. *See* Friendly, Fred

Wachenheimer, Harry, 12, 18

Wachenheimer, Samuel, 10–11, 12

Wachenheimer, Therese Friendly, 10–11, 13, 62; activism of, 15–16, 105, 134; and FWF, 16–17, 35, 38–41; and FWF's marriage, 53–54; and Judaism, 14–16; as parent, 12, 16, 18–22

Wallace, George, 255

Wallace, Mike, 7, 179–80, 195, 254, 317, 330, 333

War Department, 32, 57, 65

Warren, Gerald, 329

Wasserman, Al, 158, 165

Watergate, 1, 5, 199, 296–97

Wead, Frank, 21

WEAN (radio station), 22–23, 25–26, 31, 33, 35, 61, 193

Weaver, Pat, 191

Webster, William, 318, 319, 326, 340

Weiss, Herman, 269

Welles, Orson, 325

Werner, Dan, 304, 307–8, 361

Wershba, Joe, 99, 106, 116, 119; at CBS, 57, 81, 122, 190, 333, 350; departure of, from CBS, 130–31; and FWF, 61, 89–90, 98, 178; and FWF at CBS, 209, 219, 231; and Murrow, 100, 121

Wershba, Shirley, 61

Westin, Av, 159, 169, 230, 255; and *PBL*, 271–73, 274–78, 281–83

Westmoreland, William, 206, 330

Westmoreland v. CBS (1985), 335–36

WETA (television station), 289–90, 292, 293–94, 359

WGBH-FM (radio station), 246

WGBH-TV, 246, 247–48, 285

Wheeler, R. A., 44

White, E. B., 55, 71, 348

White, Harry Dexter, 112, 113

White, John F. (Jack), 287, 288

White, Paul, 116, 226

White, Theodore, 50

White Paper (television program), 162, 165

Whitehead, Clay, 294–95, 304

Whiteside, Thomas, 158–59, 172

Who Said That? (radio quiz show), 61–64, 107, 348

"Who Speaks for Birmingham?" (television documentary), 153–55

Wicker, Tom, 168, 230

Wicklein, John, 275

Williams, Palmer, 81–82, 95, 123, 158, 219, 333, 349

Williams, Roger, 14, 15

Williams, Winnie, 220

Willis, Jack, 289

Wilson, Harold, 351

Wilson, Woodrow, 357

Winship, Tom, 305

Wise, Jonah B., 10

Wise, Stephen S., 13

Wiseman, Frederick, 282, 322

WJAR (radio station), 20

WNET/Channel 13 (television station), 289–90, 298, 359

Woestendiek, William, 291–92

Wolf, David, 51

Wolfe, Kenneth, 43

World News Roundup (radio program), 204

World War II, 6–8, 36, 43–47, 57–58, 105, 347, 354; European theater in, 39–41. *See also* China-Burma-India theater

Wright, J. Skelly, 300

Yanks in the Orient (radio program), 36

Young, John, 193

Zanuck, Daryl, 140

Zhou Enlai, 133

Zousmer, Jesse, 99

Zwicker, Ralph W., 122